Valuation for Arbitration: Compensation Standards, Valuation Methods and Expert Evidence

Kluwer Law International

Valuation for Arbitration: Compensation Standards, Valuation Methods and Expert Evidence

Mark Kantor

Wolters Kluwer
Law & Business

AUSTIN BOSTON CHICAGO NEW YORK THE NETHERLANDS

Published by:
Kluwer Law International
P.O. Box 316
2400 AH Alphen aan den Rijn
The Netherlands
Website: www.kluwerlaw.com

Sold and distributed in North, Central and South America by:
Aspen Publishers, Inc.
7201 McKinney Circle
Frederick, MD 21704
United States of America
Email: customer.care@aspenpubl.com

Sold and distributed in all other countries by
Turpin Distribution Services Ltd.
Stratton Business Park
Pegasus Drive, Biggleswade
Bedfordshire SG18 8TQ
United Kingdom
Email: kluwerlaw@turpin-distribution.com

ISBN 978-90-411-2735-8

International Arbitration Law Library

Series Editor Dr. Julian D.M. Lew QC

In the series *International Arbitration Law Library* this book,
Valuation for Arbitration: Compensation Standards,
Valuation Methods and Expert Evidence,
is the seventeenth title

The titles published in this series are listed at the end of this volume

Acknowledgments

A large number of individuals deserve my thanks for their considerable assistance. Their comments and criticisms have persuaded and prodded me towards a better book. Of course, flaws remain and they are mine alone.

I wish especially to thank Hew Dundas, Prof. John Gotanda, Gerry Lagerberg, Prof. Irmgard Marboe, Sophie Nappert, Michael Nolan, Sergey Ripinsky, Dianne Rudo, Thierry Senechal, Geoffrey Senogles, Richard (Rory) Walck, Prof. Thomas Walde and Prof. Louis Wells. I also to wish to thank the many participants in the Oil-Gas-Energy-Mining-Infrastructure Dispute Management (OGEMID) discussion forum for their valuable contributions.

The Georgetown University Law Center, where I teach as an Adjunct Professor, and the Columbia Program on International Investment (a joint program of Columbia Law School and The Earth Institute), where I am a Fellow, provided considerable support and assistance, and I am indeed grateful.

Portions of earlier drafts of this volume were published in the online journal *Transnational Dispute Management* (TDM, <www.transnational-dispute-management>) as Kantor, "Valuation for Arbitrators: Uses and Limits of the Adjusted Book Value Method in Energy-Related Disputes," volume 4, issue 3 (June 2007) and Kantor, "Valuation for Arbitrators: Limits and Uses of Income-Based Methods of Valuation," volume 4, issue 6 (November 2007), and in several articles as part of my "Money Column" series in *Global Arbitration Review*. My thanks to TDM and *Global Arbitration Review* for their publication consent and support.

The American Institute of Certified Public Accountants and the Chartered Institute of Arbitrators each graciously granted permission for republication of their works as appendices to this volume.

Ms. Terri O'Connell deserves special thanks for deciphering my scribbles and her unfailingly cheerful typing and administrative support.

This book is dedicated to my wife, Lawranne Stewart. She is a joy, even if she laughs at my temerity in writing on a topic that involves competence with at least basic arithmetic.

Mark Kantor

May 2008

About the Author

Until he retired at the end of 1999, Mark Kantor was a partner in the Corporate and Project Finance Groups of Milbank, Tweed, Hadley & McCloy and resident in the Washington, D.C. office. He currently serves as an arbitrator and mediator and teaches both International Business Transactions and International Arbitration as an adjunct professor at the Georgetown University Law Center. He is also a Fellow at the Columbia Program on International Investment (a joint undertaking of Columbia Law School and The Earth Institute at Columbia University). Mr. Kantor is listed in *inter alia International Who's Who of Commercial Arbitration; Guide to the World's Leading Experts in Commercial Arbitration; Chambers USA, International Arbitrators;* and *Best Lawyers in America (International Arbitration).* He is the co-chair of the DC Bar International Dispute Resolution Committee and a member of the ADR Advisory Committee for the International Law Institute. He is a member of the editorial board of *Global Arbitration Review*, the editorial board of investmentclaims.com, the board of editors of *The Banking Law Journal* and the editorial board of the *Journal of World Energy Law and Business.* Mr. Kantor is also a contributing editor of *International Legal Materials* and an associate editor of both the online Oil, Gas & Energy Law Intelligence Service and the online journal *Transnational Dispute Management.* In 1990, Mr. Kantor served as the first outside general counsel of the RTC Oversight Board, the US Federal agency with policy oversight responsibility for the savings-and-loan crisis. Further details about Mr. Kantor's background and experience can be found on the web at <http://clik.to/kantor>. Mr. Kantor can be reached at mkantor@mark-kantor.com.

About the Author

Table of Contents

Chapter 1

Valuation for Arbitration: An Introduction

How often does it happen? The issue before an arbitrator is how to value the injury to an interest in a business. Both sides have engaged experienced valuation specialists as party-appointed expert witnesses. The witnesses testify persuasively to a very large valuation (in the case of claimant's expert) or a very small valuation (in the case of respondent's expert). And each expert witness also does an excellent job highlighting the weaknesses of the evidence from the opposing expert witness. The tribunal is left with widely different valuations of damaged credibility – where is the help to find a better valuation amidst the litigation carnage?[1] As a wise litigator once said, "One expert plus one expert equals no expert."[2]

The purpose of this volume is to provide some practical help to those arbitrators. One distinguished jurist recently stated:[3]

> But I cannot shirk my duty to arrive at my own independent determination of value, regardless of whether the competing experts have provided widely divergent estimates of value, while supposedly using the same well-established principles of corporate finance. Such a judicial exercise, particularly insofar as it requires the valuation of a small, private company whose shares do not trade in a liquid and deep securities market, using a record shaped by adversaries

---

1. "All too often in appraisal actions, the Court is presented with two competing experts espousing 'wildly divergent' interpretations of the circumstances confronting the corporation. This case is no exception." *Lane v. Cancer Treatment Centers of America, Inc.*, 2004 Del. Ch. LEXIS 108, *33 (Del. Ch. 2004) (footnote omitted).
2. Quoted by David Brynmor Thomas, Esq., conversation in Prague, The Czech Republic, September 27, 2005.
3. Vice Chancellor Strine of the Delaware Court of Chancery, in *Delaware Open MRI Radiology Associates, Inc. v. Kessler*, 898 A.2d 290, 310 (Del. Ch. 2006).

> whose objectives have little to do with reaching a reliable valuation, has at best the virtues of a good faith attempt at estimation. That is what I endeavor here.

We address the following discussion particularly to the many arbitrators with sound commercial knowledge but little hands-on experience with valuation studies or EXCEL spreadsheets. We offer a number of practical suggestions to assist arbitrators in this process, but candidly they are almost all variations on three central recommendations:

- Arbitrators should engage in advance planning to assure that the expert valuation evidence helps the arbitrators reach a principled decision.
- Arbitrators should consider whether an "apples-to-oranges" mis-comparison exists. If appropriate, the arbitrator can request that the parties re-present the evidence on an "apples-to-apples" basis.
- Arbitrators should focus closely on true comparability between the business at issue in the dispute and other examples offered in the expert evidence.

From an arbitrator's perspective, a valuation decision is both a question of law and a question of fact. The law – because the arbitrator must settle upon the legal standard applicable to the valuation (full compensation, adequate compensation, reparations, restitution, actual loss, fair market value, fair value, reasonably equivalent value, lost profits, *damnum emergens, lucrum cessans,* and etc.). The facts – because each valuation will depend on the specific circumstances of the business being valued.[4] The US Internal Revenue Service offers the following practical advice:

> A determination of fair market value, being a question of fact, will depend on the circumstances in each case.... Often an appraiser will find wide differences of opinion as to the fair market value of a particular stock. In resolving such differences, he should maintain a reasonable attitude in recognition of the fact that valuation is not an exact science. A sound valuation will be based upon all the relevant facts, but the elements of common sense, informed judgment and reasonableness must enter into the process of weighing those facts and determining their aggregate significance.[5]

Arbitrators would do well to adopt a similar practical approach to valuation questions.

Our objective is not to argue for, or against, any particular standard of compensation or valuation methodology. Instead, the objective is to provide practical assistance to tribunals presented with complex business valuations in the quantum phase of a hearing. We will review a variety of tools that arbitrators may employ to reach their final compensation assessment on a more principled basis, rather than

4. "Indeed, many of the arbitral awards seem to be influenced as much by the (lack of) quality of the evidence [as] by the tribunal seeking to apply valuation principles in their theoretically pure form." Comment by Gerry Lagerberg to the author, January 2008.
5. IRS Rev. Rul. 59-60, § 3.01 (1959).

splitting-the-baby or Kentucky windage. As will become apparent, a thoughtful and proactive arbitrator can help him or herself to a considerable extent. If arbitrators and valuation professionals cooperate in the utilization of valuation methods, the arbitration community will move closer towards a common language and consistent principles – a Valuation Mercatoria.

The circumstances we discuss here arise principally in the situation where each party has engaged its own valuation expert, but are applicable as well where the tribunal engages its own expert. Legal systems have historically differed in their approach towards the use of experts in litigation proceedings. The use of party-appointed experts is the norm for many common law jurisdictions, while civil law jurisdictions often rely upon a court-appointed expert.

> There is a key difference between the two traditions in the matter of how the opinion of experts should be made available to the tribunal. The American approach is to treat expert testimony as simply another aspect of the adversarial system: each side is expected to find its own expert on a subject about which the tribunal is likely to need technical information or explanations. When, as tends to happen, those experts disagree, the tribunal is left to decide for itself which information or explanation to believe.
>
> The Continental approach is for the tribunal to appoint its own expert, who will conduct his or her own inquiry into the subject in controversy. That inquiry may be fairly elaborate, and will often include hearing from the parties or from experts put forward by the parties. The tribunal's expert then reports to the tribunal. While parties may be given an opportunity to challenge the findings of the tribunal's expert, the expert's report to the tribunal often becomes the finding of the tribunal on the subject entrusted to the expert.[6]

Practice in international arbitration regularly follows a middle path between these two approaches. Arbitrators in complex valuation disputes will commonly see party-appointed experts, while themselves often employing a tribunal-appointed expert.[7] Much of the following discussion is particularly relevant to evidence from party-appointed experts.

Throughout this book, we rely to a great extent on pronouncements of several internationally respected institutions. National valuation organizations from over fifty participating countries have established the International Valuation Standards Committee (IVSC) to publish Valuation Standards for use in financial statements and to promote their worldwide observance.[8] While best known for its real estate valuation work, the IVSC has developed guidelines and standards covering

---

6. Elsing & Townsend, "Bridging the Common Law – Civil Law Divide in Arbitration," 18 Arb. Int. 59, 63–64 (2002).
7. *See* e.g., *CMS Transmission Company v. The Argentina Republic*, ICSID Case No. ARB/01/08, Award ¶ 418 et seq. (May 12, 2005) (hereinafter, "*CMS v. Argentina*") and *LG&E Energy Corp., et al. v. Argentine Republic*, ICSID Case No. ARB/02/01, Award, July 25, 2007, at ¶ 6 (hereinafter, "*LG&E v. Argentina Final Award*").
8. *See* generally <www.ivsc.org>. Illustratively, as of November 2007 some of the member organizations of the IVSC included the *Instituto Argentino de Tasaciones*, the *Instituto Brasiliero*

all aspects of valuation, including Concepts Fundamental to Generally Accepted Valuation Principles (GAVP). The latest public iteration of valuation standards issued by the IVSC dates from 2007 (IVS 2007). The IVSC has issued as well a series of Standards and Guidance Notes, including International Valuation Standard (IVS) 1 on the Market Value Basis of Valuation and IVS 2 on Valuation Bases Other than Market Value, Guidance Notes on Valuation of Intangible Assets (GN 4), Business Valuation (GN 6), Discounted Cash Flow (DCF) Analysis for Market and Non-Market Based Valuations (GN 9) and Valuation of Properties in Extractive Industries (GN 14). The IVSC has issued as well a White Paper on Valuation in Emerging Markets.

In addition to the IVSC's valuation standards and guidance, valuation procedures adopted by the *Fédération des Experts Comptables Européens* (the representative organization for the European accountancy profession), the American Society of Appraisers (ASA) and the American Institute of Certified Public Accountants (AICPA) are especially influential.

We also employ international investment arbitration cases to illustrate valuation issues in this volume. Of course, international investment arbitral awards regularly address matters such as compensation for expropriation and breaches of international law. They are, accordingly, a fruitful source for examples. Similarly, the decisions of the United Nations Compensation Commission (UNCC) are of considerable assistance in understanding compensation for business interruption claims. The public international investment law environment, where States are invariably the respondents, is clearly subject to different pressures than national courts.[9] Legal standards may therefore develop in different directions than purely commercial disputes. However, a clearer understanding of the nuts-and-bolts of valuation methods may reduce those differences that at bottom are based on a lack of exposure to valuation procedures rather than based on legal principles.

Commercial arbitration cases also address these issues, for instance in disputes involving joint venture investors. However, most commercial arbitration awards are not publicly released. Moreover, the award summaries that are occasionally made

---

Avaliacoes, the Appraisal Institute of Canada, the China Appraisal Society, the *Verband Deutscher Pfandbriefbanken* and the *Bundesverband der Immobilien-Investment-Sachverständigen* e.V. (BIIS) (Germany), The Practising Valuers Association of India, the *Consiglio Nazionale Geometri* (Italy), the Korea Appraisal Board, the Japanese Association of Real Estate Appraisal, the National Association of Mexican Valuation Institutes, the Russian Society of Appraisers and the Russian Board of Appraisers, the South African Institute of Valuers, the Tanzania Institution of Valuers and Estate Agents, the Appraisers' Association (Turkey), The Royal Institution of Chartered Surveyors (UK), The Appraisal Institute and the American Society of Appraisers (US) and the *Sociedad de Ingenieria de Tasaciones de Venezuela*. A list of all member organizations through November 2007 can be found at Appendix 1 to this book and a current list is found on the web at <www.ivsc.org/members.html>.

9. *See*, for example, the significantly stricter test of "certainty," the use of "equitable considerations" to limit compensation awards and the apparent desire to give the benefit of the doubt to State parties rather than injured parties that has developed in investment treaty arbitrations, as discussed below in Ch. II.C, II.H and II.K.

public only rarely offer details about valuation methods. However, the valuation principles reviewed here are equally important in commercial arbitration.

Additionally, we offer cases from various US forums to illustrate valuation issues. The US judicial system, of course, has no monopoly on these issues. However, the output from US courts about valuation questions has been prolific, and the opinions of those jurists are an extremely valuable resource. For example, the Delaware Court of Chancery has developed substantial expertise in valuation matters involving dissenting shareholder appraisal cases and other shareholder valuation disputes.[10] US tax forums similarly have a long record of considering valuation issues. Working inside one of the most complex tax systems in the world, the US tax authorities have built up a body of valuation precedents out of tax disputes in such varied areas as M&A transactions, spin-offs, recapitalizations and restructurings, decedents' estate tax disputes, and valuation of executive stock options.[11] US bankruptcy courts, too, have necessarily acquired significant valuation expertise. Bankruptcy courts will, for example, regularly examine complex valuation evidence to decide if a plan of reorganization properly values the insolvent enterprise for purposes of settling creditor and shareholder claims and interests. Bankruptcy courts also assess the debtor's value to decide if a transfer of assets was made at a time when the debtor company was "insolvent" and the assets thus subject to recovery.[12]

Whether looking at international investment awards, shareholder disputes, tax controversies or bankruptcy disputes, it is important to recall that the underlying

---

10. The Delaware General Corporation Law provides that, if the controlling shares in a public company vote in favor of a merger with another company, then the remaining shareholders are also required to tender their shares to the successful acquirer. Although forced by operation of law to tender their shares, the dissenters may accept for their shares the share price offered generally by the acquirer or, in some circumstances, they instead may initiate a "fair value" appraisal proceeding under the Delaware General Corporations Law § 262 in the Chancery Court in an effort to obtain a higher price. With so many corporations established under Delaware law, it should come as no surprise that Delaware's courts have produced a large body of valuation precedents in dissenting shareholder appraisal cases. A word of caution to arbitrators relying on these cases in ordinary commercial and investment disputes; the valuation principles in the "fair value" dissenting shareholder cases are occasionally idiosyncratic. For example, as discussed in Ch. 8 below, in many US states minority discounts for lack of control and discounts for lack of marketability may not be applied in those proceedings – the situation differs from state to state. Also, Delaware law does not assign the burden of proof to either the petitioner or respondent in such proceedings. Instead, the court must reach an independent valuation of the enterprise.
11. Here too, a word of caution may be appropriate. Corporate tax advisors often mutter darkly that the US Tax Court has a pro-government, high valuation bias. The US Internal Revenue Service disputes that characterization.
12. Valuation principles employed in confirming reorganization plans, though, seek to free the reorganized debtor from the "heavy hand of the past." Moreover, the concept of "reasonably equivalent value" under the preferential transfer rules of the US Bankruptcy Code is not legally identical to "fair market value." *See In re Commercial Financial Services, Inc., v. Chase Manhattan Bank U.S.A.*, N.A. et al., 350 B.R. 559, 576 (Bankr. N.D. Okla. 2006) and cases cited therein.

purposes of particular bodies of law may differ markedly. Valuation "gathers its meaning in a particular situation from the purpose for which the valuation is being made."[13] For that reason, valuation principles developed in one field of legal endeavor should not be adopted into another field without first considering how they fit into that second field.

13. 7 Collier on Bankruptcy, *supra* n. 13, at § 1129.06[2].

Chapter 2
Basic Valuation Approaches

A central issue in many business investment disputes is whether and how the alleged conduct by the respondent injured the ongoing prospects for that business; in other words, the future stream of earnings. Valuation "is, in essence, a prophecy as to the future."[14] To assess damages suffered by a company, or to value a business based upon its value to third parties, an arbitrator or an expert must regularly answer questions about that future. What would the revenues have been? The expenses? Would additional capital have been required? How certain or reliable are those estimates?

The issue of what legal standards apply to quantum decisions by arbitrators arises over and over again in this book, both directly and indirectly. First principles are important here; as we will see, many of the disputes over the applicable legal standard for compensation can be traced back to several core questions.

- Should the objective of the quantum award be to put the injured company (or its owners) back into the position as if the investment had never been made (which might lead to a "sunk investments" remedy) or back into the position as if the investment had been made but the injurious conduct had never occurred (which might lead to a "market value" remedy)?
- Do "bright line" rules of law exist (for example, "no lost profits may be awarded unless the injured business had a track record of several years of profitability before the injury occurred") or is the measure for compensation driven by the quality of the actual evidence rather than fixed "rules of thumb" (even businesses at an early stage in development may be compensated for lost future earnings if the likelihood of those future earnings can be demonstrated with the requisite degree of persuasiveness)?

14. IRS Rev. Rul. 59–60, *supra* n. 5, at § 3.03.

- What level of evidentiary persuasiveness is required (say, "reasonable certainty" versus "preponderance of the evidence") and for what issues (the fact of lost future earnings, the amount of lost future earnings, or both)?
- Who bears the consequences of the inherently uncertain nature of estimating lost future earnings (does the party seeking compensation bear the burden of future uncertainty or does the party whose conduct prevented that future from crystallizing bear the consequences of its conduct preventing certainty of calculation)?

I THREE APPROACHES

To help answer these questions, the IVSC has published Guidance Note GN 6 on Business Valuation,[15] including a description of the three "market-based approaches" employed in business valuations.

> 1.2 Business valuations are commonly sought and performed on the *Market Value* basis of valuation....
>
> . . .
>
> 5.14 Business valuation approaches
>
> 5.14.1 *Market approach* to business valuation
>
> 5.14.1.1 The *market approach* compares the subject to similar businesses, business ownership interests, and securities that have been sold in the market.
>
> 5.14.1.2 The three most common sources of data used in the *market approach* are public stock markets in which ownership interests of similar businesses are traded, the acquisition market in which entire businesses are bought and sold, and prior transactions in the ownership of the subject business.
>
> 5.14.1.3 There must be a reasonable basis for comparison with and reliance upon the similar businesses in the *market approach*....
>
> . . .
>
> 5.14.2 *Income capitalisation* approach to business valuation
>
> 5.14.2.1 The *income capitalisation approach* estimates the value of a business, business ownership interest or security by calculating the present value of anticipated benefits. The two most common income approach methods are capitalisation of income and *discounted cash flow* or *dividends method*.
>
> . . .
>
> 5.14.3 *Asset-based business valuation* approach
>
> 5.14.3.1 In business valuation the *asset-based approach* may be similar to the cost approach used by Valuers of different types of assets.

---

15. IVSC, Guidance Note GN 6 on Business Valuation (International Valuation Standards, 8th edn 2007) (hereinafter, "IVSC Business Valuation Guidance Note").

5.14.3.2 The *asset-based approach* is founded on the principle of substitution, i.e., an asset is worth no more than it would cost to replace all of its constituent parts.

5.14.3.3 In the execution of the *asset-based approach*, the cost basis balance sheet is replaced with a balance sheet that reports all assets, tangible and intangible, and all liabilities at *Market Value* or some other appropriate current value.[16]

Three Approaches to Valuation

If a valuation professional is seeking to determine the Market Value of a business or an ownership interest in that business, three approaches are commonly accepted:

- The Income-Based Approach, using methods that convert anticipated economic benefits into a single present value amount.
- The Market-Based Approach, using methods that compare the business or business interest to similar businesses or business interests.
- The Asset-Based Approach, using methods based on the current market value of assets net of liabilities.

Within the valuation community, this categorization of approaches and methods is indeed a generally accepted valuation principle, a Valuation Mercatoria. Organizations in over fifty countries subscribe to the IVSC Principles. In particular, European, US and Canadian valuation professionals share the IVSC's methodology. As the International Glossary of Business Valuation Terms adopted by inter alia the ASA, the AICPA and Canadian valuation organizations state, valuations based on an enterprise's future stream of earnings are part of the Income (Income-Based) Approach to valuation.

> a general way of determining a value indication of a business, business ownership interest, security, or intangible asset using one or more *methods that convert anticipated economic benefits into a single present amount.*[17] (emphasis added).

16. *Id.*, at ¶¶ 1.2, 5.14. *See also* IVSC Concepts Fundamental to Generally Accepted Valuation Principles (GAVP) (International Valuation Standards, 8th edn 2007) (hereinafter, "IVSC Generally Accepted Valuation Principles (GAVP)"), at ¶ 9.0.
17. International Glossary of Business Valuation Terms (hereinafter, "International Glossary of Business Valuation Terms"), available at <www.bvappraisers.org/glossary/glossary.pdf>. The International Glossary of Business Valuation Terms has been jointly adopted by the ASA, the AICPA, the Canadian Institute of Chartered Business Valuators, the National Association of Certified Valuation Analysts and the Institute of Business Appraisers. The Glossary has been appended by the AICPA to its Statement on Standards for Valuation Services No. 1 (hereinafter "sSVS 1"), Valuation of a Business, Business Ownership Interest, Security, or Intangible

Methods within the Income Approach include the Discounted Cash Flow (DCF) method, the Adjusted Present Value (APV) method and the Capitalized Cash Flow (CCF) method (the latter also being referred to as the Capitalization of Earnings method).[18]

The *Fédération des Experts Comptables Européens* adopts the approach that earnings capacity is the best measure of the value of a business, but that other valuation approaches also play a role in appropriate circumstances. The Fédération offers the following general principles:

> 2.2 The value of a business
>
> The value of a business is based, under the assumption of purely financial objectives, on the present value of net cash flows from the business to the owner (net receipts of the owner of the business). This means that the value of the business is based solely on its ability to earn business profits for the owner.
>
> This value is based on the profits of the business, which will be achieved if the business is continued in the future and assuming the disposal of any assets not required for the operations (earnings-based value). Only in the event that the present value of profits, which would arise if the entire enterprise were liquidated (liquidation value) exceeds the value of the business as a going concern should the liquidation value be shown as the business value.
>
> On the other hand, the net asset value is, of itself, of no importance when calculating the value of a business.
>
> The calculation of the business value as capitalized earnings value can be based on capitalized earnings methodology (see section 7.2 below) or discounted cash flow techniques (see section 7.3 below).[19]
>
> As this definition of the value of a business does not depend on the size of the business to be valued the general principles for valuation of SMEs do not differ from those for the valuation of larger enterprises.
>
> Nevertheless, in valuing SMEs specific matters can arise from the fact that they often do not have substantially independent management in addition

---

Asset. As a result, members of the AICPA involved in a business valuation engagement will be bound by the definitions in the Glossary for purposes of determining their obligations under the AICPA Valuation Standard. SSVS 1 can be found at Appendix 2 to this book, and the Glossary is Appendix B to SSVA 1. The descriptions of valuation concepts developed in the Glossary are well-respected in the international arbitration community. *See* e.g., *CMS v. Argentina*, *supra* n. 7, at ¶ 402; *Azurix v. Argentina*, ICSID Case No. ARB/CAF/01/12, Award dispatched July 14, 2006, at ¶ 424 (hereinafter "*Azurix v. Argentina*"). Income-Based methods are also reviewed in Business Valuation: A Guide for Small and Medium Sized Enterprises, *Fédération des Experts Comptables Européens* (July 2001) (hereinafter "FEE SME Business Valuation Guide"), available at <www.fee.be>.

18. International Glossary of Business Valuation Terms, *supra* n. 17.
19. FEE SME Business Valuation Guide, *supra* n. 17, at 6. Risius notes that valuation professionals concur. "Generally, the old mantra of 'cash is king' applies in the valuation of most companies, as cash flow is ultimately the primary driver of value. Therefore, strong consideration should typically be given to Income and Market Approaches, which both emphasize the earnings of a company in deriving an estimate of value." Risius, *Business Valuation: A Primer for Legal Professionals*, at 142 (American Bar Association 2007).

to the owners, so that the entrepreneurial abilities of the owners are of particular importance.

US bankruptcy courts will consider any recognized valuation methodology. However, some bankruptcy courts have stated a preference for Income-Based methods like the DCF method.[20] "The criterion of earning capacity is the essential one if the enterprise is to be freed from the heavy hand of past errors, miscalculations or disaster."[21]

Of course, claims for compensation resulting from international law (such as expropriation and fair and equitable treatment) and breach of contract claims may not share insolvency law's policy objective of valuing the injured company free from past errors, miscalculations and disasters. As noted above, the meaning of valuation principles depends on the purpose for which that particular valuation is being made.[22]

In addition to Income-Based methods, the valuation community further recognizes a Market (Market-Based) Approach: a "general way of determining a value indication . . . by using one or more methods that compare the subject to similar businesses, business ownership interests, securities, or intangible assets that have been sold."[23] Valuations based on comparable sales or comparable stock transactions (what the IVSC also calls a sales comparison approach) are such methods.

The US Private Equity Industry Guidelines Group (PEIGG), for example, recommends that managers of investments in private equity portfolios look first to valuation methods within the Market-Based Approach: "For Private Equity, the market approach usually is the most appropriate."[24] The term "private equity" is defined by PEIGG as "venture, buyout, mezzanine, and other investments in private companies."[25] In the same industry but internationally, the "best practices" International Private Equity and Venture Capital Valuation Guidelines reach a similar result.

> In assessing whether a methodology is appropriate, the Valuer should be biased towards those methodologies that draw heavily on market-based measures of risk and return. Fair Value estimates based entirely on observable market data will be of greater reliability than those based on assumptions.
>
> Methodologies utilizing discounted cash flows and industry benchmarks should rarely be used in isolation of the market-based measures and then only

20. *See* Stearns, "Proving Solvency: Defending Preference and Fraudulent Transfer Litigation," 62 Bus. Lawyer 39, 378–379 and cases cited in nn. 57, 61 (2007). *See also* the cases cited in n. 415 *infra*.
21. 7 Collier on Bankruptcy, *supra* n. 13, § 1129.06[2][a] at 129–155.
22. *Id.*, at § 1129.06[2].
23. International Glossary of Business Valuation Terms, *supra* n. 17.
24. Private Equity Industry Guidelines Group (PEIGG), Updated US Private Equity Valuation Guidelines (March 2007) (hereinafter, "US Private Equity Valuation Guidelines"), available at <www.peigg.org/valuations.html>, at 4.
25. *Id.*, at 1.

> with extreme caution. These methodologies may be useful as a cross-check of values estimated using the market-based methodologies.[26]

Valuation experts also recognize an Asset (Asset-Based) Approach to valuation: "a general way of determining a value indication . . . using one or more methods based on the value of the assets net of liabilities."[27] The Adjusted Book Value (ABV) method (also known as the Adjusted Net Asset method), in which asset and liability values are adjusted to their fair market value, is one such Asset-Based method.[28] For that purpose, valuation experts often employ the substitution principle, seeking to determine the replacement cost of the relevant asset. According to the International Private Equity Valuation Guidelines, the net asset value method

> is likely to be appropriate for a business where value derives mainly from the underlying value of its assets rather than its earnings, such as property holding companies and investment businesses. This methodology may also be appropriate for a business that is not making an adequate return on assets and for which a greater value can be realized by liquidating the business and selling its assets.[29]
>
> US tax authorities, too, have looked principally to earnings-based methods since the 1950s as a tool to value operating companies and to asset-based methods as a tool to value holding companies. "[P]rimary consideration is generally given to earnings in valuing operating companies while the greatest weight is given to the consideration of assets in valuing securities underlying the holding type of company."[30]

Holding companies, of course, serve as vehicles for pools of assets like securities or real estate assets. Those asset pools are themselves often valued by reference to their earnings potential. Consequently, the underpinning for an asset-based valuation of a holding company may itself be earnings-based values for the individual assets.

These three approaches (Income-Based, Market-Based and Asset-Based) comprise the most common means that valuation experts employ to value a business. Conceptually, it should be possible to value a business on the basis of any of these three approaches. However, the choice among these approaches depends to a considerable extent on the situation of the business being valued. For example,

---

26. International Private Equity and Venture Capital Valuation Guidelines (October 2006) (hereinafter "International Private Equity Valuation Guidelines"), available at <www.privateequityvaluation.com>, at 13. The International Private Equity Valuation Guidelines were developed by the Association Française des Investisseurs en Capital, the British Venture Capital Association and the European Venture Capital and Private Equity Association. As of January 2007, thirty-five industry organizations worldwide had endorsed the International Private Equity Valuation Guidelines. *Id.* Where an expert witness was or is employed by a member of one of these organizations (or an organization endorsing the US Private Equity Guidelines) but departs from the Guidelines when presenting evidence, an arbitrator may enjoy watching the subsequent cross-examination.
27. International Glossary of Business Valuation Terms, *supra* n. 17.
28. *Id.*
29. "International Private Equity Valuation Guidelines," *supra* n. 26, at 21.
30. *Estate of David J. Levenson v. Comm'r*, 282 F.2d 581, 586 (3d Cir. 1960). *See also* Rev. Rul. 54–77, § 5 (1954).

valuations of loss-making enterprises may focus on Asset-Based methods. High growth businesses, on the other hand, are more often valued on the basis of Income-Based methods. Moreover, the quality of the evidence presented to the arbitral panel may in the end dictate the choice among methods as a practical matter. Additionally, as we discuss below in Chapters 2 VI-IX, there are times when market value methods do not fully measure the damages suffered by an injured business (whether up or down).

Arbitrators should be aware that references to the Market-Based Approach are occasionally confused with references to the similar sounding concept of market value. These are, however, different concepts; the Market-Based Approach, like the Income-Based and Asset-Based Approaches, is just one means of determining the market value of a business. As the IVSC notes, all of these approaches will produce market values: "Market-based valuations may be performed by application of the *sales comparison*, *income capitalisation* and *cost approaches* to value. The data and criteria employed in each of these approaches must be derived from the market."[31]

In mid-2007, the AICPA released its Statement on Standards for Valuation Services No. 1 (SSVS 1, or the AICPA Valuation Standard) entitled "Valuation of a Business, Business Ownership Interest, Security, or Intangible Asset"[32] (effective January 1, 2008). That AICPA Valuation Standard is binding on AICPA members undertaking an "engagement to estimate value," including in a litigation support engagement.[33] For valuation of a business, a business ownership interest or a security, SSVS 1 calls for consideration by the valuer of the Income, Market and Asset-Based Approaches. For valuation of intangible assets, the standard requires consideration of Income-Based, Market-Based and Cost-Based (i.e., reproduction or replacement costs) Approaches.[34] Unsurprisingly, the AICPA Valuation Standard endorses the capitalization of benefits (CCF) method and the DCF method as frequently used Income-Based valuation methods. For Market-Based valuations, the Standard endorses the guideline public company method, the guideline company transactions method and the guideline sale of interests in the subject company (such as ownership interests or securities). Asset-Based methods endorsed by the AICPA Valuation Standard include the "adjusted net asset method" (also known as the adjusted book value method, ABV) and, for intangible assets, replacement or restoration cost methods.[35]

---

31. IVSC, Introduction to International Valuation Standards 1,2 and 3, ¶ 4.1.3 (International Valuation Standards, 8th edn 2007) (hereinafter "IVS 2007"). *See also* IVS 2007, Standard 1, at ¶ 1.3.
32. *See* Appendix 2 to this book. SSVS 1 is also available at <http://bvfls.aicpa.org/NR/rdonlyres/672E1DD4-2304-47CA-8F34-8C5AA64CB008/0/SSVS_Full_Version.pdf>.
33. *Id.*, at ¶ 2. However, SSVS 1 is not applicable to "engagements that are exclusively for the purpose of determining economic damages (for example, lost profits), unless those determinations include an engagement to estimate value." *Id.*, at ¶ 8. Translating into plain English, it appears that AICPA members are obligated to follow SSVS 1 when valuing a business for litigation purposes (including a valuation that incorporates a lost profits component), but are not required to follow SSVS 1 if the litigation engagement is solely to calculate lost profits but not an overall business valuation.
34. *Id.*, at ¶¶ 31–38.
35. *Id.*, at ¶¶ 33–36.

Courts will regularly utilize the same terminology as the IVSC, the AICPA and valuation professionals. For example, the US bankruptcy court supervising the bankruptcy of Winstar Communications considered evidence based on each of these three approaches.

> 103. There are three standard approaches to determine the fair value of assets: the market approach, the income approach and the asset approach. . . . Although experts generally consider each of these approaches . . . not all of the approaches are appropriate or helpful in determining the proper measure of valuation. Indeed valuation, although employing broad principles of economics, is as much an art as it is a science. Each approach may yield a different result and which approach offers the best or better framework is a determination made in light of the facts of a case. Nevertheless, there are some basic tenets that guide courts in evaluating valuation evidence.
>
> . . .
>
> 112. The market approach measures the subject company's assets and those of similarly situated companies.
>
> . . .
>
> 116. [The asset approach] looks at categories of assets and determines the fair market value of those assets or categories of assets based on what it would cost to replace or reconstruct the assets, that is, their replacement cost. . . . This approach generally begins with a company's balance sheet but substitutes the fair market value of assets and liabilities in place of the book value.
>
> . . .
>
> 125. The income approach estimates the value of a company based on its earnings capacity. . . . There are two commonly used methods to conduct income approach valuation. The first, capitalized debt free method also called capitalization of earnings, is based on a company's debt free net cash flow for one year or some other discrete period. . . .
>
> 126. Under the second method, the discounted cash flow method, future earnings are projected and then discounted to present value, adjusted to reflect the risk that such earnings will not materialize.[36]

The US Internal Revenue Service similarly instructs that business valuations conducted on behalf of the IRS must follow one or more of these three approaches:

> The three generally accepted valuation approaches are the asset-based approach, the market approach and the income approach. Consideration should

36. *In re Winstar Communications, Inc.*, et al., Debtors, Bankruptcy No. 01-1430 (JBR), 2005 WL 4705075, 829-833 (Bankr. D. Del.) (December 21, 2005) (footnotes omitted). Readers familiar with the valuation decisions arising out of the US savings and loan crisis in the early 1990s should not confuse this telecommunications case with the far better known case of *U.S. v. Winstar Corporation*, 518 US 839 (1996), involving the valuation of "supervisory goodwill" of a regulated financial institution under the Takings Clause of the US Constitution.

> be given to all three approaches. Professional judgment must be used to select the approach(es) ultimately used and the method(s) within such approach(es) that best indicate the value of the business interest.[37]

Valuation methods that apply an Income-Based Approach expressly take account of future earnings capacity by seeking to forecast future income. Methods applying the Market-Based or Asset-Based Approaches may also implicitly take account of future earnings, though, because those methods incorporate market values. If the market values an asset or activity by reference to its future earnings capacity, then the chosen method will incorporate that potential into the valuation. To illustrate, valuation experts may employ the Market-Based Approach to derive the value of the business in dispute by looking at the value placed by the securities markets on publicly traded stock of a second, comparable company. In such a case, the current public stock prices of the comparable company will embody, among other matters, the accumulated views of individual stock market investors about the future earnings prospects of the comparable company. Thus, by relying on the market's stock price quotations for a comparable company, the perception of the second, comparable company's earnings potential becomes embedded in the final valuation of the first company. As a result of this reliance on the market's perception of future earnings potential, the Income-Based and Market-Based Approaches converge towards a single fundamental measure-earnings. By the way, in general terms the concepts of earnings and profits are equivalents. US and Canadian professionals tend to use the term "earnings," while Europeans appear to prefer the term "profits."

The same situation may also occur if experts use the Asset-Based Approach to valuation, depending on the assets and liabilities being valued. Tangible fixed assets like plant and equipment rarely increase in value, of course; usually, they lose value (depreciate) over a period of time. Assets like goodwill[38] and intellectual property, however, can and do appreciate (or depreciate) over time if the market begins to value those intangibles more highly (or less highly) based on business developments (including future earnings potential). Therefore, if intangibles are among the assets being measured by an Asset-Based Approach, and the value of those assets is adjusted to reflect their market values as part of the valuation process, then future earnings prospects will be incorporated into the valuation. If, however, the only assets of an enterprise being measured are the kind of assets that do not have the potential to increase in value (such as many physical assets), then even market adjustments to their book value will not incorporate

---

37. Internal Revenue Service, Part 4. Examining Process, Ch. 48. Engineering Program, section 4, Business Valuation Guidelines, ¶ 4.48.2.3.2 (07-01-2006). The US Financial Accounting Standards Board (FASB) also recognizes the role of these three valuation approaches to measure the value of enterprises. *See* Statement of Financial Accounting Standards (SFAS) No. 157, Fair Value Measurements, at ¶ 18. "sFAS 157 states that valuation techniques consistent with the market approach, income approach and/or cost approach should be used to estimate fair value." Valuation Research Corporation, Alert: Worthless to You But Valuable to a Market Participant, at 2 (September 2006). So too, the AICPA's Valuation Standard SSVS 1, *supra* n. 17, at ¶¶ 32 et seq.
38. "Goodwill" is defined in the International Glossary of Business Valuation Terms, *supra* n. 17, as "that intangible asset arising as a result of name, reputation, customer loyalty, location, products, and similar factors not separately identified."

future earnings potential. Of course, some tangible assets may also appreciate or depreciate swiftly in value because of market developments. We are all familiar, for example, with dramatic changes in oil prices! And what became of the value of a warehouse full of Windows XP the day after Windows Vista was released? Surely, those shrink-wrapped boxes no longer held their original acquisition value.

Valuation terms used by appraisers and by accountants are not always exactly the same in meaning. As the IVSC points out, the accounting term "fair value" and the valuation term "market value" are compatible, but not identical.

> The expression *Market Value* and the term *Fair Value* as it commonly appears in accounting standards are generally compatible, if not in every instance exactly equivalent concepts. *Fair Value,* an accounting concept, is defined in International Financial Reporting Standards and other accounting standards as the amount for which an asset could be exchanged, or a liability settled, between knowledgeable, willing parties in an arm's-length transaction. *Fair Value* is generally used for reporting both *Market* and *Non- Market Values* in financial statements. Where the *Market Value* of an asset can be established, this value will equate to *Fair Value.*[39]

Thus far in this Introduction, we have been using terms employed by appraisers, accountants and other valuation experts. The terminology employed by valuation experts, however, is often quite different from the terminology used in many legal systems for determining compensation. Those differences may give rise to confusion, particularly where valuation terms do not match exactly with legal terms.

Courts and arbitrators, unlike valuation experts, often speak of lost profits in addition to recovery of invested capital (*damnum emergens* and *lucrum cessans,* based upon distinctions deriving from Roman law). Prof. Gotanda has reviewed treatment of lost profits under the law in a wide range of countries, the United Nations Convention on Contracts for the International Sale of Goods (CISG) and the UNIDROIT Principles of International Commercial Contracts.

> Laws of most countries provide that, in the case of a wrongful breach of contract, an injured party is entitled to recover any net gain that was not realized because of the respondent's failure to perform its obligations pursuant to the parties' agreement. Both the CISG and the UNIDROIT Principles also provide for the recovery of lost profits in such circumstances. This principle of

---

39. IVSC Concepts Fundamental to Generally Accepted Valuation Principles (GAVP), *supra* n. 16, at ¶ 8.1 It is worth noting that there is a slight difference between "fair value" as defined in US Generally Accepted Accounting Principles (GAAP) and "fair value" as defined by the International Accounting Standards Board (IASB) in International Accounting Standards (IAS). While both IASB and the US Financial Accounting Standards Board (FASB) employ market values to measure "fair value," International Financial Reporting Standards (IFRS) 3(R), the revised international business combinations statement, continues to define "fair value" as "the amount for which an asset *could be* exchanged or a liability settled between knowledgeable, willing parties in an arm's length transaction." However, FASB's definition of "fair value" is based on the exit price; "the price that *would be received* to sell an asset or paid to transfer a liability in an orderly transaction between market participants at the measurement date."

recovery is so well settled that it can be said it has become a general rule of private international law.

All countries require that a claimant satisfy certain requirements in order to be able to recover lost profits. Many countries allow only the recovery of lost profits that were directly caused by the respondent and that were foreseeable as a probable result of the breach. The concepts of causation and foreseeability, however, vary among countries. While common law countries tend to base their foreseeability rules on *Hadley v. Baxendale,* there are still many variations. Similarly, there is no uniform rule concerning foreseeability in civil law countries. For example, the French Civil Code contains a foreseeability requirement, but it is different in theory from that under English law. By contrast, German law traditionally has not recognized the concept of foreseeability, but rather limits damages, including lost profits, through the concept of adequate causation. Both the CISG and the UNIDROIT Principles employ a foreseeability requirement that contains objective and subjective elements.

A number of jurisdictions also limit recovery to only those damages that can be proved with certainty. However, the level of proof that the claimant must show varies amongst countries. In general, the claimant must prove lost profits with reasonable certainty. In many countries, though, the certainty rule applies only to the fact that the breach resulted in claimant's loss of future revenues and not to the amount of profits it lost. The UNIDROIT Principles require that lost profits be established with a reasonable degree of certainty. By contrast, the CISG does not expressly mandate that damages be proved with certainty. However, the CISG imposes a burden on the claimant to provide evidence of damage.

As a prerequisite to the recovery of lost profits, a number of civil law countries require that the respondent be at fault in breaching the agreement. The requirement of fault can be satisfied by showing that the breach was willful or resulted from negligence. Common law countries typically do not impose such a requirement on the claimant. Similarly, the CISG and the UNIDROIT Principles do not limit lost profits to only instances involving a willful or negligent breach.

With respect to the calculation of lost profits, countries typically give the judge or, in the case of some common law countries, the jury broad authority in fixing lost profits.[40]

II ACTUAL TRANSACTION PRICE

Income-Based methods like DCF valuations are often compared or contrasted with Market-Based methods relying on comparative sales transactions or stock prices. The best evidence of a company's value, of course, may be the actual price received in an arm's-length transaction for the sale of an interest in that very

40. Gotanda, "Recovering Lost Profits in International Disputes," 36 Georgetown J. Int. Law 61, 86 (2004) (footnotes omitted). Gotanda's full discussion underlying these conclusions is found at *id.*, 63–87.

business. As the US Tax Court has stated, "While listed market prices are the benchmark in the case of publicly traded stock, recent arm's-length transactions generally are the best evidence of fair market value in the case of unlisted stock."[41]

The Best Evidence?

The best evidence of fair market value may be the price agreed between a willing buyer and a willing seller, each with knowledge of the relevant facts, in a recent arm's-length transaction.

In the *CME v. Czech Republic* dispute before a Stockholm Chamber of Commerce tribunal (hereafter, *CME Stockholm*), for example, the claimant argued that "One of the best possible indicators of an enterprise's fair market value is what an actual willing buyer thinks it is worth."[42] And in *Enron v. Argentina*, the ICSID tribunal relied upon a comparison of the concern's DCF-determined value with actual transactions to determine the post-injury value of the business at issue, the regulated activities of the gas company TGS.

> 387. In the present case there is yet another aspect that must be considered. Market transactions have taken place in respect of the Claimants' participation in TGS, both in connection with the swap that took place with Petrobras and the later sale of shares to an investment fund. Willing sellers and willing buyers in this case are thus no longer hypothetical but real enough, a situation that has turned to be meaningful in the Tribunal's findings. In fact, these transactions and in particular the sale of the Claimants' 15.2% stake in TGS, are an accurate reflection of the current market value of the company.
>
> 388. LECG [claimants' valuation expert] uses DCF for establishing both the value before the measures were taken and the current value of the Claimants' participation in that business, the difference between one and the other being the estimated losses, subject to some adjustments. While the Tribunal finds

41. *Estate of James Waldo Hendrickson v. Comm'r, T.C.* Memo 1999-278, 1999 Tax Ct. Memo LEXIS 318 at *43.
42. The claimant cited to several Iran-US Claims Tribunal awards, and Brower & Brueschke, The Iran-United States Claim Tribunal 589 (1998) to buttress this point. *CME Czech Republic B.V. v. The Czech* Republic, Final Award issued in Stockholm, Sweden, in the UNCITRAL Arbitration Proceedings, March 14, 2003, at ¶ 140. As readers may be aware, the dispute in this case was simultaneously considered by both a London-based arbitral tribunal in *Lauder v. Czech Republic*, Final Award in the Matter of an UNCITRAL Arbitration, September 3, 2001 (hereinafter, "CME London"), available at <www.investmentclaims.com>, and an arbitral tribunal in Stockholm. The London proceeding held that the Czech Republic had not breached its obligations to the investors while the Stockholm proceeding held the Czech Republic liable for breach and assessed damages. For convenience, we will refer to the Stockholm proceeding as *CME Stockholm*, to the March 14, 2003 Final Award in those proceedings as the "*CME Stockholm* Final Award" and to the Partial Award of September 13, 2001 as the "*CME Stockholm* Partial Award." Because the London tribunal concluded on the merits that no liability existed, that tribunal never reached issues of quantum.

> nothing wrong in that approach, which is commonly used and has been applied by other tribunals, it involves some degree of uncertainty in the assumptions taken into account. Because there are in this case specific transactions concerning the Claimants' participation in TGS, the Tribunal considers that the real value obtained in these transactions better reflects the current value of such participation. This is a value, which is certain and arises from market transactions. Moreover, such transactions were specifically made with the intention of mitigating losses.[43]

Courts have often preferred actual transaction data to projections developed by experts, particularly projections created with litigation in mind. In a 2004 Delaware case brought by a dissenting shareholder seeking a higher price for its shares in a troubled financial institution, the Delaware Court of Chancery rejected an earnings forecast prepared by the shareholder's expert witness that produced a higher valuation. Instead, noted the court, the board of directors of the financial institution at issue in the case had conducted a thorough effort to sell the business. Accordingly, the court held that the actual sale price established the fair value of the financial institution. The court criticized the earnings forecast preferred by the plaintiff's expert for failing to adequately account for comparability issues such as the subject company's high leverage, the impact of heightened oversight of the financial institution by regulators and the potential for litigation against the company.[44]

The US bankruptcy case of *In re Iridium Operating LLC et al (Iridium Operating LLC v. Motorola, Inc.)* illustrates as well circumstances where a court will prefer actual market data to valuation forecasts by expert witnesses. In that case, the Unsecured Creditors Committee in the bankruptcy of Iridium, a failed low-orbit satellite telecommunications system, sought to recover about 3.7 billion US dollars (USD) of transfers from Iridium to Motorola, the principal shareholder and system contractor.[45] At the time of those transfers, Iridium had successfully closed a number of financings, its public stock prices indicated substantial enterprise value and management projections, various investment bankers and advisors endorsed those positive values. Indeed, Iridium's public stock prices immediately before bankruptcy continued to show significant positive value for the business.[46]

In order to challenge this market data, the Unsecured Creditors Committee engaged valuation experts to develop a DCF forecast demonstrating that Iridium had been insolvent at the time of those transfers. Those experts recast Iridium's revenue projections, arguing that the market's decisions were based on inaccurate information, manifestly unreliable and not meaningful for a start-up company.

> The Committee asks the Court to disregard historical market data as manifestly unreliable and accept the conclusions of expert witnesses who performed a discounted cash flow analysis using adjusted cash flow projections prepared

---

43. *Enron Corporation and Ponderosa Assets, L.P. v. Republic of Argentina*, ICSID Case No. ARB/01/3, Award, May 22, 2007 (hereinafter, "*Enron v. Argentina*"), at ¶¶ 387–388.
44. *The Union Illinois 1995 Investment Limited Partnership, et. al. v. Union Financial Group, Ltd.*, 847 A.2d 340 (Del. Chancery 2004).
45. *In re Iridium Operating LLC, et al v. Motorola, Inc.*, 2007 WL 2471798 (Bankr. S.D.N.Y. August 31, 2007).
46. *Id.*, at *42 et seq.

> in contemplation of litigation. This analysis sharply reduces the estimates of projected future cash flow associated with professional business travelers to take into account the limitations of the Iridium service that rendered it unsuitable fort his target market.
>
> If the Court accepts the opinions of the Committee's experts, Iridium was insolvent or inadequately capitalized during the entire critical four-year [construction and launch] period. If the Court accepts Motorola's market valuation theory, Iridium must have been solvent, despite the fact that it was unable to generate sufficient revenue to service its debt and descended into a death spiral and collapsed into bankruptcy shortly after going into commercial service.[47]

Even though the bankruptcy court recognized that the debt and equity market had proved to be exuberant, overly optimistic, a very poor predictor, and "with hindsight . . . an unreliable indicator," the court still found the market data a more reliable picture than the litigation experts' post hoc valuations.

> After careful deliberation, the Court is persuaded that contemporaneous market data for Iridium's publicly traded securities are both consistent with substantial enterprise value and inconsistent with insolvency. The market evidence is simply too voluminous and compelling to reach any other conclusion.[48]

Arbitrators, though, do not always accept the actual sales price for a company as the best indication of value. The ICSID tribunal in *Azurix v. Argentina*, for instance, held that the USD 438.55 million fee paid by Azurix, an Enron subsidiary, to the Province of Buenos Aires in 1999 for a water concession was unreasonably high.[49] The tribunal instead concluded that a reasonable person would have paid far less for the concession. The tribunal therefore awarded damages founded on a lower 2002 fair market value figure of USD 60 million, plus verified additional subsequent capital investments, rather than the much higher actual transaction price.[50]

Similarly, the ICSID tribunal in the *Southern Pacific Properties (Middle East)* case also declined to rely upon transactions involving shares in the subject company.

> 197. In the Tribunal's view, the purchase and sale of an asset between a willing buyer and a willing seller should, in principle, be the best indication of the value of the asset. This is certainly true in the case of a perfectly competitive market having many buyers and sellers in which there are no external controls or internal monopolistic arrangements. In the present case, however, there was a very limited number of transactions and there was no market as such for the shares that were sold. The price at which the shares were sold was privately negotiated. In these circumstances, the Tribunal does not believe that the share transactions can be used to accurately measure the value of SPP(ME)'s investment in ETDC.[51]

---

47. *Id.*, at *3.
48. *Id.*
49. *Azurix v. Argentina, supra* n. 17, at ¶ 426.
50. *Id.*, at ¶ 427–429.
51. *Southern Pacific Properties (Middle East) Limited v. Arab Republic of Egypt*, ICSID Case No. ARB/84/3 at ¶ 197 (hereinafter "*SPP (ME) v. Egypt*").

III LIMITS ON FORWARD-LOOKING COMPENSATION

The Income-Based Approach expressly seeks to assess a business' future earnings. As noted above, future prospects may also become embedded inside valuations based on the Market or Asset-Based Approaches. Even when arbitrators accept in principle the use of a forward-looking valuation, though, they may still apply procedures that limit the amount recovered. The contrasting approaches towards forward-looking compensation in arbitrations and judicial proceedings reveal the limits of Valuation Mercatoria. Thus, in the well-known *Aminoil v. Kuwait* case,[52] the tribunal rejected Kuwait's argument that the proper measure of compensation for a lawful expropriation of an oil concession was the net book value of the relevant assets. Instead, the tribunal accepted claimant's argument for compensation based upon the replacement value of the business as a going concern, including lost profits. The tribunal consequently accepted in principle that future earnings prospects should form part of the damages award. However, the tribunal rejected Aminoil's argument that the best means of determining lost profits was to project forward the company's past operating history over the remaining thirty-one-year life of the concession to derive estimated profits, discounting the resulting aggregate profits back to a net present value at an appropriate discount rate. Rather, the arbitrators appear to have developed an adjusted balance sheet for Aminoil's assets as at the expropriation date. The tribunal also calculated Aminoil's total liabilities as at the same date, incorporating for this purpose a reasonable rate of return to the investor of USD 10 million per year. Deducting the total liabilities from the total asset value, the tribunal awarded the net adjusted balance sheet amount plus a rate of return until the award date as the measure of compensation. The *Aminoil* tribunal accordingly rejected an Income-Based method in favor of an Asset-Based method to determine forward-looking damages.[53]

The United Nations Compensation Commission

The United Nations Compensation Commission (UNCC) was tasked with the responsibility for determining the compensation for injury to businesses caused by the Iraqi invasion of Kuwait in 1990. The UNCC considered that, if the business could reasonably have been rebuilt and resumed, compensation could only be claimed for the loss suffered during the relevant period before the rebuilding had concluded. Consequently, the UNCC valued the impact of the interruption of business caused by the Iraqi invasion.

52. *American Independent Oil Company v. Government of Kuwait*, Award of March 24, 1982, 66 I.L.R. 518 (1984) (hereinafter referred to as "*Aminoil v. Kuwait*").

53. The *Aminoil* tribunal's approach apparently also accorded no value to the company's goodwill as an operating concern or to the prospects for the company discovering additional oil reserves in the future. Some observers have criticized the valuation approach taken by the *Aminoil* tribunal on a number of grounds. *See* Hunter & Sinclair, *Aminoil Revisited; Reflections on a Story of Changing Circumstances*, 347, 361–369, and in particular n. 105 and related text, in Weiler, *International Investment Law and Arbitration*. Leading cases from the ICSID, NAFTA, *Bilateral Treaties and Customary International Law* (Cameron May 2005) (hereinafter "Weiler").

At times, the shorter duration of injury suffered by the enterprise, and the ability of that enterprise to resume ordinary operations after a period of time, will affect a tribunal's choice of valuation methods. Illustratively, the United Nations Compensation Commission (UNCC) was established to evaluate damage claims resulting from Iraq's 1990 invasion of Kuwait. The Governing Council of the UNCC adopted a general decision, Decision 9, about principles of compensation for business losses early in its work. That Decision drew particular attention to the ability of the injured enterprise to resume its activities. "In the event that the business has been rebuilt and resumed, or that it could reasonably have been rebuilt and resumed, compensation may only be claimed for the loss suffered during the relevant period." As a result, the UNCC's approach was generally to value the impact of the interruption of the business caused by the Iraqi invasion.[54]

Decision 9 acknowledged several alternative valuation methods, including the DCF method and the price/earnings (P/E) method, a particular example of the CCF method described in Chapter 6 below. The Decision also recognized "in principle" that the value of a business "may include loss of future earnings and profits where they can be ascertained with reasonable certainty."[55] However, according to Decision 9, the valuation method for business claims resulting from the Iraqi invasion should in most cases focus on past performance rather than future-looking projections to measure the losses attributable to business interruption.

> In the case of the loss of businesses and their earning capacity resulting from the invasion and occupation of Kuwait, it can be expected that a number of such businesses can be or could have been rebuilt and resumed. The method of

---

54. Conversations with Geoffrey Senogles (now a partner in the Geneva office of LBC International Investigative Accounting) and Thierry Senechal (now at the International Chamber of Commerce Commission on Banking Technique and Practice). *See also* Senogles, *Business interruption claims, Transnational Dispute Management Special Issue on Compensation and Damages in International Investment Arbitration*, vol. 4, issue 6, available on-line at <www.transnational-dispute-management.com>. Different panels at the UNCC, though, adopted different standards. For example, the E4 Panel (which considered claims submitted by Kuwaiti private sector corporations and entities, other than oil sector and environmental claims) developed a methodology based on evidence from audited accounts. The losses suffered by the claimants were calculated by looking at the sets of accounts for the three years before the invasion. The indemnity period was also limited to one year and various adjustments would be proposed for the claimant's failure to provide "best evidence" and to avoid windfall profits after resuming operations. The UNCC took into account the UNIDROIT Principles of International Commercial Contracts in formulating its approach towards calculating compensation awards. See, e.g., Report and Recommendations made by the Panel of Commissioners concerning part 1 of the First Installment of Claims by Governments and International Organizations (Category "F" Claims"), UN Doc. S/AC.26/1997/6 (1997), available at <www2.unog.ch/uncc/reports/r97-06>, at para. 60 (citing to UNIDROIT Art. 7.4.3(3) to support the view that, in the absence of evidence of reasonable certainty, the panel was entitled to exercise its discretion in damages calculations) and para. 79 (citing to UNIDROIT Art. 7.4.8(1) to support the view that the duty of an injured party to mitigate damages is a general principle of law).
55. Decision 9, adopted by the Governing Council of the United Nations Compensation Commission, S/AC26/ 1992/9, March 6, 1992, ¶ 17 (hereinafter "UNCC Decision 9"). *See* Senogles, *Business interruption claims*, *supra* n. 54, for a fuller discussion of business interruption valuation principles.

> a valuation should therefore be one that focuses on past performance rather than on forecasts and projections into the future. Compensation should be provided if the loss can be ascertained with reasonable certainty based on prior earnings or profits. For example, the loss of any earnings or profits during the relevant time period could be calculated by a multiple of past earnings and profits corresponding to that time period.[56]

In one of its earliest recommendations, the UNCC rejected a DCF earnings valuation proffered by Saudi Arabian Texaco Inc. (SAT) because it took account of estimated losses after the restoration date of SAT's business.[57]

> 439. Based on this interpretation, the Panel concludes that where an income-producing property, i.e., an asset or a group of assets, such as a business, has been completely destroyed or irreparably damaged, the DCF method can be used to estimate the cash flows through the end of the property's expected economic life in order to value that property. Where the asset or business can be repaired or resumed, however, the DCF method will not be an appropriate measure of loss to the extent that it takes into account estimated losses beyond the restoration date of the asset or business.[58]

> . . . 446. With respect to SAT's claim, the Panel finds that SAT's valuation in its amended claim of its lost future earnings does not adhere to the standard and method stipulated by the Governing Council. SAT estimates that it would have increased its cash flows but for the invasion and bases its estimated increase predominantly on its alleged investment programme. The investment programme on which so much of SAT's business loss calculations depend is not based on past performance – it is based on the hypothetical effects of a series of plans that had not been implemented at the time of the invasion.[59]

Black Swans

"One single observation can invalidate a general confirmatory sighting of millions of white swans. All you need is one single (and, I am told, quite ugly) black bird."

In the business and international economic environment, improbable rare Black Swan events may have a large impact on the prospects of a company when they occur. Yet, because they are outside our normal range of expectations, we do not ordinarily incorporate such rare events into our estimations of business prospects.

---

56. UNCC Decision 9, *supra* n. 55, at ¶ 19.
57. *Id.*
58. Claim of Saudi Arabian Texaco, Claim No. 4000604, UNCC, *Report and Recommendation made by the Panel of Commissioners Concerning the Second Installment of "E1" Claims*, S/AC.26/1999/10 (June 24, 1999), ¶¶ 435–446 (hereinafter, "UNCC Saudi Arabian Texaco Claim").
59. *Id.*

Future earnings-based forecasts clearly have their limits. One of those, a very significant issue for international businesses, is the "Black Swan" problem. A Black Swan is a highly improbable but consequential event – very rare and very important if it happens. The evocative phrase "Black Swan" comes from the shock to Western explorers when they first sighted black swans in Australia. Before Western explorers arrived at Australia, the informed Western consensus was that all swans were white. As Taleb notes, "one single observation can invalidate a general confirmatory sighting of millions of white swans. All you need is one single (and, I am told, quite ugly) black bird."[60]

Because that Black Swan was an extreme outlier on the curve of experience for the Western public, it was outside the scope of their ordinary expectations – it was a rare event. In the business and international economic environment, improbable rare Black Swan events may have a large impact on the prospects of a company when they occur. Yet, because they are outside our normal range of expectations, we do not ordinarily incorporate such rare events into our estimations of business prospects. For instance, a business projection for an Indonesian investment in 1996 might have forecast a gradual devaluation of the Indonesian rupiah by, say, 7–8% in one year. The Asian financial crisis intervened, though, and in the earlier stages of the crisis in November 1997 the IMF anticipated a large 30% devaluation of the rupiah.[61] But between June 1997 and January 1998 the Indonesian rupiah in fact devalued by over 70%. With 20/20 hindsight, of course, it is now clear to every thoughtful observer that the Asian Financial Crisis was inevitable – just ask the talking heads on the weekend talk shows. So too, the fall of the Soviet Union; outside the realm of normal expectations in 1988, a reality by 1990, producing extremely large consequences for the value of businesses, and the object of endless "post hoc predictions."

When we consider projections of future business activities and market values (whether using the Market-Based Approach, the Income-Based Approach or the Asset-Based Approach), it is necessary to acknowledge what we do not know. Investing overmuch confidence into the accuracy of predictions is not warranted. Too often, negative Black Swans like the Great Depression or the Asian Financial Crisis, or positive Black Swans like IBM's introduction of the PC in 1981, have dramatic consequences for business valuations; consequences that were not

---

60. Taleb, *The Black Swan: The Impact of the Highly Improbable*, at xvii (Random House 2007).
61. Referring to the November 1997 program agreed between the International Monetary Fund and the Indonesian Government, a 2003 Evaluation report of the IMF's Independent Evaluation Office stated: "In line with the judgment that Indonesia was facing a moderate case of contagion, the program assumed that growth would remain positive, though it would decelerate to 5 percent in 1997/98 and 3 percent in 1998/99. Continuing the tight monetary policy already in place, combined with limited foreign exchange market intervention, was expected to bring about an appreciation of the Rupiah to a soft-edge target zone of Rp 3,000 to Rp3,500 per U.S. dollar, compared with the average of about Rp 3,600 per dollar over the period of the negotiation and about Rp 2,400 per dollar for the first six months of the year." *IMF Independent Evaluation Office, Evaluation Report: The IMF and Recent Capital Account Crises: Indonesia, Korea, Brazil*, at 13 (2003).

anticipated by expert observers just a short time previous to the event occurring. Moreover, our error rate about our own knowledge is much higher than most of us expect it would be.[62] That situation appears particularly acute when we consider the error rate of financial analysts, which is quite high.[63] One reason why forecasts suffer from high error rates is that they project assumptions across a long period of time. Errors in predicting the scope of identifiable events, such as changes in interest rates or discount rates, will play out over the entire duration of a forecast. Those errors will often have large consequences for the overall value.[64]

> Our predictors may be good at predicting the ordinary, but not the irregular, and this is where they ultimately fail. All you need to do is miss one interest-rates move, from 6 percent to 1 percent in a longer-term projection (what happened between 2000 and 2001) to have all your subsequent forecasts rendered completely ineffectual in correcting your cumulative track record. What matters is not how often you are right but how large your cumulative errors are.[65]

And what is true for significant events that are closely watched, like interest rates and currency exchange rates, is far more dramatic for rare events outside our ordinary contemplation – Black Swans.

62. Taleb, *The Black Swan*, *supra* n. 60, at 137–164.
63. *Id.*, at 145–151, 320–321 (''Financial analysts, lending, and forecasting''). San Francisco Federal Reserve Bank researchers recently wrote that ''it is common wisdom that economists are not very good at forecasting recessions. . . . We find that these forecasters have little ability to predict recessions – especially at a forecast horizon of a few quarters ahead.'' Rudebusch & Williams, *Forecasting Recessions: The Puzzle of the Enduring Power of the Yield Curve* (Federal Reserve Bank of San Francisco, July 2007) at 1. Supporting data is reviewed at id, at 5–6.
64. Note the sensitivity of DCF forecasts to the chosen discount rate, discussed at text following n. 433 *infra*.
65. *Id.*, at 149. A similar situation is playing out as this book is being published. On August 16, 2007, the US Federal Reserve Board's discount rate stood at 6.25%, before being reduced by 0.50% the next day. On March 17, 2008 (just eight months later), as a consequence of the sub-prime mortgage crisis and the significant downturn in the US economy, the discount rate had been further reduced in several steps down to 3.25% (a total drop of almost one-half in the cost of debt), with another rate cut anticipated for the end of April 2008. The Fed's target rate for overnight loans between banks was 2.25% in early April 2008, down from 5.25% in September 2007. A survey of economists at that time predicted cuts down to 1.75% in June 2008 before bottoming out (a total two-thirds expected reduction in the cost of such overnight loans in only nine months). It is highly unlikely, to say the least, that most businesses and governments incorporated such a severe economic downturn and large drop in interest rates into their business forecasts in summer 2007. Yet, the impact of the reduction in demand for goods and services and the related interest rate drop on an income projection for an enterprise is necessarily quite significant. Lest this be construed as a criticism solely of methods of valuation based on financial spreadsheets and projections, recall that the stock market price of a public company is comprised of millions of individual predictions about the future for inter alia interest rate and currency fluctuations, as is the market price for commodities like oil. As should thus be apparent, this criticism applies to all market value appraisal methods.

Moreover, unlike polls and many other statistical surveys, financial forecasts do not normally come with a "margin of error" attached to them.[66] Indeed, Taleb argues that the error rate for financial forecasts is generally more statistically important than the forecast itself.

> Go to a bank or securities-analysis training program and see how they teach trainees to make assumptions; they do not teach you to build an error rate around those assumptions – but their error rate is so large that it is far more significant than the projection itself.[67]

Financial analysts do offer potential ranges of estimation in some cases by presenting optimistic, realistic and pessimistic forecasts (Best Case, Base Case and Worst Case projections). Alternative scenarios, of course, do not afford the same information as error rates. Nevertheless, a range of estimates does serve to bracket the analyst's expectations about reasonable financial expectations.

IV UTILIZING SEVERAL VALUATION METHODS

One important practical tool for arbitrators is to seek consistent valuations across several different methodologies. Valuation methodologies are not mutually exclusive. Indeed, a central task for counsel and experts is to make arbitrators comfortable with the realization that these valuation techniques are often complementary tools. As the US Supreme Court unanimously stated in *CSX Transport., Inc. v. Georgia State Bd. of Equalization*,[68] a case challenging the valuation procedures employed by the Georgia state tax authorities to determine the market value of a railroad company's property:

> Valuation is not a matter of mathematics.... Rather, the calculation of true market value is an applied science, even a craft. Most appraisers estimate market value by employing not one methodology but a combination. These various methods generate a range of possible market values which the appraiser uses to derive what he considers to be an accurate estimate of market value, based on careful scrutiny of all the data available.... Georgia's appraiser in the instant case, for example, used three different valuation techniques – the discounted cashflow approach, a market multiple approach, and a stock and debt approach.... Appraisers typically employ a combination of methods because no one approach is entirely accurate, at least in the absence of an established market for the type of property at issue. The individual methods yield sometimes more, sometimes less reliable results depending on the peculiar features of the property evaluated. As the variation

66. Taleb, *The Black Swan*, *supra* n. 60, at 160.
67. *Id.*, at 161–162.
68. 128 S.Ct. 467 (4 December 2007).

in the state appraiser's market-value range reveals, different methods can produce substantially different estimates.[69]

Quoting its own decision in *Suitum v. Tahoe Regional Planning Agency*, the Court further noted that "Valuation of property, though admittedly complex, is at bottom just 'an issue of fact about possible market prices ... an issue district courts are used to addressing.' "[70]

If the valuations reached by two methodologies are widely inconsistent with each other, that can be a strong signal something is awry with the application of one of those methodologies in the particular case. Equally, if Market-Based, Income-Based and Asset-Based valuations (or several methods within one of these approaches) produce consistent results, arbitrators may take greater comfort from the valuations. Unsurprisingly, the US Financial Accounting Standards Board (FASB) acknowledges that multiple valuation methods will be appropriate in financial accounting valuations where a reporting unit, as distinct from individual assets and liabilities, is being valued.[71]

Valuation Methods Are Not Mutually Exclusive

Valuation methods are often complementary. If the valuations reached by two methodologies are widely inconsistent with each other, that can be a strong signal something is awry. If several valuation methods produce consistent results, arbitrators may take greater comfort from the valuations.

In the most recent tribunal award in the long-running Vivendi saga, the ICSID panel expressly noted that the claimants had offered in evidence only a DCF valuation, as part of a lost profits claim.[72] The tribunal pointed out to claimants during the hearings alternative valuation methods such as book value, replacement value, liquidation value (all as discussed in Chapter 7 below) and the method ultimately relied upon by the tribunal, investment value. However, the tribunal rejected as untimely claimant Vivendi's request for permission to submit supplemental financial information based upon the valuation methods mentioned by the tribunal.[73] The Vivendi tribunal then searched the existing record for

69. *Id.*, at 472.
70. *Id.*, at 473.
71. SFAS No. 157, *Fair Value Measurements*, at ¶ 19 (September 2006).
72. *Compania de Aguas del Aconquija S.A. and Vivendi Universal S.A. v. Argentine Republic*, ICSID Case No. ARB/97/3, Award, August 20, 2007 (hereinafter "*Vivendi 2007*"), at ¶ 8.1.4. *See also id.*, Schedule A, Letter of Dr. Claudia Frutos-Peterson, Secretary of the Tribunal, at ¶ 11.
73. *Id.*, at ¶¶ 8.1.6–8.1.9.

financial information to support its award entitling Vivendi to recover amounts invested in its local Argentine water company (CAA).[74]

Different valuation approaches are in fact often embedded inside a single valuation. In *Enron Corporation v. Argentina,*[75] for example, the ICSID tribunal applied a DCF estimate to calculate the value of an investment prior to Argentina's emergency measures and an actual sales transaction with a third party to calculate the value after giving effect to the impact of the Argentine measures. Then, the tribunal compared those measures against the stock market valuation of the company for verification.[76] That procedure was conceptually appropriate since, as we have already discussed, both Income-Based and Market-Based methods are market value measures of value.

Of course, if an expert develops a valuation based on several different approaches, then a crucial issue is how to weight the various results. One US bankruptcy court somewhat irritably refused to readjust weights, instead rejecting the expert's proffered testimony entirely.

> It has not escaped the Court's attention to the fact that the values derived from applying the other two methods were higher than that from the DCF method. By reducing the weights of the results from the other methods, once again [the expert] shoved the data to a lower value. This Court is not prepared to adopt the suggestion in the plaintiffs' supplemental memorandum that it should either change the assigned weights or adopt the highest of the three values. Either the valuation is reliably prepared or it is not; this Court does not serve to control against the plaintiffs' expert witness' bias in order to save its case in chief. If a court of record cannot rely upon its "officers" [i.e., counsel] to ensure it that their retained experts prepare valuation reports in as objective and unbiased manner as can reasonably be achieved under the current state of the appraisal art, then those officers will suffer the adverse consequences from an excess of vigorous advocacy that impairs the truth-seeking duties of the court. The whole point of experts is to assist the court in determining the relevant facts, not in adding to the court's burden in having to redeem unreliable testimony by its own lights.[77]

In *In re Exide Technologies*, a US bankruptcy case, the court rejected the business valuation expert's unequal weighting of the DCF and Comparable Company

---

74. In *Vivendi 2007*, the claimant investors offered a lost profits claim based on a DCF valuation. During the hearings, the tribunal "invited Claimants to direct it to the portions of the existing record that were relevant to possible alternative approaches to calculating damages (e.g. liquidation value, book value, replacement value or amounts invested)." Following an inquiry by counsel, the tribunal president clarified that the panel was not inviting the introduction of new evidence. *Id.* Nevertheless, the claimants sought to introduce new evidence after the conclusion of the merits hearing to buttress alternative approaches to the calculation of damages. The tribunal rejected the offer as untimely, disregarded the DCF valuation as insufficiently certain to support a lost profits claim, and awarded recovery only of sunk investment costs based upon "incomplete" evidence of invested capital. *id.*, at ¶ 8.1.1 et seq. and Schedule A.
75. *Enron v. Argentina, supra* n. 43.
76. *Id.*, at ¶¶ 389, 424–428.
77. In re *Med Diversified, Inc. v. Addus Healthcare, Inc.*, 346 B.R. 621, 633 (Bankr. E.D. N.Y. 2006).

methodologies. Instead, the court held in that case, when multiple methods are employed in a business valuation, each should be given weight in the valuation analysis.[78] In contrast, the Delaware Chancery Court in a 2004 appraisal case accepted several alternate valuations based on different methods, each of which had its own shortcomings. The court gave lowest weight to a method the court considered less reliable in the circumstances.

> If CTCA had more extensive historical financial data or if its management forecasts were more liable, both of which would significantly enhance confidence in the DCF analysis, the difficulties in finding "comparables" or making adjustments to correlate "somewhat comparable" companies would support a decision to rely exclusively upon the DCF. Because of the shortcomings impairing the DCF approach, some input from a different methodology may yield a more accurate fair value.
>
> In the context of CTCA, the preferable approach is to perform a comparable company analysis and account for its shortcomings by giving it relatively minimal weight in relation to the result of the DCF process.[79]

Significant differences in the values produced by different methods, though, raise issues about acceptability of the valuations. For example, what should an arbitrator think if an expert witness offers a detailed DCF value of USD 100 million for a petroleum company, but other publicly traded petroleum companies in the same market and at the same time have dramatically depressed stock prices? The discrepancy between the expert's DCF forecast and the stock market's forecast raises serious questions about either the reliability of the DCF forecast (and underlying assumptions) or the true comparability of the stock prices used in the comparison. On the other hand, if the value of comparable petroleum companies based on their current stock prices is consistent with the expert's DCF forecast, then that consistency is useful confirmation about the reliability of the DCF valuation and the accuracy of the chosen comparables.[80]

In fact, when an operating business is valued as a going concern by means of a method within the Asset-Based Approach, the IVSC advises that use of the asset-based method should be accompanied by valuations from the Market-Based or Income-Based Approaches as well.

---

78. *In re Exide Technologies*, 303 B.R. 48, 65 (Bankr. D. Del. 2003).
79. *Lane v. Cancer Treatment Centers of America, Inc., supra* n. 1, at 126–127.
80. That is exactly the problem faced by a US bankruptcy court in In re Iridium, *supra* n. 45, where market prices showed considerable enterprise value for a satellite communications system that promptly filed for bankruptcy. Several courts have reviewed several valuations based upon different methodologies, and reached a final valuation by averaging the results. *See* e.g., *Gotham Partners, L.P. (Gotham III) v. Hallwood Realty Partners*, L.P., 855 A.2d 1059, 2003 Del. Ch. LEXIS 73 (2003) (averaging the results of a comparable company transaction, DCF and "net asset value" valuations, and the actual transaction price in a dissenting shareholder proceeding)

> The *asset-based approach* should not be the sole valuation approach used in assignments relating to operating businesses appraised as going concerns unless it is customarily used by buyers and sellers. In such cases, the Valuer must support the selection of this approach.[81]

V MARKET VALUE

Each of these valuation methods considers market value, whether utilizing an Income-Based, Market-Based or Asset-Based Approach.[82] As the IVSC notes, "[b]usiness valuations are commonly sought and performed on the *Market Value* basis of valuation."[83] Investment treaties, courts and commercial codes in many countries routinely acknowledge that the proper measure of compensation for injury to business interests is the impact on the company's market

81. IVSC Business Valuation Guidance Note, *supra* n. 15, at ¶ 5.14.3.5. Similarly, many US bankruptcy courts have stated a preference for Income-Based valuation methods. *See* Stearn, "Proving Solvency: Defending Preference and Fraudulent Transfer Litigation," *supra* n. 20, at 378–379 and nos 57 61. *See also* the cases cited at n. 415 *infra*.
82. *Id. See also* text *supra* associated with n. 31. In some disputes in the US courts, one side may argue for a "fair value," rather than a "fair market value." The term "fair value" has a specific accounting meaning under Generally Accepted Accounting Principles (GAAP), which is generally quite similar to "fair market value." However, "fair value" may also have a specific, but somewhat different, meaning under "appraisal" provisions of state laws in the United States. When the phrase "fair value" derives from appraisal provisions of corporations laws adopted in US states, a dissenting minority shareholder may demand payment for its shares in an acquisition on the basis of a judicially-determined appraisal of "fair value," rather than the price offered by the acquirer in the merger. Caveat Emptor – "fair value" as determined by appraisal statutes under corporations laws in the United States is not precisely the same thing as "fair market value" in valuation terminology or "fair value" in accounting terminology. If one party in an arbitration is arguing "fair market value" while the other party is insisting on "fair value," the difference may be lie in, among other matters, the allocation of the burden of proof or the presence or absence of a discount for lack of marketability or a discount for lack of control (a minority discount). Many corporations laws and courts do not apply such discounts to the value of stock held by dissenting shareholders in "fair value" cases for "equitable reasons." *See* e.g., American Bar Association Model Business Corporations Act (1984), § 13.101(4) ("Fair value means the value of the corporation's shares determined . . . (iii) without discounting for lack of marketability or minority status.") These discounts are discussed in more detail *infra* in Ch. 8. *See also U.S. Inspect v. McGreevy*, 57 Va. Cir. 511, 525–528, 2000 Va. Cir. LEXIS 524 (November 27, 2000), and cases cited therein.
83. IVSC Business Valuation Guidance Note, *supra* n. 15 at ¶ 1.2. Even when "market value" is the accepted test, though, important differences in the application of that test between various bodies of law should be recognized. Briefly, "fair value" is employed in US financial reporting. "Fair Value" reflects market value and the assumptions of willing buyers and sellers (market participants). That approach contrasts with "investment value," which reflects value to a particular investor (buyer or seller). "Fair market value" is employed for US tax purposes. The FASB considers "fair value" and "fair market value" to be conceptually the same. However, the FASB also notes the large body of case law interpreting the "fair market value" standard in tax cases, and therefore has chosen to not simply adopt the tax concept into financial accounting. "Navigant Capital Advisors, LLC, Valuation Viewpoints: The Valuation Newsletter of Navigant Capital Advisors," at 2 (issue 1, 1st Quarter 2006).

value.[84] Similarly, arbitral panels often start from a foundation of fair market value. The ICSID arbitrators in *CMS v. Argentina* (involving a gas transportation company), for example, began their analysis by relying on the definition of fair market value offered by the ASA:

> the price, expressed in terms of cash equivalents, at which the property would change hands between a hypothetical willing and able buyer and a hypothetical willing and able seller, acting at arms length in an open and unrestricted market, when neither is under compulsion to buy or sell and when both have reasonable knowledge of the relevant facts.[85]

Market Value

Market Value is defined as the estimated amount for which a property should exchange on the date of valuation between a willing buyer and a willing seller in an arm's-length transaction after proper marketing, wherein the parties had each acted knowledgeably, prudently and without compulsion. Particularly for real estate valuations, a fundamental aspect of a market valuation is the principle of "highest and best use," defined as the most probable use of a property that is physically possible, appropriately justified, legally permissible, financially feasible, and which results in the highest value of the property being valued.

The International Valuation Standards Committee's guidelines, Concepts Fundamental to Generally Accepted Valuation Principles (GAVP), define "Market Value" along lines very similar to the definition found in the *CMS v. Argentina* award:

> [Market Value is the] estimated amount for which a property should exchange on the date of valuation between a willing buyer and a willing seller in an arm's-length transaction after proper marketing wherein the parties had each acted knowledgeably, prudently and without compulsion.[86]

---

84. See text *supra* associated with n. 175. *See* also, e.g., *CMS v. Argentina*, *supra* n. 7, *CME Stockholm* Partial Award, *supra* n. 42, at ¶¶ 618, 624, *CME Stockholm* Final Award, *supra* n. 42, at ¶¶ 490–493 and *Azurix v. Argentina*, *supra* n. 17. But also *see* the useful discussion of the difference between "fair market value" and "reparations" in Marboe, "Compensation and Damages in International Law – the Limits of 'Fair Market Value,'" 7 *Journal of World Investment & Trade* 723, 729–735 (2006).
85. *CMS v. Argentina*, *supra* n. 7, at ¶ 402 (describing the ASA definition as "internationally recognized"). *See also Azurix v. Argentina*, *supra* n. 17, at ¶ 424. The definition employed by the *CMS* and *Azurix* panels is found at International Glossary of Business Valuation Terms, *supra* n. 17.
86. IVSC Concepts Fundamental to Generally Accepted Valuation Principles (GAVP), *supra* n. 16, at ¶ 5.2, and IVS 2007, Standard 1, Market Value Basis of Valuation, *supra* n. 31, at ¶ 3.1. The operative phrases within this definition are considered in *id.*, at ¶ 3.2.

The US Internal Revenue Service (IRS) uses a substantially similar definition. As the IRS points out in its guidance on considerations to be taken into account when valuing shares of the capital stock of closely held corporations: "Court decisions frequently state in addition that the hypothetical buyer and seller are assumed to be able, as well as willing, to trade and to be well informed about the property and concerning the market for such property."[87]

Fair market value measures the value of the business between a willing and able hypothetical seller and a willing and able hypothetical buyer. At times, it may be necessary to determine the value to a particular investor, not a generalized hypothetical party. Valuation professionals employ the term "Investment Value" for such valuations, to distinguish that standard of value from fair market value. For example, management and advisers for a potential acquirer of a business may take into account the synergies available to the potential acquirer from the acquisition, synergies that may not be available to competing bidders. In those circumstances, the Investment Value of the business to the potential acquirer may be different (possibly higher) than the fair market value of the business to a hypothetical buyer.[88] Many court and arbitral awards use the term "fair market value" when in fact applying an Investment Value standard.

Another fundamental aspect of a market valuation is the principle of "highest and best use."[89] The IVSC defines that concept as follows: "The most probable use of a property which is physically possible, appropriately justified, legally permissible, financially feasible, and which results in the highest value of the property being valued."[90]

In light of this principle, valuation experts are not limited solely to the current use of the valued property. Instead, they are bound to consider feasible uses that increase value. One US court has noted, though, a reasonableness test serves to limit the principle of "highest and best use." "In determining its highest and best use, the trial referee must consider whether there was a reasonable probability that the subject property would be put to that use in the reasonably near future."[91] Accordingly, a valuation expert will consider not solely the current use of property in the valuation, but the feasible and lawful use, that results in the highest value for the property. That principle is subject, however, to a limiting condition; only if there is a reasonable probability that use will be employed in the reasonably near future. Similarly, use of the property must be "legally permissible." That limitation requires, for example, the valuation to consider the impact of restrictive covenants in shareholder agreements. The most obvious illustrations of the "highest and best use" principle lie in the valuation of real property; subject to zoning and

87. IRS Rev. Rul. 59-60, *supra* n. 5, at § 2.02.
88. Risius, *Business Valuation: A Primer for Legal Professionals*, *supra* n. 19, at 11–12.
89. IVSC Concepts Fundamental to Generally Accepted Valuation Principles (GAVP), *supra* n. 16, at ¶ 6.7 ("The concept of highest and best use is a fundamental and integral part of *Market Value* estimates.").
90. *Id.*, at ¶ 6.3.
91. *Northeast Connecticut Economic Alliance, Inc. v. ATC Partnership*, 256 Conn. 813, 829 (2001), quoting *Robinson v. Westport*, 222 Conn. 402, 406 (1992).

other permitting requirements, is the property at Tenth and G Streets, N.W. in downtown Washington, D.C. best valued for the existing liquor store or as available for redevelopment into a commercial office building? The principle is potentially also applicable, however, to other types of investments and property.

Not all legal compensation standards adopt the "highest and best use" standard, however. As the California appellate decision in *Redevelopment Agency of the City of San Diego v. Mesdaq*[92] illustrates, the owner of a business (the Gran Havana) located on condemned property is entitled by California statute to compensation for "loss of goodwill." However, the valuation "must provide a fair estimate of actual value and cannot be based on 'hypothetical' or speculative uses of a condemned business."[93] The appellate court in that dispute overturned the trial court's decision to accept evidence valuing the Gran Havana store as an "eating and drinking establishment," rather than the existing cigar store with limited food sales. That approach, held the appeals court:

> turned the principles of Section 1263.510 [the "lost goodwill" standard] – a desire to compensate a business owner for the unique attributes of a condemned business – on its head by valuing not the particular characteristics of Mesdaq's business, but those of a better, maximized business.[94]

The *Gran Havana* decision is a useful reminder that valuation takes its purpose from the particular legal framework, not strictly from business valuation principles.

> When determining the market value of an enterprise, the US Tax Court lists the following factors to be considered . . . :
>
> (a) The nature of the business and the history of the enterprise from its inception.
>
> (b) The economic outlook in general and the condition and outlook of the specific industry in particular.
>
> (c) The book value of the stock and the financial condition of the business.
>
> (d) The earning capacity of the company.
>
> (e) The dividend-paying capacity.
>
> (f) Whether or not the enterprise has goodwill or other intangible value.
>
> (g) Sales of the stock and the size of the block of stock to be valued.
>
> (h) The market value of stocks of corporations engaged in the same or similar lines of business having their stocks actively traded in a free and open market, either on an exchange or over-the-counter.
>
> [Rev. Rule 59–60, 1959-1 C.B. at 238–239.].[95]

92. *Redevelopment Agency of the City of San Diego v. Mesdaq*, 2007 WL 2460022 (Cal. App. 4 Dist., August 31, 2007).
93. *Id.*, at *9.
94. *Id.*, at *10.
95. *Estate of James Waldo Hendrickson v. Comm'r, supra* n. 41, at *45. The US Tax Court's list is "virtually identical" to the list found in the US Estate Tax Regulations at § 20-2031-2(f).

Arbitral tribunals applying public international law also often focus on fair market value. Crawford's Commentaries on the International Law Commission's 2001 Draft Articles on Responsibility of States for Internationally Wrongful Acts point out that "[c]ompensation reflecting the capital value of property taken or destroyed as a result of an internationally wrongful act is generally assessed on basis of the 'fair market value' of the property lost."[96] International arbitral tribunals regularly use fair market value as a touchstone to calculate compensation in a variety of causes of action. Thus, two prominent international lawyers described the approach of the parties and the arbitral panel toward an expropriation claim in the *Santa Elena* ICSID case as follows:[97]

> Having determined that international law governed the dispute, the Tribunal turned to the issue of valuation. While the parties were basically in agreement that "full compensation" was to be paid and should be based on the "fair market value" of the property according to its "highest and best use," they did not agree on the application of that principle to the facts in the case at hand.

Equally, the ICSID tribunal in the recent *CMS v. Argentina* award concluded that the proper approach to calculating compensation for damages caused by breach of Argentina's "fair and equitable treatment" and "umbrella" obligations under the US – Republic of Argentina bilateral investment treaty, was "by resorting to the standard of 'fair market value.'"[98] In the *Azurix v. Argentina* award, the ICSID tribunal concluded that compensation with respect to causes of action alleging breaches of the "fair and equitable," "full protection and security" and "arbitrary measures" standards in the US – Argentina BIT would be determined on the basis of fair market value.[99] So too, the tribunal in *Enron v. Argentina* determined

---

96. Crawford, *The International Law Commission's Articles on State Responsibility: Introduction, Text and Commentaries* (2002) (hereinafter "Commentaries") at 255 (¶ 22), citing to several Iran-US Claims Tribunal awards, the World Bank Guidelines on the Treatment of Foreign Direct Investment (the World Bank's legal framework for the treatment of foreign investment) and the Energy Charter Treaty.
97. Brower & Wong, *General Valuation Principles: The Case of Santa Elena*, 747, 760, in Weiler, *supra* n. 53.
98. *CMS v. Argentina*, *supra* n. 17, at ¶¶ 410–411.
99. *Azurix v. Argentina*, *supra* n. 17, ¶ 424. The *Azurix* panel awarded compensation based upon the "fair market value" of the purchase price for the concession (USD 60 million) rather than the actual sum expended by Azurix to acquire the concession (USD 438.55 million). *Id.*, at ¶¶ 425–430. *See* generally cases and other sources cited in Marboe, *Compensation and Damages in International Law – The Limits of "Fair Market Value," supra* n. 84, at 729–732. Not all tribunals considering a cause of action for breach of the "fair and equitable" standard in international investment law have employed a market value test. In the NAFTA cases of *S.D. Meyer, Pope & Talbot* and *Feldman,* the arbitrators "exercised considerable discretion in fashioning what they believed to be reasonable approaches to damages consistent with the requirement of NAFTA." *Marvin Roy Feldman Karpa v. United Mexican States*, ICSID Case No. ARB/CAF/99/1, Award 6 December 2002, at ¶ 197. *See also LG&E v. Argentina Final Award, supra* n. 7, discussed *infra* at text associated with n. 144 et seq.

damages for breach of a "fair and equitable" claim and an "umbrella clause" by resorting to fair market value.[100]

The latest *Vivendi* award, however, illustrates that arbitrators occasionally use the term fair market value in a manner that would not be recognized by valuation professionals. There, the tribunal ruled that "it is appropriate to assess compensation, *at least in part*, based on the fair market value of the concession."[101] The panel noted, though, that "[a]t international law, depending on the circumstances arising in a particular case, there are a number of ways of approximating fair market value."[102] After rejecting a DCF "lost profits" valuation for lack of certainty, the tribunal settled on the wasted investments by Vivendi in the Argentine water company as the measure of loss. Historical investment costs, however, are clearly not a measure of the current market value of an asset – the price a willing buyer would pay a willing seller in an arm's length transaction on the valuation date. The *Vivendi 2007* tribunal, therefore, employed a non-market measure of compensation despite holding that fair market value was the proper compensation standard.[103]

Readers should note that the "market value" compensation principle, contains an implicit assumption about the treatment of Black Swan "rare events" like a future catastrophic event (such as macroeconomic collapse in the host State or a tsunami), or an extraordinarily positive event (such as a government act creating for the investment a de facto monopoly position in a large protected market). As discussed previously, future "rare events" are incorporated into a market valuation only insofar as the market price at the valuation date (rightly or wrongly) considers the prospects for the future rare event.[104]

To understand this conceptual underpinning to fair market value, let us consider the situation of a macro-economic crisis like the Asian financial crisis of the late 1990s. Assume that a hypothetical 1995 upstream petroleum investment in Southeast Asia has 999 chances in one hundred of making USD 1 million in 1997 and a one in a thousand chance of losing USD 10 billion (the invested capital) in 1997.[105] The probability (i.e., frequency) of the USD 1 million profit is 999/1,000 and the investor's expectation of that profit is USD 999,000 (USD 1 million times 999/1,000). In contrast, the probability of the USD 10 billion loss is one in a thousand, but the expectation of loss is surprisingly larger than the same investor's

---

100. *Enron v. Argentina*, *supra* n. 43, at ¶¶ 359–363, 380.
101. *Vivendi 2007*, *supra* n. 72, at ¶ 8.2.11 (footnote omitted). The reference to "at least in part" was, according to the panel, related to Vivendi's need to fund the investment's on-going costs after expropriation. *Id.*, at n. 409.
102. *Id.*, at ¶ 8.3.3.
103. *See* Carroll, *Through the Looking-Glass: And What Alice Found There*, Ch. VI at 364 (M.F. Mansfield & A. Wessels 1899).
104. *See* generally Taleb, *Fooled by Randomness* (2nd edn Random House Trade Paperback Edition 2005). Taleb argues that we systematically underestimate the potential for rare events in our personal, business and political lives. *See also* Taleb, *Black Swan*, *supra* n. 60, at 100 et seq.
105. This example is based upon a similar "gambling" example in Taleb, *Fooled by Randomness*, *supra* n. 104, at 98–99.

expectation of profit for the venture – USD 1 million (USD 10 billion times 1/1,000). That result derives from a combination of the very small size of the extremely likely profit compared with the extremely large size of the very unlikely catastrophic event, as well as the relative probabilities of the two scenarios.

In 1995, though, participants in petroleum projects in Southeast Asia (sponsors, lenders, host States, international development banks and Western export credit agencies alike) essentially disregarded the potential for a macroeconomic crisis. Thus, their market value for petroleum projects at that time would have ignored the prospects for such a catastrophic event.[106] Therefore, the market value of our hypothetical project in 1995 would not have mirrored these profit and loss expectations. Of course, by December 1997, the perception by market participants was dramatically different in the wake of the massive currency depreciations and growth reversals in the region, and the corresponding serious declines in petroleum prices. A market valuation of the same petroleum project in December 1997 would therefore be noticeably lower, because the "rare event" had in fact crystallized.

Black Swans, it should be recalled, need not always be of the negative variety; they can be positive as well. For instance, Taleb notes in his book *The Black Swan* that Viagra, a notable commercial success, was meant to be a hypertension drug.[107] The rarity of such events does not mean that their impact should be disregarded; from an arbitrator's perspective, the issue is whether both the probability and the potential impact of Black Swan events have been taken into consideration in the valuation. "Although unpredictable large deviations are rare, they cannot be dismissed as outliers because, cumulatively, their impact is so dramatic."[108]

Arbitrators may wish to take this point into account when, for example, considering the proper discount rate for a DCF calculation.[109]

Why then do courts, tribunals and commentators adopt the market value principle as a proper legal basis for computing compensation? A public policy choice is at work here. Recall the circumstances that give rise to the claim by an investor in the first place. The enterprise in question has been injured; the opposing party is the party whose conduct gave rise to the injury (whether lawfully, in the case of a lawful expropriation, or unlawfully in the case of a breach of law or contract). Thus, as between the injured party and the party whose actions caused

106. We know this because the average rates charged by international lenders to borrowers in that region during the relevant period clearly did not reflect any expectation of upheaval. For example, the average spread over 3-month LIBOR for international project finance borrowings (among the riskiest of transactions) in emerging Asia/Pacific countries in 1995 was only 119.8 basis points (1.198%), clearly reflecting that the international financial community did not anticipate the catastrophic Asian financial crisis that commenced in June 1997. *See* Jorge and Gondanecz, the term structure of credit spreads in project finance, Revised Draft: November 2005, at Table A1, 48, available at <www.fmpm.ch/docs/9th/papers_2006_web/9175.doc>. As Taleb argues, we underestimate the potential for catastrophic events. *See* text associated with n. 62 *supra*. Said another way, we are a surprisingly optimistic species.

107. *See also* Taleb's brief account of a biotech company and other illustrations at Taleb, *The Black Swan*, *supra* n. 60, at 170, 206–208.

108. *Id.*, at 236.

109. *See* Ch. 4.I *infra*.

the injury, legal systems often choose as a public policy matter not to allocate to the injured party any greater prospect for the future rare event than the market attributed to that future event on the valuation date.

As we discuss in more detail below, legal systems also incorporate other compensation principles that may limit or enhance the amount of compensation (such as taking events subsequent to the date of injury into their computations or controlling for mis-valuations by applying principles of unjust enrichment and other equitable considerations). Often those adjustment principles are in practice employed by an arbitral tribunal to take into account the consequences of the future rare event.

The market value principle can itself be employed as well on occasion to calculate a reduced amount, not just a high amount. For example, in *Azurix v. Argentina*,[110] the investor invested capital of at least USD 438.55 million in 1999 to obtain a water concession in Argentina (the "Canon" payment to the Argentine authorities for the concession). Based on inter alia a comparison with other bids in the 1999 auction, the tribunal determined that Azurix had dramatically overpaid. The tribunal further concluded that the value to a well-informed investor of that project in early 2002 would have been USD 60 million (i.e., that the market value of the investment, from the perspective of a reasonable third party, would not have exceeded USD 60 million). Therefore, the tribunal rejected the actual 1999 invested capital (the "Canon" payment amount of USD 438.55 million) in favor of its 2002 market value amount of USD 60 million to calculate the loss to the investor resulting from Argentina's breach of international investment law.

To the opposite effect, the ICSID tribunals in *ADC v. Hungary*[111] and *Siemens v. Argentina*[112] both departed from the position that the date of injury is the valuation date; in each case, to increase the compensation amount in recognition of the host State's unlawful treatment of the investment.

One useful way to think about why Market-Based "comparables" analyses may produce valuation results different from an Income-Based DCF projection is to consider the difference in their underlying assumptions about the reliability of the markets. In a comparables analysis involving multiple transactions (for example, stock prices for public companies), the valuation assumes that the markets are correct on average, even if they may be wrong about individual stocks or transactions. By contrast, DCF projections "assume that markets make mistakes, that they correct these mistakes over time, and that these mistakes can often occur across entire sectors or even the entire market."[113] The spectacular rise and equally spectacular fall of NASDAQ stock prices in the late 1990s and early 2000s perfectly illustrates why comparables valuations can easily differ from DCF computations.

---

110. *Azurix v. Argentina*, *supra* n. 17, at ¶¶ 414, 419–426.
111. *ADC Affiliate Limited and ADC & ADMC Management Limited*, ICSID Case No. ARB/03/16 Award, October 2, 2006 (hereinafter, "*ADC v. Hungary*"), at ¶¶ 496–499.
112. *Siemens A.G. v. The Argentine Republic*, Award, January 17, 2007, ICSID Case No. ARB/02/8, at ¶¶ 386–389 (hereinafter, "*Siemens v. Argentina*").
113. *Id.*, at 22.

VI CONTRACT-BASED DAMAGES

"Market Value" is not, of course, the only business valuation standard available to arbitrators, even if it is the dominant valuation standard. If the business being valued is a "single asset" company, such as a sole power plant, then arbitrators may be faced with two conceptually different ways of looking at compensation for lost value; either the impact on fair market value of the enterprise or the impact on the value of contractual performance. A power project, for example, may involve a single crucial power purchase agreement that is expected to produce the revenue stream for the entire company. If the offtaker defaults under that power purchase agreement, and there is no revenue to pay the project finance indebtedness or recover equity investments, then the entire company fails.[114] Calculations based on market value and on performance of the power purchase agreement will not necessarily each achieve the same number in such circumstances; a breach of contract measure of damages will recover the "benefit of the bargain" under the power purchase agreement regardless of how the effect of the breach alters the market value of the company. "There is no basis to assume that the value of contractual performance in accordance with the contract's terms will be equal to the fair market value of the contract – indeed it may be higher or lower."[115]

Thus, in addition to market value measures of compensation, it is useful to identify common approaches to measures of damages for breach of contract or a commercial tort (delict).[116] In the rare case, a court may order disgorgement of profits by a wrongdoer to prevent that party from benefiting from misconduct regardless of the quantum of loss suffered by the injured party – a restitutionary measure of damage. Restitution "has as its objective not the enforcement of contracts through the protection of a party's expectation or reliance interests but the prevention of unjust enrichment through the protection of his restitution interest."[117] However, the normal function of business damages is compensatory; to compensate the injured party for loss caused by the other party's breach of duty. "The initial assumption is that the injured party is entitled to full compensation for his actual loss."[118]

114. Such power purchase agreements were central to the claims in *Patuha*, *Himpurna*, *Hubco v. Pakistan*, *Tanzania Electric Supply Company, Limited v. Independent Power Tanzania Limited*, ICSID Case No. ARB/98/8, Final Award (June 22, 2001), and *Karaha Bodas*, for example.

115. Smutny, *Principles Relating to Compensation in the Investment Treaty Context*, paper delivered at the Investment Treaty Arbitration Workshop at the International Bar Association Annual Conference, Chicago, September 19, 2006, at 210 (hereinafter, "Smutny").

116. *See*, e.g., Restatement (Second) of Contracts, § 347 (expectancy interest), § 349 (reliance interest) and § 371 (restitution) (1981), 3 Farnsworth, Contracts, § 12.1 at 149–150 (reliance interest) and 150–151 (restitution) (2nd edn 1990), Cosenza, *Co-Invest at Your Own Risk: An Exploration of Potential Remedial Theories for Breaches of Rights of First Refusal in the Venture Capital Context*, 55 Am. U. L. Rev. 87, 112–115 (2005).

117. Restatement (Second) of Contracts, *supra* n. 116, at Ch. 16, Topic 4, Introductory Note.

118. *Id.*, at Ch. 16, Topic 2, Introductory Note.

For this compensatory purpose, courts in breach of contract cases will commonly award an amount that will restore the injured party to the economic position he expected from performance of the contract. This approach is known as the "expectation measure" of damages (or, the "benefit-of-the-bargain" measure).[119] If it is not feasible to measure this expectancy interest, or the court determines that it is not desirable to employ an expectancy measure, then the court may award breach of contract damages to restore the injured party to the economic position he had occupied at the time the contract was entered into by the parties; the "reliance interest" measure of damages.[120]

Contract Measures of Damages

Courts will often measure damages in a breach of contract case on the basis of the principle of restitution, compensation of the reliance interest or compensation of the expectancy interest.

Restitution has, as its objective, the prevention of unjust enrichment.

Damages based upon the reliance interest seek to restore the injured party to the economic position he would have occupied at the time the contract was entered into by the parties.

Damages based upon the expectancy interest seek to restore the injured party to the economic position he expected from performance of the contract – the "benefit of the bargain."

Business losses may be caused by tortious conduct such as a misrepresentation or tortious interference with contract, as contrasted with breach of a contractual duty. In such circumstances, the measure of compensation is normally designed to place the injured party in the position he would have occupied if the tort had not occurred. Accordingly, the court may order recovery of direct losses (such as the amount expended in mitigation) and consequential damages (such as lost profits).

Where the object of the injurious conduct involves a contract, but the misconduct involves either breach of that contract or a business tort, then contract-based and tort-based measures of quantum may produce significantly different results depending on whether the contract would have been a good bargain or a bad bargain for the injured party. To illustrate, let us look at an example. Assume that a turbine dealer agrees to sell to an equipment broker a refurbished used Rolls Royce power turbine for USD 100 million. The selling dealer informs the equipment broker that the turbine to be refurbished will be a genuine Rolls Royce turbine, manufactured at Rolls Royce's original manufacturing facility in accordance with Rolls Royce's exceptionally high standard of quality. Refurbishment

119. *Id.*, at § 347.
120. *Id.*, at § 349.

will take about one year. Once the refurbished turbine is delivered, the broker reasonably expects to be able to resell the turbine to an electricity utility for USD 150 million, because the market for turbines is growing tighter with manufacturing capacity constraints limiting the number of new turbines to be produced for an extended period – the contract is thus a good bargain for the equipment broker but by no means unsatisfactory for the turbine dealer.

At the time the turbine is to be delivered, it develops that the turbine broker had misrepresented the turbine – in fact, it is a version of the Rolls Royce power turbine manufactured under license in the Grand Duchy of Fenwick with far fewer quality controls than true RR turbines. The turbine actually delivered by the turbine dealer is therefore only worth USD 50 million. The turbine manufacturer's conduct is both a breach of the description of the turbine in the contract (a breach of contract) and a misrepresentation (a business tort).

In these circumstances, the equipment broker's breach of contract damages will be USD 100 million – it was entitled (had an expectancy interest) to an item worth USD 150 million but the item the equipment broker received was only worth USD 50 million . If, instead, the equipment broker sought recovery for tortious misrepresentation, it would only be entitled to be put back in the same position as if the tort (the misrepresentation) had not occurred. If the turbine dealer had correctly represented the turbine as a licensed turbine, then the equipment broker would not have entered into the contract at all. Accordingly, the equipment broker would be entitled to recover its USD 100 million in tort.

As that example makes clear, in the case of a good bargain a buyer may recover larger damages under a contract measure than a tort measure. But what if the contract was a bad bargain? In that case, a tort measure of damages may produce a better result for the equipment broker than breach of contract damages. If the equipment broker had overpaid for the refurbished turbine, say USD 250 million, then its contract-based damages would still be USD 150 million (giving the equipment broker the amount it expected to obtain). Damages in tort, though, would be USD 200 million (recovery of the money paid, USD 250 million, minus the value of the turbine actually received, USD 50 million). That tort-based recovery would put the equipment broker back in the position as if the correct representation had been made – no contract at all.

Of course, as we discuss in Chapter 2.XI below, the equipment broker's efforts to recover either contract-based or tort-based damages would still be subject to inter alia evidentiary issues (is the evidence of lost profits reasonably certain?), causation, foreseeability and the allocation of the burden of proof.

As is apparent, compensating an injured business or investor based on changes in market value caused by the other party's conduct awards to the injured party its expectancy interest – compensation is calculated as if the investment had been made but the injurious conduct had never occurred. In contrast, awarding to an injured investor recovery of its wasted investment ("sunk investment costs") instead protects the investor's reliance interest – compensation is calculated to put the investor back in the position as if the investment had never been made.

From a valuation analyst's perspective, contract-based damages are often calculated in one of three different ways: a before-and-after method, a yardstick method and a market-model method.[121] If the "before-and-after" method is employed, the valuer will make assessments about what would have happened during the damages period, calculated on the basis of what the business achieved before and after the injury event.[122] If, instead, the "yardstick" method is used, then the valuer will seek to calculate the results the business would have achieved based on comparable company or industry results. The importance of comparability is, of course, obvious. Finally, the "market-method" approach parallels the type of detailed projections used in DCF calculations; "the damages expert literally starts from the ground up, building a spreadsheet with assumptions about sources of revenues and expenses.... In practice, the methods will typically overlap."[123]

For each method, the duration of the damages period will be crucial. From one valuation professional's perspective:

> The end is when the company returns to profitability or level of cash flow that it would have been at had the damaging act not occurred. As you can imagine, determining the period end is seldom straightforward. Here, too, you need to assess factors such as the industry, competition, the economy, and so forth, as well as the company's prior track record, to determine when the damages "end." It may be unrealistic to carry the losses out into perpetuity, unless a business or portion of a business is unrecoverable.[124]

And, like any valuation involving forward-looking compensation, the gross amounts must be discounted back to a present value at an often contentious discount rate.

In US courts, the compensation standard for breach of contract would typically be "lost net profits." "[T]his means the contract price less cost of performance, or cost of completion, or, as it is sometimes put, 'expenses saved' as a result of plaintiff's being excused from performance by the other party's breach."[125] There are significant differences between this test and a fair market value test; most importantly, there is no reduction or discount for the risk that the contract may not be performed. A "benefit of the bargain" compensation standard will not normally discount future payments for the risk of non-performance; the defaulting party is liable to compensate fully for its default. Whether by reason of credit risk, political risk, commercial performance risk, market developments or force

---

121. Fannon, "Lost Profits Damages: A Natural Extension of Business Valuation Skills, The CPA Expert" (Spring 2001), available at <http://bvfls.aicpa.org/Resources>.
122. Or perhaps using just the "before" side if the harm precludes there bring an "after," or conversely, just the "after" side in cases (such as a "first to market" argument) where there is no "before."
123. *Id.*
124. *Id.*
125. Dunn, *Recovery of Damages for Lost Profits* (6th edn 1998), § 6.1 at 430–431. Both measures of compensation are, of course, subject to the duty to take reasonable steps in mitigation and similar limits.

majeure, though, a fair market value standard takes account of the market's perception of the likelihood of non-performance in determining compensation. Similarly, the "breach of contract" standard does not recognize an adjustment if performance under the contract would have created value beyond the four corners of the contract itself.

Duration is another issue as to which approaches may differ. "Ordinarily, damages are recoverable for the term of the contract." However, when claimants seek lost profits for breach of a long-term contract, US courts have been reluctant automatically to award damages for the full term of the contract without subjecting the issue of duration to a reasonableness test:

> [T]he judgment could be immense. The courts have generally recoiled from such awards in the few instances in which the question has been presented. The rule seems to be that lost profits can be recovered for the period of time they can be projected with reasonable certainty, although this is rarely articulated. Some projections reach forward many years and some cases award damages for the entire term of the contract however. . . . Most courts considering a claim of lost profits damages arising from a long-term contract have reduced the term for which damages may be recovered.[126]

Indeed, if the injury in question has eliminated the business entirely, then US courts may then look at a market value standard of damages rather than a lost profits computation:

> [I]f a business has not been just injured, but has been destroyed, almost all of the few cases in point hold that lost profits damages are not recoverable at all. The measure of damages is said to be the market value of the business on the date of destruction.[127]

VII DIMINUTION OF VALUE AND BUSINESS INTERRUPTION DAMAGES

If the legal compensation standard employed by arbitrators for injury to a business is not based on a complete loss of market value, common valuation alternatives include "sunk investment" amounts and "business interruption" (BI) amounts. These valuation approaches proceed from very different starting points. The "sunk investments" approach, also referred to as "wasted investments," is a measure of the reliance interest; it seeks to place the injured party in the same position as if the investment had never been made – recovery of invested sums plus a reasonable rate of return until the date of recovery. The "sunk investments" approach has no relation at all to market value – the sales amount between a willing seller and a

126. *Id.*, §§ 6.18–6.19, at 487–488. But *see* "Matter of Central Ice Cream Co.," 836 F.2d 1068 (7th Cir. 1987), in which a jury awarded plaintiffs lost profits for a twenty-year period.
127. *Id.*, § 6.24, at 500.

willing buyer. The "business interruption" approach, however, is related to current commercial values – it seeks to compensate the injured party for the diminution in value of the enterprise (lost net revenues or lost profits, depending on whether the injured party is the enterprise or its investors) for the fixed period of time necessary to allow the business to restore itself.

The impact of an injury on a business, of course, does not always result in a cessation of that business or the investor's ownership interest in the business. Instead, the business or the owner's interest may be reduced in value by the injury. Arbitrators may see compensation requests in a "diminution of value" situation based on a number of different approaches. If the event giving rise to the injury involves breach of a particular contract, then the company (or an investor on its behalf, in investment treaty cases) may present a traditional "breach of contract/lost profit" computation.[128] Two of the recent Argentine cases illustrate the strengths and weaknesses of other approaches, however; *CMS* employed a comparison of diminution in the market value of the injured company based on the difference between actual and hypothetical (but for) valuations,[129] and *LG&E* employed a "business interruption" model.[130] The two approaches, as explained below, differ in how they address the possibility that the reduction in the company's value is not permanent.

Business Interruption

A business interruption valuation seeks to calculate the amount of the temporary loss resulting from interruption of or interference with the injured business – the normal outcome is compared with the actual outcome for the affected period of time.

A "business interruption" (BI) valuation seeks to calculate the amount of the loss resulting from interrupting of or interference with the affected business: "The normal outcome is compared with the actual outcome."[131] That simple formula glosses over a number of crucial decisions that arbitrators must make when confronted with a BI claim. BI claims are regularly made under specific business interruption extensions to commercial insurance policies, and therefore the insurance community is a valuable source of information for arbitration practitioners even if the valuation dispute does not arise under a BI insurance policy. Also, as noted previously, the United Nations Compensation Commission regularly employed a business interruption methodology to calculate compensation for businesses injured by the 1990 Iraqi invasion of Kuwait. Similarly, the ICSID

128. *See* Ch. 2.VI *supra*.

129. *See CMS v. Argentina*, *supra* n. 7, at ¶¶ 422, 434. *See* generally Risius, *Business Valuation: A Primer for Legal Professionals*, *supra* n. 19, at 186–187.

130. *See LG&E v. Argentina Final Award*, *supra* n. 7.

131. Senogles, *Business interruption claims*, *supra* n. 54, at 14.

tribunal in *LG&E v. Argentina* relied upon a business interruption approach to determine compensation for the impact of Argentine unlawful regulatory conduct on LG&E's investment in three local, gas distributing companies in Argentina: *Distribuidora de Gas del Centro, Distribuidora de Gas Cuyana S.A. and Gas Natural BAN S.A.*

Several issues reoccur in any BI valuation. First, the beginning and ending dates for the valuation period. The process of identifying the beginning date for the injury assessment is similar for most methodologies, whether employing Income, Market or Asset-Based valuation approaches. However, a BI valuation must also determine the end date for valuation period – when was normalcy restored?[132]

In the insurance market, two different approaches towards BI coverage are often found; in US markets, the assessment is made until the productive capacity is restored while European insurers more commonly issue BI cover for a specified time period that may include time to rebuild sales towards pre-injury levels, not just restoring damaged productive capacity.

> For instance, in the insurance industry business interruption policy coverage is not homogenous internationally.
> - Typical US policies provide for coverage only until productive capacity is restored and covers the "Actual Loss Sustained" and thus the insured is no better off. Such US policies are often known as Gross Earnings Form (or "production form").
> - Typical European policies provide for cover within a stated indemnity period and can include a period to rebuild sales to pre-event levels. Such European policies are often known as Gross Profit Form (or "sales form").
>
> Generally in most contexts (not specifically insurance) "loss of profit" measures are based on loss of "gross" (i.e., "direct" or "variable") profits. Each measure of profit for an insured will depend on policy wording. However, for the court or the tribunal, the appropriate measure of profit lost will depend on circumstances and case facts.[133]

That same issue – when does the damage period end – will also arise in arbitration.[134] If arbitrators follow the approach incorporated into a European Gross Profit Form from the insurance industry, then the amount of compensation is likely to the larger. This difference is an important point for arbitrators to consider, and another opportunity for an apples-to-oranges miscomparison. If the dispute warrants, an arbitrator may request experts to present valuations based on both scenarios, rebuilding lost productive capacity to normal levels and rebuilding sales to normal levels.

132. "[N]ot heroics, but healing; not nostrums, but normalcy; not revolution, but restoration; not agitation, but adjustment; not surgery, but serenity; not the dramatic, but the dispassionate; not experiment, but equipoise." US President W.G. Harding, speech at Boston, Massachusetts, May 14, 1920. "Our supreme task is the resumption of our onward, normal way.... We must strive to normalcy to reach stability." Harding, Inaugural Address, Washington, D.C., March 4, 1921.

133. Senogles, *Business interruption claims*, *supra* n. 54, at 14–15.

134. *See*, e.g., *LG&E v. Argentina Final Award*, *supra* n. 7, at ¶¶ 68, 99, 101 (dividends declared prior to the end date but not paid until after the end date).

The concept of normalbusiness operations is of course another crucial determinant in a BI valuation. "[T]he investigative accountant's task is to define what is 'normal' – what would have happened in the absence of the loss event – and then compare the result with what should be taken as representing the fair actual result."[135]

Injury events, of course, arise at particular moments in a business' business or production cycle and in an economy's business cycle. BI valuations must take care to not over or under-emphasize the impact of the injury event by failing to pay attention to those issues. Moreover, if the company in question sells particular products (such as trucks or computers), then it will be important to assess if the company can draw on inventory to maintain supply. And, if so, how should inventory replenishment be addressed for compensation purposes.[136] In contrast, some businesses cannot maintain inventory – the most obvious example is an electricity project, since storing large quantities of electricity is beyond our current technology. In addition to drawing down on inventory, some companies may operate multiple production facilities or source products and services from other locations. Such shifts may serve to mitigate BI losses. The follow-on cost impact of such shifts is also part of the valuation, however.[137]

Yet another important element in a BI valuation is the treatment of a company's fixed costs. Most commonly, a business interruption valuation will focus on lost profits – loss of affected income minus the expenses that would have been (but were not) incurred to produce the lost income. That formula would ordinarily exclude fixed costs (and fixed income items like a "take-or-pay" obligation). In some circumstances, however, such as an extended business interruption period, costs that are treated as "fixed" for accounting purposes should be incorporated into the valuation. If the cause of the fixed cost (or the cause of the failure to incur the cost) is sufficiently related to the injury event, then those fixed costs are properly considered in the valuation.

> In the most general terms, loss of profit is typically taken to mean the loss of all affected income less all affected expenses. By definition, this rules out line-items that are fixed (whether fixed income or fixed costs).
>
> As one may expect this is not an absolute rule; for instance, dependant on the circumstances and (particularly) the length of period of loss, items of accounting expense commonly regarded as fixed should be brought into the analysis as having a variable element. Sometimes included in such analysis is fixed asset depreciation (given the relevant legal fact pattern and accounting circumstances). For example, this was considered in depth by the UNCC given certain circumstances in large scale petrochemical losses resulting from lengthy plant shutdowns:
>
> For a full assessment therefore reductions in so-called fixed costs (or even, reductions that it is reasonable to have expected given the circumstances)

---

135. Senogles, *Business interruption claims*, *supra* n. 54, at 17.
136. *Id.*, at 16.
137. *Id.*, at 10–11.

> should also be reviewed in case the cause of this reduction... was also sufficiently proximate to the loss event. In such a case, the reduction in these "semi-fixed" costs should be brought into the analysis by giving credit.[138]

The *CMS v. Argentina* case is an example of the first approach, comparing the estimated market value in the actual circumstances (the "pesification scenario") with a value premised on a hypothetical scenario (the "non-pesification scenario") in which Argentina did not impose its regulatory measures reducing TGN's value.[139] The difference between the two scenarios was, for the *CMS* tribunal, the amount of the damage caused by the Argentine regulatory measures. According to the *CMS* award, the overall diminution in value was quite severe – implicitly, about 97% on the DCF numbers employed by the tribunal.

The *CMS* award therefore placed upon Argentina the risk that future performance by TGN would have been better than its performance as projected in the two DCF scenarios. However, the tribunal also calculated the remaining market value of CMS's ownership interest in TGN at USD 2,148,100 , and required CMS to offer this interest to Argentina at a purchase price equal to this amount.[140] If Argentina purchased the CMS ownership interest in TGN at the price fixed by the tribunal, Argentina would hedge against this risk by itself as owner benefiting from the increased value. CMS would only benefit from this appreciation in value if Argentina chose not to exercise its option to purchase the CMS ownership interest. If, on the other hand, the two DCF scenarios relied upon by the ICSID tribunal underestimated the diminution in TGN's value, CMS would bear that risk in all cases, because the compensation award would be in final settlement of the claims by CMS.

Clearly, "causation" is an important issue in the willingness of an arbitral panel to rely on this two-scenario market value calculation. The valuation in *CMS* assumed that the difference between the pesification scenario and the non-pesification scenario was solely attributable to Argentina's regulatory measures. The *CMS* tribunal considered Argentina's arguments that the diminution in value was wholly or partly attributable either to the Argentina macroeconomic crisis[141] or to management decisions such as the amount of foreign currency debt incurred by TGN.[142] With respect to the general macroeconomic crisis, the tribunal stated that it took account of that factor in its damages computation and, with respect to the amount of foreign currency debt, the tribunal rejected the Argentine position. In addition to issues of "causation," the *CMS* two-scenario approach shared the attributes of any "market value" valuation, whether Income-Based, Market-Based or Asset-Based. Thus, the *CMS* tribunal considered, but also

138. *Id.*, at 15–16.
139. *CMS v. Argentina*, *supra* n. 7, at ¶ 434 et seq.
140. *Id.*, at ¶ 469.
141. *Id.*, at ¶¶ 248–251.
142. *Id.*, at ¶¶ 424–429.

rejected, the assertion that the pesification and non-pesification scenarios were "too speculative" to support compensations.[143]

The damages ruling in the *LG&E v. Argentina Final Award* departed from this two-scenario, market-value approach, for exactly those reasons. In that case, the injured gas companies (Cuyana, Centro and GasBan) continued to operate and pay dividends even after implementation of the Argentine regulatory measures. Also, LG&E retained its ownership interest in the companies. The *LG&E* tribunal rejected a market value approach on grounds of causation. The tribunal asked, "The question is one of '*causation*': what did the investor lose by reason of the unlawful acts?"[144] LG&E argued that the Argentine regulatory measures resulted in the destruction of 93% of the value of the companies between August 2000 and October 2002. However, the tribunal found that the value of LG&E's investment had "rebounded" since the economic crisis and that the effect of the measures on the value of the claimants' shares had not been permanent.[145] The tribunal therefore rejected loss in capital value (which it equated with loss in market value) as the basis for compensation.[146] Instead, the *LG&E* arbitrators ruled that the proper measure of damages was the reduction in dividends paid to LG&E resulting from a reduction in the companies' revenues. For the panel, the damages in the case were the amount of dividends LG&E would have received *but for* the adoption of the Argentine regulatory measures, minus dividends actually received. The tribunal limited the computation to the period from August 2000 through February 2005, holding that subsequent periods were beyond the evidence submitted in the proceedings[147] or, as discussed below, "speculative" lost future profits.[148]

The *LG&E* tribunal also rejected, in a conclusory fashion, Argentina's argument that the macroeconomic crisis was responsible in whole or in part for the reduction of dividends:

> Argentina argues that the loss in value of Claimants' investments was due to the economic collapse that affected all assets in the country and not to the alleged breaches of the tariff regime. In the Tribunal's view, it appears evident that the value of assets such as those owned by LG&E would have been negatively impacted by the economic situation. However, the Tribunal considers that the loss incurred by Claimants is the dividends they could have earned had the tariff regime not been abrogated. Respondent's conduct is the proximate cause of this loss.[149]

The *LG&E* tribunal set boundaries on the time period for which damages would be granted (August 2000 through February 2005, with an exclusion for a "state of

143. *Id.*, at ¶¶ 416, 420.
144. *LG&E v. Argentina Final Award*, *supra* n. 7, at ¶ 45.
145. *Id.*
146. *Id.*
147. *Id.*, at ¶¶ 94–95.
148. *Id.*, at ¶¶ 51, 88–91.
149. *Id.*, at ¶ 50.

necessity'' between December 2001 and late April 2003).[150] The panel decided that the issue of compensation for lost dividends after February 2005, including lost future dividends, was ''premature.'' If a diminution in value caused by the breaching party's conduct will not be permanent then, as the UNCC Governing Council pointed out in its Decision 9, ''it can be expected that [the affected business] could have been rebuilt and resumed. The method of a valuation should therefore be the one that focuses on part performance rather than on forecasts and projections into the future.''[151] Because the *LG&E* tribunal declined to consider lost profits after February 2005, the award could treat the damages computation as a form of ''business interruption'' valuation. This methodology was the manner in which the UNCC approached compensating companies for the impact of the Iraqi invasion of Kuwait. The *LG&E* award consequently followed the UNCC in applying a ''business interruption'' methodology, relying on past dividend performance up to the end of the valuation period rather than income-based changes in the three affected companies' market values.[152]

This approach is obviously founded upon the tribunal's core conclusion that the companies' losses were not permanent. That holding is open to question, since the Final Award itself noted that Argentina's regulatory measures were continuing.[153] Further, there was no indication that Argentina was willing to withdraw the offending measures.[154]

Before turning to criticisms of the market value premise, it is important to note that the definition of the enterprise being valued is a crucial, but occasionally overlooked factor. There are times when divisions within a legal entity are being valued, not the entire legal entity. In such circumstances, it will be essential for the valuation to properly isolate and (if necessary) adjust the links between that division and the remainder of the entity properly to calculate a stand-alone market value. By way of example, in *Enron v. Argentina*,[155] the Argentine pesification measures undermined the economic health of the gas transportation operations of TGN, the affected company. However, TGN also owned an LNG facility, which produced LNG for export. That latter line of business benefited from the pesification measures.

The tribunal was faced with the question of whether to net the detriments and benefits to TGN of Argentina's breach of the fair and equitable treatment provision of the US-Argentina BIT. Or, the tribunal could treat the gas

150. *Id.*, at ¶¶ 59–61.
151. UNCC Decision 9, *supra* n. 151.
152. Perhaps not surprisingly, the tribunal-appointed valuation expert was Geoffrey Senogles of LBC International Investigative Accounting. *LG&E v. Argentina Final Award*, *supra* n. 7, at ¶ 6. As a former senior UNCC staffer, Senogles was well-versed in BI methodology.
153. *LG&E v. Argentina Final Award*, *supra* n. 7, at ¶¶ 65, 88. At the time this book went to press, a request by the claimants for a supplemental ruling by the tribunal on additional damages was still pending.
154. *Id.*
155. *Enron v. Argentina*, *supra* n. 43.

transportation operations and the LNG plant separately, and assess damages based solely by reference to the impact of the pesification measures on the gas transportation business.[156] The tribunal chose to treat the gas transportation business separately, thereby substantially increasing the damage award.[157] In the *Enron* award, the panel apparently made a simple pro rata division between the transportation and LNG operations.[158] While attractive, that approach may not do justice to complex allocations such as the division between taxable profits (the successful LNG plant) and tax benefit losses (the gas transportation business) when both are combined in the same legal entity. Arbitrators may instead choose to ask the experts for a critical review of the linkages between the lines of business.

In either a lost profits or diminution of value computation, two scenarios will be employed, the "but-for" scenario and the "impaired" scenario. In each case, the scenarios will employ equivalent dates. Historic earnings must be "brought forward" to the valuation date by means of an interest rate, while future earnings are discounted back to the valuation date by means of a discount rate. The interest rate used for bringing historical amounts forward will clearly not contain the same risk factors as the discount rate used to present value future amounts. As a practical matter, the interest rate used for the historical amount is often a "risk-free" rate (such as the rate for US Treasuries) or a statutory rate for pre-judgment interest.[159]

VIII SUNK INVESTMENT COSTS AND CRITICISMS OF MARKET VALUE

While "market value" may be the dominant Valuation Mercatoria precept within the valuation community, elements of the arbitration community remain outside this consensus. Reliance upon "market value" is certainly not without its critics. One fruitful source for criticisms is found in jurisprudence and commentary in the field of international investment law. In the context of expropriation claims, for instance, discussions of fair market value calculations inevitably overlap with the perennial dispute as to whether customary international law requires compensation for an expropriation that is "prompt, adequate and effective," "fair," "just," "full," or "appropriate" or otherwise.

---

156. *Id.*, at ¶¶ 173–182, 402
157. *Id.*, at ¶ 402.
158. *Id.*, at ¶¶ 418–419.
159. Tregillis & Thompson, "Differences Between Lost Profits and Diminution of Business Value as a Measure of Damages," at 4, available to members of the AICPA's Business Valuation and Forensic Litigation Services Center at <http://bvfls.aicpa.org>.

Sunk Investment Costs and Investment Treaty Awards

Market Value is the dominant valuation principle for assessing injuries to businesses. In the context of investment treaty disputes, however, fair market value measures have been rejected in a number of cases in favor of compensation based on sunk investment costs – recovery of the "reliance interest" by seeking to put the investor back into a position as if he had never made the investment.

Some arbitrators, like some commentators, assert that market value is not the proper measure for a lawful expropriation under international law. Thus, in the quantum phase of *CME Stockholm*, Prof. Brownlie dissented from the majority on the amount of compensation to be paid by the Czech Republic for expropriating the investor's interest in a television services company. Prof. Brownlie argued that the phrase "just compensation" employed in the Czech-Netherlands bilateral investment treaty (BIT) should be interpreted to take into account the hardship a large award would cause to the Czech State.[160] In reaching his conclusions, Prof. Brownlie contrasted the "just compensation" standard in the Czech-Netherlands BIT with the fair market value standard set out in the Czech-US BIT.[161] He also argued that "appropriate compensation," rather than "full compensation," was the applicable international law standard by virtue of U.N. General Assembly Resolutions and arbitration rulings like the *LIAMCO v. Libya* and *Aminoil v. Kuwait* awards.[162] In the circumstances, Prof. Brownlie would have limited the injured investor's recovery to the amount actually invested in the expropriated venture, profits retained by the venture and not distributed to the investor and "foreseeable profits" based on a "reasonable rate of return" discounted to reflect what Prof. Brownlie described as the venture's anti-competitive dominant position.[163]

The valuation approach recommended by Prof. Brownlie provides for recovery of the reliance interest but not the expectation interest; essentially to permit the investor to recover *damnum emergens* (i.e., "sunk investment costs;" invested capital minus capital already recovered), along with a return on those sunk costs from the injury date until the recovery date at a rate the panel considers reasonable in the circumstances. The compensation amount could therefore differ significantly from the market value of the company, up or down. Unless the investment

160. *Separate Opinion on the Issues at the Quantum Phase of: CME v. Czech Republic* by Ian Brownlie, C.B.E., Q.C., at ¶¶ 23–32 (March 14, 2003). The majority award, of course, did not accept Prof. Brownlie's arguments.

161. *Id.*, at ¶¶ 110–118.

162. *Id.*, at ¶¶ 68.

163. *Id.*, at ¶ 68. Prof. Brownlie was particularly skeptical of the reliability of the DCF method utilized by the majority award, quoting at length from the Iran-US Claims Tribunal's award in *Amoco International Finance Corp. v. Islamic Republic of Iran* as to the "speculative nature" of long-term cash flow projections.

expenditures were made very recently, the impact of the conduct at issue on the market value of what was acquired with the funds may have grown or fallen depending upon a number of factors. For example, the market value of the acquired assets may depend on the nature of the asset purchased (oil and gas reserves are a good example, but so is the value of an operating television company in a competitive market) and the efficacy of the use to which it has been put. Moreover, no value is attributed in this approach to goodwill – management skills, name, reputation, customer loyalty, location and other such intangibles. Thus, the expertise developed by a company to develop its business would not be incorporated into a *damnum emergens* award. The investor would instead, by means of the award, be put back into a position as if the investment had never been made. Of course, the extent to which the other party (the defaulting or expropriating party, as the case may be) would benefit from the "uncompensated" remaining value (if any) of the investment would depend on whether the event giving rise to the injury had transferred the value of the business to that other party or had left the investor in control (if any).

European jurisprudence also occasionally questions the applicability of market value as the proper standard for compensation in some circumstances. In *James v. UK*, the European Court of Human Rights (ECHR) ruled that the European Convention on Human Rights does not "guarantee a right to full compensation in all circumstances. Legitimate objectives of 'public interest' such as pursued in measures of economic reform or measures designed to achieve greater social justice, may call for less than reimbursement of full market value."[164] Argentina proffered this statement to the tribunal in *Siemens v. Argentina*[165] as support for a compensation standard of less than full market value under the US-Argentina bilateral investment treaty. However, that ICSID tribunal rejected Argentina's argument that international investment law should follow the ECHR's perspective, observing that "Article I of the First Protocol to the European Convention on Human Rights permits a margin of appreciation not found in customary international law or the Treaty."[166]

In international investment law cases, awards often also discuss the fair market value and *damnum emergens* standards in connection with the reparations standard set out in the famous *Chorzów Factory* judgment.[167] In that case, the Permanent

164. *James v. UK*, European Court of Human Rights, 1986, 8 EHRR 123, at ¶ 48.
165. *Siemens v. Argentina*, *supra* n. 112, at ¶ 346.
166. *Id.*, at ¶ 354.
167. Case Concerning the Factory at Chorzów (*Germany v. Polish Republic*), Claim for Indemnity (Merits), No. 13, Judgment of September 13, 1928, PCIJ 1928, Series A, No. 17 (hereinafter "Chorzów Factory"). *See* generally Marboe, *Compensation and Damages in International Law – The Limits of "Fair Market Value," supra* n. 84, at 729–734. The Chorzów Factory dicta appears capable in practice of being interpreted in widely divergent fashions. Compare *CMS v. Argentina* (awarding compensation based on a DCF valuation) with *Vivendi 2007* (awarding compensation based on sunk investment costs). *See also* Valasek, "A 'Simple Scheme': Exploring the Meaning of Chorzów Factory for the Valuation of Opportunistic Expropriation in the BIT Generation," in "Transnational Dispute Management Special Issue on Compensation and Damages in International Investment Arbitration," vol. 4, issue 6, available on-line at <www.transnational-dispute-management.com>.

Court of International Justice (PCIJ) considered a situation involving breach of international law, not compensation for a lawful expropriation. The PCIJ asserted that, in such circumstances, it was appropriate to seek to place the injured party back into the situation that would have existed *but for the unlawful act.*

> The essential principle contained in the actual notion of an illegal act – a principle which seems to be established by international practice and in particular by decisions of arbitral tribunals – is that reparation must, as far as possible, wipe out all the consequences of the illegal act and re-establish the situation that would, in all probability, have existed if that act had not been committed.[168]

Note the important difference in approach between Prof. Brownlie and the *Chorzów Factory* comment. Prof. Brownlie would place the investor back into a position as if the investment had never been made. In contrast, the *Chorzów Factory* dictum focuses on putting the investor back in a position as if the investment had been made but the injury had never occurred.[169]

The highly influential International Law Commission Draft Articles on Responsibility of States for Internationally Wrongful Acts speak to these issues. Articles 31 and 36 of the ILC Articles state:[170]

> Article 31
> Reparation
>
> 1. The responsible State is under an obligation to make full reparation for the injury caused by the internationally wrongful act.
> 2. Injury includes any damage, whether material or moral, caused by the internationally wrongful act of a State.
>
> Article 36
> Compensation
>
> 1. The State responsible for an internationally wrongful act is under an obligation to compensate for the damage caused thereby, insofar as such damage is not made good by restitution.

---

168. Chorzów Factory, *supra* n. 167, at 47.
169. *See* Ripinsky, presentation on "Damnum emergens and lucrum cessans: is it relevant?" to 8th Investment Treaty Forum, British Institute of International and Comparative Law (BIICL), May 11, 2007, at 7. Papers are available by BIICL Investment Treaty Forum members at <www.biicl.com>. That is the same characterization as the description offered by Argentina of sunk investment costs in *Vivendi 2007*: "Alternatively, [wrote Argentina in its Counter-Memorial,] the Claimants may seek to be put in the position in which they would have been had they never agreed to enter into the Concession Agreement: the return to them of their investment in the Concession." *Vivendi 2007*, *supra* n. 72, at ¶ 8.3.15.
170. Official Records of the General Assembly, Fifty-sixth session, Supplement No. 10 (A/56/10), Chp. IV.E.1 (2001). The ILC Articles address only cases involving disputes between States. However, they are regularly relied upon by arbitrators, commentators and governments to illuminate standards for investor-State disputes as well.

2. The compensation shall cover any financially assessable damage including loss of profits insofar as it is established.

On their face, the ILC Articles do not resolve the question of whether, or when, use of fair market value is the appropriate standard. However, the last Reporter for the ILC Articles, Professor Crawford, has offered additional thoughts about this standard of compensation in his Commentaries on the ILC Articles.

> Compensation reflecting the capital value of property taken or destroyed as a result of an internationally wrongful act is generally assessed on the basis of the "fair market value" of the property lost. The method used to assess "fair market value," however, depends on the nature of the asset concerned.[171]

Prof. Crawford then succinctly reviewed a variety of valuation methodologies employed by arbitral tribunals in international law cases.[172] In describing these methodologies, Prof. Crawford noted the common criticisms of two oft–opposed methods, Net Book Value (i.e., book value of assets and liabilities as they appear in accounting records) and Discounted Cash Flow forecasts. With respect to the Net Book Value method, his Commentaries pointed out that "[t]he limitations of this method lie in the reliance on historical figures, the use of accounting principles that tend to undervalue assets, especially in periods of inflation, and the fact that the purposes for which the figures were produced does not take account of the compensation context and rules specific to it."[173] Prof. Crawford not only criticized the Net Book Value method. He criticized the DCF method as well.

> The [DCF] method analyses a wide range of inherently speculative elements, some of which have a significant impact on the outcome (e.g. discount rates, currency fluctuations, inflation figures, commodity prices, interest rates and other commercial risks). This has led tribunals to adopt a cautious approach to the use of the method. Hence although income-based methods have been accepted in principle, there has been a decided preference for asset-based methods.[174]

While debate may continue as to whether customary international law calls for fair market value, net book value or other value standards in international investment claims, States in practice have increasingly conceded the central role of market value as the measure of compensation for lawful expropriations in the texts of their investment treaties. Article 7(2) of the 2001 bilateral investment treaty between Cuba, no friend to the market economy, and Mexico is instructive in this regard:

> *La indemnizacion sera equivalente al valor de mercado o, a falta de dicho valor, al valor real que tenga la inversion expropiada inmediatamente antes*

---

171. Commentaries, *supra* n. 96, at 255 (¶ 22).
172. *Id.*, at 255–258 (¶¶ 22–26).
173. *Id.*, at 257 (¶ 24) (footnotes omitted). As explained fully in Chap. 7, Net Book Value (in contrast to Adjusted Book Value) is not in any event a measure of market value.
174. *Id.*, at 258 (¶ 26) (footnotes omitted). The contrast between the preference among international investment tribunals for Asset-Based methods and the preference among valuation organizations and professionals for Income-Based methods is striking.

> *de que la expropiacion se haya llevado a cabo, y no reflejara cambio alguno en el valor debido a que la intencion de expropiar se haya concocido con antenoridad a la fecha de expropiacion. Los criterios de valuacion incluiran el valor comente, el valor del activo, incluvendo el valor fiscal declarado de la propiedad de bienes tangibles, y otros criterios que resulten apropiados para determinar el valor de Mercado o el valor real, segun corresponde.*[175]

Cuba's willingness to accept market value as the primary compensation standard, and Mexico's insistence upon that standard on behalf of Mexican investors, clearly illustrates what those two States believed was necessary to attract and protect investors.

In addition to expropriation claims, investment treaty cases in which a State is held to have breached its fair and equitable treatment obligation under international law also have not approached the compensation calculation in a consistent fashion. As Smutny explains, "damages for a treaty violation are not necessarily focused on an assessment of market value – they are focused on the particular injury caused by the unlawful act. While there may be cases in which a reasonable measure of loss suffered is the fair market value of the subject property, there may also be cases in which awarding the market value of property does not compensate for the loss."[176] The *S.D. Myers v. Canada*[177] NAFTA tribunal, for example, looked to the *Chorzów Factory* reparations test for its damages standard. *S.D. Myers* concluded that Canada's temporary closure of the Canada-US border to exports from Canada of PCB-contaminated waste materials violated the fair and equitable treatment commitment in NAFTA. The award went through a twelve-step procedure to calculate the economic impact on the investor of the temporary border closure. Those steps included calculating the investor's net income stream lost to third party competitors during the temporary closure period, the net income stream lost to third parties after the closure period but attributable to the adverse impact on the investor's market position caused by the closure, and the lost net income stream during the closure period for business the investor failed to fulfill by virtue of the closing but not lost to third parties.

In *MTD v. Chile*,[178] by way of contrast, the claimant investor sought recovery of its investment expenditures (minus the residual value of the property at issue).

175. "Acuerdo Entre Los Estados Unidos Mexicanas y La Republica de Cuba para La Promoción y Protección Reciproca de las Inversiones," available on the investment treaty database maintained by UNCTAD at <www.unctad.org>. The English translation reads as follows (author's translation): "The indemnification will be equivalent to the market value or, in the absence of this value, to the real value of the expropriated investment immediately before the expropriation has been carried out, and will not reflect any change in the value because the intention to expropriate has become known prior to the date of expropriation. The estimate criteria will include the current value, the value of the assets, including the declared fiscal value of the property of tangible goods, and other appropriate criteria to determine the market value or the real value, as the case may be."

176. Smutny, *supra* n. 115, at 20.

177. *S.D. Myers v. Canada*, UNCITRAL Case, First Partial Award, November 13, 2000.

178. *MTD Equity Sdn. Bhd. and MTD Chile, S.A. v. Republic of Chile*, ICSID Case No. Arb/01/7, Final Award, May 25, 2004 (hereinafter "*MTD v. Chile Award*").

The panel accepted MTD's approach, but partially reduced the award for business risks assumed by the investor. Additionally, the recent ICSID arbitral tribunal in *PSEG v. Turkey*[179] rejected a fair market value test both because the applicable treaty only proposed that test for lawful expropriations and because the underlying facts did not, in the tribunal's view, suit use of the fair market value test. Yet another recent case, *CMS v. Argentina*,[180] concluded that applying the expropriation standard of fair market value made sense, though, even if the relevant investment treaty did not specify application of that standard to breach of a fair and equitable treatment obligation. And in the *LG&E v. Argentina Final Award*, as discussed, the tribunal rejected fair market value as the valuation standard for a fair and equitable treatment breach in favor of actual losses based upon lost dividends up to a date prior to the award.[181]

Other recent Argentine awards may not offer any more consistency than *MTD, PSEG, CMS, LG&E* and *S.D. Meyers*. The arbitrators in *Siemens v. Argentina*[182] decided that Argentina had breached both the treaty's expropriation obligation and the treaty's "fair and equitable" obligation. That panel calculated the amount due to the investor on the basis of the *Chorzów Factory* standard. The award focused on the book value of Siemens' investment expenditures. The panel rejected a lost profits claim as "very unlikely to have ever materialized." In *Azurix v. Argentina*,[183] though, the tribunal looked to the fair market value of the investment expenditures by Enron (not their book value) for a fair and equitable treatment breach.

The European Court of Human Rights also expressly departed from market value in its judgment awarding compensation for the taking by Greece of the estates and personal property of the former King of Greece and family members.[184] The ECHR distinguished between a lawful taking and an unlawful taking, reiterating that the Republic's taking of the former Royal properties was lawful. In the circumstances, the ECHR referred to "legitimate objectives of public interest" and to "equitable considerations" as support for its conclusion to base valuation of the estates on a "so-called objective, or tax value, which is arrived at by application of a [Greek] statutory formula for valuation."[185] That objective value was far less than the market value calculated by either the Greek Government's or the former Royal family's valuation experts. Therefore, although the Government's own

---

179. *PSEG v. Turkey, PSEG Global, Inc. and Kenya Ilgin Elektrik Uretim ve Ticaret Limited Sirketi v. Republic of Turkey*, ICSID Case No. ARB/02/5, Award of January 19, 2007 (hereinafter, "*PSEG v. Turkey*").
180. *CMS v. Argentina, supra* n. 7.
181. *See* text associated with n. 144 et seq. For a general discussion of compensation for a "fair and equitable" claim, *see* Hobér, "Fair and Equitable Treatment – Determining Compensation," in *Transnational Dispute Management Special Issue on Compensation and Damages in International Investment Arbitration*, vol. 4, issue 6, available on-line at <www.transnational-dispute-management.com>.
182. *Siemens v. Argentina, supra* n. 112.
183. *Azurix v. Argentina, supra* n. 17.
184. *Case of the Former King of Greece & Others v. Greece*, Application No. 25701/94, Judgment 28 November 2002.
185. *Id.*, at ¶¶ 78, 86–94.

valuation experts had reported a market value of 550,526,779 euros (EUR) for the properties, the ECHR assessed compensation by reference to an "objective" tax value of (apparently) about EUR 250,000,000.[186] The ECHR further reduced that sum by unpaid taxes,[187] resulting in an aggregate final award of EUR 13,200,000, plus simple interest, "on an equitable basis."[188]

If the arbitral panel determines that, in the circumstances, the proper measure of compensation should be based on recovery of an investor's "sunk investment costs," that calculation comprises two elements: (i) the amount of sums invested; and (ii) the rate of return to be awarded on the invested sum from the investment date until the award date. As discussed above, when a tribunal awards "sunk investment costs" it is seeking to place the investor back in the same position as if the lost investment had never been made (the reliance interest). If that investment had not been made, then the investor would of course have placed the invested sum instead in a different investment, not put the money under its proverbial mattress. The rate of return from the investment date to the award date reimburses the investor for the sums the investor would have earned from the alternative investment during that period of time.

In making its determination about the proper rate of return for the period, the arbitral panel will confront the question of whether that rate should be based on a rate of return for a debt investment, a rate of return for an equity investment or some other rate of return. Put another way, to decide the applicable rate of return on the sunk investment amount for the investment-to-award period of time, the arbitrator must in effect decide the nature of the alternative investment that would have been made by the investor if the lost investment had never been made in the first place. Would that investor have, for example, placed the invested sum in an investment in a safe debt instrument like a LIBOR deposit, an investment with a rate of return consistent with the overall stock market or an investment with a rate of return similar to the enterprise at the center of the dispute? Or, rather than looking at market comparables for this purpose, should the arbitrator instead look at the historical internal rates of return for that investor's other investments, in order to incorporate into the compensation calculation the investor's own success or failure in business ventures. That latter approach would recognize management's skill in selecting successful investments (Warren Buffett and CalEnergy?) or its track record of "picking dogs" (Enron and Azurix?).

Because those various rates of return will differ noticeably, the arbitrator's decision about the nature of that alternate investment will have significant consequences for the total amount of the compensation award. Illustratively, according

186. *Id.*, at ¶ 92–94. The judgment is noticeably unclear about the exact "objective" value employed by the ECHR.

187. *Id.*, at ¶ 98–100. The ECHR was equally ambiguous regarding the actual tax amount determined by the Court.

188. *Id.*, at ¶ 100.

to Goldman Sachs economists the average annual pre-tax rate of return on equity capital from 2001 through 2004 was about 9.5% in Germany, about 10.5% in the US and about 12% in the then-European Union member states (other than Germany).[189] At the same time, the rate for USD three-month LIBOR deposits during the same period averaged about 2.1%.[190] If, though, the investment in question was a private power project in a developing country, investors may have expected an average annual pre-tax equity rate of return of 20% or more. Applying those possible rates of return to an invested sum of USD 100 million for an arbitration award issued four years after the date of investment, the differing compensation amounts will be as follows.

Recovery of USD 100 Million Investment Awarded Four Years After Investment Date, No Compounding

Source of Rate	*Annual Rate of Return (2001–2004)*	*Total Award (USD 100,000,000 plus four-year return from investment date to award date, with no compounding)*
USD LIBOR	2.1%	USD 108,400,000
German Equity Returns	9.5%	USD 138,000,000
US Equity Returns	10.5%	USD 142,000,000
EU Equity Returns (other than Germany)	12.0%	USD 148,000,000
Hypothetical Power Project	20%	USD 180,000,000

The compensation amounts based on those alternative rates of return will, naturally, increase further if the arbitrator decides that the chosen rate of return should be compounded.[191] The compounding questions are "would the investor have reinvested its annual returns on the invested sum periodically during the investment-to-award interval and, if so, for what period(s) and for what rate(s) of return?" If the arbitrator settles on annual compounding at the same rate of return, then the amounts will grow significantly, especially for the higher return rates.

189. Broadbent, Schumacher & Schels, *No Pain Without Gain – Germany's Adjustment to a Higher Cost of Capital*, Goldman Sachs *Global Economics Paper No. 103* at 5 (corrected and revised version February 26, 2004).

190. Based on data from "Series Title: United States – Money Market – 3-month Libor interbank USD deposit rate – Last trade price or value – US dollar, provided by ECB: Percent per year," available at Economagic.com, <www.economagic.com>.

191. *See* Ch. 9.V *infra*.

Recovery of USD 100 Million Investment Awarded Four Years After Investment Date, Compounded Annually at the Same Rate of Return

Source of Rate	*Annual Rate of Return (2001–2004)*	*Total Award (USD 100,000,000 plus four-year return from investment date to award date, compounded annually)*
USD LIBOR	2.1%	USD 108,668,323.85
German Equity Returns	9.5%	USD 143,766,095.06
US Equity Returns	10.5%	USD 149,090,205.06
EU Equity Returns (other than Germany)	12.0%	USD 157,351,936
Hypothetical Power Project	20%	USD 207,360,000

IX NO MARKET EXISTS

Although "market value" is regularly the starting point for valuing a business, sometimes a relevant market for the company at issue might not exist.

> In many instances no appropriate market can be found for the property or entitlement in question. This occurs for many reasons, ranging from the fact that no one is buying or selling property of the kind involved, to the fact that a monopoly may control prices. There would almost never be a "market" in real property, only sales of more or less comparable properties. Businesses, opportunities and trade secrets might theoretically be bought and sold, but unique advantages and risks again make standard market prices unlikely. So in many cases, market value, one of the most common bases for damages decisions, is not an existing fact but a legal construct or even a convention.[192]

192. Dobbs, *Law of Remedies*, at § 3.5 (2nd edn 1993). *See*, e.g., *Phelps Dodge Corp. v. Islamic Republic of Iran*, Award No. 217-99-2, March 19, 1986, 10 US C.T.R. 121 ¶ 30 (1986): ("There was no market for Phelps Dodge's shares in November 1980.") Writing in *The New York Times*, Peter S. Goodman considered the problems of determining a market value in the US during December 2007 when "a general state of uncertainty seizes many markets. Would-be deal makers are sitting tight and waiting for the murkiness to clear, which has slowed the economy." Goodman, When the Price Isn't Right, *The Sunday New York Times*, Week in Review at 1 (9 December 2007). Goodman pointed to significant slowdowns in markets for US residential real estate (a casualty of the subprime mortgage "crisis"), television and movie media (resulting from a Hollywood screenwriters' strike), the record industry (arising out of technology-driven changes in the music distribution system) and the services of Alex Rodriguez, the New York Yankees baseball player known as A-Rod (caused by the impact of globalization and new technologies on the marketable value of a world-recognized athlete's name). With regard to real estate, Goodman commented: "Now, buyers and sellers are effectively boycotting the pretend auctioneer, unwilling to believe what he has to say." *Id.*, at 3. And more generally: "The economy is waiting for markets to absorb the new possibilities and settle on prices that make enough sense to enough people that buying and

The absence of a trading market for the specific assets being valued occurs regularly with respect to equity interests in closely held companies.

> **No Market Exists**
>
> In many cases, market value is not an existing fact, but instead a legal construct. That situation occurs regularly with respect to equity interests in closely held companies. There is often no established market for sales of interests in such companies. Arbitrators will therefore search for substitutes within the Income-Based Approach, the Asset-Based Approach or the Market-Based Approach to valuation.

Often, arbitrators will be called upon to determine the value of the equity investment in an enterprise where the enterprise is owned by a small number of investors. In such circumstances, an actual market for the equity may not exist.

> The result of this situation is that little, if any, trading in the shares takes place. There is, therefore, no established market for the stock and such sales as occur at irregular intervals seldom reflect all of the elements of a representative transaction as defined by the term "fair market value."[193]

The absence of a market for a company's assets may also be at issue. The claimant investor in *CME Stockholm* argued that the DCF method is appropriate "where no active market for the assets exists."[194]

If an actual market does not exist, though, arbitrators and the parties will search for substitutes. Accordingly, arbitral tribunals may consider "comparable sales, income produced by the property, replacement costs, cost of obtaining a functional substitute, risks of loss and chances of gains,"[195] as well as other data for constructing this substitute market. The comparable companies and transactions methods, as well as the DCF, CCF and APV methods, each of which is discussed in some detail in this volume, can all be seen as efforts to construct a hypothetical market for the business at issue when a directly demonstrable market value for the subject business is not available. It is worth noting, of course, that if no actual market exists and no realistic comparable or substitute is available, those circumstances may in fact signal that the market value of the relevant business is

---

selling can start up anew." *Id.* Such market seizures may, of course, be short run events or become long term collapses, depending on the particular situation. See also Cowan, Economic View: It's Hard to Thaw a Frozen Market, The New York Times, Sunday Business at 5 (March 23, 2008), noting fluctuations over a short period of time in Bear Stearn's stock price from USD 170 to USD 2: "What is distinctive today is the drying up of market liquidity – the inability to buy and sell financial assets – caused by a lack of good information about asset values."

193. IRS Rev. Rul. 59–60, *supra* n. 5, at § 2.03.
194. *CME Stockholm* Final Award, *supra* n. 42, at ¶ 161. Brower & Brueschke, *The Iran-United States Claims Tribunal* 589 (1998), makes the same point.
195. *CME Stockholm* Final Award, *supra* n. 42, at ¶ 161.

zero (particularly for unique assets).[196] The objective of the valuation, however, is to determine the loss suffered by an injured party. The business may still have loss of value for which compensation is appropriate even though comparable measurement tools are not usable. In such circumstances, an Income-Based method such as a DCF calculation may be warranted.

These concerns are of particular importance in underdeveloped economies. The International Valuation Standards Committee has issued a White Paper addressing the special circumstances of valuations in emerging market economies; such as an inadequate legal framework, difficulties in obtaining information, greater economic volatility, outdated national valuation standards, lack of trained valuation experts, external pressures, excessive or insufficient government intervention, and transition towards the recognition of intangible property.[197] Where insufficient market data exists in an emerging economy to support fully a market value, the IVSC considers "depreciated replacement cost" to be an acceptable substitute "for the *Market Value* of specialized property or property with a limited market."[198] The IVSC does require that the use of such a non-market value be clearly identified, that the limitations of the replacement (substitution) value estimate be clearly identified and that the expert pay particular attention to the consequences of inconsistent use of market data and non-market data in the same valuation.[199] Note that, for the IVSC, the concept of replacement (substitution) value is a market value, not a book value. Even in emerging markets, the IVSC instructs that "*Market Value* must be recognized as the fundamental basis of value."[200] The concept of "depreciated replacement cost" is most applicable for tangible assets, not business ownership interests. The concept of "replacement" or "substitution" value, however, is applicable to business interests, as will become apparent from the discussion in Chapter 7 of Asset-Based valuation methods.

X SUBSEQUENT EVENTS

Naturally, the date as of which the value of a business is determined will significantly affect the ultimate amount to be awarded. By far, the common legal approach to calculating compensation values the impact of the injury as of the date of harm. That approach, therefore, disregards events subsequent to the injury, whether positive or negative. The recent events in Argentina illustrate the importance of identifying the valuation date. The economic, political and regulatory

196. Although, in situations such as the Argentine economic crisis it may be argued that the country bears responsibility for the absence of realistic comparables as a result of its own actions. Therefore, the absence of comparables is not in all cases a signal that the business had no value.
197. IVSC, *International Valuation White Paper: Valuation in Emerging Markets* (July 1, 2001) at ¶ 1.3.
198. *Id.*, at ¶ 3.3.3.
199. *Id.*, at ¶ 3.3.3.
200. *Id.*, at ¶ 4.1.1.

events being considered by the *CMS v. Argentina*[201] and *LG&E v. Argentina*[202] tribunals were substantially identical, as were the events being considered in the claim brought by Enron Corp. to the US Overseas Private Investment Corporation (OPIC) in OPIC's *Ponderosa Assets* political risk insurance claims determination[203] and before an ICSID tribunal in *Enron v. Argentina.*[204] Despite all four decisions looking essentially at the same Argentine regulatory measures, the *CMS* tribunal set the valuation date for compensation as of August 17, 2000, OPIC in the *Ponderosa Assets* claim as of January 6, 2002 and the ICSID tribunal in *Enron v. Argentina* as of December 31, 2001. The *LG&E* tribunal set the valuation date as August 2000, but with a carve out for a "state of necessity" from December 2001 until the end of April 2003. The choice among these four dates clearly affected the valuations by many tens, if not hundreds, of millions of dollars.

The US Internal Revenue Service has pointed out the links among general economic circumstances, the particular circumstances of the property being valued, and the valuation date for that property:

> The fair market value of specific shares of stock will vary as general economic conditions change from "normal" to "boom" or "depression," that is, according to the degree of optimism or pessimism with which the investing public regards the future at the required date of appraisal. Uncertainty as to the stability or continuity of the future income from a property decreases its value by increasing the risk of loss of earnings and value in the future. The value of shares of stock of a company with very uncertain future prospects is highly speculative. The appraiser must exercise his judgment as to the degree of risk attaching to the business of the corporation which issued the stock, but that judgment must be related to all of the other factors affecting value.[205]

Illustrations abound of the principle that events subsequent to the valuation date are to be disregarded. For breach of contract claims, the great weight of authority worldwide holds that the date of injury is the proper valuation date.[206] Solvency valuations for US preferential transfer cases are also conducted as of the transfer

---

201. *CMS v. Argentina, supra* n. 7.
202. *LG&E v. Argentina Final Award, supra* n. 7.
203. "OPIC Memorandum of Determinations, Expropriation Claim of Ponderosa Assets, L.P., Argentina, Contract of Insurance No. D733" (August 2, 2005), available at <www.opic/gov/claims/report/index.asp>.
204. *Enron v. Argentina, supra* n. 43.
205. IRS Rev. Rul. 59-60, *supra* n. 5, at § 3.02.
206. Similarly, for conversions of tangible property in the US ,"[t]he general rule requires the courts to assess market value of a damaged, destroyed or converted chattel at the time of the harm." Dobbs, *Law of Remedies, supra* n. 192, at § 5.13(2). *See also Estate of James Waldo Hendrickson v. Comm'r, supra* n. 41, at *42 ("For Federal estate tax purposes, the fair market of the subject property is generally determined as of the date of the death of the decedent; ordinarily, no consideration is given to any unforeseeable future event that may have affected the value of the subject property on some later date. *See* § 20-2031-1(b), Estate Tax Regs."). But *see Energy Capital Corp. v. United States*, 302 F.3d 1314 (Fed. Cir. 2002), calculating damages by discounting lost profits to their present value as of the date of judgment.

date. Such valuations may include information known as of that date, as well as information knowable as of the date, "such as fraud or errors in the debtor's internal records."[207] As Stearn cautions, though, "the difficulty may lie in ascertaining what information was and was not knowable."[208]

So too, the AICPA's Valuation Standard SSVS 1. According to SSVS 1, the valuation professional generally should consider "circumstances existing at the valuation date and events occurring up to the valuation date." Subsequent events, i.e., conditions that were not known or knowable at the valuation date, would not ordinarily be incorporated into a valuation consistent with SSVS 1 "because a valuation is performed as of a point in time – the valuation date – and the events . . . occurring subsequent to that date, are not relevant to the value determined as of that date."[209] If a valuation is meaningful to the intended user beyond the valuation date, though, then SSVS 1 contemplates that the subsequent events may be disclosed in a separate section of the valuation report for informational purposes only.[210]

The *Fédération des Experts Comptables Européens* also instructs European accountants to focus on the information available on the valuation date. "When the date of the valuation and the time at which the valuation is carried out are different, only information should be considered which could have been obtained with due care at the valuation date."[211]

Similarly, international expropriation law traditionally calls for calculation of compensation by reference to the value of the expropriated property immediately prior to the expropriation. By way of example, the Cuba-Mexico bilateral investment treaty previously quoted provides for compensation determined at the value of the investment immediately before the expropriation was carried out. That position comports with recent arbitration awards, for instance the ICSID award in *Santa Elena v. Costa Rica*. In *Santa Elena*, the tribunal rejected claimant's argument for determining the expropriated property's value as of the date of the award (by which time the potential use of the property as a resort had been more fully revealed).[212] Instead, the tribunal held that compensation for the expropriation would be calculated as of the date the expropriation was effected. As a result, the *Santa Elena* tribunal held that "factors that arose thereafter . . . must be disregarded."[213]

207. Stearn, "Proving Solvency: Defending Preference and Fraudulent Transfer Litigation," *supra* n. 20, at 375.
208. *Id.*
209. SSVS 1, *supra* n. 17, at ¶ 43.
210. *Id.*
211. FEE SME Business Valuation Guide, *supra* n. 17, at 11.
212. *Compania del Desarollo de Santa Elena, S.A. v. Costa Rica*, ICSID Case No. ARB/96/1, Final Award (February 17, 2000), 15 ICSID Rev.–FILJ 169 (2000) (hereinafter, "*Santa Elena v. Costa Rica*"), at ¶¶ 76–83.
213. *Id.*, at 84.

One area in which subsequent events must necessarily be taken into account is steps taken by the injured party to mitigate its injuries. As the tribunal in *Enron v. Argentina* has pointed out:

> 200. While the principle that damages are specifically related under the Treaty to the date prior to the events giving rise to the claim is correct, this is not to mean that events taking place after that date are not relevant for a determination of compensation, as happens for example when a given transaction is made to minimize damages. This too will be considered by the Tribunal in the context of valuation.[214]

Moreover, the general principle that events occurring subsequent to the injury date are to be disregarded in a compensation computation is not always respected. Some courts and tribunals have held that subsequent events may on occasion be taken into account when calculating compensation.[215] Others have permitted subsequent information to be employed to test the reasonableness of valuation date information. For example, the claimant in the *CME Stockholm* proceeding asserted that using the injury date for the valuation was "settled law." However, the claimant also argued that the tribunal could look at the investment's actual subsequent performance to test the reasonableness of the company's earlier pre-injury forecasts, which CME was asking the tribunal to use as a basis for computing quantum:

> Settled law makes clear that the Tribunal's valuation of the Claimant's investment in CNTS based on the company's market value should be accomplished by reference to conditions at the time of loss, since a willing buyer would not have known what future events would bring in negotiating a purchase with a willing seller at that time.... Nevertheless, comparison of CME's projections against actual results for the period since the forecasts were prepared reinforces the reasonableness of using those forecasts in valuing CNTS.[216]

Courts will also look to subsequent events as a means of validating an appraisal made on conventional "injury date" grounds, but not as a replacement for the general rule. Accordingly, the US Court of Appeals for the Third Circuit has commented:

> A company's actual subsequent performance is something to consider when determining *ex post* the reasonableness of a valuation, *see Moody*, 971 F.2d at

214. *Enron v. Argentina*, *supra* n. 43, at ¶ 200. *See* the discussion of mitigation at Ch. 2.XI.6 *infra*.
215. *See* Marboe, *Compensation and Damages in International Law: The Limits of "Fair Market Value,"* *supra* n. 84, at 751–753 (discussing Chorzów Factory, the European Court of Human Rights *and Amco v. Indonesia* for damages on account of unlawful conduct). *See also* Zeller, *Damages under the Convention on Contracts for the International Sale of Goods* at 83–84 (Oceana Pub. 2005): "There is an argument to suggest that the time of calculating damages should be at the time the contract is breached. However, a determination of damages at that time is difficult, as the full extent of the breach is not clear. The ripple effect of the breach must be taken into consideration and that is best left as long as possible."
216. *CME Stockholm* Final Award, *supra* n. 42, at ¶ 131.

> 1074, but it is not, by definition, the basis of a substitute benchmark, *R.M.L.*, 92 F.3d at 155 (criticizing "[t]he use of hindsight to evaluate a debtor's financial condition").[217]

While the investor in the *CME* Stockholm proceedings regarded the choice of the injury date for the expropriation valuation date as "settled law," it also argued that the tribunal should adjust the information it would take into account in that valuation to exclude the impact by that time of events that proved to have been part of the expropriatory conduct.

> The correct SBS valuation of CNTS for the purpose of this proceeding is its valuation of CNTS freed from uncertainty over CNTS' future entitlement to [exclusivity to use, exploit and benefit from the license for TV Nova], since valuations for the purposes of compensation after a taking should be made without reference to diminutions in value associated with the previously sown seeds of the ultimate taking (here, the 1996 forced amendment of the CNTS MOA) or with the threat of the taking.[218]

Numerous investment treaties similarly instruct arbitrators to exclude from the value of the expropriated asset the impact on the asset's market value of the expropriatory conduct itself. For example, as noted above, the Cuba-Mexico bilateral investment treaty provides that the market value: "*y no reflejara cambio algun en al valor debido a que la intencion de expropriar se haya concocido con antenoridad a la fecha de expropriacion.*"[219]

Similarly, the 2004 Model Canadian Foreign Investor Promotion and Protection Agreement establishes the following compensation standard for expropriations.

> Such compensation shall be equivalent to the fair market value of the expropriated investment immediately before the expropriation took place ("date of expropriation"), and shall not reflect any change in value occurring because the intended expropriation had become known earlier.[220]

There are several possible approaches towards events occurring after the injury date:

(i) exclude them entirely from consideration;
(ii) include them solely to the extent a reasonable person, on the injury date, would have taken into account on that date the prospect of that future event [the common result];

217. *VFB LLC v. Campbell Soup Company*, 482 F.3d 624, 631 (3rd Cir. 2007).
218. *Id.*, at ¶ 143.
219. *Acuerdo Entre Las Estados Mexicanos y La Republica de Cuba para La Promoción y Protección Reciproca de las Inversiones*, *supra* n. 175. The English translation (author's translation) is "will not reflect any change in the value because the intention to expropriate has become known prior to the date of expropriation."
220. Available at <www.international.gc.ca/tna-nac/what_fipa-en.asp#structure>. To the same effect, *see also* Article 6.2(c) of the 2004 US Model Bilateral investment Treaty and Article III.2 of the 1994 Model US Bilateral Investment Treaty.

(iii) move the valuation date forward to include events that have occurred by the time of the award; or
(iv) leave the injury date as the valuation date, but adjust the compensation amount to reflect events occurring by the time of the award.

The difference between option (iii) and option (iv) may lie inter alia in currency fluctuations and in the date from which interest begins to accrue on the compensation amount.

Taking Account of Events Subsequent to the Injury

The common legal approach to calculating compensation values the impact of the injury as of the date of harm, and disregards subsequent events. Courts or arbitrators will include the prospect of subsequent events to the extent a reasonable person, on the injury date, would have taken the prospect of that future event into account on that date. In some cases, though, courts and arbitrators have either moved the valuation date forward to include events that have occurred by the time of the decision or have left the valuation date untouched, but adjusted the compensation amount to reflect events occurring by the time of the decision.

Recently, two investment treaty cases have departed from the "injury date" rule. In both of those cases, the tribunal held that the offending State conduct was unlawful under international law, in addition to being expropriatory. Relying on the *Chorzów Factory* standard of reparations, the tribunals accordingly took into account post-expropriation injuries in awarding compensation. The ICSID tribunal in *ADC & Hungary*[221] held that the Hungarian Government had expropriated the interests of the ADC claimants in the operating concession for the Budapest Ferihagy International Airport on January 1, 2002. The tribunal awarded compensation with a valuation date, however, of September 30, 2006, the date of the tribunal's award. As a result, the claimants were awarded the benefit of the significant increase in value of the airport concession that became apparent over the intervening 4-3/4 years. The arbitrators in *ADC v. Hungary* thus differed with the traditional rule that expropriation compensation is determined as of the date of expropriation, not the award date. Their predicate for that conclusion was a ruling that Hungary's expropriation of the operating rights was unlawful under the Hungary-Cyprus bilateral investment treaty (BIT).

The Hungary-Cyprus BIT calls for "just compensation" to be paid on account of a non-discriminatory expropriation taken in the public interest and consistent with due process. Like the Cuba-Mexico BIT and many other investment treaties, Article 4.2 of the Hungary-Cyprus BIT, in turn, specifies that: "The amount of

221. *ADC v. Hungary*, *supra* n. 111.

compensation must correspond to the market value of the expropriated investment at the moment of expropriation'' The ICSID panel interpreted that provision, however, to address only lawful expropriations – to the panel, the BIT was silent as to the proper compensation standard under international law if the expropriatory measure was not taken in the public interest, was effected without due process, was discriminatory and was not accompanied by payment of just compensation. The *ADC* tribunal held that Hungary failed to satisfy ''each and every one'' of those tests – the expropriation was, said the panel, not for a public purpose, without due process, discriminatory and without any compensation at all. The tribunal turned therefore to the reparations standard in the *Chorzów Factory* case. ''[R]eparation must, as far as possible, wipe out all of the consequences of the illegal act and re-establish the situation which would, in all probability, have existed if that act had not been committed.''

The *ADC* arbitrators described as ''almost unique'' the circumstances of a substantial increase in the value of the airport concession that unfolded between the expropriation date and the award date. In light of those circumstances, the panel concluded that the *Chorzów Factory* reparations standard required compensation for the unlawful Hungarian conduct to be computed as of the award date (set at September 30, 2006), rather than the expropriation date of January 1, 2002. Thus, according to the tribunal, the award captured the increase in value subsequent to the unlawful expropriation to ''put the Claimants in the same position as if the expropriation had not been committed.''

Although the arbitrators in *ADC* considered their circumstances almost unique, four months later the ICSID arbitrators in *Siemens v. Argentina* took a similar approach towards post-expropriation injuries. In that case, Siemens sought recovery of the fair market value of its expropriated investment (SIT), calculated for valuation purposes with effect immediately before the expropriation date of March 18, 2001. Moreover, because the tribunal had ruled that Argentina's conduct was wrongful as a matter of international law, Siemens also sought additional compensation under the *Chorzów Factory* standard ''to wipe out all the consequences of the illegal act and re-establish the situation which would, in all probability, have existed if the act had not been committed.'' Siemens argued that, while the value of the investment expropriated was not affected by the question of whether that expropriation was lawful, the amount of compensation owing to the investor could be significantly affected. Thus, said Siemens, the value of SIT at the expropriation date would be a legal floor, and additional consequential damages were appropriate to satisfy the *Chorzów Factory* standard. Accordingly, Siemens asked for a USD award of the book value of expropriated assets, including intangibles, plus ''the lost future profits that the enterprise would have gained had it been allowed to continue to operate.''[222]

Interestingly, Siemens appears to have claimed future lost profits (*lucrum cessans*) rather than seeking to include a goodwill component as part of SIT's

---

222. *Siemens v. Argentina*, *supra* n. 112, at ¶ 326.

book value. That choice that may have backfired when the panel refused Siemens' lost profits claim. The *Siemens* tribunal rejected the request for lost profits on the grounds that the amounts were "very unlikely to have ever materialized." The tribunal, though, did accept Siemens' proposed book value method of valuation on the basis of actual investments – the tribunal thus followed a classical reliance interest approach of *damnum emergens* (sunk investment costs). However, the arbitrators also held that, "[u]nder customary international law, Siemens is entitled not just to the value of its enterprise as of May 18, 2001, the date of expropriation, but also to any greater value that enterprise has gained up to the date of this forward, plus any consequential damages."[223] In particular, the tribunal decided to award compensation in USD rather than Argentine pesos (ARS), "in the context of the requirement that the consequences of the illegal act be wiped out. It would hardly be so," ruled the tribunal, "if the parity of the currency would be added as yet another risk to be taken by the investor after it had been expropriated."[224]

Similarly, in the case of *Amco Asia v. Indonesia (Amco II),* the ICSID tribunal awarded compensation as of the date of the award, not the date of breach. The tribunal reasoned:

> It may, on one view, be the case that in a lawful taking, Amco would have been entitled to the fair market value of the contract at the moment of dispossession. In making such a valuation, a tribunal in 1990 would necessarily exclude factors subsequent to 1980. But if Amco is to be placed as if the contract had remained in effect, then subsequent known factors bearing on that performance are to be reflected in the valuation technique.[225]

In *ADC* and *Siemens*, subsequent events served to increase the amount to be awarded by the tribunals. The *Amco Asia* tribunal, though, relied upon events subsequent to the expropriation date to adjust the amount of compensation payable by Indonesia.

---

223. *Id.*, at ¶ 352. The *Siemens* tribunal thus reached the same conclusion as the *ADC v. Hungary* tribunal regarding the impact on the compensation date from concluding that the expropriatory conduct violated international law. However, by awarding only sunk costs (lost expenditures) in USD, and rejecting the lost profits claim, the tribunal effectively refused to recognize any value resulting from the successful completion of the telecoms project (whether characterized as an increase in market value of the assets, know how, intangibles or goodwill). In light of the tribunal's express reliance on the Chorzów Factory standard, this aspect of the resulting compensation award is difficult to understand.
224. *Id.*, at ¶ 361. Similarly, the *Vivendi 2007* tribunal cited with approval the ruling by the Permanent Court of Arbitration in the *Lighthouse Arbitration (France v. Greece)* that "an injured party has the right to receive the equivalent at the date of the award suffered as a result of the illegal act and ought not to be prejudiced by the effects of a devaluation that takes place between the date of the wrongful act and the determination of the amount of compensation." *Vivendi 2007*, *supra* n. 72, at ¶ 8.4.5.
225. *Amco Asia v. Indonesia* (Amco Asia II), 1 ICSID Rev.–FILJ 569, ¶ 186. But *see* Ball, "Assessing Damages in Claims by Investors Against States," 16 ICSID Rev.-F.I.L.J. 408, 417 (2001), criticizing *Amco's* determination of damages at the date of the award as "unsupportable and arbitrary . . . [and] an anomaly and unreliable."

In addition to international arbitral tribunals, the US Supreme Court has asserted in its famous "Book of Wisdom" comment in the *Sinclair Refining* case that post-injury events may at times appropriately be considered when calculating damages.

> The law will make the best appraisal that it can, summoning to its service whatever aids it can.... At times the only evidence available may be that supplied by testimony of experts as to the state of the art, the character of the improvement, and the probable increase of efficiency or saving of expense.... But a different situation is presented if years have gone by before the evidence is offered. Experience is then available to correct uncertain prophecy. Here is a book of wisdom that courts may not neglect. We find no rule of law that sets a clasp upon its pages, and forbids us to look within.... To correct uncertain prophecies [for a breach of contract or a tort claim] is not to charge the offender with elements of value nonexisting at the time of his offense. It is to bring out and expose to light the elements of value that were there from the beginning.[226]

As the Supreme Court in effect recognized in *Sinclair Refining*, all estimates are uncertain. If good evidence of performance subsequent to the injury event does exist, a court (or an arbitral tribunal) may reasonably conclude that the actual business track record is useful information to be taken into account. That approach may be particulary sensible when some of the key assumptions underpinning an injury-date valuation prove with 20-20 hindsight, to have been significantly wrong.

Like the US Supreme Court, the House of Lords in the UK has also on occasion taken into account events occurring after the breach date when assessing damages. In *Golden Strait Corp. v. Nippon Yusen KK (The Golden Victory)*,[227] the breach date under a long-term charter party agreement was December 2001. The injured party sought damages for the remainder of the charter party contract period, through December 2005. However, the charter party contained a provision permitting either party to terminate the contract in the event of war between the US and Iraq and calling for arbitration of disputes. Faced with the need to calculate damages for the 2001 breach, the arbitrator concluded that the charter party would have been cancelled pursuant to that provision upon the outbreak of the Iraq war in March 2003. On review, the Court of Appeals upheld that valuation principle, accepting the argument that ignoring the impact of the subsequent 2003 war would have resulted in unjustly enriching the vessel owners for a loss it was now apparent they would not have suffered.[228]

The House of Lords considered the case and upheld the ruling of the arbitrator and the Court of Appeal. While acknowledging that calculating damages as of the injury date was the general rule, Lord Scott pointed out in his speech that the

226. *Sinclair Refining Co. v. Jenkins Petroleum Process Co.*, 289 US 689, 698 (1933) (citations omitted).
227. [2007] UKHL 12.
228. [2005] EWCA Civ. 1190.

general rule was subject to many exceptions and qualifications. He then quoted with approval from the *Bwllfa* case (a condemnation case):

> Lord Halsbury at 429 rejected the proposition that "because you could not arrive at the true sum when the notice was given, you should shut your eyes to the true sum now you do know it, because you could not have guessed it then" and Lord Robertson said at 432, that "estimate and conjecture are superseded by facts as the proper media concluded;" and, at 433, that "as in this instance facts are available, they are not to be shut out." Their Lordships were not dealing with a contractual, or tortious, damages issue but with the quantum of compensation to be paid under the Waterworks Clauses Act 1847. Their approach, however, is to my mind as apt for our purposes on this appeal as to theirs on that appeal.[229]

The prospect of unjust enrichment of the ship owners clearly played an important part in this decision. Lord Brown, for example, noted in his speech that the effect of the owners' argument would be to extend the general rule "at the plain expense" of a "fundamental principle: to restore the injured party to the same position he would have been in but for the breach, not substantially to improve it."[230]

The European Court of Human Rights has also considered post-expropriation events in valuing expropriated property under the European Convention of Human Rights. The ECHR "has repeatedly awarded amounts that took into account the increase in value of unlawfully expropriated property between the time of dispossession and the date of the judgment."[231]

Regardless of the date chosen, any market-value measure that assesses compensation as of a particular date (whether the injury date or the award date) will necessarily encounter the risk that the market prices at the chosen date prove not to be representative. Markets experience booms and busts. As former US Federal Reserve Board Chairman Alan Greenspan famously pointed out in 1996, "[H]ow do we know when irrational exuberance has unduly escalated asset values, which then become subject to unexpected and prolonged contractions as they have in Japan over the past decade?"[232] Arbitrators have faced that issue repeatedly in the

---

229. *Golden Strait Corp. v. Nippon Yusen KK* (the Golden Victory), *supra* n. 227, Lord Scott of Foscote, at ¶ 36. To the same effect, Lord Carswell at ¶ 66 and Lord Brown at ¶ 80. Lords Bingham of Cornwall and Walker of Gestingthorpe strongly dissented.
230. *Id.*, Lord Brown at ¶ 83.
231. Marboe, *Compensation and Damages in International Law – The Limits of "Fair Market Value,"* *supra* n. 84, at 752, citing to *Belvedere Alberghiera S.r.l. v. Italy*, E.C.H.R. No. 31524/9630, October 2003, ECHR 2000-vi, at ¶ 32, *Motais de Narbonne v. France*, E.C.H.R. No. 48161/99, May 27, 2003, at ¶ 19, and *Terazzi S.R.L. v. Italy*, E.C.H.R. No. 27265/95, October 26, 2004, at ¶ 37.
232. "The Challenge of Central Banking in a Democratic Society," remarks by Chairman Greenspan to The American Enterprise Institute for Public Policy Research, Washington, D.C., on 5 December 1996. *See* the discussion of *In re Iridium* at text associated with n. 45 *infra* for an illustration of high market values that proved to be wholly unrealistic.

past few years, often when presented with dot.com damages requests based upon market expectations from 1999 through early March 2000. The technology-heavy NASDAQ Composite index peaked on March 10, 2000 at over 5,048. By April 14, less than five weeks later, the NASDAQ Composite had plunged to 3,221, a drop of over 37%, and it steadily kept falling thereafter. A valuation date prior to that collapse would incorporate into a market-based valuation the extremely positive market assessments prevailing at the time. In contrast, a valuation date in late 2000 would incorporate the extremely negative market assessment prevailing at that later date. The risk of choosing a "boom" date or a "bust" date is embedded in any legal principle that calls for a market value to be determined by reference to a specific date for that market. The technical solution, to employ market values from a broader range of time in order to "normalize" numbers, is not normally embraced by legal systems.

XI COMMON LEGAL LIMITS TO COMPENSATION

Even when fair market value is accepted as the basic valuation principle for measuring an injury to an investment, legal systems routinely recognize a number of countervailing or limiting principles. As thoughtful readers will appreciate, many of these principles overlap in significant part.

Legal Principles Limiting Compensation

A checklist of common principles includes the following.

- Market Value "Too Speculative";
- Not a "Going Concern";
- Lack of Foreseeability;
- Lack of Causation and Comparative Fault;
- Burden of Proof;
- Mitigation;
- Unjust Enrichment and Other Equitable Considerations.

We consider a number of these principles in turn below.

1 Market Value Too Speculative

Many legal systems reject consideration of lost earnings opportunities when the future prospects of the enterprise are too "speculative" or "uncertain" to support such an award. As the tribunal in the *Amoco* case observed: "One of the best settled rules of the law on international responsibility of States is that no reparation for speculative or uncertain damage can be awarded (op. cit. para. 238)."[233]

National laws and international law do not require that future revenues, expenses or profits be proved with absolute certainty.[234] Nor does life generally. As Bertrand Russell has commented that "[t]he demand for certainty is one which is natural to man, but is nevertheless an intellectual vice."[235] However, at some point the impact of future uncertainties undermines the persuasiveness of estimates of future business results.[236] Thus, Article 7.4.3 of the UNIDROIT Principles of International Commercial Contracts requires that injury be established "with a reasonable degree of certainty."

Article 7.4.3
(Certainty of harm)

1. Compensation is due only for harm, including future harm that is established with a reasonable degree of certainty.
2. Compensation may be due for the loss of a chance in proportion to the probability of its occurrence.
3. Where the amount of damages cannot be established with a sufficient degree of certainty, the assessment is at the discretion of the court.

Legal systems establish different thresholds for proof to recover lost profits.[237] US law, for example, recognizes that an injured party may generally recover in breach of contract cases for loss of future profits so long as the fact of lost profits has been proven with "reasonable certainty." Thus, the US Restatement of Contracts sets out the following principle:

233. *Amoco International Finance Corp. v. Islamic Republic of Iran*, No. 310-56-3, Partial Award of July 14, 1987, Iran-US C.T.R. 189, at ¶ 238 (hereinafter "*Amoco v. Iran*").
234. "The only way to escape uncertainty in awarding compensation is to employ methods – such as book value – that are irrelevant to economic value because they focus on the past and not the future." Lieblich, "Determining the Economic Value of Expropriated Income–Producing Property in International Expropriations," 8 J. Int. Arb. 37, 77 (1991). As the *Vivendi 2007* tribunal stated, "it is well settled that the fact that damages cannot be fixed with certainty is no reason not to award damages when a loss has been incurred. In such cases, approximations are inevitable; the settling of damages is not an exact science." *Vivendi 2007, supra* n. 72, at ¶ 8.3.16 (footnotes omitted). *See also* the cases cited at *id.*, nn. 420, 421.
235. Russell, "Philosophy for Laymen," *Unpopular Essays* at 38 (Routledge 1996).
236. *See* Delaware Open MRI Radiology Associates, *P.A. v. Kessler, supra* n. 3, at 332 ("Without a reliable estimate of cash flows, a DCF analysis is simply a guess.").
237. As Prof. Gotanda has noted in a paper presented at the British Institute of International and Comparative Law's 8th Annual Investment Treaty Forum symposium on Damages in International Investment Law, "under the UNIDROIT Principles and under some laws, where the amount of damages cannot be established with sufficient degree of certainty, the assessment is at the discretion of the tribunals." Gotanda, "Assessing Damages in International Commercial Arbitration: A Comparison with Investment Treaty Disputes," (May 11, 2007) at 2–3. *See also* UNIDROIT Principles of International Commercial Contracts, Art. 7.4.4(3).

352. Uncertainty as a Limitation on Damages

Damages are not recoverable for loss beyond an amount that the evidence permits to be established with reasonable certainty.

COMMENTS & ILLUSTRATIONS: Comment:

a. Requirement of certainty. A party cannot recover damages for breach of a contract for loss beyond the amount that the evidence permits to be established with reasonable certainty.... Courts have traditionally required greater certainty in the proof of damages for breach of a contract than in the proof of damages for a tort. The requirement does not mean, however, that the injured party is barred from recovery unless he establishes the total amount of his loss. It merely excludes those elements of loss that cannot be proved with reasonable certainty. The main impact of the requirement of certainty comes in connection with recovery for lost profits. Although the requirement of certainty is distinct from that of foreseeability (§ 351), its impact is similar in this respect...

Doubts are generally resolved against the party in breach. A party who has, by his breach, forced the injured party to seek compensation in damages should not be allowed to profit from his breach where it is established that a significant loss has occurred. A court may take into account all the circumstances of the breach, including willfulness, in deciding whether to require a lesser degree of certainty, giving greater discretion to the trier of the facts. Damages need not be calculable with mathematical accuracy and are often at best approximate.... This is especially true for items such as loss of good will as to which great precision cannot be expected.... Furthermore, increasing receptiveness on the part of courts to proof by sophisticated economic and financial data and by expert opinion has made it easier to meet the requirement of certainty.[238]

Similarly, Article 1149 of the French Civil Code authorizes recovery of lost profits, subject to the requirements that such damages have been "foreseeable" at the time of contracting unless the breach was willful (Article 1152) and that the damages be the "immediate and direct result of the breach" (Article 1284).[239]

Careful lawyers may seek to draw a distinction between, first, the level of certainty that must be shown regarding whether profits would have been made but for the injury to the business and, second, the level of certainty required for computation of those lost profits. Many courts do not require the same level of certainty

238. Restatement (Second) of Contracts, § 352 (citations omitted). The Restatement notes that lost profits in contract cases must be proved with reasonable certainty, but that less certainty will normally be required for damages in a tort case. Moreover, the Restatement states that doubts are generally resolved against the party in breach.

239. Quoted in *Patuha Power Ltd. (Bermuda) v. PT.* (Persero) Perusahaan Listruik Negara (Indonesia), Final Award, 14 Mealey's Int. Arb. Rep. B-1 (1999) (hereinafter "*Patuha v. PLN Final Award*"), ¶ 403, noting similarities between comparable provisions of the Indonesian and French Civil Codes.

for the amount of damages, as compared with the fact of damages. As Dunn states in a leading US treatise:

> It would be misleading to discuss the "reasonable certainty" rule without stating its most important qualification. Those courts that have gone further than a simple statement that "reasonable certainty" is required have almost invariably recognized that the rule applies only to the *fact* of damages, not to the *amount* of damages. Proof of the fact of damages in a lost profits case means proof that there would have been some profits. If plaintiff's proof leaves uncertain whether plaintiff would have made any profits at all, there can be no recovery. But once this level of causation has been established for the *fact* of damages, less certainty (perhaps none at all) is required in proof of the *amount* of damages. While the proof of the *fact* of damages must be certain, proof of the *amount* may be an estimate, uncertain or inexact.[240]

Prof. Gotanda argues that requiring a high level of certainty for the amount of damages unfairly burdens the injured party and benefits the party whose conduct has made it so hard to calculate the loss:

> I believe that the amount of lost profits does not need to be established concretely or with certainty. That would place an almost insurmountable burden on the claimant and benefit the party who caused the damage and prevented the claimant from being able to prove concretely its loss. In order to be entitled to lost profits, the claimant must show with reasonable certainty that profits would have been made absent the respondent's actions. Once a claimant is able to show with reasonable certainty the fact of loss of profits, the claimant then needs only to provide a basis upon which a tribunal can reasonably estimate the extent of the claimant's loss of profits. This approach strikes a balance between the need for evidence upon which a tribunal may base an award of lost profits and the recognition that the difficulty in proving damages stems from the respondent's action.[241]

---

240. Dunn, *Recovery of Damages for Lost Profits, supra* n. 125, § 1.6, at 17 (emphasis in original). This statement is followed by five pages of US citations. *See also id.*, § 5.1, at 382–383; and the comment by the ICSID tribunal in *Vivendi 2007, supra* n. 72, at ¶ 8.3.3, noting that the awards relied upon by the claimant in their submissions distinguished the level of certainty required for the future probability of lost profits – the fact of probability as opposed to the amount. According to Gotanda, "Damages in Private International Law," 326 Recuil des cours 77 (Hague Academy of International Law, Martinus Nijhoff 2007), "the certainty rule applies to only the fact of damages, not to the amount of damages" in a wide range of jurisdictions, including England (*id.*, at 102), Belgium and other European civil law countries "generally" (*id.*, at 111), Canada (*id.*, at 117), the United States (*id.*, at 127), Brazil and other Latin American civil law countries "generally" (*id.*, at 131), Australia and New Zealand (*id.*, at 135) and India (*id.*, at 138).
241. Gotanda, "Assessing Damages in International Commercial Arbitration: A Comparison with Investment Treaty Disputes," at 4–5 (footnotes omitted), presented at British Institute for International and Comparative Law May11, 2007 8th annual Investment Treaty Forum. *See also* Paulsson, "The Expectation Model," at 60, in Derains & Kreindler (ed.), *Evaluation of Damages in International Arbitration* (ICC Institute of World Business Law 2006); Gotanda, "Recovering Lost Profits in International Disputes," *supra* n. 40, at 61.

The level of certainty required to show that an injured party would have realized future earnings is obviously affected if some future contingency must occur before those profits will crystallize. Conduct of another party (for example, breach of contract) may prevent the business activity from proceeding to the point in time when that contingency would be expected to crystallize. The injured claimant in such a case may then seek to recover for the "loss of the chance" to earn that profit. The UNIDROIT Principles of International Commercial Contracts acknowledge that compensation may be appropriate in such circumstances. Moreover, the UNIDROIT Principles prescribe that the basis for compensation should be the probability that the lost opportunity would have occurred. Thus, UNIDROIT Article 7.4.3(2) provides that compensation in such circumstances is to be computed on the basis of the likelihood of the chance crystallizing: "(2) Compensation may be due for the loss of a chance in proportion to the probability of its occurrence."

As the UNIDROIT Official Comments to Article 7.4.3(2) put it, compensation for the loss of a chance is proportionate to the probability of the chance coming to fruition. Compensation for a lost chance is due:

> obviously only in proportion to the probability of its occurrence; thus, the owner of a horse which arrives too late to run in a race as a result of delay in transport cannot recover the whole of the prize money, even though the horse was the favorite.[242]

Employing the illustration of an improperly delayed tender for the construction of an airport, the UNIDROIT Official Comments specify that the amount of compensation for the lost opportunity to win the tender will require a comparison with the tenders that were admitted for consideration and the degree of probability that the injured competitor's tender would have been accepted by the offeror. "The compensation will therefore be calculated as a proportion of the profit which it [the injured competitor] might have made."[243] The Official Comments follow this illustration by pointing to Article 7.4.3(3) for the measure of damages, stating that "rather than refuse any compensation or award nominal damages, the court is empowered to make an equitable quantification of the harm sustained."[244]

The damages rule in Article 7.4.3(2) for the loss of a chance directly addresses a difficult issue in many arbitrations; what to do when it is clear that the conduct in question has impaired the value of a business, but there is a lack of good evidence about the extent of that impairment (i.e., the measurement of the lost value). In the "lost opportunity" situation, of course, the absence of that evidence is attributable to the conduct of the other party. The same issue, though, will exist in many business valuation situations as well. It is noteworthy that, in the lost opportunity

242. Official Comment to UNIDROIT Principles of International Commercial Contracts, Article 7.4.3, ¶ 1.

243. *Id.*, at ¶ 2.

244. *Id.*, Cases considering compensation for the loss of a chance under Article 7.4.3(2) may be found in the UNILEX database at <www.unilex.info/dynasite.cfm?dssid=2377&dsmid=13621&x=1>.

context, the UNIDROIT Principles do not instruct arbitrators in those circumstances to forego the effort to compute quantum. Instead, Article 7.4.3(2) expressly instructs arbitrators to determine the probability of the contingency. That effort clearly calls for the exercise of judgment by the arbitral panel. Probabilities and proportions, and equitable quantification, may thus play a role in the computation of lost profits that would in any event have been subject to future contingencies.

Not all bodies of law afford compensation for a lost chance. According to an opinion of the CISG Advisory Council, damages for loss of a chance are not ordinarily recoverable under the general damages provision of the CISG, Article 74.[245] However, the CISG Advisory Council qualifies this conclusion, asserting that the prohibition of damages under the CISG for a lost opportunity will not apply if the injured party has

> purposely entered into a contract in order to obtain a chance of earning a profit. In such a case, the chance of profit is an asset, and, when a party chooses to enter into a contract to obtain such a chance, the party is entitled to compensation when the promisor unjustifiably does not perform. Otherwise, a promisor could breach that contract with impunity and avoid ''liability solely on the basis of the [aggrieved party's]'' difficulty of proving loss where it is clear at the time of formation that such loss would be impossible to prove with reasonable certainty.[246]

As is apparent from the foregoing, one important task facing an arbitrator is to decide the degree of certainty supporting a claim for lost future opportunities.

Reasonable Certainty

A commonly accepted standard for awarding forward-looking compensation (the expectancy interest) is that damages must be proved with reasonable certainty. Courts, arbitrators and commentators differ as to whether both the fact of lost profits and the amount of lost profits must meet the reasonable certainty standard, or if only the fact of lost profits must satisfy this standard. Some investment treaty arbitral tribunals have set the ''reasonable certainty'' threshold very high.

The *Vivendi 2007* ICSID award illustrates the factual circumstances that may cause a tribunal to consider a future earnings-based valuation too uncertain to support an award. Vivendi, the investor, presented a DCF valuation. Vivendi offered evidence that the water company (CAA) to be valued was not a start-up, was a

245. ''CISG Advisory Council Opinion No. 6, Calculation of Damages under CISG Article 74,'' 2006 *Nordic Journal of Commercial Law*, issue 2, at ¶ 3.15.
246. *Id.*, at ¶ 3.16 (footnotes omitted), quoting Murray on Contracts, Lexis Nexis 4th edn 2001, § 121. Authorities from the US, the UK and Belgium are cited at ¶ 3.16 n. 75.

revenue-generating enterprise and had a 65% recovery rate on its first invoices. Vivendi also provided evidence of high invoice recovery rates for other utilities in the same region. The ICSID panel, though, considered that evidence insufficient. Claimants assertions that the concession operated as going concern before, during and after CAA's tenure border on the fanciful.[247] For this purpose, the tribunal defined a "going concern" as "a business enterprise with demonstrable future earning power."[248] The tribunal pointed out that, prior to Vivendi taking over, the concession had covered only 30% of its revenues, had been "looted" by the provincial government, its operations deteriorated steadily, it could not provide services to cover the population growth rate, and it ran an average deficit of USD 17 million. The tribunal quoted claimants themselves that the concession "was not financially viable."[249] According to the tribunal, CAA (the Vivendi investment vehicle) never made a profit during its July 1995 to August 1997 tenure as operator (or the so-called "hostage period" when CAA was required to continue operating the concession after termination until October 1998). Moreover, CAA only had a positive accounting book value during this period because it was required by the Argentine authorities to carry as an asset on its books USD 55 million "of unpaid (and largely uncollectible) customer invoices."[250]

The *Vivendi 2007* panel commented that "the absence of a history of demonstrated profitability does not absolutely preclude the use of DCF valuation methodology."[251] To overcome the absence of a record of profits, however, the arbitrators concluded that a claimant must provide "convincing evidence of its ability to produce profits in the particular circumstances it faced:"[252]

> A claimant which cannot rely on a record of demonstrated profitability requires to present a thoroughly prepared record of its (or others) successes, based on first-hand experience (its own or that of qualified experts) or corporate records which establish on the balance of the probabilities it would have produced profits from the concession in question in the face of the particular risks involved, other than those of Treaty violation.[253]

The calculation of lost future earnings may be particularly challenging for business enterprises that have not yet begun production. Equally, it is challenging to forecast lost revenues for companies that are selling their products into an uncertain, illiquid market, especially if the company does not have binding purchase commitments in hand.[254] A start-up company hoping in the future to sell its products into an illiquid

247. *Id.*, at ¶ 8.3.6.
248. *Id.*
249. *Id.*
250. *Id.*, at ¶ 8.3.7.
251. *Id.*, at ¶ 8.3.8.
252. *Id.*, at ¶ 8.3.8.
253. *Id.*, at ¶ 8.3.8.
254. *See Levitt v. Islamic Republic of Iran*, 14 Iran-US Cl. Trib. Rep. 191 (1987), which involved the business of selling housing units in Iran. *See also* cases cited in Gotanda, "Recovering Lost Profits in International Disputes," *supra*, n. 40, at 94 n. 180.

market and without binding purchase commitments is, of course, triply difficult to analyze. In those circumstances, it is very hard to derive earnings forecasts for that company by means of comparisons with the market performance of competitors. For US courts, the extent of tangible business activity is an important factor.

> When the courts label a damages projection as speculative, this is something more than a mere catchall for a negative result. The unifying idea in the cases cited seems to be that the claimed losses derived not from an enterprise or activity that has come into existence, but from plans that never went further than anticipation. Recovery of lost profits damages on these tenuous facts has consistently been denied. If the business exists only in the contemplation of plaintiff, proof of lost profits is likely to be speculation. Nonetheless, if plaintiff can point to some tangible activity, past or present, the likelihood of recovery increases.[255]

In the arena of international investment law, a somewhat stricter test has been applied by some tribunals. Crawford's Commentaries on the ILC Articles summarize the various rulings in the following fashion:

> In cases where lost future profits have been awarded, it has been where an anticipated income stream has attained sufficient attributes to be considered a legally protected interest of sufficient certainty to be compensable. This has normally been achieved by virtue of contractual arrangements or, in some cases, a well-established history of dealings.[256]

For at least one tribunal, even the presence of a contractual basis for future revenues was insufficient if the contract in question does not contain the requisite level of commitment by the buyer of the company's products. The arbitral tribunal in *Petrobart Limited v. The Kyrgyz Republic* focused on the absence of an enforceable guarantee of purchases under a long-term petrochemicals contract:

> Even if the Arbitral Tribunal were inclined to entertain Petrobart's future profit claim, such claim must nevertheless fail. Neither the Contract nor Petrobart's contract with Uzneftegazdobicha is an "outputs" contract. That is to say, these contracts do not bind Petrobart to purchase from Uzneftegazdobicha, and they do not bind KGM to purchase from Petrobart. They are both contracts that provide a mechanism for Petrobart and KGM, respectively, to order shipments of gas condensate and to pay for those shipments when they are delivered. KGM could have stopped ordering gas condensate at any time. As such, Petrobart has no legitimate expectation interest in potential future profits.[257]

---

255. Dunn, *Recovery of Damages for Lost Profits*, *supra* n. 125, ¶ 728 at 607.
256. Commentaries, *supra* n. 96, at 260.
257. *See Petrobart Limited v. The Kyrgyz Republic*, Arbitral Award, March 29, 2005 Arb. No. 126/2003, "Arbitration Institute of the Stockholm Chamber of Commerce," available at <http://ita.law.uvics.com>.

In contrast to the circumstances in *Petrobart*, a company (even a start-up company) may have already entered into a long-term enforceable sales contract with a creditworthy purchaser. Examples of such long-term sales contracts include multi-year liquefied natural gas contracts and power purchase agreements – such "output" contracts naturally reduce the risk that the covered products will be unable to find willing buyers at commercially reasonable prices. If the arbitrator is satisfied that the necessary pre-conditions for payments under that contract will be fulfilled, then an Income-Based calculation of damages for lost future earnings or a breach of contract lost profits claim may be reasonably certain even though development of the business did not proceed very far before the dispute arose.

Of course, even if a binding output contract exists, the project may not yet have completed development. Until it is up and running, the project is not capable of generating revenue – for example, a power project cannot sell electricity to a power purchaser and obtain any income unless and until construction has been completed. The potential for successful completion of the investment will be affected by commercial risks, such as the prospects for delays in construction or technical difficulties. Similarly, political and natural *force majeure* events may impede fulfillment of that object as well. Moreover, even after the investment is operating the value of a long-term output purchase agreement will depend on the creditworthiness of the purchaser. In the author's experience, those impediments have not prevented an admittedly illiquid market from developing for the buying and selling of equity interests in projects under development. Of course, the buy-sell prices for such ownership interests will reflect the market's perception of the uncertainties surrounding the business' value, up or down. Indeed, the infamous Hubco power project in Pakistan successfully offered its shares publicly on the Karachi and London Stock Exchange long before physical completion of the power plant, and those shares traded regularly at market prices.[258] Similarly, the Al Manah project in Oman completed a successful initial public offering of equity shares on the Muscat stock market even before the project's construction and long-term debt financing was in place, and in that case too the shares traded regularly in a liquid market. While there is no official listing of the private sale of ownership interests in projects under development, project finance trade periodicals such as *Power in Asia, Power in Europe, Project Finance* and *Project Finance Monthly* routinely report on such transactions. It is therefore apparent that market valuations for companies at early stages in development may indeed exist.

258. According to the Hub Power Company Limited October 5, 1994 Offering Memorandum for Global Depository Receipts, at the time of the IPO in October 1994 completion of the first Unit was scheduled for June 1996 and completion of the entire plant was not expected before March 1997.

Market Value Measures for Companies with a Limited Track Record

Companies at an early stage in their business life may be especially difficult to value. However, it is not unusual for investors to buy and sell interests in such businesses. It is therefore apparent that a market value for such interests (or for the entire business) can be estimated by means of methods within the Income-, Market and Asset-Based Approaches. For example, the discount rate in a DCF valuation may be increased or the goodwill component of an Adjusted Book Value valuation may be decreased, in each case to reflect the uncertainties facing the business. The valuation challenge is to determine a principled and reliable basis for that increase or decrease.

Concerns in international investment cases over the "speculative and uncertain" nature of lost profits are not limited to companies at an early stage in their business lives. Illustratively, the enterprises at issue in the *LG&E v. Argentina* dispute all had track records of dividends covering several years prior to the imposition by Argentina of its pesification measures. Moreover, those companies continued to pay dividends throughout the period up to the ICSID hearing and award in that case, albeit at a level the tribunal held to have been impaired by the unlawful Argentine regulatory measures. Despite having evidence of prior dividends from 1993 through 2005 at hand,[259] the *LG&E* tribunal rejected the investor's claim for future dividends because "future loss to the Claimants is uncertain and any attempt to calculate it is speculative."[260]

As discussed below, the DCF, APV and CCF valuation methods can also accommodate such uncertainties by "risk-adjusting" the discount rate used to calculate the present value of the future stream of projected earnings. If such risks create too much uncertainty, though, some tribunals may decide to reject such an Income-Based method computation as insufficiently certain to sustain a damage award for lost future earnings. For example, in a dispute involving a start-up company, the arbitrators in the ICSID case of *PSEG v. Turkey*[261] did not accept claimants' arguments in favor of recovering lost profits under a Concession Contract for a power project. The start-up nature of the project played a significant role, as did a gap in the Concession Contract with respect to pricing terms. The panel stressed Turkey's "convincing" argument that "in cases where lost profits have been awarded ... this measure has been based on a long history of operations." The claimants tried valiantly to distinguish that line of cases, pointing to the payment obligations of the Turkish Ministry of Energy and Natural Resources under the

259. *LG&E v. Argentina* Final Award, *supra* n. 7, at § 74 (referring to "average annual dividends for the 1993–2001 period") and ¶ 108 (listing "actual dividends paid Aug. 2000 – Feb. 2005").
260. *Id.*, at ¶ 90. The *LG&E* case represents perhaps the most stringent test of "reasonable certainty" of the many investment treaty cases considering requests for lost profits.
261. *PSEG v. Turkey*, *supra* n. 179.

Concession Contract to provide the requisite certainty to support a lost profits claim. The Tribunal acknowledged that, in a proper case, binding contractual revenue obligations could overcome the absence of an operating history for the investment, just not on the *PSEG* facts:

> The Tribunal would have no difficulty with this proposition, because in fact a self-contained and fully detailed contract can well determine a basis for the calculation of future profits. However, the Tribunal must also note that in many long-term contracts it is most difficult if not impossible to calculate such future profits with certainty, particularly if the contract is subject to adjustment mechanisms and other possible variations with time.... Even assuming that none of these difficulties existed, in this case the exercise becomes moot because the parties never finalized the essential commercial terms of the Contract.[262]

The approach taken by the *PSEG v. Turkey* tribunal can be construed to set a high barrier to successful lost profits claims by start-up companies, even if there is a binding off-take agreement. For private power projects, though, long-term power purchase agreements with take-or-pay tariffs have begun to disappear in many countries in favor of short-term market-based pricing (so-called "merchant" power plants), even if the purchases are effected under a long-term umbrella contract. Some years ago, that trend became common as well in several other industries where long-term contracts are customary but a trading market exists; for example, LNG purchases, pipeline transportation contracts, oil & gas sales, and mining and other natural resource supply agreements. The test offered by the *PSEG v. Turkey* panel is capable of being interpreted to question the viability of lost profits claims for a start-up company with a long-term contract unless the contract in question does not have a price adjustment clause – an increasingly rare situation.

As should be apparent, a tendency on the part of tribunals to decline to award future-looking damages on the basis of insufficient certainty often shows up in claims by investors against States – claimants face a high burden of proof requirement. By way of comparison, in US breach of contract cases "doubts are generally resolved against the party in breach." In shareholder appraisal cases in the Delaware courts under the Delaware corporations law, yet another approach prevails. Neither disputing party bears the burden of proof. Instead, the court is charged to reach an independent valuation.[263] In contrast, international investment law cases like *LG&E* and *PSEG* betray a noticeable desire on the part of the arbitrators to look for means of minimizing the compensation payable by the breaching host State. For example, in addition to the *LG&E, PSEG* and *Petrobart* awards, in *Levitt v. Islamic Republic of Iran,*[264] a well-known Iran-US Claims Tribunal

262. *Id.*, at ¶ 312.
263. *See* text associated with n. 355 *infra*.
264. *Levitt v. Islamic Republic of Iran, supra* n. 254. *See also* cases cited in Gotanda, "Recovering Lost Profits in International Disputes," *supra* n. 40, at 94 n. 180.

case involving a contract for the construction and sale of 2,500 housing units, the panel entirely denied recovery of lost profits as too speculative in the circumstances.[265]

> 56. In the present instance, however, the basis of the claim . . . is highly speculative. While a profit margin of 18 percent appears in the proposal documents submitted for approval and later attached to the letter of intent signed by MHUD [the Iranian Ministry of Housing and Urban Development], no such provision was carried into the Contract itself. By the time the contract came to an end only the initial stages of clearing and grading had been completed, and no construction work had begun on buildings. The project had therefore reached only a very early stage.
>
> 57. Initially, the prospects looked favorable. The level of interest shown by prospective purchasers before the revolution was encouraging, and government approval had been given for the grant of the mortgage financing. Indeed, HO [the Housing Organization of Iran] was obliged by the terms of the Contract to use its best endeavors to obtain such financing. The demand for such housing might well have survived the events of the Revolution. However, the evidence indicates that ICC [International Construction Company, the builder] would have experienced considerable difficulties in proceeding with the major phases of the construction under the prevalent conditions of disruption and unrest, particularly in view of the fact that it was the first such project Mr. Levitt had undertaken in Iran. It is most unlikely that the project could have been completed according to the time schedule originally envisaged, or that the cost would not have been greatly increased by difficulties in providing supervision by the Levitt organization and in obtaining imported materials.
>
> 58. For these reasons the Tribunal finds that the Claimant has not established with a sufficient degree of certainty that the project would have resulted in a profit. The claim in this respect is therefore dismissed.

The *Levitt* Tribunal concluded that the expropriation by Iran of the housing enterprise had occurred after the events of the Iranian Revolution. Accordingly, the Tribunal factored the impact of the Revolution into its view of the venture's future prospects. Also, the enterprise in *Levitt* did not have any commitments from either the Iranian government or prospective purchasers of the housing units to buy the units once constructed.

Similarly, in 1987 Chamber Three of Iran-US Claims Tribunal completely rejected in the *Amoco* case the use of cash flow projections to identify market value. In that panel's view, the projections in the case were too speculative for reliance. Going further, though, the Tribunal also stated: "As a projection into the future, any cash flow has an element of speculation associated with it, as recognized by the Claimant. For this reason it is disputable whether a tribunal can use it

---

265. *Levitt v. Islamic Republic of Iran, supra* n. 254, at ¶¶ 56–58.

at all for the valuation of compensation."[266] The underlying joint venture company (Khemco) in that case had conducted profitable commercial operations from 1970 through 1977, the last full year of production prior to the Iranian Revolution. By late December 1980, Amoco's interests in Khemco had been expropriated.[267] Chamber Three concluded that the expropriation was "lawful." In determining the amount of compensation to be awarded, the tribunal held that Amoco was not entitled to compensation calculated in reliance upon the DCF method.[268] The *Amoco* award severely criticized the use of the DCF method as speculative, unrelated to the replacement value of the underlying elements of the enterprise and potentially leading to unjust enrichment of the injured party.[269]

> 239. The element of speculation in a short-term projection is rather limited, although unexpected events can make it turn out to be wrong. The speculative element rapidly increases with the number of years to which a projection relates. It is well known, and certainly taken into account by investors, that if it applies to a rather distant future a projection is almost purely speculative, even if it is done by the most serious and experienced forecasting firms, especially if it relates to such a volatile factor as oil prices. Such projections can be useful indications for a prospective investor, who understands how far it can rely on them and accepts the risks associated with them; they certainly cannot be used by a tribunal as the measure of a fair compensation.

Prof. Wells too raises the issue of inherent uncertainty in the course of criticizing the damages awarded in the arbitration brought by Karaha Bodas Company. That case involved breach by Indonesian state-owned entities Pertamina and PLN of a thirty-year take-or-pay Energy Sales Contract and Joint Operation Contract for the development and operation of a geothermal power project.[270] The Indonesian government halted the project in question early in its construction. Prof. Wells states:

> Projecting the stream of earnings for 30 years requires some heroic assumptions, especially for a project that has not yet been completed and thus has no

---

266. *Amoco v. Iran*, *supra* n. 233, at 262. Despite *Amoco*, of course, since 1987 numerous arbitral tribunals have in fact used a DCF computation for the valuation of an injured enterprise. *See* text associated with n. 284 et seq. and n. 417 et seq. Smutny, *supra* n. 115, at 12, asserts that the fact DCF analyses necessarily require "projections and estimates . . . based upon degree of speculation does not render them *per se* too speculative as a basis for award." In this context, she points out that the World Bank Guidelines on the Treatment of Foreign Direct Investment, as well as a number of investment treaties, expressly mention that DCF forecasts may be an appropriate measure of value. She also comments that DCF forecasts are widely used by business to fix "real" market values.
267. *Amoco v. Iran*, *supra* n. 233.
268. *Id.*, at ¶ 132.
269. *Id.*, at ¶¶ 228–232, 239.
270. Wells, "Double Dipping in Arbitration Awards? An Economist Questions Damages Awarded to Karaha Bodas Company in Indonesia," 19 Arb. Int. 471, 474–475 (2003) (hereinafter, "Wells"). The case is *Karaha Bodas Company L.L.C. v. Perusahaan Pertambangan Minyak Dan Gas Bumi Negara (Pertamina)* and PT. PLN (Persero), Final Award (18 December 2000) (hereinafter, "Karaha Bodas Final Award").

track record; in some cases, such projections are essential, as uncertain as they might be; but there are advantages in seeking another approach when another is feasible.

Prof. Wells suggests instead that damages in that case should have been limited to the investor's reliance interest – recovery of invested sums, plus interest thereon (or possibly lost profits) from the investment date until payment (i.e., *damnum emergens* or "investment costs"). The successful claimant could then reinvest that amount in other profit-making ventures. Prof. Wells says:

> When the investment is very recent, or still in the process of being made, there is an obvious and often easier alternative to using NPV [the net present value] of future cash flow to determine FMV [the fair market value]. If the project was expected to generate "normal" rates of return for the business, then the amount of investment itself provides a reasonable starting point for determining FMV. In most cases, the FMV of recently acquired assets is unlikely to be substantially different from the cost of those assets. Cost of investment will approximate what a buyer might pay; moreover, the investor who receives his investment back can invest the sum in another project, earn normal returns, and be equally well off. For most unfinished projects, this should end the calculations.[271]

Prof. Wells' comment that "sunk investment costs" may be the appropriate measure "when the investment is very recent, or still in the process of being made," is consistent with business valuation practices. As the International Private Equity Valuation Guidelines point out, "Where the Investment being valued was itself made recently, its cost will generally provide a good indication of Fair Value."[272] There is no binding valuation rule to help us understand what is meant by "recent" in these circumstances. However, private equity investors often employ a one-year rule of thumb to determine if the investment was made sufficiently recently to justify relying on the cost of investment for valuation purposes: "This length of period will depend on the specific circumstances of the case, but should not generally exceed a period of one year."[273]

---

271. Wells, *supra* n. 270, at 475. *Smutny* points out that "strictly speaking . . . where there is a high degree of uncertainty as to what future revenues and costs would be, the discounted cash flow method simply calls for application of a higher discount factor to reflect the greater risk that the predicted level of profits in fact would be achieved. What tribunals tend to do in such cases, however, rather than simply apply a very high discount factor, is revert to another means of measuring the fair market value of the enterprise or property." Smutny, *supra* n. 115, at 13. Wells, though, would equate compensation based on the fair market value of the *Karaha Bodas* investment with restoring the parties to a position that would have existed if the investment had never been made.
272. "International Private Equity Valuation Guidelines," *supra* n. 26, at 14.
273. *Id.*, at 26. *See also id.*, at 15, 25. *See also* Question 14 of the FAQs regarding the "International Private Equity Valuation Guidelines," at <www.privateequityvaluation.com/faq.php#14> (recommending that the Valuer assess the appropriateness of continuing to rely on the price of the investment for "fair value" purposes even before the one year period has ended, if circumstances so warrant).

If an arbitral panel adopts that approach, then no incremental value will be accorded to development and construction activities for an unfinished project beyond the acquisition cost of paying for those activities.[274] Such assets and activities may include completed feasibility studies, successful testing of geothermal reserves, construction plans and specifications, construction contracts, any partial construction work and, most importantly, execution of binding offtake agreements with take-or-pay commitments from the offtaker.[275] A "sunk investment costs" or reliance interest approach to compensation covers the out-of-pocket costs attributable to these matters, but it does not take into account (of course without double counting) the impact up or down of such expenditures on the market value of the investment from the perspective of a willing buyer – willing seller.

Changes in Value After the Investment Is Made

A reliance-interest measure of compensation based on "sunk investment costs" will not take account of the impact on the market value of the investment (up or down) resulting either from the activities funded by the invested capital or economic, political and social changes subsequent to the investment date. For example, in the capital invested in a prospective gold mine is employed to undertake feasibility studies, the results of those feasibility studies (gold vs. no gold) will significantly affect the market value of the enterprise. Similarly, the impact of macroeconomic events after the capital has been invested (high GDP growth vs. recession) will also significantly affect the investment's market value.

The possible scenarios appear to be:

(i) the "work done" created no incremental value (wasted effort, gold-plating, non-arm's length transactions, and so on);[276]

274. Crucial to Prof. Wells' approach is the assertion that "the FMV of recently acquired assets is unlikely to be substantially different from the cost of those assets." For consideration of that proposition, *see* the discussion of Adjusted Book Value in Ch. 7 *infra*. As to whether the assets of the Karaha Bodas project were "recently acquired," *see* the next succeeding footnote.

275. It is clear from the *Karaha Bodas Final Award* that, at a minimum, the project entered into binding take-or-pay project agreements with Indonesian State enterprises in 1994, spent significant sums on geothermal exploration and drilling in 1995–1997, developed infrastructure at the project site and trained technical staff. *See* Karaha Bodas Final Award, *supra* n. 270, at ¶¶ 5, 9, 86, 105. The project company gave a notice of resource confirmation to support 60 MW of electrical power in September 1997, a notice of intent to develop 110 MW in December 1997 and a subsequent notice of resource confirmation for 210 MW in December 1997. The Indonesian side objected during the arbitration to the credibility of these notices. The project was suspended by the Indonesian Government two days after the first notice, revived in November 1997 and indefinitely suspended again in January 1998. The continuing suspension was affirmed in March 1998. The project company brought its arbitration claim less than two months later.

276. "[I]f some of the investment was wasteful, or represented over-invoiced transactions with affiliates, the market value would be less than the amount invested. Indonesians claimed that

(ii) the "work done" created incremental value,[277] meaning that work was retained by the project company but could not be converted into value because the actions of the host State prevented the project company from realizing on that value (for example, the host State prohibited further development of the project, regardless of who might own it);
(iii) the "work done" created incremental value and the host State acquired that value as part of the measures taken by the host State (say, a classic expropriation); and
(iv) the "work done" created incremental value, that work was retained by the project company and the work could be transferred to a third party (for instance, the project-in-development could be sold to a third party who would be lawfully entitled to complete the project).

It is clear that scenario (i) should produce no additional payments to the project company beyond "sunk costs." Moreover, one may argue that in such a situation the compensation should in fact be reduced because the project's market value had diminished.[278] Thus, the compensation could be determined on the basis of the lower "market value" of the investment, not the higher "sunk costs." That is what the ICSID tribunal did in *Azurix v. Argentina*;[279] Azurix paid USD 438 million to the Government for a concession having a market value determined by the tribunal to be only USD 60 million not long afterwards. In that case, the Argentine authorities actually benefited from the wasted sums because they comprised an above-market-value purchase price paid by Azurix to the Government for the concession. Similarly, in scenario (iv) the project company retains the incremental value in a realizable fashion, although perhaps the State's regulatory conduct has reduced value by forcing the project company into a "fire sale." The company clearly should not be double compensated for the value it retains. Scenarios (ii) and (iii), though, involve situations where the market value of the property obtained by means of the investment was greater than the amount of the invested capital. By reason of sweat equity, goodwill, changes in market values for tangible or intangible property and the like, the investment has grown in value as a result of movement forward on the project. If that value was, at the time, freely transferable to a willing buyer in an arm's length transaction, then a market value for those assets could be established.[280]

---

this was the case in KBC." *Id.* The *Karaha Bodas* tribunal rejected the request by the Indonesian side that the project company's capital expenditures be reviewed for their reasonableness.

277. "[I]f the investor brought some kind of technology or other intangible asset to the project that added to its future cash flow but was not reflected in the investment figures, the project might have an FMV greater than the reported investment." *Id.* In this connection, note that under accounting principles the value of contract rights (such as take-or-pay power purchase agreements), and other intangibles are normally recorded (if at all) at their out-of-pocket acquisition costs on balance sheets, regardless of their current market values. *See* Ch. 7.II *infra*.
278. *See* Wells' comment at n. 276 *supra*.
279. *See* text associated with nn. 49 and 110 et seq. *supra*.
280. One common way for a project developer to realize on the value of an unfinished project with future prospects is to sell equity in the project company to third party investors before the

The *Karaha Bodas* tribunal, though, declined to limit damages solely to "sunk investment costs". The *Karaha Bodas* award illustrates circumstances where an arbitral tribunal may feel comfortable awarding damages for forgone earnings even if the business was at a very early stage in its development when disaster struck. Importantly, there are significant factual distinctions between *Levitt* and *Karaha Bodas* that help illustrate differences in how some tribunals have applied a "reasonable certainty" test. Unlike the situation in *Levitt,* the Karaha Bodas project had the benefit of a thirty-year take-or-pay USD promise from PLN, an Indonesian government enterprise. Tariff payments by PLN under that Energy Sales Contract were based on a pre-agreed pricing formula, subject to continued availability of the power. By specifying that the Indonesian side must pay in USD, the parties contractually allocated to the Indonesian State enterprises the risk of USD-Rupiah exchange rate fluctuations. The obligations of PLN to purchase and pay the project company for the electricity were effectively guaranteed under the project documents by Pertamina, Indonesia's State-owned oil and gas monopoly. Pertamina was by far the greatest single contributor of hard currency foreign exchange to the Indonesian economy and the most creditworthy Indonesian State enterprise. Unlike most State entities, Pertamina controlled valuable assets (oil and gas) that could be sold for hard currency in international markets. It also maintained bank accounts and other assets outside Indonesia. By express contract terms, Pertamina and PLN (not the project company) absorbed political force majeure risks. Further, if the Karaha Bodas geothermal project was successfully constructed to meet the contractual performance standards, the project documents allocated significant operating risks to the Indonesian respondents. Also of importance, operating costs for a geothermal power unit like the Karaha Bodas facility are comparatively small; the power project would not need separately to purchase the geothermal resource providing the plant's fuel. In contrast, a coal-fired or gas-fired thermal power plant must continually purchase its fuel supplies at market prices and then seek to recoup that fuel supply expense from its power purchasers. Therefore, if the Karaha Bodas power project was successfully constructed, future expenses would be predictable and relatively low. None of these supporting circumstances was present for the *Levitt* housing project.

Also, after reviewing the evidence presented by both sides, the *Karaha Bodas* arbitrators concluded that debt financing would have been available for the project. The arbitrators additionally specifically stated that they took the potential for delays in construction and the risk of less-than-expected geothermal reserves into account when calculating damages. Accordingly, the arbitrators expressly held that the risks of the project failing to be constructed properly and on a timely basis were accounted for in their analysis. While the language of the final award was noticeably less than crystal, it would appear that the tribunal equitably reduced

---

project is completed. *See* the discussion of Hubco Power Company in Pakistan, the Al Manah Project in Oman and other projects at text associated with n. 258 *supra*.

the amount of the damages award (rather than increasing the discount rate in a DCF analysis) to account for these development risks.[281]

Unlike the tribunal's approach in *Karaha Bodas*, but like *Levitt*, the tribunal in *Metalclad Corp. v. United Mexican States* entirely rejected future-looking damages. In that NAFTA Chapter 11 arbitration award, the arbitrators held that the preliminary stage at which a waste treatment project was injured by Mexican governmental conduct justified recovery of invested capital, but not lost profits. In the NAFTA tribunal's view, the company's lack of an established track record did not support use of a DCF valuation encompassing lost future earnings.[282] The *Metalclad* tribunal stated that "the fair market value of a going concern which has a history of profitable operation may be based on an estimate of future profits subject to a discounted cash flow analysis," citing to the *Benvenuti and Bonfant v. Congo* and *AGIP v. Congo* ICSID awards. However, the arbitrators held that the waste treatment facility in the case did not satisfy those standards.[283]

In contrast, the arbitrators in the recent *CMS v. Argentina* and *Enron v. Argentina* awards (who shared the same chair) rejected arguments that Income-Based valuation methods were inherently too speculative.[284] So too, the arbitrators in *ADC v. Hungary*.

---

281. The *Karaha Bodas* panel identified a number of risks against which the project agreements offered no contractual protection to the project company; a higher cost of capital than estimated in the company's original projections, delays in plant construction and operation and lower-than-expected geothermal reserves leading to potentially larger required investments or higher operating costs. Karaha Bodas Final Award, *supra* n. 270, at ¶ 134. The panel then noted that these risks could be accounted for by increasing the discount rate in DCF projections, but that doing so would imply that it was possible to translate such risks into a discount rate reduction "with a sufficient degree of certainty." *Id.*, at ¶ 135. The tribunal rejected adjusting the discount rate in favor of exercising its "inherent power" to assess damages; "The too many variables involved by such evaluation process suggests that different approach should be taken which, after duly considering these various factors, would entail a significant reduction of the Claimant's lost profits claim. The Arbitral Tribunal, after careful consideration of all elements involved in this analysis as enumerated above, and in the exercise of its inherent power to assess the quantum of damages on the basis of the evidence submitted by both parties, fixes at U.S. $150 million (one hundred and fifty million US dollars), the amount of lost profits to which the Claimant is entitled." *Id.*, at ¶ 136. While the choice of language obviously could be clearer, it appears that the *Karaha Bodas* panel significantly reduced the total damages that would otherwise have been calculated under DCF computations. Moreover, the panel did so in a manner that does not permit a reader of the award to recreate the calculation. The ambiguity in the panel's computation of damages has invited criticism by commentators. E.g., Wells, *supra* n. 270 (arguing, though, that the damage award in the case still appears to be excessive).
282. *Metalclad Corp. v. United Mexican States*, ICSID Case No. ARB(AF)/97/1 (August 30, 2000). The *Metalclad* tribunal stated that "the fair market value of a going concern which has a history of profitable operation may be based on an estimate of future profits subject to a discounted cash flow analysis," citing to the *Benvenuti & Bonfant v. Congo* and *AGIP v. Congo* ICSID awards. *Id.*, at ¶ 119.
283. *Id.*, at ¶ 119, again citing to the *Benvenuti & Bonfant v. Congo* and *AGIP v. Congo* ICSID awards.
284. *CMS v. Argentina*, *supra* n. 7, at ¶ 416.

> 502. Like many other tribunals in cases such as the present one, the Tribunal prefers to apply the DCF method, although it is mindful of the Respondent's admonishment that:
>
> "*international tribunals have exercised great caution in using the [DCF] method due to its inherently speculative nature.*"[285]

The tribunal in the *Patuha* and *Himpurna* cases also relied upon DCF forecasts, saying: "There is no reason to apologize for the fact that this approach involves approximations; they are inherent and inevitable. Nor can it be criticized as unrealistic or unbusinesslike; it is precisely how business executives must, and do, proceed when they evaluate a going concern."[286] Paulsson, the chair of the *Patuha* and *Himpurna* tribunals, offers a succinct explanation:

> Adjudicators have struggled since time immemorial with the limits of compensable damages, yet the concepts are not complex. At the one extreme are damages which demonstrably arise as the evidently direct consequence of the wrongful act. At the other extreme, there are damages which are insufficiently established either in fact or as a matter of causation. They are typically referred to as "too remote," "unforeseeable" or "speculative." In between there is an area of indirect damages which are controversial.
>
> That they may be recovered in beyond cavil. The difficulty is the permanent haze that overlies the boundary between what is *too remote* and what is merely indirect.[287]

Indeed, in the seminal public international law judgment in the *Chorzów Factory* case, the Permanent Court of International Justice determined to hold an expert inquiry (which was never concluded) on the valuation issues in that dispute. In its instructions for purposes of that expert inquiry, the Court explicitly focused on the need to consider the "goodwill and future prospects" of the enterprise, determined as of the injury date and again as of the judgment date.

> [T]he Court, before giving any decision as to the compensation to be paid by the Polish Government to the German Government, will arrange for the holding of an expert enquiry, in conformity with Article 50 of its Statute and actually with the suggestions of the Applicant. This expert enquiry, directions for which are given in an Order of Court of to-day's date, will refer to the following questions:
>
> I. A. What was the value, on July 3rd, 1922, expressed in Reichsmarks current at the present time, of the undertaking for the manufacture of nitrate products of which the factory was situated at Chorzów in Polish Upper Silesia, in the state in which that undertaking (including the lands, buildings, equipment, stocks and processes at its disposal, supply and delivery contracts,

285. *ADC v. Hungary, supra* n. 111, at ¶ 502.
286. *Patuha v. PLN Final Award, supra* n. 239, at ¶ 487.
287. Paulsson, "The Expectation Model," *supra* n. 241, at 59 (footnotes omitted).

> *goodwill and future prospects*) was, on the date indicated, in the hands of the Bayerische and Oberschlesische Stickstoffwerke?
>
> B. What would have been the financial results, expressed in Reichsmarks current at the present time (profits or losses), which would probably have been given by the undertaking thus constituted from July 3rd, 1922., to the date of the present judgment, if it had been in the hands of the said Companies?
>
> II. What would be the value at the date of the present judgment, expressed in Reichsmarks current at the present time, of the same undertaking (Chorzów) if that undertaking (including lands, buildings, equipment, stocks, available processes, supply and delivery contracts, *goodwill and future prospects*) had remained in the hands of the Bayerische and Oberschlesische Stickstoffwerke, and had either remained substantially as it was in 1922 or had been developed proportionately on lines similar to those applied in the case of other undertakings of the same kind, controlled by the Bayerische, for instance, the undertaking of which the factory is situated at Piesteritz?
>
> The purpose of question 1 is to determine the monetary value, both of the object which should have been restored in kind and of the additional damage, on the basis of the estimated value of the undertaking including stocks at the moment of taking possession by the Polish Government, *together with any probable profit that would have accrued to the undertaking between the date of taking possession and that of the expert opinion.*
>
> On the other hand, question II is directed to the ascertainment of the present value on the basis of the situation at the moment of the expert enquiry and leaving aside the situation presumed to exist in 1922.
>
> This question contemplates the present value of the undertaking from two points of view: firstly, it is supposed that the factory had remained essentially in the state in which it was on July 3rd, 1922, and secondly, the factory is to be considered in the state in which it would (hypothetically but probably) have been in-the hands of the Oberschlesische and Bayerische, if, instead of being taken in 1922 by Poland, it had been able to continue its supposedly normal development from that time onwards.[288]

The *CMS v. Argentina* award illustrates two analytically separate concerns about assertions that earnings forecasts are speculative; whether the projections are in general too speculative for reliability and whether particular revenue or expense estimates within a specific project are individually too speculative. Argentina attacked the use of a DCF forecast in those proceedings as too uncertain generally to support a damages valuation. The tribunal, however, held otherwise: "DCF techniques have been universally adopted, including by numerous arbitral tribunals, as an appropriate method for valuing business assets. . . . Finally, there is

288. Chorzów Factory, *supra* n. 167, at 51–52 (emphasis added). Note as well the statement by the PCIJ about determining probable profit between the injury date and the expert opinion date. The PCIJ's language is sufficiently unclear that it has led to a small cottage industry of commentary in the subsequent 80+ years.

adequate data to make a rational DCF valuation of TGN [the Argentine gas transmission company].''[289]

The tribunal, though, did accept Argentina's specific argument that the DCF projections should cease at 2027, the initial termination date for TGN's gas transmission license, rather than continuing an additional ten years later under an extension clause included in the license. In so ruling, the tribunal noted:

> [T]he license is very clear about the fact that this right is conditional and subject to a number of steps, both substantive and procedural, which might or might not take place. As it would be impossible to establish at present whether these conditions might be met, the Tribunal is persuaded by the respondent's argument that no damages should be considered beyond the year 2027.

Thus, the tribunal held that a particular element of the DCF computation was too speculative to be incorporated into the computation.

In the *CME Stockholm* award, in comparison, the arbitrators accepted that renewal of a television broadcast license would have occurred in the ordinary course. Therefore, the panel held that renewal of the broadcast license should be incorporated into the valuation in that case. The tribunal was persuaded by evidence of actual practice.

> Generally, broadcasting licenses in Europe are renewed as a matter of ordinary administrative practice and the parties could identify to the Tribunal only one known case (an English broadcasting license) in Europe in which a broadcasting license was not renewed, although the license requirements were fulfilled by the license owner.[290]

On that basis, the *CME Stockholm* panel did not treat renewal of the television license as too uncertain or speculative for inclusion in the valuation.[291] The contrast between the ''ordinary course'' renewal in *CME Stockholm* and the ''impossible to establish'' ruling in *CMS*, echoes the probability test for lost opportunities employed in UNIDROIT Article 7.4.3 discussed above in Chapter 2.XI.1.

Commentators contrast the reluctance of some international arbitral tribunals to accept lost future earnings valuations with the regular acceptance of the same methods by valuation experts and national courts. As previously mentioned, the *Fédération des Experts Comptables Européens* adopts the view that the Income-Based Approach is the best measure of a business' value. US courts also regularly

289. *CMS v. Argentina*, *supra* n. 7, at ¶ 416.

290. *CME Stockholm* Final Award, *supra* n. 42, at ¶ 605. The *CME* case is, of course, controversial because of the differing liability decisions reached by the London and Stockholm panels. We do not offer a view on that question. The *CME Stockholm* panel reached and addressed the compensation issue, and the arguments and conclusions in the quantum phase are instructive as to valuation methods.

291. *See* Dunn, *Recovery of Damages for Lost Profits*, *supra* n. 125, at § 6.23, for a review of US cases considering whether recovery for an option period is appropriate or too speculative for lost profits damages to be assessed.

rely on Income-Based methods like the DCF method. In the case of Delaware courts, acceptance of Income-Based methods of valuation did not occur instantaneously. As late as 1975, the Court of Chancery was unwilling to utilize DCF forecasts for judicial valuation despite acceptance of the methodology in the financial community.

> The defendant objected . . . for the reasons that (1) the discounted cash flow valuation is not relevant or material to valuation in an appraisal proceeding and (2) such projections of cash flow were too conjectural and speculative. . . . I agree.[292]

By the early 1980s, however, the dam had broken. Thereafter, the Delaware Court of Chancery rapidly moved to rely upon DCF forecasts to appraise the value of companies in dissenting stockholder cases.[293] Similarly, in real estate appraisal cases the Delaware Supreme Court had by 1987 decisively rejected arguments against the "income capitalization method as speculative and fraught with unsupported projections of both income and expenses."[294] It is noteworthy that the change in attitude by the Delaware courts coincided with the rapid spread of computer technology into the fields of business and finance, since DCF computations rely heavily on spreadsheet software. Once financial advisors had access to the computational power of such programs as EXCEL to develop future earnings forecasts, courts in the US soon followed suit. The DCF method has now become a primary valuation technique in the Delaware courts.[295]

2 Not a Going Concern

If the enterprise being valued is not a "going concern," investment tribunals are unwilling to project forward for estimated revenues and expenses of operation. Instead, many tribunals will either award the Adjusted Book Value (ABV) of the enterprise or order recovery of the "sunk costs" (i.e., the invested capital) together with a reasonable rate of return.[296] If the business is truly insolvent, then "in cases

---

292. *Frick v. American President Lines, Ltd.*, 1975 Del. Ch. LEXIS 236, *10 (Del. Ch. 1975).
293. *See*, e.g., cases cited in n. 53 of *Onti v. Integra Bank*, 751 A.2d 904, 916 (Del. Ch. 1999).
294. *See Seaford Associates, L.P. v. Board of Assessment Review*, 539 A.2d 1045 (Del. 1987).
295. *See Andalaro v. PFPC Worldwide*, 2005 Del. Ch. LEXIS 125, *35 (Del. Ch. 2005) (the Delaware Court of Chancery "prefer[s] to give it [the DCF method] great, and sometimes even exclusive, weight when it may be used responsibly.") The advent of the computer, in addition to making forecasting easier, may also have enveloped projections in an overly optimistic cloak of certainty; "the projection takes on a life of its own, losing its vagueness and abstraction and becoming what philosophers call reified, invested with concreteness; it takes on new life as a tangible object." Taleb, *The Black Swan*, *supra* n. 60, at 158.
296. *See*, e.g., *Benvenuti & Bonfant, Ltd. v. Congo*, ICSID Case No. ARB/77/2, Award of August 8, 1990; *Asian Agricultural Products Ltd. v. Sri Lanka*, ICSID Case No. ARB/87/3, Award of June 21, 1990 (hereinafter "*AAPL v. Sri Lanka*"); *Phelps Dodge Corp. v. Islamic Republic of Iran*, *supra* n. 192; *Sola Tiles, Inc. v. Islamic Republic of Iran*, Award No. 298-317-1, 14 Iran-US C.T.R. 223 (1987); and *Thomas Earl Payne v. Islamic Republic of Iran*, Award No. 245-335-2, 12 Iran-US C.T.R. 3 (1986).

where the business is not a going concern, so-called 'break-up,' 'liquidation' or 'dissolution' value is generally employed."[297] The comments of the tribunal in *Phelps Dodge Corp. and Overseas Private Investment Corporation v. Islamic Republic of Iran*[298] illustrate how some arbitral panels employ a "going concern" limitation.

> 30. The Tribunal cannot agree that SICAB had become a "going concern" prior to November 1980 so that such elements of value as future profits and goodwill could confidently be valued. In the case of SICAB, any conclusions on these matters would be highly speculative. While no diminution in value should be made because of the anticipation of a taking, the Tribunal could not properly ignore the obvious and significant negative effects of the Iranian Revolution on SICAB's business prospects, at least in the short and medium term. There was no market for Phelps Dodge's shares in November 1980. The value of SICAB would clearly be reduced if it were not to have continued access to technological expertise. Thus, any purchaser of Phelps Dodge's shares would either have to have been a company, like Phelps Dodge, with the necessary technical expertise which it could make available to SICAB, or the price would have to have been much reduced. Given the continued availability of such expertise, however, the Tribunal believes that SICAB, although laden with a considerable burden of debt, could reasonably have been expected to become profitable in the long term, given its well-equipped factory and given that its debt was owed to one of the principal shareholders. Nevertheless, SICAB's short-term prospects would certainly have been seen in November 1980 as sufficiently uncertain to require a considerable discounting of the anticipated long-term profits. The refusal of both Phelps Dodge and NKT to participate in the 1977 capital increase of SICAB suggests that, even then, SICAB's prospects were less than certain. Moreover, the speculative nature of future profits was recognized in the Minutes of the meeting of SICAB's Board of Directors on 26 June 1978, where it was noted that efforts must be made to obtain preferential consideration from the Government of Iran, as SICAB was expected to be dependent on government orders to 60 or 70 percent and could not be viable if it failed to obtain sizable government orders.

Thus, in *Phelps Dodge* the Iran-US Claims Tribunal declined to award value for goodwill or lost profits because the enterprise (SICAB) was not a going concern.

Similarly, in the *Sola Tiles* award, the Iran-US Claims Tribunal rejected claimant's request for goodwill and lost profits as a component of recovery. In light of the general political, social and economic changes in Iran resulting from the Iranian Revolution in 1978, the tribunal concluded that

> [t]he impact of such developments on the value of the goodwill element of Simat's business by the time of the expropriation in 1979 must have been

297. Commentaries, *supra* n. 96, at 257 (¶ 25).
298. *Phelps Dodge Corp. v. Islamic Republic of Iran*, *supra* n. 192, at ¶ 30.

> dramatic. Given the picture that emerges, Simat's prospects of continuing active trading after the Revolution were not, in the view of the Tribunal, such as to justify treating Simat as a "going concern" so as to assign any value to goodwill. The decision to assign no value to Simat's goodwill suggests a similar result as to future lost profits, which also depend upon the business prospects of a going concern.[299]

International investment arbitration awards are not the only decisions to be skeptical about the use of future earnings capacity to value a company with only a limited history. In *Lane v. Cancer Treatment Centers of America, Inc.*, a dissenting shareholder case, the Vice Chancellor of the Delaware Court of Chancery commented (without using the phrase "going concern"): "One can reasonably have doubts about the ability of a DCF analysis to capture accurately the fair value of an emerging company with an earnings history of less than two years."[300]

Still, the opposing experts in *Lane* both proffered DCF valuations to the court and the Vice Chancellor adopted the DCF methodology to reach his "fair value" decision.

Some tribunals have required a relatively extended period of operations before concluding that an enterprise is a going concern. In the *Sola Tiles* dispute, the tribunal concluded that the business in question (Simat) was not a going concern because, inter alia, "Simat had the briefest past record of profitability, having shown a loss in 1976, its first year of trading, and a small profit the next year."[301] The panel in *Sola Tiles* decided that the expropriation date was November 1978. Simat, thus, had been operating for almost three years before the expropriation date. The NAFTA tribunal in *Metalclad Corp. v. The United*

299. *Sola Tiles, Inc. v. Islamic Republic of Iran, supra* n. 296, at ¶ 64. *See also Thomas Earl Payne v. Islamic Republic of Iran, supra* n. 296, at ¶¶ 35–36, essentially rejecting goodwill and lost profits claims in light of the impact of the Iranian Revolution on the companies' prospects prior to the expropriation. Interestingly, and in contradiction of *Sola Tiles*, the *Thomas Earl Payne* tribunal also expressly concluded that the companies at issue in that case remained "going concerns" at the time of their expropriation.

300. *Lane v. Cancer Treatment Centers of America, Inc., supra* n. 1, at *93.

301. *Sola Tiles, Inc. v. Islamic Republic of Iran, supra* n. 296, at ¶ 64. Similarly, the ICSID tribunal in *Autopista Concesionada de Venezuela, C.A. v. Bolivarian Republic of Venezuela*, ICSID Case No. ARB/00/5, Award of September 23, 2003 (hereinafter "*Aucoven v. Venezuela*"), also denied a DCF valuation on the basis that the investment "had no record of profits." But *see* World Bank: *Report to the Development Committee and Guidelines for the Treatment of Foreign Direct Investment*, adopted September 21, 1992 ("a 'going concern' means an enterprise consisting of income-producing assets which has been in operation for a sufficient period of time to generate the data required for the calculation of future income and which could have been expected with reasonable certainty, if the taking had not occurred, to continue producing legitimate income over the course of its economic life in the general Circumstances following the taking by the State)." Unlike the "two or three year" period found in the *Metalclad* and *AAPL v. Sri* Lanka awards, the World Bank Guidelines focus on "a period of time" sufficient to "generate the data required" to show future income with reasonable certainty, rather than a somewhat arbitrary fixed time period for profitable operations. That distinction may be particularly important for claims by start-up companies supported by long-term contract rights.

Mexican States quoted with approval from *Sola Tiles* and *AAPL v. Sri Lanka*, asserting that a minimum period of two or three years of continuing market presence was required before an enterprise would be treated as a going concern.

> 120. However, where the enterprise has not operated for a sufficiently long time to establish a performance record or where it has failed to make a profit, future profits cannot be used to determine going concern or fair market value. In *Sola Tiles, Inc. v. Iran (1987)* (14 Iran-U.S.C.T.R. 224, 240–42; 83 I.L.R. 460, 480–81), the Iran-U.S. Claims Tribunal pointed to the importance in relation to a company's value of "its business reputation and the relationship it has established with its suppliers and customers." Similarly, in *Asian Agricultural Products v. Sri Lanka* (4 ICSID Reports 246 (1990) at 292), another ICSID Tribunal observed, in dealing with the comparable problem of the assessment of the value of good will, that its ascertainment "requires the prior presence on the market for at least two or three years, which is the minimum period needed in order to establish continuing business connections."[302]

Similarly, the *Southern Pacific Properties (Middle East)*[303] award ruled that a significant operating history was required to support reliance on a DCF valuation. In that case, property developers had already sold 386 lots (6% of the total expected lot sales). The panel held that track record was insufficient:

> 188. In the Tribunal's view, the DCF method is not appropriate for determining the fair compensation in this case because the project was not in existence for a sufficient period of time to generate the data necessary for a meaningful DCF calculation. At the time the project was cancelled, only 386 lots – or about 6 percent of the total – had been sold. All of the other lot sales underlying the revenue projections in the Claimants' DCF calculations are hypothetical. The project was in its infancy and there is very little history on which to base projected revenues.
>
> 189. In these circumstances, the application of the DCF method would, in the Tribunal's view, result in awarding "possible but contingent and indeterminate damage which, in accordance with the jurisprudence of arbitral tribunals, cannot be taken into account. (Chorzow Factory case, Series A, No. 17, 1928, at 51).[304]

Consistent with cases such as *Metalclad, AAPL, Phelps Dodge, Sola Tiles* and *Southern Pacific Properties (Middle East)*, the Romanian Government as respondent summarized its understanding of this going concern line of cases in *Noble*

302. *Metalclad Corp. v. United Mexican States, supra* n. 282, at § 120. *See also AAPL v. Sri Lanka, supra* n. 296, at 292; and *Aucoven v. Venezuela, supra* n. 301, at § 362 ("Aucoven had no record of profits and . . . it never made the investments in the project nor built the Bridge required by the Concession Agreement.")
303. *SPP (ME) v. Egypt, supra* n. 51.
304. *Id.*, at ¶¶ 188–189. It is noteworthy that the *SPP (ME) v. Egypt* tribunal employed the language found in the World Bank Guidelines: "a sufficient period of time to generate the data necessary."

Ventures v. Romania: "Under international law, an enterprise may be considered a going concern only if it has a recent history of profitability from which to project future profits with a reasonable degree of certainty."[305]

Several Years of Profitability? Why?

A number of investment treaty awards have held that forward-looking compensation is only payable if the business was a going concern at the time of injury, and further that the business is only a going concern if it has a record of several years of profitability. This use of the term "going concern" is contrary to well accepted usage of that term by accountants, valuation professionals, regulators and the business community. The term "going concern" is more properly contrasted with "liquidation value." Tribunals employing the term "going concern" to mean several years of profitability are in reality worried about establishing forward-looking compensation "with reasonable certainty."

The definition of "going concern" employed in these awards, however, is clearly different from the usage of that term by accountants, appraisers, tax authorities and valuation experts – as it would automatically eliminate, for example, companies still engaged in development of their facilities and companies showing recent losses due to heavy development or capital expenditures intended to grow their business activities. For valuation professionals, there is an important difference between, on the one hand, a business that is making and will continue to make significant losses and, on the other hand, a business that either has not yet had a chance to realize on its potential or is facing a downturn that is likely temporary. In *Phelps Dodge*, illustratively, the enterprise (SICAB) would clearly have been a going concern for accounting purposes at the time of its expropriation; the tribunal, in fact, expressly stated that SICAB had a "well-equipped factory" and that "SICAB, although laden with a considerable burden of debt, could reasonably have been expected to become profitable in the long run." To valuation professionals, those enterprises *were* going concerns. Thus, the International Glossary of Business Valuation Terms defines "Going Concern" as "an ongoing operating business enterprise" and "Going Concern Value" as

> the value of a business enterprise that is expected to continue to operate into the future. The intangible elements of Going Concern Value result from factors such as having a trained work force, an operational plant, and the necessary licenses, systems, and procedures in place.[306]

305. *Noble Ventures, Inc. v. Romania*, ICSID Case No. ARB/01/11, Award, October 5, 2005, at ¶ 228.
306. International Glossary of Business Valuation Terms, *supra* n. 17.

Under accounting principles in the US, the UK and elsewhere, and applicable regulatory standards, there is no requirement of a continuous record of profitability for a company to be deemed a going concern. Instead of requiring a "recent operating history/record of profitability," accountants contrast going concern with liquidation;[307] for example, a continuously loss-making situation that results in the business ceasing to be a viable entity. Under International Accounting Standard (IAS) 1, a company's management is required to assess an enterprise's ability to continue as a going concern. Pursuant to IAS 1, companies are considered to be "going concerns" unless they are at risk of shutting down entirely. The International Accounting Standards Board explains that

> [w]hen preparing financial statements, management shall make an assessment of an entity's ability to continue as a going concern. Financial statements shall be prepared on a going concern basis unless management either intends to liquidate the entity or to cease trading, or has no realistic alternative but to do so.[308]

Similarly, the International Standards on Auditing also contrast a going concern with a liquidation scenario:

> Under the going concern assumption, an entity is ordinarily viewed as continuing in business for the foreseeable future with neither the intention nor the necessity of liquidation, ceasing trading, or seeking protection from creditors pursuant to laws or regulations.[309]

In the United States, where US accountants and regulatory authorities follow US Generally Accepted Accounting Principles (GAAP) and Generally Accepted Auditing Standards (GAAS) rather than International Accounting Standards and International Auditing Standards, the concept of "going concern" is again not tied to a "recent record" of profitability or any particular duration of operations. Instead, it is linked to the ability of the enterprise to pay its debts in the ordinary course of business – similar to the test of insolvency for recovery of preferential transfers under US bankruptcy law.

> Continuation of an entity as a going concern is assumed in financial reporting in the absence of significant information to the contrary. Ordinarily, information that significantly contradicts the going concern assumption relates to the entity's inability to continue to meet its obligations as they become due without substantial disposition of assets outside the ordinary course of business, restructuring of debt, externally forced revisions of its operations, or similar actions.[310]

---

307. International Accounting Standard (IAS) 1, at ¶ 3(2).
308. International Accounting Standards Board, Technical Summary, IAS 1 Presentation of Financial Statements, available at <www.iasb.org/NR/rdonlyres/80B373BF-BB16-45AB-B3F7-8385CD4979EA/0/IAS1.pdf>.
309. International Standard on Auditing (ISA) 570, "Going Concern" (Effective for audits of financial statements for periods ending on or after December 31, 2000), at ¶ 3.
310. AU section 341, The Auditor's Consideration of an Entity's Ability to Continue as a Going Concern, Effective for audits of financial statements for periods beginning on or after January 1, 1989, unless otherwise indicated, at § 341.01.

Valuation experts approach the meaning of "going concern" in a manner similar to that adopted by accountants, again contrasting a going concern with a liquidation. The AICPA's Valuation Standard SSVS 1, unsurprisingly, incorporates the Glossary's definitions. The International Valuation Standards Committee, similarly, states that "[t]he premise of a going concern serves as an alternative to the premise of liquidation. Adoption of a going concern premise allows the business to be valued above liquidation value and is essential to the development of *Market Value* for the business."[311]

The case of *In re Williams Securities Litigation*,[312] offers an example of a situation in which troubled circumstances surrounding a company proved to be insufficient to justify a claim that accountants should have questioned whether a company was a going concern under US Generally Accepted Accounting Standards (GAAS). Williams Group Co. was caught up in the telecommunications industry meltdown and ultimately filed for bankruptcy in late April 2002. In a US securities fraud class action brought on behalf of public shareholders of Williams Group, the plaintiffs alleged that the company's accountants, Ernst & Young (E&Y), had failed to qualify their opinion for the company's audited 2000 financial statements to indicate doubt as to whether Williams Group was a going concern. In particular, the plaintiffs complained that, by the time of the opinion letter, it was apparent that Williams Group could have to restructure its finances and operations. For the court, though, that was insufficient. The court summarized the plaintiff's allegations and then rejected the claim, as follows:

> Plaintiffs also contend that E & Y failed to modify its audit opinion language, thus departing from GAAS, to indicate that there was substantial doubt that WCG could continue as a "going concern" for twelve months beyond December 31, 2000. According to AU § 341, one of AICPA's professional standards, E & Y, in conducting an audit of WCG's financial statements in accordance with GAAS, was required to evaluate whether there was substantial doubt as to WCG's ability to continue as a going concern for a reasonable period of time, not to exceed one year from the date of the financial statements. . . . AU § 341.01 and AU § 341.02. . . . Continuation of an entity as a going concern is assumed in the absence of significant information to the contrary. Information that significantly contradicts that assumption relates to the entity's

311. IVSC Business Valuation Guidance Note, *supra* n. 15, at ¶ 3.19.2 (emphasis in original). Indeed, basic legal dictionaries employ the same distinction. *See* Merriam-Webster's Dictionary of Law (1996): "going concern value: the value of the assets of an enterprise or of the enterprise itself considered as an operating business and therefore based on earning power and prospects rather than on the value of the same assets or the same business in the event of liquidation." That approach is also found in the ordinary legal definition of "going-concern value" found in Black's Law Dictionary, 7th edn 1999, at 1549 ("The value of a commercial enterprise's assets or the enterprise itself as an active business with future earning power, as opposed to the liquidation value of the business or its assets. Going-concern value includes, for example, goodwill.").
312. *In re Williams Securities Litigation*, 2007 WL 2007987 (N.D.Okla., July 6, 2007).

> inability to continue to meet its obligations as they become due without substantial disposition of assets outside of the ordinary course of business, restructuring of debt, externally forced revisions of its operations, or similar actions. *Id.* at AU § 341.01. Plaintiffs contend that the evidence establishes the existence of factors clearly indicating that substantial doubt existed about WCG's ability to continue as a going concern as of December 31, 2000. These factors, plaintiffs argue, portended that WCG would have needed to restructure its debt, dispose of assets and restructure its operations in order to meet its obligations in 2001. In support of this claim, plaintiffs point out that less than seven days after the April 2001 spin-off, WCG began working with The Blackstone Group to look at strategies to restructure its balance sheet. Less than two months later, in June of 2001, WCG attempted a capital spending freeze to control expenditures and announced a 10 percent lay off of its work force. Subsequently, in August of 2001, WCG bought back some of its long term debt in an attempt to restructure its balance sheet. Plaintiffs contend that these attempts at restructuring, shortly after the spin-off, show that WCG was not a going concern as defined by GAAS as of year-end 2000.
>
> E & Y contends that during the audit, it reviewed WCG's liquidity position, considered WCG's specific characteristics within the telecom industry and obtained a management representation letter from WMB confirming its financial support of WCG. As a result of this review and based upon its professional judgment, it concluded that there was no substantial doubt about WCG's ability to continue as a going concern for twelve months beyond December 31, 2000. Based upon the evidence in the record, including WMB's assurance of funding for WCG in 2001 as long as the spin-off did not occur, and Lehman Brothers' opinion that if the spin-off occurred it would not materially impair WCG's ability to fund its future capital needs, E & Y contends that plaintiffs' claim that there was substantial doubt about WCG's ability to continue as a going concern as of year-end 2000 is untenable. In addition, E & Y argues that plaintiffs' going concern argument is undermined by the indisputable fact that WCG did indeed continue as a going concern beyond December 31, 2001.
>
> E & Y also challenges plaintiffs' argument that WCG's "restructuring," which occurred months after the audit, shows substantial doubt that WCG was a going concern, contending that there is no evidence in the record to show that, to stay in business, WCG was forced to sell assets to meet its obligations as they became due.
>
> The court concludes that plaintiffs have not presented evidence sufficient under the minimal Rule 56 standard to show a material misrepresentation or omission by E & Y as to WCG's status as a going concern.[313]

The US Securities Exchange Commission (SEC), the UK Financial Services Authority (FSA), the Board of Governors of the Federal Reserve System and other financial services regulatory bodies adopt the accounting definition of "going concern" for

313. *Id.*, at *79–80.

their manifold supervisory responsibilities.[314] Regulatory authorities, such as securities and banking regulators, enforce compliance by companies, appraisers and accountants alike with these standards. Thus, the SEC requires that audits of companies whose securities are registered for public sale in the US must be audited in conformity with generally accepted auditing standards, including the "going concern" standard.

> § 78j-1. Audit requirements
>
> (a) In general. Each audit required pursuant to this title of the financial statements of an issuer by a registered public accounting firm shall include, in accordance with generally accepted auditing standards, as may be modified or supplemented from time to time by the Commission –
>
> ...
>
> (3) an evaluation of whether there is substantial doubt about the ability of the issuer to continue as a going concern during the ensuing fiscal year.[315]

Similarly, the UK's FSA requires auditors of public companies to apply these "going concern" standards as part of their obligatory disclosures to the FSA when "the auditor reasonably believes that the person concerned is not, may not be or may cease to be a going concern."[316]

Other financial services regulators also adopt and implement this approach to the definition of a going concern. In the US, for example, the choice between conservatorship and receivership for a distressed bank is based in part on the distinction between operating that bank as a going concern (even though it is suffering such a severe crisis that the US Government has already stepped in as conservator to operate the bank) and a liquidation sale. "A conservator operates or disposes of an institution as a going concern while a receiver has the power to liquidate and wind up the affairs of an institution."[317] So too, the statutory liquidator of an insurance company in the UK:

> Unless the court otherwise orders, the liquidator must carry on the insurer's business so far as it consists of carrying out the insurer's contracts of long-term insurance with a view to its being transferred as a going concern to a person who may lawfully carry out those contracts.[318]

---

314. Other examples abound, and for far more countries than just the US and the UK.
315. 15 USCS § 78j-1.
316. Financial Services and Markets Act 2000 (Communications by Auditors) Regulations 2001, SI 2587, s. 2(1)(c).
317. Banking Law, § 49.03 F.D.I.C.'s Conservatorship and Receivership Powers (Matthew Bender and Company, Inc. 2007, online at LEXIS-NEXIS). *See also* 12 U.S.C. § 204 ("The Comptroller of the Currency (in consultation with the Board of Directors of the Federal Deposit Insurance Corporation when the Corporation is appointed conservator) is authorized to examine and supervise the bank in conservatorship as long as the bank continues to operate as a going concern.").
318. Financial Services and Markets Act 2000, Ch. 8, s. 376 (Eng.) 376(2).

Similarly, the UK Financial Assistance Scheme for pensions links insolvency and a company's inability to continue as a going concern.

> (3A) Where the scheme manager is satisfied that the employer in relation to an occupational pension scheme is unlikely to continue as a going concern, the scheme manager may treat an insolvency event as having occurred in relation to that employer.[319]

And the English Companies Act 2006 also provides that:

> a payment out of capital by a private company for the redemption or purchase of its own shares is not lawful unless . . . the directors have formed the opinion that . . . the company will be able to continue to carry on business as a going concern (and will accordingly be able to pay its debts as they fall due) throughout that year.[320]

Indeed, Governments regularly define going concerns as an ongoing business enterprise regardless of the length or profitability of its prior history, or at least their tax authorities do so. For instance, the US Internal Revenue Service's Business now-superseded Valuation Guidelines actually appended the International Glossary of Business Valuation Terms (including their definitions of going concern and "going concern" value quoted above).[321]

Start-up companies and companies engaged in the development or construction stages of their activities, of course, do generally satisfy these accounting, valuation and regulatory standards as a going concern. Google Inc. illustrates the potential of mistaking a requirement of several years of regular profits for the test of whether a business is a going concern. Google was born in 1998 but did not become profitable at all until some time in 2003. If the "recent history of profitability" test correctly measures when Google became a going concern, then Google likely did not satisfy that test until at least 2005 or later. However, Google went public in August 2004 in an IPO registered with the SEC, with the required certification by its accountants that it was a going concern under US GAAP at that time. Google also listed on the London Stock Exchange in late September of 2004, again with the required "going concern" attestation. Within two months after its 2004 IPO, the stock market capitalization of Google was over USD 50 billion. Indeed, by November 2005, that capitalization had reached USD 127 billion. And, of course, the market value of Google has continued to grow steadily since then. It would seem surprising, to say the least, for international investment law to assert that Google was not a going concern in 2004.

---

319. U.K. Financial Assistance Scheme Regulations 2005, SI 1986, s. 13.
320. Companies Act 2006 (c. 46), Part 18, Ch. 5 §§ 713(1), 714(3)(h). Numerous other examples of the incorporation of the accounting and auditing conception of "going concern" into US, UK and European regulatory arrangements exist, but space constraints prevent a longer listing.
321. Internal Revenue Service, Part 4. Examining Process, Ch. 48. Engineering program, section 4. Business Valuation Guidelines, ¶ 4.48.4, Exhibit BVG-1.

Valuation experts are accustomed to occasionally applying Income or Market-Based methods even to development-stage companies in appropriate cases.[322] Arbitrators should be sensitive to the point that a company not yet generating revenue might still be a going concern, particularly if it has (as discussed in Chapter 2.XI.2 above) the benefit of a binding output purchase commitment from a purchaser.[323]

Cases from the Iran-US Claims Tribunal like *Sola Tiles* and *Phelps Dodge* illustrate circumstances where a reasonable prior operating history existed, but a dramatic rare event (there, the Iranian Revolution) occurred just prior to the valuation date. The occurrence of the rare event persuaded the arbitrators that reliance upon that prior history was inappropriate. The enterprise now faced a highly uncertain future and the past could not provide guidance. Similarly, the power project company in *Karaha Bodas* had no prior history of profits because the project was brought to a halt early in its development. The Karaha Bodas project, however, did have the benefit of a long-term USD take-or-pay contract from the most creditworthy State enterprise in Indonesia, as well as only limited construction and financing risk. In *Karaha Bodas,* the arbitrators were persuaded that the company did have a sufficiently certain future to support its forward-looking damages claims. The arbitrators founded their conclusion principally on the fact that project was supported by a binding long-term offtake agreement with predictable purchaser volumes and prices, the off-taker was creditworthy, the agreement allocated force majeure risks to the offtaker and the risks of raising capital and properly constructing the facility were in the panel's view adequately covered. By regulatory, accounting and valuation standards, though, the businesses in all three of these disputes (*Sola Tiles*, *Phelps Dodge* and *Karaha Bodas*) would have been going concerns at the time of the events giving rise to their compensation claims.

As Smutny points out more generally with respect to compensation decisions by investment treaty tribunals:

> The measure of fair market value is a question of economics and/or accounting and is not (or should not be) a function of any bright-line legal rule. It is unfortunate that much of the jurisprudence and commentary in this area seems to reflect confusion about economic and accounting concepts which in turn lead to a confused (and/or confusing) discussion of the applicable legal rules.[324]

---

322. *See* e.g., Valuation Research Corporation, Valuation Researcher Alert: Valuation for s. 409A Purposes Can Also Satisfy Financial Reporting Requirements (February 2006), discussing inter alia the use of the DCF method and comparable sales or stock transactions as a means of valuing development-stage companies. Valuation Research Corporation notes in its Alert, however, that "[f]or very early-stage companies, we often consider a cost or asset-based valuation approach."

323. *See* Ch. 2.XI.2 *supra*.

324. Smutny, *supra* n. 115, at 10. Smutny further notes "Although assessing compensation is not strictly a legal determination, there are legal constraints to the analysis." *Id.* She offers principles of causation, evidentiary rules and the "too speculative" limitation as illustrations of such constraints.

Concluding that an enterprise is a going concern for valuation or accounting purposes does not by itself resolve whether future cash flows can be estimated with the level of certainty necessary to support a forward-looking compensation award. Candidly, these "going concern" international investment cases are best understood as declining to grant an investor compensation for future earnings because the arbitrators were concerned that projecting future earnings would be too speculative and uncertain in the particular circumstances. Their concern about the uncertainty of the projections was reinforced by a track record that was in the tribunal's judgment irrelevant, erratic or simply too short for comfort. The international investment cases, though, misapply the term "going concern" to refer to qualms about projecting a limited history of past performance into compensation for lost future earnings. Arbitrators should not emulate Humpty Dumpty.

> When I use a word, "Humpty Dumpty said in a rather scornful tone, it means just what I choose it to mean – neither more nor less."
>
> "The question is," said Alice, "whether you can make words mean so many things."
>
> "The question is," said Humpty Dumpty, "which is to be the master – that's all."
>
> Alice was too puzzled to say anything, so after a minute Humpty Dumpty began again.[325]

The term "going concern" has an established meaning for the accounting and valuation professions and financial regulators, as well as in the business community. That established meaning distinguishes an ongoing business from a liquidation. It would be far better for all if arbitrators and international law commentators did not use the phrase "going concern" in a manner that creates confusion among participants in the valuation process. The real issue in cases like *Phelps Dodge, Sola Tiles* and *Metalclad* was whether projected future earnings were too uncertain in the circumstances to justify a compensation award, not whether the enterprise was a going concern.

3 FORESEEABILITY

The principle of foreseeability also limits damages awards in many jurisdictions, as well as under the U.N. Convention on Contracts for the International Sales of Goods, the US Restatement of Contracts and the UNIDROIT Principles of International Commercial Contracts.[326] The foreseeability standard in Art. 7.4.4 of the UNIDROIT Principles is illustrative.

325. Carroll, *Through the Looking-Glass: And What Alice Found There*, *supra* n. 103, at 364.

326. *See* United Nations Convention on Contracts of the International Sale of Goods Art. 74; Restatement 2d, Contracts § 351. *See also Amco Asia Corporation v. Indonesia*, Award of November 20, 1984, 24 ILM 1022 (1985) (excerpts), 1 Int. Arb. Rep. 601 (1986) (stating that damages "should be limited to reparation for direct and foreseeable harm").

Article 7.4.4
(foreseeability of harm)

> The non-performing party is liable only for harm which it foresaw or could reasonably have foreseen at the time of the conclusion of the contract as being likely to result from its non-performance.

According to the Official Comments to the UNIDROIT Principles, the concept of unforeseeability is linked with the "reasonable certainty" standard. Note that the UNIDROIT Principles do not follow the approach used by some civil law jurisdictions, assessing damages without regard to their foreseeability if the breach was due to willful misconduct or gross negligence. Therefore, argue the UNIDROIT Official Comments, a narrow interpretation of foreseeability is appropriate.

> The concept of foreseeability must be clarified since the solution contained in the Principles does not correspond to certain national systems which allow compensation even for harm which is unforeseeable when the non-performance is due to willful misconduct or gross negligence. Since the present rule does not provide for such an exception, a narrow interpretation of the concept of foreseeability is called for. *Foreseeability relates to the nature or type of the harm but not to its extent unless the extent is such as to transform the harm into one of a different kind.* In any event, foreseeability is a flexible concept which leaves a wide measure of discretion to the judge.
>
> What was foreseeable is to be determined by reference to the time of the conclusion of the contract and to the non-performing party itself (including its servants or agents), and the test is what a normally diligent person could reasonably have foreseen as the consequences of non-performance in the ordinary course of things and the particular circumstances of the contract, such as the information supplied by the parties or their previous transactions.[327]

The US Restatement (Second) of Contracts takes a somewhat different approach towards foreseeability. The Restatement distinguishes in section 351 between losses flowing from breaches in the ordinary course of events, on the one hand, and losses flowing from special circumstances, on the other hand. The Restatement also confirms the authority of a court in breach of contract cases to limit damages for foreseeable loss to avoid disproportionate compensation:

> Section 351 Unforeseeability and Related Limitations on Damages:
>
> . . .
>
> 2) Damages are not recoverable for loss that the party in breach did not have reason to foresee as a probable result of the breach when the contract was made.
> 3) Loss may be foreseeable as a probable result of a breach because it follows from the breach

327. Official Comments to UNIDROIT Principles of International Commercial Contracts, available at <www.unilex.info/dynasite.cfm?dsmid=13637>.

a) in the ordinary course of events, or
b) as a result of special circumstances, beyond the ordinary course of events, that the party in breach had reason to know.

4) A court may limit damages for foreseeable loss by excluding recovery for loss of profits, by allowing recovery only for loss incurred in reliance, or otherwise if it concludes that in the circumstances justice so requires in order to avoid disproportionate compensation.[328]

The official Comments to Restatement section 351 make clear that the foreseeability by the defaulting party of the loss need only have been "probable," not "necessary." Moreover, the Restatement test for foreseeability is an objective "reasonable person" standard, not the subjective perspective of the defaulting party:

> The mere circumstance that some loss was foreseeable, or even that some loss of the same general kind was foreseeable, will not suffice if the loss that actually occurred was not foreseeable. It is enough, however, that the loss was foreseeable as a probable, as distinguished from a necessary, result of his breach. Furthermore, the party in breach need not have made a "tacit agreement" to be liable for the loss. Nor must he have had the loss in mind when making the contract, for the test is an objective one based on what he had reason to foresee. There is no requirement of foreseeability with respect to the injured party.[329]

The Comments to the Restatement's foreseeability rule further illustrate the concepts of "damages in the ordinary course of events" and "damages resulting from special circumstance."

> Loss that results from a breach in the ordinary course of events is foreseeable as the probable result of the breach.... Such loss is sometimes said to be the "natural" result of the breach, in the sense that its occurrence accords with the common experience of ordinary persons. For example, a seller of a commodity to a wholesaler usually has reason to foresee that his failure to deliver the commodity as agreed will probably cause the wholesaler to lose a reasonable profit on it.... Similarly, a seller of a machine to a manufacturer usually has reason to foresee that his delay in delivering the machine as agreed will probably cause the manufacturer to lose a reasonable profit from its use, although courts have been somewhat more cautious in allowing the manufacturer recovery for loss of such profits than in allowing a middleman recovery for loss of profits on an intended resale.... The damages recoverable for such loss that results in the ordinary course of events are sometimes called "general" damages.
>
> If loss results other than in the ordinary course of events, there can be no recovery for it unless it was foreseeable by the party in breach because of special circumstances that he had reason to know when he made the contract.... For example, a seller who fails to deliver a commodity to a

328. Restatement (Second) of Contracts, § 351.
329. *Id.*, at Comment a.

> wholesaler is not liable for the wholesaler's loss of profit to the extent that it is extraordinary nor for his loss due to unusual terms in his resale contracts unless the seller had reason to know of these special circumstances.... Similarly, a seller who delays in delivering a machine to a manufacturer is not liable for the manufacturer's loss of profit to the extent that it results from an intended use that was abnormal unless the seller had reason to know of this special circumstance.

The Restatement's Comment (f) to section 351 also makes plain the role equitable considerations occasionally play in the application of foreseeability principles. Comment (f) cautions, though, that such considerations are less likely to be imposed in a commercial context.

> *Other limitations on damages.* It is not always in the interest of justice to require the party in breach to pay damages for all of the foreseeable loss that he has caused. There are unusual instances in which it appears from the circumstances either that the parties assumed that one of them would not bear the risk of a particular loss or that, although there was no such assumption, it would be unjust to put the risk on that party. One such circumstance is an extreme disproportion between the loss and the price charged by the party whose liability for that loss is in question. The fact that the price is relatively small suggests that it was not intended to cover the risk of such liability. Another such circumstance is an informality of dealing, including the absence of a detailed written contract, which indicates that there was no careful attempt to allocate all of the risks. The fact that the parties did not attempt to delineate with precision all of the risks justifies a court in attempting to allocate them fairly. The limitations dealt with in this Section are more likely to be imposed in connection with contracts that do not arise in a commercial setting. Typical examples of limitations imposed on damages under this discretionary power involve the denial of recovery for loss of profits and the restriction of damages to loss incurred in reliance on the contract. Sometimes these limits are covertly imposed, by means of an especially demanding requirement of foreseeability or of certainty. The rule in this Section recognizes that what is done in such cases is the imposition of a limitation in the interests of justice.[330]

4 Lack of Causation and Contributory Fault

Compensation is, of course, payable only for the consequences of injuries caused by the breaching party's conduct. The injured claimant, therefore, has the burden of demonstrating that the claimed quantum flowed from that conduct. Shelves of books and papers contain discussions of the fundamental role the principle of

330. *Id.*, at comment (f).

"causation" plays in determining both liability and compensation. While this volume is not the place to repeat those detailed analyses, we cannot overemphasize the crucial role causation performs in valuation issues. The claimant must satisfy the tribunal that the causal relationship is sufficiently close (i.e., not "too remote") to satisfy the applicable standard of causation. Also, injury to an enterprise may derive from several sources. "Causation" principles can cover a number of a number of issues, such as the issues of multiple, intervening and contributory causes and limits to legal responsibility such as "proximate cause vs. but-for causation" and "foreseeability."[331] Above, we addressed foreseeability issues. Here, we address issues of possible multiple or intervening causes. In addition, even though the breaching party did in part cause the damage, the injured party too may bear responsibility for the injury in part, and thus contributory fault may reduce or eliminate the claimed compensation.

The facts of the case will, of course, dictate what events must be considered for purposes of causation. Macro events, illustratively, may affect the market generally, whether a market-wide contraction or growth burst, a dramatic change in interest rates or oil prices worldwide, or a country-wide crisis such as occurred in Argentina. One experienced valuation professional relates the story of party expert valuations in an investment treaty arbitration for which he was serving as the tribunal-appointed valuation expert. The claimant asserted that the loss in question could be measured by a reduction in the value of majority investments in certain businesses during a particular period. However, the claimant's proposed stock market valuations failed to take account of overall market trends at the time.

> What was missing from the analysis was any recognition of the significant "corrections" that occurred in global stock markets in the same period. The reasons for these global stock market falls were in no way connected to the loss event in dispute.[332]

Issues of causation were, as discussed above,[333] crucial to the approach taken by the tribunal in *LG&E v. Argentina* towards damages. The tribunal rejected a fair market value approach towards damages, despite concurrence by both parties in that approach.[334] Instead, the tribunal concluded it must address the "actual loss" suffered by the investor "*as a result of*" Argentina's conduct. The question is one of "causation;" what did the investor lose by reason of the unlawful acts?[335] For the *LG&E* panel, the answer to that question was lost dividends for a specified duration, not a permanent diminution in market value.[336]

331. Walde & Sabahi, *Compensation, Damages and Valuation in International Investment Law* (International Law Association, 2007), at 35–36, available at <www.ila-hq.org>.
332. Senogles, *Business Interruption Claims*, *supra* n. 54, at 12.
333. *See* text associated with n. 144 et seq. *supra*.
334. *LG&E v. Argentina Final Award*, *supra* n. 7, at ¶ 33.
335. *Id.*, at ¶ 45.
336. *See* text associated with n. 144 et seq. *supra*.

Similarly, micro events may be an essential part of the causation analysis. For example, a key component of harm to a business might be traceable to delays in construction of an essential facility. Were those delays attributable to the respondent's conduct or to other problems on the project's critical path, or to a combination of circumstances?

Crawford's Commentaries to the ILC's Articles point out that "the subject matter of reparation is, globally, the injury resulting from and ascribable to the wrongful act, rather than any and all consequences flowing from an internationally wrongful act."[337] As Smutny explains, legal principles about causation:

> operate to incorporate a sense of proportionality into the obligation to make reparation for wrongful acts as they require tribunals to make determinations about the reasonableness of requiring one party or the other to bear the burden of losses when they occur.[338]

As the Commentaries note, Article 39 of the ILC Articles provides that, with respect to an international claim brought by a State, "account shall be taken of the contribution to the injury by willful or negligent action or omission of the injured State or any person or entity in relation to whom reparation is sought."[339] In application, though, respondent states have not been noticeably successful in attributing the injury to general economic circumstances. In *CMS v. Argentina,* the tribunal rejected Argentina's argument that Argentina's general economic crisis caused the investor's losses, rather than particular government conduct alleged by the investor.[340]

The ICSID tribunal in *Enron v. Argentina* offered a more subtle approach.

> 232. Yet, the Tribunal bears in mind that a major crisis indeed there was. While these unfortunate events do not in themselves amount to a legal excuse, neither would it be reasonable for the Claimants to believe they are not affected by some of the effects. The economic balance of the license was clearly affected by the crisis situation, and just as it is not reasonable for the licensees to bear the entire burden of such changed reality neither would it be reasonable for them to believe that nothing happened in Argentina since the License was approved. This is something the Tribunal will duly take into account in considering the compensation that follows such finding of liability and how the crisis period influences its determination.[341]

In practice, both tribunals (which shared the same chair) took account of the impact of the Argentine emergency in the specifics of their compensation decisions. Thus,

---

337. ILC Articles on State Responsibility, Art. 31, comment (9).
338. Smutny, *supra* n. 115, at 4.
339. Commentaries, *supra* n. 96, at 240.
340. *CMS v. Argentina, supra* n. 7, at ¶ 152 et seq. The tribunal rejected Argentina's arguments about causation in the course of its decision about liability and did not revisit that rejection when it turned to calculating damages.
341. *Enron v. Argentina, supra* n. 43, at ¶ 232.

in *CMS* the tribunal adjusted demand and tariff values in light of the crisis[342] and in *Enron* the tribunal extended the tariff adjustment period in the DCF projections for six years to accommodate the impact of the emergency.[343] The ICSID tribunal in *LG&E v. Argentina*, comparatively, concluded that Argentina's conduct was the "proximate cause" of LG&E's losses, even though LG&E's investments "would have been negatively impacted by the economic situation."[344]

In *CME Stockholm*, the Czech Republic argued during the quantum phase of those proceedings that the investor had "failed to prove causation." The Czech Republic argued that the investor had "contributed to the destruction of CNTS' participation in TV Nova" in numerous respects. Accordingly, said the Republic, the claimant investor was precluded from recovering compensation by virtue of its contributory negligence.[345] The *CME Stockholm* panel rejected that argument on the particular facts, but did not dispute the principle. In addition, the Czech Republic argued that the investor had not demonstrated that "the loss of its entire business was a foreseeable consequence of the conduct of the Media Council."[346] It appears from the *CME Stockholm* Final Award in that case that the Republic considered the causation issue to be integrally related to foreseeability; the Republic argued that: "the Czech Republic can only be liable for those actual losses, that are reasonably foreseeable consequences of the Treaty violations."[347]

Unlike the arbitrators in CME Stockholm, though, the panel in *Lauder v. Czech Republic*[348] (hereinafter "CME London") concluded on exactly the same facts that the conduct of CME's local Czech partner, Dr. Zelezny, was the principal cause of CNTS's losses. Moreover, the CME London tribunal held that Dr. Zelezny's conduct was not attributable to the Czech Republic. Accordingly, the famously contrasting decisions in CME Stockholm and CME London on identical facts were in large measure attributable to the differing views of the two panels as to causation for the injuries suffered by CNTS.

The *MTD v. Chile*[349] dispute also involved issues of contributory fault. In the late 1990s, MTD sought to develop a mixed-use planned community south of Santiago, Chile. The project failed when the Chilean government declined to

342. *CMS v. Argentina, supra* n. 7, at ¶ 443–448.
343. *Enron v. Argentina, supra* n. 43, at ¶ 414–415.
344. *LG&E v. Argentina* Final Award, *supra* n. 7, at ¶ 50. However, the tribunal accepted Argentina's "state of necessity" argument for the period from December 2001 until late April 2003, and consequently removed that time period from the damages computation. Therefore, the economic collapse was reflected to some extent in the ultimate quantum, just by a different device.
345. *CME Stockholm* Final Award, *supra* n. 42, at ¶ 300.
346. *Id.*, at ¶ 294. The Republic also argued that termination of a related Service Agreement was "unforeseeable and not proximate consequences" of the 1996 forced amendment of the CNTS Memorandum of Association. *Id.*, at ¶¶ 320, 376.
347. *Id.*, at ¶ 292.
348. *CME London, supra* n. 42.
349. *MTD v. Chile Award, supra* n. 178; and MTD Equity Sdn. Bhd. and MTD Chile, *S.A. v. Republic of Chile*, Decision on Annulment, March 21, 2007 (hereinafter, "MTD Annulment Decision").

rezone the project site from agricultural land in order to permit the project. MTD thereafter brought claims for recovery of its capital expenditures before an ICSID tribunal pursuant to an investment treaty between Chile and Malaysia. MTD alleged that the Chilean government had, by entering into foreign investment contracts with MTD, created and encouraged a strong expectation that the project was feasible from a regulatory viewpoint. The investor further asserted that the Chilean government subsequently disapproved the location of the project, but only after MTD had irrevocably committed its investment monies. The ICSID tribunal ruled in favor of MTD in the merits portion of its Final Award, but split the damages between MTD and Chile 50:50.

> By an award of 25 May 2004, the Tribunal . . . held, on the one hand, that Chile had breached its obligation of fair and equitable treatment under Article 3(1) of the BIT but, on the other hand, that the Claimants had failed to protect themselves from business risks inherent in their investment in Chile. Responsibility for the loss being equally divided, the Tribunal concluded that the Respondent should pay 50% of the assessed damages, viz., US $5,871,322.42, plus compound interest, and that each party should pay its own costs and 50% of the costs of arbitration.[350]

The ICSID panel made no effort in its final award to set out an express basis for its 50:50 split on account of contributory fault as compared with, say, a 70:30 or 20:80 split. Chile then sought annulment of the award pursuant to the ICSID Convention. Chile's arguments about the 50:50 damages decision were based on two grounds found in the ICSID Convention; serious departure from a fundamental rule of procedure and failure to state reasons. In substance, though:

> What the Respondent challenges in these proceedings is the conclusion that MTD's damages should be reduced only by 50% on account of this finding [that MTD failed adequately to protect itself against regulatory risk]. In its view the real and evident cause of the Claimants' loss was their failure to conduct adequate due diligence prior to signing the [land purchase] contract with Mr. Fontaine. On that basis, imposing 50% of the responsibility on Chile was both arbitrary and unexplained.

Indeed, Chile argued in its submissions to the Annulment Committee that the ICSID arbitrators had improperly decided the damages allocation issue *ex aequo et bono*. The Annulment Committee, however, declined in its February 2007 Decision to annul the damages award. First, the Committee pointed out that Chile had not, and could not properly, challenge the tribunal's power to employ the doctrine of contributory fault to allocate responsibility for damages between the parties. The Annulment Committee referred to ILC Article 39 for this purpose, which provides for contribution in disputes between States:

> Article 39: Contribution to the injury

350. MTD Annulment Decision, *supra* n. 349, at ¶ 39.

> In the determination of reparation, account shall be taken of the contribution to the injury by wilful or negligent action or omission of the injured State or any person or entity in relation to whom reparation is sought.

Then, the *MTD v. Chile* Annulment Committee turned to the actual 50:50 allocation. The Committee explained that estimating the impact of contributory fault was a difficult task. Thus, arbitrators were entitled to a "range of estimation "for their damages awards in such cases, especially with respect to investment treaty claims.

> The Committee agrees with the Respondent that some further reasons for a 50:50 split of damages could have been offered at this stage. But the Tribunal had already analysed the faults on both sides in some detail, holding both to be material and significant in the circumstances. As is often the case with situations of comparative fault, the role of the two parties contributing to the loss was very different and only with difficulty commensurable, and the Tribunal had a corresponding margin of estimation. Furthermore, in an investment treaty claim where contribution is relevant, the respondent's breach will normally be regulatory in character, whereas the claimant's conduct will be different, a failure to safeguard its own interests rather than a breach of any duty owed to the host State. In such circumstances, it is not unusual for the loss to be shared equally. International tribunals which have reached this point have often not given any "exact explanation" of the calculations involved. In the event, the Tribunal having analysed at some length the failings of the two parties, there was little more to be said – and no annullable error in not saying it.[351]

Like the ILC Articles mentioned in the *MTD v. Chile* Annulment Decision, the principle of contributory fault is also found in the UNIDROIT Principles of International Commercial Contracts. Article 7.4.7 provides:

> Where the harm is due in part to an act or omission of the aggrieved party or to another event as to which that party bears the risk, the amount of damages shall be reduced to the extent that these factors have contributed to the harm, having regard to the conduct of each of the parties.

Article 7.4.7 focuses on the extent to which the injured party's conduct contributed to the harm. Not all international bodies of law follow that approach towards the impact of contributory fault on a compensation decision. For instance, the CISG sets out a contribution principle in different terms. The CISG instead focuses on the extent to which the contributory fault by the injured party caused the failure to perform giving rise to the injury, not the extent of the resulting damage. CISG Article 80 specifies that contributory fault is linked to the precedent liability issue. "A party may not rely on a failure of the other party to perform, to the extent that such failure was caused by the first party's act or omission."

---

351. *Id.*, at ¶ 101 (footnote omitted).

Although egregious issues such as fraud, misrepresentation, corrupt payments or unlawful conduct on the part of the injured party are usually presented as a defense to liability in the first place, those circumstances may also form the basis for an contributory fault attack on the amount of damages to be paid by the breaching party. Notably, allegedly unlawful conduct on the part of an investor is an issue that arises repeatedly in investment treaty disputes – in the jurisdiction phase, on the merits and again to determine quantum.

5 Burden of Proof

In most legal systems, the injured party has the burden of proof generally as to damages. However, some national courts have given the benefit of the doubt to the injured party, allocating the risk of evidentiary uncertainty to the breaching party. Thus, for damages resulting from breaches of contract the US Restatement (Second) of Contracts states: "Doubts are generally resolved against the party in breach. A party who has, by his breach, forced the injured party to seek compensation in damages should not be allowed to profit from his breach where it is established that a significant loss has occurred."[352] As we have discussed, on the other hand, a forecast of future income may contain inherent uncertainties. Moreover, it is common to place the burden of proof on the moving party. Some arbitral tribunals have accordingly on occasion reversed this allocation. As the *Patuha v. PLN* Final Award illustrates: "Thus doubts have been resolved equitably in favor of the debtor."[353]

Who Bears the Burden of Proof?

Ordinarily in legal systems, the burden of proof lies with the moving party. In some circumstances, however, equitable consideration triggers a shift in the burden. In the area of damages, equitable considerations may cut both ways.

Thus, the U.S. Restatement (Second) of Contracts provides that, for damages in breach of contract cases, "doubts are generally resolved against the party in breach." The justification for this position is that the party who caused the injury should not be allowed to benefit from its conduct (especially if that very conduct was the reason for the difficulties in computing damages).

In contrast, the *Patuha v. PLN* award illustrates when the circumstances of an impoverished country, beset by economic crisis, move the arbitrators in the opposite direction: "Thus doubts have been resolved equitably in favor of the debtor."

352. Restatement 2d, Contracts § 352, Comment a.
353. *Patuha v. PLN* Final Award, *supra* n. 239, at ¶ 486. *See also id.*, at ¶ 482.

The burden of proof was an issue in the *Chorzów Factory* dispute as well. In that case, the German Government presented evidence of economic injury to the factory affected by Polish governmental conduct. However, the PCIJ ruled that Germany, the injured party, had failed to satisfy its burden of proof with respect to certain damages elements.

> The Court must however observe that it has not before it the data necessary to enable it to decide as to the existence and extent of damage resulting from alleged competition of the Chorzów factory with the Bayerische factories; the Court is not even in a position to say for certain whether the methods of the Bayerische have been or are still being employed at Chorzów, nor whether the products of that factory are to be found in the markets in which the Bayerische sells or might sell products from its own factories. In these circumstances, the Court can only observe that the damage alleged to have resulted from competition is insufficiently proved.[354]

The particular objectives behind the need for the valuation obviously affect how the burden of proof is allocated. For example, in an appraisal valuation under corporations law, the Delaware Court of Chancery has a statutory obligation to reach an independent valuation. Unlike commercial or investment arbitration, therefore, in a Delaware shareholder appraisal action each side has the burden of proving its own valuation position. "No presumption, favorable or unfavorable, attaches to either side's valuation, including the actual merger price."[355] On the other hand, where the objective of the valuation also involves a conclusion as to whether the conduct of one party was improper, Delaware courts are not reluctant to employ the burden of proof for equitable purposes. So, in a "squeeze-out" merger case where the court concludes that the transaction was "unfair" to the minority shareholders, the Delaware Court of Chancery will "resolve doubts, at the margin, in favor of the . . . minority shareholders who were involuntarily squeezed out."[356] The differing burden of proof rules in Delaware appraisal actions are yet one more reminder that valuation cases from one area of dispute should not automatically be transferred into another area of dispute without careful thought.

---

354. Chorzów Factory, *supra* n. 167, at 56. *See also Generation Ukraine v. Ukraine*, ICSID Case No. ARB/00/9, Award of September 16, 2003, at ¶ 19; *GAMI Investment, Inc. v. The Government of the United Mexican States*, Final Award of November 15, 2004, at ¶¶ 83–85. In the *MTD v. Chile Award* the sole arbitrator reduced the damages owing by Chile because the claimant investor had failed to clarify important terms of the privatization contract at issue in the dispute. *MTD v. Chile* Award, *supra* n. 178, at ¶¶ 242–243.

355. *Pinson v. Campbell–Taggart, Inc.*, 1989 Del. Ch. LEXIS 50, *19, 1989). *See also Gonsalves v. Straight Arrow Publishers, Inc.*, 793 A.2d 312, 16, 198 Del. Ch. LEXIS 45, **8 (Del. Ch. 1998). "In a statutory appraisal proceeding, unlike typical judicial proceedings, each side has the burden of proving its respective valuation position by a preponderance of the evidence." *Crescent/Mach I Partnership, L.P. v. Turner*, 2007 WL 1342263 at *9 (Del. Ch. May 2, 2007), citing to *M.G. Bancorporation, Inc. v. LeBeau*, 737 A.2d 513, 520 (Del. 1999).

356. *Delaware Open MRI Radiology Associates v. Kessler*, *supra* n. 3, at 313.

6 Mitigation

Again following national legal principles and international law, many arbitral tribunals recognize the responsibility of an injured party to take reasonable measures to mitigate its losses.[357] The principle of mitigation is by no means limited to breach of contract cases. Illustratively, in *Enron v. Argentina*, the ICSID tribunal expressly took account of the sale of a portion of the claimants' investment (and an option for sale of the remainder), as well as transfer of an affected contract, even though the transactions occurred years after the complained-of injuries.[358]

So too, the Czech Republic argued in *CME Stockholm* that the investor had failed in its obligation to mitigate losses. The Republic noted that the tribunal had fixed March 1999 as the time of expropriation, but had further held that the Republic had also earlier breached the Treaty in 1996 when the Czech Media Council improperly forced an amendment of CNTS' Memorandum of Association. According to the Czech Republic, the duty of CME to mitigate losses arose "from the moment it was aware of the circumstances giving rise to the breach."[359] Since that event occurred in 1996, argued the Republic, the increase in shareholding by the investor between 1996 and 1999 was a breach by CME of its obligation to mitigate injury and should be disregarded in calculating compensation.[360] The Tribunal acknowledged the mitigation principle but rejected the Republic's position on the facts.[361]

Respondent States also made mitigation arguments in *CME Stockholm* and the ICSID cases of *Middle East Cement Shipping and Handling Co. v. Republic of Egypt,*[362] and *Amco Asia v. Indonesia.*[363] While asserted unsuccessfully in those cases, the arbitral tribunals did recognize in each case that the principle would be applicable in appropriate circumstances in investment disputes.[364]

357. The principle of mitigation is accepted throughout common law systems for both commercial and tort law. However, many civil law systems do not establish a general duty of mitigation or limit that duty to particular areas of law such as torts/delicts. The principle of mitigation is, however, accepted in a number of instruments adopted throughout the civil law world, such as Article 77 of the U.N. Convention on Contracts for the International Sale of Goods and Article 7.4.8 of the UNIDROIT Principles for International Commercial Contracts 2004. As discussed in n. 74 *supra,* the UN Compensation Commission looked to UNIDROIT Art. 7.4.8 as support for the existence of a duty to mitigate damages as a generally accepted principle of law.

358. *Enron v. Argentina, supra* n. 43, at ¶ 387 ("such transactions were specifically made with the intention of mitigating losses").

359. *CME Stockholm* Final Award, *supra* n. 42, at ¶ 303.

360. *Id.*, at ¶ 301–303.

361. *Id.*, at ¶¶ 481 et seq.

362. *Middle East Cement Shipping and Handling Co. S.A. v. Egypt*, ICSID Case No. ARB/99/6, Award of April 12, 2002, at ¶¶ 166–171.

363. *Amco Asia Corporation and others v. Republic of Indonesia*, ICSID Final Award, June 5, 1990, Case No. ARB/81/8, and Decision and Rectification of October 17, 1990.

364. *See also CME Stockholm* Final Award, *supra* n. 42, at ¶ 301 et seq., *Starrett Housing Corp. v. Islamic Republic of Iran*, Award No. 314-24-1), Final Award August 14, 1987, 16 Iran-US C.T.R. 112, [201 ¶ 277] (1987), *Phillips Petroleum v. Islamic Republic of Iran*, Award No. 425-39-2 (June 29, 1989), 21 Iran-US C.T.R. 79, ¶¶ 111–165 (1989), *Amoco v. Iran, supra* n. 233, at 255 (¶ 217), *INA Corp. V. Islamic Republic of Iran*, Award No. 184-161-1, 8 Iran-US C.T.R. 373 at 380; *Kuwait Airways Corp. v. Iraqi Airways Company*, [2002] EWHC 1626 (Comm.), ¶ 58 (July 31, 2002).

The UNIDROIT Principles express the mitigation obligation in the following manner.

Article 7.4.8
(Mitigation of harm)

1. The non-performing party is not liable for harm suffered by the aggrieved party to extent that the harm could have been reduced by the latter party's taking reasonable steps.
2. The aggrieved party is entitled to recover any expenses reasonably incurred in attempting to reduce the harm.

As Komarov explains, the doctrine of mitigation as applied in common law jurisdictions addresses three circumstances.

> First, a party injured upon the occurrence of a breach of contract may not hold the contract breaker responsible in respect of losses that he could reasonably have avoided. Second, expenses reasonably incurred in avoiding or minimizing a loss resulting from breach of contract may be charged to the contract breaker. Third, regardless of whether an injured party in the circumstances had to mitigate, any action he takes after the breach of contract, which in fact avoids or minimizes the loss, will serve correspondingly to diminish the contract breaker's liability in damages.[365]

The concepts of mitigation and contributory negligence are treated separately in common law forums. In some civil law systems, on the other hand, the mitigation principle is intertwined with concepts of contributory negligence.[366]

One issue that may arise is the question of whether the injured party has a duty to take all reasonable measures to mitigate its injuries or only that the mitigation measures it has taken in fact have been reasonable in the circumstances. Zeller has asserted that "courts and tribunals [in CISG cases] simply ask whether the prudent business person has taken all reasonable steps, and has done all he can to keep costs to the breaching party to a minimum."[367] Other authority, in comparison, only requires that the steps taken by the injured party have been reasonable, not that that the injured party have exhausted all reasonable steps.

ICC Case No. 7006[368] illustrates the application of the mitigation duty to a long-term contract. In that case, an ICC tribunal granted only one year of lost profits for the injury to a seller. The distributor of the seller's goods breached

365. Komarov, Mitigation of damages, at 40, in Derains & Kreindler, *Evaluation of Damages in International Arbitration*, *supra* n. 241.
366. Taniguchi reviews the differences in approach towards mitigation across a number of national systems, including civil law jurisdictions like Germany and France where the mitigation duty derives from principles of contributory negligence. *See* Taniguchi, *The Obligation to Mitigate Damages*, at 79 et seq., in Derains & Kreindler, *supra* n. 241.
367. Zeller, *Damages under the Convention on Contracts for the International Sale of Goods*, at 114 (Oceana 2005).
368. XVIII Yearbook Comm. Arb. 44, 58 (1993).

its obligations under an exclusive distribution agreement several years before scheduled termination of that agreement. The tribunal concluded that, by the end of one year after receiving formal notice of termination from the distributor, the seller would have found in mitigation an alternate means for distributing its products into the relevant market. Consequently, the ICC tribunal awarded damages only for the first future year under the contract.

Similarly, mitigation principles underlay the decision by the United Nations Compensation Commission to reject the DCF method in favor of a compensation standard based on historical earnings in the claim against Iraq by Saudi Arabian Texaco Inc. arising out of the 1992 Iraqi invasion of Kuwait

> where the asset or business can be repaired or resumed, however, the DCF method will not be an appropriate measure of loss to the extent that it takes into account estimated losses beyond the restoration date of the asset or business.[369]

7 Unjust Enrichment and Other Equitable Considerations

The arbitrator, of course, is not obligated to make a compensation award that results in unjust enrichment of either the breaching or the injured party. Commonly, courts and arbitrators apply the doctrine of "unjust enrichment" to require a breaching party to disgorge the benefits of its misconduct, even at the risk of overcompensating the injured party.[370] In addition, though, a tribunal may also employ the principle of "unjust enrichment" to prevent the injured party from benefiting from the too-strict application of compensation principles. As quoted above in Chapter 2.XI.3, the US Restatement explicitly recognizes the occurrence of this phenomenon in its Official Comments about foreseeability.[371] The application of the international law doctrine of "abuse of rights" to reduce the damages in the *Patuha* and *Himpurna* awards may as well have been an instance of arbitrators acting to prevent what they saw as unjust enrichment of the investor and impoverishment of the respondent State.[372] Also, arguably, tribunals that have taken into account adverse events subsequent to the date of injury may have done so to avoid unjustly enriching the successful claimant. In light of these cases, some argue for enrichment as a principle ranking equally with fair market value and restitution for purposes of determining compensation in international investment arbitration disputes.[373]

---

369. UNCC Saudi Arabian Texaco Claim, *supra* n. 58, at ¶ 439.
370. *See* the discussion in *Azurix v. Argentina*, *supra* n. 17, at ¶¶ 434–437.
371. *See* text *supra* associated with n. 330.
372. *See*, e.g., *Patuha v. PLN Final Award*, *supra* n. 239, at ¶ 429. *See* Paulsson, "The Expectation Model," *supra* n. 241, at 71–75. Also note, in this context, the comments of *Chamber Three of the Iran-U.S. Claims Tribunal in Amoco v. Iran*, *supra* n. 233, at ¶¶ 225, 231, 258–259.
373. The usage of the terms "enrichment" and "restitution" in such discussions is obviously inconsistent with the usage of the term "restitution" in discussions of the principles underlying damages remedies in the US Restatement (Second) of Contracts and elsewhere. Compare Ch. 2.VI *supra*.

In principle, there would even be a third possibility of valuation, namely the "enrichment" standard. It has been argued that the measure of compensation upon expropriation should not concentrate on what the affected person has lost but on what the State has gained from the appropriation. This "enrichment" standard, however, has not been widely accepted in international law. It would represent a subjective standard, in this case from the perspective of the expropriating State.[374]

Equitable Considerations

The use of equitable considerations in the computation of compensation amounts is not uncommon, even if it is not always admitted. The principle is expressly recognized in the jurisprudence of the European Court of Human Rights. It also lies just beneath the surface of many judicial and arbitral decisions.

In several proceedings, tribunals have employed more general "equitable considerations" to reduce the amount to be awarded against a developing country, without detailing those considerations.[375] As noted above, the *Patuha* and *Himpurna* panel did so expressly, as did the European Court of Human Rights (ECHR) in its judgment about the value of expropriated properties of the former Greek Royal family. Indeed, Article 50 of the European Convention on Human Rights permits the ECHR to award "just satisfaction" for a breach of the Convention, including when deciding compensation for expropriation. In several cases, the ECHR has limited expropriation awards on the basis of "satisfaction équitable."[376] So too, the final arbitrator in the *LIAMCO* proceedings, who awarded damages in between two competing valuations as a "measure of equitable compensation."[377]

374. Marboe, *Damages and Compensation in International Law – the Limits of "Fair Market Value," supra* n. 84, at 732 (footnote omitted).

375. Prof. Hanotiau catalogues cases relying on equitable considerations in assessing damage in "La Détermination et L'evaluatation du dommage reparable: principles generaux et principles en emergence, in Gaillard" (ed.), *Transational Rules in International Commercial Arbitration* at 209 et seq. (ICC Pub. No. 480, 4, 1993).

376. Marboe, *Compensation and Damages in International Law – The Limits of "Fair Market Value," supra* n. 84, at 752, citing to *Belvedere Alberghiera S.r.l. v. Italy*, E.C.H.R. No. 31524/9630, October 2003, ECHR 2000-vi, at ¶ 32, *Motais de Narbonne v. France*, E.C.H.R. No. 48161/99, 27 May 27, 2003, at ¶ 19, and *Terazzi S.R.L. v. Italy*, E.C.H.R. No. 27265/95, October 26, 2004, at ¶ 37.

377. *Libyan American Oil Company (LIAMCO) v. Libyan Arab Republic*, 20 I.L.M. 1, 159–160 (1981). *See also Amoco v. Iran, supra* n. 233, at 256; Rubins & Kinsella, International Investment, Political Risk and Dispute Resolution: A Practitioner's Guide (Oceana Publications, Inc. 2005), at 257–258.

Other arbitral panels have arrived at compensation awards that have "taken account, in the traditional formulation, of 'all relevant circumstances.'"[378] As we have pointed out throughout, complex valuation calculations are rarely free from some level of uncertainty or judgment calls. Insistence on rigorous reasoning for compensation decisions in international investment awards is, in fact, a relatively new phenomenon.[379] Of course, arbitrators are only rarely authorized by the parties to decide a dispute *ex aequo et bono* or as *amiable compositeur*. Nevertheless, "the arbitrators can evaluate the damages by an *appreciation souveraine* or by making equity in order to make an overall judgment of various damages when they are not precisely identified, but when it is proven that damages have been suffered."[380] Moreover, the absence of express party authorization to resolve a valuation issue equitably may not prove an impenetrable barrier to an arbitrator's employment of equitable principles. As Kreindler candidly points out, "various techniques (interpretation) exist to arrive at the equitable solution desired by the arbitrator, even if he does not so state."[381]

The question of whether use by an arbitrator of equitable considerations to assess compensation is an improper exercise of the arbitrator's discretion has come before national courts. The Milano Corte di Appello has acknowledged that arbitrators occasionally take equitable considerations into account in their damages awards. The Corte di Appello refused, however, to overturn an arbitral award on that basis. Instead, the Court rejected an argument that the use of equitable considerations in such circumstances constituted an unauthorized *ex aequo et bono* decision by the arbitrators.[382] Similarly, the Annulment Committee in the *MTD v. Chile* dispute declined to annul the damages award by the ICSID tribunal as an unauthorized *ex aequo et bono* decision, despite the fact that the tribunal had split the damages on a 50:50 basis for contributory fault without seeking to justify that allocation.[383]

In *Sempra Energy International v. Argentine Republic*,[384] Argentina argued for a compensation calculation based upon the extent to which the investor had successfully recovered its investment and received a profit return before the

---

378. *Patuha v. PLN* Final Award, *supra* n. 239, at ¶ 484.
379. Walde & Sabahi, *Compensation, Damages and Valuation in International Investment Law*, ILA Committee on International Law of Foreign Investment, at 4, 13–16. Even today, the level of rigor in compensation decisions is often limited. *See*, e.g., Karaha Bodas Final Award, *supra* n. 270, and MTD v. Chile Award, *supra* n. 178.
380. Kreindler, Introduction at 19, in Derains & Kreindler, *supra* n. 241.
381. *Id.*, at 19.
382. *Virgilio De Agostini, et al. v. Milloil SpA, et al., Corte di Appello [Court of Appeal], Milan,* March 24, 1998, XXIII-1998 ICCA Yearbook of Commercial Arbitration (1998).
383. MTD Annulment Decision, *supra* n. 349, at ¶¶ 76, 101. At a more detailed level, it is also interesting to note that the discount rate selected by the arbitrators in the *Patuha* and *Himpurna* disputes was 21%, almost exactly midway between the 8.5% discount rate sought by the claimants and the 33.7% discount rate sought by the respondents. *See also* the cases cited in the "splitting the baby" discussion at Walde & Sabahi, *supra* n. 379, at 16.
384. *Sempra Energy International v. Argentine Republic*, ICSID No. ARB/02/16, Award, Dispatched September 28, 2007.

valuation date. If the investor had already fully recovered its investment and earned a profit before the injury event, asserted Argentina's expert witness, then the tribunal should order no additional compensation. While not discussed in the award, the underlying theory appears to have been that the investor would be unjustly enriched by receiving additional sums, since the investor had already received back its investment together with a reasonable rate of return before the injury event occurred.

The ICSID tribunal rejected the Argentine argument: "The problem at hand under the Treaty and the License is not to judge whether the companies have been fairly remunerated in the past but to determine what they were worth in 2001 given their prospects over the remaining years of the licenses."[385] The result in *Sempra* is not surprising. The Argentine argument, if accepted, would mean for example that materially reducing the value of the historically most successful companies by a breach of international law produces no compensation to the former owners, while breaches of international law harming companies that have not yet reached a revenue-generating stage, or with a continuing record of losses, produces the largest compensation awards. The respective values of the companies to arm's-length buyers (i.e., their fair market values) before the unlawful conduct would most likely be the exact opposite; companies with successful track records being worth much more to a prospective buyer than companies with no track record or, worse, a record of losses.

385. *Id.*, at ¶ 413.

Chapter 3
Comparability

Experts will offer valuation reports or testimony in arbitration proceedings based upon one or more of the following well-known valuation methods; Comparable Public Companies, Comparable Sales Transactions, Comparable Prices for Equity Interest, the Discounted Cash Flow (DCF) method, the Adjusted Present Value (APV) method, the Capitalized Cash Flow (CCF) method and the Adjusted Book Value (ABV) method. We now turn to a discussion of those methods, starting with methods based on the concept of "comparability." The objective of a comparability analysis is to attribute to the company being valued the characteristics of the other, comparable company. If that other company is truly comparable to the first company, then the benefits, risks and other attributes of the second company may appropriately be ascribed to the first company.

"Comparability" is, naturally, the foundation for valuation by reference to "comparable companies," "comparable transactions" and "comparable sales of equity interests." As explained in Chapter 4.I below, comparability is also important inter alia to the specification of discount rates for methods within the Income-Based Approach (such as DCF, APV and CCF valuations), as well as the computation of "betas" for the Capital Asset Pricing Model (CAPM) used to identify equity risk premiums for those methods.

Comparability, though, is at the heart of Market-Based methods of valuation; principally, the "comparable companies," "comparable transactions" and "comparable sales of interests" methods. Valuation experts will regularly value a business by identifying the price at which a similar business was recently sold in an arm's-length transaction between a willing buyer and a willing seller. Comparing the sales prices of similar businesses is often an effective valuation method for markets where large numbers of single asset companies exist, with a considerable number of sales transactions – markets with a large number of relatively simple – to-analyze companies. Finding such transactions is, of course, a difficult task. Most importantly, the two businesses must truly be comparable. Is a Spanish telecommunication company in fact comparable with a Colombian telecoms enterprise? Is a "merchant" power project in Virginia comparable with a power project located in Indonesia that has a long-term power sales contract with the State-owned utility? Are the circumstances surrounding two farm equipment manufacturers comparable, or are they in different geographic, product or regulatory markets? As we discuss below, questions such as these are central to an arbitrator's conclusion that two companies are sufficiently similar to justify treating them as comparable for valuation purposes.

Most stock market valuations are based on the use of comparable companies and "market multiples" derived from their performance, as are many M&A and other corporate transactions valuations. There are several reasons for this popularity. A comparables valuation involves far fewer open assumptions;[386] it can be completed quickly and inexpensively; comparables valuations are intuitively easy to understand and simpler to explain than Income-Based valuations; and the comparables valuation is "much more likely to reflect the current mood of the market, since it is an attempt to measure relative and not intrinsic value."[387]

The International Private Equity Valuation Guidelines consider that the use of an earnings multiple like EBIT or EBITDA to value an investment "is likely to be appropriate for an Investment in an established business with an identifiable stream of continuing earnings that can be considered to be maintainable." However, those Guidelines also hold that earnings multiples may be appropriately used for companies with negative earnings "if the losses are considered to be temporary and one can identify a level of 'normalised' maintainable earnings."[388]

Detractors note that market multiples reflect current market prices and attitudes. If all comparable stocks (say, dot.com stocks) are up, then the use of market multiples in such circumstances may produce a higher valuation than an Income-Based computation of the same company at the same time. The reverse is equally true if stocks in the sector are down.[389]

Market Multiples

Most stock market valuations are based on the use of comparable companies and "market multiples" like EBITDA. Comparables valuations are more likely to reflect the current mood of the market (up or down). Using "market multiples" of comparable companies measures relative values, not intrinsic values. Moreover, the choice of the comparable company and the "market multiple" is crucial to the reliability of this valuation method.

386. But, as we discuss in this part, there are a number of less transparent assumptions embedded inside the expert's choice of comparables and the market multiple used.
387. Damodaran, Relative Valuation, available at <http://pages.stern.nyu.edu/~adamodar/New_Home_Page>, (hereinafter, "Damodaran Relative Valuation"), at 1–2.
388. "International Private Equity Valuation Guidelines," *supra* n. 26, at 15.
389. Damodaran Relative Valuation, *supra* n. 387, at 2.

There are four basic steps.

- Define the multiple consistently and measure it uniformly across the companies being compared.
- Consider if the multiple is distributed in a reliable fashion across the industry and the market generally.
- Determine what fundamentals drive the chosen multiple and how changes in those fundamentals affect the multiple.
- Find the proper comparables and control for differences.

Of course, the use of comparable companies and market multiples has corresponding weaknesses. Most obviously, an incorrect choice of comparables can produce valuations based on non-comparable risk, growth and cash flow numbers. These factors are simply different for, say, a regional electricity utility company vis-à-vis a single-asset merchant power plant. The very detail of Income-Based projections like DCF forecast creates considerable transparency about many decisions by the expert. In contrast, the assumptions about how and why a particular company is comparable and, even more importantly, why other companies in the same sector were omitted from the expert's comparability analysis, are far less transparent until cross-examination by counsel occurs.

Similar questions arise regarding an expert's choice of a "market multiple" – the choice, for instance, among EBIT, EBITDA, price-to-book value, price-to-sales, etc. In the dot.com world, illustratively, companies with negative earnings and low revenues were occasionally (and, with 20/20 hindsight, unsuccessfully) valued by a multiple based on the ratio of stock price-to-hits on the company's website.

> [T]he lack of transparency regarding the underlying assumptions in relative valuations makes them particularly vulnerable to manipulation. A biased analyst who is allowed to choose the multiple on which the valuation is based or to pick the comparable firms can essentially ensure that almost any value can be justified.[390]

Arbitrators can evaluate the reliability of a "comparable companies" valuation by focusing on several core questions.

> There are four basic steps to using multiples wisely and for detecting misuse in the hands of others. The first step is to ensure that the multiple is defined consistently and that it is measured uniformly across the firms being compared. The second step is to be aware of the cross sectional distribution of the multiple, not only across firms in the sector being analyzed but also across the entire market. The third step is to analyze the multiple and understand not only what fundamentals determine the multiple but also how changes in these fundamentals translate into changes in the multiple. The final step is finding

390. *Id.*

> the right firms to use for comparison, and controlling for differences that may persist across these firms.[391]

A common procedure for measuring the value of an enterprise involves determining the value of a comparable company based upon the relationship between the comparable company's earnings (or a similar test) and the market value of that company (based on its stock price) at the relevant valuation date; illustratively, the "Price/Earnings" test referred to by the United Nations Compensation Commission or a ratio of stock price to EBITDA (Earnings Before Interest, Taxes, Depreciation and Amortization).[392] Once the market capitalization of the comparable company has been identified, the valuation then proceeds to identify a ratio of that company's earnings to that market capitalization. If, say, the stock market capitalization of a company is USD 100 million and it has an EBITDA of USD 10 million, then the EBITDA multiple for a ratio of EBITDA-to-total capitalization is 10X. The expert would then determine the EBITDA of the disputed company at the heart of the arbitration, and apply the same 10X multiple to determine the market value to a third party of that company. Of course, like all financial computations, the expert must have good numbers for the components of EBITDA in order to offer a useful valuation. As a US bankruptcy court explains:

> The key components of a comparable company analysis are the Debtor's EBITDA (i.e., earnings before interest, taxes, depreciation and amortization) and the selection of an appropriate multiple to apply to the EBITDA to arrive at enterprise value. The appropriate multiple is determined by comparing the enterprise value of comparable publicly traded companies to their trailing twelve months EBITDA. A subjective assessment is required to select the comparable companies and, here, the parties agree about which comparable companies are more appropriate to use.[393]

The strengths and weaknesses of EBITDA as an appropriate "market multiple" are reviewed in Chapter 6.II below.

The very titles of these methods for valuing businesses disclose the central challenge for arbitrators – finding sufficient comparability to justify employing the value of the comparable company as a basis for arriving at the value of the business being appraised. Perhaps identical comparability exists in the hypothetical world

---

391. *Id.*, at 5.

392. UNCC Decision 9, *supra* n. 55, at ¶ 17. *See* Ch. 6.II *infra* for a review of EDIT and EDITDA.

393. *In re Exide Technologies*, *supra* n. 78, at 61. Of course, there is no legal requirement that the measure of the EBITDA of the comparables be fixed at 12 months' historical earnings. Other courts and experts have used longer or shorter historical periods, as appeared appropriate in the particular circumstances. *See* e.g., *Sporborg v. City Specialty Stores, Inc.*, 123 A.2d 121, 1956 Del. Ch. LEXIS 99 (Del. Ch. 1956) (rejecting one year trailing earnings in favor of average of past five years' earnings). In addition, multiples other than EBITDA may also be considered, such as EBIT, EBITDAR, sales, price per foot and our favorite, price per website hits. *See* Ch. VI.B *supra*.

of theoretical economists and university professors but, in the real world of arbitration, no other enterprise likely will be precisely comparable with the company at the heart of the dispute. As the Delaware Court of Chancery has noted:

> The utility of the comparable company approach depends on the similarity between the company the court is valuing and the companies used for comparison. At some point, the differences become so large that the use of the comparable company method becomes meaningless for valuation purposes.[394]

Whether we are looking at the stock prices and performance of comparable companies or the sales price for interests in comparable companies, the same questions arise about the true comparability of the companies in question (size, products, location, markets, regulatory environment, capital structure, management and so on). Additionally, highly liquid capital stock of a publicly traded company differs in important respects from the more-difficult-to-sell capital stock or partnership interests of a privately held company. Further differences come into play in valuing the sale of an entire company (or a controlling block of shares) based upon the trading prices for sales of individual non-controlling shares of capital stock of a public company. There are a number of challenges involved in either translating public stock prices into values for private companies or extrapolating individual stock prices into values for a controlling position in an entire company. The practical question, therefore, is how close? If the chosen companies do not parallel the company at issue in the dispute, the valuation is skewed:

> [I]ts [the expert's report] main flaws, which lead to an exaggerated value for CTCA, can be traced to the comparable companies he selected and how he determined which financial ratios to rely upon in extrapolating from CTCA's data. First, the companies he selected as comparable were far less risky and far more successful than CTCA and, thus, investors naturally would pay higher multiples for a share of ownership in those companies.[395]

The IVSC Business Valuation Guidance Note instructs valuation experts to consider several factors when determining if a reasonable basis for comparison exists.[396]

- The businesses should be in the same industry or in an industry that responds to the same economic variables.
- Similarity to the subject business in terms of qualitative and quantitative business characteristics.
- Amount and verifiability of data on the similar businesses.
- Whether the price of the similar business represents an arm's-length transaction.

---

394. *In re Radiology Associates, Inc.*, 611 A.2d 485, 490, 1991 Del. Ch. LEXIS 234, **10 (Del. Ch. 1991).
395. *Lane v. Cancer Treatment Centers of America, Inc.*, *supra* n. 1, at *123.
396. IVSC Business Valuation Guidance Note, *supra* n. 15, at ¶ 5.14.1.3.

Comments by a judge in a case entitled *U.S. Inspect Inc. v. McGreevy*[397] (relating to the value of a home inspection business), about one expert's [Richman's] criticisms of another expert's [Estabrook's] comparability analysis demonstrate three important distinctions often considered in a comparability analysis; public company vs. private company, overall size differences, and comparability of the products offered by the companies.

> Richman responded that Estabrook's market approach was flawed because it was premised upon the misconception that the six comparable companies chosen by Estabrook were true comparables. On this issue, the court agrees with Richman. Notwithstanding Estabrook's attempts to link USI [the company being valued] to his chosen comparables, the court finds these companies have almost no similarity to USI for a number of reasons. First, each of the six companies has its stock traded on a public exchange. To the contrary, USI is a closely held corporation whose outstanding shares are owned by less than fifteen people. As of December 31, 1998, USI employed approximately 300 individuals. On the same date, Service Master employed 45,000 people, Ecolab employed 10,000, and Rollins employed 8,934. Moreover, in 1998 Radonic's [the relevant USI business unit's] net sales totaled approximately 25 million dollars. That same year, ADM Industries' net sales were 1.5 billion, Building One's totaled in excess of 809 million, Ecolab's approximated 1.9 billion, Maintenance America's exceeded 760 million, Rollins' fell just short of 550 million and ServiceMaster's exceeded 4.7 billion. Nor was there true comparability in the types of services provided by USI and Estabrook's chosen comparables. None of ADM Industries, Building One Services or Group Maintenance America provide home inspection services, which constitute the vast majority of USI's business. Ecolab provides various services to its customers, none of which are supplied by USI. Rollins primarily provides pest control services to its customers while USI provides no such services. And, although ServiceMaster does provide home inspection services, Estabrook was unable to provide any estimate of how much of ServiceMaster's total business its home inspection division provides.[398]

The US tax authorities, among the strongest proponents of a comparable companies valuation method, have given considerable attention to determining comparability among companies. The US Internal Revenue Service requires that comparability be based on lines of business.[399] The tax authorities, however, have recognized that other factors, such as the markets being served, are important criteria. In *Estate of Gallo*,[400] for instance, the business at issue was a wine

---

397. *U.S. Inspect Inc. v. McGreevy*, *supra* n. 82.
398. *Id.*, at 533.
399. IRS Rev. Ruling 59–60, *supra* n. 5, at 4.
400. *Estate of Gallo v. Comm'r*, 50 T.C. 470 (1985).

producer; the US Tax Court accepted evidence of value for brewers, distillers, soft-drink bottlers and well-known consumer food producers.

In addition to the questions that arise as to whether particular companies were properly treated as true comparables in an analysis, the expert may be asked to explain why other, potentially comparable companies have been excluded from the valuation. In *Heilig Meyers Company v. Internal Revenue Service*,[401] the US Fourth Circuit Court of Appeals upheld a bankruptcy court's conclusion that an expert witness "was unable to provide any explanation for how she came to base the WACC [Weighted Average Cost of Capital] analysis on the stock of seven particular consumer credit card companies out of the dozens of such companies that exist."[402] Competing experts will often present valuations based on comparable companies carefully selected to emphasize a party's preferred result. Cross-examination and thoughtful arbitrator questions are the best deterrents for such conduct.

Comparability Issues

Important issues in selecting comparable companies for the valuation include the following:

- When did the comparable valuations occur?
- Public companies vs. private companies.
- Do the comparables offer their products or services in similar markets?
- Geographic location.
- Size.
- Capital structure.
- Debt and non-cash elements of the package of consideration.

The following non-exhaustive checklist of issues may help establish whether proposed comparables are in fact sufficiently comparable to justify relying upon them to value the business involved in the dispute. Like the other checklists in this volume, many of the listed items overlap with each other in practice. Each of the comparability issues discussed below is relevant to valuations derived from each of comparable sales transactions, comparable sales of equity interests and the stock prices of comparable companies.

I TIMING

When did the comparable valuation events occur? What intervening events affect comparability? The judge in *U.S. Inspect* acknowledged an important aspect of true

401. *Heilig Meyers Company v. Internal Revenue Service*, 2007 WL1417158 (4th Cir. 2007).
402. *Id.*, at *8.

comparability, the date when comparability for each company is measured. Note the phrases in the court's opinion – "As of December 31, 1998," "on that same date" and "[t]hat same year." When comparing sales transactions or stock prices involving different companies (even if those companies are themselves truly comparable with each other), it is crucial to determine if intervening events between the first measurement date and the subsequent second measurement date affect that comparability. For example, a sale of a company operating a US wireless telecommunications license in 1999 is not easily compared with a sale in 2001 of a second company holding a similar US license. As is well known, the market values of telecoms companies in the US collapsed starting in 2000. More prosaically, changes over time in macroeconomic factors like interest, inflation, growth and foreign exchange rates can obviously undermine comparability as well.

II PUBLIC vs. PRIVATE

If the disputed business is a private company, do the comparables also involve private companies? If some of the events or stock prices involve public companies, how does the ability of the public company to access public capital markets for financing affect the relative valuations. (Up or down? Within what range?) Experts will almost never offer an exact figure in response to such a question. But if asked to do so, they may be willing to testify as to a range of possible impacts. Obtaining such testimony can often help arbitrators narrow the differences between conflicting expert valuations.

III PRODUCTS AND SERVICES MARKETS

Do the comparables offer their products or services in similar markets? The author is aware of one arbitration in which the company at issue was a single "merchant peaker" power generation project having no long-term power contracts (i.e., making only day-by-day sales, and therefore exposed to upward and downward movements in the current market sales price for electricity). The claimant offered up a well-known US electricity utility as a comparable. Close examination of the electricity utility's financial statements revealed, however, that 43% of that utility's aggregate revenues came from power transmission and distribution (i.e., totally different services from power generation) or under long-term fixed power supply contracts that protected against current price fluctuations (i.e., a significantly different buyer-seller relationship). Of the 21% of revenues that incorporated merchant power plants like the company being valued, the utility's financial statements surprisingly defined the scope of that business activity to cover power plants *with* long-term power sales contracts, so long as less than three-quarters of the power produced by such a plant was covered by the long-term contracts. In other words, a plant qualified as a merchant plant under this definition even if 74% of its power sales *were* covered by long-term sales contracts protecting against price fluctuations! By contrast, the "merchant peaker" power plant at issue in the arbitration had no long-term power sales contracts at all. The difference, of course, was whether buyers were committed to purchase the power (long-term sales contracts) or free to choose other sellers (day-by-day sales). In sum, only some unidentifiable portion of 21% of the allegedly comparable electricity utility's revenues related to electricity sold into a comparable market on similar terms. All of the remaining revenues related to either sales of electricity based on a substantially different sales arrangement (long-term purchase commitments at pre-agreed prices) or to sales of entirely different services. Needless to say, the comparability of the electricity utility with the merchant power plant was not evident.

As noted above, the trial judge in *U.S. Inspect v. McGreevy* found that some of the alleged comparables in that case offered services not provided by the company in dispute (e.g., pest control services versus home inspection services). Others did not offer at all the home inspection services that constituted the vast majority of the disputed company's business. Arbitrators should ask the experts about the make-up of the products or services offered by the comparables. In the previously mentioned "merchant peaker" arbitration, over 19% of the revenue of a second allegedly comparable electricity utility proposed by the expert proved to be attributable to telecommunications services, having nothing at all to do with electricity. Other unquantified business activities of that second alleged comparable business again included electricity transmission and distribution services, as well as owning coal mines and investing in gas, water and desalination businesses. The more diversified the array of products and services offered by one company, the harder it will be to justify that company as a comparable for a second company with more focused business activities, especially if size disparities amplify the impact of that diversification.

IV GEOGRAPHIC LOCATION

Geography can encompass, among other matters, differences in market characteristics, political, tax and regulatory regimes, currency risks and other macroeconomic differences. Again, the "merchant peaker" arbitration offers an illustration. That power plant was located in the United States. Another of the comparables proffered by the expert witness was an electricity utility in Southern Europe, with no business activities in the US and the great majority of its revenues denominated in Euros. Yet a fourth alleged comparable was a US company, but with over 70% of its total revenues derived from sources outside the US (including a number of developing countries). The circumstances facing the two comparables were noticeably different from the risks faced by the US power plant at issue in the dispute. The US power plant, unlike the proposed comparables, involved strictly US customers paying solely in USD, regulated entirely by US regulators. Arbitrators can question experts closely on these issues. Particularly if the proposed comparables are public companies, this type of information is available from a company's annual reports, prospectuses and other public filings made with securities regulatory authorities like the US Securities Exchange Commission and the UK Financial Services Authority. Those filings are often appended to expert reports, but in the far back among the exhibits where arbitrators do not always venture unescorted.

V SIZE

Size matters, most importantly for market share and for purposes of obtaining financing from commercial lenders or trade creditors. As the discussion in Chapter 4.I below about size premiums for discount rates demonstrates, smaller companies often face a different risk profile from larger companies. By how much do the sizes of the comparable companies differ? How do the experts think that size differential affects the relative valuations? (Again, up or down? Within what range?)

VI CAPITAL STRUCTURE

Some companies have extremely complex capital structures or a relatively high debt-to-equity leverage ratio. Different enterprises, led by their management and investors, have different sensitivities to risk. Companies are particularly aware of the risks created by adding debt to the capital structure. Capital structure decisions by companies accordingly depend upon many factors, such as business risk, the tax and accounting consequences of adding or reducing debt (e.g., the tax deductibility of interest payments on debt in some countries), financial flexibility and the impact of leverage on risk and profits. The capital structures of private companies may be especially complicated, with some equity investors often entitled under their shareholder agreements to preferred returns on their invested capital while other equity investors are subordinated until the first investors have reached the pre-agreed target returns.[403] Moreover, investors will often invest their equity into private companies in the form of deeply subordinated debt to take advantage of preferential tax, accounting and other legal advantages. Arbitrators should make sure any such differences are incorporated into the valuations – for example, a 25% shareholder is not necessarily entitled to 25% of the value of the company if that minority shareholder has agreed to subordinate its equity returns to the prior fulfillment of a minimum target rate of return for the majority investor. Therefore, the stock price paid for that 25% partially subordinated interest will require

403. *See*, e.g., *La Prairie Group Contractors (International) Ltd. v. CE Cascenan, Ltd.*, et al. (hereinafter, "*LaPrairie Group v. CE Casecnan*"), Tentative Phase I Trial Decision at 2, Case No. CE-02-409959, Superior Court of the State of California, County of San Francisco (May 27, 2005), affd in part and overruled in part by the California Court of Appeal, First District, Division 1 (February 21, 2007) (under Stockholders Agreement, stock ownership among shareholders in Philippine hydropower project to be readjusted if earnings do not meet principal sponsor's target internal rate of return).

adjustment before being compared to a common shareholder interest in a second company even if the companies themselves are comparable. Similarly, the specific terms of subordinated debt contributed by a project sponsor may determine whether that investment is treated equally and ratably with equity investors or is entitled to priority returns.[404]

VII DEBT AND NON-CASH CONSIDERATION

Naturally, arbitrators need to consider the entire package of consideration passing between the parties to a transaction. That consideration in an M&A transaction effected by means of an asset sale often includes, for example, the assumption by the acquirer of liabilities. The total purchase price for a company may therefore require taking account of how much debt was assumed (or forgiven) in connection with a comparable sales transaction, not merely the cash exchanged between the parties. In addition to assuming or forgiving liabilities as part of the overall purchase price, other non-cash compensation may also play a role. The claimant investor in *Noble Ventures v. Romania* commented on the importance of non-cash consideration in quantum calculations in its submissions to the ICSID tribunal.

> 92. Second, in his calculation of fair market value, [Romania's expert witness] ignored all elements of consideration other than the fixed cash price. SOF's [the Romanian State Ownership Fund's] own documents, however, demonstrate that it considered the variable cash consideration, the proposed investments, the environmental and social obligations as part of the value received from the sale to Noble Ventures. Similarly, when APAPS [the Romanian privatization authority] resold CSR [the company being valued] in 2004, its press release described the purchaser's commitment of 14 million Euros in investments and assumption of debts of 10 million Euros as key benefits of the transaction, even though the cash consideration was 1 Euro.[405]

In comparisons between the stock prices of two public companies, arbitrators also should be sensitive to comparisons between two companies with widely differing debt profiles. To illustrate, in the early 1990s most international project financings of power projects in developing countries had a 3:1 debt-to-equity leverage ratio

404. In the transaction at issue in *LaPrairie Group v. CE Casecnan*, California Court of Appeal, *supra* n. 403, the controlling sponsor contributed about USD 43 million of "equity" for cost overruns in the form of deeply subordinated debt. That decision came back to haunt the sponsor, when the court interpreted the "minimum rate of return" provisions in the Stockholder Agreement to not treat that deeply subordinated debt as an equity contribution for purposes of calculating returns. *Id.*, California Court of Appeal, First District, Division 1 (February 21, 2007), at Part VI. The commercial reasonableness of that court's decision is open to question in those particular circumstances.

405. *Noble Ventures, Inc. v. Romania*, *supra* n. 305, at ¶ 225. In light of the tribunal's decision against liability on the merits, the investor's contentions on these points were never addressed in the case. *Id.*, at ¶ 229.

(75% debt, 25% equity). By 1997 (just before the Asian financial crisis), though, sponsors were bringing power projects to market with debt-to-equity ratios of 4:1 or higher, an obviously riskier deal. If a 1994 project with a 3:1 leverage is offered as comparable to a 1997 project with a 4:1 leverage ratio, that type of difference can have a substantial impact on the comparison. Similarly, the repayment schedules for long-term debt owing by some companies to their creditors may extend over a substantial period of time. A longer repayment schedule for the same principal amount, of course, spreads the debt payments over a longer time frame and reduces the size of individual principal payment installments. Another company may owe the same aggregate principal amount of long-term debt, but face much larger principal payments on that debt over a shorter time frame. The second company, all other things being equal, may be a noticeably riskier investment than the first. Many solvency opinions for highly leveraged buy-outs contain a "refinancing assumption," in which the valuation expert concludes that the acquired company will be solvent after the acquisition *assuming* the acquisition debt can be successfully extended or refinanced when it matures in a few years. If that assumption proves to be incorrect, as it did for many US companies in 1989–1990, then the company will end up quickly filing for bankruptcy as its debt comes due without a source of funds for repayment.

It is also important to assure that the two companies being compared include the same types of transactions in their definitions of "indebtedness," and thus that the debt-to-equity ratios employ the same definition of debt. For instance, the characterization of leases as either finance leases (capital leases counted as debt on the balance sheet) or operating leases (expensed and thus not counted as debt) can dramatically affect how a company's debt structure is presented.[406] The manner in which a company treats leases for accounting purposes may have a very significant impact on its debt-to-equity ratio. As the Wall Street Journal noted in 2004, at the time of US Airway's 2004 bankruptcy filing, the airline's most recent audited balance sheet showed USD 3.15 billion of long-term debt.[407] That balance sheet, however, did not include US Airway's USD 7.39 billion of operating lease obligations with respect to its fleet of passenger jets. Those long-term lease obligations were not treated as "indebtedness" for GAAP purposes. Also, businesses often utilize the flexibility within accounting principles in a materially different fashion. Moreover, companies often come from countries with different accounting principles. The results can easily show up in differing definitions of debt, and thus affect comparability.

These distinctions only highlight a few of the manifold ways in which differing approaches towards indebtedness can affect a valuation. The best advice is that thoughtful questions can bring to light important comparability issues.

---

406. *See* Damodaran, Dealing with Operating Leases, Stern School of Business (undated), available at <http://pages.stern.nyu.educ/~adamodar/New_Home_Page>.
407. Weil, "How Leases Play a Shadowy Role in Accounting," *Wall Street Journal*, September 22, 2004, at A1.

Chapter 4

Important Components of DCF Valuations

Let us now turn from methods within the Market-Based Approach to valuation methods within the Income-Based Approach; first, Discounted Cash Flow (DCF) projections. As we have noted above, the DCF method is one of the most well accepted methods used for business valuations. The importance of the DCF valuation method is recognized by the issuance of a specific Guidance Note by the International Valuation Standards Committee, Guidance Note No. 9. The IVSC's DCF Guidance Note states:

> DCF analysis has gained widespread application due in part to the advancement of computer technology. DCF analysis is applied in valuations of real property, businesses and intangible assets; in investment analyses; and as an accounting procedure to estimate value in use. The use of DCF has increased substantially in institutional, investment property and business valuation sectors and is frequently required by clients, underwriters, financial advisers and administrators, and portfolio managers.[408]

The AICPA, the ASA, the Canadian appraisal profession and several other valuation organizations have agreed on a common definition of Discounted Cash Flow: "[A] method within the income approach whereby the present value of future expected net cash flows is calculated using a discount rate."[409]

Another way to describe the DCF method is that it measures the present value of the future cash flows available to equity. The cash flow available to equity is

408. IVSC, International Valuation Guidance Note No. 9, Discounted Cash Flow Analysis for Market and Non-Market Based Valuations 3 (International Valuation Standards, 8th edn 2007) (hereinafter, "IVSC DCF Guidance Note"), at ¶ 1.1.

409. International Glossary of Business Valuation Terms, *supra* n. 17.

"Net income after taxes, plus depreciation and other non-cash charges, less increases in working capital, less capital expenditures, less decreases in invested debt capital principal, plus increases in invested capital debt principal."[410]

DCF Method

The Discounted Cash Flow method thus comprises several steps:

- Estimating future cash flows of the enterprise being valued (revenues minus expenses, with certain adjustments) during a specific projection period (e.g., ten years). Adjustments may exclude non-recurring transactions, non-arm's length transactions and non-operating assets (i.e., assets not used in core operations). Non-operating assets are valued separately, however, and added to the final DCF value to reach a total value.
- Calculating the present value of those future cash flows, taking into account the time value of money and the risks faced by the investment. Each individual year of expected future return is discounted back to a present value. We then add the present values of each year to obtain the value of the investment.
- If appropriate, estimating the terminal value of cash flows arising after the end of the specific projection period (i.e., cash flow after the ten-year period)
- Aggregating the present value of the cash flows within the projection period and the present value (if any) of the post-projection period terminal value.
- Deducting the fair market value of the enterprise's debt to arrive at the net cash flow available to the equity investors.

The *Lawyer's Business Valuation Handbook* summarizes the importance of DCF valuations to the financial and business community:

> The DCF method is the predominant valuation technique employed by investment bankers to value companies for capital markets transactions or acquisitions. The discounted cash flow method is the most conceptually correct method because it captures the driving principle of valuation: Value is the present worth of future benefits. Capitalizing [*i.e.*, the CCF method discussed in Chapter 6 below] is merely a shortcut method that hopes to produce a similar result.
>
> . . . Not only is discounted cash flow the most theoretically correct valuation method, it is also the most widely practiced valuation method in the

410. IVSC Business Valuation Guidance Note, *supra* n. 15, at ¶ 3.11.3.

> world of corporate finance. Furthermore, the method is increasingly used by valuation experts and increasingly accepted by the courts (with the exception of a few family law courts, such as those in California).
>
> In both *discounting* and *capitalizing*, we are converting an expected stream of income into a present value. In other words, we are estimating what someone would pay today (or as of the effective valuation date) for some expected stream of future economic income.[411]

DCF valuations are not, of course, always appropriate. The International Private Equity Valuation Guidelines express skepticism about relying on DCF projections when other valuation methods are available.

> The Discounted Cash Flow (DCF) technique is flexible in the sense that it can be applied to any stream of cash flows (or earnings). In the context of private equity valuations, this flexibility enables the methodology to be applied in situations that other methodologies may be incapable of addressing. While this methodology may be applied to businesses going through a period of great change, such as a rescue refinancing, turnaround, strategic repositioning, loss making or is in its start-up phase, there is significant risk in utilizing this methodology.[412]

When presented with a DCF forecast, arbitrators will focus on the key assumptions and inputs in the calculations. Arbitrators will also focus on the extent to which the financial calculations are sensitive to changes in those assumptions or inputs. For example, what does an X% change in a price assumption produce in the final amount? What happens if the discount rate increases (or decreases) by Y%? What if interest rates go up (or down) by Z%? From an expert's perspective, the main work in developing a DCF projection will be to identify all of the important variables, confirm that the core assumptions are reasonable and then construct a financial model to perform the required computations. Each of those tasks must be done in a manner that persuades the arbitrator the resulting discounted cash flows are credible. To achieve that objective, the underlying evidence must be sound and the model must be reliable.

DCF analyses involve extensive spreadsheets. Compiling a DCF projection thus requires the detailed consideration of numerous individual line items in revenue and expense forecasts, as well as a myriad of assumptions. Moreover, the underlying financial models are a riot of numbers, values, and shorthand identifiers for computer calculations, where each printed spreadsheet page (itself highly complex) represents many hidden underlying, inter-linked equations. In business

411. Pratt, *The Lawyer's Business Valuation Handbook* (American Bar Association 2000), at 105 (footnote omitted). The *Lawyer's Business Valuation Handbook* has been referred to as "the leading non-academic treatise" by the Delaware Court of Chancery in *Delaware Open MRI Radiology Associates, P.A. v. Kessler*, *supra* n. 3, at 339 n. 130 (Del. Ch. 2006).

412. "International Private Equity Valuation Guidelines", *supra* n. 26, at 21. To the same effect, *see* the US Private Equity Valuation Guidelines, *supra* n. 24, ¶ 41 at 10.

transactions, DCF valuations (and other valuation methods) often cope with the potential for variations among these items by employing sensitivity analyses. It is very common, therefore, for potential investors to obtain Base Case, Best Case and Worst Case valuations of a proposed investment to test the sensitivity of the valuation to crucial variables.

Increasingly, disputes in arbitration over the value of ongoing business activities have involved competing DCF forecasts presented by the opposing parties. It should come as no surprise, though, that many arbitrators are uncomfortable with the manifold details of a DCF computation. Arbitrators often look to the experts to simplify and clarify the evidence through expert reports and testimony. Unfortunately, the substance of a DCF forecast is not simple. For example, despite the best efforts of the experts, DCF forecasts ultimately require decisions by the arbitrators on the reasonableness of assumptions. More unfortunately, too often an expert witness will confuse and complicate the presentation of the DCF analysis, rather than simplifying and clarifying it. Of course, that may be the result of skillful cross-examination by counsel or testimony by the opposing expert witness. As we noted at the beginning of this volume, arbitrators are regularly left with two widely different valuations, each having suffered heavy damage to its credibility from the litigation artillery duels.

DCF computations for a company can vary widely, depending on differing assumptions employed in the forecasts about future revenues and expenses, additional capital requirements, interest and inflation rates, currency fluctuations, the starting and ending dates for the DCF forecast period and other matters. Significantly, DCF forecasts are highly sensitive to the choice of the overall discount rate used in the formula to discount the gross income amount back to a present-value amount. DCF forecasts are also highly sensitive to the terminal value projecting the residual value to the end of the investment's life, especially if the period for the detailed projections is short (e.g., five years).

A DCF projection is only as good as its content; the "garbage in, garbage out" (GIGO) principle surely applies. Experts, judges and arbitrators alike understand this GIGO precept. Therefore, they accept (or reject) a DCF forecast based as much on the quality of the underlying evidence as on their own like or dislike for discounted cash flow analysis as a valuation method; "its just a tool."[413] The Delaware courts often give significant weight to the DCF valuation method in shareholder valuation cases.[414] Similarly, US bankruptcy courts and tax authorities

413. Comment by Gerry Lagerberg to the author, January 2008.

414. "The DCF method is frequently used in this court, and [the court] prefer[s] to give it great, and sometimes even exclusive, weight when it may be used responsibly". *Andalaro v. PFPC Worldwide, supra* n. 295, at *35. *See also Matrix Group Ltd. v. Rawlings Sporting Goods Company, Inc.*, 47 F.3d 583, 594 (8th Cir. 2007) (Delaware courts have recognized the DCF method as the "preeminent valuation methodology" in the financial community). Other relevant Delaware cases include *Cede & Co. v. Technicolor, Inc.*, 1990 Del. Ch. 259 (Del. Ch. 1990), *Gesoff v. IIC Industries, Inc.*, 902 A.2d 1130, 2006 Del. Ch. LEXIS 91 (Del. Ch. 2006), and cases cited at n. 53 of *Onti, Inc. v. Integra Bank, supra* n. 293, at 916.

regularly rely on the DCF method.[415] Also, Government entities will themselves employ the DCF method for their regulatory purposes; a fact that may prove significant to the persuasiveness of a challenge to the reliability of the DCF method in subsequent arbitral proceedings.[416]

For international investment law cases, the *CME Stockholm* arbitrators interpreted the *World Bank Guidelines on the Treatment of Foreign Direct Investment* to hold that compensation based on a DCF valuation was ''presumptively reasonable'' if the enterprise being valued was ''a going concern with a proven record of profitability.''[417] Unlike commercial cases and financial valuation practice, though, some international investment treaty tribunals have been reluctant to accept a discounted cash flow methodology to determine business value. As discussed above,[418] the *Aminoil* award declined to apply the discounted future profits evidenced proposed by the claimant oil company to determine the value of an oil

---

415. As the bankruptcy court noted in *In re Trans Max Technologies, Inc.*, 2006 WL 2571986 at *6 (Bankr. D. Nev., August 15, 2006), "entity valuation for cramdown purposes [confirmation of a reorganization plan over the objections of some creditors] typically involves some form of a discounted cash flow analysis" citing to 7 Collier on Bankruptcy, *supra* n. 13, at ¶ 1129.06[2]. Illustratively, in a period of just a few recent months, the following cases addressing a variety of US bankruptcy issues relied in whole or in part on DCF valuations: *In re Granite Broadcasting Corp.*, 2007 WL 1492465 (Bankr. S.D.N.Y., May 18, 2007); *In re American Classic Voyages Co. v. JP Morgan Chase Bank*, 2007 WL 1237828 (Bankr. D. Del., April 27, 2007); and *In re OCA, Inc.*, 2006 WL 3833929 (Bankr. E.D. La., December 29, 2006). *See also* the cases cited in In re Iridium, *supra* n. 45, at *61 n. 51 and in Stearns, "Proving Solvency: Defending Preference and Fraudulent Transfer Litigation," *supra* n. 20, at nn. 57, 61. Illustrative US tax cases, particularly cases involving the valuation of companies for estate tax purposes, include *Estate of Simplot v. Comm'r*, 112 T.C. 130 (1999); *Estate of Jung v. Comm'r*, 101 T.C. 412 (1993); *Kohler v. Comm'r*, T.C. Memo 2006-152; *Estate of Heck v. Comm'r*, T.C. Memo 2002-34; *Estate of True v. Comm'r*, T.C. Memo 2001-167; Estate of Magnin, T.C. Memo 2001-31; and *Estate of Borgatello v. Comm'r*, 2000-264. Other bankruptcy and tax examples abound.
416. *See CMS v. Argentina*, *supra* n. 7, at ¶ 416 ("DCF techniques have been universally adopted...; as a matter of fact, it was used by ENARGAS [the Argentine gas regulatory authority] in its 1996/7 tariff review.") Government agencies often employ DCF projections to assess the economic impact on businesses of regulatory measures. *See*, e.g., US Environmental Protection Agency (EPA), National Pollutant Discharge Elimination System – Proposed Regulations to Establish Requirement for Cooling Water Intake Structures at Phase III Facilities, Port II, 69 Fed. Reg. 68444, at *48 (November 24, 2004) ("EPA has conducted extensive analyses of the economic impacts of this proposed rule and the co-proposed options discussed above, using an integrated energy market model (the IPM) and an analysis of market costs and residential rates for the energy sector, and a discounted cash flow analysis model for the facility, firm, and market levels for manufacturers."). *See also id.*, at *81–82. Other examples of use by regulatory authorities of the DCF valuation method are voluminous, crossing industry and national boundaries around the world.
417. *CME Stockholm* Final Award, *supra* n. 42, at ¶ 161. *See also Enron v. Argentina*, *supra* n. 43, at ¶ 385 ("there is convincing evidence that DCF is a sound tool used internationally to value companies, albeit that it is to be used with caution as it can give rise to speculation. It has also been constantly used by tribunals in establishing the fair market value of assets to determine compensation of breaches of international law".) (footnotes omitted).
418. *See* text related to n. 53 *supra*.

concession expropriated by Kuwait. Similarly, the panel in *MINE v. Republic of Guinea* declined to utilize a DCF forecast, although it awarded lost profits damages on an alternate theory.[419] The *Tecmed*[420] tribunal, in a NAFTA "regulatory expropriation" case, also rejected a USD 52 million fair market valuation proposed by the investor based upon a DCF analysis. Among the reasons given in the award was the "protracted" duration of the fifteen-year projection period (based on the projected life of the waste disposal facility investment at issue). In addition, the panel considered the project's future revenues to be dependent on difficult-to-predict future investments. Accordingly, *Tecmed* awarded the investor USD 5.55 million, based largely upon the initial purchase price of the property plus lost profits for (it would seem) a two-year period. The tribunal also apparently adjusted the award for additional investments in the property by the investor subsequent to the purchase date. The computation basis for the per annum lost profits amount was not explained in the final *Tecmed* award.

Commentators have noted the reluctance of investment treaty arbitral panels to rely upon DCF projections for lost earnings determinations:[421]

> In rejecting the DCF method of estimating investment value, the *Tecmed* panel relied on a number of prominent arbitration awards adopting the same approach. Indeed, it is one of the puzzling aspects of contemporary investment treaty arbitration practice that tribunals have repeatedly resisted a method nearly universally recognized in the economics community as the most reliable way to estimate the fair market value of ongoing concerns. To be sure, the most common factor militating against application of DCF in these cases has been that the investment in question is not a "going concern."

Even where the arbitrators have accepted a discounted case flow valuation in a proceeding against a host State, the reluctance to award large damage amounts is obvious. For example, in the *Patuha v. PLN* award arising out of Indonesia's response to the Asian financial crisis, the arbitrators made an "equitable

419. *See* Meyer, Quintero & Shao, "The Effect of Risk on the Value of Lost International Business Profits," 7 *International Journal of Value-Based Management* 107, 109 (1994).

420. *Tecnicas Medioambientates Tecmed, S.A., v. United Mexican States*, Award, ICSID Case No. ARB (AF)/00/02 (May 29, 2000), 43 I.L.M. 133 (2004) (hereinafter "Tecmed").

421. Coe & Rubins, Regulatory Expropriation and the Tecmed Case: Context and Contributions, 597, 659 (footnotes omitted), in Weiler, *supra* n. 53, citing *Metalclad Corp. v. United Mexican States*, *supra* n. 282; *Phelps Dodge Corp. v. Islamic Republic of Iran*, *supra* n. 192; *Wena Hotels Ltd. v. Arab Republic of Egypt*, Award, ICSID Case No. ARB/98/4 (8 December 2000), 41 I.L.M. 896, 918–99 (2002); *CME Stockholm* Final Award, *supra* n. 42, at ¶ 604; and *Santa Elena v. Costa Rica*, *supra* n. 212. Among the numerous other investment awards that have declined to award lost profits are *Aucoven v. Venezuela*, *supra* n. 301; Southern Pacific Properties (Middle East) *Limited v. Republic of Egypt*, ICC Arbitration No. YD/AS No. 3493, Award of March 11, 1983; *AAPL v. Sri Lanka*, *supra* n. 296; *Benvenuti & Bonfant v. Congo*, *supra* n. 296; *AGIP S.p.a. v. The Government of the People's Republic of the Congo*, ICSID Case No. ARB/77/1, Award of November 30, 1979; *Société Quest-Africaine des Bétons Industrials (SOABI) v. Republic of Senegal*, ICSID Case No. ARB/82/1, Award of February 25, 1988; *PSEG v. Turkey*, *supra* n. 179, and *Amoco v. Iran*, *supra* n. 233.

assessment of the evidence, and, in the circumstances of this case, resolving all doubts in favour of PLN, the debtor.''[422] Moreover, the panel additionally offered an ''abuse of rights'' justification for further limiting the amount of the award.[423]

Some claim that the clash in investment treaty arbitrations between awards that compensate an investor's expectancy interest (such as earnings-based methods) and awards that compensate only an investor's reliance interest (such as sunk investment costs) may, in fact, not be founded on differing views about the reliability of the various valuation methods. Instead, as Sergey Ripinsky argued in a presentation to the Investment Treaty Forum of the British Institute of International and Comparative Law,[424] a process of ''reverse engineering'' may be occurring. Ripinsky pointed out that forward-looking valuation methods often yield a higher number than asset-based methods. The latter may be perceived by arbitrators as producing a ''fairer,'' ''moderate'' result, better balancing interests of investors and States'. His conclusion? ''Reverse engineering – first the 'fair' outcome, then the reasoning to match that outcome.''[425]

That approach, of course, is not unfamiliar to arbitrators faced with the task of reaching consensus among the members of a three-person panel. Nor is it inconsistent with the development of legal principles in common law jurisdictions.

This reluctance to rely upon a DCF analysis in investment treaty disputes is by no means universal. In the *CMS v. Argentina* award under the US-Argentina bilateral investment treaty, the tribunal rejected comparable stock prices and comparable sales price approaches. The panel's basis for that ruling was that the companies proposed for stock price comparison were in fact not comparable and that no significant evidence of comparable transactions was proffered.[426] The tribunal also chose not to apply an asset value approach on the basis that CMS, the foreign investor, was a minority shareholder in the injured company, which moreover had a record showing profits.[427] The arbitrators further rejected valuing the company on the basis of an ''options approach,'' under which the value of a company would be

---

422. *Patuha v. PLN* Final Award, *supra* n. 239, at ¶ 482. Note that *Patuha v. PLN* is not an investment treaty case.
423. *Id.*, at ¶¶ 435–458. *See also* Paulsson, "The Expectation Model," *supra* n. 241, at 10–13, defending the application of the "abuse of rights" doctrine in the circumstances.
424. Ripinsky, presentation on "Damnum emergens and lucrum cessans: is it relevant?" to 8th Investment Treaty Forum, British Institute of International and Comparative Law (BIICL), May 11, 2007. Papers are available to BIICL Investment Treaty Forum members at <www.biicl.com>.
425. *Id.*, at 8.
426. *CMS v. Argentina*, *supra* n. 7, at ¶¶ 412, 414. In *Enron v. Argentina*, *supra* n. 43, at ¶¶ 380–389, another ICSID tribunal with the same chair determined to employ a DCF valuation to calculate the value of the injured company under the ''no pesification'' scenario, and then to employ prices from actual sales/option transactions to calculate the value in the ''pesification'' scenario. The tribunal held the difference between the two scenarios to be the damages incurred by the claimant investors. *See also* the awards in *CME Stockholm*, *Starrett Housing*, and *Phillips Petroleum*.
427. *Id.*, at ¶ 413.

based on the value of its assets in alternative uses, given the single viable use of a gas transmission business.[428] The tribunal instead embraced the DCF method.

> 416. This leaves the Tribunal with the DCF method and it has no hesitation in endorsing it as the one which is the most appropriate in this case. TGN was and is a going concern; DCF techniques have been universally adopted, including by numerous arbitral tribunals, as an appropriate method for valuing business assets; as a matter of fact, it was used by ENARGAS in its 1996/7 tariff revenues. Finally, there is adequate data to make a rational DCF valuation of TGN.
>
> 417. The Tribunal also notes that in spite of the disagreement between the parties as to the appropriate application of the valuation method, experts from both sides have shared the view that DCF was the proper method in this case for determining losses that continue through a prolonged passage of time.[429]

Many arbitral tribunals find the DCF method to be difficult to apply. The arbitral tribunal in *Patuha v. PLN*, which valued an Indonesian power project on the basis of DCF forecasts, was candid about the challenges involved in DCF projections and discount rates.

> 482. Weighing the factors discussed in paragraphs 273–281 as well as the relative immaturity and modest prospects of the Patuha project, the Arbitral Tribunal holds that the most appropriate discount rate is 21%. The arbitrators make no pretense that this is the result of precise weightings of the discrete considerations that have influenced the arbitrators; nor do they wish to create the illusion that they have engaged in econometric modeling, or even calibrated costs and revenues with a time line that establishes hypotheses for the commissioning of generating Units, contingencies of reservoir evolution, and the like. Both the rate and its application reflect a series of adjustments made by the arbitrators in their equitable assessment of the evidence, and, in the circumstances of this case, resolving all doubts in favour of PLN, the debtor.
>
> 483. The Arbitral Tribunal is not aware of any instances of international arbitral tribunals carrying out their own DCF computations to replace those presented by one of the parties. Indeed, in the case of *Philips Petroleum* although the award clearly accepted the DCF methodology and contained a sophisticated discussion of its application in the context of a "careful and realistic appraisal of the revenue-producing potential of the asset" including levels of production, costs, taxes, other charges, prices, and risks, Chamber Two of the Iran-US Claims Tribunal explicitly stated that it "does not intend to make its own DCF analysis with revised components, but rather to determine and identify the extent to which it agrees or disagrees with the estimates of both parties and their experts concerning all these elements of valuation," and that in particular it would not "substitute the Claimant's discount rate with its own."

428. *Id.*, at ¶ 415.
429. *Id.*, at ¶¶ 411, 416–417 (footnotes omitted).

484. It may be objected that this approach exposes the ostensible adoption of the DCF method as something of a fig leaf. Indeed, it is difficult to connect the criticisms raised by the tribunal in the *Philips Petroleum* case against the claimant's computations with the sum in turn announced as the result of that Chamber's having taken account, in the traditional formulation, of "all relevant circumstances." True enough, the tribunal identified two kinds of factors that affected its view of the DCF calculations, namely general "equitable considerations" and "verification" by means of an alternative valuation method which looked to tangible investments and historic earnings. Nevertheless, it is legitimate to ask whether the result, in that case and often elsewhere, is not to create an illusion of scientific analysis to mask the reality of subjective approximations.

485. To be fair, there is nothing new under the sun. Lucrum cessans has always been an inexact science. As the arbitral tribunal put it in the *Delagoa Bay* case almost exactly one century ago, "such a computation made in advance on the basis of purely theoretical data cannot hope to be absolutely accurate but only comparatively likely."

486. The present Arbitral Tribunal wishes to be transparent in both its reasoning and its computations, fully recognizing the limitations of an exercise where risks, costs, and revenues are conjectural, controversial, and imperfectly synchronized. The Arbitral Tribunal has followed three lodestars: (i) the DCF method is adopted in accordance with the understanding articulated above in paragraphs 352–362; (ii) the Claimant must bear the burden of demonstrating the validity of its hypotheses; (iii) the infirmities perceived by the Arbitral Tribunal with respect to those hypotheses have resulted in a recomputation which the arbitrators fully realize is imprecise, but which seeks to avoid arbitrariness by compelling a thorough consideration of all relevant factors, all the while being conscious of erring, whenever imprecision is inevitable, in favour of PLN. Thus doubts have been resolved equitably in favour of the debtor.

487. There is no reason to apologise for the fact that this approach involves approximations; they are inherent and inevitable. Nor can it be criticized as unrealistic or unbusinesslike; it is precisely how business executives must, and do, proceed when they evaluate a going concern. The fact that they use ranges and estimates does not imply abandonment of the discipline of economic analysis; nor, when adopted by the arbitrators, does this method imply abandonment of the discipline of assessing the evidence before them.[430]

430. *Patuha v. PLN* Final Award, *supra* n. 239, (footnotes omitted). The arbitrators in *CMS v. Argentina*, *supra* n. 7, expressed similar sentiments at ¶ 420: "[S]uch estimates need not be arbitrary or analogous to a shot in the dark; with the appropriate methodology and the use of reasonable alternative sets of hypotheses, it is possible to arrive at figures which represent a range of values which can be rationally justified, even though there is general agreement that their accurateness can only be fully assessed some 22 years later."

More succinctly, Prof. Gotanda has noted that "[t]he problem with the DCF method... is that it is difficult to apply."[431]

We do not intend in this book to instruct arbitrators as to the one single correct approach to DCF forecasts. We do hope, however, to point out some issues that consistently arise. We also hope to identify some tools arbitrators may use to find common ground between the differing positions of the parties. For this purpose, we will first discuss the role of risk and the discount rate in DCF analyses. Then, we will consider some of the other important components of a DCF calculation.

I DISCOUNT RATES

Let us start at the back, and work forward. A DCF analysis seeks to determine the lost net earnings a company will suffer as a result of the legal injury that triggered the dispute. The DCF method does so by calculating that company's anticipated future stream of net cash flow over a specific future period of time, and then discounting that gross amount back to a present-value lump sum. Therefore, selecting the proper discount rate is central to a DCF valuation (and, indeed, to valuations under the APV and CCF methods discussed in chapters V and VI below).

The discount rate is the "rate of return used to convert a future monetary sum into present value."[432] Many experts take the position that the purpose behind selecting the discount rate is to identify the minimum rate of return a reasonable third party would anticipate as a condition to making the investment as of the valuation date. As Pratt explains:

> The discount rate is the expected *total rate of return* the investor requires to commit funds to the particular investment. It is market-driven in that it represents the expected rates of return available in the market on other investments that are comparable in terms of risk.[433]

If the period of a DCF forecast covers, say, ten years of future business activity going forward from the valuation date, then the DCF analysis involves forecasting the projected net cash flow of the company for each of those future ten years. The valuation will discount each of those annual amounts back to the valuation date to

---

431. Gotanda, "Recovering Lost Profits," *supra* n. 40, at 91. Cf. Amerasinghe, "Issues of Compensation for the Taking of Alien Property in the light of Recent Cases and Practices," 41 I.C.L.Q. 22, 64 (1982) ("It would seem that the assessment of full compensation is at the present time filled with variables and is certainly not a very scientific process.").

432. International Glossary of Business Valuation Terms, *supra* n. 17. *See also* The Lawyer's Business Valuation Handbook, *supra* n. 411, at 107.

433. The Lawyer's Business Valuation Handbook, *supra* n. 411, at 118. Alert readers will have already noted the importance of that ubiquitous concept "comparable" in Pratt's description. *See also* the definition of a discount rate by reference to a rate of return in IVSC DCF Guidance Note, *supra* n. 408, at ¶ 3.4. However, note the criticism of a "rate of return" approach towards discount rates discussed *infra* at text preceding n. 513.

determine the aggregate net present value of the ten years of projected future net cash flow. That present value amount would then be combined, if appropriate in the factual circumstances, with the similarly discounted net present value of an estimate of net income subsequent to the ten-year period (i.e., the "terminal value" discussed below). The cumulative sum represents the measure of the fair market value of the enterprise.

The final DCF amount can be very sensitive to differences in discount rates. In large investment disputes, a few percentage points of difference between discount rates can affect the final compensation amount by many millions of dollars. If, hypothetically, an arbitral panel concludes that a company will have had net cash flow (i.e., revenues minus expenses, with a few other fancy adjustments) of USD 10 million per annum for each of those ten years, then the aggregate gross future dollar amount of net cash flow would be USD 100 million (USD 10 million x ten years). To determine the net present value at the valuation date (i.e., the value to the injured party as of the beginning of the ten-year period) of that future stream of income, the arbitrators would select a discount rate to make the present-value computation. For instance, at a 33.7% discount rate (as proposed by respondent PLN's expert for valuing the Indonesian geothermal power project in *Patuha v. PLN*), the net present value of a ten-year income stream of USD 10 million per year will be USD 28.05 million. But if, instead, the arbitrators apply a discount rate of 8.5% (as argued for by the claimant investor's expert in the same case), then the present value of the same stream of income will be USD 65.61 million, a significant USD 37.56 million range. At a discount rate of 21% (the rate actually selected by the *Patuha v. PLN* arbitrators), the net present value of that ten-year income stream of USD 10 million per year will be USD 40.54 million.

The sensitivity of a DCF computation to the selection of the discount rate is well-illustrated by the impact of the difference between petitioner's proposed 27.43% discount rate and respondent's proposed 27.9% discount rate in *Lane v. Cancer Treatment Centers of America, Inc.*, a Delaware shareholder appraisal case. That small 0.47% range between the two discount rates resulted in a full 7% difference in the two competing valuations.[434] Similarly, in an action brought by Cinerama as a dissenting shareholder resulting from raider Ronald Perelman's acquisition of Technicolor, the competing experts valuing Technicolor disagreed as to the proper discount rate to be employed in the court's DCF valuation. Petitioner argued for a discount rate of 12.50%, while the acquirer countered with rates of 20.4% and 17.3% for different components of Technicolor. The court noted that: "[I]f one substitutes the higher discount rate used by respondent's principal expert for the lower rate used by petitioner's expert and makes no other adjustment to either DCF model the difference reduces from $49.61 a share to $20.86."[435]

Unsurprisingly, claimants argue for low discount rates and respondents argue for high discount rates. It is therefore rare to find both sides agreeing on the applicable

434. *Lane v. Cancer Treatment Centers of America, Inc.*, *supra* n. 1, at *112 n. 151.
435. *Cede & Co. v. Technicolor, Inc.*, *supra* n. 414, at *23 n. 15.

discount rate. Rubins & Kinsella thus expressed astonishment at the agreement between claimant and respondent in the *CME Stockholm* case; "inexplicably, both parties' experts concurred as to the proper discount rate to be applied."[436]

Choosing a discount rate is crucial to a DCF forecast. However, courts have not developed a single approach to determining the appropriate discount rate.

> The experts also haggle over the correct discount rate.... Testimonial feuds about discount rates often have the quality of a debate about the relative merits of competing alchemists. Once the experts' techniques for coming up with their discount rates are closely analyzed, the court finds itself in an intellectual position more religious than empirical in nature, insofar as the court's decision to prefer one position over the other is more a matter of faith than reason.[437]

Ordinarily, the valuation will apply a single discount rate to all future cash flows. It is possible, of course, to apply different discount rates to different time periods. "The investment cash flows can be assigned different discount rate[s] commensurate with the level of risk (i.e., uncertainty) of future cash flows at different points in time."[438]

To do so, though, will require the valuation professional (or the arbitrator) to exercise judgment as to when the different discount rates should be used, as well as how to calculate the different rates.

The approach taken in the US by courts to select a discount rate has often depended on the subject matter of the dispute. Illustratively, for claims on account of lost wages for injured individuals in personal injury and other employment disability cases, US courts often select a discount rate reflecting solely the rate of inflation and investment of the lost stream of income at a safe rate of return. Typically, that results in low discount rates of 2–4% and thus a large damage award. This choice of a low discount rate intentionally ignores the possibility that the injured individual might have lost his or her job anyway or be unable to easily find a new job; whether for lack of competence, because the employee's skills have become less valuable in light of business or technological developments, in a downsizing if the employer becomes distressed or the relevant industry is suffering an economic downturn, or otherwise. Instead, the choice of such a low discount rate de facto assumes that the individual will promptly be able to obtain a comparable replacement job.[439]

That approach may be attractive as a public policy matter when awarding compensation to a disabled individual. However, if an arbitrator relies upon a DCF forecast for a business venture, it makes far more sense to recognize fully in the selection of the discount rate the investment risks faced by that business venture as part of the damages computation. Otherwise, the injured investor would receive a compensation award for projected future earnings as if the receipt of those sums was guaranteed,

---

436. Rubins & Kinsella, *supra* n. 377, at 256. The agreed rate was 10.83%. *CME Stockholm* Final Award, *supra* n. 42, at ¶ 564.

437. *Delaware Open MRI Radiology Associates, P.A. v. Kessler*, *supra* n. 3, at 338.

438. Senechal, *Dealing with Uncertainty: Discounted Cash Flow (DCF) Versus Adjusted Present Value* (APV), at 4, *Transnational Dispute Management Special Issue on Energy Disputes*, vol. 4, issue 3, available on line at <www.transnational-dispute-management.com>.

439. Dunn & Harry, "Modeling and Discounting Future Damages', *Journal of Accounting" Online Issues*, January 2002, available at <www.aicpa.org/pubs/jofa/jan2002.html>.

rather than being subject to a range of uncertainties; market risks, competitive pressure, technological change, poor management, government regulatory changes, credit problems with suppliers and customers, force majeure events and the host of other normal commercial concerns that plague businesses every day. For example, even fixed monthly payments under hell-or-high-water long-term purchase contracts are subject to the credit risk that the obligor may become insolvent and the country risk that the host State in which the obligor is located will suffer war or a political or macroeconomic crisis. As we all know, nothing ever is truly guaranteed in business.

Discount Rates

The discount rate used in a DCF valuation is the rate of return used to convert future cash flows into a present value that reflects the risks associated with those cash flows. DCF valuations can be very sensitive to differences in discount rates. Common approaches used to select discount rates include the "build-up procedure" and the "Weighted Average Cost of Capital" (WACC) procedure. As part of developing discount rates, it is necessary to identify the cost of equity capital as a component of the discount rate. The cost of equity capital is often computed using the "Capital Asset Pricing Model."

Two general approaches to developing a discount rate are regularly employed by valuation experts: the "build-up" procedure and the Weighted Average Cost of Capital (WACC) procedure. In the latter case, the "cost of equity" component of the WACC is often calculated based upon the Capital Asset Pricing Model (CAPM). We discuss these procedures below.

1 Build-Up Procedure

Many valuation experts will testify that a discount rate, at a specific time and for a particular company, is comprised of at least three components, all determined as of that specific time: a "risk-free" rate, an element covering systematic (i.e., market) "equity risk," and an element covering subjective risk for that particular company.[440] These components are added, to "build up" the discount rate. When estimating a discount rate for a DCF valuation or a capitalization rate for a CCF valuation, the IVSC Business Valuation Guidance Note calls for the valuation expert to "consider such factors as the level of interest rates, rates of return expected by investors on

440. *Id.* As discussed in below in this Ch. 4.I.1, it is also common to assert that a size premium should be included for small companies and a sovereign risk premium should be included for non-domestic companies. With respect to the role of risk in discount rates, *see* generally Deutsch, Jones, Tyler & Knull, *Accounting for Uncertainty in Discounted Cash Flow Valuation of Upstream Oil and Gas Investments, Transnational Dispute Management Special Issue on Compensation and Damages in International Investment Arbitration*, vol. 4, issue 6, available on-line at <www.transnational-dispute-management.com>.

similar investments, and the risk inherent in the anticipated benefit stream."[441] The risk-free and systematic risk components together comprise the "base" discount rate, which is the "most objective and verifiable" component of the overall discount rate.

> The experts in this case have used the proxy that has found the most favor among professional appraisers: the so-called "build-up model." The build-up model begins with the core factors considered by CAPM [the Capital Asset Pricing Model, discussed below], a risk-free rate and an equity premium rate. From there, however, the build-up model begins to diverge from CAPM. Under the build-up method, beta is not considered. A size premium, used consistently with the practice of most current users of CAPM in the appraisal and valuation context, is de rigueur under the build-up model. Much more heretical to CAPM, however, the build-up method typically incorporates heavy dollops of what is called "company-specific risk," the very sort of unsystematic risk that the CAPM believes is not rewarded by the capital markets and should not be considered in calculating a cost of capital.[442]

The Compagnie des Conseils et Exports Financiers (CCEF), the French professional tax advisers' organization, has developed a form for determining discount rates in connection with French tax filings. That form is based on the "build-up" procedure. It sets out the building blocks for developing a discount rate, as well as a grid of company-specific risks and possible weightings.[443]

Elements Constituties Du Taux	*Nature Des Elements*	*Pourcentage D'estimation*
Taux de base qui ajusterait offre et demande d'actifs monétaires L.M.T.	Taux de rendement des obligations d'Etat (OAT à 10 ans)	4 à 6% actuellement proche de 5,35%
Risque général d'entreprise	Couverture du risque général d'entreprise (avec majoration pour le marché des entreprises non cotées: prime de non liquidité)	4 à 6% actuellement 4%
Risque sectoriel	Positif ou négative (par référence au risque général d'entreprise)	A apprécier +/− 50% du risque général
Risque spécifique de l'entreprise considérée	Voir grille ci-dessous	A apprécier +1 à 15%

441. IVSC Business Valuation Guidance Note, *supra* n. 15, at ¶ 5.14.2.2.2.

442. *Delaware Open MRI Radiology Associates, P.A. v. Kessler*, *supra* n. 3, at 338–339 (footnote omitted).

443. *See* Annex 3 – Calculation of the Discount Rate (CCEF), in FEE SME Business Valuation Guide, *supra* n. 17, at 47.

La grille d'evaluation du "risque spécifique d'entreprise" qui a été établie par la commission comporte 8 rubriques, et se présente ainsi (faisant reférénce à une éventuelle periode de transition avant la période dite de stabilité).

RUBRIQUES	*Pondération*	*Risque pendant la période de Transition*						*Risque pendant la période de Stabilité*					
		Nul 10%	Moyen 25%	Elevé 50%	Trés Élevé 75%	Absolu 100%	NA	Nul (1)	Moyen (2)	Eleve (3)	Trés élevé (4)	Absolu (5)	NA
1 Technologie													
2 Management													
3 Chef d'entreprise													
4 Dépendance													
5 Production													
6 Position concurrentielle													
7 Liquidité-défaillance													
8 Autres													
TOTAL													

Other checklists for building a discount rate encompassing risk-free, systematic risk and subjective risk components also exist, as the following listing by *Dunn & Harry* attests.[444]

Unsystematic or Subjective	Market risk	– Barriers to market entry;
		– Market size or share constraints;
		– Strength of competition;
		– Buyer project or service acceptance;
		– Shifting buyer preferences.
	Financial risk	– Illiquidity;
		– Unfavorable contractual; obligations;
		– Excessive debt.
	Management risk	– Depth of management talent;
		– Key employee dependence;
		– Management's past experience with product or service.
	Product risk	– Key supplier dependence;
		– Obsolescence;
		– Reliance on specific patents and licenses;
		– Lack of productive capacity;

444. Dunn & Harry, "Modeling and Discounting Future Damages," *supra* n. 439, at Exhibit 1: Discount Rate Risk Considerations.

		– Commercial impracticality of production.
	Company sales	– Key customer dependence;
		– Lack of product diversification;
		– Lack of geographic sales; diversification.
	Business	– General economic conditions environmental risk;
		– Government regulation.
"Base" rate	Systematic risk	– General equity risk premium;
		– Beta coefficient for the subject; industry to modify the general equity risk premium;
		– Company size premium.
	Risk-free	– US Treasury coupon bond, note or bill yield.

As the foregoing list makes clear, the "base" rate includes the cost of debt plus the incremental cost of partially employing equity funds (rather than debt) to finance the capital costs of the enterprise. The expert valuer then adds specific risks attributable to the company and industry to arrive at the total discount rate.

The cautious arbitrator will wish to be assured that the build-up rate incorporates an inflation factor. For USD cash flow forecasts, the "risk-free" component of a discount rate is generally a comparable US Treasury debt security of a similar tenor. As anyone familiar with the business pages of the newspaper knows, the yield to maturity for a US Treasury security will include both a "real rate of return" and the expected rate of inflation over the life of that security. Accordingly, the "risk-free rate" already incorporates an adjustment for inflation, and no separate inflation adjustment to the discount rate is appropriate.

Valuation professionals also point out the relationship between the currency in which the cash flow analysis is conducted and the debt security chosen for the risk-free rate. It is the currency of the calculation, not the location of the investment, that is determinative.

> The risk free rate used to come up with expected returns should be measured consistently when the cash flows are measured. Thus, if cash flows are estimated in nominal U.S. dollar terms, the risk free rate will be the U.S. treasury bond rate. This also implies that it is not where a project or firm is domiciled that determines the choice of a risk free rate, but the currency in which the cash flows on the project or firm are estimated. Thus, Nestle can be valued using cash flows estimated in Swiss Francs, discounted back at an expected return estimated using a Swiss long term government bond rate, or it can be valued in British pounds, with both the cash flows and the risk free rate being British pound rates. Given that the same project or firm can be valued in difference currencies, will the final results always be consistent?

> If we assume purchasing power parity, then differences in interest rates reflect differences in expected inflation. Both the cash flows and the discount rate are affected by expected inflation; thus, a low discount rate arising from a low risk free rate will be exactly offset by a decline in expected nominal growth rates for cash flows, and the value will remain unchanged.
>
> If the difference in interest rates across two currencies does not adequately reflect the difference in expected inflation in these currencies, the values obtained using the different currencies can be different. In particular, projects and assets will be valued more highly when the currency used is the one with low interest rates relative to inflation. The risk, however, is that the interest rates will have to rise at some point to correct for this divergence, at which point the values will also converge.[445]

Arbitrators will wish to make sure that competing experts are using the same debt security as the basis for their "risk-free" rate. For example, if the duration of the DCF forecast is ten years, with equal annual USD cash flow amounts, one expert might use ten-year US Treasury Bonds for the risk-free rate. The opposing expert, however, may use a US Treasury Bond with a maturity shorter than ten years (say, seven years), on the grounds that ten equal annual cash flow payments over the ten-year forecast period is equivalent to an "average-life-to-maturity" of about seven years. Shorter-term Treasuries normally carry a lower interest rate than longer-term Treasures,[446] thereby reducing the discount rate and increasing the compensation award. Consequently, arbitrators should determine early in the process whether the experts are making an apples-to-apples comparison by using the same "risk-free" US Treasury rate. If not, the arbitrator may ask for the experts to re-run their numbers, using the same underlying US Treasury security to identify the "risk-free" component of the discount rate.

More controversy arises with respect to the second building block in this approach to constructing a discount rate; the systematic (i.e., market) "equity risk" component. Experts will generally testify that the purpose of this systematic equity risk measure is to add an additional element to the discount rate to account for the market risk and volatility of making an equity investment (rather than a debt investment as evidenced by the risk-free US Treasury security). This component of building a discount rate reflects systematic risk: "the risk that is common to all risky securities and cannot be eliminated through diversification."[447] General

---

445. Damodaran, Estimating Risk Free Rates, at 5–6, available at <http://pages.stern.nyu.edu/~adamodar/New___Home___Page>.

446. But not always. If the trading market for US Treasuries at the valuation date shows an "inverted yield curve," that means short-term Treasury securities are yielding at that time a higher rate of return than longer-term Treasuries. An "inverted yield curve" is not the ordinary situation, but it does occur from time to time. If the valuation date is a date on which the yield curve is inverted, long-term interest rates embedded into a valuation may be lower than short-term rates; yet another reminder of the importance of the valuation date.

447. International Glossary of Business Valuation Terms, *supra* n. 17. The International Glossary further states: "The measure of systematic risk in stocks is the beta coefficient." *Id.* For an

equity market risks include factors such as the volatility of the equity market and an adjustment for business size.

Thus, the AICPA and ASA define "Equity Risk Premium" as "a rate of return added to a risk-free rate to reflect the additional risk of equity instruments over risk free instruments (a component of the cost of equity capital or equity discount rate."[448] It would of course be extraordinary for the discount rate used in determining the value of an equity investor's interest in a company to fall below the rate at which the subject company can borrow debt from commercial sources on an arm's-length basis at the relevant valuation date. As the panel in *CMS v. Argentina* noted, "while it is true that the risk borne by shareholders is also borne by debt holders, it is well recognized that shareholders bear a significantly larger risk, because their claims are residual."[449]

Equity Risk Premium

An equity investment in a business is acknowledged to be riskier than a debt investment in the same business. Discount rates for investments must therefore incorporate a component to reflect this equity risk premium; a rate of return added to a risk-free rate to reflect the additional risk of equity instruments over risk-free instruments. For U.S. markets, experts often rely on data from Ibbotson Associates for this purpose.

For US markets, data research companies collect detailed historical information about the general public equity (systematic) risk premium, as well as the incremental impact of size on the general equity risk premium. Ibbotson Associates is a well-known source of that data. When US data is relevant, arbitrators should not be surprised to see Ibbotson data presented in support of an expert's build-up of a discount rate. Naturally, just like everything else in the identification of the risk premium for a discount rate, Ibbotson data is not free from technical controversy.[450]

explanation of the beta coefficient, *see* the discussion of the CAPM method of calculating discount rates above at Ch. 4.I.3.

448. International Glossary of Business Valuation Terms, *supra* n. 17.

449. *CMS v. Argentina*, *supra* n. 7, at ¶ 454.

450. The Lawyer's Business Valuation Handbook, *supra* n. 411, at 121. *See* further the sources identified in *id.*, n. 4 for a technical discussion of some of the controversies. Some have argued that the equity risk premium produced from Ibbotson data is too high, pointing the finger principally at "success" and "survivorship" biases. *See*, e.g., Dimson, Marsh & Staunton, Global Evidence on the Equity Risk Premium, The Journal of Applied Corporate Finance, vol. 15, No. 4 (Summer 2003). For the period 1900–2002, Dimson, Marsh & Staunton find US equity risk premiums as follows: relative to T-Bills, a geometric premium of 5.3% and an arithmetic premium of 7.2%; relative to T-Bonds, a geometric premium of 4.4% and an arithmetic premium of 6.4%. *Id.*, at Table 1.

Experts often rely on Ibbotson Associates' data to identify the general equity (systematic) risk premium in the US markets. Ibbotson bases its systematic risk data on a comparison of historical US public stock market returns and historical US Treasury securities yields. The firm offers that data in three series; thirty-day, five-year and twenty-year comparisons. The relatively easy access to this data, and its regular usage in the valuation field, may help explain why many DCF valuations employ a five-year projection period;[451] relying on the data from the Ibbotson five-year historical time series to calculate the cost of capital makes life easier for the valuation expert.

To illustrate the size of a systematic equity risk premium in the US public stock markets, the following table summarizes Ibbotson Associates' data on risk premiums for publicly traded stocks in the US, relative to US Treasury Bills and Bonds, for different time periods.[452]

Risk Premium for Equity

	STOCKS – T. BILLS		*STOCKS – T. BONDS*	
	Arithmetic	Geometric	Arithmetic	Geometric
1926–1997 (50 years)	9.05%	7.13%	7.73%	6.10%
1962–1997 (35 years)	6.21%	5.64%	5.55%	5.48%
1981–1997 (15 years)	11.56%	12.02%	9.56%	9.07%

There are "surprisingly large differences" in the US historical equity premiums that experts use in their reports, even though many analysts rely on the same Ibbotson Associates database of historical US stock returns. The differences are largely explained by the difference in time periods used, the use of arithmetic versus geometric averages of stock returns (or, in plain words, whether the average returns are compounded annually) and the choice of short-term Treasury Bills or long-term Treasury Bonds as the risk-free rate.[453] With respect to time periods, Ibbotson Associates data is available back to 1926. Some experts use the entire data series back to 1926, while others use fifty, twenty-five, ten or even five-year periods for their historical stock returns. The differences are significant. Moreover, the choice between arithmetic or geometric averages also affects those differences – the arithmetic average is the simple arithmetic mean of the series of annual returns while the geometric average is the compounded annual average return for that series. When the "risk-free rate" is deducted from the equity returns to arrive at the equity risk premium, the choice of the risk-free rate will also affect the final number. Shorter-term Treasury securities usually carry lower interest rates

451. *See* Cost of Capital Quarterly, published quarterly by Ibbotson Associates.
452. Damodaran, Estimating Equity Risk Premiums, <http://pages.stern.nyu.edu/~adamdar/New_Home_Page>, at 8–9.
453. *Id.*, at 5–8.

than longer-term Treasury Securities. Therefore, the use of short-term Treasury Bills for the risk-free rate will normally produce a higher equity risk premium than would the use of long-term Treasury Bonds. The situation may cry out for ''apples-to-apples'' questions.

As previously discussed in Chapter 2.III above,[454] it is important to be aware of error rates in connection with financial projections. It is possible to identify a standard error rates for US equity risk premiums based on the annual standard deviations in US stock prices. As reported by Damodaran, between 1926 (the date from which the data has been kept) and 1997 that annual standard deviation has been 20%. Therefore, standard error rates can be demonstrated for the following time periods; 8.94% for a five-year period, 6.32% for a ten-year period, 4.00% for a twenty five-year period and 2.83% for a fifty-year period.[455] Although already high by statistical practices, these error rates are probably underestimated to some extent. The error rates assume that annual stock returns over time are not correlated with each other. If annual returns are correlated to some extent, as seems likely, then the standard error is understated.

If a longer time period is used, then arbitrators should be aware that two underlying assumptions become difficult to support; by averaging equity premiums over an extended period of time, we assume that investors' risk premiums have not changed over that time period and that the average risk investment in a diversified portfolio remained stable during that period. As Damodaran politely points out: "We would be hard pressed to find anyone who would be willing to sustain this argument with fervor.''[456] Additionally, relying on the longer time periods may also incorporate data that predates fundamental market changes, such as the dramatic growth in depth and liquidity seen by US and international stock markets in our lives. Looking at too long of a period may mask the impact of those changes to the overall economy on a going-forward basis. However, the solution to these problems, using a more recent and shorter time period, has easily spotted problems as well. Notably, shorter periods have ''unacceptably high'' standard error rates.[457] Also, using the longer time periods may be more representative, because the extended duration picks up crashes, booms, bull markets, bear markets and other possible outcomes (including historical Black Swan events).[458] If the period is too short, it may not be representative of the range of outcomes the company could face in the future, particularly large unpredictable deviations. There is no consensus answer to the choice of which historical periods to look at for the purpose of identifying an equity risk premium.

We have, so far, been considering equity premiums derived from US stock market data. Arbitrators should be cautious, of course, if an expert relies on US market data sources to value a business that does not seek capital from sources for

454. *See* text associated with n. 62 et seq. *supra*.
455. Damodaran, Estimating Equity Risk premiums, *supra* n. 452, at 6.
456. *Id.*, at 9.
457. *Id.*
458. *See* text associated with n. 60 et seq. *supra*.

which the US markets are relevant. If, however, the arbitrator accepts the proposition that a discount rate is a reasonable investor's expected total rate of return,[459] then US market data can certainly be relevant in appropriate circumstances even if the investment is not in the US and the investors are not from the US In many cases, though, experts and arbitrators must look to non-US data. However, if the problems in determining an equity risk premium are serious for the US equity market, they are far more daunting for non-US markets. For companies in developing and transition economies, the difficulties are obvious; their stock markets rarely have a reliable history of more than a decade, include only a limited number of issuers and are highly illiquid. Moreover, insider trading, lack of transparency and market manipulation can be serious issues, and regulatory enforcement can be unpredictable. Volatility of returns can be extreme.

Even if we are considering developed markets outside the US, problems remain. The error rates for calculating stock market returns in major non-US developed equity markets may be more serious than for the US market. Apart from the UK, trading in some of the major non-US markets was, until recently, historically dominated by shares of only a few companies and was quite thin. Moreover, the duration of the available data for those markets is in many cases far shorter than for the US market, which exacerbates the error rate issue.

Differences among the various studies of non-US markets may be quite large. Damodaran estimated premiums as follows for some of the major markets: Australia, an average equity risk premium of 1.48%; France, at 2.34%; Germany, at −0.80%; Italy, at −2.35%; Japan, at 3.04% (but just think what that number would be if the data extended beyond 1996 to 2000); Switzerland, at 3.38%; and the UK, at 4.61%.[460] In contrast, for the period 1900–2002, Dimson, Marsh & Staunton estimated equity premiums in the same markets relative to Treasury Bonds as follows: Australia, a geometric premium of 6.0% and an arithmetic premium of 7.6%; France, a geometric premium of 3.6% and an arithmetic premium of 5.8%; Germany (excluding the hyperinflation years of 1922–1923), a geometric premium of 5.7% and an arithmetic premium of 9.0%; Italy, a geometric premium of 4.1% and an arithmetic premium of 7.6%; Japan, a geometric premium of 5.4% and an arithmetic premium of 9.5%; Switzerland, a geometric premium of 1.2% and an arithmetic premium of 2.9%; and the U.K, a geometric premium of 3.8% and an arithmetic premium of 5.1%. For the same period, by way of comparison, Dimson, Marsh & Staunton measures US equity premiums relative to Treasury Bonds as a geometric premium of 4.4% and an arithmetic premium of 6.4%.[461]

Also of importance, in the twentieth century the US stock markets were among the most successful equity markets in the developed world. Therefore, reliance on US equity risk premiums for non-US enterprises carries a "success bias" element.

---

459. *See* text associated with n. 432 *supra*.

460. Damodaran, Estimating Equity Risk Premiums, *supra* n. 452, at 10–11. In reviewing these average equity risk premiums, note that the standard error rates for each of the mentioned markets for the period from 1970–1996 exceeded 5%.

461. Dimson, Marsh & Staunton, *supra* n. 450, at Table 1.

In addition, a "survivorship" bias may exist; to what extent are failed companies excluded from the data? Globally, the potential for a "survivorship" bias also exists for markets. As Dimson, Marsh & Staunton point out with respect to their own study for 1900–2002, "we still focus on markets that survived, omitting countries such as Poland, Russia, or China whose compound rate of return was −100%. Although these markets were relatively small in 1900, their omission probably leads to an overestimate of the worldwide risk premium."[462]

To resolve these problems arising from reliance on historical stock returns, some valuation experts argue instead for relying on an "implied equity risk premium" based on the present value of expected dividends, growing at a constant rate. That technique relies on current investor expectations rather than historical stock returns. Once the valuation identifies the "investor expected returns on equity" (i.e., current investor expectations for investment returns), the valuer then calculates the equity risk premium by deducting the "risk-free" debt rate from the expected rate of return.[463] Valuers can create a similar formula based on cash flow expectations, rather than dividend expectations, to encompass investor expectations for returns from stock buy-backs, sales of the company, sales of equity interests or other non-dividend returns. Illustratively, if the valuation analyst concluded that, on the valuation date, equity investors expect a total return of 10% on their capital and the risk-free debt rate on that date is 4%, then the "implied equity risk premium" is 6%.

The "implied equity risk premium" formula does not rely on historical stock returns. Accordingly, valuations can use the technique to estimate equity risk premiums for any market for which estimates of investor return expectations and expected growth rates can be obtained. Of course, arbitrators will recognize that the estimates of investor expected returns and the expected growth rate estimate are crucial assumptions underlying this technique. Often, those estimates are highly subjective.

These issues are compounded when the size of the company comes into the equation. Most experts conclude that small companies in general are riskier than large companies. By increasing the systematic component of a discount rate for a small company premium, we increase the discount rate, thereby decreasing the size of the eventual compensation award. Many analysts separately compute a "size premium," while others incorporate the risks associated with the size of a business into their calculation of the subjective risk premium.

> Extensive empirical studies have shown that smaller companies tend to have higher risks than larger companies. Although controversial, most observers believe this is true. Because of this higher risk, such companies have a higher cost of capital.[464]

---

462. *Id.*
463. Damodaran, "Estimating Equity Risk Premiums," *supra* n. 452, at 10–11.
464. The Lawyer's Business Valuation Handbook, *supra* n. 411, at 121. *See also* Ogier, Rugman & Spicer, The Real Cost of Capital: A Business Field Guide to Better Financial Decisions at 266–274 (FT Prentice Hall 2004).

The existence of a size premium for small companies is not without its critics, however. Arbitrators therefore should not be surprised of the opposing experts dispute the existence of a size premium before the tribunal.

Size Premium

Smaller companies tend to have higher risks than larger companies, according to empirical studies. Therefore, valuation professionals may introduce a "size premium" into the computation of a discount rate, increasing the discount rate or small companies in recognition of the increase in risk. For U.S. markets, experts again often look to data from Ibbotson Associates. Not all experts accept that a size premium exists. Moreover, the proper use of a size premium for non-U.S. markets, particularly for companies in developing countries, is controversial.

Dimson, Marsh & Staunton have tried to calculate both worldwide equity risk premiums and equity risk premiums individually for sixteen countries for which data was available across the period 1900–2002, all of them (other than South Africa) currently developed countries.[465] They found the average equity risk premiums to be as follows: relative to T-Bills, a geometric premium of 4.5% and an arithmetic premium of 6.9%; relative to T-Bonds, a geometric premium of 3.8% and an arithmetic premium of 5.9%. Based on the Dimson, Marsh & Staunton data, the most successful equity markets in the past century were Australia, Germany (but excluding the hyperinflation of 1923–1923), Japan, South Africa and Sweden. Their data identifies lower equity premiums in the US and UK than found in other studies, including Ibbotson Associates data for the US

Here too, many experts look to data compiled from US markets by Ibbotson Associates to calculate size premiums if data for the particular market is not available. *Gesoff v. IIC Industries, Inc.*[466] is one of the very few cases to consider whether the detailed information available from US stock markets about small-company equity premiums can usefully be applied to valuations of non-US companies. The US holding company (IIC) at issue in that dissenting shareholder appraisal case was an investment company. IIC owned a Hungarian hotel business listed on the Budapest stock exchange (Danubius), another listed Hungarian company (Agrimill) engaged in agricultural products processing, an Israeli heavy equipment distribution

465. Dimson, Marsh & Staunton, *supra* n. 450, at Table 1. Note that this data is based on indexes expressed in USD. As a result, the results will be affected by the important question of whether the local currency depreciated (results lower) or appreciated (results higher) against the USD during the twentieth century. The individual countries are Australia, Belgium, Canada, Denmark, France, Germany, Ireland, Italy, Japan, The Netherlands, South Africa, Spain, Sweden, Switzerland, the United Kingdom and the United States.

466. *Gesoff v. IIC Industries, Inc.*, *supra* n. 414.

(ITE) and a company engaged in multi-product goods distribution throughout Africa (Balton). For a US company, Ibbotson data pointed to a 5.33% small-company risk premium. Should that data be relied upon for valuations of the non-US companies? According to the Delaware Court of Chancery:

> [T]he finance literature . . . is deeply conflicted, and indeterminate, on the correct application of such premium in foreign valuations. As multiple important sources have noted, the small-size premium almost certainly does not apply in a uniform way in all markets. Rather, local factors and local conditions necessarily change whether a corporation can expect to experience the higher risk and higher returns that small corporations evidence in the U.S[467]

After reviewing the available research studies, the Court concluded that:

> The general weight of the scholarship, in summary, seems to be that the small-size premium might well apply in the same way as in the U.S. in more highly developed foreign markets, and would not apply to the same extent, or at all, in newly developing markets.

Applying these principles, the Court ruled that a small-company equity premium was not appropriate for Balton, which sold its products into the African market. The Court did apply the full US small-company premium to Agrimill and ITE. The Court devoted special attention to Danubius, which formed part of the index for the Budapest Stock Exchange and was a Hilton Hotels licensee. The Court applied a 2.41% small-company equity premium to Danubius, in light of those facts, rather than the full 5.33% premium derived from the Ibbotson US data.[468]

The third component in the "build-up" approach to selecting a discount rate addresses subjective risks. That component covers those aspects of a particular company that distinguish an investment in that company from a generic investment in the equity stock market generally. Such individualized risks include the company's specific market and regulatory risks, financial risks, management strengths and weaknesses, product and technological circumstances and similar concerns. To illustrate, a company selling products that will rapidly become obsolete due to expected technological change faces a different risk profile than a company selling products for which technological innovation is rare.

Subjective Risks in the Build-Up Procedure

The most often questioned aspect of developing a discount rate by means of the build-up procedure is the component reflecting those aspects of a particular company that distinguish an investment in that company from a generic equity investment, the "subjective risks" component.

467. *Id.*, at 1160, **86.
468. *Id.*, at 1161, **88–90.

The risk of an oil well going dry, for example, is a specific risk, while the risk of increases in oil prices worldwide because of supply constraints is a systematic risk. Similarly, the risk of a strike by a union at a factory is an individual risk, but the risk of increased labor-management strife in a country resulting from decreases in real wages for blue collar workers in that country is a systematic risk. Courts are occasionally skeptical of the motives behind an expert's determination of the subjective risk component of a discount rate.

> The calculation of a company-specific risk is highly subjective and often is justified as a way of taking into account competitive and other factors that endanger the subject company's ability to achieve its projected cash flows. In other words, it is often a back-door method of reducing estimated cash flows rather than adjusting them directly. To judges, the company specific risk premium often seems like the device experts employ to bring their final results into line with their clients' objectives, when other valuation inputs fail to do the trick.[469]

Measuring such subjective risks as of the valuation date is very challenging. Many expert witnesses will look to the market practice of investment bankers and valuation experts in the particular industry to validate their efforts to estimate the subjective risk component of a discount rate for a company within that industry. Investment bankers may have prepared their own forecasts for the company in dispute in connection with an underlying transaction before the dispute arose. Often, of course, bankers will prepare such forecasts when that company is seeking finance in the capital markets, considering an M&A transaction or contemplating an initial public offering of its capital stock (an IPO). Similarly, contemporaneous business valuations are often obtained for tax purposes such as a step-up in basis as part of an acquisition or to value a decedents' estate. The bankers will have used a discount rate as part of their own present value calculations for those forecasts. The rate chosen by the bankers may prove to be persuasive evidence during a later arbitration after the venture has collapsed.

The party seeking a lower discount rate will commonly argue that many of the company-specific risks addressed in the third building block of the discount rate (subjective risks) have already been addressed within the specific revenue and expense items embedded inside each year's number in the projection period. The risk of credit problems with customers, for example, may already be taken into account when estimating a company's annual revenues by incorporating a customer default rate into the computation. Similarly, the risk of technological change may be taken into account in estimating R&D expenses or the capital cost of upgrading production facilities to remain competitive. If these risks are already taken into account when developing the revenue and expense estimates, then is it double counting to include them in the discount rate?[470] As the *Fédération*

---

469. *Delaware Open MRI Radiology Associates, P.A. v. Kessler, supra* n. 3, at 339.
470. *See In re Doctors Hospital of Hyde Park, Inc.*, 360 B.R. 787, 861–862 (Bankr. N.D. Ill. 2007), reviewing whether company specific issues such as depth of management, fraud,

des Experts Comptables Européens advises: "the uncertainties relating to future business profits can be reflected in the valuation by two means: as a deduction from the expected amount of business profits (safety equivalent method or profit deduction method) or as an uplift to the discount rate (interest uplift method, risk premium method)."[471] The Czech Republic also pointed out in *CME Stockholm* that two possible methods may be used to factor this risk and uncertainty into a DCF analysis. "First, the cash flows . . . could be adjusted downwards to reflect the reduced prospects of achieving the original projected cash flows. Second, the risk and uncertainty could be determined by an increase in the discount rate used."[472]

In a fashion similar to the advice of the Fédération, the FASB's Statement of Financial Accounting Standards (SFAS), No. 142 compares two different approaches towards selecting a discount rate to determine present value of a specific asset or liability; the "traditional approach" and the "expected cash flow approach." SFAS No. 142 establishes US accounting standards for valuing goodwill and other intangible assets in a business combination, Appendix E to SFAS No. 142 (excepts from FASB Concepts Statement No. 7) lists several components of a present value measurement, four of which may be relevant to a discount rate:

. . .

b. Expectations about possible variations in the amount or timing of [future] cash flows
c. The time value of money, represented by the risk-free rate of interest
d. The price for bearing the uncertainty inherent in the asset or liability
e. Other, sometimes unidentifiable, factors including illiquidity and market imperfections.[473]

If the discount rate for present value of the asset or liability is to be determined in accordance with the "traditional" approach then, just as is the case in the build-up procedure, under FSAS No. 142 all of these components should be taken into account to select the discount rate.[474]

FASB Concepts Statement No. 7 further contrasts a single "best estimate" of those cash flows (coupled with the "traditional" approach to determining the discount rate) with use of several possible cash flow futures to which probabilities have been assigned (coupled with determining the discount rate solely on the basis of the time value of money).[475] The FASB found that "expected cash flow" approach to be a more effective measurement tool in many cases, because it

management's reputation, unreliability of financial statements and the effect of Federal legislation were, or were not, "baked into" the beta factor affecting the equity risk premium in a CAPM analysis.

471. FEE SME Business Valuation Guide, *supra* n. 17, ¶ 6.2 at 21.
472. *CME Stockholm* Final Award, *supra* n. 42, at ¶ 334.
473. SFAS 142, Financial Accounting Standards Board, as amended (June 2001), at Appendix E, E1, incorporating ¶ 39 of FASB Concepts Statement No. 7.
474. *Id.*, at ¶ 40.
475. *Id.*

"used all expectations about possible cash flows instead of the single most-likely cash flow."[476]

> 45. The Board found the expected cash flow approach to be a more effective measurement tool than the traditional approach in many situations. In developing a measurement, the expected cash flow approach uses all expectations about possible cash flows instead of the single most-likely cash flow. For example, a cash flow might be $100, $200, or $300 with probabilities of 10 percent, 60 percent, and 30 percent, respectively. The expected cash flow is $220.[477] The expected cash flow approach thus differs from the traditional approach by focusing on direct analysis of the cash flows in question and on more explicit statements of the assumptions used in the measurement.[478]

Given the large number of variables within the revenue and expense projections, the practical problem with the FASB's approach is that it may generate tens, if not hundreds of alternative cash flow futures. The computations, as well as the subjective judgments involved in creating the alternative cash flow futures, may be daunting.

Business managers and bankers developing revenue and expense estimates try, of course, to take a realistic approach towards formulating their projections, rather than assuming the best situation – doing otherwise would quickly put them into the ranks of the unemployed.[479] Indeed, as described above, investment bankers often prepare several sets of financial projections showing different risk cases (Best Case, Base Case, Worst Case). The contemporaneous revenue and expense forecasts of a company and its financial advisors therefore clearly do incorporate subjective estimates of risk. Consequently, some experts advise that the discount rate in a DCF forecast should exclude subjective risks. Instead, say these experts, each individual revenue and expense item should be carefully adjusted in the financial model to reflect the expert's professional views about the probabilities of risk crystallizing with respect to each such item.[480] Equally, some parties will argue in the arbitration proceedings that the managers have already in fact adjusted the financial model to reflect those risk assessments. Therefore, no additional subjective component should be incorporated into either the cash flow estimates or the computation of the discount rate under the "build-up" procedure –

---

476. *Id.*, at ¶ 45.
477. (100 USD × .1) + (200 USD × .6) + (300 USD × .3) = 220 USD. The traditional notion of a best estimate or most-likely amount in this example is 200 USD (the 60% scenario).
478. *Id.*, at ¶ 45–46.
479. Projections "should reflect the results expected to be achieved by the company. In other words, the projections should not be 'ultra-conservative' or 'overly optimistic,' but rather, realistic expectations." Risius, *Business Valuation: A Primer for Legal Professionals*, *supra* n. 19, at 73–74.
480. *See* Dunn & Harry, "Modeling and Discounting Future Damages," *supra* n. 439, at 49. *See also United States v. 1,629.6 Acres of Land*, 360 F. Supp. 147, 152 (D. Del. 1973) for an example of a valuation estimate in which the income stream was risk-adjusted and the capitalization rate was not adjusted for those risks.

according to this argument, the cash flow estimates should be used without change and the discount rate should not include a company-specific risk premium.

Company-specific risk premiums do not, in all cases, have to be positive. Although not commonly found in evidentiary presentations, "[i]f the company being valued has specific attributes that make it a less risky investment than what has been reflected in the other premiums, then a negative company specific risk premium would be appropriate."[481]

In addition to the risk-free rate, systematic risk component and subjective risk component, the valuation may also address sovereign risks. If a USD-based discount rate is being employed to value a business not based in the United States, then it also becomes necessary to adjust the risk-free component of the discount rate to reflect the sovereign risk of the host State of the investment. One common "build-up" procedure is to determine the country risk premium involved by looking to the country risk premium of the country's USD sovereign debt over the USD risk-free rate. Some valuation professionals, though, will base their country risk premiums for equity investments not solely on the interest rate margin ("spread") for sovereign bonds over US Treasuries, but also include an adjustment for the difference in the volatility (uncertainty) between the equity and debt markets in that country. The purpose of that adjustment is to reflect the greater general uncertainties in equity returns compared with debt returns, but not caused by events that result in debt defaults. Such an approach will increase the equity risk premium and thus the discount rate used in the business valuation. For instance, Damodaran calculated the June 1998 interest rate spread between Brazilian sovereign debt and US Treasuries as 2.00% (based on Standard & Poor's country ratings). However, after adjusting for the difference between volatility in the Brazilian equity index and the Brazilian Brady Bonds, he calculated the Brazilian resulting country equity risk premium as 6.29% (a substantial increase over the 2.00% debt margin).[482] The ICSID panel in *Enron v. Argentina* appears to have accepted this distinction between sovereign default risk and country volatility.[483] Critics of this approach note that it produces inconstant results. Other country risk adjustment approaches include an empirical analysis of credit ratings (particularly for emerging market countries), the addition of a country risk premium to the cost of equity based on sovereign debt spreads, and adjustments to both the risk-free rate for debt and, if required to the equity market premium within the cost of equity.[484]

---

481. Risius, *Business Valuation: A Primer for Legal Professionals*, *supra* n. 19, at 91.
482. Damodaran, Estimating Equity Risk Premiums, *supra* n. 452, at 14–15. Even then, the cost of equity can vary widely in light of other calculation assumptions. Following his calculation of the equity risk premium with a volatility adjustment, Damodaran then computed three different "cost of equity" numbers for a Brazilian pulp and paper manufacturer (15.68%, 13.92% and 10.53%) based on differing assumptions about that company's exposure to Brazilian country risk. *Id.*, at 15–17.
483. *Enron v. Argentina*, *supra* n. 43, at ¶¶ 119–121, 148–150, 377–378.
484. *See* generally Ch. 6: International WACC and Country Risk, in Ogier, Rugman & Spicer, The Real Cost of Capital: A Business Field Guide to Better Financial Decisions, *supra* n. 464.

Country Risk Premium

Valuation professionals will also consider a country risk adjustment as a component of the discount rate. One common procedure is to determine the country risk premium by looking to the country risk premium of the particular country's USD sovereign debt over the USD risk-free rate. That approach does not, however, account for the difference in volatility (uncertainty) between the equity and debt markets in that country. Particularly for countries with underdeveloped and illiquid equity markets, that difference in volatility can add significantly to the size of the country risk premium.

Once the country risk premium is calculated, an equity risk premium is then added to reflect systematic equity risk plus the company's subjective risk characteristics.[485] Thus, building a USD discount rate for a company based outside the US will involve four components: the risk-free USD rate, an adjustment for host-State sovereign risk, an adjustment for systematic risks (including a small company adjustment, if appropriate), and an adjustment for company-specific subjective risks. Of course, it will be important to make sure the sovereign risk component and small company adjustment in the proposed discount rate are not double-counted in other risk components.

2 Weighted Average Cost of Capital (WACC)

Rather than "building up" a discount rate, a popular alternative approach for computing a discount rate is to utilize the Weighted Average Cost of Capital (WACC) for the company in dispute (or the WACC of its comparables). For example, the discount rate employed by experts for both claimant and respondent in the DCF valuations considered by the *CME Stockholm* tribunal was based upon the enterprise's WACC.[486] This approach considers that the proper discount rate should approximate the balance between risks and benefits that third-party investors and lenders would reach if they were called upon to make new equity investments and new loans to the company at the beginning date of the DCF forecast (the valuation date).

The WACC method estimates the future cost to the company of borrowing new debt (on an after-tax basis if the company is capable of utilizing a tax deduction for its interest expense),[487] as well as the future cost to the company of

485. This was essentially the approach taken by one expert in *CMS v. Argentina*, *supra* n. 7, at ¶ 454.
486. *CME Stockholm* Final Award, *supra* n. 42, at ¶¶ 160, 164.
487. "Since the interest on debt is deductible for tax purposes, an after-tax interest rate is used in the WACC calculation." Risius, *Business Valuation: A Primer for Legal Professionals*, *supra* n. 19, at 92–93.

obtaining new equity capital. The cost of equity capital for the company is calculated separately from the cost of the debt capital, often on the basis of the Capital Asset Pricing Model (CAPM) discussed below in Chapter 4.I.

The valuation then proportionately weights the cost of debt and the cost of equity to determine the all-in cost of capital to the company (the WACC). The resulting WACC is used as the discount rate for the DCF calculation.[488]

Weighted Average Cost of Capital (WACC)

The WACC procedure for computing a discount rate considers that the proper discount rate should approximate the balance between risks and benefits that arm's-length third party investors and lenders would reach if they made new equity investments and new loans to the company at the valuation date. The WACC procedure estimates the future cost to the company of borrowing those new loans and the future cost to the company of obtaining that new equity capital. The valuation then proportionately weighs the cost of that new debt and the cost of that new equity to determine the WACC.

In the world of business finance, the WACC is very important for a number of interconnected reasons; as a discount rate, to determine if a company is covering its cost of funds for its current projects, and to set the minimum threshold (the "hurdle rate") for moving forward with new projects.

- First . . . , it is used as the discount rate to bring projected future cash earnings to their present values.
- Second, it is used to test whether the company is earning its cost of capital on existing projects.
- Third, it defines the hurdle rate for proposed new projects.

488. The WACC/CAPM procedure for calculating the cost of capital is regularly used in Delaware appraisal cases, as well as US bankruptcy and tax cases. Among the many cases relying on CAPM and WACC to obtain a discount rate for a DCF valuation, a small sampling includes *Andalaro v. PFPC Worldwide*, *supra* n. 295; *In re Radiology Associates, Inc.*, *supra* n. 394; *Onti v. Integra Bank*, *supra* n. 293; *Cede & Co. v. Technicolor, Inc.*, *supra* n. 414; *Lane v. Cancer Treatment Centers of America, Inc.*, *supra* n. 1; *Delaware Open MRI Radiology Associates, P.A. v. Kessler*, *supra* n. 3; In re Exide Technologies, *supra* n. 78; *Gilbert v. M.P.M. Enterprises, Inc.*, 1998 Del. Ch. LEXIS 60 (Del. Ch. 1998); *Hintmann v. Fred Weber, Inc.*, 1998 Del Ch. LEXIS 26 (Del. Ch. 1998); *MacLane Gas Co., L.P. v. Ensearch Corp.*, 1992 Del. Ch. LEXIS 255 (Del. Ch. 1992); *Union Illinois 1995 Investment Limited Partnership v. Union Financial Group, Ltd.*, *supra* n. 44; *In re Emerging Communications, Inc.*, 2004 Del. Ch. LEXIS 70 (Del. Ch. 2004); *Cede & Co. v. JRC Acquisition Corp.*, 2004 Del. Ch. LEXIS 12 (Del. Ch. 2004); *Cede & Co. v. Medipoint Healthcare, Inc.*, 2004 Del. Ch. LEXIS 124 (Del. Ch. 2004); and *In re PNB Holding Co.*, 2006 Del. Ch. LEXIS 158 (Del. Ch. 2006). Similarly lengthy lists of US bankruptcy cases and tax decisions can easily be compiled.

> Think of the cost of capital as the investor's opportunity cost at the company's level of risk. It is the return an investor can expect to receive by investing in another company of comparable risk.[489]

Given the important role WACC calculations play to help companies understand if their existing projects are covering their capital costs and if new projects will meet minimum profit requirements, it is no surprise that arbitrators often see evidence in a dispute based on the WACCs used by companies in their regular business planning activities.

To calculate a company's WACC, the arbitrator must know the cost to the company for each source of the company's capital. The WACC is the weighted average of those costs. The weighting is proportionate to the portion that comes from each of those sources of capital. If the business has only one type of debt capital (say, a bank loan) and one type of equity capital (say, common stock), then the standard formula for calculating the WACC is straightforward.[490] The WACC will equal:

The ratio of the amount of debt to the amount of total capital	$\frac{\text{Debt}}{(\text{Debt}+\text{Equity})}$
multiplied by the interest rate (i) on the debt	times i
plus	plus
The product of that same debt-to-total capital ratio	$\frac{\text{Debt}}{(\text{Debt}+\text{Equity})}$
multiplied by the rate of return (r) on equity	times r

Neither life nor the WACC is quite that simple, however. First, the interest payable on loans and other debt is usually tax deductible by the company. Payment of dividends by the company on its equity is, however, not usually tax deductible. The cost to the company of debt capital and equity capital need to be put on the same basis for a WACC calculation, by correcting the cost of debt for the tax savings to the company deriving from the tax deductibility of interest payments. So, the WACC computation will include a tax adjustment. If the pre-tax interest rate payable on the debt is 10%, the company has a 40% tax rate and the company has sufficient income to utilize fully its interest tax deduction, then the after-tax cost of the debt capital will be 6%.

Then, the valuation must further take account of any situation where the company's capital structure is not a simple "bank loan plus common stock"

---

489. Dickie, Financial Statement Analysis and Business Valuation for the Practical Lawyer (2nd edn American Bar Association 2006) at 261.
490. Several variations on the standard formula exist, including the Modigliani-Miller WACC model (which takes account of interest tax shields discounted at the cost of debt) and the Miles-Ezzel WACC model (which discounts the first year's interest tax shield at the cost of debt, but subsequent years' interest tax shields at the unleveraged cost of equity). The details of these models are beyond this simple book, but we refer interested readers to Ogier, Rugman & Spicer, The Real Cost of Capital: A Business Field Guide to Better Financial Decisions, *supra* n. 464, at 217 et seq. for further information.

picture. What if the company has both bank debt and publicly-traded bonds? For "traded" debt like public bonds, the rate of return is not the nominal interest rate printed on the face of the bonds. Instead, the rate of return will be corrected to the "yield to maturity" of the bonds based on the price at which the bonds currently trade in the market. In addition, there may be several levels and types of debt, each with its own cost of capital; senior secured loans, senior unsecured loans, subordinated bonds, convertible bonds, and etc. That formerly simple WACC formula must be rewritten to separately account for the cost of each type of debt capital.

And then there is the equity capital side of the equation. Just like situations involving multiple layers of debt, many companies have several layers of equity capital; common stock, preferred stock, warrants and other variations. Moreover, if the company is not a corporation, but rather a partnership, the variations are limited only by the ingenuity of the businesspeople and lawyers involved in negotiating the allocation of contributions, risks and opportunities among the partners.

One last factor should also be considered – will be debt-to-equity leverage ratio for the business remain the same for the entire DCF projection period or will it change over time? If the expert persuades the arbitrator that the relationship between debt and equity will not remain static for the life of the DCF projection, it is not sufficient to just change the ratio and leave the rest of the formula untouched. It will also be necessary to acknowledge that the cost to the company of both its debt capital and its equity capital will change as well. The reason is simple; the increase in the company's proportionate debt burden creates risks and thus costs:

> [A]s the company increases its leverage, (1) its borrowing costs rise, and (2) the risk to which the equity is exposed rises and the shareholders expect a higher return, which means a higher cost of equity for the company. In short, as the leverage rises, the costs of debt and equity rise. It is a dynamic relationship.[491]

Arbitrators may be attracted to the WACC as a means of avoiding the subjective judgments involved a "build-up" discount rate. For companies with outstanding equity and debt securities in liquid capital markets (i.e., with debt and equity securities that are regularly traded in public securities markets), the experts can calculate market equity return requirements and market interest rates for the company by reference to then-current trading prices for those securities in the securities market. Many companies, however, do not have outstanding regularly traded equity and debt securities. Indeed, private companies (especially in developing countries) often rely on debt and equity financings for which little market trading data is available – the markets are very thin (illiquid), trading is restricted by securities laws, and not much public information exists. Consequently, an expert employing a WACC measure for a discount rate will look to the trading prices of equity and debt securities of comparable companies, thereby raising again

491. *Id.*, at 262.

the exact same comparability issues noted already in Chapter 3 above. In such cases, the arbitrators should carefully consider the comparability of the cost of capital data relied upon by that expert to calculate the WACC measure.

It is important to point out that the discussions above about small company size and country risk adjustments to discount rates must also be taken into account for a discount rate developed on the basis of the WACC method.

Naturally, if there is existing information about a company's cost of debt, then that information will often prove to be the basis for the computation of the cost of debt capital. If, however, it is necessary to develop a projected cost of debt capital, then the valuation expert will look first to the same base rate for debt we discussed above in connection with the "build-out" procedure.

3 Capital Asset Pricing Model (CAPM)

Like the "build-up" procedure, the WACC method begins by identifying a risk-free rate and an equity premium.[492] Both the "build-up" procedure and WACC look to the same sources of data for risk-free rates and equity premiums. However, the CAPM procedure for calculating the cost of equity in a WACC rejects the use of a subjective risk component. Instead, the CAPM procedure adjusts the equity premium to take account of the extent to which the stability of the equity of the company in question (or its comparables, if the company itself does not have publicly traded stock) varies from the stability of the trading values of the equity stock market as a whole (i.e., the particular investment's "volatility"). The CAPM procedure is widely accepted in the valuation community and in US case law.[493]

The CAPM method attempts to measure the difference between the equity risk of the particular assets held by the company in question (say, power plants) and the equity risk of investing in a hypothetical portfolio of diversified assets.[494] The idea underlying that approach is to isolate the risks attributable to the particular business activity in which the company is engaged. In the field of corporate finance, CAPM is "considered by many to be the most theoretically correct model for estimating an equity discount rate."[495] CAPM is accordingly the "equity cost of capital" model

---

492. *Delaware Open MRI Radiology Associates, P.A. v. Kessler*, *supra* n. 3, at 338–339.
493. "While there are other models to determine equity, CAPM is probably the most widely used." In re Exide Technologies, *supra* n. 78, at 64 n. 32 (quoting Pantaleo & Ridings, "Reorganization Value," 51 Bus. Law. 419, 437 (1996). The Fédération des Experts Comptables Européens also supports the use of CAPM to make a market-based determination of the risk premium in a discount rate. FEE SME Business Valuation Guide, *supra* n. 17, ¶ 6.2 at 12 and § 7.3.2.5 at 30.
494. The CAPM formula is as follows: "Cost of Equity = R(f) + (Beta × [R(m) – R(f)], where 'R(f)' is the risk-free rate, 'beta' is the beta (volatility measure) of the target's equity securities, and 'R(m)' is the expected return on a market portfolio consisting of a large number of diversified stocks." In re American Classic Voyages Co., 2007 WL 1237828, at *11 n. 19 (Bankr. D. Del. 2007), quoting from Pantaleo & Ridings, "Reorganization Value," 51 Bus. Law. 419, 433 (1996).
495. The Lawyer's Business Valuation Handbook, *supra* n. 411, at 105.

most commonly used by corporate finance practitioners. However, CAPM's seemingly technical quantitative process can hide a number of difficult assumptions about the applicability of the underlying securities market data. Arbitrators should therefore be aware that the CAPM method is not without its professional critics.

Calculating the Cost of the Equity Component Of a Discount Rate

The Capital Asset Pricing Model (CAPM) seeks to isolate the risks attributable to a particular business activity, as compared with the equity markets as a whole. CAPM is in part a substitute for the "subjective risks" component of the build-up procedure for computing a discount rate. Because the CAPM procedure relies on data from public companies, its use for small closely held companies raises challenges.

The US Tax Court, for example, has been skeptical of the use of WACC and CAPM to value small closely held companies with little possibility of going public – an instance where comparability once again comes into play. If the business being valued is a private company, then of course no public trading data will be available. In such circumstances, experts employing CAPM will look to public comparables for the private company. And, of course, the exact same comparability issues we reviewed in three above arise once again.[496] Moreover, volatility adjustments for small companies tend to be higher than volatility adjustments for large companies (resulting in higher discount rates and lower valuations). It may be difficult indeed to find a large publicly traded company that is comparable to a small private company for purposes of determining the volatility of the closely held private company's equity.[497]

A basic difference between the CAPM procedure and the "build-up" procedure for determining the equity premium lies in the use of an adjustment (a "coefficient") to the general equity (systematic) risk premium. That coefficient is called a "beta." Beta measures the sensitivity (volatility) of the rate of return on an individual security (or a portfolio of securities) to general rates of return in the public stock markets.[498] Looking again at US markets, valuation experts

496. Indeed, the alleged "comparables" criticized Ch. 3.III were presented by an expert seeking to justify their use to develop betas for a CAPM-based discount rate. *See* In re American Classic Voyages, *supra* n. 494, at *11–12, for an instance of an unsuccessful attack on the comparability of companies chosen by an expert for use in a CAPM procedure.

497. *See Estate of James Waldo Hendrickson v. Comm'r*, *supra* n. 41.

498. "The computation of beta is a linear regression of the rate of return on a given security (or portfolio of securities) on the market return for a series of time periods. If returns for the subject go up and down about the same degree as the market, then beta equals 1.0. If the returns tend to be more volatile in response to market moves (that is, go up more than the market when the market goes up and down more than the market when the market goes down), then beta is greater than 1.0. Conversely, if the returns tend to be less volatile in response to changes in

commonly refer to S&P 500 data for information about general rates of return for US public stocks. Note that the use of a "beta" to adjust general equity returns for volatility will also have an impact on the calculation of the "size premium" and the subjective company specific premium (if any). Indeed, for adjustments to the size premium in the US markets resulting from the beta calculation, our friend Ibbotson Associates publishes a series of data called *Size Premium in Excess of CAPM.*[499] Accordingly, using the CAPM procedure to calculate the cost of equity capital in a WACC computation has an impact on all of the elements employed to develop a discount rate, other than the risk-free rate.

In CAPM, theorists tell us that the beta should measure the additional risk added to a portfolio of diversified equity investments by including that particular investment within the portfolio. The equity risk premium, in turn, should measure the additional return the investor will require before investing in a portfolio that contains such an investment, as compared with a risk-free investment. In practice, though, valuation analysts calculate betas on the basis of the local stock market index, not a theoretical diversified equity portfolio. Then, the valuation estimates the equity risk premium by comparing the historical premiums earned by stocks over the returns of risk-free debt securities (usually, government securities like Treasuries) over long periods of time.[500]

Once the expert calculates the beta (the volatility modifier), the general equity (systematic) risk premium is multiplied by that beta. "Equity beta" is calculated by comparing the movement in the returns of a company's stock (or the stock of a company comparable to the subject company) against the movement in the returns of the stock market as a whole, which for calculation purposes is assigned a benchmark beta of one. For example, if a company's stock generally increases 2% in price when the market increases by 1%, the stock would have a beta of 2.0 (two divided by one). If the beta is greater than 1.0, greater uncertainty increases the systematic risk premium and thus increases the discount rate. Similarly, if the beta is less than 1.0, then the uncertainty is lower than the general market, and accordingly the systematic risk premium (and thus the discount rate) is reduced.

As previously mentioned, many adherents of CAPM do not believe it is appropriate to add any company–specific premiums to a CAPM analysis, other than a size premium. Other experts disagree, though, and occasionally we see an expert argue in litigation for a company or industry-specific adjustment to a WACC discount rate derived from CAPM.[501] Adjustments to the specific company (subjective) risk premium are, unsurprisingly, more subjective, just as they are

---

market returns, the beta is less than 1.0." The Lawyer's Business Valuation Handbook, *supra* n. 411, at 123. The volatility is normally measured for the last three to five years, reinforcing the tendency for DCF projection periods to cover five years in many analyses.

499. Ibbotson provided non-beta-adjusted size premia up through its Stocks, Bonds, Bills, and Inflation (SBBI) 1994 Yearbook. Since then, Ibbotson has provided beta-adjusted size premia, starting with its SBBI 1995 Yearbook.

500. Damodaran, Estimating Equity Risk Premiums, *supra* n. 452, at 4–5.

501. *See* e.g., *The Union Illinois 1995 Investment Limited Partnership v. Union Financial Group, Ltd.*, *supra* n. 44, at 354–355 and n. 28.

in the "build-up" procedure. Arbitrators presented with an argument for a company or industry-specific adjustment within a CAPM analysis should be sensitive to the possibility that the volatility measured by a beta adjustment might in the circumstances overlap with the risks covered by the subjective risk premium. However, the volatility measured by beta does not automatically exclude a separate subjective risk premium for that specific company's risks. Pratt's advice is:

> Be careful to ensure that the analyst is not double-counting risk factors already captured by beta and the size premium. For example, are the subject company's weaknesses in management depth, breadth of company base, and other such elements any more limited than the companies from which the size factor was estimated?[502]

One issue should be easy for the arbitrator to spot although it is complex to explain – again, an apples-to-oranges issue. To determine the relative volatility of the company's stock in order to calculate the cost of equity capital, the CAPM valuation expert may also have to take account of the differing debt profiles of the company and the comparable(s). For this purpose, CAPM employs concepts known as "equity betas," "debt betas" and "asset betas" as measuring tools. The "asset beta" is the final adjustment coefficient; it measures the volatility in financial returns of a target firm, and is calculated based on "equity betas" and "debt betas."

Unless the company's own stock is publicly traded, the equity beta for a particular company is calculated based on the equity betas of other companies in a business comparable to the company at issue in the proceeding. However, companies have different debt profiles, some with much more debt than equity while others have proportionately much less debt. The CAPM expert will need to make adjustments to the raw "equity beta" for differences in the debt profiles of the various companies from which the equity beta has been derived. Otherwise, the numbers would not be comparable. The expert will separate out the effects of the differing debt financings by means of a process known as "unlevering." Unlevering is necessary if the debt burden of the target company is different from the debt burden of the comparables; higher debt levels generally lead to higher equity betas. Accordingly, to permit comparisons between companies with different debt profiles, equity betas are unlevered to approximate the equity beta of a company that has no debt. The valuation expert will then reintroduce debt into the computation by "relevering" the beta to take into consideration the debt level projected for the company in dispute, thus taking account of the particular debt profile of the subject company as compared with the industry's general circumstances.[503]

Readers will be pleased to know that they are not required to comprehend fully the use of betas in CAPM to understand this discussion. However, for a CAPM

---

502. *Id.*, at 125.

503. For an illustration of this process, *see* BTR Dunlop Holdings, Inc. v. Comm'r, T.C. Memo 1999-377, at 18–19, 22 (November 15, 1999), a US tax case in which competing experts offered valuations of Schlegel Corporation and its UK and German subsidiaries in connection with the tax consequences of Schlegel's acquisition by BTR Dunlop in 1998).

analysis to work properly, the equity betas and debt betas must derive from comparable sources – yes, that word again! By "unlevering" and "relevering," an expert witness will adjust the subject company's equity beta by "weighting" it to account for the debt-to-equity ratios of the companies the expert considers comparable to the business in dispute, based upon the market value of their equity. However, that procedure offers avenues for miscalculation.

For example, if the stock prices of the comparables (i.e., the market values of equity ownership interests in the comparables) have crashed, as happened for shares in many US companies in 2000–2002, then as a simple matter of arithmetic that event dramatically reduces the portion of total capitalization of that company attributable to equity (i.e., stock). This occurred because the stock market capitalization of the company collapsed by virtue of the collapse in share prices. To illustrate, if the price-per-share for the stock of the comparable company was USD 10 the day before the collapse and USD 5 after the collapse, and the company has 10 million shares outstanding, then the equity capitalization of that company was halved from USD 100 million to USD 50 million at a stroke – after all, stock prices are market values. In contrast with stock prices, however, the principal amount of the company's outstanding debt remained the same despite the stock price collapse, even though the likelihood of the company repaying that full face amount may have been reduced significantly by the same events that gave rise to the stock price crash. Thus, the "face" principal amount of the company's debt remained unchanged in such circumstances. However, the market value of that same debt may have also dropped just like the market value of the company's equity shares.

Why have we forced the reader to endure this technical description? In the situation we discuss, if the expert is using a market value number for the equity side of the formula for the business, but a "face amount" number for the debt side of the same business, the resulting valuation will be improperly skewed. Arbitrators should be careful to ask whether adjustments on one side of the measure (e.g., the equity) have been matched by comparable adjustments on the other side of the measure (e.g., the debt). If not, the expert is offering an apples-to-oranges comparison. Here too, early attention by the arbitrator to this possibility may result in corrected, and more reliable, DCF forecasts.

Another important potential apples-to-oranges miscomparison may be found in the choice of the debt beta used by the expert to adjust the raw cost of equity numbers for differing debt profiles. CAPM expert witnesses often use an assumed debt beta from investment funds that hold only portfolios of debt securities. This approach makes sense, because it is difficult to obtain detailed public information about actual debt betas from comparable companies – even for public companies, much of their debt is privately held and not publicly traded. Equity betas, on the other hand, are usually based directly on publicly available information about the actual stock prices of publicly traded comparable companies. However, if the credit rating for the chosen debt fund is different from the credit ratings of the comparables, that mismatch may then result in a serious exaggeration of the asset beta, the final measure of volatility, when the raw equity beta is adjusted by means of the debt beta – the chosen debt fund is not comparable to the comparables.

For example, an expert witness in one recent arbitration used an "assumed debt beta" derived from US mutual funds. Those particular mutual funds held a broad range of corporate debt securities rated "BB" by Standard & Poor's credit rating service. At the same time, though, the expert used an equity beta derived from several public companies in an industry suffering severe economic pressures at the time. Those comparables had significantly lower credit ratings than the mutual funds; two had B-ratings, one had a BBB-rating, one had a CCC rating and the last had a D-rating. The consequence of this mismatch between a risky equity beta and a less risky debt beta for use with respect to the same company was to de-emphasize the riskiness of an equity investment in that company, resulting in an artificially lower discount rate (and thus a larger compensation award). Arbitrators can control this practice by asking about the comparability of the securities used to derive the equity and debt betas, and requiring experts to use comparable sources in the same industry and with the same credit ratings.

Arbitrators may on occasion be presented with calculations of an equity discount rate based upon a procedure called the "French-Fama" procedure. As explained above, CAPM uses a single factor, beta, to determine the volatility of the investment compared with the market as a whole. In contrast, the "French-Fama" procedure employs three factors for that purpose; classical beta, an adjustment for small-capitalization stocks versus large-capitalization stocks, and an adjustment for stocks with high book value-to-price (so-called "value stocks") versus their opposite (so-called "growth stocks"). The argument used by proponents of the "French-Fama" procedure to calculating equity discount rates is that "small cap" stocks and value stocks historically tend to do better in the US stock markets. Therefore, say these advocates, the formula for calculating equity premiums and volatility should recognize and adjust for that reality. Opponents respond by pointing out that no consensus explanation exists for the phenomenon. The application of the "French-Fama" procedure to non-US companies is, of course, especially challenging due to limited availability of data.

4 Weighting the Debt and Equity Capital Costs

Once the cost of debt capital and the cost of equity capital are determined, the expert must then "weight" the two costs on the basis of a debt-to-equity ratio to arrive at the WACC. One common criticism of the use of WACC is that the method assumes the selection of the relative "weights" between the cost of equity and the cost of debt remains the same for the life of the company. If the company is likely to pay down its debt rapidly or significantly increase its debt load (i.e., alter its debt-to-equity ratio), that assumption may be unwarranted. For example, some companies borrow heavily to finance a large acquisition, and then pay down that debt fairly rapidly. Arbitrators may be faced with competing analyses, one in which the expert specifies a particular optimum life-long ratio of debt to equity for the company, and the other in which the opposing expert argues that the mix between debt and equity should vary over the life of the business. Unsurprisingly, the answer to this disagreement is not found in theory, but rather in the particular characteristics of the company and the quality of the evidence.

Additionally, using WACC may overvalue a company by under-discounting the portion of a company's net cash flows that benefits solely the equity investors (i.e., cash flows that are not shared with debt investors). We consider this problem and its possible solutions in Chapter 4.II below. While more complex, it is certainly possible to use different discount rates for different phases of the company's DCF projection period or different components of the company's net cash flow. One purpose behind using different discount rates is to reflect projected future changes over time in the company's debt-to-equity relationship and the resulting changes over time in the costs of debt and equity capital.

Weighting the Debt and Equity Components

One common criticism of WACC is that the method assumes the selection of the relative "weights" between the cost of equity and the cost of debt remains constant for the life of the business. Some companies, however, do not have a constant debt-to-equity ratio throughout their business lives. It is possible to use different discount rates for different phases of a company's life, if warranted to adjust for this situation.

Disputes exist as to whether the proper measure of the debt for this ratio is its book value or its market value.[504] Also, the selection of "weights" between debt and equity may expose a difference between experts about which debt-to-equity ratio is appropriate, particularly if the valuation relates to a controlling interest in the investment. If the interest being valued is a minority ownership interest, then the valuation ordinarily relies upon the subject company's actual capital structure.[505] However, in the case where a controlling interest in the company is being valued, some experts utilize the subject company's actual debt-to-equity ratio while other experts utilize instead a debt-to-equity ratio that is average for the industry. The rationale for employing an industry average rather than the actual capital structure is that one of the prerogatives of controlling a company is the ability to change its capital structure.[506]

Without seeking to resolve this debate, we do note two points for arbitrators to consider. First, the shareholder agreements for some private companies grant contractual rights to minority investors that limit the ability of the controlling investor to alter unilaterally the company's capital structure. If such minority protection rights exist, the persuasiveness of the rationale for employing an industry-average

504. *See* Mandron, "The WACC: A Minefield," *Business Valuation Review* (March 2005).
505. *The Lawyer's Business Valuation Handbook*, *supra* n. 411, at 130.
506. *Id.*

capital structure must obviously be considered in light of the specific minority rights granted in the shareholders agreement.

Second, using an industry average for a company rather than its actual capital structure can easily alter the cost of the company's debt and equity. As the percentage of the overall capital structure attributable to debt increases,

> the risk is increased for both the debt and the equity, thus increasing the cost of each component. A common error is to hypothesize a much greater percentage of debt with no increase in the cost of debt or equity, thus lowering the computed WACC and reaching an unattainably inflated indicated value for the company.[507]

Accordingly, if an arbitrator is presented with an industry-average WACC rather than a WACC based on the subject investment's actual debt-to-equity capital structure, the arbitrator may wish to ask questions about changes to the rate of return the company must now offer to attract debt and equity capital.

5 Contemporaneous Business Forecasts

The "build-up" and WACC methods for deriving a discount rate both have strengths and weaknesses. Experts accordingly do not always develop a discount rate quantitatively as suggested by these methods. Instead, as mentioned in Chapter 4.I.1(v) above, an expert may look to discount rates employed by financial analysts who had earlier been engaged to produce valuations for significant corporate transactions involving the subject company. Companies routinely obtain such valuations before making investments. Companies will also obtain valuations to buttress their tax positions, including to support stock options and to establish the adjusted tax basis of assets acquired in certain M&A deals. In the US bankruptcy context, some courts "entertain a *de facto* presumption as to the reasonableness of management's projections made at or about the time of the questioned transactions and unbiased by litigation incentives."[508] For the *In re Iridium* court, the test of the reliability of management projections was whether they were "reasonable and prudent when made."[509] Moreover, the court commented that contemporary investment banker analyses confirming the validity of management projections were an indicator of reasonableness.[510]

In many cases, undertaking an initial public offering (IPO), selling new equity on debt, engaging in an M&A transaction or undertaking other large transactions may require detailed earnings forecasts. Similarly, contemporaneous business valuations may be required as a practical matter to comply with applicable law.

507. *Id.*
508. Stearn, Proving Solvency: Defending Preference or Fraudulent Transfer Litigation, *supra* n. 20, at 380. *See* the discussion of cases at *id.*, 380–381 nn. 64–67.
509. In re Iridium, *supra* n. 45, at *57.
510. *Id.*

For example, companies in the US at all stages of development have since 2005 been obtaining independent valuations to set the strike price for employee stock options to avoid adverse income tax consequences under section 409A of the US Internal Revenue Code.

Prospective financing sources regularly require companies to provide detailed projections of their expected revenues and expenses as a precondition to committing to provide financial support. In fact, such projections are often required as a precondition to even considering the proposed financing. For instance, the Project Finance Division of the Export-Import Bank of the United States (Ex-Im Bank) requires inter alia the following financial information at the very beginning of the application process for limited-recourse project finance loans, including projections on an expected (base) case, optimistic (best) case and pessimistic (worst) case basis.

> 5. Projected annual financial statements covering the period from project development through final maturity of the proposed Ex-Im Bank financing, to include balance sheet, profit and loss, source and application of funds statements, and debt service ratios. Projections should include a sensitivity analysis for not only the expected scenario, but pessimistic and optimistic cases as well.
>
> This information should also be provided electronically in Lotus 123 or Excel. The structure of the financial model should be in a format that is user friendly. Ex-Im Bank must be able to review and adjust the assumptions in the model.
>
> 6. Assumptions for the financial projections, including but not limited to the basis for sales volume and prices; operating and administrative costs; depreciation, amortization and tax rates; and local government policy on price regulation.
>
> 7. Market information to include ten years of historical price and volume data; present and projected capacity of industry; product demand forecast with assumptions; description of competition and projected market share of the project as compared to the shares of the competition; identity and location of customers; and marketing and distribution strategy.[511]

Experts and arbitrators alike therefore often look to "at the time" forecasts by the enterprise or its bankers as a useful source for DCF valuations. Thus, the claimant investor in the *CME Stockholm* proceedings argued that management forecasts developed prior to the Czech Republic's alleged breach of international law were reasonable in the circumstances and should be relied upon by the arbitrators. To support this conclusion, the claimant asserted that the tribunal should be influenced by the responsible character of the estimates in those forecasts, incorporation of a margin of error and the business incentives for management to make accurate predictions in the forecasts.[512]

---

511. Fact Sheet: Ex-Im Bank's Approach to Project Finance, at 7, available at <www.exim.gov/pub/txt/ebd-p-01.doc>.

512. *CME Stockholm* Final Award, *supra* n. 42, at ¶ 134 ("The 1999 Forecasts presented a reasonable prediction of future results. Responsible estimation, incorporation of margins to

Contemporaneous Business Forecasts

Experts do not always rely on the build-up or WACC procedures to develop a discount rate. If "at the time" business forecasts from management or investment advisors are available, valuation professionals and courts will often look to the discount rates used in those forecasts. In using such contemporaneous forecasts, arbitrators should be aware of the dates of the internal data and the purposes behind those particular forecasts.

Such studies will be helpful to the arbitrator in validating expert testimony. When relying on those forecasts, though, the arbitrator must be sensitive to, among other matters: the dates of the studies (markets can change quickly); the dates of the revenue and expenses assumptions embedded within the studies (which themselves may derive from much earlier and possibly outdated market studies); and the purposes behind those documents. After all, exceptionally positive financial analyses are occasionally employed to persuade a potential buyer or lender to part with its money, but negative analyses by project sponsors may not see the light of day. Similarly, conservative analyses are occasionally developed by the majority owner of a company to justify a low buy-out price for shares held by minority investors or to minimize taxes.

A number of issues arise if the compensation decision in an arbitration relies upon valuations undertaken for a different purpose and at a different time. For example, experts argue as to whether the "rate of return" sought by prospective investors in a company is equivalent to the proper discount rate for application in a DCF analysis. On the one hand, investors (and their investment bankers) clearly consider all of the components of the discount rate in developing their target rates of return. They will only invest in a company whose DCF forecasts meet their minimum return requirements. On the other hand, the rates of return required by a particular investor may reflect the specific circumstances of that investor, not just the rate of return demanded generally in the market for an investment.

Some investors are comfortable investing in assets with, say, a 15% per annum rate of return, while other investors will not invest unless a proposed investment is expected to return a higher rate, say 20% per annum. If that is the case, then the minimum rate of return specified by that investor (or its bankers) to invest in the target company may not necessarily be an accurate proxy for the discount rate in a DCF projection. However, evidence of a common approach towards target rates of return among participants in a particular industry may

---

account for error and the monetary incentive to predict accurately make the 1999 Forecasts a solid and appropriate foundation from which to determine CNTS's 1999 market value.") Note, however, that Prof. Brownlie criticized reliance on the forecasts as speculative in his Separate Opinion. *See* Brownlie, Separate Opinion dated March 13, 2003 *supra* n. 160 at ¶¶ 66–71, 107–109.

have a significant practical impact as evidence of a common risk assessment. That rate of return, thus, may still be a very useful guide as to the perception held by investors of the riskiness of investing in the company at issue in the dispute.

Arbitrators also should be cautious when relying solely on the discount rates employed by investors or bankers in an earlier financial analysis. It is essential to consider the impact of supervening events between the date of that analysis and the date of injury. Financial analyses for a proposed investment transaction are usually prepared before that transaction occurs. Therefore, the risks reflected in those rates comprise the entire set of risks a company will face for the duration of the investment period. In contrast, the injury to the investor triggering the arbitration claim typically occurs at some point after the investment has been made. Accordingly, the investor's rate of return before making the investment often "takes account of risks which have already been successfully overcome"[513] by the time the injury occurs.

To illustrate, if a prospective investor in a "greenfield" power project targets a 20% internal rate of return (IRR) when evaluating a prospective investment, the risk profile embedded in that rate includes, inter alia, the risks that debt financing for the project might not successfully be raised or that project's construction might founder before the expected completion date. If the injury at issue in the dispute has occurred during the operating phase of the project, after permanent debt financing has been raised and successful construction of the project has concluded, then those important financing and construction risks will have already been overcome before the event giving rise to the dispute occurs. Thus, the investor's risk at the time of the valuation may very well have been reduced substantially from the time the investment was originally conceived.

On the other hand, supervening events may equally have made the investment much riskier; given the 2001 collapse in the telecommunications market, bankers who used a 13% discount rate in early 2000 for an international telecoms project would use a substantially higher rate just one year later.

We will now turn from discount rate issues to consider other common issues in a DCF valuation.

II DIRECT EQUITY VS. INDIRECT EQUITY (TOTAL INVESTED CAPITAL) METHODS

There are several Income-Based procedures for valuing an equity interest in a business concern. Two that are often considered are called the "indirect equity value" (or "Total Invested Capital") and the "direct equity value." These procedures differ in the manner they treat the debt of the business being valued. The "indirect equity value" is calculated as the enterprise value minus the market value of the business' debt, computed inter alia based on the WACC discount rate. The "direct equity value," in contrast, calculates the net cash flow of the business after giving effect to debt payments, and then discounts the result based on a discount

513. *Patuha v. PLN Final Award*, *supra* n. 239, at ¶ 480.

rate derived solely from the cost of equity capital. When the value of the entire business is determined by projecting and then discounting the cash flows available to all investors (debt and equity), with the value of the debt capital then being subtracted to arrive at the equity value of the business, that procedure is called the "indirect equity" or "Total Invested Capital" method. The *Fédération des Experts Comptables Européens* describes these procedures as follows:

> Whereas the market value of equity is determined indirectly as the difference between the enterprise value and the market value of debt using the weighted average cost of capital (WACC) and the adjusted present value method (APV), the equity method determines the market value of equity by discounting cash flows net of cost of debt using the return on equity (cost of equity). The concepts of weighted average cost of capital and adjusted present value are based on gross values (enterprise value methods), whereas the concept of direct calculation of the value of equity is based on net capital. Regardless of the difference in the method used, the individual DCF procedures result in the same values.[514]

The indirect equity (Total Invested Capital) procedure is the most commonly used application of an Income-Based Method.[515] Properly applied, as the *Fédération des Experts Comptables Européens* asserts, the "direct equity" and "indirect equity" procedures should "result in the same values." The difference between the indirect equity (Total Invested Capital) application and the direct equity application lies with the underlying assumptions: "If internally consistent assumptions are utilized, however, the results indicated should be consistent no matter which application is used."[516] If opposing experts present substantially different valuations, one relying on Total Invested Capital and the other on Direct Equity, the thoughtful arbitrator will ask the experts to clarify and justify their competing assumptions.

Direct Equity vs. Indirect Equity
(Total Invested Capital)

The "indirect equity value" method (also known as Total Invested Capital) calculates the enterprise value minus the market value of the business' debt, and then discounts the resulting amount by means of the WACC (or a built-up discount rate). The "direct equity value" method, in contrast, calculates the net cash flow of the enterprise after giving effect to debt payments, and then discounts the resulting amount by means of a discount rate based solely on the equity cost of capital. The resulting DCF amounts should be the same if the debt-to-equity ratio of the enterprise remains constant throughout the business' life.

514. FEE SME Business Valuation Guide, *supra* n. 17, ¶ 7.3.1 at 28.
515. Risius, *Business Valuation: A Primer for Legal Professionals*, *supra* n. 19, at 67.
516. *Id.*, at 66–67.

However, use of a WACC as part of the "indirect equity" procedure to set the discount rate can lead to misestimating the value of a business if the valuation expert is not careful. Recall that, to calculate the equity value of a business, the valuation expert will determine the annual net cash flows of the company and its terminal value. Then, those amounts are discounted back to their present values at the selected discount rate (here, WACC or a rate derived from the build-up procedure). Once that discounted amount is determined, the principal amount of the company's debt is then subtracted to arrive at the company's equity value. The WACC contains an implicit assumption: that the net cash flows to all invested capital (both debt capital and equity capital) are shared proportionately between the invested debt and the invested equity. If the debt-to-equity ratio is 40:60, 40% of the cash flows go to debt and 60% to equity. "In other words, if the lenders put up 40% of the required investment, they will receive 40% of all future cash flows, be they negative or positive, small or large. Shareholders will get the remaining 60%."[517]

That assumption is only correct, however, up to the level necessary to satisfy the rights of the lenders (the so-called "required" cash flows). Lenders, of course, are owed a fixed maximum amount of principal. Cash flows beyond the amounts necessary to service that debt (the so-called "excess" cash flow) belong entirely to the equity. Only the equity investors "should benefit (suffer) from positive (negative) excess cash flows."[518] That same assumption, of course, may have been incorporated into a discount rate derived from the build-up procedure. If the WACC is employed as the discount rate without taking account of this phenomenon, then the weighted average cost of both the higher cost of equity capital and the lower cost of debt capital will be used to discount that "excess" cash flows (in addition, of course, to the "required" cash flow). The effect of applying the lower combined debt-equity rate to the "excess" cash flows would improperly be to increase the present value of that portion of the company's net cash flows. This situation will occur, of course, if the principal amount of debt reduces through pay downs or if the capital of the company grows without a corresponding increase in debt. If the proportion of the company's capital that is debt stays constant (because of refinancings, for example), then the proportionality problem will not arise.

There are several possible means of adjusting the valuation procedure to address this proportionality problem. Some of these proportionality adjustments continue to employ the WACC for all cash flows (with adjustments), while others do not. One such procedure is an iterative method in which the WACC is successively adjusted to reflect the different proportionate sharing of cash flows between debt and equity capital. This procedure yields an approximation of the proper rates. However, the iterative approach suffers from technical weaknesses and unrealistic assumptions, particularly if the company's earnings are expected to grow over time.[519] The iterative solution faces particular problems when the business'

517. Mandron, The WACC: A Minefield, *supra* n. 504, at 14.
518. *Id.*, at 15, 21.
519. *Id.*, at 15–18.

cash flows are growing or the proportion of its capital attributable to debt and to equity changes over time.[520]

A second, more technically accurate procedure is to split the cash flows into a "required" component and an "excess" component. The WACC is then utilized as the discount rate solely for the "required" cash flows. The cost of equity capital (calculated, say, by means of CAPM) is utilized as the discount rate for the "excess" cash flows and the terminal value.[521]

A third means of resolving this proportionality problem involves replacing the WACC as the discount rate with the cost of equity capital and altering the cash flow formula. The panel in *CMS v. Argentina* used this procedure, the "direct equity method." To achieve this result, the valuation will first compute the net cash flows to the equity investors (including as liabilities in those cash flows, of course, scheduled payments of principal and interest on the debt). That sum is then discounted to its present value at the cost of equity (not the lower WACC). The principal amount of the company's debt is then added back to that amount to determine the full enterprise value. As the *CMS v. Argentina* panel noted, using the "direct equity method" can result in a substantial difference when compared with the original WACC computation (not, though, with a WACC calculation that has been adjusted to address the proportionality problem); in the *CMS* case, the difference was USD 40 million.

> 480. There are two recognized ways of computing the value of a firm and its securities on a DCF basis. One can start computations with the cash flows to the firm before interest and debt repayments, discount such flows at the weighted average cost of capital (the "WACC") and add the discounted cash flows to the firm to establish its value, then, the value of debt is subtracted and the residual value is the value of equity ("the indirect equity value"). Alternatively, one can compute first the cash flows to equity (cash flows from operations, minus interest and debt repayments), discount them at the cost of equity ("COE") and add the discounted cash flows to equity to establish the value of equity ("the direct equity value") then, one adds the value of debt to establish the value of the firm. The Tribunal has been advised that, by and large, analysts have tended to favor the first method. This approach was taken by Mr. Wood-Collins [the investor's expert] but he appears to have applied it in a circular way. Having computed the cash flows to equity and the cash flows to creditors, he then adds them up and discounts them at the weighted average cost of capital (the "WACC"); the sum of these discounted cash flows represents the value of the firm, from which the value of the debt is subtracted to arrive at the present value of equity. In fact, Mr. Wood-Collins goes from equity to debt to the firm and then back to equity.
>
> 481. The Tribunal does not see the need for this detour and shares the view of its own experts that having computed the cash flows to equity, Mr. Wood-

520. *Id.*, at 13, 15–21.
521. *Id.*, at 14–15.

> Collins needed then only to discount them at the cost of equity ("COE") to obtain the present value of TGN's equity.
>
> 482. The distinction between the two methods of computing value is not a purely academic matter. In general, under the first method, the computed value is larger than under the second one, because the WACC implicitly assumes that shareholders and creditors will receive a proportional share according to the weights included in the WAC of the firm's cash flows. Such appears to be the case when cash flows to the firm are larger than or equal to what the creditors are due and such was the result of the calculations made by Mr. Wood-Collins in this case, where the Tribunal has calculated, on the basis of Mr. Wood-Collins' hypotheses, a net difference of some USDS $40 million between the two methods.
>
> 483. In making its own calculations, the Tribunal will use the second method (the direct equity value).[522]

If properly computed, the "splitting" procedure and the "direct equity method" should result in the same value, and the iterative procedure should reach an approximation of that value.[523]

III PROJECTION PERIODS

The chosen duration of the projection period in a DCF forecast will affect the significance of the "terminal value" factor discussed in Chapter 4.IV below; the shorter the projection period, the larger the proportion of the total net amount that will be attributable to the post-projection period calculated by reference to the "terminal value." Indeed, the shorter the DCF projection period, the closer the calculation resembles the CCF method discussed below. The overall value of a business can be significantly affected by the terminal value. Accordingly, the duration of the projection period may be crucial.

Court and arbitral decisions differ widely in their choice of a projection period for a DCF forecast. If the company at issue is heavily dependent on a particular long-term contract (for example, a twenty-year power purchase agreement or concession contract), then sufficient data will often also exist to enable a valuation expert to make revenue and expense assumptions for the duration of that contract. It would not be unusual, therefore, to see a DCF forecast with a duration of "construction period plus 20 years." for a power project that has a twenty-year take-or-pay power purchase agreement commencing upon completion of the project's construction. Unsurprisingly, if management or bankers prepared a contemporaneous DCF forecast for an underlying transaction, it is common for the parties and their experts simply to adopt the duration of that forecast period for their compensation evidence in the subsequent arbitration.

522. *CMS v. Argentina*, *supra* n. 7, at ¶¶ 420–433.
523. Mandron, The WACC: A Minefield, *supra* n. 504.

Duration of DCF Projection Periods

If the company at issue is heavily dependent on a particular long term contract or the valuation is based on "at the time" management or financial advisor business forecasts, courts and experts often use the same period for their compensation decisions. Conceptually, the length of the projection period should be for the number of years in which the company's growth rate is predicted to be noticeably higher or lower than its expected long-term growth rate. In practice, if no long-term contract or contemporaneous business forecast is used as a basis, experts often use easy-to-understand periods of five or ten years.

The arbitral panel in *CMS v. Argentina* took an approach along those lines. The arbitrators employed a projection period for their DCF computation that ended upon the termination of the government-issued license to operate a gas transmission line in 2027.[524] Although the license acknowledged a potential ten-year extension to 2037, the tribunal eliminated that extension from the projection period as speculative.[525] The DCF projection period in *CMS* thus was equal to the original duration of the license. The ICSID tribunal in *MINE v. Republic of Guinea*[526] rejected the use of the DCF method to value a bauxite shipping contract as too speculative as well. Nevertheless, the tribunal awarded lost profits to MINE by employing the profits from another venture and extrapolating those profits for a ten-year time period, rather than the full duration of the thirty-year shipping contract at issue in that dispute.[527] Among the reasons motivating the *MINE* tribunal to

524. *CMS v. Argentina*, *supra* n. 7, at ¶ 439.
525. *Id.*
526. 4 ICSID Rep. 61, 75–76 (1997).
527. The *MINE* tribunal has been heavily criticized for failing to understand valuation principles: "The Tribunal initially rejected MINE's projections of future lost profits as too speculative, since the MINE venture had never earned any profits. The Tribunal then awarded damages, using the profits of the other venture over its two year life and projecting these profits over the expected ten year life of the MINE venture. The Tribunal then added a sum for simple interest (from the date of the breach to the date of the judgment) and costs. The Tribunal ignored the present value of the lost profits and simply summed the future expected profits based upon two years of history of another venture, which may or may not have been the same as the proposed MINE venture. Further, the Tribunal ignored the concept of compound interest and used simple interest to compute the amount due as damages. In effect, this type of damage computation may or may not make the claimant (MINE) whole. This Tribunal, just as the one in *Amoco,* demonstrates that it does not understand the principles of valuation and how it should be applied in order to adequately compensate the plaintiff. Since the Tribunals fail to deal with the concept of present value in their cases, these cases provide little guidance on the determination of discount rates or interest rates." Meyer, Quintero & Shao, The Effect of Risk on the Value of Lost International Business Profits, *supra* n. 419, at 109 (footnotes omitted). *See* text associated with n. 266 et seq. *supra* for a discussion of the valuation approach taken in the *Amoco* case.

limit the period to ten years was the presence of an early termination provision in the shipping contract.

National courts too have considered the proper duration of an earnings forecast. In *Estate of Charles A. Borgatello v. Comm'r of Internal Revenue*,[528] a US estate tax case, the US Tax Court considered the length of the cash-flow period for a DCF valuation of a real estate holding company whose assets comprised shopping centers. The court compared the evidence of the estate's expert (Holden, who presented a seven-year analysis) and the IRS' expert (Marx, who argued for ten years). The Tax Court settled on the longer period, based upon the characteristics of the particular location of the shopping centers and real estate market practice:

> Another area of disagreement among the experts is the appropriate duration of the cash-flow period. Mr. Holden uses a 7-year cash-flow period whereas Mr. Marx uses a 10-year cash-flow period. Mr. Holden justifies his 7-year period on the basis of, inter alia, market uncertainties and the fact that as the cash-flow period is extended into the future, the analysis becomes less reliable. Mr. Holden also notes that real estate markets tend to flow in 7-year cycles. Mr. Marx points out that a 10-year cash-flow period is supported by information from local brokers and national real estate publications. Although 7 years may be a reasonable cash-flow period in some cases, we are inclined to follow the trends of the Montecito-Santa Barbara real estate market. We find, therefore, that Mr. Marx's estimate of a 10-year cash-flow period is persuasive because it follows more closely Santa Barbara's real estate norms.

Perhaps unsurprisingly, the effect of selecting the longer period was to increase the valuation and thus the estate taxes.

Conceptually, the length of the projection period should be the number of years in which the company's growth rate is projected to be noticeably higher or lower than its normalized long-term growth rate.[529] However, such figures are rarely offered. Instead, most valuations use easy-to-understand periods of five, ten, etc., years or follow the periods selected in contemporaneous business forecasts.

The potential for mitigation has also played a role in setting the duration of a lost profits/cash flow analysis. In one ICC arbitration, the panel awarded lost profits for only one year, calculated on the company's income stream from a breached contract for the year. In that dispute, the parties had entered into a three-year exclusive distribution agreement. The distributor terminated the agreement early without cause. The ICC arbitrators held that the successful claimant could have obtained alternate distribution services to mitigate its losses after one year.[530] In contrast, another ICC tribunal awarded lost profits for the full forty months of an agency and distribution contract.[531] In that case, the claimant wine

528. T.C. Memo 2000-264, 2000 Tax Ct. Memo LEXIS 309, 80 T.C.M. (CCH) 260, T.C.M. (RIA) 54013 (August 18, 2000, amended August 21, 2000).
529. Risius, *Business Valuation: A Primer for Legal Professionals*, *supra* n. 19, at 73.
530. ICC Final Award, Case No. 7006, 1992, 18 Y.B. Com. Arb. 58 (1993).
531. ICC Final Award, Case No. 5946, 1990, 16 Y.B. Com. Arb. 97 (1991).

producer was held to have improperly terminated the agreement. As a result, the arbitrators awarded the distributor lost profits damages for the full remaining term of the contract.

Most enterprises, of course, do not have long-term output purchase contracts, but are expected to have an indefinite life. As a conceptual matter, valuation experts will testify that the proper projection period for such an investment is "until the company is expected to reach a steady growth state,"[532] with periods subsequent to the specific projection period addressed by the "terminal value" factor discussed below. Once the company stabilizes in its competitive environment, the company's returns are expected to approximate the returns in the economy generally.[533] Absent a specific reason to choose a different duration, experts often employ a five-year projection period in such circumstances. As a practical matter, the use of five-year projection periods in the US may be attributed in part to easy access to important data used to establish discount rates; five-year US Treasury securities data and five-year equity premium and small company data from Ibbotson Associates. "The specific forecast period typically runs from three to ten years, with five years being common."[534]

In addition to the duration of the forecasts, it is crucial for arbitrators to pay attention to the beginning date for the projection period (i.e., the valuation date), since the discount rate and other indicia of risk are usually determined as of that date. Thus, the DCF forecast for an international telecommunications company in June 2000 could be substantially more favorable than a DCF forecast for the same company as of January 2001 – in the intervening months, significant overcapacity in the telecoms markets became evident, revenue estimates for virtually all telecoms companies plummeted significantly, several telecom firms filed for bankruptcy and risk factors increased noticeably.

If the arbitrators determine on a valuation date that is not consistent with the beginning date utilized in the expert evidence, then the expert's evidence might be disregarded.[535] Unless the arbitrators and the parties are prepared to accept the possibility that the panel may make its compensation determination without much

532. Dickie, Financial Statement Analysis and Business Valuation for the Practical Lawyer, *supra* n. 489, at 284.

533. The Lawyer's Business Valuation Handbook, *supra* n. 411, at 114.

534. *Id. See also Crescent/Mach I Partnership, L.P. v. Turner, supra* n. 355, at *10 (footnotes omitted): "In its projections before the merger, Holdings' [the acquisition company's] management used a five-year projection period. Delaware courts frequently use a five-year period. The Petitioners offer best practices guides that recommend using 7–10 year projection periods. Taylor [Petitioner's expert] offers evidence that some of the variables in the model (*e.g.*, capital expenditures, net operation glosses, depreciation, and amortization) would benefit from a longer projection period in order to reach a steady state. However, the Petitioners admit that the effect of these variables on the final outcome is of low magnitude. More significant, however, is Turner's [Respondent's] defense of five-year projections: regular changes in the soft drink market make longer projections unreliable."

535. This situation arose in the *Santa Elena v. Costa Rica* case, where the claimant presented a 1993 property appraisal and a fair market DCF analysis commencing on December 31, 1997. The panel instead concluded that the operative valuation date was May 5, 1978, rendering claimant's expert evidence irrelevant. *See* Brower & Wong, *supra* n. 97, at 767.

support from expert evidence, it is prudent to plan ahead for this possibility if the valuation date is in dispute.

IV TERMINAL VALUE

Ordinary businesses are expected to have an indefinite life – they do not disappear at the end of some fixed period of time. Operating companies, of course, do not lose the entirety of their value at the conclusion of a DCF forecast's projection period. Instead, they continue operating and generating income, which must be accounted for in a proper valuation. The purpose of a "terminal value" factor in a DCF valuation is to enable a potential investor (or an arbitrator) to identify the remaining economic value of the company after the end of the chosen projection period. As described in the *CME Stockholm* award, a terminal value covers "the period thereafter [after the Forecast Period] in perpetuity for which period an estimation of the value of the business at the end of the Forecast Period was made (the 'terminal value' or 'continuing value') which takes account of the future prospects at the time."[536] The combination of the present value of the net cash flow for the DCF projection period and the present value of the terminal value should result in a complete valuation of the company, regardless of the chosen duration of the projection period. This terminal value, by the way, is called the "residual" in some valuations – the two terms have the same meaning here.

Terminal Value Computations

Apart from the selection of the discount rate, perhaps the most significant variation in DCF valuations comes from the calculation of the terminal value; the present value of the remaining economic value of the business after the projection period ends. For valuations based on short projection periods, the portion of the total DCF amount attributable to the terminal value amount can be a very high proportion of the total amount. One simple way to think of the terminal value is as the amount the business would be worth if sold at the end of the specific projection period, discounted back to the valuation date.

As the *Fédération des Experts Comptables Européens* states:

> For the more immediate first phase, which often covers a manageable period of time of three to five years, the accountant normally has access to sufficiently detailed forecast data.... The years covering the subsequent, second phase are normally based on more or less general projections of the detailed forecasts made for the first phase. Consideration should be given as to whether the assets and liabilities, financial and earning position of the business being

536. *CME Stockholm* Final Award, *supra* n. 42, at ¶ 572.

> valued after the detailed forecast period remain in a so-called steady state or whether the annual business profits still change, but reflect a constant or constantly-growing amount of business profits.[537]

One simple way to think of the "terminal value" is as the amount the business would be worth if it was sold at market value at the end of the specific projection period, discounted back to a present value as of the valuation date.

To estimate this terminal value, a popular method that experts may apply (known as the Gordon Growth or constant growth model) is to take the free cash flow from the last year in the projection period (i.e., year five in the case of a five-year DCF projection period or year ten in the case of a ten-year DCF projection period).[538] To that year's free cash flow number, the expert will apply a "perpetual growth rate" to reflect continued growth in company revenues. According to the Gordon Growth model, the "terminal value" is equal to the free cash flow in the "terminal year" (here, year five or year ten) *divided* by the sum of the capitalization rate minus the expected growth rate.

$$\frac{\text{Final Projected Year Cash Flow Times (1 Plus Long-Term Cash Flow Growth Rate)}}{\text{(Discount Rate Minus Long-Term Cash Flow Growth Rate)}}$$

The expert then calculates a present value for the resulting amount based upon the chosen discount rate.[539]

For purposes of deciding which year(s) should form the base for a "terminal value" calculation, the IVSC advises valuation experts to look to the "practices of investors in the market, and Valuers should mirror those practices and fully disclose the method chosen."[540]

Perpetual Growth Rate

If the terminal value is calculated based on the Gordon Growth Model, the selection of the company's "perpetual growth rate" will be a critical decision. The Gordon Growth Model makes a crucial assumption that the future growth after the specific projection period will occur at a constant rate. Arbitrators should be wary of proposed "perpetual growth rates" well in excess of the national growth rate plus the expected inflation rate. In addition, arbitrators should closely scrutinize the revenue and expense numbers in the last year of the projection period (the numbers used in the terminal value computation) to make sure they are representative amounts.

537. FEE SME Business Valuation Guide, *supra* n. 17, at ¶ 5.3.
538. "Free cash flow" is, by the way, a slightly different number from the "net cash flow" number used in the DCF projections themselves.
539. *BTR Dunlop Holdings, Inc. v. Comm'r*, *supra* n. 503, at 20–21.
540. IVSC DCF Guidance Note, *supra* n. 408, at ¶ 5.1.

In a recent Eighth Circuit decision, a prominent US appellate court rejected an argument that including a terminal value amount in a damages award was improper because it was inherently speculative. The case, *Matrix Group Ltd. v. Rawlings Sporting Goods Company, Inc.*,[541] involved breach by Rawlings of an exclusive license agreement permitting Matrix to use Rawling's trademark on sports bags. In a jury trial, the jury awarded Matrix damages for breach of the license agreement on the basis of the discounted present value of the cash flow under the license agreement. That damages award included a "terminal value" component. The District Court eliminated the terminal value amount from the damages award. In doing so, the trial court relied on Rawlings' argument that "speculation is necessarily involved in estimating terminal value because revenue lost over an infinite period of time could be included."[542]

The Eighth Circuit Court of Appeals, however, rejected this analysis and restored the terminal value component to the damages award. The appellate court began its review by noting that the law applicable to the license agreement (Delaware law) "disapproves of speculative damages . . . but damages need only have a reasonable basis, they need not be absolutely certain."[543] The appellate court specifically acknowledged the role of a terminal value in a DCF computation. "Calculating the value of an asset at liquidation or disposition is a necessary part of discounted cash flow analysis, which the Delaware courts have recognized as 'the preeminent valuation methodology' in the financial community."[544]

Moreover, the Court of Appeals also recognized the propriety of the Gordon Growth model for calculating terminal values:

> In her valuation Smith [Matrix's expert] used what is called the "constant growth" or "Gordon growth" model, which assumes constant growth of an asset and then discounts this value to arrive at the present value of the terminal value. . . . The constant growth model which Smith employed has been specifically recognized as an accepted way to determine terminal value. *See* Prescott Group Small Cap, L.P. v. Coleman Co., 2004 WL 2059515 at 14 (Del. Ch. Sept. 8, 2004).[545]

The appellate court declined to accept Rawlings' characterization of a terminal value as necessarily speculative, responding that "[t]he constant growth model is entirely different from calculating damages based on an infinite series of periodic cash flows, for its formula is meant to estimate the cash available from a disposition of the asset."[546] The court then concluded that the jury could reasonably have

541. *Matrix Group Ltd. v. Rawlings Sporting Goods Company, Inc., supra* n. 414.
542. *Id.*, at 593.
543. *Id.* (citations omitted).
544. *Id.*, at 594.
545. *Id.*
546. *Id.* The Eighth Circuit decision also rejected Rawlings' argument that a terminal value calculation is only proper for valuing businesses in shareholder appraisal cases, not for breach of long-term contracts like the exclusive license agreement: "Rawlings argues that the cases in which recovery for terminal value was allowed are distinguishable because they involved

accepted the expert's testimony, and held that the District Court erred by excluding the "terminal value" component of the damages award.

The US bankruptcy court case of *In re Nellson Nutraceuticals, Inc.*[547] also recently considered the calculation of the "terminal value" factor. In that case, four party-appointed experts each utilized the DCF method to calculate the Debtor's enterprise value. Three of those experts employed a "terminal value" using EBITDA as the unit of comparison to measure free cash flow in the DCF projection period. However, the fourth expert employed EBITDA minus capital expenditures as his unit of comparison. The DCF projections for all experts covered the six-year period from 2006 through 2011. Illustrating the importance of the "terminal value" factor, the Bankruptcy Court noted that

> Mr. Harris's [the fourth expert's] calculation of the Debtors' terminal value under his DCF analysis has a material impact on his ultimate conclusion as to the Debtors' enterprise value. Indeed, the terminal value of $274.7 million used under Mr. Harris's DCF analysis accounts for approximately 68% of Mr. Harris's concluded enterprise value of the Debtors' of $404.5 million.[548]

Observers will see that the Gordon Growth model makes a crucial assumption – future growth (if any) after the projection period is assumed to occur at a constant rate.

> The procedure preferred by most appraisers for developing the estimate of the terminal value is to use the capitalization model, usually the constant growth capitalization model. In other words, the implied assumption is that, after the specific forecast period, the business's net cash flow will continue to grow at some average annual compound rate.[549]

The size of the perpetual growth rate used in the Gordon Growth model reflects the valuation expert's expectations for the company's growth of the company after the end of the DCF forecast period.[550] The higher the expert's growth projection, the larger the final terminal value amount.

---

statutory stock appraisal. The agreement here, however, like shares in a corporation, was expected to generate income for an indefinite period. Rawlings gives no reason why the financial principles applied to one revenue producing asset like stock should not be applied to another like a license agreement." *Id.*

547. *In re Nellson Nutraceuticals, Inc.*, et al, 2006 WL3479293 (Bankr. D. Del. 2006).

548. *Id.*, at *8. Similarly, on the basis of a five-year DCF projection period, 70% of one expert's proposed valuation of a healthcare company was attributable to the terminal value factor. *See* In re *Med Diversified, Inc. v. Addus Healthcare, Inc.*, *supra* n. 77, at 632–633. In another Delaware case, *Cede & Co. v. Technicolor, Inc.*, *supra* n. 414, at *90, the difference between a constant (last forecast year) cash flow and cash flow perpetually growing at 5% produced a 16.56 USD per share difference in final value in the *Technicolor* shareholder dispute.

549. The Lawyer's Business Valuation Handbook, *supra* n. 411, at 114.

550. "Cimasi [a valuation expert] used the Gordon Growth Model to place a value on the remaining period of ownership after post acquisition year 5, 'under which the net cash flow from the final period [wa]s grown' by the selected growth rate of four percent. . . . The Court was never provided with an explanation of why the rate of 4% was used as a growth rate in the terminal

> The discounted cash flow model obviously is very sensitive to the amounts of income projected beyond the projection period. The reviewer should inquire whether projections used were prepared during the normal course of business or in connection with a transaction for buyers or lenders (often optimistic) or for justifying the price to be paid (perhaps pessimistic).[551]

Clearly, the larger the perpetual growth rate used in the terminal value formula, the larger the compensation award. US courts in "dissenting shareholder" cases often apply a perpetual growth rate equal to the expected *nominal* growth in the national economy (i.e., the expected real growth rate adjusted for the expected inflation rate) plus whatever incremental company – or industry-specific growth increment (if any) the court deems appropriate in the particular circumstances.[552] "Real" growth and interest rates signify growth or interest rates *excluding* inflation. "Nominal" rates, in comparison, incorporate an inflation factor. Employing a nominal growth rate avoids double counting for inflation, since the inflation rate is embedded inside the discount rate as well. Using only the economy's real growth rate would improperly reduce the final amount.[553]

The size of the terminal value is directly related to the growth rate selected by the expert. Some experts, unsurprisingly, focus on a low or zero growth rate.

> I find Baehr's assumption that no growth would occur beyond the projected five-year period unreasonable; it must be assumed that CTCA would continue to grow at least at the rate of inflation. Thus, I will assume a 5% growth rate for perpetuity.[554]

---

period. He testified that he considered this rate 'conservative in that we recognized that this was a huge growth industry.' Tr., August 26, 2005, at p. 163. He never explained why he felt the need to use a conservative figure in valuing a business in what he described as a huge growth industry. He has simply not given the Court enough information to determine whether the 4% growth figure used was a reliable figure. In light of all of the other flaws in applying this method, the Court cannot simply give deference to professional judgment in determining the growth figure in this instance, which represented over 70% of his value determination under the DCF method." In re *Med Diversified, Inc. v. Addus Healthcare, Inc., supra* n. 77, at 637 (footnotes omitted).

551. The Lawyer's Business Valuation Handbook, *supra* n. 411, at 116.
552. Kotain and Weirs, Fundamentals of Business Valuation and their Application in Legal Disputes, at 4 (March 20, 2002), available on line at <www.rkvaluation.com/articles/index.html>.
553. Dickie, Financial Statement Analysis and Business Valuation for the Practical Lawyer, *supra* n. 489, at 287.
554. *Lane v. Cancer Treatment Centers of America, Inc., supra* n. 1, at *117. Federal Reserve Board Governors would be appalled by this judge's blithe assumption in 2004 of a continuing 5% inflation rate for the US economy. *See*, in contrast, *Delaware Open MRI Radiology Associates, P.A. v. Kessler, supra* n. 3, at 337 (Del. Ch. 2006): "Mitchell assumed a constant perpetuity growth rate of 4%. Reed assumed a perpetuity growth rate of 3%. As between the two, I find Mitchell's rate more realistic. Reed essentially assumed no real growth in the value of Delaware Radiology after the projection period, which I believe is unduly pessimistic. Mitchell captures a modest increment of growth for the MRI Centers above the growth of the entire economy that is realistically achievable, and I adopt his perpetuity assumption."

Arbitrators should also be cautious in accepting very high perpetual growth rates, well in excess of the national growth rate plus the expected inflation rate. The US economy helps illustrate the reason, as Dickie explains:

> In estimating a growth rate, a common mistake is to assume an unrealistically rapid rate of growth. After adjusting for inflation (that is, in real terms), the growth of the U.S. economy has averaged 2% to 3%, reflecting the 1% average growth rate in the population plus increases in the living standard. Consider that if a company grows more rapidly than the economy's real rate of growth plus the inflation rate, and if it does so in perpetuity, then at some point, its value will be infinite, and eventually its revenues will constitute almost the entire economy. To be sure, it would be a very long time before that happened, but the point remains that one should be quite skeptical of assumed real growth rates in excess of about 2%. Thus if the expected inflation rate is 3.5%, one ought to be leery of assumed nominal growth rates much in excess of 5.5%.[555]

Naturally, arbitrators will recognize that these numbers should differ depending on which economy's growth and inflation rates are employed. GDP growth rates differ from country to country, and are subject to significant ups and downs over a period of years. Moreover, a portion of any country's real economic growth rate is directly attributable to the extent to which that country's population grows. Patterns of population growth worldwide are in the midst of dramatic change, making reliance on historical population growth rates as a component of a country's overall economic growth rate potentially improper. As the United Nations Conference on Trade and Development (UNCTAD) has recently reported: "[T]he world population is in the midst of an unprecedented transformation brought about by the transition from a regime of high mortality and high fertility to one of low mortality and low fertility."[556] Countries differ markedly as to their location within this demographic transition. Illustratively, UNCTAD's medium variant estimate is that China's population will grow by about 4.5% in the aggregate between 2007 and 2015. Conversely, over the same period Germany's population is forecast by UNCTAD to decrease by about 1%, Japan's by slightly more than 1% and Russia's by more than 4.2%.[557] Those disparities should not be ignored when making growth assumptions for a "terminal value," nor should historical population and living standards growth rates be accepted without scrutiny. The impact of the population decreases in our future on a country's overall economic growth rate remains to be seen.

555. *Id.*, at 286–287. "It is common for the long-term growth rate utilized in the DCF method to be reasonably close to long-term inflationary expectations. . . . In addition to inflationary expectations, it is also appropriate to consider the long-term expected real growth in the macro-economy beyond inflation." Risius, *Business Valuation: A Primer for Legal Professionals*, *supra* n. 19, at 83–84.
556. UNCTAD, World Population Prospects: The 2006 Revision – Population Aging (2007).
557. Based on *id.*, at Table A.2.

Dickie's comment that a high perpetual growth rate would eventually result in the valued business exceeding the size of the entire US economy was the subject of litigation in the US bankruptcy case of *In re Nanovation Technologies, Inc.* The court in that case rejected the comment, pointing out that a perpetual growth rate was intended as a tool "to compensate for the inability of the analyst to gradually reduce growth over a period of years beyond the discrete period in the DCF analysis," not as a "literal representation of how the analyst expects the subject company to actually grow in the future."[558] As the court also pointed out, after a period of time (in that case, about twenty years), by virtue of the discount rate in a present value analysis, the growth rate no longer has a significant impact on value.[559] Therefore, the theoretical complaint that the value of the company will constitute the entire economy at some future date does not have practical impact on valuations.

The *Nanovation Technologies* case also illustrates the use of a declining growth curve in a terminal value computation, rather than a single growth rate. The experts justified that approach (although disagreeing on its implementation) as a result of expectations about high early future growth in the relevant industry, photonics.[560]

Apart from the Gordon Growth model, several other approaches to calculating the "terminal value" factor exist. Experts often employ a multiple of earnings like EBIT or EBITDA.[561]

> An alternative procedure to estimate terminal value is to use estimated market multiples applied to some measure of the company's economic income projected for the year following the end of the discrete forecast period. An example would be to estimate net income for the year following the forecast period and use a price earnings ratio to estimate the terminal value. If valuing the entire invested capital rather than just the common equity . . . then one might use a multiple of earnings before interest and taxes [EBIT], or a multiple of earnings before interest, taxes, and depreciation [EBITDA]. This procedure is commonly used by investment bankers.[562]

Like the Gordon Growth model, the use of market multiples to calculate a terminal value also often makes the simplifying assumption that the post-projection future will be constant.

> A frequently used assumption is that market multiples will remain the same as on the effective valuation date. However, they probably won't. Markets change, especially markets for specific industries. For example, if an industry

558. In re Nanovation Technologies, Inc., 364 B.R. 308, 327 (Bankr. N.D. Ill. 2007).
559. "That is why the trustee's big theme that KPMG's [the expert's] selection of a growth rate of 15% will ultimately compound into a value that exceeds the gross national product is naïve and ignores present value principles of the discounted cash flow method." *Id.*, at 329.
560. *Id.*, at *329–330, 351–352.
561. *See* Ch. 6.II for a more complete discussion of the components of EBITDA and EBIT.
562. The Lawyer's Business Valuation Handbook, *supra* n. 411, at 117.

> is in a high-growth stage now, that is usually reflected in high market multiples. When the industry reaches more of a steady state, market multiples are not likely to be as high. Even if the analyst assumes that multiples in a high-growth industry will decline, the level of multiples at any future date is hard to predict.[563]

In *Crescent/Mach I Partnership, L.P. v. Turner*,[564] the Delaware Chancery Court was faced with competing terminal value computations, one based on the Gordon Growth Model and the other based on an EBITDA multiplier. The choice was especially significant because the terminal value in that case (using a five-year DCF projection period) "comprise[d], unfortunately, roughly three-quarters of the final valuation under both parties' models."[565] The court chose to rely on the Gordon Growth Model, rather than the EBITDA multiplier, because "a good industry comparison is crucial if a multiplier methodology is employed, but the Respondent has not established that appropriate comparables are available."[566] *Crescent/Mach I* thus makes clear the importance of comparability in terminal value calculations based on market multiples like EBITDA.

Just like the practice of using Market-Based and Income-Based valuation methods to check each other, so too experts often use both the Gordon Growth model and a market multiple to double-check their results.

> If the analyst uses the constant growth model to estimate the terminal value, the reviewer can check to see whether the market multiples implied by the terminal value are reasonable. If the analyst uses market multiples to estimate the terminal value, the reviewer can check to see whether the capitalization rate implied by the terminal value is reasonable.[567]

A few pointers for arbitrators may be helpful in assessing proposed terminal values. First, what if the only valuable asset of a company is a concession or sales contract with a fixed termination date? In such circumstances, the company will obtain no revenue whatsoever after that termination date unless the other party voluntarily agrees to renew the contact or there is an alternate buyer available to enter into a replacement contract. One example might be a ten-year public mining concession. Once that concession expires, the company loses the right to exploit the mine. Some experts, of course, might argue that the company could reasonably expect the concession contract to be renewed, in which case a terminal value component could be appropriate for the DCF computation. If the arbitrator concludes, on the other hand, that renewal of the concession is speculative, then adding a terminal value to the calculus would not be appropriate.[568] So, in *CMS v. Argentina* the

563. *Id.*
564. *Crescent/Mach I Partnership, L.P. v. Turner*, *supra* n. 355.
565. *Id.*, at *14 (footnotes omitted).
566. *Id. See* Ch. 3 for a detailed discussion of "comparability."
567. The Lawyer's Business Valuation Handbook, *supra* n. 411, at 117–118.
568. *See*, e.g., *CMS v. Argentina*, *supra* n. 7, at ¶ 439, rejecting the inclusion of a ten-year license extension option in the projection period.

arbitrators declined to consider a ten-year extension to a gas transmission concession despite an extension option in the Argentine license. In making that decision, the arbitrators in effect concluded that it was not appropriate in the circumstances to attribute value to the investment (TGN) beyond the term of the original license ending 2027. Unsurprisingly, there is no evidence in the *CMS v. Argentina* award that the arbitrators employed a terminal value in their DCF calculations. In the *CME Stockholm Final Award*, by way of contrast, the arbitrators accepted that "broadcasting licenses in Europe are renewed as a matter of ordinary administrative practice."[569] In such a case, use of a terminal value factor would be warranted despite the termination date in the original license.

If a project reverts free of cost to the host government at the end of the operating period established by the project concession, then no terminal value would seem to be appropriate.[570] An obvious example is the difference between a "build-own-operate-transfer" (BOOT) project and a "build-own-operate" (BOO) project. In the case of a BOOT project, the project owner is legally obligated to transfer the project at no cost to the host government at the end of the concession period. Therefore, the investors are not entitled to a residual value after the end of the concession. In contrast, the investors in a BOO project continue to own the facility after the concession has expired. Therefore, a BOO facility may still have residual value to its owners after the expiry of the concession.

Of course, this kind of concern does not exist for a well-established company with diversified sources of revenues. In those circumstances, it is reasonable to assume that the company will in fact continue to operate and generate revenue and profits or losses, as the case may be, for many years after the end of the projection period. If the current owners chose to sell the company at the end of, say, a five-year specific projection period, the company would surely fetch some price from a third-party buyer (its fair market value at that time). Business valuations of such companies, accordingly, routinely include terminal value factors.

Second, if a terminal value is appropriate in the circumstances, the arbitrators might wish to pay special attention to the specific details of the last year of the DCF projection period. That last year is the year from which the free cash flow amount used in the perpetual growth calculation is often taken.[571] The chosen year should

---

569. *CME Stockholm* Final Award, *supra* n. 42, at ¶ 605.

570. *See* Wells, *supra* n. 270, at 474, discussing the terms of the thirty-year Joint Operating Contract and Energy Sales Contract between Karaha Bodas Corp. and two Indonesian state enterprises. Similarly, nothing in the *CMS v. Argentina* award suggests that the DCF forecast in that case contained a terminal value after the 2027 expiration of the company's gas transmission license despite the presence of a ten-year conditional extension clause in the license. A thoughtful expert might, of course, argue that some residual value is still appropriate in those circumstances because the project operator has unique know how and expertise to operate those particular facilities, and thus may be able to successfully negotiate for contract or license extensions covering the remaining useful life of the project. Such an argument would naturally be met with the counter-argument that the proposition is "speculative."

571. "Terminal value is calculated by adjusting cash-flows *in the final period* to represent the future cash-generating capability of the company." *BTR Dunlop Holdings, Inc. v. Comm'r*, *supra* n. 503, at 20 (emphasis added).

be normal, rather than unusual. If, for example, the year chosen for the "terminal year" is at the top or the bottom of a business cycle, then the resulting calculation may produce exaggerated results. "Many industries – including the steel, chemical, and auto industries – are cyclical, and using a terminal year at the top or bottom of the cycle is likely to be misleading."[572]

As the US bankruptcy court in *In re Nellson Nutraceuticals* noted, the terminal value is highly sensitive to the estimates contained in the chosen year.

> Mr. Harris [Debtors expert valuation witness] testified that his terminal value relies entirely on the Debtors estimate of capital expenditures for 2011 – the final year of the Debtors long range business plan. Mr. Harris further testified that the Debtors' capital expenditures are highly volatile from year-to-year, they have varied drastically in the past, and they will continue to do so in the future. All the experts agree that, while EBITDA and EBIT also vary from year-to-year, they are less volatile than a company's capital expenditures.[573]

In some projections (particularly management analyses prepared at the commencement of a project), the cash flow amount in the last year may not accurately reflect a company that will continue operations after the end of that year. Let us use the mining concession as an example again. If a valuation expert hired by the project investors prepared cash flow forecasts at the beginning of the ten-year concession, it is highly unlikely that the projections for year ten would show any anticipated capital expenditures. After all, why would the investors make capital investments during year ten, and then hand the mine back to the concessionaire on December 31 of that year complete with the brand new capital equipment! As a result, the expense figures in year ten of the DCF forecast will be lower than for other years, thereby increasing free cash flow for that particular year. What if, though, it is clear to the arbitrators that the mining concession will be renewed indefinitely and, consequently, a terminal value is appropriate? By using that year ten free cash flow amount in the terminal value calculation, the valuation effectively (and inaccurately) will assume that same low year ten capital expenditures for each subsequent year following the projection period. The assumption of lower capital expenditures in year ten (and thus a higher terminal value) is obviously incorrect. In circumstances where the company will continue to operate the mine, the investors will instead cause the company to make capital expenditures in year ten that

---

572. Dickie, Financial Statement Analysis and Business Valuation for the Practical Lawyer, *supra* n. 489, at 284. *See also* FEE SME Business Valuation Guide, *supra* n. 17, at ¶ 5.3 (forecast assumptions in first phase need to be checked for their relevance in projecting earnings for terminal value calculation).

573. *In re Nellson Nutraceuticals, Inc*. et al, *supra* n. 547, at *9. *See also CME Stockholm* Final Award, *supra* n. 42, at ¶ 576. "Taking into account that experts almost agreed on the perpetuity growth rate of 3.4%/4%, the large difference between the experts' calculations derive from the gap of the projected cash flows for the years 2006, 2007 and 2008 and the further calculation of the continuing value (or terminal value) based on the cash flow in 2008." As the court noted, "[t]he substantial gap between the experts" valuations for the year 2008, therefore, became dominating for the experts' valuation results. *Id.*, at ¶ 577.

are normal for continuing operations, rather than reducing year ten expenses in anticipation of withdrawal at year's end.

The same issue will arise, of course, for several other items in the year ten revenue and expense assumptions for the mine, such as depreciation and amortization, long-term marketing expenses, hiring bonuses for new employees and other expenditures that make commercial sense only if mining activities continue in the future. One mistake worth noting relates to the amounts for capital expenditures and depreciation expenses in the year(s) used as the base for the terminal value calculation. Since depreciation expenses are tied to the purchase of fixed assets (i.e., capital expenditures), it is not feasible for depreciation expenses to exceed capital expenditures in perpetuity. If, however, the amount of depreciation expenses in the chosen year happens to exceed the amount of capital expenditures in the same year, that is exactly what would happen. Therefore, arbitrators should scrutinize those numbers closely to ensure this mistake does not occur.[574]

Accordingly, if the arbitrator determines that a terminal value is appropriate, it is important to inquire carefully whether the expert valuations should alter some of the revenue and expense assumptions embedded in the cash flow numbers for the last year of the projection period are realistic in the circumstances.[575] Even if the cash flows for the final year are not unusual, some financial experts will average several years of cash flows as the basis for a terminal value calculation, to normalize for variations from ordinary operations.

A terminal value may not be the only way of computing the remaining value of a company after the detailed projection period. If the business is expected to be sold at the end of the detailed DCF forecast period, then the *Fédération des Experts Comptables Européens* recommends calculating the expected sales value (minus related costs) rather than a terminal value of future earnings.[576]

V TAXES

Another common dispute in DCF analyses is whether the discount rate and cash flow estimates should be made on a pre-tax or after-tax basis; i.e., how should the analysis reflect the successful claimant's responsibilities to pay income taxes.[577]

574. Risius, *Business Valuation: A Primer for Legal Professionals*, *supra* n. 19, at 82.
575. It may, of course, be appropriate to adjust historical earnings information for particular items that should not be projected on a going-forward basis. The Fédération des Experts Comptables Européens offers a checklist, including eliminating earnings from assets no longer used in the business, adjusting for changes in accounting policy, and recalculation of expenses such as taxes and bonuses that are based on income levels. *See* FEE SME Business Valuation Guide, *supra* n. 17, ¶ 7.2.2.1 at 24.
576. *Id.*, ¶ 7.3.2.3 at 29. The FEE does not recommend any particular procedure for calculating the expected sales value. Accordingly, the expert may end up using the Gordon Growth Model for that purpose in any event.
577. Clearly, the cash flow estimates in a DCF projection must always reflect the separate obligation of the company itself to pay its own income and other business taxes before computing net cash flow available to the equity investors.

International Accounting Standard 36 specifies that a discount rate should be a pre-tax rate.[578] However, the IVSC DCF Guidance Note makes the point that, if another measure of income is used within the revenue and expense projections (e.g., after-tax), then the discount rate should be appropriately matched – the valuation must be based on an apples-to-apples computation.[579]

The *Fédération des Experts Comptables Européens* takes a clear stand on this issue, when valuing a company from the perspective of the owners of a business. According to the Fédération, both income taxes of the business and the owners' personal income taxes should be included in the calculation, because the valuation for that purpose "is determined by the amount of net cash flows to an investor which is freely available to that investor."[580] Note, however, that the Fédération does not consider in this recommendation the potential impact to the investor of paying income taxes on sums awarded in an arbitration award embodying the compensation obligation. The Fédération also asserts that the actual tax burden of the owner should be used, taking into account the owner's specific tax status, rather than using a standard tax rate.[581] Here, the Fédération is looking to the Investment Value of the concern in the hands of a particular investor, not the reasonable third-party buyer required by the definition of market value.[582]

The issue is whether to use pre-tax income amounts and discount rates or post-tax income amounts and discount rates. To understand the magnitude of this issue, a 26%pre-tax rate of return is equivalent to a 16% after-tax rate of return at a 40% income tax rate. As we have previously explained, the impact of using a 16% discount rate in a DCF valuation rather than a 26% rate can be enormous. Contrary to the view of the Fédération des Experts Comptables Européens, many experts will offer testimony regarding lost earnings and profits on a pre-tax basis to avoid double counting the taxes payable on the arbitration award. In contrast, some experts will argue instead that arbitrators should compute damages on an after-tax basis, employing an after-tax discount rate. The resulting present value of the after-tax cash flow would then be "grossed up" to a pre-tax damage award by dividing the after-tax damage award by 1 minus the current marginal tax rate.[583] If properly implemented, this procedure too will avoid double counting the tax burden. Because of the many variables involved in establishing the investor's marginal tax rates now and into the "DCF future," though, many experts prefer to employ pre-tax amounts and discount rates.

578. International Accounting Standard (IAS) 36, at ¶ 55.
579. IVSC DCF Guidance Note, *supra* n. 408, at ¶ 4.3.
580. FEE SME Business Valuation Guide, *supra* n. 17, ¶ 4.4.1.3 at 12–13, ¶ 6.3 at 22–23.
581. *Id.*, ¶ 4.4.25 at 15.
582. The IVSC refers to such as valuation as "*Investment Value, or Worth.* The value of property to a particular investor, or a class of investors, for identified investment or operational objectives." This subjective concept relates specific property to a specific investor, group of investors, or entity with identifiable investment objectives and/or criteria. IVS 2007, Standard 2, Bases Other Than Market Value, *supra* n. 31, at ¶ 3.1.
583. Meyer, Fitzgerald & Moini, "Loss of Business Profits, Risk, and the Appropriate Discount Rate," 4 J. Legal Econ. 27, 34–35 (1994).

We offer no opinion as to the correct choice between the pre-tax and the after-tax procedures. However, we do wish to remind arbitrators again of the need for an apples-to-apples comparison. If one expert is employing a pre-tax approach, while another expert is employing an after-tax approach (grossed-up for income taxes), arbitrators should consider requesting the party-appointed experts to show the impact on their valuations of employing the alternate method. Moreover, if the value of comparable sales transactions or comparable public stock valuations is also in evidence, arbitrators will wish to assure as well that equivalent tax treatment has been used in those valuations to assure comparability of the evidence. It is of course important to remind an expert witness using the after-tax method to gross-up the resulting lower present value cash flow amount for income taxes. Otherwise, the successful claimants will be paying income tax on the compensation award, which itself was reduced on account of that taxation – an obvious instance of double counting.

Another tax issue is noteworthy. Arbitrators should pay attention to the specific tax rates utilized by the experts. In any tax calculation, there are at least two potentially important tax rates; the corporate income tax rate charged by the host jurisdiction to the business itself and the income tax rate payable by the investor. If the compensation measurement is made by reference to the amount at which an independent third party would value the disputed company, then it is appropriate to use customary marginal corporate income tax rates for the first calculation (the investment's corporate taxes). The ASA and the US Internal Revenue Service, for example, employ this procedure as part of their fair market value test. Investment bankers follow the same approach when developing transaction projections.

In Delaware, courts often look to the company's historical tax rate. However, historical tax rates paid by the subject company may not always be the best evidence of the tax rate that should be used by a valuation expert as the "going forward" tax rate in DCF projections of future cash flow. If circumstances have changed that make the historical tax rate inappropriate for use in projections of the future, then the court will be prepared to depart from the company's historical tax rate. For example, in a statutory appraisal case involving the acquisition of a Dr Pepper bottling company by Cadbury Schweppes and the Carlyle Group; the expert for the acquirer (Collins) relied on a 40% tax rate based on historical taxes and comparable companies.[584] The opposing expert, Taylor, argued for a 38.11% tax rate. The Chancery Court stated that "[w]hen available and reliable, the historical tax rate will likely be appropriate."[585] However, the court pointed out that, "owing to its history of rapid expansion, an applicable historical tax rate for Holdings [the company being valued] is not apparent."[586] The court further noted that the models employed by both experts failed to account properly for taxes at the level of the

584. *Crescent/Mach I Partnership, L.P. v. Turner, supra* n. 355, at *11.
585. *Id. See also Cede & Co. v. JRC Acquisition Corp., supra* n. 488, at *10.
586. *Crescent/Mach I Partnership, L.P. v. Turner, supra* n. 355, at *10.

individual states involved (California and Texas).[587] In the circumstances, the court exercised its "equitable judgment"[588] to select 39% as the rate.

> In effect, neither side has proved an appropriate tax rate. The evidence supports an inference that the appropriate rate lies within a range of 38.11% to 40%. Therefore, the Court finds, based on a weighing of the reasonable inferences from the evidence produced at trial, that the appropriate tax rate projection is 39%.[589]

Similarly, the Delaware Court of Chancery recently rejected an argument that a company's historical annual tax rate of 17.8% should have been used in a DCF computation, rather than a 38% tax rate based on statutory rates. As the Chancery Court pointed out, the subject company's "annual historical tax rates for 2001–2005 were significantly lower than the 38% used in management projections or the 40% used in Houlihan Lokey's [the valuation firm's] discounted cash flow analysis only because of losses and loss carry forwards during that period."[590] Since the tax impact of those losses was exhausted by the time of the period covered in the DCF forecast, the company's tax burden during the forecast period would revert to rates that are more ordinary. The Court therefore employed ordinary corporate tax rates, not the much lower historical 17.8% rate.

It is, of course, necessary to investigate what tax rates actually apply in the host jurisdiction – US rates are not appropriate for, say, German companies. In the United States, the marginal corporate tax rate for third-party valuations is usually set at about 40%, summing US Federal, State and local corporate income taxes (and taking into account the Federal deduction for State and local taxes in accordance with standard tax practice). In international arbitrations, of course, the experts should be cautious in using US marginal tax rate assumptions without first considering whether the taxpayer will likely face such a tax framework.

There is a final point to note about the impact of taxes on comparisons between comparable companies located in different countries. Some countries, like the US, rely principally on a corporate income tax. Other countries, like many European states, rely heavily on value added taxes. In comparing earnings, cash flow amounts or multiples, it is essential to make sure that the valuations take account of potential differences in revenue and estimates related to the manner in which a country taxes the activities of enterprise with its jurisdiction.

Turning from the enterprise itself to taxation of the investor, what if the universe of prospective investors must have specific non-generic tax characteristics? Translating that question into plain English by means of an example, what if a US investment is a "Subchapter S corporation" – that is, the company is subject to a requirement that all of its investors be individuals (rather than an enterprise) in order for the company itself to maintain preferred tax treatment? In such

587. *Id.*
588. *Id.*, at *10 n. 64.
589. *Id.*, at *10.
590. *Abrons v. Maree*, 2006 WL 3502908 (Del. Ch. 2006) at *6.

circumstances, a different approach may be appropriate because the particular characteristics of that type of investor will be relevant to the business' fair market value.[591]

The specific tax characteristics of an enterprise have played a role in valuing companies in Delaware dissenting shareholder cases. In *In re Radiology Associates, Inc.*, the court considered the petitioner's argument that the cash flow value of the subject company should be increased to account properly for its Subchapter S (non-taxable) status. The court rejected the particular methodology for making the adjustment proposed by the claimant, but employed an alternate methodology to modify the cash flows so as to recognize the impact of the tax-advantaged status of the Subchapter S business.[592] In *In re Doctors Hospital Of Hyde Park, Inc.*, though, a US bankruptcy court ruled that, for purposes of determining if a Subchapter S hospital was insolvent, it was proper to "tax effect" the company as if it was subject to ordinary taxation (a "C" corporation).[593] According to the bankruptcy court, the first step in valuing an ownership interest in a Subchapter S corporation is to determine if the interest being valued is a minority or a controlling interest. If a controlling interest is being valued, then there should be no difference in value between an S corporation and a C corporation, because the purpose of the insolvency analysis would be to determine the value of the debtor enterprise to a theoretical buyer, "regardless of the nature of the buyer." Since the expert was valuing the entire company, concluded the court, use of ordinary tax rates rather than Subchapter S tax-advantage rates was appropriate. It is not clear whether that approach would be appropriate outside a bankruptcy context.

VI YEAR-END CONVENTION VS. MID-YEAR CONVENTION

A company's revenues and expenses, of course, do not arrive uniformly throughout the year. For example, retail sales in department stores in the United States are heavily weighted towards the last six to seven weeks of the calendar year, the Thanksgiving-to-New Years holiday buying season. In fact, the Friday after Thanksgiving in late November, one of the year's busiest shopping days, is popularly known as "Black Friday" because it is traditionally the date on which retailers shift from the "red" (losses) into the "black" (profits) for the year. Similarly, as many lawyers know, a disproportionately large percentage of the income of a law firm with a significant deal practice will arrive in the last two

591. *See*, for example, *Herlitzke v. Herlitzke*, 2006 WL 2971804 (Wis. Ct. App. 2006), at ¶ 12, affirming a decision by the lower court to accept one party's valuation in a divorce proceeding because that valuation took into account the tax consequences of being a minority shareholder in a Subchapter S corporation.

592. *See* e.g., *In re Radiology Associates, Inc.*, *supra* n. 394, at 494–495; *Delaware Open MRI Radiology Associates, P.A. v. Kessler*, *supra* n. 3, at 326–331.

593. In re Doctors Hospital of Hyde Park, Inc., *supra* n. 470, at 856–857.

months of the year, because clients press hard to close outstanding transactions before their own year-ends. Valuation experts do not think it is practical, however, to apply varying discount rates to DCF cash flow forecasts within different portions of the same fiscal year. The experts, therefore, often make a choice between applying the discount rate to the final net cash flow amount at year-end or instead utilizing an averaging technique called the "mid-year convention."[594] Under the year-end convention, the projected cash flow for the first year in the projection period is discounted from the last day of the first year. The projected cash flow for the second year is discounted from the last day of the second year. Subsequent years are treated similarly. In contrast, under the mid-year convention "the first year's projected cash flow is discounted over a half year (i.e., to =.5)," not the full year. "[T]he second year's projected cash flow is discounted over one and a half years (i.e., to =1.5), and so on."[595]

Compared with a year-end computation, using the mid-year convention will have the effect of accelerating some income and thus slightly increasing the compensation award. In contrast, treating all income as arriving at year-end may have the effect of deferring the timing of some income actually received earlier in the year. Thus, the amount of the award would be slightly decreased if the company actually receives a substantial part of its income earlier in the year. Practicality, rather than theory, often determines the choice an expert makes between these two approaches, as a US estate tax dispute about the value of a famous California champagne house illustrates.

> The parties agree that (1) approximately 60 percent of Korbel's champagne sales occur during the last quarter of the calendar year and (2) as much as 20 percent of such sales occur during the last week of December. Since Korbel's revenues are not spread evenly throughout the year, we are unconvinced that Dr. Spiro's use of the midyear convention results in a more accurate valuation than Dr. Bajaj's use of the yearend convention. We adopt the yearend convention.[596]

Arbitrators should question the experts as to which procedure was employed in the opposing valuation reports, again seeking an apples-to-apples comparison.

A word of caution to arbitrators who have discovered the many present-value calculators on the Web, and are using them to test the sensitivity of net cash flow amounts against different discount rates. Those websites do not disclose whether they utilize year-end or mid-year procedures. Most, however, appear to be set up so that only year-end computations are possible. Therefore, if the expert witness in a particular proceeding is using the mid-year convention and the internet-savvy arbitrator is testing those valuations on the Web for different discount rates, the arbitrator's results will differ as a result.

---

594. *U.S. Inspect, Inc. v. McGreevy*, *supra* n. 82, at 524. *See also Kleinwort Benson Ltd. v. Silgan*, 1995 Del. Ch. LEXIS 75, No. CIV.A. 11107, 1995 WL 376911 (Del. Ch. June 15, 1995).

595. Risius, *Business Valuation: A Primer for Legal Professionals*, *supra* n. 19, at 75 (2007). Risius asserts that most valuation professionals employ the mid-year convention. *Id.*

596. *Estate of Heck v. Comm'r*, *supra* n. 152, at *43.

VII ENTERPRISE VALUE, EQUITY VALUE AND BUSINESS SEGMENTS

An arbitrator may be presented with an "enterprise" valuation rather than an "equity" valuation. An "enterprise" valuation is the common equity value of a business plus debt at market value plus the market value of any minority interests plus the market value of any preferred equity minus cash and cash equivalents. The cash and cash equivalents are deducted, by the way, because an enterprise's value is the sum of its equity value and its net liabilities; the cash is deducted from the debt to arrive at the net liability amount. In contrast, an "equity" valuation is essentially the value to the equity investors of the entire enterprise, but adjusted further to reflect the fact that an equity investor is subordinated to the claims of the debt holders of the company. If the issue before the arbitrators involves measuring the loss of value suffered by an equity investor as a consequence of injury to the underlying business, then the "equity" valuation is clearly the proper measure of the company's value.

Enterprise Value vs Equity Value

If the issue before the arbitrators involves measuring the loss of value suffered by an equity investor as a consequence of injury to the underlying business, the "equity value" is the proper measure of value, the "enterprise value" adjusted to reflect the fact that equity investors are subordinated to claims by the debt holders of the company. Said another way, equity investors are entitled to all the cash flows after the debt holders are fully paid.

At times, of course, the impact of the injury may be felt only by one segment of an enterprise. In that situation, the tribunal will be faced with the question of whether the company is divisible for purposes of valuation and, if so, the impact of that division on the equity investment in the business. The ICSID tribunal in *Enron v. Argentina*[597] faced that issue. In the particular circumstances of that case, the arbitrators concluded that the regulated and non-regulated businesses should be separated for both liability and valuation purposes.

> 176. The Tribunal realizes that there are two different approaches to this question. Looked at from the point of view of the value of equity as expressed in shares, the Respondent's argument has merit. In fact, shares are not divisible and represent an interest in a company as a whole. Their stock market transactions are priced considering this whole, for better or worse. If stock market valuation is chosen as the appropriate method to determine the value of the

597. *Supra* n. 43.

company and eventual compensation for losses, the integration of regulated and non-regulated activities is the natural consequence.

177. There is, however, another approach. The only purpose of the claims brought to the Tribunal is to obtain compensation for losses allegedly suffered as a consequence of government measures. These measures refer only to a sector of activity which is subject to regulation. It follows that if regulated tariffs were the source of the complaint, it is only the consequence of the measures in respect of such tariffs that should be compensated. Conversely, it is quite evident that if the non-regulated sector had been affected by government measures, a claim to the effect that tariffs of the regulated activity should be increased to compensate for that loss would not be admissible. Valuation methodologies do exist so as to measure the damage on an individual sector of the business.

. . .

181. . . . The Tribunal thus concludes that the regulated and the non-regulated sectors of TGS are to be kept separate and independent for the purpose of this claim.[598]

VIII DOUBLE COUNTING

The challenges involved in coming to grip with a DCF valuation are compounded by confusion in adapting modern business valuation techniques to long-standing legal categories for components of a compensation award. The "old Roman law tradition"[599] divides damages components into *damnum emergens* (recovery of reliance interest amounts for the "loss suffered" or "sunk costs," such as lost investment capital) and recovery of the expectation interest as *lucrum cessans* (lost profits). That conceptual division continues today for breach of contract damages in many jurisdictions and in the UNIDROIT Principles of International Commercial Contracts.[600] In some business valuation disputes,[601] arbitrators have awarded both an amount equal to the invested capital as *damnum emergens* and an amount based on DCF projections as *lucrum cessans.* However, the potential for double recovery of invested capital can arise if recovery of sunk

598. *Id.*, at ¶¶ 176–177, 181.

599. Tallon, Damages, Exemption Clauses, and Penalties, 40 Am. J. Comp. L. 675, 677 (1992).

600. *Id. See* UNIDROIT Principles of International Commercial Contracts Art. 7.4.2(1).

601. Wells argues that the *Karaha Bodas* tribunal fell into this error. *See* Wells, *supra* n. 270. Smutny too criticizes the use of *damnum emergens* and *lucrum cessans* ("classically applied to the determination of heads of damages potentially available for breach of contract and tort claims") to determine the economic value of expropriated property. She comments that the discussion of those concepts in expropriations claims "reflects either non-acceptance of fair market value as the standard of compensation, a confused sense of how to determine the fair market value of income-generating assets [citing to the *Amocov. Iran* case], or simply claims for damages owing for tort or breach of contract that are considered as well." Smutny, *supra* n. 115, at 15 (footnote omitted).

investment costs is combined with a DCF valuation. An Income-Based Approach like a DCF forecast calculates the net present value of *all* cash flows an equity investor will receive, including the component of those cash flows that constitutes a recovery by the investor of invested capital (sunk investment costs) as well as the component that constitutes a return on that equity capital (gross profits to the investor). If the arbitrator awards recovery of the invested capital as *damnum emergens* and also separately awards the net present DCF amount as *lucrum cessans*, the investor's recovery will double count the invested capital.

Double Counting

If arbitrators are not wary, dividing a compensation analysis into a reliance interest (*damnum emergens*) and an expectancy interest (*lucrum cessans*), but using a single DCF forecast, can result in double counting. Similar double counting issues may result from the treatment of interest in the award. Also, double counting can occur if the valuation attributes independent value to a piece of equipment and to the revenue-generating contract for use of that equipment by a third party. The valuations should either rely solely on the DCF valuation or adjust the reliance and expectancy components to back out any double counting.

Crawford raises this concern in his Commentaries on the ILC Articles: "A particular concern is the risk of double-counting which arises from the relationship between the capital value of an enterprise and its contractually based profits."[602] That same risk of double counting can apply as well to the value of equipment (i.e., an asset value) and associated contracts that generate revenue by using that equipment (i.e., an income value). Thus, in the Iran-US Claims Tribunal case of *Shahin Shaine Ebrahimi v. Islamic Republic of Iran*, the tribunal stated:

> The Expert was adamant that it was inappropriate to add the net present value of a company's profit margin on its outstanding contracts to the value of its tangible assets. The Expert indicated that "[t]o include in the valuation of [Gostaresh Maskan] both the value of the equipment and the cash flows that this equipment is likely to produce involves double counting." The Expert further pointed out that "this does not imply that the existence of these contracts is irrelevant to the value of [Gostaresh Maskan], but only that the value of the contracts cannot be regarded as additional to that of the assets."[603]

The net cash flow of a DCF forecast includes recovery of the investments made by investors in the business out of the cash flow available for distribution to equity

602. Commentaries, *supra* n. 96, at 258 (¶ 26).
603. *Shahin Shaine Ebrahimi v. Islamic Republic of Iran*, Award No. 560-44-3, 30 Iran-US C.T.R. 170, ¶ 159 (1994).

investors (i.e., the recovery of invested equity capital). Thus, it would be double counting for arbitrators to award a successful claimant recovery of its invested equity and also to award as "lost profits" the full present value of the discounted net cash flow of the company. Instead, the award should either provide for DCF damages alone or provide for recovery of invested capital and DCF net future earnings, with a rather complicated adjustment to remove the recovered capital from the earnings computation.[604] If arbitrators do rely upon the categories of sunk investment costs and lost profits to calculate compensation, it will be necessary to back out of an Income-Based forecast any amounts attributable to invested capital separately recovered as *damnum emergens* to avoid such double counting.[605]

Translating the Roman law concepts of *damnum emergens* and *lucrum cessans* collectively into an investment valuation is, consequently, a very challenging exercise. A prudent arbitrator may prefer to not subdivide the overall commercial valuation data into the two legal categories of *damnum emergens* (reliance interest) and *lucrum cessans* (expectation interest). Instead, if the parties have offered evidence of the overall market value of a business concern, the arbitrator may choose to focus on a single valuation method that captures both recovery of invested capital and a return on that capital.

Another double-counting risk to be noted by arbitrators may result from the treatment of interest in an award with both *damnum emergens* and *lucrum cessans* components. If the arbitrators' award properly computed lost profits (*lucrum cessans)*, it will be important to assure that any separately computed award for recovery of invested capital (*damnum emergens*) does not provide for accrual of interest on that invested capital from the date of investment until the award date. Accrual of interest in that situation is improper "simply because the capital sum cannot be simultaneously earning interest and generating profits."[606]

Still another case of double counting is sometimes incorrectly asserted. Critics of forward-looking compensation awards point out that, as soon as the successful claimant receives the awarded amount, it will immediately reinvest that amount in another profit-making venture. Therefore, argue these critics, the investor is getting a double profit recovery; once as part of the DCF-based award and a second time through reinvestment of the awarded sum.[607]

---

604. *See Patuha v. PLN Final Award, supra* n. 239, at ¶ 360. *See also* Wells, *supra* n. 270, at 474–475.
605. As Paulsson says, "The central idea is surpassingly simple. Once there is an award of *damnum emergens*, there must be a corresponding debit before any *lucrum cessans* is recoverable". Paulsson, "The Expectation Model", *supra* n. 241, at 62. The *Karaha Bodas* award expressly stated that it took account of the risk of double counting. However, that award does not explain the process used by the arbitral panel to avoid double counting, and therefore is easily criticized. *See* Wells, *supra* n. 270, at 474. CCF and ABV valuations are subject to the same risk as DCF valuations in this regard, to the extent they incorporate amounts attributable to invested capital.
606. Commentaries, *supra* n. 96, at 202 (¶ 33).
607. *See*, e.g., Bowett, Claims Between States and Private Entities: The Twilight Zone of International Law, 35 Catholic L. Rev. 929, 941 (1986); Wells, *supra* n. 270, at 475.

However, if the purpose of a compensation award is "to re-establish the situation that would, in all probability, have existed if that act [the unlawful injury] had not been committed,"[608] then the alleged double recovery does not occur. The DCF amount represents the sum of future earnings for the investor, just received early in a lump sum and reduced to reflect that early receipt by "present valuing" the gross amount at the specified discount rate. If the injury had not been committed, and therefore the claimant had received those earnings periodically in the future, the claimant at the time of receipt would have reinvested those periodic payments in other profitable ventures. The receipt of a lump sum award just means that the reinvestment occurs earlier. And the receipt of a reduced lump sum (the discounted present value) means that reinvestment of the smaller lump sum should not produce greater profits from reinvestment than would have been the case if the reinvestment had instead occurred in the ordinary course of the business; periodically in the future and in a larger aggregate amount. If the DCF amount is properly discounted to a present value sum, no double recovery will occur.[609]

IX SPECIFIC FORECAST ITEMS: NON-OPERATING ASSETS, INTEREST, FOREIGN EXCHANGE RATES AND MINORITY INTERESTS AS ILLUSTRATIONS

In addition to the more general elements discussed above, a DCF cash flow forecast will naturally also be affected by the expert's estimates of the amounts to put into each individual revenue or expense line item. With perhaps hundreds of line items to consider, it is sensible to limit ourselves to a few examples – treatment of non-operating assets, the role of interest rates[610] and foreign exchange rates in the forecasts, and the value of a company's minority ownership interests in other companies.

1 NON-OPERATING ASSETS

As previously mentioned, non-core assets of a business are excluded from the cash flow computation. Non-core assets (i.e., non-operating assets) have value, of course, and must therefore be separately accounted for in the valuation. For Income-Based methods like DCF, CCF and APV, the income and expenses

608. Chorzów Factory, *supra* n. 167, at 47.
609. Walde & Sabahi, *supra* n. 331, at 23, have also argued that selection of an overly low discount rate (neglecting the risk associated with the investment) in a DCF projection will lead to "double recovery." If the chosen discount rate for a DCF forecast is too low, then the resulting present value amount will be too high. Equally, if the chosen discount rate is too high, then the resulting present value amount will be too low and the claimant will be undercompensated.
610. We will leave to others a discussion of the perennially popular issue of whether simple or compound interest on the compensation amount should be awarded. We do consider computation issues for post-award interest in Ch. 9 below.

associated with the non-operating assets must be isolated and excluded from cash flow projections. For Market-Based methods like comparative stock prices and sales transactions, revenues and expenses from non-operating assets must also be isolated and excluded. The excluded assets should then be separately valued using standard valuation procedures for those assets, and added back to reach a total valuation. Moreover, the impact of non-operating assets should also be excluded from the numerator and denominator of any market multiples drawn from comparable companies or comparable transactions; otherwise, the non-core operations of the comparable would be included as a factor in the valuation of the business even though the non-operating assets of the comparable likely are not central to the activities of the business being valued or relevant to comparability.[611]

Risius illustrates the procedure for isolating the impact of non-operating assets by means of a manufacturing company with two divisions, North America and Asia.[612] In the example, the Asian division is scheduled for liquidation because of poor performance. To properly value the manufacturing company, the valuation identifies the cash flow of the North American division using a 5X EBITDA method. Separately, the valuation calculates the liquidation value (not the EBITDA value) of the Asian division. The two values are then added together to reach the total enterprise value.

Occasionally, experts offer different lists of non-operating assets to be excluded from the company's core operations. Typically, a non-operating asset is one that can be removed from the company without impairing its ability to conduct business. Common examples may include excess vacant land, marketable securities and fixed assets held in a poorly performing division of the business that is going to be liquidated.[613] The determination of whether an asset is part of core operations and properly included, or a non-operating asset and properly excluded, depends on the specifics of each business and the available evidence.

2 Interest Rates

Projected interest amounts comprise a cash flow expense item. The amount, of course, is subject to variation depending on the interest rate selected for use in the projections. Arbitrators should inquire as to whether competing DCF valuations

---

611. Risius, *Business Valuation: A Primer for Legal Professionals*, *supra* n. 19, at 124–126. Similarly, AICPA Valuation Standard SSVS 1, at ¶ 41, instructs valuation analysts, when valuing a controlling interest using an Income-Based method, to exclude from the value of the operating assets any non-operating assets, non-operating liabilities, or excess or deficient operating assets. Those excluded items should then be added to the value of the operating entity. If, however, a non-controlling ownership (e.g., minority) interest is being valued, then the valuation analyst must consider whether or not to exclude those items, "depending on the valuation analyst's assessment of the influence exercisable by the non-controlling interest." No exclusion is appropriate, though, for valuations employing Asset-Based methods.
612. Risius, *Business Valuation: A Primer for Legal Professionals*, *supra* n. 19, at 125–126.
613. *Id.*

contain comparable interest rate assumptions. If the valuations offered by opposing parties differ widely in their interest rate assumptions, then it may be appropriate for the arbitrators to request that the parties re-run their projections with common interest rate assumptions, to promote comparability of the competing forecasts. That same approach may be sensible as well for other material aspects of the debt load of the company, including the estimated principal amount, tenor and schedule of repayments for that debt.

Arbitral panels are naturally reluctant to substitute their own views as to the reasonableness of expenditure choices made by the company.[614] As the arbitrators in the *Karaha Bodas* dispute explained:

> 100. With regard to the Respondents' other argument alleging that part of KBC's expenditures totaling US $32.2 Million (Thirty Two Million and Two Hundred Thousand U.S. Dollars) were wasteful as a result of its poorly conceived and inefficient exploration program which conferred no benefit on PERTAMINA according to the Respondents' Expert Reports submitted in the present proceedings, the present Arbitral Tribunal is in full agreement with the rule clearly stated by the Himpurna Arbitral Tribunal, according to which:
>
> *"In the case of a breach of contract, the wasted cost is what the Claimant has spent in reliance on the agreement, without reference to how judicious or providential those expenditures turned out to be" (Himpurna California Energy Ltd – Bermuda Case, Final Award, § 445 at pp. 130–131).*
>
> Indeed, the Respondents' breach has deprived the Claimant's expenditures of any value for the Claimant. The Respondents are not entitled to question now their original appropriateness since they have put the Claimant in a position where it cannot take any advantage of them for the benefit of the Project and demonstrate in concreto their usefulness.
>
> 101. Accordingly, the Claimant has as a matter of principle to be compensated for all the proven sunken costs which were incurred with regard to activities carried out in reality, without any need to enter into an ex post facto debate about whether such expenditures were reasonable and profitable or not. In other words, the Claimant is entitled to recover all costs and investments adequately proven and directly related to the works undertaken in implementation of the Contracts concluded with the Respondents.
>
> 102. The same test applies with regard to the expenditures paid to KBC's local shareholder PT Sumarah and which are claimed by the Respondents to be questionable. Nothing in the records sustains any accusation of impropriety with regard to PT Sumarah involvement as a publicly disclosed shareholder of KBC whose name appears on the Financial Statements and Reports submitted to both Respondents. The sums received by the said local Partner as

614. *See Patuha v. PLN Final Award*, *supra* n. 239, at ¶¶ 369–372. But *see Azurix v. Argentina*, *supra* n. 17, at ¶¶ 240, 413, 426–429, where the tribunal concluded that Azurix dramatically overpaid for an Argentine water company.

> "financing expenses" and "head office expenses" were openly declared and contained in the expenditures communicated to the Respondents and which did not raise any objection until recently in the course of the present proceedings. The mere fact that the said expenses took the form of an agreed percentage does not imply dissimulating improper payments. Hence, the Arbitral Tribunal considers the allegations about the unwarranted nature of such payments unfounded, and consequently rejects the objection to their reimbursement.[615]

Of course, arbitrators may have fewer qualms about verifying whether the expenditures were in fact incurred.[616] In those situations, interest computations may play a role in calculating the amount of capital invested in an enterprise. In many projects, for example, the equity investors will initially provide capital in the form of deeply subordinated development-phase loans to the company rather than equity contributions. The disbursed sums from such development-phase loans are applied to the payment of goods and services used for the benefit of the company. Therefore, such loans properly constitute invested capital. Like any other loans, those development-phase loans will accrue interest at an interest rate agreed between the borrower and the affiliated lender. When the project reaches financial close and independent lenders disburse their own debt financing, the equity investors will often capitalize their development-phase loans, together with the accrued and unpaid interest, by foregoing their right to payment of the outstanding principal of the development-phase loans and accrued interest thereon. Instead, the investors will treat the sums as invested equity capital.

By itself, that is perfectly legitimate commercial behavior designed to protect the investor from competing third-party creditors of the project during the development phase. However, if the investor controls the company, the rates and other terms upon which interest has accrued on those development-phase loans may not have been negotiated in an arm's length manner. In such circumstances, the arbitrator may wish to pay particular attention to the interest rate specified for the development-phase loans. For example, the author is familiar with a power project financing where the sponsor selected an artificially fast compounding period for interest accruing on the development-phase loans. The project was founded upon a power purchase agreement containing a fixed tariff. The tariff in the power purchase agreement incorporated a pre-agreed rate of return based on the amount of the sponsor's equity contribution. The controlling sponsor provided cash in the sum of about USD 5,000,000 as development-phase capital for two years in the form of deeply subordinated loans, all prior to borrowing from commercial lenders. When the commercial loans were finally disbursed, the total amount of the development-phase loans and interest accrued thereon was capitalized as the sponsor's

615. Karaha Bodas Final Award, *supra* n. 270, at ¶¶ 100–102.

616. In *Siemens v. Argentina*, the Argentine Republic sought appointment of a tribunal expert to verify actual expenditures of invested capital recorded on the company's audited financial statements. The tribunal, though, rejected that request in light of the audited nature of the financial statements and the absence of convincing evidence that the sums were not properly spent. *See* text associated with n. 857 et seq. *infra*.

equity contribution (i.e., the basis for the pre-agreed rate of return under the power purchase agreement). Promissory notes accruing interest at 8% per annum, a perfectly reasonable rate at that time, evidenced the development-phase loans. However, closer inspection revealed that the 8% interest on the notes was stated to be payable monthly during the development period, with the interest accruing during each month being capitalized as additional principal at the end of the month (i.e., compounded monthly). For the next month, interest accrued at the 8% rate on the new larger capitalized sum, and so on for each month until financial close. Thus, the 8% notes compounded monthly during the development phase for about twenty-four months.

The effect of that monthly compounding was to increase the sum of invested capital by a significant amount, enabling the controlling investor to receive its pre-agreed rate of return under the tariff on a clearly higher capital amount despite actually having disbursed a lower cash amount. At 8% simple interest, the sponsor's effective rate of return would have been 16% for the two-year development phase of the project. At annual compounding, the effective rate of return would have been 16.64%. If semi-annual compounding had been employed instead, the sponsor's effective rate of return would have been 16.99%. But by compounding monthly for the two-year period, the sponsor showed a 17.29% effective rate of return. The sponsor's capitalized equity contribution therefore comprised the original USD 5 million plus an amount calculated as the 17.29% rate of return thereon for the two years. Over the power project's twenty-year concession period and for large enough invested amounts, the dollar value of those differences can be significant (more than enough to pay an arbitrator's fees!). Faced with such a situation in an arbitration, a careful arbitrator would seek testimony as to the reasonableness of monthly compounding in the circumstances.[617] If the arbitrator concluded that interest had been compounded too frequently, then the next issue would be how to correct the calculation to value properly the company.

A similar issue arose in the *Siemens v. Argentina* proceeding. As explained by the *Siemens* tribunal, "*prima facie*, capitalization of interest during the development phase of an investment is normal practice." In that project, Siemens contributed only 27 million ARS as equity capital to the investment (SITS) but over ARS 225 million as debt capital. Interest on the debt capital accrued and compounded at different rates and times; three-month rollover credit at 12.08% in 1998–1999, twelve-month rollover credit in 2000 at 9% and again three-month rollover credit in 2001 at 14%. The tribunal held that capitalization of those development-phase loans was appropriate. However, the tribunal determined that interest on the development-phase loans to be included in the capitalized

617. In this situation, a development loan was made to an investment vehicle, with interest on the loan compounding monthly. Those circumstances are quite different from the issue of compounding pre- or post-award interest on the compensation granted by the arbitral panel. The commercial circumstances with respect to compound interest on a development-phase loan do not necessarily mirror the commercial re-investment and policy issues governing post-default interest.

amount should be calculated on the basis of a 2.35% interest rate (based on Siemens' cost of borrowing, hedged by potential interest rate swaps). The tribunal therefore capitalized only a percentage of interest on the development phase loans in the proportion that the assumed cost of borrowing (2.35%) bore to the interest rate charged to SITS (12.08% for 1998–1999, 9% for 2000 and 14% for 2001). The equity contribution amount accepted by the tribunal therefore included the principal amount of Siemens' development loans plus only that reduced portion of the accrued interest on the development loans.[618]

3 Foreign Exchange Rates

For cross-border transactions, both revenue and expense estimates can also be very sensitive to the foreign exchange rates selected for the projections. In the *CMS v. Argentina* dispute, the ICSID tribunal selected a foreign exchange conversion rate of ARS 2.97/USD 1, rather than the ARS 3.59/USD 1 rate proposed by the claimant – about a 17.3% appreciation in value for the Argentina peso.[619] The tribunal calculated the investor's compensation in that case as the difference between a "no pesification" scenario and the reduced value of the investment after giving effect to Argentina's pesification measure. With revenues and operating expenses denominated in ARS (after pesification), but the company's debt still payable in USD, the tribunal's choice of a more favorable exchange rate produced noticeably greater net cash flows and thus a smaller difference between the two scenarios. The effect of the tribunal's foreign exchange rate decision was to reduce the compensation award in that case by many millions of dollars.

4 Minority Interests

There are times when an income measure such as DCF does not fully capture the market value of an operating company. Some assets held by the company have value, but do not generate cash that shows up in cash flow (revenues minus expenses). One example is the ownership by the company of a minority shareholding in another company. The only impact of that minority interest on cash flow would be either the receipt of dividends, if the issuer of the stock paid dividends on those shares, or the receipt of the proceeds of disposition of the minority interest,

618. *Siemens v. Argentina*, *supra* n. 112, at ¶¶ 370–372. It appears in the tribunal's revised computation that interest in excess of 2.35% was written off, that interest on the development-phase loans at 2.35% was capitalized, and that the compounding dates were left unchanged. The award is silent as to whether the panel's choice of a 2.35% rate as the "hedged" cost of Siemens' borrowing included or excluded the cost of the up-front fees paid by Siemens to obtain the hedges. Given market interest rates at the time, though, it seems likely the tribunal excluded the cost of up-front fees for the hedges. Those up-front fees should certainly have been included to determine Siemens' "all in" cost of borrowing, not excluded.

619. *CMS v. Argentina*, *supra* n. 7, at ¶ 449.

if the company being valued disposed of the shares. The minority interest may have significant value, however, whether or not the issuer of the shares is paying dividends. Many companies do not pay dividends even though an acquirer would pay a large sum to purchase an ownership interest in that company – the fair market value of the minority interest. Therefore, to obtain a complete picture of the fair market value of the company at issue in the dispute, it will be necessary to add to the final valuation the fair market value of assets such as the minority interest that are not captured by a cash flow test.

Chapter 5

Adjusted Present Value (APV) Method

Increasingly, valuation experts are employing a valuation method within the Income-Based Approach known as the Adjusted Present Value (APV) method. APV is normally used as a variant of the DCF method, but does not employ a weighted average cost of capital (WACC) calculation. By utilizing the APV procedure, the valuation can separate out and account for the tax attributes of debt and the incremental bankruptcy risk created by adding additional debt.[620] The APV method can be used as an adjustment, by the way, to a CCF valuation as well.

The DCF method and the APV method both seek to measure the same fair market value of a company, the company's "enterprise value." In Chapter 4, we discussed a method in which the enterprise value of the company is essentially equal to the market value of its equity plus the market value of its debt. When valuation professionals use the APV method, they measure the company's enterprise value as the value of the company without debt (the "unlevered enterprise") plus the present value of the tax savings from the company's debt.[621]

620. FEE SME Business Valuation Guide, *supra* n. 17, ¶ 7.3.3 at 30. *See also* Senechal, Dealing with Uncertainty: Discounted Cash Flow (DCF) Versus Adjusted Present Value (APV), *supra* n. 438.

621. *Id.*, at 4.

Adjusted Present Value (APV)

The APV method is a variant of the DCF method, but does not employ WACC. An APV valuation estimates

- the expected cash flow of the enterprise (just like the DCF/WACC method;
- the unleveraged cost of equity (often using CAPM);
- the expected future capital structure of the enterprise;
- the discount rate to be applied to the reduction in income taxes that results from the enterprise taking a tax deduction for interest expense on its debt (the so-called 'tax shield');
- the incremental bankruptcy risk created through the incurrence of additional debt;
- the long-term growth rate of the enterprise's free cash flow and its debt;
- the discount rate for the tax shield;
- the equity cost of capital as the discount rate for the other components of the APV valuation.

The APV method keeps the company's debt amount fixed over time. In contrast, the DCF/WACC method keeps the debt-to-equity ratio fixed over time.

An APV valuation of a company calls for estimates of (i) expected cash flow (like the DCF/WACC method), (ii) the unleveraged cost of equity (often using a CAPM procedure for that purpose), (iii) the expected future capital structure of the company, (iv) the discount rate to be applied to the "tax shield" (a "tax shield" is the reduction in income taxes that results from taking an allowable deduction from taxable income, here the deduction for interest expenses on debt), (iv) the incremental bankruptcy risk created through the incurrence of additional debt and (v) the "steady-state long-term growth rate of free cash flow and debt" for the company. Senechal offers the following suggestions to help determine when use of the APV method or the DCF/WACC method is more appropriate in a particular case.[622]

- If a firm's leverage ratio (debt to total assets) is constant, then the DCF/WACC method is easier as only one discount rate needs to be calculated.
- If a firm's leverage ratio is not constant, then it is easier to use the APV method.

622. Senechal, Dealing with Uncertainty: Discounted Cash Flow (DCF) Versus Adjusted Present Value (APV), *supra* n. 438, at 4.

- If a firm's leverage ratio changes over time, then the WACC discount rate will have to be continually recalculated, which can be extremely cumbersome.
- To calculate the tax shields under the APV method, one needs to know the firm's marginal tax rate.[623]

The APV method employs a discount rate for the tax shields that will be different from the discount rate derived from the cost of equity capital. Therefore, arbitrators will wish to understand in detail how the expert has derived the tax shield discount rate used in the valuation evidence. In addition, the changes in the projections to reflect a company's changes in its future debt-equity capital structure will be a crucial item of estimation, since those changes will affect the difference (if any) between a valuation generated on the basis of a DCF/WACC methodology and on the basis of an APV valuation. Finally, the APV method calls for an estimation of the "effect of borrowing the amount [of debt] on the probability that the firm will go bankrupt." That probability estimate will be another critical difference between a DCF/WACC valuation and an APV valuation of the same company.

As is apparent, to use the APV method it is necessary to first compute the value of the "unlevered enterprise." To do so, the valuation will calculate the company's operating free cash flow; which is the "[f]ree cash flow of the company after tax assuming the company is financed entirely with equity. This is net of capex [capital expenditures] and tax, but not depreciation and interest. The tax is calculated without the interest tax deduction."[624] Once the operating cash flow is determined, it is discounted to a present value at an "unlevered" discount rate; i.e., at a rate derived solely from the (normally higher) cost of equity capital alone.

Then, the valuation makes a separate calculation to determine the present value of the debt tax shield. One simple way to do this is to multiply the company's corporate tax rate by the market value of its debt. While that formula helps to show the importance of the debt tax shield, it is not always useful for a credible valuation because it relies on two assumptions; that the company will always be profitable enough to pay the full corporate tax rate each year and that the amount of the company's debt will be fixed in perpetuity.[625] Of course, if a WACC calculation of the company's discounted cash flow is used instead, a different problematic assumption is often made; that the company's debt will always be a constant proportion of company value.[626] In that case, the WACC procedure will incorporate the impact of the debt tax shield by using a lower discount rate, the averaging of the higher equity cost of capital and the lower debt cost of capital. However, for the APV method, the discount rate used to calculate the present value of the tax savings (the debt tax shield) may be different from WACC. If, unlike the WACC

---

623. *Id.*, at 5.
624. *Id.*, at 5.
625. *Id.* In essence, this formula assumes the company will be profitable but never grow. One example of such a company, though, is a single asset power project enterprise with a long-term power purchase agreement.
626. *See* text associated with n. 491 *supra*.

method, the company's leverage ratio may change over time, then the debt tax shield has to be forecast year by year to reflect projected shifts in that ratio.[627] If the valuation expert decides the tax shield has the same risk as the company's operating cash flows, then the proper discount rate will be the unlevered (cost of equity) rate. If, though, the amount of debt is not expected to vary with the success of the company, then the proper discount rate may be the debt rate.

Finally, the valuation will also deduct an amount calculated as the incremental bankruptcy risk created through the incurrence of additional debt. The sum of the unlevered enterprise value less debt, adjusted for the positive addition for the interest tax shield and the negative deduction for bankruptcy risk, will be the equity valuation for the enterprise.

As Senechal remarks:

> The adjusted present value is equal to the sum of the value of the unleveraged company and the value of tax shield less the present value of financial distress costs. Each of these components is discounted at different rates representing the different risks. APV is obtained in three steps. First, we begin by estimating the value of the firm with no leverage. We then consider the present value of the interest tax savings generated by borrowing a given amount of money. Finally, we evaluate the effect of borrowing the amount on the probability that the firm will go bankrupt.[628]

Proponents argue that the APV method improves upon traditional DCF calculations because APV will take direct account of financing and tax benefits such as the tax deductibility of interest.

To illustrate how important the tax deduction for interest expense can be to the value of a business, let us look at a somewhat oversimplified example. Multiplying the amount of the debt by the tax rate is, as noted above, one means of assessing the value of the debt tax shield. If 30% of a company's capital is debt and that company faces a 40% corporate tax rate, then the debt tax shield would contribute 12% to the company's total value. If the company's leverage doubles to 60%, which is still well below the leverage ratio for many project finance companies and other highly-leveraged entities, then the tax shield contributes almost a quarter of the company's value, 24%.[629] This sensitivity of a company's market value to tax benefits helps explain why tax lawyers and accountants are so well paid!

The value of a debt tax shield is the tax savings to the debtor, here the company, of making interest payments on debt as compared with making the same amount of payments as dividends on equity. In *Citizens Federal Bank, FSB v. U.S.*, the US Court of Federal Claims awarded the claimant damages for

---

627. Cooper & Nyberg, Cooper & Nyborg, Valuing the Debt Tax Shield, NHH Dept. of Finance & Management Science Discussion Paper No. 2007/15 (March 27, 2007), available at <http://papers.ssrn.coom/sol3/papers.cfm?abstract_id=979910>, at 24.

628. Senechal, Dealing with Uncertainty: Discounted Cash Flow (DCF) Versus Adjusted Present Value (APV), *supra* n. 438, at 3.

629. Cooper & Nyberg, Valuing the Tax Shield, *supra* n. 627, at 2.

the lost "tax consequences" of being required by the US Government to exchange subordinated debt for preferred stock pursuant to the Financial Institutions Reform, Recovery and Enforcement Act of 1989 (FIRREA) in contravention of prior Federal regulatory and contractual assurances.[630]

> It is well-established that "tax consequences" are "an element of damages when they are reasonably foreseeable and flow from the breach." . . . Accordingly, the court held that Citizens is entitled to damages sustained from the loss of its interest tax shield. . . . The evidence adduced at trial demonstrated the amount of such damages, $14.615 million, to a reasonable degree of certainty.[631]

The APV valuation isolates the net effect of using debt as a source of capital on the company's value, by considering both the benefits and the costs of borrowing. One primary benefit of borrowing, as compared with financing a company solely through equity capital, is a tax benefit – interest paid on the debt by the company is tax deductible in most countries. The APV analysis therefore considers the present value of the interest tax savings to the company generated by borrowing a given amount of money.[632] The APV method will consider as well the costs of the borrowing. Apart from the differences between the rate of return on debt as compared with the rate of return on equity capital, the most significant cost of relying on debt finance rather than equity finance is the added risk that the enterprise will become bankrupt because it is carrying more liabilities.

Under the APV method, the valuation forecast will keep the company's debt amount fixed over time. Tax benefits are computed based on this debt amount and form part of the cash flow calculations. The expected bankruptcy cost is also based upon this fixed debt amount. In contrast, in the WACC procedure the company's debt-to-equity ratio, not the debt amount itself, is kept fixed over time. If a company is growing, then of course, the company will need to borrow additional debt sums to maintain the same debt-to-equity ratio.

Attention to the role of interest tax shields has grown with the increases in the leveraged acquisitions during the past few years, reviving an acquisition technique that led to the LBO boom of the 1980s and a number of prominent insolvencies at the end of that decade. In the US, valuation of an interest tax shield has become more complicated since the 2003 income tax cuts introduced different tax rates for dividends than for interest.[633] Moreover, the picture is complicated if a tax system is not perceived as permanent; for example, the risk that the 2003 US tax cuts will be reversed in the future has to be taken into account in any separate debt tax shield valuation.

---

630. *Citizens Federal Bank, FSB v. U.S.*, 66 Fed. Cl. 179 (June 30, 2005).
631. *Id.*, at 78.
632. For a useful discussion of how to value a tax shield from interest expense, *see* Cooper & Nyborg, Valuing the Tax Shield, *supra* n. 627.
633. Similar differences between tax rates for dividends and for interest exist in other countries with an "imputation" tax system under which investors are permitted to claim back part of the corporate tax when dividends are distributed, such as Australia, France and Germany.

> In some cases where the tax system currently favors dividends over interest, such as the U.S. at the present time [2007], that tax regime may not be expected to continue. Valuing the debt tax shield for a company involves predicting the net tax saving from interest for the indefinite future. The use of a net tax saving significantly less than the full corporate tax rate requires that the tax system favor equity returns – for example, due to a lower tax on dividends than interest – one case where this clearly applies is in those countries that have had imputation tax systems for a long time, such as Australia, France, and Germany. This was also the case in the U.K. prior to the unexpected change in the tax system in 1997.[634]

Arbitrators will need to be satisfied that the APV forecast takes account of both the benefits and the costs of additional borrowings. WACC and APV address differently the issue of bankruptcy costs (i.e., the risk that the enterprise will be more likely to become insolvent because it has more debt). The APV approach enables the valuation to consider both direct and indirect bankruptcy costs. But, "[i]n practice, analysts who use APV add the expected tax benefits from debt to the unlevered firm value and all too often ignore expected bankruptcy costs (which are difficult to estimate)."[635]

A 1993 US estate tax dispute illustrates one of the few litigated cases in which tax shields were explicitly considered as a reduction to enterprise value. In that case, the family's expert valuation witness (May) employed what the US Tax Court called an "Unlevered Capital Factor" analysis, which adjusted a CCF valuation by separately calculating the impact of tax shields but not addressing incremental bankruptcy risk.[636] May calculated the value of Hutchens Industries, Inc. (HII), the nation's then-largest manufacturer of trailer-truck suspensions, by using an unleveraged capitalization rate (which thus incorporated a discount rate based on the equity cost of capital, not the weighted average cost of debt and equity capital). Then, among other adjustments, he added back to the CCF amount the present value of tax shields for inter alia HII's debt of 2,083, 619.[637] May reached a final enterprise value for HII of USD 17,820,000, including a present value amount for the tax shields of USD 406,358. The tax shields therefore constituted about 2.3% of HII's value, based on less than 12% debt capital (a very low proportion of debt to equity).

To our knowledge, the APV method has not yet made its way into any published arbitration awards; it is, of course, only a matter of time.[638]

---

634. Cooper & Nyborg, Valuing the Debt Tax Shield, *supra* n. 627, at 10–11.
635. Damodaran, The Adjusted Present Value Approach, available at <http://pages.stern.nyu.edu/~adamodar/New_Home_Page/valquestions/apv.htm>. *See*, illustratively, *Lewis G. Hutchens Non-Marital Trust v. Comm'r*, T.C. Memo 1993-600 (16 December 1993).
636. *Lewis G. Hutchens Non-Marital Trust v. Comm'r*, *supra* n. 635, at *44 et seq.
637. *Id.*, at *45.
638. But *see* Senechal, Dealing with Uncertainty: Discounted Cash Flow (DCF) Versus Adjusted Present Value (APV), *supra* n. 438 ("APV methodologies are now commonly used in litigation for estimating the pecuniary value of damage in investment disputes"). Senechal discusses the use of both APV and DCF/WACC methods in a recent international arbitration proceeding involving an Eastern European investment to manage hotels and other tourist facilities.

Chapter 6

Capitalized Cash Flow (CCF) Method

I INTRODUCTION

Where historical earnings information is available for a business, an expert may seek to project future earnings on the basis of that prior earnings information. The expert may thus employ the Capitalized Cash Flow (CCF) method (also known as the Capitalization of Earnings method). Like the DCF method, a CCF valuation is an Income-Based method. Valuation experts often prefer to employ the CCF method for companies with significant intangible assets and few fixed assets.[639] For situations where the investment's income is expected to grow at a steady rate based on past experience, a CCF valuation will (i) identify the historical income amount (often, either last year's EBITDA, or another "market multiple," or an average of that multiple over the past several years), (ii) *multiply* that income amount by the rate at which the income amount is expected to grow in the future and then (iii) *divide* the resulting sum by a discount rate minus the same expected growth rate.

> In capitalizing, instead of projecting each future increment of income and dividing it by the discount rate compounded for some number of years into the future, we select a single expected number and simply divide that number by a rate of return that we call a *capitalization rate*.[640]

A CCF valuation relies on a company's historical income amounts. Consequently, the reliability of the CCF method depends crucially on the reliability of those historical figures. If those amounts are misstated (Enron or Parmalat?), then the

639. *See Gonsalves v. Straight Arrow Publishers, Inc.*, *supra* n. 355, at 319, n. 18.
640. The Lawyer's Business Valuation Handbook, *supra* n. 411, at 108.

resulting CCF valuation will be correspondingly wrong. If the historical income amounts are, for whatever reason, not a good predictor of future income amounts, then again the CCF valuation will prove inaccurate. Investors and acquirers, particularly in the private equity field, regularly rely on the CCF method of valuation for their business transactions.[641] Thus, arbitrators often will see CCF evidence when those transactions give rise to disputes.

Capitalized Cash Flow (CCF) Method

In the Capitalized Cash Flow (CCF) Method (also know as the Capitalization of Earnings Method), the valuation identifies the company's historical income amount (often, that company's EBITDA or, if not available, the EBITDA of a comparable company). That income amount is multiplied by the rate at which the income amount is expected to grow in the future (the growth rate). The resulting sum is then divided by a discount rate minus the growth rate (the capitalization rate). The discount rate for a CCF valuation is computed in the same fashion as a DCF discount rate. A CCF valuation is proper if the future is expected to look like the past. The CCF valuation is particularly sensitive to the choice of the historical income number, the choice of the discount rate and the choice of the growth rate.

Just like the DCF method, the CCF method can be applied on the basis of either Indirect Equity (Total Invested Capital) or Direct Equity procedures.[642]

Under the indirect equity (Total Invested Capital) procedure, the numerator of the multiple will be the sum of the market value of equity and interest-bearing debt. That sum is divided by the chosen multiplier (e.g., EBITDA) to determine the multiple for total invested capital. To calculate the equity value of the company, the valuation subtracts interest-bearing debt from the total.[643] Conversely, under the direct equity application, the numerator is solely the market value of equity. That amount is divided by the chosen multiplier (e.g., EBITDA) to determine the multiple for the equity value.

Perhaps an illustration that employs a 3% short-term growth rate, a 3% long-term growth rate and a 13% discount rate, will make this all more concrete. Let us assume that the International Arbitration Centre, Ltd. (IAC) had EBITDA last year (2007) of USD 1,000,000, and we are seeking to value the company on a CCF basis in 2008. We expect IAC's growth rate in earnings for the indefinite future to be 3% per annum. In our wisdom, we have determined that IAC's weighted average cost of capital (and thus the discount rate in our example) is 13%. The process for

641. "International Private Equity Valuation Guidelines," *supra* n. 26 at 15–18; US Private Equity Valuation Guidelines, *supra* n. 24, ¶¶ 35–40 at 9.
642. *See* Ch. 4.II.
643. Risius, *Business Valuation: A Primer for Legal Professionals*, *supra* n. 19, at 98–99.

specifying the discount rate used in this calculation is, by the way, the same as the process used for selecting the discount rate in the DCF method. Consequently, the prediction of a future growth rate for the company's income is tempered by the use of a discount rate incorporating the risks and uncertainties faced by the company. The formula for calculating the present value of the International Arbitration Centre by means of the CCF method would be:

$$\text{IAC's Present Value} = \frac{\text{USD } 1{,}000{,}000\ (1 + .03)}{(.13 - .03)} = \frac{\text{USD } 1{,}030{,}000}{.10} = \text{USD } 10{,}300{,}000$$

More fully, the CCF formula is as follows:

A.	Debt-free Distributable Cash Flow (last year)	USD 1,000,000
B.	Growth Rate	3.0%
C.	Debt-Free Distributable Cash Flow (One-Year Forward) C = A × (1 + B)	USD 103
D.	Discount Rate	13.0%
E.	Long-Term Growth Rate	3.0%
F.	Capitalization Rate (F = D – E)	10.0%
G.	Enterprise Value (C/F)	USD 10,300,000

Now, dear readers, you know how to calculate the market value on a CCF basis of the ICC Court of Arbitration, the LCIA and the AAA's International Centre for Dispute Resolution!

The measure of estimated cash flow and the capitalization rate are both crucial to the CCF method. Like all of the other valuation methods we assess, the CCF method involves implicit assumptions: in the case of a CCF valuation, either that the cash flow amount being capitalized will forever remain constant *or* that the cash flow amount being capitalized will increase or decrease, as the case may be, in perpetuity at a constant annually compounded rate. To obtain the capitalization rate, the expert will determine a discount rate in the manner previously discussed in Chapter 4.I. If the valuation is based upon the capitalized cash flow increasing or decreasing at a constant annual compounded rate, then the capitalization rate will equal the chosen discount rate minus the long-term growth rate for the investment (in the case of annual increases) or plus the long-term rate of decrease (in the case of annual decreases). As a related matter, the IVSC Business Valuation Guidance Note points out that the capitalization rate used in a CCF valuation must be consistent with the approach used for cash flow – pre-tax or post-tax.[644]

644. IVSC Business Valuation Guidance Note, *supra* n. 15, at ¶ 5.14.2.1.1, ¶ 5.14.2.2.5.

The expected growth rate from the company's income is embedded into the capitalization rate and is normally an expected annualized rate for the entire life of the investment. Usually, that growth rate will include within it expected inflation. Consequently, the choice of a growth rate for use in the CCF capitalization rate is extremely important. "If this growth rate is overestimated, then the capitalization rate is underestimated, the resulting value is overestimated, and vice versa."[645]

For many investments, we can reasonably expect their income to increase over time. If the growth rate for that income stream can be specified at a fairly steady rate over a long period of time, then that projected growth rate can be applied to the income amount to produce a valuation amount that takes the business' expected future growth into account. Of course, the first concern any reasonable person would raise with respect to this valuation method is that the uncertainties involved in predicting future growth rates for a company make the selection of a "reasonably steady growth rate" potentially unrealistic. The CCF method anticipates and addresses this objection to some extent; the income amount is multiplied by the capitalization rate. That capitalization rate in turn incorporates the estimated growth rate and a discount rate. The risk factors (i.e., uncertainties) that are embedded inside the discount rate (as we have discussed in Chapter 4.I above) are thus also found within the discount rate used in the CCF method. Similarly, if the valuation is based on capitalization rates determined from market transactions, then the uncertainties taken into account by actual market players in their transactions will also be embedded inside the chosen capitalization rate. Accordingly, the prediction of a steady rate of growth in income is adjusted to some extent in each case to reflect inter alia commercial and political uncertainties.

The CCF method appears on its face to be a simpler valuation computation, and is inherently attractive for that reason. The valuation will often compute average earnings for several preceding years (to "normalize" for peaks and valleys). Then, the expert will calculate the capitalization rate in order to project into the future the enterprise's stream of earnings based upon that historical earnings record. The CCF method is thus most useful when the future is expected to be similar to the past. However, if the business is potentially facing either a downturn or an upturn, then, as the disclaimers in those advertisements about investment funds say, "past results are no guarantee of future performance."

CCF valuations can also be used in conjunction with comparable businesses. Reliable past earnings information for the company being valued may not exist. If the valuation expert obtains historical earnings from other, similar companies (rather than the actual past earnings of the subject investment itself), then the CCF capitalization rate will not be calculated on the basis of the discount rate minus the expected growth rate. Instead, to preserve comparability, the capitalization rate in such circumstances will be based on the discount rate embedded inside the comparable transactions, as calculated by the expert. Additionally, if the income amount is based on comparable companies rather than the subject

645. The Lawyer's Business Valuation Handbook, *supra* n. 411, at 127–128.

investment's historical earnings, valuation experts will commonly use an "earnings" amount such as EBITDA to determine the company's historical cash flow, rather than the "net cash flow" amount ordinarily used in DCF valuations.

Moreover, it may be necessary to review and adjust revenue and expense numbers, just like the case of a DCF valuation. The AICPA Valuation Standard SSVS 1 instructs valuation analysts conducting a CCF valuation to consider:

- Normalization adjustment
- Nonrecurring revenue and expense items
- Taxes
- Capital structure and financing costs
- Appropriate capital investments
- Noncash items
- Qualitative judgments for rules used to compute discount and capitalization rates
- Expected changes (growth or decline) in future benefits (for example, earnings or cash flows).[646]

The use of the CCF method is especially sensitive to several important variables, including the selection of the unit of comparison (like EBITDA), the duration of the period over which that earnings measure is based, the adjustments (if any) made to the calculated earnings amounts, and the choice of the capitalization rate. As the Delaware Court of Chancery pointed out in its valuation of Straight Arrow Publishers (SAP), the publisher of the famous rock-and-roll magazine *Rolling Stone*:

> The legitimacy of this formula depends on the validity of at least four key decisions: 1) the choice of an appropriate earnings measure (*e.g.*, EBIT, EBITDA); 2) the selection of the historical time period on which the measure is based; 3) the determination of which adjustments, if any, should be made to the earnings measure to reflect items such as non-recurring expenses; and 4) the determination of an appropriate capitalization rate. In this case, all of these decisions are inseparably intertwined, for each depends on which view of SAP one accepts: that of the phoenix soaring out of the ashes or that of Icarus rising dangerously towards the sun.[647]

II MARKET MULTIPLES

Once comparablesfor a CCF comparison are identified, the valuation must then translate the transaction(s) involving the comparable investment into a value for the investment being valued.

---

646. SSVS 1, *supra* n. 17, at ¶ 33.a.
647. *Gonsalves v. Straight Arrow Publishers, Inc.*, *supra* n. 355, at 319.

> 189. A market multiples approach takes a particular financial or operating statistic of a publicly traded company and establishes a ratio between that statistic and the value of the company.... For example, a valuation consultant can look at the value of a public company and compare that value to its revenues over the past 12 months or its estimated revenue for the next year. The ratio between those statistics and the company's known value is called a "multiple." Each type of ratio is known as a "pricing fundamental." By looking at a number of pricing fundamentals for a number of "comparable" companies, an analyst can choose an appropriate multiple to apply to his or her subject company. The analyst can then use the multiple he or she has selected by applying his or her judgment aided by examination of the multiples shown by comparable companies. The analyst takes the equivalent statistic for the subject company and by applying the ratio selected derives an indicated value for the subject company....
>
> 190. A market multiples analysis requires the valuation consultant to make three decisions. First, the consultant must identify publicly traded companies that are sufficiently comparable to the subject company to make them acceptable "guideline" companies. Second, the consultant must identify appropriate ratios, or "pricing fundamentals" from which a value of the subject company can be derived. Finally, the consultant must consider the ratios shown by the guideline companies and select a ratio that, in the consultant's judgment, is appropriate to apply to the subject company.[648]

It is then necessary to agree on the "pricing fundamental" or "unit of comparison."[649] The valuation expert will derive the fair market value of the business in dispute by determining the value of the comparable and attributing to the disputed business the same proportionate value by means of the unit of comparison – the "market multiple." In choosing among various "units of comparison," it is also important to consider the purpose of the CCF valuation. For example, if the Direct Equity "flavor" of the CCF method is being used, a price-to-earnings (P/E) multiple may not be relevant to debt holders. The earnings of a company (also known as net income) are net of interest expense (i.e., calculated after deduction of interest expenses on debt). Since none of the company's net income would thus be available for scheduled debt payments, debt-holders do not see the P/E ratio as a very useful measuring tool for their purposes.

CCF valuations do not simply adopt the numbers from previous years without adjustment. Among the necessary adjustments are non-recurring events, non-arm's length transactions and non-operating assets (i.e., assets not used in core operations).[650]

Common CCF units of comparison for the indirect equity (Total Invested Capital) procedure include EBITDA, EBIT, revenues, and total assets, in each

648. In re Nanovation Technologies, Inc., *supra* n. 558, at 331.
649. The Lawyer's Business Valuation Handbook, at 144 et seq.
650. Risius, *Business Valuation: A Primer for Legal Professionals*, *supra* n. 19, at 69.

case measured against the market value of total invested capital. Common CCF units of comparison for the Direct Equity procedure include earnings, earnings before taxes, and the book value of shareholders equity, in each case measured against the current price of equity (i.e., its market value).[651]

For real estate transactions, illustratively, the "price per square foot" is a common unit of comparison. The multiplier most commonly preferred by acquirers in M&A transactions is EBITDA (or its sister, EBIT), which measures the gross cash flow of the business before interest and taxes. EBITDA means "Earnings Before Interest, Taxes, Depreciation and Amortization." EBIT is simply a similar earnings measure, but does not exclude depreciation and amortization. By excluding depreciation and amortization, EBITDA eliminates potential distortions from differing asset depreciation policies employed by the two companies being compared. The application of EBITDA (or EBIT) to comparable transactions is a common instance of the Market-Based Approach to valuation and the CCF method of the Income-Based Approach.[652]

Comparisons between businesses (rather than single assets) can employ a variety of different units of comparison. Common multipliers beyond EBITDA and EBIT include sales, discretionary earnings, debt-free net income, debt-free cash flow and the book value of invested capital (adjusted or not).[653] Readers will note that many of these tests eliminate interest-bearing debt as part of the measurement, thereby seeking to mitigate the impact of the issues noted in Chapter 3. VII above as to the comparability of the debt profiles of the businesses being compared. An expert may employ several different market multiples to compare two different companies, with the purposes of bringing to light any possible inconsistencies hidden by one test but uncovered by another test.

To find the market value of the company at the center of the dispute, the expert witness will seek to determine the transaction price of acquiring the comparable company as a multiple of the unit of comparison – if, say, the stock market capitalization of a company is USD 100 million and it has an EBITDA of USD 10 million, then the EBITDA "multiple" for a ratio of EBITDA-to-total capitalization is 10X. The expert would then determine the EBITDA of the disputed company at the heart of the arbitration, and apply the same 10X multiple to determine the market value to a third party of that company. Of course, like all financial computations, the expert must have good numbers for the components of EBITDA in order to offer a useful valuation.

Because EBITDA (or EBIT) is often used as the multiplier for enterprise valuations, it is worth reviewing the use of that unit of comparison in a little

651. *Id.*, at 100.
652. *Id.*, at 145.
653. *Id.*, at 145–146. *See CME Stockholm* Final Award, *supra* n. 42, at ¶ 146, for a valuation based upon "station operating cash flows" as the multiple ("a measure closely similar to EBITDA"). The *CME Stockholm* panel adopted this valuation as part of its quantum decision. *See id.*, at ¶¶ 519–549. Another popular (but ultimately unsuccessful) unit of comparison during the dot.com boom was price per website hits.

more detail. As stated above, EBITDA is a cash-flow measure of earnings that excludes expenses from interest, taxes, depreciation and amortization (i.e., Earnings (E) before deductions for ITDA). Alternatively, EBITDA can be described as the company's operating income, with expenses for depreciation and amortization subtracted out. EBITDA therefore tests the ability of a company to service its debt burden out of cash flow (but including the non-cash items of depreciation and amortization).

EBITDA

EBITDA (earnings before deductions for interest, taxes, depreciation and amortization) is often used as a multiplier for CCF valuations, as well as "comparable companies" valuations. EBITDA has known limitations as a financial tool, especially for industries where regular and large capital expenditures are called for or that face rapid technological change. EBITDA is also sensitive to the choice between capitalizing or expensing expenditures. Capitalizing an expenditure, rather than treating it as an expense, can significantly increase a company's total valuation amount.

Earnings, interest and taxes are ideas familiar to lawyers. However, many arbitrators (like, candidly, the author) find the concepts of depreciation and amortization confusing. Depreciation is an expense recorded on a company's financial statements associated with the cost of fixed assets (i.e., property, plant and equipment). Under GAAP accounting, when equipment or other fixed assets are acquired, the total purchase price is *not* recorded as an expense when paid. Instead, the purchase price is "expensed" through depreciation over the economic life of the relevant asset. Amortization is a similar concept, expensing the purchase price of an intangible asset (not a fixed asset) over the economic life of that intangible.[654]

An example from Dickie's *Financial Statement Analysis and Business Valuation for the Practical Lawyer*[655] may help explain depreciation. As Dickie points out, ordinary individuals equate the terms "costs" and "expenses," but accountants do not. Accountants divide expenditures into two categories, those that are currently "expensed" when incurred and those that are "capitalized" when incurred. Depreciation is the process of reducing the value of a "capitalized" asset on a company's financial statements on a year-by-year basis. When an expenditure for an asset is "capitalized," the cost is immediately placed on the company's balance sheet and "expensed" partially each year over the expected life of the asset. Thus, in Dickie's example, he spent USD 10 for lunch and USD 30 for a shirt (given such low prices, obviously not in New York, London or Paris). His

654. Risius, *Business Valuation: A Primer for Legal Professionals*, *supra* n. 19, at 43 n.1.
655. Dickie, Financial Statement Analysis and Business Valuation for the Practical Lawyer, *supra* n. 489, at 33, Sidebar 2.3.

accountant treated the cost of lunch as a current expense. The accountant therefore simply deducted that entire USD 10 cost from the company's revenues during the year Dickie bought the lunch. However, the accountant assumed that the shirt would have a substantially longer useful economic life than the lunch. So, the accountant treated the shirt as a "capital asset." He therefore placed the USD 30 cost of the shirt on Dickie's balance sheet as an asset and depreciated the amount of that asset (i.e., reduced that amount in the first and each subsequent year by deducting a portion of that amount as an expense in that year) over the two-year expected usable life of that shirt. At the end of the two-year period, the value of the shirt asset on Dickie's balance sheet reached zero. As Dickie also notes in his illustration, GAAP and tax law offer a number of alternate means of depreciating the capital asset; for example, expensing the asset in a "straight line" over its expected usable life or by accelerating the expensing more quickly (e.g., the "sum of the years" digit method). Tax laws often permit more rapid depreciation of capital assets than GAAP. The result of a difference between GAAP and tax treatment, by the way, will be a deferred tax liability.[656]

While the various different methods for depreciating a capital asset are certainly beyond the scope of this volume, it is surely important to recognize the impact of the basic choice between "expensing" and "capitalization" on valuations. If an asset is capitalized rather than expensed, the amount of the company's assets are increased and its current liabilities are reduced. The legal woes of WorldCom Corporation demonstrate the potential risks of mischaracterization.[657] For about one year, WorldCom capitalized its "line costs" (the costs of transmitting voice and data over the networks of other telecoms companies) rather than expensing them. Line costs were WorldCom's single largest operating outlay. Shifting those costs from current expenses into capital assets dramatically improved the cash flow position (and profits) WorldCom presented on its financial statements. A US federal court later held that accounting for the line costs as a capital expense was fraudulent and thus a criminal violation of US securities laws. Several WorldCom senior officers are currently serving prison sentences as a result. Additionally, members of WorldCom's board of directors settled the eventual civil class action claims against them individually for USD 54 million plus interest.

Not all depreciation choices, of course, risk potential jail sentences. GAAP affords companies considerable latitude with respect to their methods of accounting for depreciation of assets (or depletion, in the case of oil and gas or other natural resource reserves).[658] Moreover, GAAP also offers companies flexibility in choosing the length of time over which the assets in question will be depreciated. Companies naturally choose the method that best suits their individual purposes. Depreciation therefore is excluded from an EBITDA analysis to improve comparability between companies that may pursue different (but equally lawful) depreciation approaches.

---

656. *Id.*
657. *Id.*, at 34–35, 181–182.
658. The Lawyers Business Valuation Handbook, *supra* n. 411, at 243.

Several issues arise if an expert witness presents such a valuation method to the tribunal. First, EBITDA has some known limitations as a financial tool. EBIDTA was originally used for financial analysis to evaluate companies facing economic stress. Use of EBITDA was extended to calculate the value of companies in leveraged buy-outs in the 1980s, and then to a very broad group of companies in the 1990s. The dotcom boom/bust at the end of the 1990s, however, exposed a number of EBITDA's limits. For example, EBITDA is a better measurement for companies with longer assets lives. If, instead, the target company holds assets with shorter economic lives generally or is in an industry faced with rapid technological change, then EBITDA may not be a good measurement tool for the company. And, as the WorldCom story illustrates, EBITDA can also be manipulated through aggressive accounting. In mid-2000, Moody's Investors Services released a Special Comment about the utility of EBITDA.[659] That report summarized its conclusions as follows.

- The use of EBITDA and related EBITDA ratios as a single measure of cash flow without consideration of other factors can be misleading.
- EBITDA is probably best assessed by breaking down its components into EBIT, Depreciation, and Amortization. Generally speaking, the greater the percentage of EBIT in EBITDA, the stronger the underlying cash flow.
- EBITDA is relevant to determining cash flow in its extremis. EBITDA remains a legitimate tool for analyzing low-rated credits at the bottom of the cycle. Its use is less appropriate, however, for higher-rated and investment grade credits particularly mid-way through or at the top of the cycle.
- EBITDA is a better measurement for companies whose assets have longer lives – it is not a good tool for companies whose assets have shorter lives or for companies in industries undergoing a lot of technological change.
- EBITDA can easily be manipulated through aggressive accounting policies relating to revenue and expense recognition, asset writedowns and concomitant adjustments to depreciation schedules, excessive adjustments in deriving "adjusted pro-forma EBITDA," and by the timing of certain "ordinary course" asset sales.
- We find the ten critical failings of using EBITDA to be the following:
  1. EBITDA ignores changes in working capital and overstates cash flow in periods of working capital growth.
  2. EBITDA can be a misleading measure of liquidity.
  3. EBITDA does not consider the amount of required reinvestment – especially for companies with short lived assets.
  4. EBITDA says nothing about the quality of earnings.

659. Moody's Investors Services, Special Comment, Putting EBITDA in Perspective: Ten Critical Failings of EBITDA as The Principal Determinant of Cash Flow (June 2000) (hereinafter, "Moody's Special Comment").

5. EBITDA is an inadequate standalone measure for comparing acquisition multiples.
6. EBITDA ignores distinctions in the quality of cash flow resulting from differing accounting policies – NOT all revenues are cash.
7. EBITDA is not a common denominator for cross-border accounting conventions.
8. EBITDA offers limited protection when used in indenture covenants.
9. EBITDA can drift from the realm of reality.
10. EBITDA is not well suited for the analysis of many industries because it ignores their unique attributes.[660]

Therefore, arbitrators may not wish in all circumstances to rely solely on EBITDA as a measure of the value of comparable companies, especially for industries where regular and large capital expenditures are called for or that face rapid technological change.

Second, even when EBITDA is a proper tool for comparing business values, it is still important to consider apples-to-oranges comparability questions. For example, depreciation of capital expenditures plays a strong role in determining a company's income numbers. If the comparable has a different "capital expenditures" profile than the target company, then the use of an acquisition or stock price multiple based on the EBITDA of one company with a strongly different picture of future capital expenditures than the second company the result will be an inaccurate comparison between the two companies. The business being valued may make capital equipment purchases only rarely, with the equipment in question having a long expected life. In contrast, the allegedly comparable company may purchase capital equipment far more often and that equipment may be short-lived. Experts can test for this problem by producing analyses employing both EBITDA and EBIT. If the relationship between the target company and the comparable remains proportionately the same, then the arbitrator may have more confidence that the capital expenditures profiles of the two companies are similar.

Legal differences between countries may also affect comparability of EBITDA/EBIT multiples. Healthcare costs are a useful example. Many countries rely heavily on public funding of employee healthcare, while other countries look towards corporate or individual contributions to a much greater extent. Comparing the EBITDA's of companies from two countries that differ significantly in this respect may produce an apples-to-oranges miscomparison. If a company in one country makes significant contributions to employee healthcare programs, while another company in a second country (but otherwise identical) looks to government-funded healthcare programs for its employees, then the first company will face a higher operating expense burden. Consequently, the company carrying its own

660. *Id.*, at 1. The Special Comment further briefly considered the strengths and weaknesses of EBITDA as a cash-flow measure for ten separate industries, ranging from "deathcare" to "petroleum exploration & production" companies. *Id.*, at 20–22.

healthcare expenses will record a lower EBIT/EBITDA than the second company. That second company may, of course, very well be assessed a higher tax burden than the first company, since the government-sponsored healthcare program available to its employees will be paid out of that country's tax receipts. However, EBIT/EBITDA measure a company's earnings *before* taxes. Thus, there is no EBIT adjustment for an increase (if any) in the company's tax burden to fund the Government-sponsored program.

The impact of differing sources for healthcare funding is particularly obvious among Western European, UK and US companies. In the UK, for example, public spending in 2004 comprised 83.4% of total healthcare spending.[661] Germany funded 78.5% of its total healthcare spending from public money, and France 76%.[662] By contrast, the US funded only 44.9% of its healthcare spending in 2004 from public funds.[663] Moreover, the disparities in income tax rates among those countries are not allocated proportionately with their differing approaches to healthcare spending. According to KPMG's annual survey of corporate tax rates, in January 2004 the average corporate tax rate in the UK was 30%, in Germany 39.58%, in France 34.33% and in the US 40%.[664] However, the UK, Germany and France all employ to differing degrees Value Add Tax (VAT) assessments, which are not used in the US.[665]

Accordingly, if an arbitrator is presented by an expert with EBIT/EBITDA comparisons between companies in different States, it may be appropriate to inquire whether any adjustments are necessary to reflect differing sources of employee healthcare expenses or other significant Government spending programs for employees. Similarly, the valuation comparison should take account of differing tax burdens and means of assessing taxes.

Another potential apples-to-oranges issue arises in international arbitrations if the company in dispute and the comparable employ different accounting rules. This risk can arise if one of the companies uses aggressive accounting techniques, while the other uses a conservative accounting approach – Enron and Parmalat, thus, may not be good EBITDA comparables for other companies! More prosaically, this risk also exists if one business uses GAAP from one country (say, US GAAP), but the other business uses GAAP from a different country – the two GAAPs may have gaps between them.

661. "Health Public Spending as % of total," OECD Health Data 2004, on-line at <www.nationmaster.com>.
662. *Id.*
663. *Id.*
664. KPMG Annual Corporate Tax Rate Survey_January 2004, at 3–4, on-line at <www.kpmg.com.sg/publications/tax_CorptaxSurvey2004.pdf>.
665. As we all know, there are significant national differences in tax bases and reliance on payroll, social security, net wealth, VAT, sales/turnover and other non-income taxes, as well as income taxes imposed on individuals. Cross-border corporate income tax burden comparisons are therefore especially challenging.

For example, Moody's Investors Services analyzed the EBITDA of a Colombian wireless telecommunications company for 1997 and early 1998.[666] Colombian GAAP permitted the wireless company to capitalize marketing and subscriber acquisition costs, rather than expensing them as would be the case under US GAAP. The earnings of the Colombian company were therefore stated at a much higher number on its balance sheet than would have been the case under US GAAP. As a result, EBITDA under Colombian GAAP similarly produced a significantly larger number than would have been the case under US GAAP. Because of the impact of this accounting difference on a company's reported earnings, employing the EBITDA multiple of the Colombian wireless company to value a similar US wireless company would produce distorted results.[667]

Exhibit 11 ($'s in millions)

Celumovil S.A.: EBITDA Can Differ As A Result Of Cross-Border Accounting Conventions

	December 1997	6 Months June 1998
Operating Income	84.3	65.6
Depreciation and Amortization	13.4	7.1
Colombian GAAP EBITDA	**97.7**	**72.7**
Handset Subsidy Expense	8.1	21.2
Sales Commission Expense	16.3	18.0
Colombian GAAP EBITDA Before Subscriber Acquisition Costs	**122.1**	**111.9**
Cash Handset Subsidies	(48.4)	(64.4)
Cash Sales Commissions	(50.6)	(44.3)
Colombian GAAP EBITDA After Subscriber Acquisition Costs	**23.1**	**3.2**
Add-back of Cash Sales Commissions	50.6	44.3
Amortization of Sales Commissions	(23.6)	(34.2)
Amortization of R&D Expense	(1.2)	(0.6)
US GAAP EBITDA	**48.9**	**12.7**

Depreciation and amortization principles may also differ significantly among many accounting systems, again leading to distortions if EBITDA/EBIT numbers from one accounting system are applied without adjustment for a company subject to a different accounting system. In addition, accounting systems generally offer a company considerable flexibility in depreciating fixed assets. If two companies utilize that flexibility in markedly different manners, then it may be necessary to make adjustments to avoid another apples-to-oranges comparison.[668]

Another accounting issue that affects earnings-based multipliers such as EBITDA is the means by which a company accounts for its inventory.[669]

---

666. Moody's Special Comment, *supra* n. 659, at 16–17.
667. *Id.*, Exhibit 11 at 17.
668. Risius, *Business Valuation: A Primer for Legal Professionals*, *supra* n. 19, at 101, noting that, if two companies are identical except that one employs GAAP flexibility to depreciate identical fixed assets faster than the other, then the calculated price-earnings (P/E) ratios of the two companies will be different. "But from a cash flow standpoint, and thus from a market value standpoint, this difference in accounting for depreciation is not relevant." *Id.* (footnote relating to tax impact omitted).
669. *Id.*, at 106.

Some companies use LIFO (Last-in-First-Out) while others use FIFO (First-in-First-Out). Apart from tax issues, the choice between LIFO and FIFO should not affect operating cash flow of a company. However, the choice between the two methods does affect GAAP financial statements. Comparisons between two otherwise identical companies may therefore need to be adjusted if one uses LIFO while the other uses FIFO inventory accounting.

III TIME PERIODS

Two time periods are particularly important for proper use of the CCF method; first, the time period over which the valuation calculates the historical earnings of the business at the center of the dispute and, second, the time period for the historical earnings measure from comparable companies. To normalize prior historical cash flow results, some analysts use a three or five-year average or weighted average. If the company is experiencing significant growth, significant declines or extraordinary events, though, the use of the longer period without scrutiny may be inappropriate.

In its valuation of the company that owned *Rolling Stone* magazine, the Delaware Court of Chancery was asked to choose between earnings based on one year of the company's earnings (1985) or earnings based on a five-year period ending in 1985. The choice was obviously fact-intensive. The petitioner (seeking a higher valuation):

> believed that this one-year period (rather than the longer time period) was justified because SAP's [the company] earlier years' earnings were distorted by the inclusion of relatively unsuccessful ventures that SAP had sold or dissolved by the time of the merger, and because only the earnings base of 1985 truly reflected the success of the Repositioning Plan.[670]

In contrast, the respondent (arguing for a lower valuation) employed a longer five-year earnings period based "on the belief that a shorter period would place too much emphasis on the peak years' profits or contain figures too varied to average. He also felt that the value of SAP as a going concern should be valued by focusing on SAP's earnings as a whole, rather than just the earnings of Rolling Stone."[671]

Recall that the court viewed this choice as reflecting two competing visions of the company; "the phoenix soaring out of the ashes [the earlier years being irrelevant] or that of Icarus rising dangerously towards the sun [the earlier years being an indicator of long-term problems.]." The Court concluded that a five-year earnings base was appropriate to reflect "the nature of the enterprise as an enterprise with a *consistent history of attempts to diversify.*"[672] However, to acknowledge the

---

670. *Id.*, at 320.
671. *Id.*
672. *Id.*, at 323 (emphasis in original).

successful impact of SAP's Repositioning Plan by 1985, the Chancellor applied progressive weighting to the impact of the years in the earnings base, so that 1985 earnings were given five times the weight of 1981 earnings.[673] As the *Rolling Stone* case demonstrates, for some disputes the selection of the proper duration of measurement can significantly affect the resulting valuation.

673. *Id.* A five-year period is common for valuations, but neither law nor valuation standards require any particular fixed time period – the proper period is a ''representative'' period. ''When asking for historical financial statements on the subject property, one should endeavor to study statements during a *relevant period*. The most commonly used period is five years. However, conceptually, the relevant period covers the most recent period of time immediately prior to the valuation date during which the statements represent the company's general operations.'' Pratt, Reilly & Schweihs, ''Valuing a Business: The Analysis and Appraisal of Closely Held Companies,'' at 62 (4th edn Prentice Hall 2000).

Chapter 7

Asset-Based Methods, Particularly Adjusted Book Value (ABV)

Now that we have reviewed both Market-Based and Income-Based valuation methods, we turn our attention to the last of the three approaches, Asset-Based methods. One of the most widely used Asset-Based methods is "Adjusted Book Value" (ABV), also known as "Net Asset Value."

I INTRODUCTION

A company with a large asset base, such as the known reserves of an oil & gas exploration and production company, is often valued on the basis of the individual values of the assets owned by the company, net of its liabilities – its "Adjusted Book Value." The first step in computing that value is to determine the accounting "book value" of the assets and liabilities of the enterprise. Subsequent steps include identifying assets and liabilities not found on an accounting balance sheet and then revaluing all asset and liabilities to their market values.

Adjusted Book Value (ABV)

The Adjusted Book Value (ABV) method requires calculation of the difference between a business's total assets (net of depreciation, depletion and amortization) and its total liabilities, including material assets and liabilities not found on accounting balance sheets, in each case adjusted to their fair market values.

The ABV method is most appropriate for start-up companies, holding companies and other asset-intensive businesses, and companies that may not be viable operating companies.

ABV is a method for determining fair market value. Many assets and liabilities are recorded on balance sheets at their acquisition cost, not their market values. The ABV method requires that those items be adjusted to their current market values.

In addition, many assets (such as fully depreciated assets, internally developed intellectual property, good will and other elements of "going concern value") may not be found on a company's accounting balance sheet. So too, with many liabilities (such as environmental liabilities, contingent liabilities and liabilities for corporate capital gains taxes on appreciated assets). These items also need to be included in the valuation, again adjusted to their current market values.

As a starting point for this computation, the *IVSC Business Valuation Guidance Note* defines "Book Value" as:

> [w]ith respect to a business entity, the difference between total assets (net of depreciation, depletion, and amortization) and total liabilities of a business as they appear on a balance sheet. In this case, *book value* is synonymous with *net book value*, *net worth* and *shareholder's equity.*[674]

Then, those book values are adjusted to their market values to produce a current valuation. Importantly, while there are important exceptions,[675] many assets are presented at their historical value on financial statements prepared in accordance with generally accepted accounting or regulatory accounting principles, not at their market values. Increasingly, accounting principles are moving towards current values and away from historical acquisition costs. For example, US Statement of Financial Accounting Standards (SFAS) No. 157, Fair Value Measurements, and International Accounting Standard 19 now require periodic revaluations of investments held on the books of private equity funds. The US Private Equity Industry Guidelines Group, for example, recommends that valuations of investments in private equity portfolios generally be updated quarterly to comply with SFAS 157.[676] On those revaluation dates, the fund must adjust the book value of the investments to their "fair value" at current market prices. As this trend continues, more and more assets are being carried

674. IVSC Business Valuation Guidance Note, *supra* n. 15, at ¶ 3.3.2.

675. For example, financial assets held for trading by financial institutions are normally "marked to market." SFAS 157 requires the use of "Fair Value" for such assets, not historical cost. In fact, for a brief period of time in the 1990s, US tax law permitted (but did not require) sellers of nonfinancial goods and services to employ mark-to-market accounting for their customer accounts receivable. *See Heilig Meyers Company v. Internal Revenue Service, supra* n. 401, at *1.

676. US Private Equity Valuation Guidelines, *supra* n. 24, ¶ 10 at 2. As part of its joint "business combination" project with the International Accounting Standards Board (IASB), starting with fiscal years after 15 December 2008 the Financial Accounting Standards Board (FASB) in the US will also now require companies (and thus their accountants) to determine the value of an acquired business at "fair value" (i.e., at current value, not at historical cost). *See* SFAS 141 (R), Business Combinations, and SFAS 160, Non-controlling Interests in Consolidated Financial Statements, both effective for fiscal years after 15 December 2008.

on an accounting balance sheet at current values rather than at cost. As a result, the gap between GAAP and IAP, on the one hand, and market values, on the other hand, will diminish. Still, significant differences exist today, especially for items that are not financial assets. As a reminder, the International Glossary of Business Valuation Terms defines "Adjusted Book Value" to mean: "[A] method within the asset approach whereby all assets and liabilities (including off-balance sheet, intangible, and contingent) *are adjusted to their fair market values.* [NOTE: In Canada on a going concern basis.]"[677] (emphasis added).

Adjusted Book Value is thus generally the difference between the values of an enterprise's assets and liabilities, where the book values of those assets and liabilities have been adjusted to reflect current market values. This approach is commonly used for companies whose value lies largely in tangible, easily saleable assets – petroleum in tanks, for instance. Shipping companies, illustratively, may own a number of vessels. Similarly, real estate companies and hotel companies may also hold interests in numerous properties. The values of those individual assets may be ascertainable from market data. Additionally, book value may be employed where no alternative value can be established in the market.

As we have discussed, courts in the US often prefer to use Income-Based or Market-Based Approaches when valuing operating companies. Still, *The Lawyer's Business Valuation Handbook* offers a list of situations where US courts will instead look to the Asset-Based Approach for valuations.

In doing so, the accountant must recognize the "fair value" of both acquired assets and assumed liabilities. Similarly, accountants will have to measure the acquisition of a non-controlling interest in a business at "fair value." Importantly, contingent assets and contingent liabilities being acquired in a business combination will also now be valued under SFAS 141 (R) at "fair value" at the time of acquisition. Therefore, accountants will have to come to a current value for amounts that may or may not be paid/received even though that amount will depend upon the resolution of future uncertain events. Accounting for in-process research and development expenses is also moving towards "fair value" standards, and will have to be valued at current values and expensed at the acquisition date. *See* SFAS 141 (R). The FASB has expanded the definition of a "business" employed for these accounting purposes to cover development-stage entities; an enterprise "that is capable of being managed to provide a return to investors or economic benefit to owners, members, or participants." *See* Valuation Research Corporation, Alert: FASB Issues Business Combination Statement, at 1 (January 2008). The result of these new rules will be a significant expansion in "fair market" valuations for accounting purposes in connection with M&A transactions and other business combinations, including valuations of minority interests, development-stage enterprises and contingent liabilities. As a consequence, we can anticipate considerable attention being paid by the accounting and valuation professions and audited companies to valuation techniques in these areas as the business community comes to grips with the need to undertake a much more extensive array of "fair value" valuations for fiscal years after December 15, 2008. Unlike SFAS 141(R), the newly adopted International Financial Reporting Standards (IFRS) business combination standard IFRS 3(R) will not always require minority non-controlling interests in such circumstances to be recorded at "fair value." Instead, the reporting company will have the option to do so. Still, whether in the US (where such "fair value" treatment will be mandatory under GAAP for fiscal years after December 15, 2008) or in Europe (where such treatment will be permitted under IAS come July 1, 2009), arbitrators can expect to see accountants valuing minority interests at "fair value" on financial statements far more often once these new standards become fully effective.

677. International Glossary of Business Valuation Terms, *supra* n. 17.

- start-up companies;
- holding companies, financial institutions, agricultural businesses, and other asset-intensive businesses;
- marital estate valuations of companies or practices in which all goodwill is personal, and the state's case law does not consider personal goodwill as a marital asset;
- companies that may not be viable as operating companies.[678]

Because of the principle of "Highest and Best Use" previously discussed, the Asset-Based Approach is also applied when the value of the assets of an operating company are greater than the value of the company based on its anticipated cash flow. For example, if a company is not expected to generate positive cash flow, the highest value of that company may result from the sum of the market values of the company's assets net of liabilities.[679]

The International Valuation Standards Committee advises that the Asset-Based Approach should be considered in valuations of controlling interests in businesses involving either an investment or holding company or a business being valued on a basis other than a going concern premise.[680] Moreover, the IVSC specifies that the Asset-Based Approach should not generally be the sole valuation approach for operating businesses appraised as going concerns. When an operating business is valued as a going concern by means of a method within the Asset-Based Approach, the IVSC advises that use of the asset-based method should generally be accompanied by valuations from the Market-Based or Income-Based Approaches as well.

> The *asset-based approach* should not be the sole valuation approach used in assignments relating to operating businesses appraised as going concerns unless it is customarily used by buyers and sellers. In such cases, the Valuer must support the selection of this approach.[681]

The *Siemens v. Argentina* tribunal distinguished, in its view, the circumstances where book value is appropriate from situations where the DCF method is employed.

> Usually, the book value method applied to a recent investment is considered an appropriate method of calculating its fair market value when there is no market for the assets expropriated. On the other hand, the DCF method is applied to ongoing concerns based on the historical data of their revenues and profits; otherwise, it is considered that the data is too speculative to calculate future profits.[682]

Adjusted Book Value, as explained in Chapter 2.I above, is a means of determining fair market value. However, as discussed below, valuation professionals do not consider unadjusted book values, recorded on financial statements in accordance with accounting precepts, to be related in any way to market values.

---

678. The Lawyer's Business Valuation Handbook, *supra* n. 411, at 172.
679. Risius, *Business Valuation: A Primer for Legal Professionals*, *supra* n. 19, at 129–130.
680. IVSC Business Valuation Guidance Note, *supra* n. 15, at ¶ 5.14.3.4.
681. *Id.*, at ¶ 5.14.3.5.
682. *Siemens v. Argentina*, *supra* n. 112, at ¶ 355.

As we explain further along in this chapter, the assets and liabilities of the business being valued must be adjusted as part of the ABV method to their market (replacement) values. The IVSC notes that the Asset-Based Approach "is founded on the principle of substitution, i.e., an asset is worth no more than it would cost to replace all of its constituent parts."[683] The historical cost to a company of acquiring its properties is not normally an accurate indicator of the current market value of those assets at the valuation date, unless the date the property was acquired is quite close to the valuation date. To illustrate, the prices that willing buyers are prepared to pay for petroleum or real estate assets have fluctuated, and undoubtedly will continue to fluctuate, widely from time to time. However, considerable current information is available in spot and futures markets about current prices for oil, gas and other petroleum products. Similarly, information is available in many real estate markets about, for example, the current price per usable square feet/meters for comparable commercial office space. Accordingly, valuation experts will utilize that current data, rather than the historical acquisition cost recorded as book value on the company's financial statements, to obtain the value for the company's underlying petroleum or real estate assets. Similar illustrations for other assets abound.

Valuation experts generally seek to determine the "replacement value" of the assets to calculate ABV. The replacement cost procedure seeks to identify the current market price of comparable assets in replacement of the injured assets. For replacement valuations, the ABV method values a company based upon the "in-use" value of the company's net operating assets. As the *Fédération des Experts Comptables Européens* explains, the "net asset value" is "the replacement value of all existing intangible and tangible assets and liabilities used in the business."[684]

However, the *Fédération des Experts Comptables Européens* also concludes that "the net asset value is, of itself, of no importance when calculating the value of a business."[685] Many assets and liabilities are simply not found on a company's balance sheet, particularly certain intangible assets and goodwill. Therefore, the valuation must be adjusted to take account of the current value of those omitted items. If that is not done, then in the words of the Fédération, "being a net partial replacement value, [the computed value] does not have a direct relationship to future business profits. Hence, it does not have a value function as such."[686] The Fédération discourages the use of ABV by European accountants to value small

683. IVSC Business Valuation Guidance Note, *supra* n. 15, at ¶ 5.14.3.2.
684. FEE SME Business Valuation Guide, *supra* n. 17, at ¶ 8.3 at 35.
685. *Id.*, at ¶ 2.2 at 6. Smutny lists a number of considerations, such as the choice between capitalization and expensing assets, inflation adjustments and depreciation deductions, that "limit the evidentiary value of this measure [book value] significantly." Smutny, *supra* n. 115, at 13–14. As noted by the arbitrators in *Enron v. Argentina*, *supra* n. 43, at ¶ 382, "The book value of TGS stake is by definition valid for accounting purposes but, as noted by LEGC [claimants' expert], fails to incorporate the expected performance of the firm in the future." Of equal importance, it usually also fails to incorporate current performance as well.
686. FEE SME Business Valuation Guide, *supra* n. 17, at ¶ 2.2 at 6.

and medium-size enterprises unless the use of ABV "is specifically laid down in the terms of engagement for the valuation report."[687]

For reasons that make good sense to accountants (and perhaps to mere mortals), not all assets and liabilities are found on a company's balance sheet prepared in accordance with GAAP or IAP. Pratt's *Lawyer's Business Valuation Handbook* offers a useful, non-exhaustive list of off-balance sheet assets and liabilities to be considered when adjusting a company's balance sheet for an ABV valuation.[688]

- assets fully depreciated but still in useful service;
- inventory or accounts receivable written off by accounting policy but still saleable or collectible;
- intellectual property developed internally and therefore expensed instead of capitalized;
- work force in place, systems, and similar elements of "going-concern value;"
- goodwill;
- expected proceeds or costs relating to existing or potential lawsuits;
- environmental liabilities;
- liabilities for corporate capital gains taxes on appreciated assets.

We would add contingent, unmatured liabilities to that list (such as the market value of off-balance sheet Enron-type debt if that debt can "spring back" onto the balance sheet in certain situations). Some of these assets and liabilities, of course, may be of such an uncertain or contingent nature that identifying a reliable value will prove not to be feasible in the circumstances.

The valuation expert will seek to determine what a prudent purchaser would pay for the subject company's assets, with the proceeds used to pay off outstanding liabilities of the company. To the extent the existing assets of the business have less utility than new assets by virtue of deterioration or obsolescence, that reduced value will be reflected in the hypothetical sales price for the asset to the prudent purchaser. Tangible assets like drilling rigs are illustrative; the current value of a drilling rig combines the impact of supply and demand factors with the impact of deterioration of the particular rig as it ages. The expert's source of information about the hypothetical sales price for an asset is often the arm's length price for similar assets in the market. As with the "comparable companies" and "comparable transactions" methods, therefore, the reliability of the replacement cost valuation method depends heavily on the comparability of the replacement assets with the assets at issue in the dispute. Here too, careful inquiry by arbitrators about such crucial matters as location and market characteristics can help illuminate the worth of evidence about the value of alleged replacement assets.

Additionally, the careful arbitrator will consider whether the expert witness has sufficient expertise to offer evidence about the replacement value for the particular class of assets at issue in the testimony. An individual who is qualified

687. *Id.*
688. The Lawyer's Business Valuation Handbook, *supra* n. 411, at 169.

to testify as to replacement cost for, illustratively, a pool of marketable securities in a holding company may not have the requisite expertise to testify as to the replacement value for a pool of real estate properties held in another holding company.

Because using ABV requires extensive modifications both to convert balance sheet historical numbers into market values and to value off-balance sheet items, the Delaware courts are leery of relying on Asset-Based values if reliable Income-Based information is available.

> First, except for corporations with significant natural resource assets or with significant non-operating assets, the Delaware courts generally have refrained from weighing the asset prong heavily in applying the Delaware Block Method [a combination of the Asset Approach, the Market Approach and the Income Approach] when the earnings valuation method appears reliable.... Further, in this case, Mr. Stryker's [the expert's] analysis incorrectly did not include an amount for goodwill.... Thus, I give no weight to Mr. Stryker's asset valuation because Delaware courts generally have not weighed the asset prong heavily and because Mr. Stryker calculated an asset value that more closely reflected Radiology's liquidation value than its going-concern value.[689]

As we explain below, intangible assets, particularly the goodwill of a successful operating company, may be undervalued by the Adjusted Book Value method unless careful attention is paid to assets not found on an accounting-based balance sheet. ABV is accordingly not easily applied to businesses that are heavily dependent on goodwill or other intangibles. For example, in an unpublished opinion a Virginia State court rejected the use of the ABV method to value a medical practice, contrasting the effective use of ABV for real estate companies with the attempted application of the ABV method in that case to medical services.[690] As that court surely thought, it is hard indeed to compute the replacement (substitute) value of a doctor when intangibles like reputation and bedside manner play such a crucial role in the success or failure of medical practice.

For purposes of an ABV valuation, valuation experts will adjust the historical cost numbers in a company's records (the book value), to reflect their current market value. Before turning to the problems that may result if historical book values are used, we should note the circumstances where *unadjusted* book values may be appropriate. As the tribunal in the *Aminoil* case (involving, inter alia, petroleum reserves) stated: "[T]he net book value method may be suitable when it is a case of a recent investment, the original cost of which is not far from that of the present replacement cost. But when that is not so, other methods are indicated."[691] It is important to note, though, that relying on unadjusted book values does not obviate the need for a valuation professional to consider whether off-balance sheet assets and liabilities should also be included in the company's Asset-Based valuation.

---

689. *In re Radiology Associates, Inc., supra* n. 394, at *29–30.
690. *Gardner v. Gardner*, Case No. 0468-04-3 (Va. App. January 11, 2005), *reported in* Valuation Case Digest vol. VII, issue 3, at 8 (2005).
691. *Aminoil v. Kuwait, supra* n. 52, at 1377, § 165 (1982).

If the investment expenditures are not so closely related in time to the valuation as to justify relying on the amount specified in the company's financial statements, valuation experts will criticize the use of *unadjusted* book value to determine the injury to a business investment:

> A significant shortcoming of the book value method, and a key reason why it isn't used more often, is that, due to inflation, the cost of the same assets might be greater at present than when the company acquired them (or lower in some cases, such as computing power), although this isn't evident from the financial statements. Further, even if one were to use replacement cost rather than actual historic cost, the company might not actually buy the very same assets were it to replace them currently. Clearly in the case of telecommunications equipment and computers, a company would generally not do so. Even in more stable industries such as shipping, the company might acquire more up-to-date assets. Hence, even adjusting for present costs of the assets requires judgment calls not universally agreed upon. Indeed, the GAAP book value of the asset might be quite different from the market value of the asset. Examples of assets that can be difficult to value include real estate that has appreciated and brand names or other intellectual property not displayed on the balance sheet.
>
> The single greatest limitation of the book value method is that it ignores the value management may have added to the assets. The whole point of management is to make the assets worth more than their cost. By building and training a work force, by developing a reputation in the marketplace, by learning how to produce the goods or services at low cost, by creating opportunities for expansion, and in other ways, management (and past managements) should have – and in most cases has – created value in excess of the cost or book value of the assets.[692]

The damages award in *Siemens v. Argentina* may have fallen into this trap. In that case, the arbitrators rejected a lost profits claim as too speculative and awarded investment expenditures (the reliance interest in "sunk costs") to Siemens.[693] The venture in question had largely completed its engineering and development of an immigration control, personal identification, and electoral information system (including national identity cards), had begun production of the identity cards and had reached the operations stage for the immigration control subsystem.[694] Clearly, therefore, management had added value to the enterprise beyond the out-of-pocket invested sums. Whether characterized as goodwill, know how or other intangibles, the tribunal does not appear to have taken that incremental value into account in its compensation award.

---

692. Dickie, Financial Statement Analysis and Business Valuation for the Practical Lawyer, *supra* n. 489, at § 8.2(a). *See also* Risius, *Business Valuation: A Primer for Legal Professionals*, *supra* n. 19, at 23: "One of the most common mistakes that many attorneys make with respect to the valuation of a business enterprise is assuming that the accounting-based book value of a company is equivalent to market value. That is simply not an accurate assumption."

693. *Siemens v. Argentina*, *supra* n. 112, at ¶ 355 et seq.

694. *Id.*, at ¶ 81–92.

II HISTORICAL AMOUNTS, INTANGIBLES AND GOODWILL

For arbitrators to understand this criticism of *unadjusted* book value, we should first consider what asset and liability numbers are actually set out on a company's balance sheet pursuant to Generally Accepted Accounting Principles (GAAP) or International Accounting Principles (IAP). US GAAP generally requires long-lived fixed assets, like capital equipment or a factory, initially to be recorded on the company's balance sheet at their *acquisition cost.* That cost amount is then reduced by depreciation over the asset's useful life.[695] However, the accounting treatment of *intangible* assets on the books of a company is a far more complicated exercise that has significant implications for a book value appraisal. The IVSC reminds valuation professionals that intangible assets must be incorporated into a proper valuation of an enterprise.

> 5.10.7.1 Intangible value may be embodied in identifiable intangible assets such as patents, trademarks, copyrights, brands, know-how, databases, etc.
>
> 5.10.7.2 Intangible value may also be contained in undifferentiated assets, often called "*goodwill.*" Note that goodwill value in this context is similar to goodwill in the accounting sense in that both are the residual value (historical cost in accounting terms) after all the other assets have been taken into account.
>
> 5.10.7.3 If the business has intangible assets, the Valuer must ensure that the value of the intangibles is fully reflected, whether the identifiable intangible assets have been valued separately or not.[696]

US GAAP and IAP call for intangible assets that have "finite" useful lives to be recorded at their acquisition cost and then amortized over their useful lives; such assets include patents, trademarks, copyrights and franchises.[697] Intellectual property, of course, often comprises an important component of value for many companies. Once finite intangibles have been fully amortized, they show zero value on a company's books even if they continue to have significant market value. If the

---

695. Dickie, Financial Statement Analysis and Business Valuation for the Practical Lawyer, *supra* n. 489, at § 2.2(d).
696. IVSC Generally Accepted Valuation Principles (GAVP), *supra* n. 16, at ¶ 5.10.7.
697. Dickie, Financial Statements and Business Valuation for the Practical Lawyer, *supra* n. 489, at § 2.2(c). The values of tradenames and trademarks too are not found on an accounting-based balance sheet, unless that name or mark was obtained as part of an acquisition. Risius, *Business Valuation: A Primer for Legal Professionals*, *supra* n. 19, at 24. With the adoption of revisions to International Accounting Standards IAS 38 in 2004, companies using IAS have the option to measure the value of intangible assets on their financial statements after their acquisition either at cost or revalued periodically at fair value by reference to an active market. IAS 38 acknowledges, though, that active markets for intangible assets will be uncommon. As a result, most companies will continue to carry intangible assets on their IAS-compliant books at cost (minus amortization and impairment losses).

market value of such an asset is greater than its amortized book value, however, the company's balance sheet does not automatically reflect that increased value.

> Some assets, such as Coca-Cola's secret formula, don't even appear on its balance sheet at all. Microsoft's Windows has no material presence on its balance sheet yet has a market value in the billions of dollars. The product lines of pharmaceutical companies, except where they have been acquired, also have no material presence on balance sheets because the R&D needed to create them has been expensed. Yet many of these products have multi-billion dollar values.[698]

If the intangible asset (say, the Coca-Cola secret formula) is ever acquired by another company then, pursuant to accounting principles, the acquirer will have to record the acquired intangible asset (the Coca Cola formula) on its books at its fair value (generally, the new acquisition cost). The acquirer will not employ on its own balance sheet the formula's historical cost previously recorded on the balance sheet of the seller before the acquisition transaction. Except for such acquisition situations, however, the book value of an intangible asset is recorded on a company's balance sheet at its original cost, minus amortization and reduced for any impairment of value.[699] Thus, as noted above, some intangible assets end up having little or no balance sheet value, despite enormous market value. If an asset with substantial market value has been expensed, depreciated, or amortized to zero, it may not even be reflected at all on the company's balance sheet – exactly like the Coca Cola formula and Microsoft's Windows trademark.

Book Accounting Principles

Several features of GAAP accounting principles deserve particular attention to explain criticisms of unadjusted book value as a valuation methodology.

Intangible assets are generally recorded on an accounting balance sheet at their historical acquisition cost and then amortized. Once intangible assets with finite useful lives have been fully amortized, they show zero value on a company's balance sheet even if they continue to have significant market value.

Goodwill is generally recorded on accounting balance sheets at historical acquisition cost, even if the market value of goodwill has changed due to developments subsequent to the acquisition date.

Tangible assets are generally recorded on accounting balance sheets at their historical acquisition cost and then depreciated. Many tangible assets, such as oil and gas reserves and office buildings, have market values significantly different from their depreciated acquisition cost.

698. Dickie, Financial Statement Analysis and Business Valuation for the Practical Lawyer, *supra* n. 489, at § 3.1(d), Sidebar 3.4 (footnotes omitted).
699. *Id.*, at §§ 3.2(c) & 3.2(d).

Management of a company exercises judgment under GAAP in deciding whether contingent liabilities should be included on an accounting balance sheet and, if so, the amount of liability. Management of a company exercises judgment under GAAP in the choice of depreciation and amortization amounts for many assets.

Liabilities are generally recorded on an accounting balance sheet at their face amount. The market value of those liabilities may differ significantly by reason of macroeconomic and other events.

Increasingly, accounting principles are moving from historical acquisition cost towards periodic revaluations to reflect current values. As that trend continues, the gap between GAAP and market values will diminish.

An example may help clarify. An English biotech company, Alpha, may spend 5 million United Kingdom pounds (GBP) to develop and patent a drug. However, in the circumstances only 1 million GBP qualifies as a development cost under UK GAAP. Accordingly, the book value of the drug on Alpha's balance sheet will be 1 million. GBP. The drug proves to be very successful, so less than a year later Alpha is able to sell the patent and all related drug rights to Bravo, also an English company, for 800 million GBP. Internally, Bravo's management would have been prepared to pay up to 1 billion GBP for the drug rights, but other bidders for the patent withdrew from the bidding process before the price rose to that level. Under UK GAAP, the book value of the drug rights on Bravo's financial statements will now be 800 million GBP, the acquisition cost to Bravo, not the original 1 million GBP cost or the full 1 billion GBP Bravo was prepared to pay. Then Charlie, a third English company, promptly acquires Bravo in a corporate take-over for many billions of Pounds Sterling. Once the acquisition has been consummated, Charlie allocates 1.2 billion GBP of the overall take-over price (the acquisition price) to the book value of the drug rights on its (Charlie's) balance sheet.[700]

As this example makes clear, the original 1 million GBP book value on Alpha's financial statements for the drug rights did not reflect either the actual development costs for the drug or its market value before the sale to Bravo. In addition, the difference between the book value for the drug rights on Bravo's balance (800 million GBP) and the value of the same drug rights on Charlie's balance sheet after the take-over (1.2 billion GBP) may not reflect a change in market value for the drug rights. Rather, it reflects Charlie's judgment about how to allocate the overall purchase price for acquiring Bravo. That allocation will, of course, be made within a range of reasonable asset values that management could have selected as the value of the drug rights. The choice within that range may have been influenced by tax and other issues unrelated to market value; not that anyone

700. This example is taken from the presentation by Simon de Quidt, "Methods of Valuation: which method for which case?" given on May 11, 2007 to the 8th Investment Treaty Forum of the British Institute of International and Comparative Law (BIICL). Papers are available to BIICL Investment Treaty Forum members at <www.biicl.org>.

would ever admit to such conduct. Similar results occur under US GAAP and International Accounting Principles.

Goodwill is another very important asset for which book value and market value may differ significantly. The *IVSC Business Valuation Guidance Note* defines "goodwill" as "[f]uture economic benefits arising from assets that are not capable of being individually identified and separately recognized."[701] The IVSC further defines "Transferable Goodwill" as:

> That intangible asset that arises as a result of property-specific name and reputation, customer patronage, location, products, and similar factors, which generate economic benefits. It is inherent to the specialized trading property, and will transfer to a new owner on sale.[702]

Goodwill is the value of the company not directly attributable to a specific identifiable asset, whether net working capital or tangible or intangible assets. As the International Glossary of Business Valuation Terms points out, the term "goodwill" reflects such intangibles as name, reputation, customer loyalty and location.[703] Many intangible assets, like patents and contract rights, within an enterprise can be specifically valued. What is left over in a company's value, after allocating to specific assets, is goodwill. Working backwards, "the business enterprise value is computed and the value of the net working capital, tangible assets and intangible assets is subtracted from the total enterprise value. The amount of value remaining pertains to the goodwill associated with the business."[704] Illustratively, if the market value of Google today is USD 200 billion (measured as total public shares multiplied by today's share price), tangible assets

701. IVSC Business Valuation Guidance Note, *supra* n. 15, at ¶ 3.21.1.
702. *Id.*, at ¶ 3.21.3.
703. International Glossary of Business Valuation Terms, *supra* n. 17.
704. Risius, *Business Valuation: A Primer for Legal Professionals*, *supra* n. 19, at 172–173. *In Davison v. Margolin, Winer & Evens*, LLP, 2007 WL 703108 (N.Y. Sup. Ct. March 8, 2007), a New York court held that a malpractice claim against an accounting firm for improper valuation of a 50% interest in a medical practice being dissolved was an improper collateral attack on the arbitration award that had adopted the valuation. In that case, the shareholders agreement for the medical enterprise provided for appointment of an independent valuation expert to value dissolution of the practice. If the parties could not agree on the identity of that expert, an arbitrator would make the appointment. The parties disagreed on both the proper valuation and the identity of the expert. One side (Davison) contended that goodwill was not properly included in the valuation, and thus the medical practice was worth only 3,600 USD. The other side (Ratner) contended that goodwillshould be included, and thus the practice was worth more than 1 million USD. The arbitrator adopted the valuation of the independent expert (Margolin, Winer & Evens, LLP), who included goodwillin the valuation. Davison, the disappointed party, failed in his efforts to prevent confirmation of the arbitration award in the New York courts. Then, Davison brought a malpractice and breach of contract action against Margolin, Winer & Evens, arguing that the allegedly erroneous appraisal had resulted in Davison paying an inaccurate amount to his former partner Ratner. However, the court rejected that malpractice claim as just an effort to rehash the failed attack on the arbitration award itself.

comprise 15% of that value, intangible assets comprise 60% and networking capital 10%, then the residual goodwill would be 15% of Google's market value.

The US Internal Revenue Service counsels that whether or not the enterprise has goodwill or other intangible value is fundamental to a careful valuation.[705] Equally, in international investment law, the PCIJ's *Chorzów Factory* judgment expressly instructed the expert inquiry to consider goodwill and prospects.[706] Calculating the ABV of a company without attributing any value to goodwill is closer to a liquidation valuation than a going concern valuation.[707] Goodwill is, in some respects, treated for book value purposes like intangible assets on a company's balance sheet. In other respects, though, it is not. Again pursuant to US GAAP and IAP, goodwill is recorded at cost. Like intangible assets, if a company is acquired by another company, then goodwill on the acquired company's balance sheet is adjusted to reflect its fair value at the time of the acquisition. However, since US GAAP changes in 2001, goodwill (unlike finite intangibles such as contract rights) is no longer amortized in the US – it is considered instead to not have a finite life.

The FASB has recognized the interplay between the accounting rule requiring adjustment of the book values of goodwill and intangibles when a company is acquired, on the one hand, and valuation methods, on the other hand. Statement of Financial Accounting Standards (SFAS) No. 142[708] asserts that "[a] present value technique is often the best available technique with which to estimate the fair value of a group of net assets (such as a reporting unit)."[709]

In the Information Age, it is disconcerting (to say the least) to find valuations that do not fully reflect the value of management, know how, intellectual property and other information assets.

The difficulties with unadjusted book values are not limited solely to intangible assets. Fixed assets, too, may raise serious valuation issues. If a factory or other capital equipment continues to operate successfully even after its book value has been depreciated to zero, it clearly has value. As Pratt noted, an ABV valuation must account for "assets fully depreciated but still in useful service."[710] Moreover, many tangible assets (whether or not fixed assets) may increase in

705. IRS Rev. Rule 59–60, *supra* n. 5, at §§ 4.01(f) and 4.02(f).

706. *See* text associated with n. 288 *supra*.

707. *In re Radiology Associates, Inc.*, *supra* n. 394, at *29–30. In the context of distressed companies and bankruptcy proceedings, many bankruptcy courts are reluctant to place great reliance on large values for goodwill. *See* cases cited at n. 10 of Stearn, "Proving Solvency: Defending Preference and Fraudulent Transfer Litigation," *supra* n. 20, at 362.

708. SFAS 142, Financial Accounting Standards Board, as amended (June 2001).

709. *Id.*, at ¶ 24. Note that regulatory accounting principles may require a company to carry asset and liability values on its balance sheet that are not commercially reasonable. The *Vivendi 2007* panel rejected Argentina's argument in favor of book value because "CAA's book value at this time distorts the economic reality due to the fact that CAA was required to carry a U.S. $55 million asset of unpaid (and largely uncollectible) customer invoices." Vivendi 2007, *supra* n. 72, at ¶ 8.3.7. *See also id.*, at ¶ 8.3.14.

710. The Lawyer's Business Valuation Handbook, *supra* n. 411, at 169.

market value over the years, but remain valued for GAAP and International Accounting Principles purposes at their original acquisition cost.

> Examples of assets that have a fair value well above their GAAP values are: trees owned by forest products companies, which are on the books as seedlings but that have been growing in size and value ever since they were planted; brandy that is being distilled but is on the books at the cost of the grapes; and buildings which were built decades ago and have been fully depreciated yet have substantial market values.[711]

Moreover, despite the fond hopes of many arbitrators and commentators, looking to asset values rather than income-based methods does not eliminate the subjectivity of business valuations. The proper amount to be shown on a balance sheet for many items calls for the exercise of judgment by the company's management and its accountants. An obvious example is the amount of a reserve or provision for contingencies or partial losses such as a defaulted long-term contract. For accounting purposes, management must exercise judgment to decide whether the value of the contract has been impaired and, if so, by what amount. Other examples, perhaps less obvious to non-accountants but quite crucial, include: (i) whether and when a contingent liability should be included on the balance sheet and, if so, the amount to be included (Enron's infamous "Raptor" off-balance sheet financings comes to mind); and (ii) the allocation of the cost of acquiring a large number of assets in a single transaction across the various assets being acquired (the "Charlie" illustration above). If the assets in question are owned by a company that has been acquired, sold, and acquired again repeatedly, as is occasionally the case in our modern economies, then the book value of an asset on the financial statements of the current owner may in fact reflect a series of prior historical judgment calls.

Yet another exercise of judgment that finds its way into book values is the process of depreciating the value of an asset over its usable life. Depreciation principles for many accounting systems afford the company significant flexibility, including as to the duration of the asset's usable life, the amount of depreciation and the schedule for depreciation. The value of a partially depreciated asset on a company's financial statements will reflect that exercise of judgment by the company's management.

These examples show that, except by purest chance, the historical book value of intangible assets, goodwill and many tangible assets simply will not reflect their real values at the time the business is being valued. *Pratt, Reilly & Schweihs* put the point bluntly: "There is no theoretical support, conceptual reasoning, or empirical data to suggest that the value of a business enterprise (under any standard of value) will necessarily equal the company's accounting book value."[712]

---

711. Dickie, Financial Statement Analysis and Business Valuation for the Practical Lawyer, *supra* n. 489, at § 3.1(d), Sidebar 3.4.

712. Pratt, Reilly & Schweihs, Valuing a Business: The Analysis and Appraisal of Closely Held Companies, *supra* n. 673, at 308.

III LIABILITIES

Any Asset-Based valuation must deduct a business' liabilities to arrive at an enterprise value. Assets, though, are not the only balance sheet items that may need to be adjusted for market value in an ABV analysis. On occasion, liabilities too require adjustment.

> Sometimes long-term debt has a market value different from its face value. If a company has borrowed long term and interest rates have risen, then the market value of its long-term debt will have declined. This is not recognized under GAAP unless the company is acquired. In that event the liabilities, as well as the assets, are brought onto the books of the acquirer at their FMVs.[713]

Troubled companies and highly leveraged enterprises, such as project finance companies, are especially sensitive to this situation.

Similarly, a contingent liability (like a guarantee, a repurchase obligation or a litigation risk) is not normally disclosed on a balance sheet unless and until it is probable that the liability will be incurred and the amount of the loss can be reasonably estimated.[714] Thus, many contingent liabilities simply never show up on a balance sheet, but can certainly affect a company's value in the marketplace. The sudden appearance of hundreds of millions of dollars of contingent obligations on Enron's balance sheet from the "Raptor" financings, when it became probable that those contingent liabilities would in fact crystallize, was of course a precipitating event in Enron's spectacular bankruptcy.

In the course of estimating the current value of a liability, the objective of the valuation is to determine the value of the assets (usually cash) required to either (i) settle the liability with its holder or (ii) transfer the entity to an acquirer of comparable creditworthiness.[715] To do so, experts often seek to identify the price at which third parties are willing to hold the obligor's liabilities as assets (e.g., to purchase a promissory note evidencing the liability).

> For example, the proceeds from a loan are the price that a lender paid to hold the borrower's promise of future cash flows as an asset. Similarly, the fair value of a bond payable is the price at which that security trades, as an asset in the marketplace.[716]

Not all liabilities are readily transferable. For instance, manufacturers may sell their products accompanied by a performance warranty. That warranty is, of course, a liability of the manufacturer. If the product might become subject to a

---

713. *Id.*, at § 4.2(b). Note that, in a US preferential transfer case, liabilities will be valued at their face amount (not their market value) regardless of whether the debtor was a going concern. Stearn, Proving Solvency: Defending Preference or Fraudulent Transfer Litigation, *supra* n. 20, at 381–382.
714. Dickie, Financial Statement Analysis and Business Valuation for the Practical Lawyer, *supra* n. 489.
715. FASB Concepts Statement No. 7, at ¶ 75.
716. *Id.*, at ¶ 76.

general recall for defects, the aggregate of the contingent warranty liabilities can become quite large. The beneficiary of the warranty (i.e., the asset holder) is unlikely to sell the warranty rights to a third party separate from the related products (leaving to one side the somewhat unusual economics of US class actions). Other liabilities, such as environmental liabilities, are not held by specifically identifiable holders. Environmental liabilities, too, can be quite large. In such cases, valuation experts may instead attempt to estimate the price that the obligor would have to pay for a third party to assume the obligor's liability.[717]

The creditworthiness of the obligor under a liability is obviously central to its value. Further, the credit standing of an obligor can, and often does, change over time. Changes in credit standing, as well as changes over time in market interest rates, may be reflected in the discount rate employed to determine the present value of the liability. Just like assets, though, it is also possible to employ an "expected cash flow" approach, comparing a range of default probabilities to calculate the expected current market value of the liability.[718]

In light of these accounting principles for the book value of assets and liabilities, even a properly audited balance sheet will not show a company's market value: "[T]he fair market values may differ markedly, up or down, from the GAAP values."[719] As this discussion makes clear, looking at a company's balance sheet without adjustments for market value creates a risk of serious errors in valuation. It bears repeating here that the Adjusted Book Value method, as employed by organizations such as the IVSC, the Fédération des Experts Comptables Européens, FASB, the ASA and the AICPA, contemplates adjusting assets and liabilities (including off-balance sheet, intangible and contingent liabilities) to their current values.[720]

IV VALUATIONS BY CATEGORIES

When an ABV valuation has been completed, the resulting report will differ from the business' original accounting balance sheet in two important ways: the balances in the original asset and liability accounts will have been revalued to their current values and a number of new asset and liability accounts may (indeed, likely will) have been added to reflect items not found in the original accounting-based financial statement. To revalue assets from their book values to their market

717. *Id.*, at ¶ 77.
718. *Id.*, at ¶ 82.
719. *Id.*
720. *See* e.g., International Glossary of Business Valuation Terms, *supra* n. 17. The Fédération focuses on the "in use" value, not the "fair market value." FEE SME Business Valuation Guide, *supra* n. 17, at 35 ("in use value of net operating assets"). "In use" value is the value a specific property has for a specific use to a specific user and is the same as the IVSC concept of "Investment Value or Worth." *See* IVSC Concepts Fundamental to Generally Accepted Valuation Principles (GAVP), *supra* n. 16, at ¶ 9.3.3.

values, the first step will be to separate out individual categories of accounts. One common categorization is as follows:

1. Financial asset account categories (e.g., cash, accounts receivables, prepaid expenses, inventory).
2. Tangible personal property (e.g., machinery and equipment, furniture and fixtures, trucks and automobiles).
3. Real estate (e.g., land, land improvements, buildings, building improvements).
4. Intangible real property (e.g., leasehold interests, easements, mineral exploitation rights, air and water rights, development rights, and so on).
5. Intangible personal property (e.g., patents, trademarks, copyrights, computer software, trade secrets, customer relationships, going-concern value, goodwill, and so on).
6. Current liability account categories (e.g., accounts payable, taxes payable, salaries payable, accrued expenses, and so on).
7. Long-term liability account categories (e.g., bonds, notes, mortgages, and debentures payable, and so on).
8. Contingent liabilities (e.g., pending tax disputes, pending litigation, pending environment concerns, and so on).
9. Special obligations (e.g., unfunded pensions, earned vacations or other leaves of absence, ESOP repurchase liabilities, and so on).[721]

The valuation would then determine which existing assets and liabilities on the balance sheet need to be revalued to current values.

The next step is to address off-balance sheet items. For the reasons explored above, unrecorded tangible and intangible assets then need to be identified for valuation; examples include intangible assets created internally by the business (e.g., Windows) and tangible assets that have been either expensed (rather than capitalized) or fully depreciated even though they still have economic value. Machinery tools, dies and molds often fall into the latter category.

Similarly, off-balance sheet and contingent liabilities need to be identified for inclusion in the appraisal. Contingent liabilities are not, for accounting purposes, typically recorded on the company's balance sheet. However, material contingent liabilities are usually discussed in the footnotes to audited financial statements. Examples including material pending litigation, income tax claims and environmental claims. Arbitrators should exercise caution, though, before deciding that all material contingent liabilities have been identified in those footnotes. Once again, the Enron story is a useful reminder that the legal and accounting standards for even footnote disclosure of contingent liabilities may be susceptible to widely differing interpretations.

---

721. Pratt, Reilly & Schweihs, Valuing a Business: The Analysis and Appraisal of Closely Held Companies, *supra* n. 673, at 309–310.

Having identified all relevant assets and liabilities, the valuation will proceed to create a value-basis balance sheet; for example, a balance sheet showing fair market values for the assets and liabilities at the valuation date. Looking at common categories of assets, it may be helpful to list out the means of revaluing that the expert can utilize.

- Financial Assets – Accounts and notes receivable would usually be valued at the present value of their collection (i.e., their net realizable value).
- Real Estate – Valuation professionals will choose among several appraisal approaches; the replacement cost approach (based on the principle of substitution), the income capitalization approach and the sales comparison approach.
- Intangible Real Estate – This category refers to leasehold interests, possessory rights such as permits, exploration rights, air or water rights, mineral exploration rights, development rights, easements and similar rights relating to the use or exploitation of real estate. While the same three approaches are available as would be the case for real estate itself, the replacement cost (substitution) approach is usually not relied upon for intangible real estate interests, since the cost of the underlying property is normally not relevant to the user.[722]
- Tangible Personal Property – For tangible merchandise inventory, appraisers will commonly look to the cost of reproduction, comparative sales or the income method. Other tangible property is often valued on the basis of the principle of substitution; for example, at replacement cost, depreciated for physical deterioration and with an allowance for obsolescence of the property.
- Intangible Personal Property – The scope of intangible assets is vast and, given the growth of technology and service-oriented economies, growing. As previously discussed, many intangible assets are simply not found are GAAP or IAS balance sheet. Pratt, Reilly & Schweihs offer the following categorization of intangible assets.
- technology-related (e.g., engineering drawings and technical documentation);
- customer-related (e.g., customer lists and customer relationships);
- contract-related (e.g., favorable supplier or other product/service contracts);
- data processing-related (e.g., computer software, automated databases);
- human capital-related (e.g., employment agreements, a trained and assembled workforce);
- marketing-related (e.g., trademarks and trade names);
- location-related (e.g., leasehold interests, certificates of need);
- goodwill-related (e.g., going-concern value);

722. *Id.*, at 324.

– engineering-related (e.g., patents, trade secrets);
– literary-related (e.g., literary copyrights, musical composition copyrights).[723]

Like other assets, the market, income and cost approaches are all theoretically available to value an intangible asset. However, it is difficult to use the market approach, since individual intangible assets are not normally sold separately from an overall business. Certain financial assets and intangible real estate assets, however, do often sell separately and therefore may be valued on the basis of comparable market transactions.

Replacement cost is also a viable valuation procedure for intangibles:

> The replacement cost of an intangible is the cost to create, at current prices, an asset having equal utility to the subject. This duplicate would be created using the same materials, standards, design, layout, and quality of workmanship used to create the original intangible. An intangible's reproduction cost encompasses all of the deficiencies, "superadequacies," and obsolescence that exist in the subject intangible asset. Many of these conditions or characteristics are inherent in the subject and, therefore, incurable.[724]

Thus, the difference between replacement cost and reproduction cost for an intangible asset will be its "incurable functional and technological obsolescence."

Lastly, of course, intangible assets may be valued on an income basis. Intangible assets can serve to either increase the business' revenues (e.g., sell more products) or decrease the business' costs (e.g., incur lower labor or material expenses). Either consequence is an addition to the value of the business that may appropriately be valued on an income basis.[725] Double-counting is a risk, though. The expert witness (or the arbitrator) must assure that the stream of economic benefit associated with the intangible asset is not also assigned to another asset. In the Iran-US Claims Tribunal case of *Shahin Shaine Ebrahimi v. Islamic Republic of Iran*, the tribunal-appointed expert "was adamant that it was inappropriate to add the net present value of a company's profit margin on its outstanding contracts to the value of its tangible assets."[726]

For valuations based on fair market value, it may help to look at the revenue or expense item in question from the perspective of a willing, able and fully informed potential buyer. Would that hypothetical buyer consider the amount of the item reasonable?

723. *Id.*, at 326.
724. *Id.*, at 331.
725. *Id.*, at 329.
726. *Shahin Shaine Ebrahimi v. Islamic Republic of Iran*, *supra* n. 603, at ¶ 159.

V DOUBLE COUNTING

Like the case of DCF valuations, double counting may also be an issue in ABV calculations. A company may, for example, make a provision in its financial books on account of the risk of future termination of a material contract to which the company is a party, especially if that contract is in dispute. That provision, in effect, preserves cash to protect against the contingency of a future termination of the contract by writing off the relevant amount. In doing so, the company thus has reduced its current profits and held back cash for expected future losses. The provisioned amount is, of course, an asset on the books of the company. Therefore, the provisioned amount would be included in any sum of assets in an ABV computation. However, the conduct at issue in the dispute may itself have prevented performance of that particular contract. A private power project may, for instance, make provision for termination of an important but troubled power purchase agreement. If that power purchase agreement is later terminated in disputed circumstances, the company's claim for compensation will relate directly to that agreement. If damages are subsequently awarded by the arbitral panel for losses calculated on the basis of future performance of the frustrated contracts, then "the provisioning for risks related to Contract termination would lead to double counting and is disallowed for purposes of the book value calculation."[727]

Cash reserves are found as well in many other circumstances, including debt service and major maintenance reserve accounts required by project finance lenders. Arbitrators should look carefully at the function of cash reserves and the nature of the claimed injury in the dispute, to assure that double counting does not inadvertently occur in the final awarded amount.

VI LIQUIDATION VALUE

No discussion of asset valuation methods is complete without addressing "Liquidation Value." Like ABV, Liquidation Value is a method within the Asset-Based Approach. "*Liquidation value* means the net amount that can be realized (after liquidation expenses) in either an orderly or a forced sale of the business assets or some portion of them."[728]

Because most companies have greater value in continued use as an enterprise, the Liquidation Value method usually does not provide the most useful valuation of the company.[729] As *Collier on Bankruptcy* notes, liquidation value is "nearly always considerably less than the going concern value."[730] "In liquidations, the

727. *Siemens v. Argentina*, *supra* n. 112, at ¶ 374.
728. The Lawyer's Business Valuation Handbook, *supra* n. 411, at 13.
729. Dickie, Financial Statement Analysis and Business Valuation for the Practical Lawyer, *supra* n. 489, at 291.
730. Collier on Bankruptcy, *supra* n. 13, at ¶ 547.04.

value of most intangible assets (e.g., goodwill) tends towards zero, and the value of all tangible assets reflects the circumstances of liquidation."[731]

However, liquidation value is appropriate "if at the time in question the business is so close to shutting its doors that a going concern standard is unrealistic."[732] Continued operations, though, may enable the company to preserve "any positive difference between the going concern value of the business and the liquidation value."[733]

> **Liquidation Value**
>
> "Liquidation value" is the net amount that can be realized in either an orderly sale or a forced sale. Liquidation value is appropriate if use of "going concern value" is unrealistic. The chosen liquidation premise (either an orderly sale or a forced sale) will significantly affect the valuation amounts. Both an orderly sale and a forced sale involve selling on an asset-by-asset basis.

The asset value determined by Liquidation Value is the realizable value from the sale of the individual asset, net of associated liabilities and of transportation costs, sales commission and other transaction expenses. If, illustratively, an aircraft is sold at Liquidation Value, its value will be the sales price for the aircraft, minus any loans secured by the plane, the cost of ferrying the plane and transferring it to the buyer. Like ABV, the realizable value is again a market value, not a book value. Importantly, that value is determined by a sale to a third party on a basis consistent with the underlying liquidation premise, either an orderly disposition or a forced sale.[734] The chosen liquidation premise will clearly affect the value given to the asset by a willing buyer. Recall that the definition of "fair market value" presumes a willing buyer and a willing seller. A sale upon liquidation, in contrast, may not involve a willing seller, but rather a seller forced by necessity to sell, even if the sales price is lower than the seller might have expected, or forced to sell by operation of law. The definition of "fair market value" also assumes that both parties have reasonable knowledge of the relevant facts. In a liquidation, the prospective buyer has reasonable knowledge of the circumstances facing the distressed seller. Accordingly, the buyer in a liquidation context will have leverage to extract a favorable, and lower, price for the individual asset.

As defined by valuation professionals, both an orderly disposition and a forced sale involve selling on an asset-by-asset basis. In comparison, the disposition of a

731. IVSC Business Valuation Guidance Note, *supra* n. 15, at ¶ 5.7.1.1.
732. In re Vadnais Lumber Supply, Inc., 100 B.R. 127, 131 (Bankr. D. Mass. 1989). *See also Gilman v. Scientific Research Prods. Inc. of Del.* (In re Mama D'Angelo, Inc.), 55 F.3d 552, 555 (10th Cir. 1995); Collier on Bankruptcy, *supra* n. 13, at ¶ 547.12.
733. Collier on Bankruptcy, *supra* n. 13, at ¶ 1100.01.
734. The Lawyer's Business Valuation Handbook, *supra* n. 411, at 11.

going concern ordinarily involves the sale of the overall business (including its goodwill). As a result, all Liquidation Values are based on an asset-by-asset sale, not on the sale of an overall business. Therefore, the goodwill value associated with an ongoing entity will be absent – no value is attributable in liquidation to such factors as managerial skills, business name, customer loyalty and the like. For that reason, the Liquidation Value method will ordinarily not be employed to value a business for which goodwill or going concern value has commercial importance.

The speed with which those individual sales occur is dictated by the value premise. In the case of an orderly disposition of the assets of a business, the valuation premise is that all of the assets of the business will be sold individually "and that they will enjoy normal exposure to their appropriate secondary market"[735] In contrast, the valuation premise underlying a forced sale is that the assets will be sold individually "and that they will experience less than normal exposure to their appropriate secondary market."[736] Rapid sales in a forced liquidation, of course, usually result in lower sales prices.

If an operating enterprise is generating losses (or only minimal pre-tax profits), then the Liquidation Value of the business may exceed its value as a profit-generating entity. Dickie tells the story of Alexander's, the New York department store chain that filed for bankruptcy in 1995.[737] At the time of its bankruptcy filing, Alexander's was unable to pay its debts out of revenues in the ordinary course of business – it was insolvent. The company's most valuable assets were in fact "the buildings housing its 11 stores and the land under them, particularly the block-long parcel in Manhattan, across the street from Bloomingdale's flagship store on the upper East Side."[738] As Dickie relates, the market value of those real estate assets exceeded Alexander's going concern value because the retail operations of the various department stores on those sites had, sadly, a negative value. Thus, Liquidation Value exceeded going concern value in that case. Recall that market value includes the principle of "highest and best use." If the business has greater value in liquidation than as a going concern, the valuation expert will appropriately employ Liquidation Value despite the fact that the company is a going concern. Smutny also comments that an Income-Based valuation resulting in a low or negative value may not mean the subject property is worthless. "It may simply mean that it may not have meaningful value as a profit generating venture in comparison to other possible investments. It may have a liquidation value or value in some other respect."[739]

735. *Id.*

736. *Id.*

737. Dickie, Financial Statement Analysis and Business Valuation for the Practical Lawyer, *supra* n. 489, at 69–70, Sidebar 3.4.

738. *Id.*, at 70.

739. Smutny, *supra* n. 115, at 13 n. 32.

Chapter 8
Discounts

Once an equity value has been established, it may still be necessary to reduce that value to reflect discounts for minority interests or for lack of marketability, among others. The AICPA's Valuation Standard SSVS 1 instructs valuation analysts to consider whether valuation discounts or premiums should be included in a business valuation. In particular, SSVS 1 notes discounts for lack of marketability (DLOM) and for lack of control (DLOC).[740] These two discounts "taken together, can easily make the value of a minority interest less than half the value of a proportionate share of the value of the business as a whole."[741] Alternatively, in some

740. SSVS 1, *supra* n. 17, at ¶ 40.

741. The Lawyer's Business Valuation Handbook, *supra* n. 411, at 196. In addition to the DLOC and DLOM discounts discussed below, other discounts occasionally found in business valuations at the enterprise level include a key person discount, a portfolio discount, a trapped capital gains discount, a litigation risk discount and an environmental risk discount. *See*, e.g., *Hodas v. Spectrum Technology, Inc.*, 1992 Del. Ch. LEXIS 252, *13 (Del. Ch. 1992) (key man discount warranted). Shareholder-level discounts occasionally asserted include voting versus nonvoting shares and a blockage discount. Readers interested in a summary of these various discounts may wish to look at The Lawyer's Business Valuation Handbook, *supra* n. 411, at 220–225. *See* also International Glossary of Business Valuation Terms, *supra* n. 17. Arbitrators should be sensitive to the potential that the use of a discount is already accounted for in another aspect of the valuation. For example, does a requested discount for lack of voting rights overlap with a DLOC? Does a requested "key person" discount overlap with a size premium in an Income-Based discount rate? The answers will vary from case to case. Arbitrators should also be sensitive to industry practice and accounting requirements; for example, to comply with US GAAP and in particular the "fair value" rules of SFAS 157, US private equity industry valuation guidelines do not permit use of a blockage discount for share in publicly-traded companies. *See* US Private Equity Valuation Guidelines, *supra* n. 24, ¶ 44

circumstances, if the calculated equity value is a minority value, it may become necessary to increase the value by a "control premium:"

> A common question often asked of valuation practitioners by attorneys is what the typical range of valuation discounts are that apply to the valuation of a minority interest in a privately held company. It is not possible to answer this question without first asking a clarifying question – discount from what?[742]

We look here at the minority discount, also known as the Discount for Lack of Control (DLOC), and the marketability discount, known as the Discount for Lack of Marketability (DLOM). The DLOC and the DLOM are occasionally combined by valuation analyses into a single discount. However, it has become much more common to distinguish the two discounts and account for them separately.[743] A US Tax Court decision in 1982 explained the distinction between the two discounts in the following terms:

> In their arguments, neither petitioner nor respondent clearly focuses on the fact that two conceptually distinct discounts are involved here, one for lack of marketability and the other for lack of control. The minority shareholder discount is designed to reflect the decreased value of shares that do not convey control of a closely held corporation. The lack of marketability discount, on the other hand, is designed to reflect the fact that there is no ready market for shares in a closely held corporation. Although there may be some overlap between these two discounts in that lack of control may reduce marketability, it should be borne in mind that even controlling shares in a nonpublic corporation suffer from lack of marketability because of the absence of a ready private placement market and the fact that flotation costs would have to be incurred if the corporation were to publicly offer its stock.[744]

The following Chart 8.1 may help readers to place the location of these discounts and their relationship to the measure of value being used in the valuation.

---

at 11; "2007 Updated Private Equity Valuation Guidelines Frequently Asked Questions," <www.peigg.org/images/2007__March_Updated_US_PE_Valuation_Guidelines.pdf>, at ¶¶ 19, 20.

742. Risius, *Business Valuation: A Primer for Legal Professionals*, *supra* n. 19, at 147.

743. *Id.*, at 197.

744. *Estate of Andrews v. Comm'r*, 79 T.C. 938, 953 (1982).

Chart 8.1. Relationship of Discounts to Equity Value

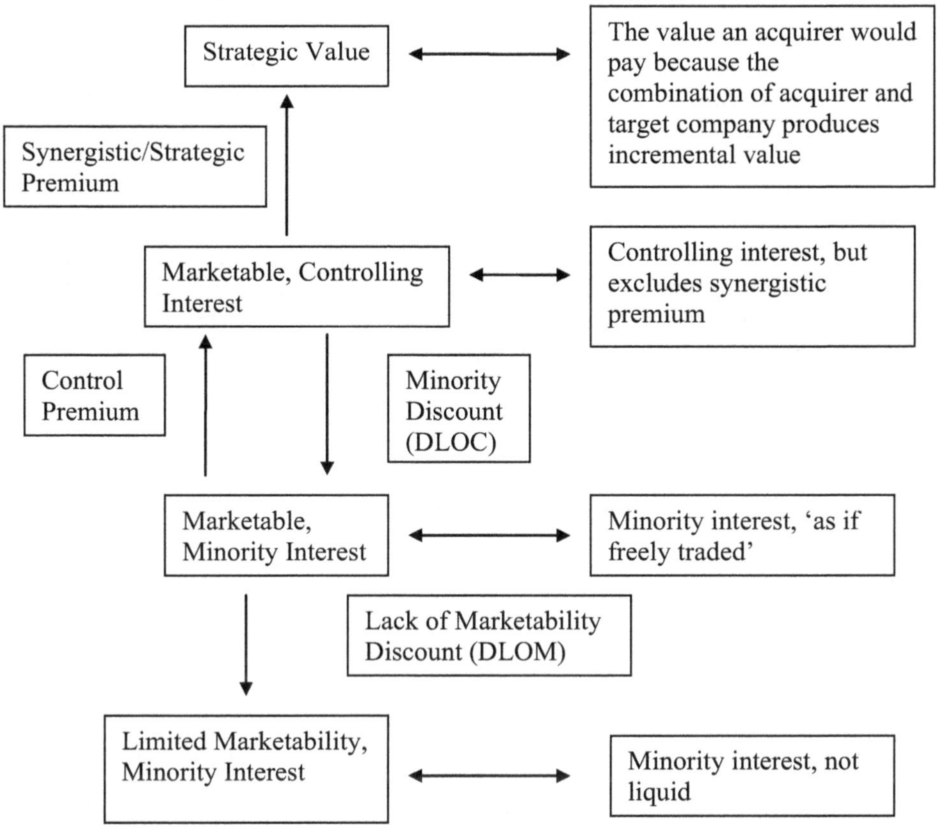

Asset-Based valuation methods assume that the investor has the ability to dispose of the company's assets. Accordingly, an Asset-Based valuation presumes a "controlling interest" basis. If the arbitration involves the valuation of a minority interest in a company, the valuation should consider whether a DLOC or DLOM is warranted.[745] Income-Based methods like DCF, CCF and APV, in contrast, may be calculated on either a controlling or minority-interest basis. The valuation expert must therefore first determine which basis, controlling or minority, was used before deciding if a DLOC or DLOM is appropriate. To produce a controlling-interest valuation, the cash flows would first be adjusted for changes (if any) to reflect how a controlling owner would run the business.

One such dispute arbitrators may face is whether, in connection with a Market-Based "comparable companies" valuation, the enterprise value is a controlling-interest value or a minority-interest value. If the comparable company is a public company and its value is derived from its stock price, then the resulting value is "a minority-interest level of value because the multiples are based on minority

745. Risius, *Business Valuation: A Primer for Legal Professionals*, *supra* n. 19, at 150.

transactions of stock."[746] If Google, Inc. is presented as a public company comparable to the business being valued in the arbitration, and the multiplier is stock price-to-earnings (the P/E ratio), the price component of that ratio is the current trading price for one share of stock in Google, clearly a minority interest. Therefore, argue these experts, a value based on Google's P/E ratio is a minority-interest value, and no DLOC is appropriate.

Other experts challenge this position. They argue that public companies like Google are subject to significant shareholder, analyst and regulatory review. Consequently, those companies are operated in an efficient fashion. As a result, these experts assert, the values resulting from individual stock prices are the same as what a controlling owner would pay.[747] A third set of contenders argue that the multiples should be treated neutrally with respect to this issue. Instead, just as is the case for Income-Based methods, the numbers underlying the multiplier (earnings, revenues, assets, etc.) should be scrutinized to determine if they require adjustment to reflect how a controlling owner would run the business.[748]

Arbitrators may therefore anticipate that contending experts will present this question to the tribunal for decision; perhaps an instance of the blind leading the deaf. Since valuation professionals have not yet resolved this dispute among themselves, arbitrators must do the best they can based upon the evidence before them and the advocacy of counsel.

I MINORITY DISCOUNT (DLOC)

Some sales transactions do not involve the sale of an entire company, but rather the sale of a minority interest in that company. Arbitrators should be particularly cautious about simply extrapolating the value of an enterprise from the sales price for a minority interest on a straight-line basis. Purchasers may pay a control premium for a controlling interest in a company. The same concept is often called a discount for lack of control ("*DLOC*") when backing into the value for a minority non-controlling interest based upon information about sales of controlling interests; a DLOC is "an amount or percentage deducted from the pro rata share of value of 100% of an equity interest in a business to reflect the absence of some or all of the powers of control."[749]

Discount for Lack of Control (DLOC)

The Discount for Lack of Control (DLOC) is an amount or percentage deducted from the sale of the minority non-controlling equity interest in the business to reflect the absence of some or all of the powers of control. Experts often differ widely on the range of minority discounts that may be appropriate.

746. *Id.*, at 152.
747. *Id.*
748. *Id.*
749. IVSC Business Valuation Guidance Note, *supra* n. 15, at ¶ 3.14.

Additionally, both majority and minority ownership interests in private companies are often bound by contractual governance or transferability restrictions under shareholder agreements. Those contractual restrictions can materially affect valuations (up or down).[750] An arbitrator may seek assurance that the expert valuation evidence properly accounts for such restraints where they exist. A valuation expert may be neglecting important contractual transfer restrictions or inappropriately conflating ordinary contract provisions into transfer restrictions. Here again, questioning of the expert witness will clarify whether an apples-to-apples comparison is being offered.

Even where no special contractual restrictions apply, experts often differ widely on the range of minority discounts or control premiums that may be appropriate. Indeed, some experts may even question the need for a minority discount or control premium at all. Common sense tells us, though, that purchasers in an arm's-length transaction will pay more for a controlling investment in a company than a non-controlling share. Valuation experts therefore may testify in US proceedings to a range for a DLOC (when calculating the value of a minority interest derived from sales of controlling interests in comparable transactions) of 15% to 40%, an obviously wide range. Damodaran has recently surveyed some of the more important studies; his conclusion for US markets is that "[t]here is clear evidence that practitioners apply control premiums in private company transactions, ranging from 15 to 20% for a majority stake; conversely, this translates into an equivalent discount for a minority stake."[751]

A number of valuation professionals argue that, if the DCF valuation relies upon market stock price data to develop the discount rate, then it is necessary to add a "control premium" because stocks trade in the market at a "minority price." Therefore, according to these experts, reliance on that market data inside the DCF computation results in an implicit minority discount. The Delaware courts are skeptical. In *Lane v. Cancer Treatment Centers of America, Inc.*, the Court of Chancery quoted with approval Pratt's rejection of that argument.

---

750. *See* IRS Rev. Rul. 59–60, § 8 (1959) (discussing the impact of restrictions on transfer of stock covered by a shareholders agreement in the context of US estate and gift taxes).

751. Damodaran, The Value of Control: Implications for Control Premia, Minority Discounts and Voting Share Differentials at 58, available at <http://pages.stern.nyu.edu/~adamodar/New__Home__Page>. Another possible source of information about the size of a DLOC is studies of closed-end investment funds. Closed-end funds are publicly-traded companies that hold and trade portfolios of other publicly-traded securities; and are prominent examples. Surprisingly, numerous research studies show that publicly-traded shares of closed-end funds typically trade at a discount compared to the aggregate value in the open market of the securities within their portfolios. Many researchers believe the discount reflects the shareholder's lack of control over the underlying securities in the portfolio. Therefore, the discount can be argued to be a proxy for a DLOC. Median discounts for a closed-end fund are lower than discounts shown for control premium studies; typically 5–15%. Risius, *Business Valuation: A Primer for Legal Professionals*, *supra* n. 19, at 156. Ogier, Rugman & Spicer consider that the "general guidance" for valuing a minority stake in a publicly traded company is a minority discount of 10–15%. Ogier, Rugman & Spicer, The Real Cost of Capital: A Business Field Guide to Better Financial Decisions, *supra* n. 464, at 264.

> Some analysts believe that the income approach always produces a publicly traded minority basis of value because the Capital Assets Pricing Model (CAPM) and the buildup model develop discount and capitalization rates from minority transaction data in the public markets. This is a very common and highly flawed conclusion. *There is little or no difference in the rate of return that most investors require for investing in a public, freely tradable minority interest versus a controlling interest.*[752]

While the use of market data to develop a discount rate might not have required a "control premium" adjustment in *Lane*, the same was not true for the values produced by the comparable companies analysis in the same case.[753] Accordingly, the court added a premium to the comparable companies analysis to adjust for the minority discount, but not to the DCF analysis.[754]

II DISCOUNT FOR LACK OF MARKETABILITY (DLOM)

In addition to a minority discount, determining the disputed company's value based on stock prices may also require the arbitrator to consider the impact on that value of the liquidity or illiquidity of the equity interest in the disputed company – whether the market for that particular equity interest is so shallow that it impedes the ability to find ready buyers. In many cases, the expert will derive the value of a private company by looking to the price of publicly traded stock of comparable companies. This is not surprising, of course, since it is very difficult to obtain stock price information for private companies. Stock price information for public companies, in contrast, is by definition publicly available.

However, one of the purposes behind taking a company public is to enhance the marketability of the stock by creating a deep, highly liquid market for that stock, protected by a credible securities regulatory framework like the ones that exist in the US, UK and Western European securities markets. Such liquidity clearly enhances the value of shares, by making it much easier for a shareholder quickly to sell the shares if necessary. Public securities markets also assist buyers and sellers alike with clear price information. Additionally, the level of investor and regulatory scrutiny of public companies is higher than for private companies. In comparison, capital stock of private companies may be harder to resell. The market for securities issued by private companies is far less deep, delays may occur as a result of searching for potential buyers and the reassurance offered by independent regulatory and analyst oversight is lower. Moreover, privately held

752. *Lane v. Cancer Treatment Centers of America, Inc.*, *supra* n. 1, at 118, quoting Pratt, Business Valuation Discounts and Premiums, at 30 (John Wiley & Sons, Inc. 2001) (emphasis in original).
753. *Id.*, at 129, citing to Travelocity.com, Inc., 2004 Del Ch. LEXIS 75, 2004 WL 1152338, at *8.
754. "Although this Court has tended to apply a control premium on the order of 30%, Cimasi advocated, on behalf of Lane, a 20% premium. The Court does not consider the premium advocated by Cimasi unreasonable and, thus, will adopt it." *Id.*, at 130 (footnotes omitted).

shares of a company are often subject to transfer restrictions found in shareholder agreements (preemption rights). As a result, prices for stock in private companies are often lower to reflect these impediments.

Valuation practices in the business world thus often call for application of a discount for lack of marketability (DLOM). For example, the International Private Equity Valuation Guidelines expect that a marketability discount may be employed to value an ownership interest in a private business. Those Guidelines note that "[a] discount in the range of 10% to 30% (in steps of 5%) is generally used in practice, depending on the particular circumstances."[755] Many expert valuation witnesses will accordingly testify to a DLOM when considering the value of equity in a private company."an amount or percentage deducted from the value of an ownership interest to reflect the relative absence of marketability."[756]

Again, the IVSC definition of a DLOM is similar: "An amount or percentage deducted from an equity interest to reflect lack of marketability."[757]

Discount for Lack of Marketability (DLOM)

A Discount for Lack of Marketability (DLOM) is an amount or percentage deducted from the value of an equity interest to reflect the relative absence of marketability. In the U.S., the benchmark against which a DLOM is measured is common stock registered with the SEC and having an active trading market. Experts often differ widely on the range of DLOM's that may be appropriate.

The benchmark in the US against which a lack of marketability discount is measured is common stock securities registered with the US Securities and Exchange Commission and having an active trading market.[758] The experts, though, may disagree about whether a DLOM from comparable public stock prices is applicable to equity interests in a closely held company like a joint venture. Further, the experts may also disagree about the size of the DLOM that is appropriate, and the available research again shows a very wide range. Numerous academics and other valuation experts have researched this issue for US markets. The following discount numbers should be used cautiously; no research study is definitive and, of course, use of US data in international disputes is never simple. In the US market,

755. "International Private Equity Valuation Guidelines," *supra* n. 26 , at 19. As another illustration of practices in the private equity industry, for an investment as part of an initial public offering in shares of a publicly-traded company that are subject to a "lock-up" preventing trading, "[i]n the case of a six-month lock-up period, in practice a discount of 20% to the market price is often used at the beginning of the period, reducing to zero at the end of the period." *Id.*, at 24.

756. International Glossary of Business Valuation Terms, *supra* n. 17.

757. IVSC Business Valuation Guidance Note, *supra* n. 15, at ¶ 3.29.

758. The Lawyer's Business Valuation Handbook, *supra* n. 411, at 207 et seq.

however, research studies have compared freely transferable public stock of a company with so-called "restricted" stock of the same company (for example, stock granted to senior executives of the same company as part of their compensation package). For restricted stock studies, the average discount have ranged from the low twenties to about 45%, with "the majority clustering around 35 percent."[759] Studies of initial public offerings (IPOs) have also offered some guidance, with a majority range of 32–75% for the DLOMs.[760] The size of the company may significantly affect lack of marketability discounts, with research studies of restricted stock showing mean discounts of 32.9% for very small companies with revenues under USD 10 million annually, ranging downward to an average discount of 14.9% for larger companies with revenues over USD 100 million.[761] Some experts will conclude that restricted stock studies are a more reliable means of estimating a DLOM than IPO studies.[762] Naturally, the use of US market studies to guide arbitrators in making decisions about discounts for non-US companies is fraught with comparability challenges. Yet, disregarding the impact of marketability on the value of an ownership interest just because the business at issue is from a country for which research studies are not yet available creates as well the potential for error.

If the evidence in an arbitration warrants considering a DLOM, the arbitrator should be sensitive to several points. First, as we have previously pointed out, many shareholder agreements contain contractual provisions that increase the value of the covered stock; for example, "tag-along rights" guaranteeing a minority shareholder the ability to sell its shares along with a controlling shareholder to the same buyer and at the same price. In some industries, the only likely buyer of a business is a company that wishes to acquire a controlling interest. The presence of tag-along rights or a put provision may thus enhance the marketability of stock held by minority investors in such circumstances. Other common provisions of a

---

759. *Id.*, at 209. *See also Estate of James Waldo Hendrickson v. Comm'r*, *supra* n. 41, at *74–75, referring generally to evidence of "several empirical studies that, on average, support the application of marketability discounts in the range of 30 to 45 percent." As Ogier, Rugman & Spicer point out, the US restricted securities studies show differing results depending on the stringency of US securities law restrictions on trading of the stock. Studies covering periods before 1990 suggest an average discount for restricted stock of 30–35%. The US loosened its trading restrictions for restricted stock somewhat in 1990 and later. Studies since 1990 suggest that the discount has fallen to 20–30% (or even to 15% based upon the latest changes to the US restricted stock trading rules). Ogier, Rugman & Spicer, The Real Cost of Capital: A Business Field Guide to Better Financial Decisions, *supra* n. 464, at 259. Arbitrators must therefore be sensitive to the dates of studies relied on by experts and whether the restrictions on the stock at that time were comparable to the restrictions in the case before the arbitral panel.

760. *See* Damodaran, Marketability and Value: Measuring the Illiquidity Discount, at 30–31, available at <http://pages.stern.nyu.edu/~adamodan/New__Home__Page>.

761. The Lawyer's Business Valuation Handbook, *supra* n. 411, at 209, referring to Oliver & Meyers, "Analysis of Restricted Stocks of Public Companies: 1980–1995," The Management Planning Study (Ch. 12) in Mercer, Quantifying Marketability Discounts (1997).

762. Damodaran criticizes the IPO studies, saying "it seems likely that what these studies conclude is a marketability discount is reflective of other factors." Damodaran, Marketability and Value: Measuring the Illiquidity Discount, *supra* n. 760, at 31.

shareholders agreement, like "drag-along rights," puts and calls, rights of first refusal and rights of first offer, will also significantly affect valuations (again, both up and down).[763] And many shareholder agreements contain outright restrictions on share transfers that bind not only the original signatories but also subsequent permitted transferees. If such provisions are present, arbitrators should expect expert valuation witnesses to testify to their impact on the company's valuation.

Second, the individual characteristics of the business at issue in the dispute will certainly affect the discount. As an illustration, for companies located in countries like the US where the sale of an ownership interest in a business may attract tax on accumulated capital gains, potentially large corporate tax obligations for significant accumulated capital gains may be a factor taken into account in calculating a DLOM. Similarly, the presence of substantial net operating losses, and the resulting attractive US tax benefits, may enhance marketability of some companies.

III OVERLAP

Both conceptually and in practice, the DLOC and the DLOM may overlap.[764] The presence of contractual rights and restrictions in shareholder agreements affecting both control and marketability will enhance this potential overlap. Arbitrators must be sensitive to the risk of double discounting, and make adjustments necessary to prevent that result. Illustratively, the US Tax Court applied a combined 35% DLOM and DLOC to the value of a "Subchapter S" corporation engaged in the liquor business (Korbel, well known for its champagne), taking into account for that purpose both the Subchapter S status of the company and the effect of a contractual right of first refusal in the shareholder arrangements.[765]

Overlapping Discounts

A DLOC and a DLOM may overlap, both conceptually and in practice. Arbitrators must therefore be sensitive to the risk of double counting. Also, DLOC's and DLOM's are not additive. Instead, they are multiplicative; they are taken one after another in sequence.

763. "Both Drs. Bajaj and Spiro also believe that the ROFR [right of first refusal] would reduce value, but disagree both as to rationale and quantum. We are satisfied that some amount of discount is attributable to the ROFR and that 10 percent is an appropriate discount for both the ROFR and the purchaser's minority status, given Dr. Spiro's addition of a 10-percent discount for Korbel's status as an S corporation." *Estate of Heck v. Comm'r, supra* n. 152, at *53.

764. "[T]here may be some overlap between these two discounts in that lack of control may reduce marketability." *Estate of Andrews v. Comm'r, supra* n. 744, at 953 (1982).

765. *Estate of Heck v. Comm'r, supra* n. 152, at *53.

Minority and marketability discounts are not additive. They are normally multiplicative; that is to say, they are taken one after another in sequence.[766] If, say, the value of "control" shares in a company is USD 10 per share, the minority discount (DLOC) is 25% and the marketability discount (DLOM) is also 25%, the valuation calculation would be:[767]

USD 10.00	Control Value
−2.50	Less: DLOC (.25 x USD 10.00)
USD 7.50	Marketable Minority Value
−1.875	Less: DLOM (.25 x 7.50 USD)
USD 5.625	Per Share Value of Limited Marketability, Minority Shares

Arbitrators do not, of course, always accept DLOCs and DLOMs. The ICSID panel in *ADC v. Hungary* rejected the application of either discount to the valuation of the ADC entities' minority interest in an expropriated airport operating concession. With respect to the discount for lack of marketability, the arbitrators stated:

> As is currently pointed out by Dr. Spiller of LECG [the investor's expert], an illiquidity discount is usually associated with privately held companies that have erratic or volatile cash flows. Regulated entities, such as the Project Company, do not typically attract an illiquidity discount because of the relatively stable cash flows associated with them. This is also shown by BAA's acquisition of Budapest Airport Rt. [the successor airport operator] on December 22, 2005 which did not involve an illiquidity discount.[768]

The *ADC v. Hungary* arbitrators also rejected application of a DLOC, asserting that "no such discount is required to be applied since ADC Affiliate had adequate shareholder protections in the Project Agreements."[769] The award does not make clear whether the "shareholder protections" were specific minority shareholder voting protections of the type often found in shareholder agreements or the entirety of contract rights granted to the ADC entities under the Project Agreements, including "rate of return" protections and fixed management fees.

If an expert witness testifies to a specific discount but the underlying support identifies a range of potential discount values, the experts can be encouraged to explain how and why the particular discount was selected from within that range.

---

766. "[W]e note that as a general proposition the application of a minority discount and discount for marketability is multiplicative rather than additive. *See* Trugman, Understanding Business Valuation: A Practical Guide to Valuing Small to Medium-Sized Businesses 286 (1998)." *Id.* at *33. *See also* The Lawyer's Business Valuation Handbook, *supra* n. 411, at 198.
767. Based upon Exhibit 13-1 in *id.*, at 198.
768. *ADC v. Hungary*, *supra* n. 111, at ¶ 512. These comments appear to apply concerns over the stability of cash flows and the appropriate discount rate for a DCF valuation towards the separate issue of a DLOM for illiquidity in the market for selling the investment itself.
769. *Id.*

Ultimately, even the most adamant expert witness will acknowledge that determination of these discounts is inexact. Arbitrators must live with a high level of uncertainty when grappling with the difficult issues created by DLOCs and DLOMs. Ignoring the potential for such discounts is, though, improper in appropriate cases.

Chapter 9
Checklist for Interest

Courts and commentators commonly acknowledge that interest has three functions; compensating the injured party, preventing the other party from being unjustly enriched and encouraging timely resolution of disputes.

> There are three reasons for requiring a respondent to pay interest to a claimant that has succeeded on its damages claims. The first rationale is to fully compensate the claimant by restoring it to the position it would have enjoyed if the breach had not occurred. In this context, the payment of interest recognizes that, by refusing to pay the claimant immediately, the respondent has deprived the claimant of the ability to invest the sum owed. Thus, interest compensates the claimant for the loss of the use of its money because of this delay.
>
> The second reason for awarding interest is to prevent unjust enrichment of the respondent. Respondents that retain the use of money owed to the claimants during the resolution of the dispute are said to have unfairly benefited from its use. They are receiving the earning capacity of the borrowed money without compensating the claimants for the loss of its use. The respondents thus should pay the opportunity cost of the money withheld to the claimants.
>
> The third reason for awarding interest is that it promotes efficiency. Without interest, claimants will not be fully compensated for their loss. As a result, respondents may be insufficiently deterred, may not try to avoid future litigation, and, indeed, may even take steps to delay the resolution of the dispute because respondents profit from the use of claimants' money while the dispute is being resolved. This possibility may also cause claimants to be over-deterred and to take excessive precautions to avoid future litigation. Thus, interest awards encourage parties both to avoid disputes and, if they do occur, to resolve them in a timely manner.[770]

770. Gotanda, "Compound Interest in International Disputes" (2004) Oxford U. Comp. L Forum 1 at ouclf.iuscomp.org, text following n. 20 (footnotes omitted).

Much has already been written elsewhere about the proper approach towards the rate of interest on the awarded sum.[771] Instead of repeating that work, we simply offer the following checklist of issues that arbitrators face in making their decisions about the proper interest rate to be applied to award amounts.

Checklist of Issues Related to Interest

A number of computation issues affect the rate of interest on the awarded sum.

- legal sources of interest calculations;
- the currency of the interest rate;
- fixed or floating interest rates ;
- the day count (e.g., "Actual/360" or "30/365");
- compounding;
- beginning dates for interest accrual.

I LEGAL SOURCES OF INTEREST CALCULATIONS

The first question, of course, is whether there is a contractual agreement between the parties on the proper interest rate and, if so, is it binding for purposes of the arbitration? If there is no binding contract rate, is there a statutory or treaty-based interest rate and, if so, is that legal rule binding on the arbitration? The authority of the arbitral panel to award interest may vary depending upon whether the question arises with respect to pre-award interest, post-award/pre-confirmation interest or post-confirmation interest.[772] The US Federal Arbitration Act and the UNCITRAL Model Law on International Commercial Arbitration are both silent as to the issue of post-award interest. The English Arbitration Act 1996, though, specifically addresses the authority of arbitrators in this area, permitting the arbitral tribunal

771. *See*, e.g., Senechal, "Time Value of Money: A Case Study, in Transnational Dispute Management Special Issue on Compensation and Damages in International Investment Arbitration," vol. 4, issue 6, available on-line at <www.transnational-dispute-management.com>. *See also* Colón & Knoll, "Prejudgment Interest in International Arbitration, in Transnational Dispute Management Special Issue on Compensation and Damages in International Investment Arbitration," vol. 4, issue 6, available on-line at <www.transnational-dispute-management.com>, at 6. "When a tribunal is faced with the issue of determining an award of prejudgment interest, it must make, at the very least, the following three important determinations: 1. The period over which prejudgment interest is to run; 2. The prejudgment interest rate; and 3. The compounding frequency. In addition, if the damage and award are in different currencies, a tribunal must also determine when to convert these currencies."

772. *See* Coe, International Commercial Arbitration: American Principles and Practice in a Global Context at 297–299 (Transnational Publishers 1997); Gotanda, Awarding Interest in International Arbitration, 90 Am. J. Int. Law 40 (1996).

to grant "simple or compound interest from such dates, as such rates and with such rests as it considers meets the justice of the case:"

> 49. (1) The parties are free to agree on the powers of the tribunal as regards the award of interest.
>
> (2) Unless otherwise agreed by the parties the following provisions apply.
>
> (3) The tribunal may award simple or compound interest from such dates, at such rates and with such rests as it considers meets the justice of the case.
>
> (a) on the whole or part of any amount awarded by the tribunal, in respect of any period up to the date of the award;
>
> (b) on the whole or part of any amount claimed in the arbitration and outstanding at the commencement of the arbitral proceedings but paid before the award was made, in respect of any period up to the date of payment.
>
> (4) The tribunal may award simple or compound interest from the date of the award (or any later date) until payment, at such rates and with such rests as it considers meets the justice of the case, on the outstanding amount of any award (including any award of interest under subsection (3) and any award as to costs).
>
> (5) References in this section to an amount awarded by the tribunal include an amount payable in consequence of a declaratory award by the tribunal.
>
> (6) The above provisions do not affect any other power of the tribunal to award interest.

Statutes in many jurisdictions, of course, specify the applicable interest rate on court judgments; jurisdictions differ as to whether those statutes cover arbitration awards. Moreover, extensive case law and commentary discuss whether those statutes and applicable arbitration law limit the authority of arbitrators to grant post-award interest and whether the ability to award interest is an inherent remedial power of the arbitrator. A thoughtful arbitrator may ask the parties for their views at an early stage in the proceedings, before it is obvious who will win the dispute.

Occasionally, the interest rate is addressed by the applicable arbitration rules. The ICC, UNCITRAL and ICSID arbitration rules are currently silent as to interest. Proposals have been made to include express authorization of interest in the forthcoming revision of the UNCITRAL Rules. Article 28(4) of the American Arbitration Association's International Arbitration Rules provides that 'the tribunal may award such pre-award and post-award interest, simple or compound, as it considers appropriate, taking into consideration the contract and applicable law.' The LCIA Arbitration Rules also expressly authorizes interest. Rule 26.6 states in relevant part:

> The Arbitral Tribunal may order that simple or compound interest shall be paid by any party on any sum awarded at such rates as the Arbitral Tribunal determines to be appropriate, without being bound by legal rates of interest imposed by any state court, in respect of any period which the Arbitral Tribunal determines to be appropriate ending not later than the date upon which the award is complied with.

More generally, the AAA's Commercial Arbitration Rules provide in Article 43 that the arbitrator "may grant any remedy or relief that the arbitrator deems just and equitable and within the scope of the agreement of the parties."

II CURRENCY

Arbitrators will also be called upon to decide what currency is associated with the proper interest rate. Obviously, base rates for different currencies can vary widely. In the NAFTA *S.D. Meyers, Inc. v. Canada* award, the arbitrators awarded compensation in Canadian dollars (CAD). Then, the panel was faced with the question of whether to order interest at a prevailing CAD rate or, because the claimant SDMI would have converted its CAD revenues immediately into USD in the ordinary course of its business, at a prevailing USD rate. The panel chose to employ a CAD rate, because it was the currency of the lost revenue stream and the award:

> 304. The rate of interest to be applied is closely connected with the question of the currency of account in which the award of compensation is made.
>
> 305. On the one hand, the currency in which SDMI operated was US$ and no doubt all income received into SDMI's bank account in Ohio would have been converted into that currency. On the other hand, based on the bids made to potential Canadian customers (and the revenue from the seven completed contracts), the currency of account of the transactions between SDMI/MYERS Canada and their Canadian customers was (or was to be) CAN$. On balance, the Tribunal considers that the currency of account of the lost income stream is more closely connected with the loss and damage suffered by SDMI than the working currency of SDMI in Ohio. Accordingly, the Tribunal determines that the currency of the compensation awarded in this Second Partial Award should be CAN$.
>
> 306. It follows that the interest rate to be applied should be related to the standard Canadian prime rates applicable from time to time during the relevant period. The relevant period shall be the date of the Notice of Arbitration to the date of payment of the Award. Such interest shall be compounded annually.[773]

III FIXED OR FLOATING

To what "money market" is it appropriate for arbitrators to look as a possible source of a base rate of interest (LIBOR, prime, Bank of England rate, Federal Reserve discount rate, etc.)? And should interest be "fixed" or "floating?"[774]

---

773. *S.D. Myers, Inc. v. Canada*, UNCITRAL (NAFTA) Second Partial Award (Damages), 21 October 2002, at ¶¶ 304–306. *See* Colón & Knoll, Prejudgment Interest in International Arbitration, *supra* n. 771, at 18–21, for a discussion of foreign currency adjustments.

774. *See* Colón & Knoll, Prejudgment Interest in International Arbitration, *supra* n. 771, at 14–16.

Moreover, if the base rate for interest is a floating rate such as LIBOR (the London Interbank Offered Rate), rather than a fixed per annum rate, what mechanism should be built into the award to avoid future calculation disputes between the parties about the impact of fluctuations in that floating rate? Some arbitral panels seek to specify a floating rate for post-award interest, but do so in such a succinct manner that calculation issues persist. For example, one recent award ruled:

> [T]he most appropriate benchmark which will compensate adequately an international company such as PSEG Global is the 6 month average LIBOR plus 2 per cent per year for each year during which amounts are owing. The interest shall start running on the date specified below until payment of the Award. Interest shall be compounded semi-annually.[775]

That interest rate formula leaves open several computation issues. Those issues include (i) identifying the market sources from which the LIBOR rate quotes are to be obtained and averaged and (ii) whether the arbitrators intended the parties to take all of the daily LIBOR rates during the post-award period and average them or to take the average of the LIBOR rates on the first day of that period and each six-month date thereafter. LIBOR-based loan agreements and deposit contracts, by the way, typically employ the latter approach. However, it is by no means clear whether the arbitrators intended to follow the finance markets in their calculation practices.

LIBOR rate quotes are publicly available from several sources, including individual reference banks, the Dow Jones Telerate screen and the Reuters screen. International loan documents employ a far more precise approach to interest calculations than the approach found in arbitration awards, undoubtedly because the question of interest calculations is central to a lender's reason for entering into the loan transaction. Illustratively, CE Casecnan Energy and Water Company, Inc., a Philippine project company, issued its LIBOR+3% Floating Rate Notes in 1996 to finance a Philippine hydropower and irrigation project. Those Notes contain an extremely detailed interest rate provision that is consistent with market practice for USD LIBOR financings:

> [A]nd to pay interest on the unpaid portion of the principal amount [of the Note] at the interest rate set forth above [LIBOR+3.00%] (the "*Interest Rate*") from the most recent Interest Payment Date (as defined below) to which interest has been paid or duly provided for or, if no interest has been paid or duly provided for, from the Issue Date set forth above [the date the Note was initially issued], quarterly in arrears on each February 15, May 15, August 15 and November 15 in each year (the "*Interest Payment Date*"), commencing February 15, 1996, until the principal amount is paid in full or payment thereof is duly provided for. The period from and including the Issue Date set forth above to and including the first Interest Payment Date and each successive period from but excluding an Interest Payment Date to and

775. *PSEG v. Turkey*, *supra* n. 179, at ¶¶ 348.

including the next succeeding Interest Payment Date is herein called an "Interest Period." On the second Business Day (but, as to the determination of the initial Floating Rate Note Interest Rate, four calendar days) prior to the commencement of each Interest Period (an "Interest Determination Date"), the Trustee shall determine what, if any, offered rate for U.S. dollar deposits for the applicable Interest Period appears on the Designated LIBO Page (as defined below) as of 11:00 a.m. (London time) on such Interest Determination Date; *provided* that, if such information is not available on the Designated LIBO Page, the Trustee shall determine a rate from information supplied to the Trustee by a nationally-recognized reporting service for similar information acceptable to the Trustee. The Interest Rate for such Interest Period shall be 300 basis points above such offered rate (or, if the offered rate is not available, the rate determined from information supplied by such nationally-recognized reporting service), rounded upwards, if necessary, to the nearest 1/16th of 1%, as determined by the Trustee. "Designated LIBO Page" means the display designated as "British Bankers Association Interest Settlement Rates" ("BBA"), currently page 3750, on the Dow Jones Telerate Service (or such other page as may replace the "BBA" page on that service for the purpose of displaying London interbank offered rates of major banks).

The above clause shows extreme sensitivity towards the risk that LIBOR rate quotes may not be available from the expected source. That concern reflects international banks' experience with the 1974 Herstatt Bank crisis, when many banks encountered severe difficulties in obtaining LIBOR quotes.

Most arbitration practitioners would find the level of complexity and precision found in the CE Casecnan provision unnecessary and, perhaps, daunting. Even outside the international financial community, though, interest rate provisions in sophisticated business transactions are more precise than most arbitration awards. For instance, the default interest rate provisions for one oil concession joint bidding agreement called for LIBOR +2% compounded monthly.

The amount not paid by the Defaulting Party shall bear interest from the date due until paid in full at the Agreed Interest Rate.

"Agreed Interest Rate" means interest compounded on a monthly basis, at a fluctuating rate per annum equal to the one (1) month term LIBOR rate for U.S. dollar deposits published by the Wall Street Journal or, if not so published, by the Financial Times of London, plus two percent (2%), applicable on the first Working Day prior to the due date of payment and thereafter on the first Working Day of each succeeding one (1) month term.

"Working Day" means a day on which the banks are customarily open for business in Dubai, United Arab Emirates.[776]

776. As a technical matter, it would be appropriate to add a "day count" to this provision; i.e., "at a fluctuating rate per annum, calculated on the basis of a year of 360 days and the actual number of days elapsed, equal to. . . ."

The arbitrator could include in the award a clause modeled on the interest rate provisions from the joint bidding agreement, as follows:

> Interest shall accrue on any unpaid portion of the amount awarded in Paragraph XX above from [insert beginning date] until paid in full, [compounded on a monthly/quarterly/semi-annual basis,] at a fluctuating rate per annum, calculated on the basis of a year of 360 days and the actual number of days elapsed, equal to the [one/three/six] month term LIBOR rate for U.S. dollar deposits published by the Wall Street Journal or, if not so published, by the Financial Times of London, [plus X%], applicable on the first New York banking day prior to [insert beginning date] and thereafter on the first New York banking day of each succeeding [one/three/six] month term.

Arbitrators will be pleased to know that they need not draft their awards with quite the level of detail required by international banks. Still, reference to publicly available quotations may indeed be useful. That will be especially true if the arbitrators anticipate the parties may take the award into other forums for an extended period of time. An arbitrator can easily (sic) incorporate into the award a more technically correct interest rate provision by cross-referencing to definitions commonly accepted by the international financial community. The widely used interest rate definitions in the ISDA (International Swaps and Derivatives Association, Inc.) 2006 Definitions for interest rate and currency swaps may also be useful to arbitrators here who wish a more precise interest computation, along the lines of provisions in finance documents. ISDA drafted its 2006 Definitions to establish objective, self-operating interest rate quotations from publicly available sources. In addition, the ISDA 2006 Definitions contain useful fallback rates if the chosen base rate is not being quoted by reason of an emergency. ISDA offers floating and fixed interest rate definitions for many of the major tradable currencies in the world and, for each currency, a variety of potential base rates.[777] For example, ISDA's definitions of USD LIBOR derived from the Reuters screen reads as follows:

> (xx) "USD_LIBOR-LIBO" means that the rate for a Reset Date will be determined on the basis of the offered rates for deposits in U.S. Dollars for a period of the Designated Maturity which appear on the Reuters Screen LIBO Page as of 11:00 a.m., London time, on the day that is two London Banking Days preceding that Reset Date. If at least two rates appear on the Reuters Screen LIBO Page, the rate for that Reset Date will be the arithmetic mean of such rates. If fewer than two rates appear, the rate for that Reset Date will be determined as if the parties had specified "USD-LIBOR-Reference Banks" as the applicable Floating Rate Option.
>
> (xxi) "USD-LIBOR-Reference Banks" means that the rate for a Reset Date will be determined on the basis of the rates at which deposits in U.S.

777. ISDA also offers useful inflation indexes for twenty-three countries in a different set of definitions, the 2006 ISDA Inflation Derivatives Definitions.

> Dollars are offered by the Reference Banks at approximately 11:00 a.m., London time, on the day that is two London Banking Days preceding that Reset Date to prime banks in the London interbank market for a period of the Designated Maturity commencing on that Reset Date and in a Representative Amount. The Calculation Agent will request the principal London office of each of the Reference Banks to provide a quotation of its rate. If at least two such quotations are provided, the rate for that Reset Date will be the arithmetic mean of the quotations. If fewer than two quotations are provided as requested, the rate for that Reset Date will be the arithmetic mean of the rates quoted by major banks in New York City, selected by the Calculation Agent, at approximately 11:00 a.m., New York City time, on that Reset Date for loans in U.S. Dollars to leading European banks for a period of the Designated Maturity commencing on that Reset Date and in a Representative Amount [an amount comparable to the amount of the award].[778]

Thus, to incorporate ISDA's "USD-LIBOR-LIBO" rate into an arbitration award, the arbitrator can include the following clause to require interest to accrue at LIBOR as quoted on the Reuters screen:

> Interest shall accrue on the amount awarded in Paragraph XX above [if compounding, add "together with unpaid interest thereon as provided in this Paragraph YY accrued and added to the unpaid amount so awarded at the end of each [three-month, six-month, etc.] period,"] for each day from [insert beginning date] until the date such amount is paid in full at a per annum interest rate equal to "USD-LIBOR-LIBO" (as such term is defined in the International Swaps and Derivatives Association, Inc. (ISDA) 2006 Definitions) [*plus* X%, if the arbitrators wish to assess a margin over LIBOR] with a "Designated Maturity" of [select duration for LIBOR; e.g., one month, three months, six months] and "Reset Dates" of [insert beginning date] and thereafter the last day of each succeeding "Designated Maturity" period. If required, the "Calculation Agent" shall be [name of bank] and the Calculation Agent shall select the Reference Banks.

As the forgoing clauses indicate, any time arbitrators elect to use a floating rate, the award must further choose between a shorter-term base rate and a longer-term base rate. For example, three-month LIBOR, six-month LIBOR or nine-month LIBOR? Arbitrators should be aware that there is a link here with the issue of compounding interest – it would be unusual to choose, say, twelve-month LIBOR as the base interest rate but to compound interest semi-annually, because breaking a twelve-month LIBOR funding deposit contract before its maturity triggers indemnification costs owing by the depositor to the deposit bank.

---

778. Similar ISDA floating rate definitions are currently available for USD CD rates, constant maturity, US Treasury securities, commercial paper, Fed Funds, Bond Equivalent Yield, Prime, Treasury bills and several other popular interest rate options. Comparable ISDA rate definitions are currently available for euros, sterling, yen, dollar, the Canadian dollar, the Australian dollar, the Singaporean dollar, the South African rand, the Swiss franc and other popular currencies.

The UNIDROIT Principles on International Commercial Contracts propose in Article 7.4.9 that the short-term bank rate for loans to prime borrows should be employed for default payments:

> Article 7.4.9 (*Interest for failure to pay money*)
>
> (1) If a party does not pay a sum of money when it falls due the aggrieved party is entitled to interest upon that sum from the time when payment is due to the time of payment whether or not the non-payment is excused.
>
> (2) The rate of interest shall be the average bank short-term lending rate to prime borrowers prevailing for the currency of payment at the place for payment, or where no such rate exists at that place, then the same rate in the State of the currency of payment. In the absence of such a rate at either place the rate of interest shall be the appropriate rate fixed by the law of the State of the currency of payment.
>
> (3) The aggrieved party is entitled to additional damages if the non-payment caused it a greater harm.

The Official Comments to Article 7.4.9 explain that the theory underlying the chosen rate is "the rate at which the aggrieved party will normally borrow the money which it has not received from the non-performing party. That normal rate is the average bank short-term lending rate to prime borrowers prevailing at the place for payment for the currency of payment."

The language used in that Article raises obvious calculation questions. Most importantly, no single rate for short-term loans to prime business borrowers is generally published. However, the US Board of Governors of the Federal Reserve System does publish on its website (at <www.federalreserve.gov/releases/cp>) a "daily commercial paper release;" the US dollar market rates for the previous banking day for one-day, seven-day, fifteen-day, thirty-day, sixty-day and ninety-day commercial paper. Obviously, commercial paper is not a bank loan. Commercial paper is, though, now the principal form of short-term unsecured commercial finance for prime US corporate borrowers. To employ a commercial paper rate, an interest clause in an arbitration award for interest payments would need to specify the particular duration of the commercial paper from among those six published maturities, since their rates differ.

Moreover, the Federal Reserve "daily commercial paper" release sets out those rates for four separate categories of credit ratings used by Moody's Investors Service and Standard & Poor's – AA non-financial, A2/P2 non-financial, AA financial and AA asset-backed. The first two of those credit rating categories deal with business borrowers rather than financial borrowers. Any of these rating categories could be used to craft an interest clause in an award. However, if the maturity of the relevant commercial paper and the credit rating category are not both specified in a clause referring to the Federal Reserve's "daily commercial paper release," then the parties to the arbitration will not be able to determine what rate was selected by the arbitrator.

In light of the complexities surrounding floating rate interest calculations, it is no surprise that many arbitrators prefer fixed rate interest provisions. A technically correct clause setting post-award interest at a fixed rate would read as follows:

> Interest shall accrue on any unpaid portion of the amount awarded in Paragraph XX above [if compounding, add "together with unpaid interest thereon as provided in this Paragraph YY accrued and added to the unpaid amount so awarded at the end of each [three-month, six-month, etc.] period,"] for each day from [insert beginning date] until the date such amount is paid in full at an interest rate of X% per annum, calculated on the basis of a year of [360/365] days and the actual number of days elapsed.

IV DAY COUNT

Will interest accrue on the basis of the "Actual/360" rate, the "Actual/365" rate or the "30/360" rate? And what the heck is the difference?

Each of these "day counts" is used in the financial markets for calculating interest. The "Actual/360" rate calls for calculation of interest based on a "year" of 360 days and the actual number of days elapsed. That computational basis for interest is known as the "bank rate," and is regularly employed in domestic money markets in the US, and many European countries. The "bank rate" is also used to calculate LIBOR USD interest rates. In contrast, the "Actual/365" rate calculates interest on a "year" of 365 or 366 days, as the case may be (i.e., in accordance with the common calendar) and the actual number of days elapsed. That approach to interest calculation is used inter alia in domestic money markets in the UK (but not for LIBOR USD), many Commonwealth countries, Japan and Belgium. The international fixed rate bond market, however, employs the "30/360" rate, which is based upon a "year" of 360 days and twelve equal 30-day months (to facilitate coupon-clipping in the old days when bonds had physical coupons).

To exacerbate our confusion, for the bank rate, interest starts to accrue on the second day of the relevant period, and the last day of the first period is also the first day of the second period.[779] However, interest calculated on the bond rate accrues from the first day of the monthly period to and including the last day of that period. Clear, yes?

Do these differences matter? Well, if interest accrues on an award at 8% per annum simple interest for 365 days on a USD 100,000,000 award, a calculation based on the bank rate (Actual/360) will accrue USD 111,111 more interest for the same period than if interest was based on Actual/365 (an effective annual rate of 8.111% rather than 8.0%). At least one arbitrator's fees? Of course, if post-award

779. Even more methods of calculating interest for a "year" are found at <www.financial.org/support/developerfunc/mathref/daycount.htm>.

interest is compounded monthly, quarterly or semi-annually during that year, the differential will be even larger. Rather than re-invent the wheel, arbitrators may prefer to follow the day-count convention in the finance markets for the particular base rate they select.

V COMPOUNDING

Should interest compound? That question has occupied the attention of innumerable arbitrators and counsel, as well as commentators.[780] As Senechal points out, "today, there is no uniform standard of practice for applying interest and calculating present day values. In the finance industry, trade usage has developed over the years but, in arbitration and litigation, a uniform set of rules has not yet emerged."[781] He offers the following trade usages with respect to interest compounding from the world of finance as help for arbitrators, but not as a legally binding standard in arbitration proceedings.

> The following trade usage can be of some help to determine the application of interest rates but not enough to set a standard:
>
> 1. Bonds are often compounded on a yearly or semi-annual basis. Corporate bonds are most frequently payable on the semi-annual basis.
> 2. Mortgage loans generally refer to semi-annual compounding (but sometimes the monthly compounding basis is used, i.e., in the US market).
> 3. Most financial institutions worldwide award interest on a daily (and sometimes bi monthly) compounded basis for money on deposit.
> 4. Continuous compounding is not widely used. In financial engineering, the valuation of derivatives may use continuous compounding.[782]

We will not intervene in the debate over whether compounding is appropriate. If, though, the arbitrators answer this question "yes," over what period should

---

780. *See* e.g., Gotanda, "Compound Interest in International Disputes" *supra* n. 770, surveying interest compounding practices in judicial systems in common law and civil law countries worldwide, including 16 countries and the European Union. In *Vivendi 2007*, the ICSID tribunal made a non-exhaustive review of previous investment arbitration awards and found seven awards granting compound interest and three granting simple interest. Vivendi 2007, *supra* n. 72, at n. 432. *See also* Wilson, Cain & Gray, "ICSID Arbitration Awards and Cost, Transnational Dispute Management," vol. III, issue 5 (December 2006), available at <www.transational–dispute-management.com>, reviewing 14 awards, the majority of which awarded compound interest; and Walde & Sabahi, *supra* n. 331, at 41 ("In fact, most recent awards provide for compound interest – in spite of earlier practices against awarding compound interest.").

781. Presentation by Thierry Senechal at International Chamber of Commerce Conference on Arbitration and Expertise: Use of Experts in International Arbitration, January 11, 2008, at 8.

782. *Id.*

compounding occur (for instance, monthly, quarterly, semi-annually or annually)? The impact of compounding or not compounding can be quite high. If a USD 100,000,000 award accrues interest at 8% for a 365-day year, here is the effect of successively more frequent compounding over a single year.

Period	*Formula*	*Sum*	*Effective Rate*
Annual	USD 100,000,000 × (1+0.08)	= USD 108,000,000	8.000%
Quarterly	USD 100,000,000 × $(1+\frac{0.08}{4})^4$	= USD 108,243,000	8.243%
Monthly	USD 100,000,000 × $(1+\frac{0.08}{12})^{12}$	= USD 108,300,000	8.300%
Weekly	USD 100,000,000 × $(1+\frac{0.08}{52})^{52}$	= USD 108,322,000	8.322%

As the frequency of compounding increases from annual towards weekly, so does the effective interest rate. However, the effective rate will increase more slowly as compounding occurs more frequently. For the same example, the effective rate for daily compounding would be 8.327% for our example and the total would be USD 108,327,000 – a mere USD 5,000 increase over weekly compounding. The commercial and public policy issues that affect the choice of a post-award compounding period are, of course, different in several respects from the issues affecting the choice of a pre-award compounding period. Notably, pre-award compounding may involve a comparison with commercial re-investment and sources of funding less relevant to post-award practice.

VI BEGINNING DATES FOR INTEREST ACCRUAL

In some cases, arbitrators may not easily be able to establish a precise date of loss. The arbitrators will need to determine, notwithstanding, the date from which interest will begin to accrue. For example, when faced with this issue in connection with lost profits claims the United Nations Compensation Commission (UNCC) ordinarily selected the mid-point of the loss period as the operative date.[783] Similarly, the ICSID tribunal in *Siemens v. Argentina* had to decide on the starting date for interest accruing on "post-expropriation costs" incurred on multiple dates. The tribunal ruled that identifying each date for calculation purposes "would not be practicable." Accordingly, the tribunal selected January 1, 2002, being the date "by which most of these costs had been incurred."[784] Similarly, for interest on

783. UNCC, Report and Recommendations Made by the Panel of Commissioners Concerning the First Installment of "E2" Claims, at ¶ 287, S/AC.26/1998/7 (July 3, 1998). *See also* UNCC Saudi Arabian Texaco Claim, *supra* n. 58, at ¶¶ 497.

784. *Siemens v. Argentina, supra* n. 112, at ¶ 397.

unpaid bills for services rendered in 1999, the tribunal commenced interest accrual on January 1, 2000 regardless of the dates of the individual bills.[785]

VII MISCELLANEOUS QUESTIONS

Arbitrators will be faced with numerous other interest calculation questions. Four arise regularly, and call upon the arbitrator to exercise his or her judgment:

(i) Is a "margin" or "spread" over the chosen base rate (whether fixed or floating) appropriate to compensate for risks or lost opportunities?

(ii) If the arbitral panel determines that the proper base rate is the injured party's "cost of funds" or individual borrowing rate, how is that to be determined? Is it solely the cost of the claimant's short-term working capital funds, the all-in cost of the claimant's debt funding, the all-in cost of the claimant's total capital, or something else?

(iii) If the arbitral tribunal determines that the proper rate incorporates the "benefits" of "hedging" against interest or currency fluctuations, what is the "cost" of such "hedging?"[786] Interest rate hedging contracts like swaps, caps and collars may lower a company's nominal interest rate. However, the company will pay the hedge provider an up-front fee to obtain the hedge, in addition to periodic payments. The company must incorporate those fees into the computation of the all-in cost of borrowing.

(iv) Should the tax benefits or tax costs associated with interest be taken into account? Most courts and arbitral panels, of course, decline the invitation to wade into this swamp.[787]

---

785. *Id.*

786. *See id.*, at ¶ 370, for an example of an arbitral tribunal that incorporated the benefits of hedging but perhaps not the costs.

787. *See* Colón & Knoll, Prejudgment Interest in International Arbitration, *supra* n. 771, at 22 (footnotes omitted): "If the claimant's country taxes interest as it accrues (whether or not it is received), the claimant is better off receiving a lump sum award of prejudgment interest because it did have to pay tax earlier on the interest as it accrued. In addition, if the award would have been taxable, the claimant would have been able to have invested only the after-tax proceeds and consequently would not have earned as much interest. In both of these cases, the multiplier should be adjusted to compensate the claimant properly. In spite of the conceptual correctness of making such adjustments, we are not aware of any courts or tribunals that have done. The one court that addressed the issued declined to make such an adjustment."

Chapter 10

What Can the Careful Arbitrator Do?

Thus far in this book, we have pointed out a number of issues with the evidence about company valuations. Our suggestions for how arbitrators can manage these challenges have focused on applying two tools:

- Asking enough questions to determine if an ''apples-to-oranges'' miscomparison exists, and requesting experts to re-present their data to enable an appropriate ''apples-to-apples'' comparison.
- Focusing closely on true comparability, whether between companies or transactions employed in a ''comparables'' analysis or within the details of a DCF, APV, CCF or ABV analysis.

We now turn towards other tools that an arbitrator may employ to encourage experts to present realistic company valuations generally. Many of the tools described in this book contemplate arbitrators taking an active role in structuring the evidentiary process for compensation decisions. That approach by no means attracts a consensus. Questioning by an arbitrator may not sit well with many members of the international arbitration community. Nor may such tools as requests by the arbitrators for lists of material differences,[788] ''hot-tubbing''[789] or multiple scenarios and sensitivity analyses.[790]

> English-speaking lawyers familiar with the (mildly) inquisitorial ways of commercial arbitration may not appreciate the extent to which some legal traditions may view questioning or other active intervention by fact-finders as possible indicators of prejudgment or a lack of neutrality.[791]

---

788. *See* text associated with n. 798 et seq. *infra*.
789. *See* text associated with n. 842 et seq. *infra*.
790. *See* text subsequent to n. 802 *infra*.
791. Crook, Fact-Finding in the Fog: Determining the Facts of Upheavals and Wars in Inter-State Disputes, paper presented at 4th Annual ITA-ASIL Annual Conference (Washington, D.C., March 28, 2007), at 17–18.

Consequently, we caution arbitrators to think carefully about the particular circumstances of a case before employing the tools discussed in this Chapter 10. It makes good sense for an arbitrator to determine first if the objectives can be achieved by less intrusive means. Moreover, some of these proposed measures can be quite costly to the parties, even if not seen as intrusive. We therefore recommend that arbitrators consider whether, and when, to employ these devices; they may be best applied only in those cases where the economic stakes justify the out-of-pocket outlays and the consequences of an extended trial.

The relative reliability of valuation evidence will, of course, differ from case to case and from legal system to legal system. Some civil law systems, for example, give precedence to documentary evidence over oral testimony, while some common law practitioners pay particular attention to oral witness testimony.[792] For arbitrators, it is helpful in assessing expert valuation evidence to understand how valuation professionals weigh documentary evidence when developing their valuations. One experienced valuation practitioner, Geoffrey Senogles, offered his own personal assessment, as follows:

> The following represents a set of very general practical, personal comparative guidelines on documentary evidence:
> - Documents are *better* than verbal assertions/confirmations.
> - Documents prepared by an independent third party are *better* than those prepared by the claimant/insured/defendant/insurer.
> - Documents prepared contemporaneously (and prior to/immediately following the loss event) are *better* than those prepared after the date the claim was submitted.
> - Documents prepared absent any prospect of a claim are *better* than those created in response to (or with knowledge of) the extant claim.
> - Documents audited by a reputable professional firm of accountants are *better* than accounts not subject to this outside review (however limited in practice).
> - Original documents are *better* than photocopies or electronic formats.
>
> The use of the adjective's comparative form *better* attempts to make clear that the issue of evidence is inherently subjective. Notice the avoidance of the superlative form *best*.[793]

I ADVANCE PLANNING

The first and foremost tool available to an arbitrator is advance planning. Thoughtful advance planning can materially reduce the litigation costs of the parties in the arbitration, as well as clarifying the evidence for the arbitrators.

792. Townsend & Elsing, "Bridging the Common Law – Civil Law Divide in Arbitration," *supra* n. 6, at 62.
793. Senogles, *Business interruption claims*, *supra* n. 54, at 18.

The potential for advance planning with respect to valuation date disputes illustrates the point. The arbitrator's decision about the applicable valuation date is one obviously important preliminary step in the compensation determination. In *CMS v. Argentina,*[794] the Claimant argued for a valuation date of August 2000, claiming treaty breaches from that date. The Respondent asserted that the alleged treaty breaches occurred, if at all, no earlier than January 2002. The tribunal selected August 17, 2000 as the date of the treaty breaches and therefore as the valuation date. That difference had large consequences for calculating compensation in the case, because the Argentine economic crisis deepened significantly between August 2000 and January 2002. If the DCF calculations in that dispute had been made as of January 2002 rather than August 2000, then the revenue estimates for the company as of the valuation date would likely have been lower, the inflation and foreign exchange rates different and the discount rate may have been higher. And, of course, there would have been 1½ years less of foregone revenue to compensate. Those changes could have potentially reduced the compensation award by a large amount.[795]

Valuation Date and Advance Planning

The choice of the valuation date can materially affect the amount of compensation to be awarded. If the choice of date is in controversy, advance planning by the arbitrators can be of significant assistance to the parties and the arbitral tribunal.

How does this relate to "advance planning"? At a minimum, arbitrators can focus the parties on the impact of differing valuation dates. The tribunal may ask up front if a dispute exists over the applicable date. The arbitrators may also request the parties to insure that their experts provide valuation evidence to assist the tribunal regardless of how the tribunal decides the dispute over the valuation date. Such an approach would have avoided the situation in which the claimant in *Santa Elena v. Costa Rica*[796] found itself. In that ICSID case, the claimant presented a 1993 property appraisal and a fair market DCF analysis based on a December 31, 1997 valuation date. The panel ruled instead that the operative valuation date was May 5, 1978. The effect of this ruling was to make the claimant's expert evidence irrelevant.

One prominent business valuation treatise reminds valuation professionals about the need in such circumstances to seek advice from their instructing counsel.

794. *CMS v. Argentina, supra* n. 7, at ¶¶ 396–397.
795. The Argentine cases have in fact not settled on a consistent date, with consequences for compensation in the hundreds of millions of Dollars. *See* text associated with n. 201 *et seq. supra*.
796. *Santa Elena v. Costa Rica, supra* n. 212.

> In some litigated cases, the valuation date itself is an issue to be resolved by the court. In such situations, the appraiser must be prepared to address the valuation as of several dates, sometimes without knowing until after the judgment is rendered which date the court determines to be relevant. Since the choice of valuation date in such cases will be a legal matter, the attorney for whom the expert appraiser will be testifying should take the responsibility, as part of defining the assignment, of considering all the potentially applicable valuation dates and instructing the appraiser to be prepared to address the value as of each date. Sometimes a court will give an advance ruling on the valuation date to avoid the expense of appraisers doing valuations as of dates that the court will not deem relevant.[797]

By taking steps to highlight this issue early in the proceedings, the arbitrators may become aware that their choice among potential valuation dates will materially alter the valuation evidence. If the size and complexity of the case warrants, then the tribunal might consider bifurcating the arbitration hearings into two phases, liability and quantum, and deciding the valuation date issue as part of the first phase.

Bifurcation, of course, is often more appropriate in complex cases where the liability issue itself may be dispositive. Moreover, the decision to bifurcate a case into liability and quantum phases has significant cost and tactical consequences for the parties. For example, the impact of bifurcation on the pre-hearing document production process can be significant. The burden of document production as to liability issues is often borne equally by the claimant and the respondent, without easily predictable advantage or disadvantage to either of the parties. The claimant, however, is more likely to have documents bearing on its own alleged damages than the respondent. Once liability is determined, consequently, a successful claimant (not the respondent) will normally bear the principal burden of document production with respect to the damages it claims to have suffered. If the arbitral panel bifurcates the proceedings into liability and quantum phases, the approach of a party towards the breadth of document production for the damages phase of the arbitration may be noticeably different than its attitude towards document production for the liability phase. In particular, a respondent may have greater incentive to make broad document requests in the quantum phase than in the liability phase, since the risk of reciprocal broad requests by the claimant is likely to be lower. If, on the other hand, the arbitration is not bifurcated by the arbitrators, then there is a higher risk to respondent that its own broad document requests motivated by damages issues will be met with equally broad requests by the claimant covering liability issues. Arbitrators thus should never lightly undertake bifurcation of a proceeding.

The valuation date is not the only matter that benefits from attention at the beginning of a case. Early in the proceedings, it may become apparent to the

797. Pratt, Reilly & Schweihs, Valuing a Business: The Analysis and Appraisal of Closely Held Companies, *supra* n. 673, at 27.

arbitrators that the parties will be presenting expert valuations differing widely in approach or results. Arbitrators can take prompt steps towards clarifying those differences and identifying the underlying assumptions from which the differences derive. For example, it may be helpful for the arbitrators to request from the experts a list of the material matters as to which they disagree. Similarly, as soon as practicable after the arbitrator becomes aware of important "apples-to-oranges" situations, the arbitrators should consider whether to request the experts to provide valuations on an "apples-to-apples" basis. By acting quickly on such matters, an arbitrator may be able to obtain evidence that is more easily compared and contrasted. If the arbitrator awaits the oral hearings to make these requests, time and cost pressures and other countervailing considerations can adversely affect the ability of the arbitrator to elicit such useful information. Moreover, simple fairness suggests acting early, in order to assure that the parties have fair notice and an opportunity to be heard on the revised valuations.

Managing the Expert Report Process

Experts may be asked to present their reports in draft form to the opposing party, with a view to narrowing differences before final reports are submitted to the arbitral tribunal.

Arbitrators may request opposing experts who have submitted expert reports to develop and submit lists of agreed matters and of material differences.

With the reports and the lists in hand, the arbitral tribunal may then request supplemental valuation reports seeking the use of more comparable methodologies and assumptions. However, arbitrators should be very sensitive to the costs involved.

One possible approach would be to specify in an early procedural order that the party-appointed experts should develop in advance an agreed list of issues. Article 5.3 of the IBA Rules for the Taking of Evidence in International Commercial Arbitration provides for a list of matters as to which the contending experts agree. That Article provides:

> The Arbitral Tribunal in its discretion may order that any Party-Appointed Experts who have submitted Expert Reports on the same or related issues meet and confer on such issues. At such meeting, the Party-Appointed Experts shall attempt to reach agreement on those issues as to which they had differences of opinion in their Expert Reports, and they shall record in writing any such issues on which they reach agreement.

A list of agreed matters is welcome, of course. The arbitrators may wish as well, though, for a list of the important *dis*agreements. Additionally, the panel may hope for a bona fide attempt by the experts to narrow their differences. In this regard, an arbitrator might also note with interest one of the Guidelines for Expert Witnesses in proceedings in the Federal Court of Australia:[798]

> If experts retained by the parties meet at the direction of the court, it would be improper conduct for an expert to be given or to accept instructions not to reach agreement. If, at a meeting directed by the court, the experts cannot reach agreement on matters of expert opinion, they should specify their reasons for being unable to do so.

If the panel orders such procedures, the parties in turn may seek an order preventing either party from eliciting testimony at the hearings about statements and other conduct by the experts at that meeting.

The English Protocol for the Instruction of Experts to give Evidence in Civil Claims (the CJC Protocol)[799] instructs the court to establish an agenda for a pre-trial discussion among experts. The CJC Protocol also provides that the parties may not instruct their experts to avoid reaching agreement. To the frustration of many of the clergy, the parties' lawyers may only be present at the expert discussion if all sides mutually so agree or the court so orders. Also, the content of the expert discussions is not available for use at trial absent mutual agreement of the parties:

> 18.6 The agenda should indicate what matters have been agreed and summarise concisely those which are in issue. It is often helpful for it to include questions to be answered by the experts. If agreement cannot be reached promptly or a party is unrepresented, the court may give directions for the drawing up of the agenda. The agenda should be circulated to experts and those instructing them to allow sufficient time for the experts to prepare for the discussion.
>
> 18.7 Those instructing experts must not instruct experts to avoid reaching agreement (or to defer doing so) on any matter within the experts' competence. Experts are not permitted to accept such instructions.
>
> 18.8 The parties' lawyers may only be present at discussions between experts if all the parties agree or the court so orders. If lawyers do attend, they should not normally intervene except to answer questions put to them by the experts or to advise about the law.[6]
>
> 18.9 The content of discussions between experts should not be referred to at trial unless the parties agree (CPR 35.12(4)). It is good practice for any such agreement to be in writing.
>
> [6] *Hubbard v. Lambeth, Southwark and Lewisham HA* [2001] EWCA 1455.

Unlike judicial practice in the UK and elsewhere, commonly used arbitration rules do not address such details. The Chartered Institute of Arbitrators has stepped into

---

798. Guidelines for Expert Witnesses in proceedings in the Federal Court of Australia, ¶ 3.1 (last amended March 2004).

799. "Civil Justice Council, Protocol for the Instruction of Experts to give Evidence in Civil Claims" (June 2005), available at <www.justice.gov.uk/civil/procrules_fin/contents/form_section_images/practice_directions/pd35_pdf_eps/pd35_prot.pdf>.

the space to offer an optional Protocol for the Use of Party-Appointed Expert Witnesses in International Arbitration (the CIArb Protocol). The CIArb Protocol is clearly based upon the CJC Protocol used in the English civil courts. The CIArb Protocol contemplates that party-appointed experts will hold an early pre-trial discussion. At that discussion, the CIArb Protocol calls for the experts to seek to reach agreement on the issues on which they are to give an opinion, the tests or analyses to be conducted and the manner in which they are to be conducted.[800] Thereafter, the CIArb Protocol requires the experts jointly to prepare for the arbitrators and the parties a report of that discussion setting out areas of agreement and disagreement.

> (b) Following such discussion, the experts shall prepare and send to the Parties and to the Arbitral Tribunal a statement setting out:
> (i) those issues upon which they agree and the agreed opinions they have reached on those issues;
> (ii) those tests and analyses which they agree need to be conducted and the agreed manner for conducting them;
> (iii) those issues upon which they disagree and a summary of their reasons for disagreement; and
> (iv) the tests and analyses in respect of which agreement has not been reached as to whether they shall be conducted and/or the manner in which they should be conducted, and a summary of their reasons for disagreement.[801]

The CIArb Protocol specifies that the content of the expert discussions shall be without prejudice to the respective positions of the parties. Also, except for the required joint statement, the content of the expert discussions "shall not be communicated to the Arbitral Tribunal unless the parties mutually agree thereto."[802]

With a list of differences in hand, and after reviewing the expert reports themselves, the arbitrator can then present to the parties a pre-hearing request for supplemental valuation reports (if appropriate). Such a request might ask the experts to employ more comparable methodologies and assumptions. Naturally, that request by an arbitrator should be without prejudice to the ability of each party to argue in favor of its original methodology and assumptions. Arbitrators should be cautious, of course, to avoid pre-judging fact-intensive issues like asset replacement costs, DCF discount rates and revenue and expense estimates prior to the evidentiary hearing. Accordingly, the tribunal might consider structuring such a request as "sensitivity tests," in order to appreciate the impact on one expert's opinion of accepting important elements of the opposing expert's valuation procedures. Be aware, though, of the potentially large cost to the parties of such a process, in time and in resources of experts and counsel alike. Be aware, also, of the

---

800. *The Chartered Institute of Arbitrators Protocol for the Use of Party-Appointed Expert Witnesses in International Arbitration*, at Art. 6.1 (hereinafter "CIArb Protocol"). *See* Appendix 3 to this book. Also available to Chartered Institute members at <www.arbitrators.org>.
801. *Id.*, at Art. 6.1(b).
802. *Id.*, at Art. 6.2.

impact on an arbitrator's own reading responsibilities; asking for experts to re-run their financial analyses to incorporate several alternatives in multiple categories (e.g., three possible discount rates, two different sales estimates and two different capital expenditures estimates) may generate hundreds, if not thousands, of spreadsheet pages!

II RANGES OF ESTIMATES: AUDIT TRAIL

Many criticisms of a valuation reduce, but do not eliminate, the reliability of that valuation. Questions about the true comparability of proposed comparables may expose important differences between the company and potential comparables. Nevertheless, the differences may not cause arbitrators to disregard that evidence entirely. For example, the Delaware Court of Chancery has on occasion considered valuations based on several different scenarios.

> Specifically, the court believes that using a scenario analysis, averaging conservative and optimistic possibilities, is the most appropriate valuation technique for a company in the somewhat uncertain position of IIC at the time it was to be valued.[803]

In such circumstances, arbitrators can narrow the identified differences by asking the experts to estimate the impact of adjustments necessary to account for the differences and to provide ranges of impact when precise estimation is beyond reach. Here too, a request by an arbitrator for such information should be made sufficiently far in advance to produce useful data on a basis consistent with due process considerations.

As discussed at length elsewhere in this volume, many cases consider whether the evidence presented is sufficiently certain to support a forward-looking compensation award. A separate question can be raised before the arbitrators about the accountability of the expert for the records and sources of information upon which that valuation is based and its ties with the evidence presented in the case. As one expert has explained, "it is crucial to have an audit trail in place to ensure that the origin of estimates is easily traceable to the evidence provided."[804] An audit trail may be central to several tasks of the arbitral panel; (i) linking the proposed valuations back to evidence in the record of the case and (ii) isolating for arbitral review those elements of the valuation that are ultimately based on the judgment and opinion of the expert witness.

To achieve this objective, arbitrators may wish to make sure early in the proceedings that the parties have instructed their experts to maintain sufficiently detailed records to enable the panel to test the veracity, accuracy and completeness of the underlying data. With respect to tribunal-appointed experts, the arbitral

803. *Gesoff v. IIC Industries, Inc., supra* n. 414, at 1157.
804. Special thanks to Thierry Senechal for drawing attention to this point.

panel may usefully include an "audit trail" instruction in that expert's terms of reference.

III STANDARDS OF CONDUCT FOR PARTY-APPOINTED EXPERTS

In many judicial systems, the expert's duty to the court overrides any duty to the client. In the UK, for example, the seminal English case of *National Justice Compania Naviera S.A. v. Prudential Assurance Co. Ltd.* (The Ikarian Reefer)[805] clearly stated this precept. The *Ikarian Reefer* guidelines have been summarized as follows:

- Expert evidence presented to the court should be, and should be seen to be, the independent product of the expert uninfluenced by the exigencies of litigation.
- An expert witness should provide independent assistance to the court by way of objective and unbiased opinion to matters within this expertise.
- An expert witness should never assume the role of an advocate.
- An expert witness should not omit to consider material facts that could detract from his concluded opinion.
- An expert witness should make it clear when a particular question or issue falls outside his expertise.
- If, after exchange of reports, an expert changes his view on a material matter, having read the other side's expert's report or for any other reason, such change of view should be communicated . . . to the other side without delay, and when appropriate, to the court.[806]

Reacting to concerns about rising costs and litigation delays, a 1996 report known as the Woolf Report[807] criticized the prevailing approach towards experts in the courts of England and Wales for producing "hired guns". According to the Woolf Report, the then-existing adversarial system in the courts also encouraged efforts to overwhelm opposing parties faced with an imbalance of financial resources. The Woolf Report recommended a series of changes to practice in England and Wales respecting party-appointed experts. A key recommendation of the Report was that the expert should owe a primary duty to the court, not the party engaging him: "Fundamentally, [Lord Woolf's] reforms were based on the notion that the expert

805. [1993] 2 Lloyd's Rep. 68. *See also* Rule 35.3, Civil Procedure Rules (CPR) of England and Wales.
806. Cain & Twombley, "Expert Witness: Their Duties and Responsibilities, Geomatics World," vol. 10, issue 4 (May-June 2002), on-line at <www.pvpubs.com./archives.asc>. *See*, generally, Dundas, "Experts in International Arbitration," paper presented at XXth Annual ICC Symposium of Arbitrators, Paris, France (March 14, 2005), and cases cited in Appendix 1 thereto.
807. Right Hon. Lord Woolf MR, *Access to Justice: Final Report to the Lord Chancellor [of] the Civil Justice System in England and Wales*, 1996.

has an overriding duty to assist the court impartially and independently, and not to advocate the case of the party by whom he/she is retained.''[808]

Standards of Conduct for Party-Appointed Experts

The standards of conduct for party-appointed experts differs significantly from legal system to legal system. Many civil law systems do not rely heavily on party-appointed experts. In the UK and many other countries, the expert owes a primary duty to the court. In the U.S., the role of party-appointed experts is more adversarial. There is no consensus regarding the standards of conduct for party-appointed experts in arbitration proceedings. In the valuation field, many professional organizations establish standards of conduct for their members when acting as expert witnesses.

The Woolf Report triggered considerable change in the English approach towards expert evidence, with the courts adopting inter alia Rule 35.3 of the Civil Procedure Rules of England and Wales. Incorporating the central tenets of the Woolf Report, Rule 35.3 imposed on expert witnesses a primary obligation towards the court. Most recently, the Civil Justice Council's Protocol for the Instruction of Experts to give Evidence in Civil Claims[809] addresses the balance between the duty of reasonable skill and expertise an expert owes to his or her engaging party and the overriding duty owed to the court:

> 4. Duties of Experts
>
> 4.1 Experts always owe a duty to exercise reasonable skill and care to those instructing them, and to comply with any relevant professional code of ethics. However when they are instructed to give or prepare evidence for the purpose of civil proceedings in England and Wales they have an overriding duty to help the court on matters within their expertise (CPR 35.3). This duty overrides any obligation to the person instructing or paying them. Experts must not serve the exclusive interest of those who retain them.
>
> 4.2 Experts should be aware of the overriding objective that courts deal with cases justly. This includes dealing with cases proportionately, expeditiously and fairly (CPR 1.1). Experts are under an obligation to assist the court so as to enable them to deal with cases in accordance with the overriding objective. However the overriding objective does not impose on experts any duty to act as mediators between the parties or require them to trespass on the role of the court in deciding facts.

808. Jones, Use of independent experts in arbitration: Independent experts – the common law approach, paper presented at International Bar Association Annual Conference, Prague, The Czech Republic, September 25–30, 2005.
809. *Supra* n. 799.

4.3 Experts should provide opinions which are independent, regardless of the pressures of litigation. In this context, a useful test of "independence" is that the expert would express the same opinion if given the same instructions by an opposing party. Experts should not take it upon themselves to promote the point of view of the party instructing them or engage in the role of advocates.

4.4 Experts should confine their opinions to matters which are material to the disputes between the parties and provide opinions only in relation to matters which lie within their expertise. Experts should indicate without delay where particular questions or issues fall outside their expertise.

4.5 Experts should take into account all material facts before them at the time that they give their opinion. Their reports should set out those facts and any literature or any other material on which they have relied in forming their opinions. They should indicate if an opinion is provisional, or qualified, or where they consider that further information is required or if, for any other reason, they are not satisfied that an opinion can be expressed finally and without qualification.

4.6 Experts should inform those instructing them without delay of any change in their opinions on any material matter and the reason for it.

4.7 Experts should be aware that any failure by them to comply with the Civil Procedure Rules or court orders or any excessive delay for which they are responsible may result in the parties who instructed them being penalised in costs and even, in extreme cases, being debarred from placing the experts' evidence before the court. In Phillips v. Symes Peter Smith J held that courts may also make orders for costs (under section 51 of the Supreme Court Act 1981) directly against expert witnesses who by their evidence cause significant expense to be incurred, and do so in flagrant and reckless disregard of their duties to the Court.

A number of other jurisdictions and organizations impose a similar requirement that experts owe an overriding duty to the judge (or tribunal); see, for example, the Federal Court of Australia's Guidelines for Expert Witnesses, the EuroExpert Code of Practice and the Code of Practice for Experts Issued jointly by the Academy of Experts and the Expert Witness Institute.[810] Further, like the English court in *Phillips v. Syme,*[811] the New South Wales Law Reform Commission has pressed for courts to consider imposing sanctions on experts who breach court-adopted codes of conduct.

This critical English approach towards party-appointed experts also extends to their fee arrangements. For example, case law and practice in English court

810. *See* The Code of Practice for Experts, online at the website of the Academy of Experts, <www.academy-experts.org/cprac.html>; Federal Court of Australia, "Guidelines for Expert Witnesses in Proceedings in the Federal Court of Australia" (June 6, 2007), available at <www.fedcourt.gov.au/how/prac_direction.html>; and "EuroExpert Code of Practice," available at <www.euroexpert.de/en/Code-of-practice/341>.

811. [2004] EWHC 2230 (CH).

proceedings reject compensating a party-appointed expert based on a success fee. In *Regina (Factortame Ltd. and others) v. Secretary of State for Transport, Local Government and the Regions (No. 8),*[812] the Court of Appeal asserted that giving of evidence by an expert on the basis of a contingent fee was "highly undesirable." According to that Court, consent to receive expert evidence on such a basis should only be given in rare circumstances.[813] The New South Wales Law Reform Commission has also urged courts to discourage success-based fees for experts.[814] US courts similarly are very skeptical of success fees for expert witnesses. A US bankruptcy court in New York explained that skepticism:

> The Belinsky submission was seriously undermined by the fact that his compensation from the Preferred Holders is contingent on the total consideration to be received by the Preferred Holders under a confirmed plan. Belinsky admitted that he did not understand that it is highly unusual for an expert witness fee to be contingent on the results of his testimony, and that a court is entitled to discredit anything said by an expert compensated by such an arrangement.[815]

As the arbitration community is aware, *Ikarian Reefer* and the Woolf Report have influenced the approach taken by many international arbitral panels. However, none of the best-known international arbitration rules directly addresses the responsibilities a party-appointed expert may owe to the tribunal. Additionally, the respected IBA Rules on the Taking of Evidence in International Commercial Arbitration largely sidestep the issue. Article 5 of those Rules, which relates to party-appointed experts, does require each expert report to contain an affirmation of the truth of its contents. Article 5 also requires the experts to appear for testimony at oral hearings unless the parties mutually agree otherwise. Significantly, though, Article 5 does not address whether a party-appointed expert must be independent and impartial or owe any duty to the tribunal.

Article 5 – Party-Appointed Experts

1. A Party may rely on a Party-Appointed Expert as a means of evidence on specific issues. Within the time ordered by the Arbitral Tribunal, a Party-Appointed Expert shall submit an Expert Report.
2. The Expert Report shall contain:
   (a) the full name and address of the Party-Appointed Expert, his or her present and past relationship (if any) with any of the Parties, and a description of his or her background, qualifications, training and experience:

812. [2002] EWCA Civ. 932 [2003].
813. The White Book of Civil Procedure states as well at ¶ 3.5.3.3 that "although not expressly covered by the Rules or Practice Direction, it would clearly not be acceptable to the court for an expert witness to be paid any form of contingency arrangement."
814. Jones, *supra* n. 808.
815. *In re Granite Broadcasting Corp.*, *supra* n. 415, at *20 (citations omitted).

(b) a statement of the facts on which he or she is basing his or her expert opinions and conclusions,
(c) his or her expert opinions and conclusions, including description of the method, evidence and information used in arriving at the conclusions:
(d) an affirmation of the truth of the Expert Report; and
(e) the signature of the Party-Appointed Expert and its date and place.

3. The Arbitral Tribunal in its discretion may order that any Party-Appointed Experts who have submitted Experts Reports on the same or related issues meet and confer on such issues. At such meeting, the Party-Appointed Experts shall attempt to reach agreement on those issues as to which they had differences of opinion in the Experts Reports, and they shall record in writing any such issues on which they reach agreement.
4. Each Party-Appointed Expert shall appear for testimony at an Evidentiary Hearing, unless the Parties agree otherwise and the Arbitral Tribunal accepts this agreement.
5. If a Party-Appointed Expert does not appear without a valid reason for testimony at an Evidentiary Hearing except by agreement of the Parties accepted by the Arbitral Tribunal, the Arbitral Tribunal shall disregard his or her Expert Report unless, in exceptional circumstances, the Arbitral Tribunal determines otherwise.
6. If the Parties agree that a Party-Appointed Expect does not need to appear for testimony at an Evidentiary Hearing, such an agreement shall not be considered to reflect an agreement as to the correctness of the content of the Expert Report.

Unsurprisingly, the CIArb Protocol for the Use of Party-Appointed Expert Witnesses in International Arbitration follows English practice in requiring that experts should provide assistance to the arbitrators rather than advocating the position of their appointing party. Thus, Article 4 of the CIArb Protocol specifies inter alia that experts must be independent of their appointing party and "objective, unbiased and uninfluenced by the pressures of the dispute resolution process or by any Party."[816]

Article 4 – Independence, Duty and Opinion

1. An expert that gives evidence in the Arbitration shall be independent of the Party which has appointed the expert to give such evidence.
2. Payment by the appointing Party of the expert's reasonable professional fees for the work done in giving such evidence shall not, of itself, vitiate the expert's independence.
3. An expert's duty, in giving evidence in the Arbitration, is to assist the Arbitral Tribunal to decide the issues in respect of which expert evidence is adduced.
4. An expert's opinion should be independent, objective, unbiased and uninfluenced by the pressures of the dispute resolution process or by any Party . . . .

816. CIArb Protocol, *supra* n. 800, at Art. 4.

To reinforce these obligations, Article 8 of the CIArb Protocol sets out the form of a declaration to be signed by each party-appointed expert confirming, among other matters, the expert's independence from the appointing party and obligation to assist the tribunal.

> (a) I understand that my duty in giving evidence in this arbitration is to assist the arbitral tribunal to decide the issues in respect of which expert evidence is adduced. I have complied with, and will continue to comply with, that duty.
> (b) I confirm that I am independent of the party which has appointed me.
> (c) I confirm that this is my independent, objective, unbiased opinion which has not been influenced by the pressures of the dispute resolution process or by any party to the arbitration.
> (d) I confirm that all matters upon which I have expressed an opinion are within my area of expertise.
> (e) I confirm that I have referred to all matters which I regard as relevant to the opinions I have expressed and have drawn to the attention of the arbitral tribunal all matters, of which I am aware, which might adversely effect my opinion.
> (f) I confirm that, at the time of providing this written opinion, I consider it to be complete and accurate and constitute my true, professional opinion.
> (g) I confirm that if, subsequently, I consider this opinion requires any correction, modification or qualification I will notify the parties to this arbitration and the arbitral tribunal forthwith.[817]

Moreover, under the CIArb Protocol, a party's instructions to its party-appointed expert would not be privileged. Accordingly, those instructions may be ordered disclosed in the arbitral proceedings upon good cause being shown. The CIArb Protocol considers working papers, however, to be privileged from disclosure.

> Article 5 – Privilege
>
> 1. All instructions to, and any terms of appointment of, an expert shall not be privileged against disclosure in the Arbitration, but the Arbitral Tribunal, shall not, in relation to the instructions or terms of appointment:
>   (a) order disclosure of the instructions or appointment or any document relating thereto; or
>   (b) permit any questioning of the expert about such instructions or appointment
>
>   unless it is satisfied that there is good cause.
> 2. Drafts, working papers or any other documentation produced by an expert for the purposes of providing expert evidence in the Arbitration shall be privileged from production and shall not be discloseable in the Arbitration.[818]

817. *Id.*, at Art. 8.1.

The UK Court of Appeal in *Toth v. Jarman*[819] recently offered guidance about the mandatory nature of conflicts disclosure by a party-appointed expert. According to the Court of Appeal, the presence of a conflict would not automatically disqualify the expert. Instead, the central issue was whether the expert's opinion was sufficiently free from litigation pressure and independent from the parties.[820] Consequently, the Court of Appeal imposed a requirement that the party calling an expert to testify should disclose details of that expert's conflicts of interest at as early a stage in the proceedings as possible. Therefore, the Court set out detailed guidance in its judgment about the obligation of an expert witness to identify conflicts. In addition to presenting a curriculum vitae with employment details, the Court of Appeal asked that expert witness sign a declaration to the following effect:

(a) I have no conflict of interest of any kind, other than any I have disclosed in my report.
(b) I do not consider that any interest I have disclosed affects my suitability as an expert witness on any issue on which I have given evidence.
(c) I will advise the party by whom I am instructed if, between the date of my report and the trial, there is any change in circumstances which affects my answers to (a) or (b).

The Court of Appeal's guidance in the *Toth* judgment offers no insight into how to define "conflicts of interest." CIArb Guideline 10 on the use of tribunal-appointed experts similarly calls for a tribunal-appointed expert to submit to the tribunal and the parties "a statement of his or her independence from the parties and the tribunal," as well as a curriculum vitae.[821] Conflict of interest questions have, of course, attracted significant commentary and court attention in the potentially analogous area of arbitrator disclosure requirements and conflicts of interest. However, unlike the issue of arbitrator conflicts of interest, there is as yet little commentary or case law guidance about the grey areas of expert witness conflicts and disclosure obligations.

Effective January 1, 2008, valuation analysts who are members of the AICPA are bound by the standards with respect to objectivity and conflicts of interest contained in its Valuation Standard SSVS 1, including obligations to be impartial and free from conflicts of interest:

---

818. *Id.*, at Art. 5.
819. *Toth v. Jarman*, [2006] Civ. 1028.
820. *Id.*
821. The Chartered Institute of Arbitrators Practice Guide, Guideline 10: Guidelines on the Use of Tribunal – Appointed Experts, Legal Advisers and Assessors (2004), at ¶¶ 15–16 (hereinafter, ("CIArb Guideline 10"). *See* Appendix 4 to this book. Also available to Chartered Institute members at <www.arbitrators.org>. Similarly, the Civil Justice Council Protocol for the Instruction of Experts to give Evidence in Civil Claims, *supra* n. 799, at ¶ 7.1(f), requires establishing that "there is no potential conflict of interest," but offers no guidance as to the standard for determining what constitutes a "potential conflict of interest."

14. The AICPA *Code of Professional Conduct* requires objectivity in the performance of all professional services, including valuation engagements. Objectivity is a state of mind. The principle of objectivity imposes the obligation to be impartial, intellectually honest, disinterested, and free from conflicts of interest. If necessary, where a potential conflict of interest may exist, a valuation analyst should make the disclosures and obtain consent as required under Interpretation No. 102-2, "Conflicts of Interest", under Rule 102, *Integrity and Objectivity* (*AICPA Professional Standards*, vol. 2, ET sec. 102.03).[822]

Adoption of an overriding duty on the part of experts towards the court has not been universal in the common law world. One well-founded criticism of that approach lies in the simple recognition of the actual circumstances that prevail in an adversarial system. If court or arbitral rules require impartiality and independence from party – appointed experts, parties may be encouraged to seek experts who are partisan but appear impartial and independent. Such an approach creates incentives for experts to develop polished acting skills. The reality is often complex:

> [T]here is a tradition (English?) that the expert is presented as "independent" and with only obligations to the court. But that is largely (not completely) a fiction. The expert that is hired by one side and communicates in preparing his or her expertise exclusively with one party can not be completely independent. Independence is a relative, not an absolute concept. The expert will be pulled between the forces from one party (which can be pretty strong and insistent) and, on the other side, personal / ethical and in particular reputational concerns over appearing "professional" (and that means also ability to stand up to demands, subtle or not subtle signals from clients). The more business and clients one has and the less one needs the greater presumably the forces favoring greater (never absolute) independence. Dr. Schuetze, in the Festschrift II for KH Boeckstiegel, has therefore expressed quite reasonable doubts on the independence of the party-appointed experts, though the actual dynamics is more complicated and one can not use the binary independence / no independence matrix but rather think of concepts such as "relative independence" and "professionalism."[823]

In the United States, where the presentation of expert evidence in litigation and domestic arbitration has historically been partisan, the US Supreme Court moved in the 1993 case of *Daubert v. Merrell Dow Pharmaceuticals*[824] to shift the examination of the validity of scientific expert evidence from juries towards the control of the court. Although *Daubert* itself addressed only scientific evidence, the 1999 Supreme Court decision in *Kumho Tire Company, Ltd v. Carmichael*[825] expanded

822. SSVS 1, *supra* n. 17, at ¶ 14.
823. Posting by Prof. Thomas Walde, February 2, 2006 to "Oil-Gas-Energy-Mining-Infrastructure Dispute Management (OGEMID) Discussion List," archived at <www.transnational-dispute-management.com/members/ogemid/welcome.asp>.
824. *Daubert v. Merrell Dow Pharmaceuticals*, 509 US 579 (1993).

Daubert scrutiny to all testifying experts, whether scientific or not. This approach does not directly compare with the *Ikarian Reefer* principle that an expert witness owes a duty to assist the court. Nevertheless, the *Daubert* and *Kumho* rulings and their progeny in the US have imposed greater control over expert testimony than had previously existed. However, the nature of judicial scrutiny for valuation evidence in the US courts may differ from scrutiny of expert evidence on scientific issues. A US bankruptcy court recently offered the following views, founded on the central role of cross-examination in the US adversarial system:[826]

> [The *Daubert* case] concerned scientific evidence, which relies upon the scientific methods and should be objectively testable. Experts in disciplines that require the use of professional judgment are less likely candidates for exclusion because challenges may be ultimately viewed as matters in which reasonable experts may differ in exercising their judgment as to the appropriate methodology to employ or the appropriate variable to plug into a calculation. *See, e.g., Joy Recovery Technology,* 286 B.R. at 70 ("[a]ccounting is not an exact science. Accountants are therefore required to make judgments about how to communicate financial information. A *Daubert* hearing is not the time to fully test the validity of those assumptions."). Such matters may be and should be explored and highlighted through cross-examination of the expert and presentation of contrary evidence, not at the preliminary admissibility stage. In non-scientific disciplines, assuming that the opinion addresses a

---

825. 526 US 137 (1999). The Tenth Circuit Court of Appeals has provided the following guidance for evaluating the admissibility of expert testimony:

> "Generally, the district court should focus on an expert's methodology rather than the conclusions it generates. *Daubert,* 509 US at 595, 113 S.Ct. 2786, 125 L.Ed.2d 469. However, an expert's conclusions are not immune from scrutiny: 'A court may conclude that there is simply too great an analytical gap between the data and the opinion proffered.' *General Elec. Co. v. Joiner,* 522 US 136, 146, 118 S.Ct. 512, 139 L.Ed.2d 508 (1997) ('[N]othing in either *Daubert* or the Federal Rules of Evidence requires a district court to admit opinion evidence which is connected to existing data only by the *ipse dixit* of the expert.'). Under *Daubert,* 'any step that renders the analysis unreliable . . . renders the expert's testimony inadmissible. This is true whether the step completely changes a reliable methodology or merely misapplies that methodology.' *Mitchell [v. Gencorp, Inc.],* 165 F.3d [778,] 782 [10th Cir. 1999] (*quoting In re Paoli R.R. Yard PCB Litigation,* 35 F.3d 717, 745 (3d Cir. 1994)). It is critical that the district court determine 'whether the evidence is genuinely scientific, as distinct from being unscientific speculation offered by a genuine scientist.' *Id.*, at 783 (*quoting Rosen v. Ciba-Geigy Corp.,* 78 F.3d 316, 318 (7th Cir., 1996)). Regardless of the specific factors at issue, the purpose of the *Daubert* inquiry is always 'to make certain that an expert, whether basing testimony upon professional studies or personal experience, employs in the courtroom the same level of intellectual rigor that characterizes the practice of an expert in the relevant field.' *Kumho Tire,* 526 US at 152, 119 S.Ct. 1167, 143 L.Ed.2d 238."

Dodge v. Cotter Corp., 328 F.3d 1212, 1222–23 (10th Cir. 2003).

826. In re *Commercial Financial Services, Inc. v. Chase Manhattan Bank USA*, N.A., 2006 WL 2766084 (Bankr. N.D. Okla., September 16, 2006) at *3. It is not uncommon in US valuation cases for a suspect expert's testimony to be admitted, but given little or no persuasive weight by the court.

> factual issue of consequence to the legal regime underlying a claim or defense, where the use of professional judgment may produce a broad range of acceptable opinions, so long as the expert possesses at least one of the qualifying attributes listed in Rule 702 (specialized knowledge, skill, education, experience or training), has employed a methodology recognized in the profession or by the courts, and can identify the source of the facts and data underlying the opinion (demonstrating a connection of the opinion to the facts of the case), a probing cross-examination and presentation of opposing experts and evidence will permit the fact-finder to judge the soundness of the expert's judgment, as well as the expert's credibility and potential bias, in order to assess how much weight to accord the expert's opinion. Even unpersuasive expert testimony is admissible if it is relevant (*i.e.,* it will assist the fact-finder in resolving a disputed factual issue) and is a product of a reasonable and reliable methodology. *See Joy Recovery Technology,* 286 B.R. at 70 (as is often the case, dueling experts will assist the trier of fact in fully understanding an issue; thus, it is not the function of a *Daubert* hearing to exclude an expert merely because her conclusion ultimately may be rejected).

Codes of conduct in the valuation industry also affect an expert's duties.[827] For example, Principle 4 of the ASA's Principles of Approved Practice and Code of Ethics states that "The appraiser's primary obligation to his client is to reach complete, accurate, and pertinent conclusions and numerical results regardless of the client's wishes or instructions in this regard." If the appraiser is engaged by a party in an arbitration or other controversy, Principle 4.3 holds that

> it is unethical for the appraiser to suppress any facts, data, or opinions which are adverse to the case his client is trying to establish; or to overemphasize any facts, data or opinions which are favorable to his client's case; or in any other particulars to become an advocate. It is the appraiser's obligation to present the data, analysis, and value without bias, regardless of the effect of such unbiased presentation on his client's case.[828]

The AICPA approaches the ethical responsibilities of an accountant as expert witness in a somewhat different manner. The AICPA Professional Ethics Division's Code of Professional Conduct,[829] as adopted by the Public Company Accounting Oversight Board established by the US Congress, binds AICPA members. Interpretations of that Code by the AICPA's Professional Ethics Division reject the position that an accountant providing expert witness services is an

---

827. US organizations that issue business valuation credentials include the ASA, the AICPA, the Institute of Business Appraisers and the National Association of Certified Valuation Analysts. Risius, *Business Valuation: A Primer for Legal Professionals*, *supra* n. 19, at 7. Internationally, many of the constituent members of the IVSC will also issue business valuation credentials.

828. "ASA, Principles of Appraisal Practice and Code of Ethics," available at <www.appraisers.org/join/code_ethics.htm>.

829. Available at <www.aicpa.org/about/code/sec100.htm>.

advocate on behalf of the client. Rule 102 under the AICPA Code states that "in the performance of any professional service, a member [of the AICPA] shall maintain objectivity and integrity, shall be free of conflicts of interest, and shall not knowingly misrepresent facts or subordinate his or her judgment to others."[830] As previously mentioned, the AICPA's Valuation Standard SSVS 1 will make business valuations expressly subject to these obligations. The AICPA Professional Ethics Division's Interpretation 101 also considers the application of that Rule to an accountant's service as an expert witness:

> 101. Client Advocacy and Expert Witness Services
>
> .202 Question – Would the performance of expert witness services be considered as acting as an advocate for a client as discussed in interpretation 102-6 [ET section 102.07]?
>
> .203 Answer – No. A member serving as an expert witness does not serve as an advocate but as someone with specialized knowledge, training and experience in a particular area who should arrive at and present positions objectively.[831]

One segment of the US valuation community (appraisals for real estate transactions subject to regulation by a US federal financial institutions regulator) is subject to mandatory minimum appraisal standards as a matter of law.[832] The Uniform Standards of Professional Appraisal Practice (USPAP), as developed by the Appraisal Foundation, satisfy this obligation and it is likely that SSVS 1 will soon be confirmed as a qualifying appraisal standard as well. The USPAP standards[833] contain a legally binding Ethics Rule, including a requirement that the appraiser conduct appraisals "with impartiality, objectivity, and independence, and without accommodation of personal interests."[834] Moreover, the USPAP Ethics Rule states that:

> It is unethical for an appraiser to accept an assignment, or to have a compensation arrangement for an assignment, that is contingent on any of the following:
>
> 1. the reporting of a predetermined result (e.g., opinion of value);
> 2. a direction in assignment results that favors of cause of the client;
> 3. the amount of a value opinion;
> 4. the attainment of a stipulated result; or
> 5. the occurrence of a subsequent event directly related to the appraiser's opinions and specific to the assignment's purpose.[835]

---

830. *Id.*
831. *Id.*
832. *See* Financial Institutions Reform, Recovery and Enforcement Act of 1989 (FIRREA), §§ 1107, 1110, 12 U.S.C. §§ 3336, 3339. For a review of the development of the regulatory framework for real estate appraisers in the US, *see* Bunton, "An Overview of the Regulation of Appraisers and Accountants In the United States and Its Possible Application in the People's Republic of China" (June 2000), available at <www.appraisalfoundation.org>.
833. Available at <www.appraisalfoundation.org>.
834. USPAC Ethics Rule, effective July 1, 2006.

Also, in the US, the Pension Protection Act of 1996[836] now requires a "qualified appraisal" to substantiate the value for tax deductibility of many non-cash charitable contributions with a value exceeding USD 5,000. To be a "qualified appraisal," a "qualified appraiser" must conduct the valuation in accordance with "generally accepted appraisal standards" and applicable IRS regulations.[837] The Uniform Standards of Professional Appraisal Practice (USPAP) and the AICPA's Valuation Standard SSVS 1 should satisfy this requirement. A "qualified appraiser" must either have earned an appraisal designation from a recognized professional appraiser organization or otherwise qualify under yet-to-be-issued IRS regulations.[838]

Note that valuation experts from other professions, such as commercial and investment banking, are often *not* subject to similar codes of conduct.

If a valuation accepts inputs from counsel or a client without verification for reasonableness, serious issues may arise under applicable professional codes of conduct (if any). For example, the IVSC's DCF Guidance Note states that, if a client causes the expert to follow specific requirements that do not correspond to those for market value estimates, then the result should be identified as "Non-Market Value."[839] Moreover, the IVSC calls for the expert to "carry out sufficient research to ensure that cash flow projections and the assumptions that are the basis for the DCF model are appropriate and reasonable for the subject market."[840] The DCF Guidance Note also provides that "[i]t is the responsibility of the Valuer to ensure that the controlling input is consistent with market evidence and the prevailing market outlook. Further, the Valuer who supervises the construction of the DCF model ... is responsible for the integrity of that model in terms of ... the appropriateness of all inputs."[841]

Regardless of court rules and industry codes of conduct, expert witnesses in many arbitration proceedings will still conduct themselves as partisan advocates on behalf of the party retaining them (whether obvious or subtle). Thus, financial valuation experts in some cases have carefully assumed an unrealistic discount rate provided by counsel rather than acknowledging that rate's obvious inadequacies. For example, the author observed an accountant serving as an expert witness assume, without evident embarrassment, a 4.7% discount rate for his DCF analysis in a dispute over the value of a limited recourse power project, determined as the

835. *Id.*, at "Management." Each written appraisal report for an interest in a business enterprise with respect to a federally-related transaction must contain a signed certification that the appraiser fulfilled these requirements. *See* USPAP Standard 10-3, available at <www.appraisalfoundation.org>.
836. Pub. L. No. 109-280. These obligations do not currently apply to estate and gift taxation issues.
837. *Id.*, at § 1219.
838. Crain, "Pension Protection Act Changes Valuations for Tax Purposes," *Journal of Accountancy* at 40 (September 2007).
839. IVSC DCF Guidance Note, *supra* n. 408, at ¶ 5.4. Para. 5.9 requires the expert to follow as well the requirements of the IVSC Code of Conduct.
840. *Id.*, at ¶ 5.6.
841. *Id.*, at ¶ 5.8.

sum of 2% over the rate of inflation. The expert chose the 4.7% figure based on US employment disability cases supplied by instructing counsel. That expert also claimed, in the alternative, that a 4.01% rate for one-year US Treasury bills, with no additional adjustments for the risk of investing in the equity of a limited recourse power project, was also a reasonable discount rate for the case. Unsurprisingly, the party who benefited from a large valuation had engaged the expert in question.

Here again, an arbitrator can take early and affirmative steps to control overly partisan conduct by party-appointed experts. If the members of the tribunal are in agreement that the expert owes an overriding duty to the tribunal, arbitrators may include in an early procedural order elements of *Ikarian Reefer* as guiding principles for the attitude of the tribunal towards expert evidence. Or, the tribunal may ask party-appointed experts to subscribe to the substance of the practice code for one of the above professional organizations (or a similar organization) before submitting their expert reports or testimony, even if the experts in question are not members of the particular organization.

IV EXPERT EXCHANGES

Sometimes the arrangements for submitting expert reports and expert testimony at trial can also become highly repetitive. The process of exchanging expert reports on valuation, followed by rebuttal reports from each expert and occasionally reply reports as well, is an expensive and schedule-extending process. It also results in arbitrators reading two and perhaps three versions of much the same evidence. Moreover, oral expert testimony and cross-examination by opposing counsel at the oral hearings may in effect repeat points made in expert reports. To some extent, arbitrators can control the repetitive nature of this process by asking the experts to exchange their draft reports, and commentary on those drafts, with each other before finalizing the expert reports for submission to the tribunal. If the arbitrators couple this approach with a requirement that the competing experts produce a list of material agreements and differences following an expert 'meet and confer', then the panel may receive expert evidence much more focused on the issues truly dividing the parties.

Another practical issue is the sequence in which party-appointed valuation witnesses present their evidence at the oral hearings. Expert witnesses, testifying as part of the presentation by their appointing party of the larger case for which they have been called, may testify days, weeks or even months apart from each other. Depending on the duration of the cases presented by the parties, the gap between hearing one expert's valuation testimony and cross-examination and then hearing the opposing expert's testimony and cross-examination may limit the ability of an arbitrator to properly compare the competing evidence. Obviously, hearing transcripts mitigate this problem. However, arbitrators may also address this difficulty by scheduling the expert witnesses to testify in succession, one after the other, so that the panel can consider the valuation testimony at the same time.

Additionally, arbitrators increasingly employ an "expert confrontation" to explore differences in the proffered testimony. In such a procedure, the opposing experts have the opportunity to comment on the views of each other in a common setting. That technique is not without its critics and should only be used in carefully thought out circumstances. The leading arbitration treatise by Redfern & Hunter offers the following possible procedures.

> Another, more innovative, concept is for the experts for each party to be heard simultaneously. The experts are seated opposite or alongside each other in front of the arbitral tribunal at the same time and each is asked to comment and respond to the opinions of the others on an agenda basis. This enables individual members of the arbitral tribunal to obtain the opinions of the experts on specific issues with a degree of immediacy that is not possible where there may be an interval of several days between the particular topics being dealt with by the opposing experts.
>
> In 1998 one of the authors participated in an arbitration under the AAA's International Arbitration Rules in which a variation of this method was adopted. The expert witnesses submitted written reports as part of the Tribunal's pre-hearing briefing: they were then cross-examined and re-examined by the parties' counsel at the hearing; at the end of all the oral testimony and before the closing arguments, the Tribunal drew up an agenda of disputed "expert" matters and sat across the table from the two experts discussing the agenda items one by one in a quite informal manner; and, finally, the parties' counsel were offered an opportunity to ask further questions for clarification purposes.[842]

Tribunals may vary the format of expert confrontations to suit the particular circumstances of an individual case. One delightfully named variant is "hot-tubbing," which involves hearing all experts in a panel format. Each expert has an opportunity to present a summary of his or her views. The other expert(s) then have the opportunity to question and comment on that evidence. Counsel engage in cross-examination only after the experts have worked through their own presentations. Notably, in a "hot-tubbing" procedure, an expert may feel more comfortable acknowledging points made by the opposing expert if the role of counsel is deferred until the end of the process. Needless to say, many counsel are uncomfortable with this inversion of ordinary trial procedure. Similarly, some in the arbitration community consider these tools too interventionist for arbitrators.

842. Redfern & Hunter, "Law and Practice of International Commercial Arbitration" 6-96 (4th edn 2004) (citation omitted). The author understands from Ms. Sophie Nappert that the concept of witness conferencing is to be credited to Wolfgang Peter, a prominent Swiss arbitrator.

Expert Exchanges

"Hot-tubbing" and other forms of expert exchanges have become more common in arbitration. Arbitrators should recognize that each party will carefully prepare its party-appointed expert for these exchanges. Arbitrators should take care to manage these procedures so as to avoid inadvertently providing an advantage to an expert primarily because of that expert's greater skill at "cross-examination" and similar advocacy techniques than the opposing expert.

The arbitrator should recognize, of course, that each party will carefully prepare its party-appointed expert before stepping into the hot tub. Therefore, the expert exchange may become just as scripted as the direct and cross-examinations unless the arbitrator works to achieve less partisan interaction. The use of an expert exchange accordingly requires advance preparation by arbitrators; witness conferencing cannot replace adequate knowledge by the arbitrator of the evidence, the issues and the differences between the parties. The author has unfortunately experienced a situation where one set of experts was well scripted but the other was not. In particular, an expert who proves to be skilled at cross-examination techniques has a clear advantage over others in formats where experts question each other. In those circumstances, discipline may be required to avoid over-crediting the expert whose presentation is more polished. One useful tool for focusing the expert exchange is for the arbitrator to provide to the expert witnesses in advance a list of the items in which the tribunal has a particular interest. If the arbitrator is satisfied that an expert will answer candidly, perhaps the most searching question the arbitrator can ask the expert is: "If the other side had engaged you, would you have reached the same conclusions?" But would you believe the expert who replies 'yes'?

V OBTAINING THE FINANCIAL MODELS

Commonly, a party will present the panel with a photocopy of the final spreadsheet printout from a financial forecast, but not the spreadsheet's computer file containing the underlying financial model. In such circumstances, the arbitrator will be unable unilaterally to determine the impact of changing one line-item on the many other affected line-items in the spreadsheet. In cases where the experts offer Income-Based forecasts or similar numbers-heavy valuations, a courageous arbitrator may ask as well for the computer files containing the financial models underlying those forecasts.[843]

843. "To boldly go where no one has gone before." Capt. Luc Picard, "Star Trek: The Next Generation, Episode 1" (1987). Delaware courts may be bolder. "In fact, the Court may, instead of accepting the methodologies proposed by the parties, create its own model." *Lane v.*

Like the businesses they value, valuation methods have become far more 'IT' (information technology) intensive. In response, just like the Project Finance Division of US Eximbank does in its application process,[844] arbitrators can request that projections be provided in a user friendly format to enable the panel to consider the impact of changes to important variables. However, arbitrators are often unfamiliar with the intricacies of manipulating EXCEL spreadsheets or the detailed building blocks of an Income-Based forecast. Importantly, numerous interlinked equations are embedded into the financial models underlying a forecast. Thus, a change in one line-item of a forecast may actually affect a number of other connected line-items.[845]

To illustrate, let us assume the parties disagree about the forecast amount of capital expenditures that the company will make during a ten-year DCF projection period. One expert witness contends for an aggregate of USD 20 million spread equally over the ten-year period of the forecast. The other expert instead estimates USD 30 million, with the extra USD 10 million all occurring in the first few years. If the arbitrator accepts the second expert's views on this particular issue, but otherwise is persuaded by the remainder of the first expert's DCF forecast, the arbitrator cannot simply pencil in the new, larger capital expenditures with no other adjustments to the spreadsheet. An increase in capital expenditures may require the company to obtain additional financing, resulting in an impact on the line-item in each subsequent year for additional interest expenses and principal payments on debt. If the capital expenditures are proportionately large, an incremental increase in equity contributions may also be necessary to maintain the company's overall debt-to-equity leverage ratio. Under the company's pre-existing loan agreements, additional capital expenditures may affect a mandatory debt-to-equity leverage ratio or other financial covenants. If that has occurred, the company would be compelled to raise additional equity or take other financial steps to remain in compliance. Moreover, additional capital expenditures also have an impact on depreciation estimates, as well as corporate tax payments. The list of follow-on consequences can even include additional sales revenues and related operating expenses, if the necessary capital expenditure involves an expansion of the company's productive capacity. Each of these items is an element in the financial model. And, lest we forget, these changes may also affect the debt-to-equity ratio used in determining a WACC discount rate and the free cash flow amount used to determine the terminal value.

Arbitrators cannot intuit these relationships. They must either request the experts to provide recalculated DCF forecasts or, more boldly, obtain the computer spreadsheet files with the underlying financial models and input the capital expenditure and related changes themselves. If (and we stress 'if') the financial model

---

Cancer Treatment Centers of America, Inc., *supra* n. 1, at *58 n. 87, citing *Cede & Co. v. Technicolor, Inc.*, *supra* n. 414.

844. *See* text associated with n. 511 *supra*.

845. *See, e.g.*, *In re Radiology Associates, Inc.*, *supra* n. 394, at *13: "Since I have adjusted the proper growth rate in the discounted cash flow analysis down to 5%, I must also adjust expenses projected on a percentage of net sales basis (e.g., general administrative expenses and adjusted depreciation)."

has been properly constructed, inputting the change should result in automatic changes in many other linked line-items, resulting in recalculated numbers for each of those line-items in the DCF forecast:

> 146. When reviewing an expert opinion regarding the value of a corporation, courts frequently adjust or correct expert opinion analysis in reaching their final opinion on valuation. *See Arnold v. Baisch (In re Great Lakes Boat Repair)*, 2006 Bankr. LEXIS 2537, *2 (Bankr. W.D.N.Y. 2006) (while the court elected to go with one experts raised on cross examination); *River Valley Fitness One*, 2006 Bankr. LEXIS 345 at *42–43 (the court adopted a mid point range value for a corporation after they found that the record did not contain sufficient evidence for the court to conclude one end of a range was more likely than the other to be correct); Mirant, 334 B.R. at 824 (the court found it necessary to recalculate the value of the corporation due to out-dated data inputs); Heilig-Meyers Co. v. Wachovia Bank, N.A. (In re Heilig-Meyers Co.), 319 B.R. 447 (Bankr. E.D. Va. 2004) (the court, after reviewing two experts opinions, choose to assign their own values to each variable of an insolvency test, picking and choosing numbers from each experts valuation to reach its own conclusion); and in re Vanderveer Estates Holding, LLC, 293 B.R. 560, 577 (Bankr. E.D.N.Y. 2003) (the court elected to adopt a combination of two expert's opinions, combining the variables to calculate a new final value).
>
> 147. Thus, in this case, the Court will determine the Debtors' enterprise value by: (i) accepting the opinions of the three experts as to the Debtors' enterprise value; (ii) making adjustments to those opinions to correct for certain errors or inconsistencies; (iii) weighing the three expert opinions (as adjusted) based upon the credibility of each expert's opinion and testimony; and (iv) adjusting the weighted average of the experts' opinions to compensate for the May 2006 LRP and the Debtors' performance since June 2006.[846]

Less boldly, the arbitrator may simply wish to obtain an appreciation of the economic importance of various disputed assumptions and revenue/expense estimates. The arbitrator might therefore input argued-for changes into the DCF financial models and observe the extent to which the final present-value amounts actually differ – testing the sensitivity of the important components of the calculations. Thus, if one expert persuasively criticizes the other expert's sales forecasts are too pessimistic, the arbitrator could input a variety of possible adjustments (5% more, 10% more, 15% more, etc.) into the model to better understand the commercial impact of increased sales. Similarly, the arbitrator may wish to test the impact of changes in the discount rate on the net present value amount in a DCF calculation – 8%, 12%, 16%, and so on.

Again, the efficacy of this process will depend on whether additional manual inputs are required and whether the financial model was properly constructed. The

846. *In re Nellson Nutraceuticals, Inc.*, 2007 WL 201134 (Bankr. D. Del. January 18, 2007), at ¶¶ 146–147.

author, though, has had the experience of inputting increased sales figures into a DCF spreadsheet and seeing a *lower* net income amount pop out the other end. Diligent efforts to track all of the various embedded linkages proved fruitless, for lack of expertise; it was clear the result was backwards but not possible to determine why or to reverse the outcome. Unless the arbitrator also has the ability to look into the interlinked equations embedded in the spreadsheet file, the arbitrator will not be able to tell if additional manual inserts are required or if the model was properly constructed.

If the panel is sufficiently courageous to ask for the financial model, the party-appointed experts may become concerned about proprietary information included in their models. Many expert witnesses are professional financial advisors, who rely upon private databases of industry information to help their clients consider the pros and cons of potential acquisitions, investments and other business transactions. Those proprietary databases may represent thousands of hours spent by the expert sifting through obscure records to find well-hidden nuggets of commercially valuable information. Thus, an expert may insist that information remain confidential and not be shared with the opposing party or its expert witness. In such a case, the tribunal may need carefully to craft an order agreed with the parties. Such an order might limit the ordinary prohibition against *ex parte* contacts between party and tribunal to enable the experts to send their financial models directly to the tribunal, without sharing the model with the other party to the dispute. Alternatively, that information may be designated 'Attorneys Eyes Only'. As arbitrators will appreciate, an expert who relies heavily on such proprietary data will of course face questioning about the possible lack of transparency or reliability of the underlying data.

Even if a prudent arbitrator forgoes asking for the financial models in honest recognition of his or her limits, that arbitrator may still utilize present-value calculators on the Web to gain an understanding of the sensitivity of the final DCF or CCF damage amount to changes in the chosen discount or capitalization rate. Readers can find useful present-value Web-based calculation tools at <www.investopedia.com/calculator/NetPresentValue.aspx>, <www.business-analysis-made-easy.com/NPV-Calculator.html> and <www.pine-grove.com/financial%20calculators/npv.htm>, among other Internet locations. EXCEL and other common spreadsheet software also contain a present-value calculation equation. The arbitrator may copy the annual net cash flow amounts for each year of the DCF forecast (before discounting to a present value) into the blanks and then calculate the net present value of those annual cash flow amounts with different discount rates. As mentioned above in Chapter 4.VI, these tools normally are set up to use only the year-end convention.

VI THE TRIBUNAL-APPOINTED EXPERT

Having considered all of the foregoing issues and tools, arbitrators in appropriate cases may ultimately decide the most prudent course of action is to obtain the services of their own expert.

The Tribunal-Appointed Expert

In appropriate cases, arbitrators may employ their own expert. Several of the most popular arbitration rules authorize the use of tribunal-appointed experts. The costs of a tribunal-appointed expert may be considerable. When a tribunal-appointed expert is appointed on valuation issues, the parties may become concerned that the expert will become de facto the fourth arbitrator. Arbitrators must therefore be careful to assure that the parties have a full and fair opportunity to be heard. Arbitrators must also pay close attention to the tribunal-appointed expert's background. For many disputed matters, the arbitrators might in fact be resolving a valuation dispute simply by appointing as their expert the proponent of one school of thought, rather than a competing school.

The *CMS v. Argentina* tribunal thus appointed its own expert for valuation purposes,[847] as did the *LG&E* tribunal.[848] Similarly, Chambers of the Iran-US Claims Tribunal also relied on tribunal-appointed experts in a number of cases.[849] For instance, in the matter of *Shahin Shaine Ebrahimi v. Islamic Republic of Iran*, the panel appointed Dr. Richard A. Brealey, author of one of the most prominent valuation treatises, to review and report on the valuation of the subject business. The panel's terms of reference for Dr. Brealey, utilizing an Adjusted Book Value (ABV) methodology, stated in relevant part:

> 1. The Tribunal requires the assistance of the expert in determining the fair market value, as of 13 November 1979, of Gostaresh Maskan Company ('GMC'). The expert's valuation shall be made on the basis of fair market value, taking into account the tangible physical and financial assets of the undertaking and other elements, if any, including but not limited to, contractual and intellectual property rights, commercial prospects, goodwill, and likely future profitability. The effects of the very act of nationalization or effects of events that occurred subsequent to nationalization shall be excluded; however, prior changes in the general political, social, and economic conditions which might have affected GMC's business prospects as of the date it was taken shall be taken into account [citations omitted].

847. *See CMS v. Argentina*, *supra* n. 7, at ¶ 418 et seq.
848. *See LG&E v. Argentina* Final Award, *supra* n. 7, at ¶ 6. As discussed in Ch. 2.VII above, the damages decision in that case bore a strong family resemblance to the valuation methodology employed by the UNCC, the former employer of that expert, Geoffrey Senogles. Based on the author's inquiries, there is no reason to believe that the choice of the expert in that case dictated the results.
849. On the use of tribunal-appointed experts by the Iran-US Claims Tribunal, *see* Allinson & Holtzmann, *The Tribunal's Use of Experts, in The Iran-United States Claims Tribunal and the Process of International Claims Resolution* (Caron & Crook eds 2000).

2. For the purpose set forth above, the expert, after familiarizing itself with the documents filed by the Parties which the Tribunal, in consultation with the expert, has selected as necessary to the performance of its task, shall give its opinion as to such fair market value including:
   A. Value of fixed assets applying the appropriate index[es] and deducting actual depreciation, making such adjustments, if any, as may be appropriate in respect of (i) project expenses (vs. plant and equipment account) and (ii) allegedly fictitious transactions;
   B. Value of current assets, including but not limited to those set out below;
   C. Value of GMC's letters of credit;
   D. Value of:
      (1) accounts receivable, assuming (i) that price adjustments are applicable and, alternatively, (ii) that price adjustments are not applicable
      (2) progress payments not yet posted, including inter alia progress payments with respect to (i) New Town and (ii) NIOC;
   E. Value of other assets including, inter alia:
      (1) GE license
      (2) rights to Gypsum Mine
      (3) shares in Palayeshgar
      (4) shares in Gostaresh Blount;
   F. Value of GMC's contract backlog, taking into consideration inter alia:
      (1) assumptions regarding contract performance (GMC's capability, government payments)
      (2) applicability of price adjustments
      (3) status of contracts, i.e., were they cancelled by 13 November 1979 or not?
   G. Value, if any, of GMC's goodwill;
   H. Effects, if any, of
      (1) doubtful debt provision
      (2) whether purchases of equipment and supplies by GMC pursuant to letters of credit were properly debited to its account by issuing banks
      (3) whether NIOC (employer supplied) materials were properly credited to NIOC
      (4) taxes applicable under Iranian law to GMC's income.
   I. Possible effect, if any such effect were deemed relevant by the Tribunal, of the Claimants' shares representing a minority interest in GMC, or the Respondent's acquisition of a controlling interest in GMC.[850]

The panel accepted most of Dr. Brealey's expert findings, but disagreed with the views of their expert on certain matters: for instance, "the Tribunal does not accept the 20% discount applied by the Expert to Gostaresh Maskan's PARs [price

---

850. *Shahin Shaine Ebrahimi v. Islamic Republic of Iran*, *supra* n. 603, at n. 18 (citations omitted).

adjustment receivable claims against employers for the indexation of the nominal contract prices] owing by the expropriating debtor.''[851]

Many civil law arbitrators and judges in fact expect that the expert will be selected by, and responsive to, the panel rather than the parties.[852] In a number of international arbitrations, both party-appointed experts and tribunal-appointed experts may be used:

> [The] converging practice is to use both approaches. International arbitrators now expect to hear from experts presented by the parties, either by reading their reports or by hearing their oral testimony, or both. But arbitrators faced with conflicting expert reports may well fall back on their ability, found in most sets of arbitration rules, to appoint a tribunal expert to help them to resolve the conflict. Where the arbitrators appoint an expert, however, they commonly allow the parties the opportunity to question him after he has submitted his report. They may also allow the parties to call their own experts to take issue with the views of the tribunal's expert.[853]

Several of the most popular international arbitration rules contemplate use of tribunal-appointed experts. For example, Article 27 of the UNCITRAL Arbitration Rules authorizes appointment of a tribunal expert on the following terms:

> 1. The arbitral tribunal may appoint one or more experts to report to it, in writing, on specific issues to be determined by the tribunal. A copy of the expert's terms of reference, established by the arbitral tribunal, shall be communicated to the parties.
> 2. The parties shall give the expert any relevant information or produce for his inspection any relevant documents or goods that he may require of them. Any dispute between a party and such expert as to the relevance of the required information or production shall be referred to the arbitral tribunal for decision.
> 3. Upon receipt of the expert's report, the arbitral tribunal shall communicate a copy of the report to the parties who shall be given the opportunity to express, in writing, their opinion on the report. A party shall be entitled to examine any document on which the expert has relied in the report.
> 4. At the request of either party the expert, after delivery of the report, may be heard at a hearing where the parties shall have the opportunity to be present and to interrogate the expert. At this hearing either party may present expert

851. *Id.*, at ¶ 127.
852. *See*, e.g., Browne, Williamson & Barkacs, ''The Perspectival Nature of Expert Testimony in the United States, England, Korea and France,'' 18 Conn. J. Int. L. 55, 92-100 (2002) (Korea and France as illustrations).
853. Elsing & Townsend, ''Bridging the Common Law – Civil Law Divide in Arbitration,'' *supra* n. 6, at 64 (footnotes omitted).

> witnesses in order to testify on the points at issue. The provisions of article 25 [Hearings] shall be applicable to such proceeding.[854]

Similarly, Article 20.4 of the ICC Rules of Arbitration states that "[t]he Arbitral Tribunal, after having consulted the parties, may appoint one or more experts, define their terms of reference and receive their reports. At the request of a party, the parties shall be given the opportunity to question at a hearing any such expert appointed by the Tribunal." Article 22.1 of the AAA's International Arbitration Rules provides that "[t]he tribunal may appoint one or more independent experts to report to it, in writing, on specific issues designated by the tribunal and communicated to the parties." Article 21 of the LCIA Arbitration Rules also permits the Tribunal to appoint independent experts unless otherwise mutually agreed by the parties. Like the UNCITRAL Rule, the LCIA Rules obligate the parties to provide requested information and access to property to the Tribunal – appointed expert. Following English arbitration law in this regard, Article 21.3 of the LCIA Rules specifically addresses the costs of such an expert. That article provides for the expert's fees and expenses to be paid out of the parties' deposits and form part of the costs of the arbitration to be allocated by the tribunal between the parties, as the tribunal determines.

Not all arbitration rules address tribunal – appointed experts, however. The AAA Commercial Arbitration Rules, which are widely used in US domestic arbitrations and occasionally referenced in the arbitration clauses of international contracts as well, make no mention of an arbitral panel's authority to appoint its own expert. The ICSID Arbitration Rules are also silent, although the use of tribunal-appointed experts on valuation issues is increasingly common.

The ability of an arbitral panel to appoint its own expert may also derive from national arbitration law, rather than the applicable arbitration rules. For example, Article 26 of the UNCITRAL Model Law on International Commercial Arbitration permits the tribunal, unless the parties mutually agree otherwise, to appoint its own expert and require the parties to provide "any relevant information" to that expert. Thereafter, the parties are entitled to question the expert at the hearing and present their own experts:

> Article 26. Expert appointed by arbitral tribunal
>
> (1) Unless otherwise agreed by the parties, the arbitral tribunal
>
> (a) may appoint one or more experts to report to it on specific issues to be determined by the arbitral tribunal;

854. *See* Paulsson & Petrochilos, "Revision of the UNCITRAL Arbitration Rules (2006)," available at <www.uncitral.org/pdf/English/news/arbrules_report.pdf>, for a discussion of possible amendments to Article 27. *Paulsson & Petrochilos* recommend amending Article 27 to make explicit that the tribunal must consult with the parties before appointing its own expert and to grant the tribunal authority to compel party-appointed experts to meet and confer with the tribunal-appointed expert, or with each other, along the lines contemplated by existing English judicial procedure under CRP Rule 35. The *Paulsson & Petrochilos Report* was commissioned by the UNCITRAL Secretariat, but does not necessarily represent the official thinking of the Secretariat.

> (b) may require a party to give the expert any relevant information or to produce, or to provide access to, any relevant documents, goods or other property for his inspection.
> (2) Unless otherwise agreed by the parties, if a party so requests or if the arbitral tribunal considers it necessary, the expert shall, after delivery of his written or oral report, participate in a hearing where the parties have the opportunity to put questions to him and to present expert witnesses in order to testify on the points at issue.

The UK has followed Model Law Article 26 in Article 37 of the Arbitration Act 1996. In addition to covering the same areas as the UNCITRAL Model Law, Article 37 also addresses the costs of the tribunal-appointed expert if the arbitrators have engaged the expert on their own account, treating those costs in the same manner as arbitrator fees:

> 37. (1) Unless otherwise agreed by the parties –
> (a) the tribunal may–
> (i) appoint experts or legal advisers to report to it and the parties, or
> (ii) appoint assessors to assist it on technical matters,
> and may allow any such expert, legal adviser or assessor to attend the proceedings; and
> (b) the parties shall be given a reasonable opportunity to comment on any information, opinion or advice offered by any such person.
> (2) The fees and expenses of an expert, legal adviser or assessor appointed by the tribunal for which the arbitrators are liable are expenses of the arbitrators for the purposes of this Part.

UNCITRAL Model Law countries and the UK are by no means the only countries to grant tribunals authority to engage their own experts. As Practice Guideline 10 of The Chartered Institute of Arbitrators notes, in "other countries, notably Switzerland, France, Belgium, [and] the U.S., the parties and, in default, the tribunal's power to determine the arbitral procedure has always been interpreted as permitting the appointment of experts."[855]

Additionally, the investor-State arbitration provisions in some recent bilateral investment treaties and free trade agreements address the role of tribunal-appointed experts. Thus, the 2004 US Model Bilateral Investment Treaty contains the following provision for tribunal-appointed experts:

> Article 32: Expert Reports
>
> Without prejudice to the appointment of other kinds of experts where authorized by the applicable arbitration rules, a tribunal, at the request of a disputing party or, unless the disputing parties disapprove, on its own initiative, may appoint one or more experts to report to it in writing on any factual issue concerning environmental, health, safety, or other scientific matters raised by

855. CIArb Guideline 10, *supra* n. 821, at ¶ 2.3.

a disputing party in a proceeding, subject to such terms and conditions as the disputing parties may agree.

Pursuant to this provision, the tribunal may appoint its own expert for factual issues concerning scientific matters, unless the parties mutually disapprove. As Article 32 makes clear, the terms and conditions for that expert's engagement are also subject to mutually-agreed control by the parties. Article 42 of the 2004 Canadian Model Agreement for the Promotion and Protection of Investments is identical. There is as yet no precedential experience with such provisions to help counsel determine if the phrase 'any factual issue concerning ... other scientific matters' encompasses valuation of an investment.

The costs of a tribunal-appointed expert may be considerable. Accordingly, parties are often reluctant to see arbitrators engage an independent expert.[856] Occasionally, however, a party may specifically request the tribunal to appoint a valuation expert. In *Siemens v. Argentina*, Argentina sought the appointment by the tribunal of an expert "to analyze the accounts of SITS [the expropriated investment] and ensure that the amounts spent by SITS were spent for purposes of carrying out the Project." As the panel explained the Argentine request, "For Argentina, there is a need to show how each dollar or peso was spent and relate each dollar or peso to the item financed with it."[857] The investor opposed the Argentine request, arguing that the audited financial statements of SITS were sufficient evidence of the invested capital. The tribunal rejected the request by Argentina (over the objection of one arbitrator). In doing so, the majority noted that Argentina had failed to offer convincing evidence showing that the funds made available to SITS were not used for the intended purpose.[858]

When the tribunal does appoint its own expert, parties may be concerned that the independent expert will become de facto the fourth, and decisive, arbitrator on the compensation issue. How, ask the parties, will an arbitrator be capable of questioning the opinions of an expert the panel itself selected?[859] In addition, parties may be concerned that the opinions of a valuation expert appointed by the panel will not receive sufficient scrutiny and critical analysis, creating the potential for errors and omissions. The IBA Rules for the Taking of Evidence in International Commercial Arbitration seek to address these concerns by requiring consultations with the parties about a tribunal-appointed expert's terms of reference, mandating a statement about the expert's independence, requiring the

856. As The Chartered Institute of Arbitrators comments in CIArb Guideline 10, *supra* n. 821, at ¶ 4, "before appointing an expert ... under this Section the tribunal must first consider whether this is consistent with its duty under Section 33(1)(b) [of the 1996 Arbitration Act] to adopt procedures suitable to the Circumstances of the particular case, avoiding unnecessary delay or expense, so as to provide a fair means for the resolution of the matters failing to be determined."

857. *Siemens v. Argentina*, *supra* n. 112, at ¶ 358.

858. *Id.*, at ¶ 360. Compare Separate Opinion from Professor Domingo Bello Janeire, Arbitrator, January 30, 2007, at 1.

859. But note the rejection by the panel of certain of the advice from its own valuation expert in *Shahin Shaine Ebrahimi v. Islamic Republic of Iran*, *supra* n. 603, at ¶ 127.

expert's work to be shared with the parties and permitting examination of the expert at an evidentiary hearing:

Article 6 Tribunal-Appointed Experts

1. The Arbitral Tribunal, after having consulted with the Parties, may appoint one or more independent Tribunal-Appointed Experts to report to it on specific issues designated by the Arbitral Tribunal. The Arbitral Tribunal shall establish the terms of reference for any Tribunal-Appointed Expert Report after having consulted with the Parties. A copy of the final terms of reference shall be sent by the Arbitral Tribunal to the Parties.
2. The Tribunal-Appointed Expert shall, before accepting appointment, submit to the Arbitral Tribunal and to the Parties a statement of his or her independence from the Parties and the Arbitral Tribunal. Within the time ordered by the Arbitral Tribunal, the Parties shall inform the Arbitral Tribunal whether they have any objections to the Tribunal-Appointed Expert's independence. The Arbitral Tribunal shall decide promptly whether to accept any such objection.
3. Subject to the provisions of Article 9.2, the Tribunal-Appointed Expert may request a Party to provide any relevant and material information or to provide access to any relevant documents, goods, samples, property or site for inspection. The authority of a Tribunal-Appointed Expert to request such information or access shall be the same as the authority of the Arbitral Tribunal. The Parties and their representatives shall have the right to receive any such information and to attend any such inspection. Any agreement between a Tribunal-Appointed Expert and a Party as to the relevance, materiality or appropriateness of such a request shall be decided by the Arbitral Tribunal, in the manner provided in Articles 3.5 through 3.7. The Tribunal-Appointed Expert shall record in the report any non-compliance by a Party with an appropriate request or decision by the Arbitral Tribunal and shall describe its effects on the determination of the specific issue.
4. The Tribunal-Appointed Expert shall report in writing to the Arbitral Tribunal. The Tribunal-Appointed Expert shall describe in the report the method, evidence and information used in arriving at the conclusions.
5. The Arbitral Tribunal shall send a copy of such Expert Report to the Parties. The parties may examine any document that the Tribunal – Appointed Expert has examined and any correspondence between the Arbitral Tribunal and the Tribunal-Appointed Expert. Within the time ordered by the Arbitral Tribunal, any Party shall have the opportunity to respond to the report in a submission by the Party or through an Expert Report by a Party-Appointed Expert. The Arbitral Tribunal shall send the submission or Expert Report to the Tribunal-Appointed Expert and to the other Parties.
6. At the request of a Party or of the Arbitral Tribunal, the Tribunal-Appointed Expert shall be present at an Evidentiary Hearing. The Arbitral Tribunal may question the Tribunal-Appointed Expert and he or she may be questioned by the Parties or by any Party-Appointed Expert on issues raised by

the Parties' submissions or in the Expert Reports made by the Party-Appointed Experts pursuant to Article 6.5.

7. Any Expert Report made by a Tribunal-Appointed Expert and its conclusions shall be assessed by the Arbitral Tribunal with due regard to all circumstances of the case.

The IBA Rules thus offer the parties some protection from the risk that a tribunal-appointed expert will become the de facto judge of valuation issues, acting without the procedural shields of prior notice and an opportunity to be heard as to that expert's methodology and conclusions. Many counsel, of course, remain unpersuaded that the IBA Rules prevent that situation from actually occurring.

The Chartered Institute of Arbitrators has issued a useful Practice Guide for arbitrators relating to the use of tribunal-appointed experts.[860] By way of background, the English 1996 Arbitration Act leaves an arbitral tribunal with considerable discretion about the expert procedure. However, section 37 of the Act does require that any information, opinion or advice offered by a tribunal-appointed expert must be communicated to the parties and the parties must be afforded a reasonable opportunity to comment. The scope of the tribunal expert's terms of reference is, of course, a central issue. Duties can range from preparing questions for the arbitrators, to writing a report commenting on the reports of the party-appointed experts, to "auditing" the financial models of the other experts (a common task for lenders' experts in a project finance transaction). At its broadest, a tribunal-appointed expert may even be charged with preparing an independent financial model.

CIArb Guideline 10 draws the attention of the tribunal to the following items for consideration.

- whether or not the case is suited to the use of a tribunal appointed expert;
- if so, what are to be the expert's terms of reference;
- who is to be appointed and on what terms;
- what material is to be provided initially to the expert;
- whether the expert is to be able to seek further material or information from the parties;
- the time-table for the production of the expert's report;
- whether or in what circumstances the parties are to be entitled to call their own expert evidence or to serve their own experts reports;
- the procedure for enabling the parties to comment on the expert's report; and
- the procedure to be adopted at the hearing.[861]

860. CIArb Guideline 10, *supra* n. 821. CIArb Guideline 10 offers inter alia a checklist of items to be considered by arbitrators when deciding whether to appoint an expert (¶ 6), discusses the character of cases suited to the use of tribunal-appointed experts (¶¶ 7–9) and provides helpful guidance to arbitrators in managing both the process of appointment and the subsequent use of the expert (¶¶ 10–26).

861. CIArb Guideline 10, *supra* n. 821, at ¶ 3.

Moreover, CIArb Guideline 10 calls for the tribunal to consider an order requiring "each party to give the expert any further information or to produce any further documentation or material that the expert may require."[862] Linked to this obligation, The Chartered Institute also points out that the tribunal must establish a clear procedure "designed to ensure that any material provided by one party is seen by the other and that both sides and the tribunal know precisely what material has been provided to the expert for the purpose of drawing up his or her report."[863]

Whether or not participants employ the IBA Rules or CIArb Guideline 10 in the proceedings, arbitrators must be careful to assure that the parties have a full and fair opportunity to consider the activities of a tribunal – appointed expert. The arbitrator should not delegate to that expert the decision-making responsibilities of the arbitral panel. To police compliance with this precept, transparency becomes important. Illustratively, English arbitration law prohibits arbitrators from meeting privately with the tribunal-appointed expert, even if the participants do not discuss any evidence during that meeting.[864]

Concerns about the potential for undue influence on the part of the tribunal expert have made their way into the English courts. In the recent English case of *Brandeis (Brokers) Ltd. v. Herbert Black et al.*, the court considered a claim by one party that the conduct of a tribunal – appointed expert constituted improper delegation of part of the decision-making responsibilities of the arbitrators. The court rejected the challenge, holding that the applicable London Metals Exchange arbitration rules afforded the tribunal wide discretion under which to determine the applicable procedure. The court also held that the arbitrators did not improperly delegate their powers to the tribunal-appointed expert.

> It would be a different matter if Brandeis could establish, as it asserts, that the arbitrators effectively delegated their decision making on important questions to Mr Brazier [the tribunal-appointed expert]. That criticism, if substantiated, would amount to serious irregularity, but I reject it. The arbitrators considered Mr Brazier's evidence carefully. They accepted some parts and did not accept other parts. Their award contains their evaluation of him and of other

862. *Id.*, at ¶ 3.5.2.
863. *Id.*, at ¶ 3.5.3.
864. *See* Dundas, *Tribunal-Appointed Experts in International Commercial Arbitration: Exploring the Boundaries*, vol. 5, issue 2, *The International Arbitration News 10* (Summer 2005), discussing *Hussman (Europe) Ltd. v. Al Ameen Trade and Development Company* et al., [2000] 2 Lloyds Rep. 83, and *Brandeis (Brokers) Ltd. v. Herbert Black* et al., [2001] 2 Lloyds Rep. 359. More generally, several respected commentaries consider the principle to be of general application. *See* e.g., Schäfer, *Verbist & Imhoos, ICC Arbitration in Practice*, at 103 (Kluwer 2005), and Fouchard, Gaillard & Goldman on *International Commercial Arbitration*, at § 1293 (English edn Gaillard & Savage, Kluwer 1999). The principle is not, however, absolutist. *See Luzon Hydro Corporation v. Transfield Philippines Inc.* [2004] SCHC 204, [2004] 4 S.L.R. 705, in which a Singaporean court refused to vacate an ICC arbitral award notwithstanding direct meetings and correspondence between the tribunal and its expert on "administrative matters" such as identifying technical services, to which the parties were not privy.

> witnesses. When objections to Mr Brazier's evidence were raised, the arbitrators observed that they were conscious of their responsibility to decide disputed questions of fact. From what they said and from the terms of their award (which was carefully constructed and ran to 74 pages) I have no doubt that they conscientiously did so.[865]

In addition to being sensitive to due process and conflict of interest considerations, arbitrators must also pay close attention to the tribunal-appointed expert's background. For many disputed matters, two or more competing schools of expert thought exist. In light of the influence of a tribunal – appointed expert, it is essential for arbitrators to be sensitive to the risk of de facto resolving a valuation dispute by the simple act of appointing as their expert the proponent of one school of valuation, rather than another school. Accordingly, one very important aspect of the process of selecting a tribunal-appointed expert is the involvement of the opposing parties in the selection process. While neither party, of course, should hold a veto over the tribunal's choice, efforts by the panel to share information and obtain the views of the parties before finalizing the panel's choice will enhance the legitimacy of the evidence of the expert eventually appointed by the tribunal.[866]

We hope that the explanations and tools offered in this volume will contribute to the reliability of business valuations in arbitration proceedings. Elements of valuation principles may have reached consensus within the valuation community, but sharp differences still exist for many questions. Moreover, the arbitration community and valuation professionals divide from each other, and within themselves, on significant issues. Valuation Mercatoria remains a future prospect. Still, perhaps there is indeed help available for arbitrators in the maze comprised of comparables, DCF forecasts, capitalization rates, mid-year conventions, betas and other financial mysteries.

865. *Brandeis (Brokers) Ltd. v. Herbert Black* et al., *supra* n. 864, at ¶ 68.
866. *See* Schäfer, Verbist & Imhoos, *ICC Arbitration in Practice*, *supra* n. 864, at 103.

Appendix 1

List of Current IVSC Members, Observers and Correspondents from <www.ivsc.org/members.html>. Current as of April 13, 2008

IVSC Member

Country	*Members*
Argentina	Instituto Argentino de Tasaciones
Australia	Australian Property Institute
Austria	Austrian Institute of Property Valuation and Valuation Standards
Brazil	Instituto Brasileiro Avaliacoes
Canada	Appraisal Institute of Canada
	Canadian Institute of Chartered Business Valuators (CICBV)
China	China Appraisal Society
Colombia	Registro Nacional de Avaluadores
Czech Republic	The Czech Chamber of Appraisers
Egypt	The Egyptian Association of Real Estate Appraisers
Germany	Verband Deutscher Pfandbriefbanken
	Bundesverband der Immobilien-Investment-Sachverständigen e. V. (BIIS)
Greece	Body of Sworn-in Valuers of Greece
Hong Kong, China	Hong Kong Institute of Surveyors
India	The Practising Valuers Association of India
Indonesia	Indonesian Society of Appraisers

Country	*Members*
Ireland	The Society of Chartered Surveyors in the Republic of Ireland
	The Irish Auctioneers and Valuers Institute
Italy	Consiglio Nazionale Geometri
Japan	Japanese Association of Real Estate Appraisal
Kazakhstan	Chamber of Professional Appraisers of Kazakhstan
Kenya	Institution of Surveyors of Kenya (ISK)
Korea	Korea Appraisal Board
Latvia	Latvian Association of Appraisers
Lithuania	Lithuanian Association of Property Valuers
	Lithuanian Association of Property and Business Valuation Enterprises
Malawi	Surveyors Institute of Malawi
Malaysia	The Institution of Surveyors, Malaysia
Mexico	National Association of Mexican Valuation Institutes
The Netherlands	Raad voor Onroerende Zaken (ROZ, the Real Estate Council)
New Zealand	Property Institute of New Zealand (PINZ)
Norway	Norges Takseringsforbund
Nigeria	Nigerian Institution of Estate Surveyors and Valuers
Philippines	Institute of Philippine Real Estate Appraisers (IPREA)
Poland	The Polish Federation of Valuer's Associations
Romania	The National Association of Romanian Valuers
Russia	Russian Society of Appraisers
	Russian Board of Appraisers
	Self-Regulated Inter-Regional Appraisers Association (SIAA)
Singapore	Singapore Institute of Surveyors and Valuers
Slovenia	Slovenian Institute of Auditors
South Africa	South African Institute of Valuers
Spain	Association Espanola de Sociadades de Tasacion
Sweden	Samfundet för Fastighetsvardering
Tanzania	Tanzania Institution of Valuers and Estate Agents
Thailand	Thai Valuers Association
Turkey	Appraisers' Association
Ukraine	Ukrainian Society of Appraisers
United Kingdom	The Royal Institution of Chartered Surveyors
United States	The Appraisal Institute
	American Society of Appraisers
Venezuela	Sociedad de Ingenieria de Tasaciones de Venezuela

IVSC Observers

Country	*Observer*
Albania	The Albanian Society of Real Property Valuers
Barbados	Barbados Association of Professional Valuers
Estonia	Estonian Association of Appraisers
Finland	Finnish Association for Real Estate Valuation
Georgia	Georgian Federation of Professional Assets Valuators
	Expertise Institute for Valuation of Assets of Georgia
Luxembourg	Institut National de l'Expertise Immobiliere
Macedonia	Macedonian Appraisal Society
Slovakia	Slovak Association of Economic Appraisers

IVSC Correspondents

Country	*Correspondent*
Palestine	Palestinian Auditors and Accountants Association
Vietnam	Price Control Department, Ministry of Finance

Appendix 2

AICPA Statement on Standards for Valuation Services No. 1: Valuation of a Business, Business Ownership Interest, Security, or Intangible Asset (SSVS No. 1), Including the International Glossary of Business Valuation Terms

VALUATION OF A BUSINESS, BUSINESS OWNERSHIP INTEREST, SECURITY, OR INTANGIBLE ASSET

Introduction and Scope

1. This Statement establishes standards for AICPA members (hereinafter referred to in this Statement as *members*) who are engaged to, or, as part of another engagement, estimate the value of a **business,**[1] ***business ownership interest, security,*** or **intangible asset** (hereinafter collectively referred to in this Statement as ***subject interest).*** For purposes of this Statement, the definition of a *business* includes not-for-profit entities or activities.

2. As described in this Statement, the term ***engagement to estimate value*** refers to an engagement or any part of an engagement (for example, a tax, litigation, or acquisition-related engagement) that involves estimating the value of a subject interest. An engagement to estimate value culminates in the expression of either a ***conclusion of value*** or a ***calculated value*** (see paragraph 21). A member who performs an engagement to estimate value is referred to, in this Statement, as a ***valuation analyst.***

3. Valuation analysts should be aware of any governmental regulations and other professional standards applicable to the engagement, including the AICPA *Code of Professional Conduct* and the Statement on Standards for Consulting Services (SSCS) No. 1, *Consulting Services: Definitions and Standards* (AICPA, *Professional Standards,* vol. 2, CS sec. 100), and the extent to which they apply to engagements to estimate value. Compliance is the responsibility of the valuation analyst.

---

1. This Statement includes two glossaries. Appendix B is the International Glossary of Business Valuation Terms (IGBVT), jointly developed by the AICPA, the American Society of Appraisers (ASA), the Canadian Institute of Chartered Business Valuators, the National Association of Certified Valuation Analysts, and the Institute of Business Appraisers. The IGBVT is reproduced verbatim in Appendix B, "International Glossary of Business Valuation Terms." Appendix C provides definitions for terms included in this Statement, but not defined in the IGBVT. The terms defined in Appendix B are in boldface type the first time they appear in this Statement; the terms defined in Appendix C are in italicized boldface type the first time they appear in this Statement.

4. In the process of estimating value as part of an engagement, the valuation analyst applies **valuation approaches** and **valuation methods,** as described in this Statement, and uses professional judgment. The use of professional judgment is an essential component of estimating value.

Exceptions from This Statement

5. This Statement is not applicable to a member who participates in estimating the value of a subject interest as part of performing an attest engagement defined by Rule 101 of the AICPA Code of Professional Conduct (for example, as part of an audit, review, or compilation engagement).

6. This Statement is not applicable when the value of a subject interest is provided to the member by the client or a third party, and the member does not apply valuation approaches and methods, as discussed in this Statement.

7. This Statement is not applicable to internal use assignments from employers to employee members not in the *practice of public accounting,* as that term is defined in the AICPA *Code of Professional Conduct* (AICPA, *Professional Standards,* vol. 2, ET sec. 92. 25). (Interpretation No. 1, "Scope of Applicable Services" of *Statement on Standards for Valuation Services,* Illustrations 24 and 25).

8. This Statement is not applicable to engagements that are exclusively for the purpose of determining economic damages (for example, lost profits) unless those determinations include an engagement to estimate value. See also Interpretation No. 1, Illustrations 1, 2, and 3.

9.(a) This Statement is not applicable to mechanical computations that do not rise to the level of an engagement to estimate value; that is, when the member does not apply valuation approaches and methods and does not use professional judgment. See Interpretation No. 1, Illustration 8.

(b) This Statement is not applicable when it is not practical or not reasonable to obtain or use relevant information; as a result, the member is unable to apply valuation approaches and methods that are described in this Statement.[2]

Jurisdictional Exception

10. If any part of this Statement differs from published governmental, judicial, or accounting authority, or such authority specifies valuation development procedures or valuation reporting procedures, then the valuation analyst should follow the applicable published authority or stated procedures with respect to that part applicable

2. Unless prohibited by statute or by rule, a member may use the client s estimates for compliance reporting to a third party if the member determines that the estimates are reasonable (based on the facts and circumstances known to the member). See Interpretation No. 1, "Scope of Applicable Services" of *Statement on Standards for Valuation Services* and *Statement for Standards on Tax Services* No. 4.

to the valuation in which the member is engaged. The other parts of this Statement continue in full force and effect (Valuation Services Interpretation No. 1).

Overall Engagement Considerations

Professional Competence

11. Rule 201A, *Professional Competence,* of the AICPA *Code of Professional Conduct* (AICPA, *Professional Standards,* vol. 2, ET. sec. 201.01), states that a member shall "undertake only those professional services that the member or the member's firm can reasonably expect to be completed with professional competence." Performing a valuation engagement with professional competence involves special knowledge and skill. A valuation analyst should possess a level of knowledge of valuation principles and theory and a level of skill in the application of such principles that will enable him or her to identify, gather, and analyze data, consider and apply appropriate valuation approaches and methods, and use professional judgment in developing the estimate of value (whether a single amount or a range). An in-depth discussion of valuation theory and principles, and how and when to apply them, is not within the scope of this Statement.

12. In determining whether he or she can reasonably expect to complete the valuation engagement with professional competence, the valuation analyst should consider, at a minimum, the following:

a. Subject entity and its industry
b. Subject interest
c. **Valuation date**
d. Scope of the valuation engagement
   i. Purpose of the valuation engagement
   ii. ***Assumptions and limiting conditions*** expected to apply to the valuation engagement (paragraph 18)
   iii. Applicable **standard of value** (for example, ***fair value*** or **fair market value),** and the applicable **premise of value** (for example, going concern)
   iv. Type of valuation report to be issued (paragraph 48), intended use and users of the report, and restrictions on the use of the report
e. Governmental regulations or other professional standards that apply to the subject interest or to the valuation engagement

Nature and Risks of the Valuation Services and Expectations of the Client

13. In understanding the nature and risks of the ***valuation services*** to be provided, and the expectations of the client, the valuation analyst should consider the matters in paragraph 12, and in addition, at a minimum, the following:

a. The proposed terms of the valuation engagement
b. The identity of the client
c. The nature of the interest and ownership rights in the business, business interest, security, or intangible asset being valued, including **control** characteristics and the degree of **marketability** of the interest
d. The procedural requirements of a valuation engagement and the extent, if any, to which procedures will be limited by either the client or circumstances beyond the client's or the valuation analyst's control
e. The use of and limitations of the report, and the conclusion or calculated value
f. Any obligation to update the valuation

Objectivity and Conflict of Interest

14. The AICPA *Code of Professional Conduct* requires objectivity in the performance of all professional services, including valuation engagements. Objectivity is a state of mind. The principle of objectivity imposes the obligation to be impartial, intellectually honest, disinterested, and free from conflicts of interest. If necessary, where a potential conflict of interest may exist, a valuation analyst should make the disclosures and obtain consent as required under Interpretation No. 102-2, "Conflicts of Interest," under Rule 102, *Integrity and Objectivity* (AICPA, *Professional Standards,* vol. 2, ET sec. 102.03).

Independence and Valuation

15. If valuation services are performed for a client for which the valuation analyst or valuation analyst's firm also performs an attest engagement (defined by Rule 101 of the AICPA Code of Professional Conduct), the valuation analyst should meet the requirements of Interpretation No. 101-3, "Performance of Nonattest Services," under Rule 101, *Independence* (AICPA, *Professional Standards,* vol. 2, ET sec. 101.05), so as not to impair the member's independence with respect to the client.

Establishing an Understanding with the Client

16. The valuation analyst should establish an understanding with the client, preferably in writing, regarding the engagement to be performed. If the understanding is oral, the valuation analyst should document that understanding by appropriate memoranda or notations in the working papers. (If the engagement is being performed for an attest client, AICPA Ethics Interpretation 101-3 requires the engagement understanding to be in writing.) Regardless of whether the understanding is written or oral, the valuation analyst should modify the understanding if he or she encounters circumstances during the engagement that make it appropriate to modify that understanding.

17. The understanding with the client reduces the possibility that either the valuation analyst or the client may misinterpret the needs or expectations of the

other party. The understanding should include, at a minimum, the nature, purpose, and objective of the valuation engagement, the client's responsibilities, the valuation analyst's responsibilities, the applicable assumptions and limiting conditions, the type of report to be issued, and the standard of value to be used.

Assumptions and Limiting Conditions

18. Assumptions and limiting conditions are common to valuation engagements. Examples of typical assumptions and limiting conditions for a business valuation are provided in Appendix A, "Illustrative List of Assumptions and Limiting Conditions for a Business Valuation." The assumptions and limiting conditions should be disclosed in the valuation report (paragraphs 52(l), 68(g), and 71(m).

Scope Restrictions or Limitations

19. A restriction or limitation on the scope of the valuation analyst's work, or the data available for analysis, may be present and known to the valuation analyst at the outset of the valuation engagement or may arise during the course of a valuation engagement. Such a restriction or limitation should be disclosed in the valuation report (paragraphs 52(m), 68(e), and 71(n)).

Using the Work of Specialists in the Engagement to Estimate Value

20. In performing an engagement to estimate value, the valuation analyst may rely on the work of a third party specialist (for example, a real estate or equipment appraiser). The valuation analyst should note in the assumptions and limiting conditions the level of responsibility, if any, being assumed by the valuation analyst for the work of the third party specialist. At the option of the valuation analyst, the written report of the third party specialist may be included in the valuation analyst's report.

Development

Types of Engagement

21. There are two types of engagements to estimate value – a ***valuation engagement*** and a ***calculation engagement.*** The valuation engagement requires more procedures than does the calculation engagement. The valuation engagement results in a conclusion of value. The calculation engagement results in a calculated value. The type of engagement is established in the understanding with the client (paragraphs 16 and 17):

a. *Valuation engagement* – A valuation analyst performs a valuation engagement when (1) the engagement calls for the valuation analyst to estimate the value of a subject interest and (2) the valuation analyst estimates the value (as outlined in paragraphs 23–45) and is free to apply the valuation approaches and methods he or she deems appropriate in the circumstances. The valuation analyst expresses the results of the valuation as a conclusion of value; the conclusion may be either a single amount or a range.

b. *Calculation engagement* – A valuation analyst performs a calculation engagement when (1) the valuation analyst and the client agree on the valuation approaches and methods the valuation analyst will use and the extent of procedures the valuation analyst will perform in the process of calculating the value of a subject interest (these procedures will be more limited than those of a valuation engagement) and (2) the valuation analyst calculates the value in compliance with the agreement. The valuation analyst expresses the results of these procedures as a calculated value. The calculated value is expressed as a range or as a single amount. A calculation engagement does not include all of the procedures required for a valuation engagement (paragraph 46).

Hypothetical Conditions

22. Hypothetical conditions affecting the subject interest may be required in some circumstances. When a valuation analyst uses hypothetical conditions during a valuation or calculation engagement, he or she should indicate the purpose for including the hypothetical conditions and disclose these conditions in the valuation or calculation report (paragraphs 52(n), 71(o), and 74).

Valuation Engagement

23. In performing a valuation engagement, the valuation analyst should:

- Analyze the subject interest (paragraphs 25–30)
- Consider and apply appropriate valuation approaches and methods (paragraphs 31–42)
- Prepare and maintain appropriate documentation (paragraphs 44–45)

24. Even though the list in paragraph 23 and some requirements and guidance in this Statement are presented in a manner that suggests a sequential valuation process, valuations involve an ongoing process of gathering, updating, and analyzing information. Accordingly, the sequence of the requirements and guidance in this Statement may be implemented differently at the option of the valuation analyst.

Analysis of the Subject Interest

25. The analysis of the subject interest will assist the valuation analyst in considering, evaluating, and applying the various valuation approaches and

methods to the subject interest. The nature and extent of the information needed to perform the analysis will depend on, at a minimum, the following:

- Nature of the subject interest
- Scope of the valuation engagement
- Valuation date
- Intended use of the valuation
- Applicable standard of value
- Applicable **premise of value**
- Assumptions and limiting conditions
- Applicable governmental regulations or other professional standards

26. In analyzing the subject interest, the valuation analyst should consider financial and nonfinancial information. The type, availability, and significance of such information vary with the subject interest.

Non-financial Information

27. The valuation analyst should, as available and applicable to the valuation engagement, obtain sufficient nonfinancial information to enable him or her to understand the subject entity, including its:

- Nature, background, and history
- Facilities
- Organizational structure
- Management team (which may include officers, directors, and key employees)
- Classes of **equity** ownership interests and rights attached thereto
- Products or services, or both
- Economic environment
- Geographical markets
- Industry markets
- Key customers and suppliers
- Competition
- **Business risks**
- Strategy and future plans
- Governmental or regulatory environment

Ownership Information

28. The valuation analyst should obtain, where applicable and available, ownership information regarding the subject interest to enable him or her to:

- Determine the type of ownership interest being valued and ascertain whether that interest exhibits control characteristics
- Analyze the different ownership interests of other owners and assess the potential effect on the value of the subject interest

- Understand the classes of equity ownership interests and rights attached thereto
- Understand the rights included in, or excluded from, each intangible asset
- Understand other matters that may affect the value of the subject interest, such as:
  - *For a business, business ownership interest, or security:* shareholder agreements, partnership agreements, operating agreements, voting trust agreements, buy-sell agreements, loan covenants, restrictions, and other contractual obligations or restrictions affecting the owners and the subject interest
  - *For an intangible asset:* legal rights, licensing agreements, sublicense agreements, nondisclosure agreements, development rights, commercialization or exploitation rights, and other contractual obligations

Financial Information

29. The valuation analyst should obtain, where applicable and available, financial information on the subject entity such as:

- Historical financial information (including annual and interim financial statements and key financial statement ratios and statistics) for an appropriate number of years
- Prospective financial information (for example, budgets, forecasts, and projections)
- Comparative summaries of financial statements or information covering a relevant time period
- Comparative common size financial statements for the subject entity for an appropriate number of years
- Comparative common size industry financial information for a relevant time period
- Income tax returns for an appropriate number of years
- Information on compensation for owners including benefits and personal expenses
- Information on key man or officers' life insurance
- Management's response to inquiry regarding:
  - Advantageous or disadvantageous contracts
  - Contingent or off-balance-sheet assets or liabilities
  - Information on prior sales of company stock

30. The valuation analyst should read and evaluate the information to determine that it is reasonable for the purposes of the engagement.

Valuation Approaches and Methods

31. In developing the valuation, the valuation analyst should consider the three most common valuation approaches:

- **Income (Income-based) approach**

- **Asset (Asset-based) approach** (used for businesses, business ownership interests, and securities) or **cost approach** (used for intangible assets)
- **Market (Market-based) approach**

32. The valuation analyst should use the valuation approaches and methods that are appropriate for the valuation engagement. General guidance on the use of approaches and methods appears in paragraphs 33–41, but detailed guidance on specific valuation approaches and methods and their applicability is outside the scope of this Statement.

33. *Income Approach.* Two frequently used valuation methods under the income approach include the **capitalization of benefits method** (for example, earnings or cash flows) and the **discounted future benefits method** (for example, earnings or cash flows). When applying these methods, the valuation analyst should consider a variety of factors, including but not limited to, the following:

a. *Capitalization of benefits (for example, earnings or cash flows) method.* The valuation analyst should consider the following:
   - ***Normalization*** adjustments
   - Nonrecurring revenue and expense items
   - Taxes
   - **Capital structure** and financing costs
   - Appropriate capital investments
   - Noncash items
   - Qualitative judgments for risks used to compute discount and **capitalization rates**
   - Expected changes (growth or decline) in future benefits (for example, earnings or cash flows)

b. *Discounted future benefits method (for example, earnings or cash flows).* In addition to the items in item *a* above, the valuation analyst should consider:
   - Forecast/projection assumptions
   - Forecast/projected earnings or cash flows
   - **Terminal value**

c. For an intangible asset, the valuation analyst should also consider, when relevant:
   - Remaining useful life
   - Current and anticipated future use of the intangible asset
   - Rights attributable to the intangible asset
   - Position of intangible asset in its life cycle
   - Appropriate discount rate for the intangible asset
   - Appropriate ***capital or contributory asset charge,*** if any
   - Research and development or marketing expense needed to support the intangible asset in its existing state
   - Allocation of income (for example, ***incremental income, residual income,*** or ***profit split income***) to intangible asset
   - Whether any tax amortization benefit would be included in the analysis
   - Discounted multi-year excess earnings

- Market royalties
- Relief from royalty

Asset Approach and Cost Approach

34. A frequently used method under the asset approach is the adjusted net asset method. When using the adjusted net asset method in valuing a business, business ownership interest, or security, the valuation analyst should consider, as appropriate, the following information related to the premise of value:

- Identification of the assets and liabilities
- Value of the assets and liabilities (individually or in the aggregate)
- Liquidation costs (if applicable)

35. When using methods under the cost approach to value intangible assets, the valuation analyst should consider the type of cost to be used (for example, reproduction cost or replacement cost), and, where applicable, the appropriate forms of depreciation and obsolescence and the remaining useful life of the intangible asset.

Market Approach

36. Three frequently used valuation methods under the market approach for valuing a business, business ownership interest, or security are:

- ***Guideline public company method***
- ***Guideline company transactions method***
- Guideline sales of interests in the subject entity, such as business ownership interests or securities

Three frequently used market approach valuation methods for intangible assets are:

- Comparable uncontrolled transactions method (which is based on arm's-length sales or licenses of guideline intangible assets)
- Comparable profit margin method (which is based on comparison of the profit margin earned by the subject entity that owns or operates the intangible asset to profit margins earned by guideline companies)
- ***Relief from royalty method*** (which is based on the royalty rate, often expressed as a percentage of revenue that the subject entity that owns or operates the intangible asset would be obligated to pay to a hypothetical third-party licensor for the use of that intangible asset)

For the methods involving guideline intangible assets (for example, the comparable profit margin method), the valuation analyst should consider the subject intangible asset's remaining useful life relative to the remaining useful life of the guideline intangible assets, if available.

37. In applying the methods listed in paragraph 36 or other methods to determine valuation pricing multiples or metrics, the valuation analyst should consider:

- Qualitative and quantitative comparisons
- Arm's-length transactions and prices
- The dates and, consequently, the relevance of the market data

38. The valuation analyst should set forth in the report the rationale and support for the valuation methods used (paragraph 47).

39. *Rules of Thumb.* Although technically not a valuation method, some valuation analysts use rules of thumb or industry benchmark indicators (hereinafter, collectively referred to as **rules of thumb**) in a valuation engagement. A rule of thumb is typically a reasonableness check against other methods used and should generally not be used as the only method to estimate the value of the subject interest.

Valuation Adjustments

40. During the course of a valuation engagement, the valuation analyst should consider whether valuation adjustments (discounts or premiums) should be made to a **pre-adjustment** value. Examples of valuation adjustments for valuation of a business, business ownership interest, or security include a **discount for lack of marketability or liquidity** and a **discount for lack of control.** An example of a valuation adjustment for valuation of an intangible asset is obsolescence.

41. When valuing a controlling ownership interest under the income approach, the value of any **nonoperating assets,** nonoperating liabilities, or ***excess or deficient operating assets*** should be excluded from the computation of the value based on the operating assets and should be added to or deleted from the value of the operating entity. When valuing a noncontrolling ownership interest under the income approach, the value of any nonoperating assets, nonoperating liabilities, or excess or deficient operating assets may or may not be used to adjust the value of the operating entity depending on the valuation analyst's assessment of the influence exercisable by the noncontrolling interest. In the asset-based or cost approach, it may not be necessary to separately consider nonoperating assets, nonoperating liabilities, or excess or deficient operating assets.

Conclusion of Value

42. In arriving at a conclusion of value, the valuation analyst should:

a. Correlate and reconcile the results obtained under the different approaches and methods used.
b. Assess the reliability of the results under the different approaches and methods using the information gathered during the valuation engagement.
c. Determine, based on items *a* and *b,* whether the conclusion of value should reflect (1) the results of one valuation approach and method or (2) a combination of the results of more than one valuation approach and method.

Subsequent Events

43. The valuation date is the specific date at which the valuation analyst estimates the value of the subject interest and concludes on his or her estimation of value. Generally, the valuation analyst should consider only circumstances existing at the valuation date and events occurring up to the valuation date. An event that could affect the value may occur subsequent to the valuation date; such an occurrence is referred to as a ***subsequent event.*** Subsequent events are indicative of conditions that were not known or knowable at the valuation date, including conditions that arose subsequent to the valuation date. The valuation would not be updated to reflect those events or conditions. Moreover, the valuation report would typically not include a discussion of those events or conditions because a valuation is performed as of a point in time – the valuation date – and the events described in this subparagraph, occurring subsequent to that date, are not relevant to the value determined as of that date. In situations in which a valuation is meaningful to the intended user beyond the valuation date, the events may be of such nature and significance as to warrant disclosure (at the option of the valuation analyst) in a separate section of the report in order to keep users informed (paragraphs 52(p), 71(r), and 74). Such disclosure should clearly indicate that information regarding the events is provided for informational purposes only and does not affect the determination of value as of the specified valuation date.

Documentation

44. Documentation is the principal record of information obtained and analyzed, procedures performed, valuation approaches and methods considered and used, and the conclusion of value. The quantity, type, and content of documentation are matters of the valuation analyst's professional judgment. Documentation may include:

- Information gathered and analyzed to obtain an understanding of matters that may affect the value of the subject interest (paragraphs 25–30)
- Assumptions and limiting conditions (paragraph 18)
- Any restriction or limitation on the scope of the valuation analyst's work or the data available for analysis (paragraph 19)
- Basis for using any ***valuation assumption*** during the valuation engagement
- Valuation approaches and methods considered
- Valuation approaches and methods used including the rationale and support for their use
- If applicable, information relating to subsequent events considered by the valuation analyst (paragraph 43)
- For any rule of thumb used in the valuation, source(s) of data used, and how the rule of thumb was applied (paragraph 39)
- Other documentation considered relevant to the engagement by the valuation analyst

45. The valuation analyst should retain the documentation for a period of time sufficient to meet the needs of applicable legal, regulatory, or other professional requirements for records retention.

Calculation Engagement

46. In performing a calculation engagement, the valuation analyst should consider, at a minimum, the following:

a. Identity of the client
b. Identity of the subject interest
c. Whether or not a business interest has ownership control characteristics and its degree of marketability
d. Purpose and intended use of the calculated value
e. Intended users of the report and the limitations on its use
f. Valuation date
g. Applicable premise of value
h. Applicable standard of value
i. Sources of information used in the calculation engagement
j. Valuation approaches or valuation methods agreed upon with the client
k. Subsequent events, if applicable (paragraph 43)

In addition, the valuation analyst should comply with the documentation requirements listed in paragraphs 44 and 45. The quantity, type, and content of documentation are matters of the valuation analyst's professional judgment.

THE VALUATION REPORT

47. A valuation report is a written or oral communication to the client containing the conclusion of value or the calculated value of the subject interest. Reports issued for purposes of certain controversy proceedings are exempt from this reporting standard (paragraph 50).

48. The three types of written reports that a valuation analyst may use to communicate the results of an engagement to estimate value are: for a valuation engagement, a detailed report or a summary report; and for a calculation engagement, a calculation report.

For a Valuation Engagement

a. *Detailed Report:* This report may be used only to communicate the results of a valuation engagement (conclusion of value); it should not be used to communicate the results of a calculation engagement (calculated value) (paragraph 51).
b. *Summary Report:* This report may be used only to communicate the results of a valuation engagement (conclusion of value); it should not be used to

communicate the results of a calculation engagement (calculated value) (paragraph 71).

For a valuation engagement, the determination of whether to prepare a detailed report or a summary report is based on the level of reporting detail agreed to by the valuation analyst and the client.

For a Calculation Engagement

c. *Calculation Report:* This type of report should be used only to communicate the results of a calculation engagement (calculated value); it should not be used to communicate the results of a valuation engagement (conclusion of value) (paragraph 73).

49. The valuation analyst should indicate in the valuation report the restrictions on the use of the report (which may include restrictions on the users of the report, the uses of the report by such users, or both) (paragraph 65(d)).

Reporting Exemption for Certain Controversy Proceedings

50. A valuation performed for a matter before a court, an arbitrator, a mediator or other facilitator, or a matter in a governmental or administrative proceeding, is exempt from the reporting provisions of this Statement. The reporting exemption applies whether the matter proceeds to trial or settles. The exemption applies only to the reporting provisions of this Statement (paragraphs 47–49 and 51–78). The developmental provisions of the Statement (paragraphs 21–46) still apply whenever the valuation analyst expresses a conclusion of value or a calculated value (Valuation Services Interpretation No. 1).

Detailed Report

51. The *detailed report* is structured to provide sufficient information to permit intended users to understand the data, reasoning, and analyses underlying the valuation analyst's conclusion of value. A detailed report should include, as applicable, the following sections titled using wording similar in content to that shown:

- Letter of transmittal
- Table of contents
- Introduction
- Sources of information
- Analysis of the subject entity and related nonfinancial information
- Financial statement/information analysis
- Valuation approaches and methods considered
- Valuation approaches and methods used
- Valuation adjustments

- Nonoperating assets, nonoperating liabilities, and excess or deficient operating assets (if any)
- Representation of the valuation analyst
- Reconciliation of estimates and conclusion of value
- Qualifications of the valuation analyst
- Appendices and exhibits

The above listed report sections and the detailed information within the sections described in the following paragraphs 52–77 may be positioned in the body of the report or elsewhere in the report at the discretion of the valuation analyst.

Introduction

52. This section should provide an overall description of the valuation engagement. The information in the section should be sufficient to enable the intended user of the report to understand the nature and scope of the valuation engagement, as well as the work performed. The introduction section may include, among other things, the following information:

a. Identity of the client
b. Purpose and intended use of the valuation
c. Intended users of the valuation
d. Identity of the subject entity
e. Description of the subject interest
f. Whether the business interest has ownership control characteristics and its degree of marketability
g. Valuation date
h. Report date
i. Type of report issued (namely, a detailed report) (paragraph 51)
j. Applicable premise of value
k. Applicable standard of value
l. Assumptions and limiting conditions (alternatively, these often appear in an appendix) (paragraph 18)
m. Any restrictions or limitations in the scope of work or data available for analysis (paragraph 19)
n. Any hypothetical conditions used in the valuation engagement, including the basis for their use (paragraph 22)
o. If the work of a specialist was used in the valuation engagement, a description of how the specialist's work was relied upon (paragraph 20)
p. Disclosure of subsequent events in certain circumstances (paragraph 43)
q. Any application of the jurisdictional exception (paragraph 10)
r. Any additional information the valuation analyst deems useful to enable the user(s) of the report to understand the work performed

If the above items are not included in the introduction, they should be included elsewhere in the valuation report.

Sources of Information

53. This section of the report should identify the relevant sources of information used in performing the valuation engagement. It may include, among other things, the following:

a. For valuation of a business, business ownership interest, or security, whether and to what extent the subject entity's facilities were visited
b. For valuation of an intangible asset, whether the legal registration, contractual documentation, or other tangible evidence of the asset was inspected
c. Names, positions, and titles of persons interviewed and their relationships to the subject interest
d. Financial information (paragraphs 54 and 56)
e. Tax information (paragraph 55)
f. Industry data
g. Market data
h. Economic data
i. Other empirical information
j. Relevant documents and other sources of information provided by or related to the entity

54. If the financial information includes financial statements that were reported on (audit, review, compilation, or attest engagement performed under the Statements on Standards for Attestation Engagements [SSAEs]) by the valuation analyst's firm, the valuation report should disclose this fact and the type of report issued. If the valuation analyst or the valuation analyst's firm did not audit, review, compile, or attest under the SSAEs to the financial information, the valuation analyst should so state and should also state that the valuation analyst assumes no responsibility for the financial information.

55. The financial information may be derived from or may include information derived from tax returns. With regard to such derived information and other tax information (paragraph 53(e)), the valuation analyst should identify the tax returns used and any existing relationship between the valuation analyst and the tax preparer. If the valuation analyst or the valuation analyst's firm did not audit, review, compile, or attest under the SSAEs to any financial information derived from tax returns that is used during the valuation engagement, the valuation analyst should so state and should also state that the valuation analyst assumes no responsibility for that derived information.

56. If the financial information used was derived from financial statements prepared by management that were not the subject of an audit, review, compilation, or attest engagement performed under the SSAEs, the valuation report should:

- Identify the financial statements

- State that, as part of the valuation engagement, the valuation analyst did not audit, review, compile, or attest under the SSAEs to the financial information and assumes no responsibility for that information

Analysis of the Subject Entity and Related Non-financial Information

57. The valuation analyst should include a description of the relevant non-financial information listed and discussed in paragraph 27.

Financial Statement / Information Analysis

58. This section should include a description of the relevant information listed in paragraph 29. Such description may include:

a. The rationale underlying any normalization or ***control adjustments*** to financial information
b. Comparison of current performance with historical performance
c. Comparison of performance with industry trends and norms, where available

Valuation Approaches and Methods Considered

59. This section should state that the valuation analyst has considered the valuation approaches discussed in paragraph 31.

Valuation Approaches and Methods Used

60. In this section, the valuation analyst should identify the valuation methods used under each valuation approach and the rationale for their use.

61. This section should also identify the following for each of the three approaches (if used):

a. Income approach:
   - Composition of the representative benefit stream
   - Method(s) used, and a summary of the most relevant risk factors considered in selecting the appropriate **discount rate,** the capitalization rate, or both
   - Other factors as discussed in paragraph 33
b. Asset-based approach or cost approach:
   - *Asset-based approach:* Any adjustments made by the valuation analyst to the relevant balance sheet data
   - *Cost approach:* The type of cost used, how this cost was estimated, and, if applicable, the forms of and costs associated with depreciation

and obsolescence used under the approach and how those costs were estimated

c. Market approach:
   - For the guideline public company method:
     - The selected guideline companies and the process used in their selection
     - The pricing multiples used, how they were used, and the rationale for their selection. If the pricing multiples were adjusted, the rationale for such adjustments
   - For the guideline company transactions method, the sales transactions and pricing multiples used, how they were used, and the rationale for their selection. If the pricing multiples were adjusted, the rationale for such adjustments
   - For the guideline sales of interests in the subject entity method, the sales transactions used, how they were used, and the rationale for determining that these sales are representative of arm's length transactions

62. When a rule of thumb is used in combination with other methods, the valuation report should disclose the source(s) of data used and how the rule of thumb was applied (paragraph 39).

Valuation Adjustments

63. This section should *(a)* identify each valuation adjustment considered and determined to be applicable, for example, discount for lack of marketability, *(b)* describe the rationale for using the adjustment and the factors considered in selecting the amount or percentage used, and (c) describe the pre-adjustment value to which the adjustment was applied (paragraph 40).

Non-operating Assets and Excess Operating Assets

64. When the subject interest is a business, business ownership interest, or security, the valuation report should identify any related nonoperating assets, non-operating liabilities, or excess or deficient operating assets and their effect on the valuation (paragraph 41).

Representation of the Valuation Analyst

65. Each written report should contain the representation of the valuation analyst. The representation is the section of the report wherein the valuation analyst summarizes the factors that guided his or her work during the engagement. Examples of these factors include the following:

a. The analyses, opinions, and conclusion of value included in the valuation report are subject to the specified assumptions and limiting conditions (see paragraph 18), and they are the personal analyses, opinions, and conclusion of value of the valuation analyst.

b. The economic and industry data included in the valuation report have been obtained from various printed or electronic reference sources that the valuation analyst believes to be reliable (any exceptions should be noted). The valuation analyst has not performed any corroborating procedures to substantiate that data.
c. The valuation engagement was performed in accordance with the American Institute of Certified Public Accountants Statement on Standards for Valuation Services.
d. The parties for which the information and use of the valuation report is restricted are identified; the valuation report is not intended to be and should not be used by anyone other than such parties (paragraph 49).
e. The analyst's compensation is fee-based or is contingent on the outcome of the valuation.
f. The valuation analyst used the work of one or more outside specialists to assist during the valuation engagement. (An outside specialist is a specialist other than those employed in the valuation analyst's firm.) If the work of such a specialist was used, the specialist should be identified. The valuation report should include a statement identifying the level of responsibility, if any, the valuation analyst is assuming for the specialist's work.
g. The valuation analyst has no obligation to update the report or the opinion of value for information that comes to his or her attention after the date of the report.
h. The valuation analyst and the person(s) assuming responsibility for the valuation should sign the representation in their own name(s). The names of those providing significant professional assistance should be identified.

Representations Regarding Information Provided to the Valuation Analyst

66. It may be appropriate for the valuation analyst to obtain written representations regarding information that the subject entity's management provides to the valuation analyst for purposes of his or her performing the valuation engagement. The decision whether to obtain a representation letter is a matter of judgment for the valuation analyst.

Qualifications of the Valuation Analyst

67. The report should contain information regarding the qualifications of the valuation analyst.

Conclusion of Value

68. This section should present a reconciliation of the valuation analyst's estimate or various estimates of the value of the subject interest. In addition to a

discussion of the rationale underlying the conclusion of value, this section should include the following or similar statements:

a. A valuation engagement was performed, including the subject interest and the valuation date.
b. The analysis was performed solely for the purpose described in this report, and the resulting estimate of value should not be used for any other purpose.
c. The valuation engagement was conducted in accordance with the Statement(s) on Standards for Valuation Services of the American Institute of Certified Public Accountants.
d. A statement that the estimate of value resulting from a valuation engagement is expressed as a conclusion of value.
e. The scope of work or data available for analysis is explained, including any restrictions or limitations (paragraph 19).
f. A statement describing the conclusion of value, either a single amount or a range.
g. The conclusion of value is subject to the assumptions and limiting conditions (paragraph 18) and to the valuation analyst's representation (paragraph 65).
h. The report is signed in the name of the valuation analyst or the valuation analyst's firm.
i. The date of the valuation report is included.
j. The valuation analyst has no obligation to update the report or the conclusion of value for information that comes to his or her attention after the date of the report.

69. The following is an example of report language that could be used, but is not required, when reporting the results of a valuation engagement:

> We have performed a *valuation engagement,* as that term is defined in the Statement on Standards for Valuation Services (SSVS) of the American Institute of Certified Public Accountants, of *[DEF Company, GHI business ownership interest of DEF Company, GHI security of DEF Company, or GHI intangible asset of DEF Company]* as of *[valuation date].* This valuation was performed solely to assist in the matter of *[purpose of the valuation];* the resulting estimate of value should not be used for any other purpose or by any other party for any purpose. This valuation engagement was conducted in accordance with the SSVS. The estimate of value that results from a valuation engagement is expressed as a conclusion of value.
>
> *[If applicable]* We were restricted or limited in the scope of our work or data available for analysis as follows: *[describe restrictions or limitations].*
>
> Based on our analysis, as described in this valuation report, the estimate of value of *[DEF Company, GHI business ownership interest of DEF Company, GHI security of DEF Company, or GHI intangible asset of DEF Company]* as of *[valuation date]* was *[value, either a single*

amount or a range]. This conclusion is subject to the Statement of Assumptions and Limiting Conditions found in *[reference to applicable section of valuation report]* and to the Valuation Analyst s Representation found in *[reference to applicable section of valuation report].* We have no obligation to update this report or our conclusion of value for information that comes to our attention after the date of this report.

[Signature]

[Date]

Appendices and Exhibits

70. Appendices or exhibits may be used for required information or information that supplements the detailed report. Often, the assumptions and limiting conditions and the valuation analyst's representation are provided in appendices to the detailed report.

Summary Report

71. A summary report is structured to provide an abridged version of the information that would be provided in a detailed report, and therefore, need not contain the same level of detail as a detailed report. However, a summary report should, at a minimum, include the following:

a. Identity of the client
b. Purpose and intended use of the valuation
c. Intended users of the valuation
d. Identity of the subject entity
e. Description of the subject interest
f. The business interest's ownership control characteristics, if any, and its degree of marketability
g. Valuation date
h. Valuation report date
i. Type of report issued (namely, a summary report) (paragraph 48)
j. Applicable premise of value
k. Applicable standard of value
l. Sources of information used in the valuation engagement
m. Assumptions and limiting conditions of the valuation engagement (paragraph 18)
n. The scope of work or data available for analysis including any restrictions or limitations (paragraph 19)
o. Any hypothetical conditions used in the valuation engagement, including the basis for their use (paragraph 22)
p. If the work of a specialist was used in the valuation (paragraph 20), a description of how the specialist's work was used, and the level of responsibility, if any, the valuation analyst is assuming for the specialist's work

q. The valuation approaches and methods used
r. Disclosure of subsequent events in certain circumstances (paragraph 43)
s. Any application of the jurisdictional exception (paragraph 10)
t. Representation of the valuation analyst (paragraph 65)
u. The report is signed in the name of the valuation analyst or the valuation analyst's firm
v. A section summarizing the reconciliation of the estimates and the conclusion of value as discussed in paragraphs 68 and 69
w. A statement that the valuation analyst has no obligation to update the report or the calculation of value for information that comes to his or her attention after the date of the valuation report

72. Appendices or exhibits may be used for required information (paragraph 70) or information that supplements the summary report. Often, the assumptions, limiting conditions, and the valuation analyst's representation are provided in appendices to the summary report.

Calculation Report

73. As indicated in paragraph 48, a calculation report is the only report that should be used to report the results of a calculation engagement. The report should state that it is a calculation report. The calculation report should include the representation of the valuation analyst similar to that in paragraph 65, but adapted for a calculation engagement.

74. The calculation report should identify any hypothetical conditions used in the calculation engagement, including the basis for their use (paragraph 22), any application of the jurisdictional exception (paragraph 10), and any assumptions and limiting conditions applicable to the engagement (paragraph 18). If the valuation analyst used the work of a specialist (paragraph 20), the valuation analyst should describe in the calculation report how the specialist's work was used and the level of responsibility, if any, the valuation analyst is assuming for the specialist's work. The calculation report may also include a disclosure of subsequent events in certain circumstances (paragraph 43).

75. Appendices or exhibits may be used for required information (paragraph 72) or information that supplements the calculation report. Often, the assumptions and limiting conditions and the valuation analyst's representation are provided in appendices to the calculation report.

76. The calculation report should include a section summarizing the calculated value. This section should include the following (or similar) statements:

a. Certain calculation procedures were performed; include the identity of the subject interest and the calculation date.
b. Describe the calculation procedures and the scope of work performed or reference the section(s) of the calculation report in which the calculation procedures and scope of work are described.

c. Describe the purpose of the calculation procedures, including that the calculation procedures were performed solely for that purpose and that the resulting calculated value should not be used for any other purpose or by any other party for any purpose.
d. The calculation engagement was conducted in accordance with the Statement on Standards for Valuation Services of the American Institute of Certified Public Accountants.
e. A description of the business interest's characteristics, including whether the subject interest exhibits control characteristics, and a statement about the marketability of the subject interest.
f. The estimate of value resulting from a calculation engagement is expressed as a calculated value.
g. A general description of a calculation engagement is given, including that (1) a calculation engagement does not include all of the procedures required for a valuation engagement and (2) had a valuation engagement been performed, the results may have been different.
h. The calculated value, either a single amount or a range, is described.
i. The report is signed in the name of the valuation analyst or the valuation analyst's firm.
j. The date of the valuation report is given.
k. The valuation analyst has no obligation to update the report or the calculation of value for information that comes to his or her attention after the date of the report.

77. The following is an example of report language that could be used, but is not required, in reporting a calculation engagement:

> We have performed a *calculation engagement,* as that term is defined in the Statement on Standards for Valuation Services (SSVS) of the American Institute of Certified Public Accountants. We performed certain calculation procedures on *[DEF Company, GHI business ownership interest of DEF Company, GHI security of DEF Company, or GHI intangible asset of DEF Company]* as of *[calculation date].* The specific calculation procedures are detailed in paragraphs *[reference to paragraph numbers]* of our calculation report. The calculation procedures were performed solely to assist in the matter of *[purpose of valuation procedures],* and the resulting calculation of value should not be used for any other purpose or by any other party for any purpose. This calculation engagement was conducted in accordance with the SSVS. The estimate of value that results from a calculation engagement is expressed as a calculated value.
>
> In a calculation engagement, the valuation analyst and the client agree on the specific valuation approaches and valuation methods the valuation analyst will use and the extent of valuation procedures the valuation analyst will perform to estimate the value of the subject interest. A calculation engagement does not include all of the procedures required in a *valuation*

engagement, as that term is defined in the SVSS. Had a valuation engagement been performed, the results might have been different.

Based on our calculations, as described in this report, which are based solely on the procedures agreed upon as referred to above, the resulting calculated value of *[DEF Company, GHI business ownership interest of DEF Company, GHI security of DEF Company, or GHI intangible asset of DEF Company]* as of *[valuation date]* was *[calculated value, either a single amount or a range].* This calculated value is subject to the Statement of Assumptions and Limiting Conditions found in *[reference to applicable section of valuation report]* and to the Valuation Analyst's Representation found in *[reference to applicable section of valuation report].* We have no obligation to update this report or our calculation of value for information that comes to our attention after the date of this report.

[Signature]
[Date]

Oral Report

78. An oral report may be used in a valuation engagement or a calculation engagement. An oral report should include all information the valuation analyst believes necessary to relate the scope, assumptions, limitations, and the results of the engagement so as to limit any misunderstandings between the analyst and the recipient of the oral report. The member should document in the working papers the substance of the oral report communicated to the client.

Effective Date

79. This Statement applies to engagements to estimate value accepted on or after January 1, 2008. Earlier application is encouraged.

ILLUSTRATIVE LIST OF ASSUMPTIONS AND LIMITING CONDITIONS FOR A BUSINESS VALUATION

The valuation report or calculation report should include a list of assumptions and limiting conditions under which the engagement was performed. This appendix includes an illustrative list of assumptions and limiting conditions that may apply to a business valuation.

Illustrative List of Assumptions and Limiting Conditions

1. The conclusion of value arrived at herein is valid only for the stated purpose as of the date of the valuation.

2. Financial statements and other related information provided by *[ABC Company]* or its representatives, in the course of this engagement, have been accepted without any verification as fully and correctly reflecting the enterprise's business conditions and operating results for the respective periods, except as specifically noted herein. [Valuation Firm] has not audited, reviewed, or compiled the financial information provided to us and, accordingly, we express no audit opinion or any other form of assurance on this information.
3. Public information and industry and statistical information have been obtained from sources we believe to be reliable. However, we make no representation as to the accuracy or completeness of such information and have performed no procedures to corroborate the information.
4. We do not provide assurance on the achievability of the results forecasted by *[ABC Company]* because events and circumstances frequently do not occur as expected; differences between actual and expected results may be material; and achievement of the forecasted results is dependent on actions, plans, and assumptions of management.
5. The conclusion of value arrived at herein is based on the assumption that the current level of management expertise and effectiveness would continue to be maintained, and that the character and integrity of the enterprise through any sale, reorganization, exchange, or diminution of the owners' participation would not be materially or significantly changed.
6. This report and the conclusion of value arrived at herein are for the exclusive use of our client for the sole and specific purposes as noted herein. They may not be used for any other purpose or by any other party for any purpose. Furthermore the report and conclusion of value are not intended by the author and should not be construed by the reader to be investment advice in any manner whatsoever. The conclusion of value represents the considered opinion of *[Valuation Firm],* based on information furnished to them by *[ABC Company]* and other sources.
7. Neither all nor any part of the contents of this report (especially the conclusion of value, the identity of any valuation specialist(s), or the firm with which such valuation specialists are connected or any reference to any of their professional designations) should be disseminated to the public through advertising media, public relations, news media, sales media, mail, direct transmittal, or any other means of communication without the prior written consent and approval of *[Valuation Firm].*
8. Future services regarding the subject matter of this report, including, but not limited to testimony or attendance in court, shall not be required of *[Valuation Firm]* unless previous arrangements have been made in writing.
9. [Valuation Firm] is not an environmental consultant or auditor, and it takes no responsibility for any actual or potential environmental liabilities. Any person entitled to rely on this report, wishing to know whether such liabilities exist, or the scope and their effect on the value of the property, is encouraged to obtain a professional environmental assessment. *[Valuation*

Firm] does not conduct or provide environmental assessments and has not performed one for the subject property.

10. *[Valuation Firm]* has not determined independently whether *[ABC Company]* is subject to any present or future liability relating to environmental matters (including, but not limited to CERCLA/Superfund liability) nor the scope of any such liabilities. *[Valuation Firm]'s* valuation takes no such liabilities into account, except as they have been reported to *[Valuation Firm]* by *[ABC Company]* or by an environmental consultant working for *[ABC Company],* and then only to the extent that the liability was reported to us in an actual or estimated dollar amount. Such matters, if any, are noted in the report. To the extent such information has been reported to us, *[Valuation Firm]* has relied on it without verification and offers no warranty or representation as to its accuracy or completeness.
11. *[Valuation Firm]* has not made a specific compliance survey or analysis of the subject property to determine whether it is subject to, or in compliance with, the American Disabilities Act of 1990, and this valuation does not consider the effect, if any, of noncompliance.
12. [Sample wording for use if the jurisdictional exception is invoked.] The conclusion of value (or the calculated value) in this report deviates from the Statement on Standards for Valuation Services as a result of published governmental, judicial, or accounting authority.
13. No change of any item in this appraisal report shall be made by anyone other than *[Valuation Firm],* and we shall have no responsibility for any such unauthorized change.
14. Unless otherwise stated, no effort has been made to determine the possible effect, if any, on the subject business due to future Federal, state, or local legislation, including any environmental or ecological matters or interpretations thereof.
15. If prospective financial information approved by management has been used in our work, we have not examined or compiled the prospective financial information and therefore, do not express an audit opinion or any other form of assurance on the prospective financial information or the related assumptions. Events and circumstances frequently do not occur as expected and there will usually be differences between prospective financial information and actual results, and those differences may be material.
16. We have conducted interviews with the current management of *[ABC Company]* concerning the past, present, and prospective operating results of the company.
17. Except as noted, we have relied on the representations of the owners, management, and other third parties concerning the value and useful condition of all equipment, real estate, investments used in the business, and any other assets or liabilities, except as specifically stated to the contrary in this report. We have not attempted to confirm whether or not all assets of the business are free and clear of liens and encumbrances or that the entity has good title to all assets.

INTERNATIONAL GLOSSARY OF BUSINESS VALUATION TERMS*

To enhance and sustain the quality of business valuations for the benefit of the profession and its clientele, the below identified societies and organizations have adopted the definitions for the terms included in this glossary.

The performance of business valuation services requires a high degree of skill and imposes upon the valuation professional a duty to communicate the valuation process and conclusion in a manner that is clear and not misleading. This duty is advanced through the use of terms whose meanings are clearly established and consistently applied throughout the profession.

If, in the opinion of the business valuation professional, one or more of these terms needs to be used in a manner which materially departs from the enclosed definitions, it is recommended that the term be defined as used within that valuation engagement.

This glossary has been developed to provide guidance to business valuation practitioners by further memorializing the body of knowledge that constitutes the competent and careful determination of value and, more particularly, the communication of how that value was determined.

Departure from this glossary is not intended to provide a basis for civil liability and should not be presumed to create evidence that any duty has been breached.

American Institute of Certified Public Accountants
American Society of Appraisers
Canadian Institute of Chartered Business Valuators
National Association of Certified Valuation Analysts
The Institute of Business Appraisers

Adjusted Book Value Method – a method within the asset approach whereby all assets and liabilities (including off-balance sheet, intangible, and contingent) are adjusted to their fair market values. {NOTE: In Canada on a going concern basis}

Adjusted Net Asset Method – see **Adjusted Book Value Method.**

Appraisal – see **Valuation.**

Appraisal Approach – see **Valuation Approach.**

* Reproduced verbatim from the International Glossary of Business Valuation Terms (the Glossary), which appears at http://bvfls.aicpa.org/Resources/Business+Valuation/ Tools+and+Aids/Definitions+and+Terms/International+Glossary+of+Business+Valuation+Terms.htm. Note that the phrase, "we discourage the use of this term," that appears herein is also reproduced verbatim.

Appraisal Date – see **Valuation Date.**

Appraisal Method – see **Valuation Method.**

Appraisal Procedure – see **Valuation Procedure.**

Arbitrage Pricing Theory – a multivariate model for estimating the cost of equity capital, which incorporates several systematic risk factors.

Asset (Asset-Based) Approach – a general way of determining a value indication of a business, business ownership interest, or security using one or more methods based on the value of the assets net of liabilities.

Beta – a measure of systematic risk of a stock; the tendency of a stock's price to correlate with changes in a specific index.

Blockage Discount – an amount or percentage deducted from the current market price of a publicly traded stock to reflect the decrease in the per share value of a block of stock that is of a size that could not be sold in a reasonable period of time given normal trading volume.

Book Value – see **Net Book Value.**

Business – see **Business Enterprise.**

Business Enterprise – a commercial, industrial, service, or investment entity (or a combination thereof) pursuing an economic activity.

Business Risk – the degree of uncertainty of realizing expected future returns of the business resulting from factors other than financial leverage. See **Financial Risk.**

Business Valuation – the act or process of determining the value of a business enterprise or ownership interest therein.

Capital Asset Pricing Model (CAPM) – a model in which the cost of capital for any stock or portfolio of stocks equals a risk-free rate plus a risk premium that is proportionate to the systematic risk of the stock or portfolio.

Capitalization – a conversion of a single period of economic benefits into value.

Capitalization Factor – any multiple or divisor used to convert anticipated economic benefits of a single period into value.

Capitalization of Earnings Method – a method within the income approach whereby economic benefits for a representative single period are converted to value through division by a capitalization rate.

Capitalization Rate – any divisor (usually expressed as a percentage) used to convert anticipated economic benefits of a single period into value.

Capital Structure – the composition of the invested capital of a business enterprise; the mix of debt and equity financing.

Cash Flow – cash that is generated over a period of time by an asset, group of assets, or business enterprise. It may be used in a general sense to encompass various levels of specifically defined cash flows. When the term is used, it should be supplemented by a qualifier (for example, "discretionary" or "operating") and a specific definition in the given valuation context.

Common Size Statements – financial statements in which each line is expressed as a percentage of the total. On the balance sheet, each line item is shown as a percentage of total assets, and on the income statement, each item is expressed as a percentage of sales.

Control – the power to direct the management and policies of a business enterprise.

Control Premium – an amount or a percentage by which the pro rata value of a controlling interest exceeds the pro rata value of a noncontrolling interest in a business enterprise to reflect the power of control.

Cost Approach – a general way of determining a value indication of an individual asset by quantifying the amount of money required to replace the future service capability of that asset.

Cost of Capital – the expected rate of return that the market requires in order to attract funds to a particular investment.

Debt-Free – *we **discourage the use of this term.*** See **Invested Capital.**

Discount for Lack of Control – an amount or percentage deducted from the pro rata share of value of 100% of an equity interest in a business to reflect the absence of some or all of the powers of control.

Discount for Lack of Marketability – an amount or percentage deducted from the value of an ownership interest to reflect the relative absence of marketability.

Discount for Lack of Voting Rights – an amount or percentage deducted from the per share value of a minority interest voting share to reflect the absence of voting rights.

Discount Rate – a rate of return used to convert a future monetary sum into present value.

Discounted Cash Flow Method – a method within the income approach whereby the present value of future expected net cash flows is calculated using a discount rate.

Discounted Future Earnings Method – a method within the income approach whereby the present value of future expected economic benefits is calculated using a discount rate.

Economic Benefits – inflows such as revenues, net income, net cash flows, etc.

Economic Life – the period of time over which property may generate economic benefits.

Effective Date – see **Valuation Date.**

Enterprise – see **Business Enterprise.**

Equity – the owner's interest in property after deduction of all liabilities.

Equity Net Cash Flows – those cash flows available to pay out to equity holders (in the form of dividends) after funding operations of the business enterprise, making necessary capital investments, and increasing or decreasing debt financing.

Equity Risk Premium – a rate of return added to a risk-free rate to reflect the additional risk of equity instruments over risk free instruments (a component of the cost of equity capital or equity discount rate).

Excess Earnings – that amount of anticipated economic benefits that exceeds an appropriate rate of return on the value of a selected asset base (often net tangible assets) used to generate those anticipated economic benefits.

Excess Earnings Method – a specific way of determining a value indication of a business, business ownership interest, or security determined as the sum of a) the value of the assets derived by capitalizing excess earnings and *b)* the value of the selected asset base. Also frequently used to value intangible assets. See **Excess Earnings.**

Fair Market Value – the price, expressed in terms of cash equivalents, at which property would change hands between a hypothetical willing and able buyer and a hypothetical willing and able seller, acting at arms length in an open and unrestricted market, when neither is under compulsion to buy or sell and when both have reasonable knowledge of the relevant facts. {NOTE: In Canada, the term "*price*" should be replaced with the term "*highest price.*"}

Fairness Opinion – an opinion as to whether or not the consideration in a transaction is fair from a financial point of view.

Financial Risk – the degree of uncertainty of realizing expected future returns of the business resulting from financial leverage. See **Business Risk.**

Forced Liquidation Value – liquidation value, at which the asset or assets are sold as quickly as possible, such as at an auction.

Free Cash Flow – ***we discourage the use of this term.*** See **Net Cash Flow.**

Going Concern – an ongoing operating business enterprise.

Going Concern Value – the value of a business enterprise that is expected to continue to operate into the future. The intangible elements of Going Concern Value result from factors such as having a trained work force, an operational plant, and the necessary licenses, systems, and procedures in place.

Goodwill – that intangible asset arising as a result of name, reputation, customer loyalty, location, products, and similar factors not separately identified.

Goodwill Value – the value attributable to goodwill.

Guideline Public Company Method – a method within the market approach whereby market multiples are derived from market prices of stocks of companies that are engaged in the same or similar lines of business and that are actively traded on a free and open market.

Income (Income-Based) Approach – a general way of determining a value indication of a business, business ownership interest, security, or intangible asset using one or more methods that convert anticipated economic benefits into a present single amount.

Intangible Assets – nonphysical assets such as franchises, trademarks, patents, copyrights, goodwill, equities, mineral rights, securities, and contracts (as distinguished from physical assets) that grant rights and privileges and have value for the owner.

Internal Rate of Return – a discount rate at which the present value of the future cash flows of the investment equals the cost of the investment.

Intrinsic Value – the value that an investor considers, on the basis of an evaluation or available facts, to be the "true" or "real" value that will become the market value when other investors reach the same conclusion. When the term applies to options, it is the difference between the exercise price and strike price of an option and the market value of the underlying security.

Invested Capital – the sum of equity and debt in a business enterprise. Debt is typically *(a)* all interest-bearing debt or *(b)* long-term, interest-bearing debt. When the term is used, it should be supplemented by a specific definition in the given valuation context.

Invested Capital Net Cash Flows – those cash flows available to pay out to equity holders (in the form of dividends) and debt investors (in the form of principal and interest) after funding operations of the business enterprise and making necessary capital investments.

Investment Risk – the degree of uncertainty as to the realization of expected returns.

Investment Value – the value to a particular investor based on individual investment requirements and expectations. {NOTE: in Canada, the term used is "*Value to the Owner.*"}

Key Person Discount – an amount or percentage deducted from the value of an ownership interest to reflect the reduction in value resulting from the actual or potential loss of a key person in a business enterprise.

Levered Beta – the beta reflecting a capital structure that includes debt.

Limited Appraisal – the act or process of determining the value of a business, business ownership interest, security, or intangible asset with limitations in analyses, procedures, or scope.

Liquidity – the ability to quickly convert property to cash or pay a liability.

Liquidation Value – the net amount that would be realized if the business is terminated and the assets are sold piecemeal. Liquidation can be either "orderly" or "forced."

Majority Control – the degree of control provided by a majority position.

Majority Interest – an ownership interest greater than 50% of the voting interest in a business enterprise.

Market (Market-Based) Approach – a general way of determining a value indication of a business, business ownership interest, security, or intangible asset by using one or more methods that compare the subject to similar businesses, business ownership interests, securities, or intangible assets that have been sold.

Market Capitalization of Equity – the share price of a publicly traded stock multiplied by the number of shares outstanding.

Market Capitalization of Invested Capital – the market capitalization of equity plus the market value of the debt component of invested capital.

Market Multiple – the market value of a company's stock or invested capital divided by a company measure (such as economic benefits, number of customers).

Marketability – the ability to quickly convert property to cash at minimal cost.

Marketability Discount – see **Discount for Lack of Marketability**.

Merger and Acquisition Method – a method within the market approach whereby pricing multiples are derived from transactions of significant interests in companies engaged in the same or similar lines of business.

Mid-Year Discounting – a convention used in the Discounted Future Earnings Method that reflects economic benefits being generated at midyear, approximating the effect of economic benefits being generated evenly throughout the year.

Minority Discount – a discount for lack of control applicable to a minority interest.

Minority Interest – an ownership interest less than 50% of the voting interest in a business enterprise.

Multiple – the inverse of the capitalization rate.

Net Book Value – with respect to a business enterprise, the difference between total assets (net of accumulated depreciation, depletion, and amortization) and total liabilities as they appear on the balance sheet (synonymous with Shareholder's Equity). With respect to a specific asset, the capitalized cost less accumulated amortization or depreciation as it appears on the books of account of the business enterprise.

Net Cash Flows – when the term is used, it should be supplemented by a qualifier. See **Equity Net Cash Flows** and **Invested Capital Net Cash Flows**.

Net Present Value – the value, as of a specified date, of future cash inflows less all cash outflows (including the cost of investment) calculated using an appropriate discount rate.

Net Tangible Asset Value – the value of the business enterprise's tangible assets (excluding excess assets and nonoperating assets) minus the value of its liabilities.

Nonoperating Assets – assets not necessary to ongoing operations of the business enterprise. {NOTE: in Canada, the term used is *"Redundant Assets."*}

Normalized Earnings – economic benefits adjusted for nonrecurring, noneconomic, or other unusual items to eliminate anomalies and/or facilitate comparisons.

Normalized Financial Statements – financial statements adjusted for nonoperating assets and liabilities and/or for nonrecurring, noneconomic, or other unusual items to eliminate anomalies and/or facilitate comparisons.

Orderly Liquidation Value – liquidation value at which the asset or assets are sold over a reasonable period of time to maximize proceeds received.

Premise of Value – an assumption regarding the most likely set of transactional circumstances that may be applicable to the subject valuation; for example, going concern, liquidation.

Present Value – the value, as of a specified date, of future economic benefits and/or proceeds from sale, calculated using an appropriate discount rate.

Portfolio Discount – an amount or percentage deducted from the value of a business enterprise to reflect the fact that it owns dissimilar operations or assets that do not fit well together.

Price/Earnings Multiple – the price of a share of stock divided by its earnings per share.

Rate of Return – an amount of income (loss) and/or change in value realized or anticipated on an investment, expressed as a percentage of that investment.

Redundant Assets – see **Nonoperating Assets.**

Report Date – the date conclusions are transmitted to the client.

Replacement Cost New – the current cost of a similar new property having the nearest equivalent utility to the property being valued.

Reproduction Cost New – the current cost of an identical new property.

Required Rate of Return – the minimum rate of return acceptable by investors before they will commit money to an investment at a given level of risk.

Residual Value – the value as of the end of the discrete projection period in a discounted future earnings model.

Return on Equity – the amount, expressed as a percentage, earned on a company's common equity for a given period.

Return on Investment – See **Return on Invested Capital** and **Return on Equity**.

Return on Invested Capital – the amount, expressed as a percentage, earned on a company's total capital for a given period.

Risk-Free Rate – the rate of return available in the market on an investment free of default risk.

Risk Premium – a rate of return added to a risk-free rate to reflect risk.

Rule of Thumb – a mathematical formula developed from the relationship between price and certain variables based on experience, observation, hearsay, or a combination of these; usually industry specific.

Special Interest Purchasers – acquirers who believe they can enjoy post-acquisition economies of scale, synergies, or strategic advantages by combining the acquired business interest with their own.

Standard of Value – the identification of the type of value being utilized in a specific engagement; for example, fair market value, fair value, investment value.

Sustaining Capital Reinvestment – the periodic capital outlay required to maintain operations at existing levels, net of the tax shield available from such outlays.

Systematic Risk – the risk that is common to all risky securities and cannot be eliminated through diversification. The measure of systematic risk in stocks is the beta coefficient.

Tangible Assets – physical assets (such as cash, accounts receivable, inventory, property, plant and equipment, etc.).

Terminal Value – See **Residual Value**.

Transaction Method – See **Merger and Acquisition Method**.

Unlevered Beta – the beta reflecting a capital structure without debt.

Unsystematic Risk – the risk specific to an individual security that can be avoided through diversification.

Valuation – the act or process of determining the value of a business, business ownership interest, security, or intangible asset.

Valuation Approach – a general way of determining a value indication of a business, business ownership interest, security, or intangible asset using one or more valuation methods.

Valuation Date – the specific point in time as of which the valuator's opinion of value applies (also referred to as "Effective Date" or "Appraisal Date").

Valuation Method – within approaches, a specific way to determine value.

Valuation Procedure – the act, manner, and technique of performing the steps of an appraisal method.

Valuation Ratio – a fraction in which a value or price serves as the numerator and financial, operating, or physical data serve as the denominator.

Value to the Owner – see **Investment Value**.

Voting Control – *de jure* control of a business enterprise.

Weighted Average Cost of Capital (WACC) – the cost of capital (discount rate) determined by the weighted average, at market value, of the cost of all financing sources in the business enterprise's capital structure.

GLOSSARY OF ADDITIONAL TERMS

Assumptions and Limiting Conditions. Parameters and boundaries under which a valuation is performed, as agreed upon by the valuation analyst and the client or as acknowledged or understood by the valuation analyst and the client as being due to existing circumstances. An example is the acceptance, without further verification, by the valuation analyst from the client of the client's financial statements and related information.

Business Ownership Interest. A designated share in the ownership of a business (business enterprise).

Calculated Value. An estimate as to the value of a business, business ownership interest, security, or intangible asset, arrived at by applying valuation procedures agreed upon with the client and using professional judgment as to the value or range of values based on those procedures.

Calculation Engagement. An engagement to estimate value wherein the valuation analyst and the client agree on the specific valuation approaches and valuation methods that the valuation analyst will use and the extent of valuation procedures the valuation analyst will perform to estimate the value of a subject interest. A calculation engagement generally does not include all of the valuation procedures required for a valuation engagement. If a valuation engagement had been performed, the results might have been different. The valuation analyst expresses the results of the calculation engagement as a calculated value, which may be either a single amount or a range.

Capital or Contributory Asset Charge. A fair return on an entity's *contributory assets,* which are tangible and intangible assets used in the production of income or cash flow associated with an intangible asset being valued. In this context, *income* *or cash flow* refers to an applicable measure of income or cash flow, such as net income, or operating cash flow before taxes and capital expenditures. A capital charge may be expressed as a percentage return on an economic rent associated with, or a profit split related to, the contributory assets.

Capitalization of Benefits Method. A method within the income approach whereby expected future benefits (for example, earnings or cash flow) for a representative single period are converted to value through division by a capitalization rate.

Comparable Profits Method. A method of determining the value of intangible assets by comparing the profits of the subject entity with those of similar uncontrolled companies that have the same or similar complement of intangible assets as the subject company.

Comparable Uncontrolled Transaction Method. A method of determining the value of intangible assets by comparing the subject transaction to similar transactions in the market place made between independent (uncontrolled) parties.

Conclusion of Value. An estimate of the value of a business, business ownership interest, security, or intangible asset, arrived at by applying the valuation procedures appropriate for a valuation engagement and using professional judgment as to the value or range of values based on those procedures.

Control Adjustment. A valuation adjustment to financial statements to reflect the effect of a controlling interest in a business. An example would be an adjustment to owners' compensation that is in excess of market compensation.

Engagement to Estimate Value. An engagement, or any part of an engagement (for example, a tax, litigation, or acquisition-related engagement), that involves determining the value of a business, business ownership interest, security, or intangible asset. Also known as *valuation service.*

Excess Operating Assets. Operating assets in excess of those needed for the normal operation of a business.

Fair Value. In valuation applications, there are two commonly used definitions for fair value:

(1) For financial reporting purposes only, the price that would be received to sell an asset or paid to transfer a liability in an orderly transaction between market participants at the measurement date. *Source:* Financial Accounting Standards Board definition in Statement of Financial Accounting Standards (SFAS) No. 157, *Fair Value Measurements*, as used in the context of Generally Accepted Accounting Principles (GAAP) (Effective 2008).

(2) For state legal matters only, some states have laws that use the term *fair value* in shareholder and partner matters. For state legal matters only, therefore, the term may be defined by statute or case law in the particular jurisdiction.

Guideline Company Transactions Method. A method within the market approach whereby market multiples are derived from the sales of entire companies engaged in the same or similar lines of business.

Hypothetical Condition. That which is or may be contrary to what exists, but is supposed for the purpose of analysis.

Incremental Income. Additional income or cash flow attributable to an entity's ownership or operation of an intangible asset being valued, as determined by a comparison of the entity's income or cash flow with the intangible asset to the entity's income or cash flow without the intangible asset. In this context, *income or cash flow* refers to an applicable measure of income or cash flow, such as license royalty income or operating cash flow before taxes and capital expenditures.

Normalization. See ***Normalized Earnings*** in Appendix B, "International Glossary of Business Valuation Terms."

Pre-adjustment Value. The value arrived at prior to the application, if appropriate, of valuation discounts or premiums.

Profit Split Income. With respect to the valuation of an intangible asset of an entity, a percentage allocation of the entity's income or cash flow whereby (1) a split (or percentage) is allocated to the subject intangible and (2) the remainder is allocated to all of the entity's tangible and other intangible assets. In this context, *income or cashflow* refers to an applicable measure of income or cash flow, such as net income or operating cash flow before taxes and capital expenditures.

Relief from Royalty Method. A valuation method used to value certain intangible assets (for example, trademarks and trade names) based on the premise that the only value that a purchaser of the assets receives is the exemption from paying a royalty for its use. Application of this method usually involves estimating the fair market value of an intangible asset by quantifying the present value of the stream of market-derived royalty payments that the owner of the intangible asset is exempted from or "relieved" from paying.

Residual Income. For an entity that owns or operates an intangible asset being valued, the portion of the entity's income or cash flow remaining after subtracting a capital charge on all of the entity's tangible and other intangible assets. *Income or cash flows* can refer to any appropriate measure of income or cash flow, such as net income or operating cash flow before taxes and capital expenditures.

Security. A certificate evidencing ownership or the rights to ownership in a business enterprise that (1) is represented by an instrument or by a book record or contractual agreement, (2) is of a type commonly dealt in on securities exchanges or markets or, when represented by an instrument, is commonly recognized in any area in which it is issued or dealt in as a medium for investment, and (3) either one of a class or series or, by its terms, is divisible into a class or series of shares, participations, interests, rights, or interest-bearing obligations.

Subject Interest. A business, business ownership interest, security, or intangible asset that is the subject of a valuation engagement.

Subsequent Event. An event that occurs subsequent to the valuation date.

Valuation Analyst. For purposes of this Statement, an AICPA member who performs an engagement to estimate value that culminates in the expression of a conclusion of value or a calculated value.

Valuation Assumptions. Statements or inputs utilized in the performance of an engagement to estimate value that serve as a basis for the application of particular valuation methods.

Valuation Engagement. An engagement to estimate value in which a valuation analyst determines an estimate of the value of a subject interest by performing appropriate valuation procedures, as outlined in the AICPA Statement on Standards for Valuation Services, and is free to apply the valuation approaches and methods he or she deems appropriate in the circumstances. The valuation analyst expresses the results of the valuation engagement as a conclusion of value, which may be either a single amount or a range.

Valuation Service. See **Engagement to Estimate Value**.

INTERPRETATION NO. 1-01, "SCOPE OF APPLICABLE SERVICES" OF STATEMENT ON STANDARDS FOR VALUATION SERVICES NO. 1, VALUATION OF A BUSINESS, BUSINESS OWNERSHIP INTEREST, SECURITY, OR INTANGIBLE ASSET

Background

1. The Statement on Standards for Valuation Services (SSVS) establishes standards of performance and reporting for all AICPA members performing those valuation services that are within the scope of the Statement. When originally proposed on March 30, 2005, the Exposure Draft contained a list of questions and answers (Appendix A of the March 30, 2005 Exposure Draft) that were intended to assist members in determining if an engagement, particularly with regard to litigation or tax engagements, fell within the scope of the Statement. Through the Exposure Draft process, it was determined that the questions and answers were an integral part of the Statement and should be made authoritative. This Interpretation is part of the AICPA's continuing efforts at self-regulation of its members in valuation practice, and its desire to provide guidance to members when providing valuation services. The Interpretation does not change or elevate any level of conduct prescribed by any standard. Its goal is to clarify existing standards.

General Interpretation

2. The SSVSs apply to an engagement to estimate value if, as all or as part of another engagement, a member determines the value of a business, business ownership interest, security, or intangible asset (SSVS paragraphs 1 and 2). In the process of estimating value, professional judgment is used to apply valuation approaches and valuation methods as described in the SSVSs (SSVS paragraph 4).

3. In determining whether a particular service falls within the scope of the Statement, a member should consider those services that are specifically excluded:

- Audit, review, and compilation engagements (SSVS paragraph 5)
- Use of values provided by the client or a third party (SSVS paragraph 6)
- Internal use assignments from employers to employee members not in the *practice of public accounting* (SSVS paragraph 7)
- Engagements that are exclusively for the purpose of determining economic damages (for example, lost profits) and that do not include an engagement to estimate value (SSVS paragraph 8)
- Mechanical computations that do not rise to the level of an engagement to estimate value (SSVS paragraph 9(a))
- Engagements where it is not practical or reasonable to obtain or use relevant information and, therefore, the member is unable to apply valuation approaches and methods described in this Statement. (SSVS paragraph 9(b))
- Engagements meeting the jurisdictional exception (SSVS paragraph 10)

4. A member should be diligent in determining if an engagement falls within the scope of the Statement. Unless specifically excluded by the SSVS, if the engagement requires a member to apply valuation approaches and methods, and use professional judgment in applying those approaches and methods, the SSVS would apply. In determining the scope and requirements of the engagement, a member should consider the client's needs, or the requirements of a third party for which the valuation is intended, including governmental, judicial, and accounting authorities. In addition, a member should consider other professional standards that might apply.

Specific Illustrations

5. The following illustrations address general fact patterns. Accordingly, the application of the guidance discussed in the "General Interpretation" section to variations in general facts, or to particular facts and circumstances, may lead to different conclusions. In each illustration, there is no authority other than that indicated.

Illustrations Relating to Litigation Engagements and Certain Controversy Proceedings

6. *Illustration 1.* Do lost profits damage computations fall within the scope of the Statement?

7. *Conclusion.* No, unless the computations are undertaken as part of an engagement to estimate value (SSVS paragraphs 1,2, and 8).

8. *Illustration 2.* Is an economic damages computation that incorporates a terminal value within the scope of the Statement?

9. *Conclusion.* The use of a terminal value exclusively for the determination of lost profits is not within the scope of this statement unless that determination will be used as part of an engagement to estimate value (Illustration 1).

10. *Illustration 3.* If a start-up business is destroyed, is the e nomic damages computation within the scope of the Statement?

11. *Conclusion.* There are two common measures of damages: lost profits and loss of value. If a valuation analyst performs an engagement to estimate value to determine the loss of value of a business or intangible asset, the Statement applies. Otherwise, the Statement does not apply (*Illustration* 1). In order to determine whether the Statement applies, a member acting as an expert witness should evaluate whether the particular damages calculation constitutes an engagement to estimate value with respect to the business, business interest, security, or intangible asset or whether it constitutes a lost-profits computation.

12. *Illustration 4.* Does the Statement include any exceptions relating to litigation or controversy proceedings?

13. *Conclusion.* Yes, the Statement includes a reporting exemption for certain controversy proceedings (SSVS paragraph 50); however, there is no litigation or controversy proceeding exemption from the developmental provisions of the Statement (SSVS paragraphs 21 – 46) in circumstances in which an engagement to estimate value is performed *(Illustration 1).*

14. *Illustration 5.* Is the Statement's reporting exemption for litigation or controversy proceedings (see SSVS paragraph 50) the same as the "litigation exemption" in the AICPA attestation standards?

15. *Conclusion.* No, the so-called "litigation exemption" is provided for in the AICPA attestation standards and is further discussed in the attestation interpretations. The attestation standards do not apply to engagements in which a practitioner is engaged to testify as an expert witness in accounting, auditing, taxation, or other matters, given certain stipulated facts. This is clarified in the attestation interpretation, which states, in part, that the attestation standards do not apply to litigation services engagements when (among other requirements) the practitioner "has not been engaged to issue and does not issue an examination,

a review, or an agreed-upon procedures report on the subject matter, or an assertion about the subject matter that is the responsibility of another party." (Interpretation No. 3, "Applicability of Attestation Standards to Litigation Services," of Chapter 1, "Attest Engagements," of Statement on Standards for Attestation Engagements *No. 10, Attestation Standards: Revision and Recodification,* as revised [AICPA, *Professional Standards,* vol. 1, AT sec. 9101.34–.42].) However, unlike the AICPA attestation standards, which do not apply in any capacity to litigation or controversy proceeding situations, as discussed above, the Statement's exemption for litigation or certain controversy proceedings is an exemption from the reporting provisions of the Statement (SSVS paragraphs 47–78).

Illustrations Relating to Tax Engagements

16. *Illustration 6.* When does the Statement apply to members who determine values related to tax reporting and planning engagements?

17. *Conclusion.* The Statement applies when the member is engaged to estimate the value of a business, business ownership interest, security, or intangible asset (SSVS paragraph 1). The application of valuation approaches and methods and the use of professional judgment (SSVS paragraph 4) are required, unless an exception applies (SSVS paragraphs 5 through 10).

18. *Illustration 7.* If the sole purpose of an engagement is reporting a value in a tax return and the Statement applies to this engagement, are any separate reports (specifically, valuation reports) required to be issued? To whom are those reports required to be provided? Is a report required to be attached to the tax return? Are any specific disclosures required?

19. *Conclusion.* The Statement requires the preparation of a written or oral valuation report (SSVS paragraphs 47–78) that is communicated to the client (SSVS paragraph 47) but does not require that any report be attached to the tax return or mandate any other tax-specific disclosures. In limited circumstances, a taxing authority may require its own report, which would obviate the need for a separate valuation report (SSVS paragraph 10 and *Illustration 18*). There is also a reporting exemption for certain controversy proceedings (SSVS paragraph 50 and *Illustration 4*).

20. *Illustration 8.* Are mechanical computations of value, for example, computations using actuarial tables, excluded from the Statement?

21. *Conclusion.* Mechanical computations of value are excluded from the Statement if they do not rise to the level of an engagement to estimate value, that is, if the member does not apply valuation approaches and methods, and does not use professional judgment, as described in the Statement (SSVS paragraph 9(a)).

22. Examples of services that do **not** rise to the level of an engagement to estimate value include: *(a)* computations of a remainder interest under a grantor

retained annuity trust (GRAT) using actuarial tables; *(b)* determining the value of relatively small blocks (relative to the total amount of corporate stock outstanding) of publicly traded stock whose per share price is readily ascertainable; *(c)* preparing a tax return using the valuation of a business that was provided by a third-party appraiser, or by the client (SSVS paragraph 6); and *(d)* calculating cash "hold back" requirements for tax contingencies (SSVS paragraphs 1, 4, and 9(a)).

23. Examples of services that rise to the level of an engagement to estimate value include: *(a)* valuing a block of publicly traded stock, if the analysis includes consideration of a discount for blockage, lockup, or other contractual or market restrictions such that valuation approaches and methods are applied, and professional judgment is used to determine the fair value, fair market value, or other applicable standard of value; *(b)* valuing stock that is not publicly traded; and *(c)* computing the fair market value of assets in a charitable remainder trust (CRT), if the engagement requires the application of valuation approaches and methods, and the use of professional judgment to estimate the fair market value.

24. *Illustration 9.* Does the "jurisdictional exception" (SSVS paragraph 10) provide that an engagement to estimate value is not subject to the Statement if a member determines and reports values using procedures mandated or allowed by the Internal Revenue Code (IRC), Internal Revenue Service (IRS) regulations, court cases, or other published guidance and other sources of federal, state, and local law solely for purposes of tax return preparation and other tax services using these methods?

25. *Conclusion.* No, the "jurisdictional exception" would not exempt the engagement from this Statement, even if the engagement's sole purpose was to value a subject interest (SSVS paragraph 1) for tax reporting purposes. Only the portion of the Statement that differs from the published governmental or judicial authority is superseded for purposes of the engagement. The remainder of the Statement applies to the engagement.

26. *Illustration 10.* Is an interest in a publicly traded partnership whose shares are frequently traded considered a "security" under the Statement? Is an interest in a family limited partnership (FLP), or in another nontraded partnership, considered a "security" under the Statement?

27. *Conclusion.* Whether interest constitutes a "security" is a legal determination. However, where the value of a security is readily ascertainable, a valuation analyst does not need to apply valuation approaches and methods and use professional judgment. Accordingly, the valuation of such an interest would not be subject to the Statement (SSVS paragraphs 1 and 9(a)). An interest in a non-publicly traded partnership, such as an FLP, whether considered a security or not, is a business ownership interest. The valuation of such nonpublicly traded interest requires the application of valuation approaches and methods and the use of professional judgment, and, accordingly, would be subject to the Statement (SSVS paragraphs 1, 4, and *Illustration* 6), unless the exception under SSVS

paragraph 9(b) applies *(Illustration 13e).* If the engagement requires the valuation analyst to consider and apply adjustments, for example, valuation discounts or premiums, then the engagement would be subject to the Statement.

28. *Illustration 11.* A client engages a member to provide advice for planning purposes (such as estate planning, personal financial planning, or merger and acquisitions planning). The client holds an ownership interest in a family business being operated as a limited liability company, an interest in a private real estate limited partnership, publicly traded stock, a personal residence, and a retirement account (not an IRA). Is this a valuation engagement subject to the Statement?

29. *Conclusion.* It depends. Providing technical advice, without reference to values for the various assets, is not subject to the Statement. However, if a member calculates a value to illustrate various planning options, he or she may fall under the Statement with regard to various assets. If one or more of the assets for which value is to be determined for purposes of the plan illustrations is a business, business ownership interest, security, or intangible asset, and the client or a third party does not provide the values for these assets, or the member does not use assumed or hypothetical values as part of the overall engagement, the member performing the valuation(s) is subject to the Statement with regard to these assets (SSVS paragraph 1 and *Illustration 6*). In this example, if the member applies valuation approaches and methods and uses professional judgment to determine the value of the ownership interest in the family business or the interest in the private real estate limited partnership in order to provide planning advice, the Statement would apply. In contrast, if the client or a third party provides the values for these assets, or the member uses assumed or hypothetical values, the Statement would not apply because the member would not be applying valuation approaches and methods and using professional judgment. In addition, the exception under SSVS paragraph 9(b), where it is not practical or reasonable to obtain or use relevant information, could apply (see *Illustration 13e*). The computation of the "estimated estate tax" or other taxes once the values have been determined, assumed, or provided is not subject to the Statement, as the computation is a tax computation but would be subject to the Statement on Standards for Tax Services (*Illustration 10* at paragraph 27 of this Interpretation).

30. *Illustration 12.* There are many instances where a tax engagement involves the need for a member to estimate value. The estimation of value may not be the primary purpose of the engagement, but rather a necessary task to perform or item to consider, when making a tax determination concerning the reporting of a transaction on a tax return. Consider the following practice situations:

31. *Illustration 12a.* A member has been engaged to determine the deductibility of interest on a nonrecourse loan. Under applicable regulations, interest on a nonrecourse loan cannot be deducted if it is clear that the company will be unable to service the debt. For purposes of tax reporting, a conclusion must be reached concerning the ability of the company to service the debt. Is this considered a valuation engagement subject to the Statement?

32. *Conclusion.* This is not a valuation engagement covered by the Statement because it is not the valuation of a subject interest (SSVS paragraph 1). This example is a debt-service analysis.

33. *Illustration 12b.* There are compliance filings that require an estimate of the value of a company. For example, the "market value" of "intangible personal property," as defined by a state's taxing authority may need to be reported annually on an intangible personal property tax return. A client has a subject interest that is considered intangible personal property for purposes of the return. The member has been engaged to prepare the tax return. Is this a valuation engagement subject to the Statement?

34. *Conclusion.* It depends. If the state requires an estimation of the value of a subject interest, and the estimation of value requires the application of valuation approaches and methods and the use of professional judgment (SSVS paragraphs 1 and 4), the Statement applies. If, however, the client or a third-party appraiser provides the value of the subject interest to the member, the Statement does not apply (SSVS paragraphs 1 and 6). In addition, the exception under SSVS paragraph 9(b), where it is not practical or reasonable to obtain or use relevant information, could apply *(Illustration 13e).* Alternatively, if the state follows more informal rules where the application of valuation approaches or valuation methods are not necessary, the Statement does not apply (SSVS paragraph 4).

35. *Illustration 12c.* There are times when a member must allocate value among various assets. For example, IRC sections 1060 and 338 require the allocation to assets, based on relative values, of consideration paid. In partnership taxation, there may be allocations under IRC sections 754, 743, and 734 and special tax basis adjustments for partnerships (sales or exchanges and transfers at or upon death) may require an allocation of value among various partnership assets. Are these types of allocations engagements to estimate value subject to the Statement?

36. *Conclusion.* It depends. If one or more of the assets to which value is to be allocated is a subject interest (that is, a business, business ownership interest, security, or intangible asset), and the client or a third party did not provide the member with a value for those assets, then the member performing the allocation would be subject to the Statement, and the member is required to apply valuation approaches and methods, and use professional judgment to value those assets (SSVS paragraphs 1, 4, and *Illustration 6*), unless an exception applies (SSVS paragraphs 5–10). For example, in an IRC section 1060 allocation, after the allocation of purchase price to cash, receivables, inventory, and depreciable tangible assets, there is a residual amount of value allocable to goodwill or going concern. The mechanical assignment of the residual amount to goodwill or going concern is not subject to the Statement. However, if the member allocates this residual amount to specific intangible assets (such as to various customer-based and supplier-based intangibles), such allocation is based on the assets' relative values. Because the member applies valuation approaches and methods and uses professional judgment to value those specific intangible assets, the Statement applies.

37. *Illustration 12d.* If the member does not apply any discount and simply computes the fair market value of an interest in a family limited partnership (FLP) for tax purposes, is this a valuation engagement subject to the Statement?

38. *Conclusion.* Yes, the Statement applies if the member determines the value of the FLP or an interest in an FLP. The application of valuation approaches and methods, and the use of professional judgment are required, unless an exception applies (SSVS paragraphs 5–10). The fact that the member does not apply a discount does not exempt the engagement from the Statement (SSVS paragraphs 1–4 and 9(a)).

39. *Illustration 12e.* Would the Statement apply to the computation of the fair market value of assets in, or the computation of the required distribution of, a charitable remainder trust (CRT)?

40. *Conclusion.* It depends on the underlying assets held by the CRT. The Statement would apply only if the member determines the value of a business, business ownership interest, security, or intangible asset (SSVS paragraph 1). To the extent that the CRT holds assets that, to be valued, require the application of valuation approaches and methods, and the use of professional judgment, such as an interest in a limited liability corporation (LLC), the Statement would apply. However, if the CRT only holds publicly traded stock with a readily ascertainable value, the Statement would not apply because valuation approaches and methods and professional judgment would not be needed in the computation (SSVS paragraphs 1 and 4, and *Illustration 6*).

41. *Illustration 12f.* In circumstances in which the value of assets contributed by partners to a partnership differ from their cost basis, each difference must be tracked for tax purposes under IRC section 704(c) so that amounts of gain or loss can be properly assigned to the contributing partners. Are these types of asset value assignments valuation engagements subject to the Statement?

42. *Conclusion.* It depends. If one or more of the assets for which value is relevant under IRC section 704(c) is a subject interest that is, a business, business ownership interest, security, or intangible asset, and the client or a third party does not provide the valuation, and the member applies valuation approaches and methods and uses professional judgment to value these assets for IRC section 704(c) tax purposes, then the Statement applies (SSVS paragraphs 1 and 6, and *Illustration 6*).

43. *Illustration 12g.* A member has been engaged to perform a cost segregation study. The study involves an analysis of the costs of building a structure and the allocation of such costs to the real and personal property components of the structure so that depreciation of those components may be properly computed. Is this a valuation engagement subject to the Statement?

44. *Conclusion.* No, none of the assets constitutes a subject interest (SSVS paragraph 1).

45. *Illustration 12h.* A member has been engaged to provide advice to a company regarding the tax planning for income from discharge of indebtedness under IRC section 108. The company has advised the member that the company will be able to negotiate a settlement in complete satisfaction of an obligation at 30 cents on the dollar. Is this a valuation engagement subject to the Statement?

46. *Conclusion.* It depends. Under IRC section 108(a), gross income of the company excludes income from discharge of indebtedness only under certain circumstances. One of those circumstances is the insolvency of the company. Under IRC section 108(d)(3), insolvency results from an excess of liabilities over the fair market value of assets. If *(a)* the company must rely on the insolvency provisions of IRC section 108; *(b)* one or more of the assets for which value is relevant under IRC section 108 is a subject interest (that is, a business, business ownership interest, security, or intangible asset); *(c)* the company or a third party does not provide the valuation; and *(d)* the member applies valuation approaches and methods, and uses professional judgment to value the subject interest(s) for purposes of the IRC section 108(d)(3) insolvency determination, the Statement applies.

47. *Illustration 13.* An executor has engaged a member to prepare an estate tax return, which requires determining values for the following estate assets: *(a)* shares in a publicly traded company, "TI Corporation," whose shares are infrequently traded; *(b)* a large block of stock in "LB Corporation," a publicly traded company; *(c)* a brokerage account consisting of shares in various publicly traded companies; *(d)* "CHB Corporation," a closely held business owned by the decedent and the decedent's family; and *(e)* a 5 percent interest in "RP," a privately held rental real estate partnership. Does the Statement apply to any of the following assets owned by the estate? (See *Illustration 10* at paragraph 27 of this Interpretation regarding the valuation of a security.)

48. *Illustration 13a.* Does the Statement apply to shares in a publicly traded company, "TI Corporation," whose shares are traded infrequently?

49. *Conclusion.* It depends; although the price of a share of publicly traded stock is ascertainable from published sources, there are no definitive criteria that would indicate when the Statement applies to shares that are infrequently traded. A key consideration is the average daily trading volume of TI Corporation stock on or around the valuation date. The concept of fair market value incorporates the notions that (1) cash could have been received for the stock at the valuation date, and (2) the share price of an infrequently traded stock could decrease if a relatively large block of the stock were to be put on the market on that date. If the subject shares held by the estate do not represent a significant percentage of the daily trading volume of TI stock on or around the valuation date, and the price of a share of the stock is readily ascertainable on the valuation date, then the resulting value (the quoted share price times the number of shares owned) represents a cash price that could have been received at the valuation date for the block, and the Statement does not apply because the calculation of value is mechanical (SSVS

paragraph 9(a)). If, however, the subject shares held by the estate represent a large percentage of the average daily trading volume of the stock, the quoted market price for a share may not be adequate for purposes of determining the fair market value of the block of shares on the valuation date. In that case, the Statement applies because valuation approaches and methods need to be applied, and professional judgment needs to be used in determining the value of the block (SSVS paragraphs 1 and 4) (See *Illustration 10* at paragraph 27 of this Interpretation regarding the valuation of a security.)

50. *Illustration 13b.* Does the Statement apply to a large block of stock in "LB Corporation," a publicly traded company?

51. *Conclusion.* The answer depends on the amount of shares to be valued in relation to the average daily trading volume in LB Corporation on or around the valuation date. There are no definitive criteria that would indicate when the Statement applies to the valuation of a large block of publicly traded stock. The concept of fair market value incorporates the notion that cash could have been received from a sale of the block on the valuation date. A large block could decrease the share price if sold on the valuation date. The Statement would typically not apply to the valuation of a large block (for example, 200,000 shares) of a large and actively-traded public company. Even though the value of the estate's stock may be large in absolute terms, the daily trading volume in such stock on the valuation date may be sufficiently high that a sale of the block on the valuation date would not affect the market price of a company's shares. In such a case, the quoted market price of a share times the number of shares held by the estate may be considered to reflect the fair market value of the subject block of stock, and because it would not be the case that valuation approaches and methods would need to be applied and professional judgment used, the Statement would not apply. If, however, the large block of publicly traded shares represents a significant percentage of the daily trading volume, the Statement would apply because valuation approaches and methods would need to be applied and professional judgment used to determine the value (SSVS paragraphs 1 and 4).

52. *Illustration 13c.* Does the Statement apply to a brokerage account consisting of shares in various publicly traded companies?

53. *Conclusion.* The Statement would not apply to the determination of the value of a brokerage account consisting of publicly traded securities, except as discussed in paragraphs 49 and 51 of this interpretation. Absent certain scenarios involving infrequently traded securities or large blocks of stock, the application of valuation approaches and methods and the use of professional judgment are not necessary in that determination (SSVS paragraphs 1 and 4).

54. *Illustration 13d.* Does the Statement apply to "CHB Corporation," a closely held business owned by the decedent and the decedent's family?

55. *Conclusion.* The Statement would apply to the determination of value of CHB Corporation because valuation approaches and methods need to be applied,

and professional judgment needs to be used to determine the fair market value of the ownership interest in CHB (SSVS paragraphs 1 and 4).

56. *Illustration 13e.* Does the Statement apply to a 5 percent interest in a privately held rental real estate partnership (RP)?

57. *Conclusion.* The Statement would apply to the determination of value of the 5 percent interest in rental real estate partnership (RP) because valuation approaches and methods need to be applied and professional judgment needs to be used to determine the fair market value of the ownership of a fractional interest in a privately held partnership (SSVS paragraphs 1 and 4). However, where it is not practical or not reasonable to obtain or use relevant information and, therefore, the member is unable to apply valuation approaches and methods, the Statement would not apply. For example, the member has requested from RP's general partner financial information the member needs in order to apply valuation approaches and methods. The general partner is not responsive to the member's requests, and the due date for filing the estate tax return is near. Given the small ownership interest, and given that RP is likely a relatively small percent of the total estate, unless prohibited by statute or by rule, the member may then use the taxpayer's estimates if the member determines that the estimates are reasonable (based on the facts and circumstances known to the member) (SSVS paragraph 9(b)).

58. *Illustration 14.* Would the answers to *Illustration 13* change if the values were provided by the client or a client-engaged third party?

59. *Conclusion.* The Statement would not apply if the values were provided by the client or by a client-engaged third party because the member is not applying valuation approaches and methods and using professional judgment to determine value (SSVS paragraphs 1 and 4). However, the member would be subject to Statement on Standards for Tax Services No. 3, *Certain Procedural Aspects of Preparing Returns,* in providing appropriate due diligence with respect to the values provided to the member (see AICPA, *Professional Standards,* vol. 2, TS sec. 300). It is also recommended that the understanding between member and client in these circumstances include documentation of the fact that the member is not determining but rather is being provided with the value of the subject interest.

60. *Illustration 15.* Would the answers to *Illustration 13* change if the values were provided by an outside third-party specialist hired by the member?

61. *Conclusion.* If the member engages an outside third-party specialist to assist with the member's work, and it is the member expressing a conclusion or calculated value, the member will be applying valuation approaches and methods and using professional judgment; thus, the Statement would apply (SSVS paragraphs 1 and 4; SSVS paragraphs 20, "Using the Work of Specialists in the Valuation Engagement"). If, however, the third-party specialist is determining the value in his or her own name and providing that value to the client, and the member will not be applying valuation approaches and methods or using professional judgment (SSVS paragraphs 1 and 4, and *Illustration 6*), the Statement would

not apply, but the member would be subject to Statement on Standards for Tax Services No. 3, *Certain Procedural Aspects of Preparing Returns,* in providing appropriate due diligence with respect to the values provided (AICPA, *Professional Standards,* vol. 2, TS sec. 300).

62. *Illustration 16.* The client and the member agree that the member will value a partnership interest and then apply an "average" discount that the member is to determine (based on the results of various studies and case law). Does the Statement apply? If so, is this a valuation engagement or a calculation engagement?

63. *Conclusion.* Yes, the Statement applies because the member determined the value of the partnership interest by applying valuation approaches and valuation methods and using professional judgment. This would be considered a calculation engagement because the member and the client have agreed on the specific valuation approaches or valuation methods the valuation analyst will use and the extent of valuation procedures the valuation analyst will perform (SSVS paragraph 21(b) and *Illustration 6*).

64. *Illustration 17.* Would the Statement apply if a member has an informal conversation or communicates in writing with a client regarding the alternative tax consequences of gifting versus selling a business using a presumption of a specific value of the business?

65. *Conclusion.* No, the Statement would not apply. The member is providing tax advice using an assumed or hypothetical value of a business and is not determining value, applying valuation approaches and methods, and using professional judgment to value a business (SSVS paragraphs 1 and 4, and *Illustration 6*).

66. *Illustration 18.* Would the Statement apply to a transfer pricing study (IRC section 482) that involves the use of specific methodologies, data, terminology, and documentation requirements that are provided in the IRS regulations and procedures, and whose methodologies and documentation requirements differ from those contained in the Statement?

67. *Conclusion.* No. To the extent that the transfer pricing study applies, for example, to the valuation of inventory or services, the Statement would not apply (see SSVS paragraph 1 and *Illustration 6*). To the extent that the transfer pricing study applies to the valuation of intangible assets, the Statement would normally apply. However, because the IRS regulations require that the taxpayer reasonably calculate an arm's-length price according to the best method that is determined using third-party comparable data under explicit IRS rules and documentation procedures, and to the extent these IRS rules and procedures differ from the Statement, the jurisdictional exception (SSVS paragraph 10) would exempt the valuation of the intangible assets from the developmental provisions of the Statement (SSVS paragraphs 25–48). In addition, to the extent that the IRS regulations (such as IRS regulation section 1.6662-6(d) (2) (iii)) and procedures provide specific documentation requirements for avoiding potential penalties, and if a transfer pricing report is provided to a client according to such IRS documentation requirements, the

jurisdictional exception would apply to the reporting provisions of the Statement (SSVS paragraphs 50–78) and thus a valuation report would not be necessary.

68. *Illustration 19.* In a situation where the Statement applies to members who determine value as part of tax engagements, would the member also be required to be in compliance with the Statements on Standards for Tax Services (SSTSs)?

69. *Conclusion.* Yes, the Statement would apply only to the valuation determination and reporting aspects of the engagement but the SSTSs would apply to all aspects of the engagement. For example, even though the Statement would govern the determination of value of an applicable asset reported on a tax return, the member would also have to be in compliance with SSTS No. 1, *Tax Return Positions,* for that valuation.

70. *Illustration 21.* Do settlements or negotiations of value in offers-in-compromise or tax disputes fall under the Statement?

71. *Conclusion.* No, settlements or negotiations of value in offers-in-compromise or tax disputes are part of a tax process. However, if a member prepares a valuation in preparation for a settlement or negotiation of value, and the valuation involves the application of valuation approaches and methods and the use of professional judgment, the valuation would fall under the developmental aspects of the Statement. The settlement or negotiation process itself is not a valuation and would not fall under the Statement. In addition, the Statement's reporting exemption for certain controversy proceedings would apply as the valuation was performed specifically for the administrative matter (SSVS paragraph 50).

Illustrations Relating to Other Engagements

72. *Illustration 20.* Does determining the value of accounts receivable fall under the Statement?

73. *Conclusion.* No, accounts receivable constitute **tangible assets** under the Statement (SSVS Appendix B), and do not constitute a subject interest (SSVS paragraph 1).

74. *Illustration 22.* In the course of performing a valuation under the Statement, if a valuation analyst prepares prospective financial information (for example, as part of a discounted cash flow or discounted earnings analysis within the income approach), does this require the valuation analyst to examine or compile such information in accordance with the Statements on Standards for Attestation Engagements (SSAEs)?

75. *Conclusion.* No, Chapter 1, "Attest Engagements," of SSAE No. 10, *Attestation Standards: Revision and Recodification* (AICPA, *Professional Standards,* vol. 1, AT sec. 101), as amended (AT sec. 101.01) states that the attestation standards apply when a practitioner is "engaged to issue or does issue an

examination, a review, or an agreed-upon procedures report on subject matter, or an assertion about the subject matter . . . , that is the responsibility of another party.'' If the valuation analyst has not been engaged to examine, compile, assemble, review, or apply agreed-upon procedures to prospective financial information, and does not issue an examination, compilation, assembly, or agreed-upon report on prospective financial information, the SSAEs do not apply (SSARS 14).

76. *Illustration 23.* Under a valuation engagement, a valuation analyst is free to select any and all valuation approaches and methods the valuation analyst deems appropriate in the circumstances. Under a calculation engagement, the valuation analyst and the client agree to the specific approaches or methods the valuation analyst will use or the extent of calculation procedures the valuation analyst will perform. (SSVS paragraph 21.) Under SSVS paragraph 18, a restriction or limitation on the scope of the valuation analyst's work, or the data available for analysis may be present and known to the valuation analyst at the outset of the engagement, or may arise during the course of an engagement (and such restriction or limitation should be disclosed in the report). Is it possible to have a restriction or limitation that is of such a degree that a valuation analyst engaged to perform a valuation engagement should propose altering the engagement to be a calculation engagement?

77. *Conclusion.* Although the two engagements represent two different types of service performed by valuation analysts, the possibility exists. If, in the course of a valuation engagement, restrictions, or limitations on the scope of the valuation analyst's work or the data available for analysis are so significant that the valuation analyst believes that he or she cannot, even with disclosure in the valuation report of the restrictions or limitations, adequately perform a valuation engagement leading to a conclusion of value, the valuation analyst should determine whether he or she has the ability to adequately complete the engagement as a calculation engagement or should consider resigning from the engagement.

78. *Illustration 24.* If a member employed in industry, government, or education ''moonlights'' doing engagements to estimate value, do the Standards apply?

79. *Conclusion.* Yes, the Standard applies. By moonlighting, the member is holding him or herself out as a certified public account and as being in public practice. The Standard would apply just as it would to any other member in public practice unless one of the exceptions applies.

80. *Illustration 25.* Does the Statement apply to an assignment from an employer to an employee member not in public practice to prepare a valuation for internal financial reporting purposes?

81. *Conclusion.* No, paragraph 7 exempts internal use assignments from an employer to an employee member not in the practice of public accounting. However, if the valuation is to be used for financial reporting purposes, the employer and the employee may wish to consider whether the work will be accepted by the employer's outside auditors if the statement is not followed.

Illustrations for PFP-Specific Engagements

These illustrations assume the member has not been engaged to perform a business valuation.

82. *Illustration 26.* When does the Statement apply to members who determine values related to personal financial planning engagements?

83. *Conclusion.* The Statement applies to personal financial planning engagements when the member determines the value of a business, business ownership interest, security, or intangible asset (SSVS paragraph 1) and in the process of determining the value applies valuation approaches and methods and uses professional judgment (SSVS paragraph 4) unless an exception applies (SSVS paragraphs 5–10).

84. *Illustration 27.* If a member is engaged to provide personal financial planning services to a client and, in the course of the engagement, estimates the proceeds from a hypothetical future sale of the client's business interest, does the Statement apply?

85. *Conclusion.* No. The Statement does not apply because estimate of future sales proceeds does not in itself constitute a valuation engagement (SSVS paragraphs 1 and 4).

86. *Illustration 28. A* member is engaged to provide personal financial planning services to a client and, in the course of the engagement, estimates the proceeds from a hypothetical future sale of the client's business interest. As part of that engagement, the member shares general industry knowledge to assist the client in estimating the current value of the business interest. Does the Statement apply?

87. *Conclusion:*

(a) If, in the process of determining the current value from which the member estimates future sales proceeds, the member applies valuation approaches and methods and uses professional judgment, the Statement applies to the determination of the current value (SSVS paragraph 4). However, the Statement does not apply when the member shares general industry knowledge with the client instead of applying professional judgment.

(b) If the client or another party provides the current value, and the member does not apply valuation approaches and methods, the Statement does not apply (SSVS paragraphs 4 and 6).

(c) If the member uses a hypothetical or assumed value as the starting point for the calculation of future sales proceeds and does not apply valuation approaches and methods, the Statement does not apply (SSVS paragraphs 1 and 4). The Statement does not apply to a general discussion with the client of valuation concepts or industry price multiples based on the member's industry knowledge, which assists the client in determining a hypothetical or assumed value (SSVS paragraphs 4 and 6).

88. *Illustration 29.* The client has asked the member to prepare a personal financial plan that includes an estimate of future proceeds from a sale of the business interest at retirement. The member estimates the future proceeds based on an estimate of the business' current value by applying a rule of thumb for the business' industry, but the member does not consider the risk factors of the subject interest or exercise other professional judgment in applying the multiple. Does the Statement apply?

89. *Conclusion.* No, the Statement does not apply because the member did not use professional judgment (SSVS paragraph 4). If the member considers specific risk factors of the business interest in applying the price multiple, the Statement applies.

This Statement titled Valuation of a Business, Business Ownership Interest, Security, or Intangible Asset *was unanimously adopted by the assenting votes of the AICPA Consulting Services Executive Committee.*

Consulting Services Executive Committee 2003–2007

Dominic A. Cingoranelli, Jr., *Chair*
Lester Coffey
Marianne Pulli Evashenk
Dan H. Hanke
Bryan Eric Lundstrom
Michael E. Mares
Paul D. Milne
Paul Richard Osborne
Robert F. Reilly

Business Valuation Committee 2003–2007

Michael A. Crain, *Chair 2004–2007*
Thomas E. Hilton, *Chair 2003–2004*
Melvin Haskell Abraham
James A. Andersen
Christine P. Baker
Richard S. Barnes
William J. Bavis
Travis N. Chamberlain
Cindy Eddins Collier
Robert E. Duffy
John R. Gilbert
Robert P. Gray
Lindon A. Greene
Rudolph L. Hertlein
Yassir Karam
G. William Kennedy
Michael E. Mares
Bradley H. Minor
Robert F. Reilly
Sheri F. Schultz
Robin E. Taylor
Linda B. Trugman
Judith A. Wagner
H.Joe Wells
Carolyn J. Worth
Timothy W. York

Business Valuation Standards Writing Task Force

Edward J. Dupke, *Chair*
R. James Alerding
Gregory Forsythe
James R. Hitchner

AICPA Staff
Specialized Communities & Firm Practice Management

James C. Metzler, *Vice President*
Small Firm Interests

Stephen L. Winters,
Director
Specialized Communities
and Firm Practice
Management

Thomas M. Miller, *Technical Manager*
Business Valuation and Forensic &
Litigation Services

The AICPA gratefully acknowledges the contributions of Terry Jacoby Allen, James Feldman, Gretchen Fischbach, Nancy Gault, Michael N. Heaton, Joseph Lhotka, Debra Lockwood, Michael J. Mard, Richard I. Miller, Charles E. Landes, James S. Rigby, Jr., Marc T. Simon, James L. (Butch) Williams, Anat Kendal, Janice Fredericks, and Anthony Basile.

Appendix 3
The Chartered Institute of Arbitrators Protocol on Instructions to Party-Appointed Expert Witnesses

The Chartered Institute of Arbitrators

Protocol for the Use of Party-Appointed Expert Witnesses in International Arbitration

Preamble

1. This Chartered Institute of Arbitrators Protocol for the Use of Party-Appointed Expert Witnesses in International Arbitration (the Protocol) is intended to govern in an efficient and economical manner the preparation and giving of expert evidence in international arbitrations, particularly those between Parties from different legal traditions. It is designed to supplement the legal provisions and the institutional or ad-hoc rules according to which the Parties are conducting the Arbitration.

2. Parties and Arbitral Tribunals may adopt the Protocol in whole or in part or may use it as a guideline in developing their own procedures for the preparation and giving of expert evidence. The Protocol is not intended to limit the flexibility that is inherent in, and an advantage of, international arbitration, and Parties and Arbitral Tribunals are free to adapt it to the particular circumstances of each arbitration.

3. Each Arbitral Tribunal is encouraged to identify and establish with the Parties, as soon as it is appropriate in the Arbitration, the issues in respect of which it considers expert evidence to be appropriate.

4. The preparation and giving of expert evidence in accordance with this Protocol is intended to give effect to the following principles

- each Party is entitled to know, reasonably in advance of any Evidentiary Hearing, the expert evidence upon which the other Parties rely;
- experts should provide assistance to the Arbitral Tribunal and not advocate the position of the Party appointing them;
- there should be established before any hearing the greatest possible degree of agreement between experts.

Article 1 – Definitions

In the Chartered Institute of Arbitrators Protocol for the Use of Party-Appointed Expert Witnesses in International Arbitration.

"Arbitral Tribunal" means a sole arbitrator or a panel of arbitrators validly deciding by majority or otherwise.

"Arbitration" means the arbitration in respect of which the Arbitral Tribunal has been appointed.

"Evidentiary Hearing" means any hearing in the Arbitration whether or not held on consecutive days, at which the Arbitral Tribunal receives oral evidence.

"General Rules" means the institutional or ad-hoc rules according to which the Arbitration is being conducted.

"Party" means a party to the Arbitration, and "Parties" shall be construed accordingly.

"Protocol" means this Chartered Institute of Arbitrators Protocol for the Use of Party-Appointed Expert Witnesses in International Arbitration.

Article 2 – Use of Protocol

1. The Protocol shall govern the preparation and giving of expert evidence.

(a) whenever the Parties agree that it shall do so; or
(b) upon application by one or more Parties for party appointed expert evidence to be adduced in the Arbitration, and the Arbitral Tribunal, after consultation with the Parties, directs that the Protocol shall apply.

2. In the event of a conflict between any provision of the Protocol and any mandatory provision of law agreed by the Parties or determined by the Arbitral Tribunal to be applicable to the Arbitration, the mandatory provision of law shall prevail.

3. In the event:

(a) of a conflict between the Protocol and the General Rules;
(b) that the Protocol and the General Rules are silent on anything concerning the preparation and giving of expert evidence; or
(c) that there is a dispute as to the meaning of the Protocol;

the Arbitral Tribunal shall, after consultation with the Parties, make any necessary interpretations and shall make any directions appropriate for the preparation and giving of expert evidence in the Arbitration.

Article 3 – Permission to Adduce Expert Evidence

1. Where the Protocol is to apply, the Arbitral Tribunal shall, in consultation with the Parties and in timely fashion, direct:

(a) the issue evidence shall be adduced in the Arbitration;
(b) the number of experts in respect of each issue that shall be permitted to give evidence in the Arbitration;
(c) what tests or analyses shall be required.

2. Expert evidence shall be adduced in the manner provided for in Articles 6 and 7.

Article 4 – Independence, Duty and Opinion

1. An expert's opinion shall be impartial, objective, unbiased and uninfluenced by the pressures of the dispute resolution process or by any Party.

2. Payment by the appointing Party of the expert's reasonable professional fees for the work done in giving such evidence shall not, of itself, vitiate the expert's impartiality.

3. An expert's duty, in giving evidence in the Arbitration, is to assist the Arbitral Tribunal to decide the issues in respect of which expert evidence is adduced.

4. An expert's written opinion should:

(a) contain the full name and address, background, qualifications, training and experience of the expert;
(b) state any past or present relationship with any of the Parties, the Arbitral Tribunal, counsel or other representatives of the Parties, other witnesses and any other person or entity involved in the Arbitration;
(c) contain a statement setting out all instructions the expert has received from the appointing Party and the basis of remuneration of the expert;
(d) only address the issue or issues in respect of which the Arbitral Tribunal has given permission for expert evidence to be adduced;
(e) state which facts, matters and documents, including any assumed facts or other assumptions, have been considered in reaching the opinion;
(f) state which facts, matters and documents, including any assumed facts or other assumptions, the opinion is based upon;
(g) state the opinion(s) and conclusion(s) that have been reached and a description of the method, evidence and information used in reaching the opinion(s) and conclusion(s);
(h) state which matters the expert has been unable to reach an opinion on;

(i) state which matters (if any) are outside the expert's area of expertise;
(j) adequately reference all documents and sources relied upon;
(k) contain a declaration in the form set out in Article 8; and
(l) be signed by the expert and state its date and place.

Article 5 – Privilege

1. All instructions to, and any terms of appointment of, an expert shall not be privileged against disclosure in the Arbitration, but the Arbitral Tribunal shall not, in relation to the instructions or terms of appointment:

(a) order disclosure of the instructions or appointment or any document relating thereto; or (b) permit any questioning of the expert about such instructions or appointment unless it is satisfied that there is good cause.

2. Drafts, working papers or any other documentation created by an expert for the purposes of providing expert evidence in the Arbitration shall be privileged from production and shall not be discloseable in the Arbitration.

Article 6 – Expert Evidence

1. Within the time ordered by the Arbitral Tribunal, and save where the Arbitral Tribunal directs to the contrary, expert evidence shall be adduced in the Arbitration using the following procedure:

(a) The experts appointed by the Parties on related expert issues shall hold a discussion for the purpose of:
  (i) identifying and listing the issues upon which they are to provide an opinion;
  (ii) identifying and listing any tests or analyses which need to be conducted; and
  (iii) where possible, reaching agreement on those issues, the tests and analyses which need to be conducted and the manner in which they shall be conducted.
  (iv) if the Arbitral Tribunal so directs, the experts shall prepare and exchange draft outline opinions for the purposes of these meetings, which opinions shall be without prejudice to the Parties' respective positions in the Arbitration and privileged from production to the Tribunal.
(b) Following such discussion, the experts shall prepare and send to the Parties and to the Arbitral Tribunal a statement setting out:
  (i) those issues upon which they agree and the agreed opinions they have reached on those issues;
  (ii) those tests and analyses which they agree need to be conducted and the agreed manner for conducting them;
  (iii) those issues upon which they disagree and a summary of their reasons for disagreement; and

(iv) the tests and analyses in respect of which agreement has not been reached as to whether they shall be conducted and/or the manner in which they should be conducted, and a summary of their reasons for disagreement.

(c) Following such statement:
   (i) any agreed tests and analyses shall be conducted in the agreed manner;
   (ii) any agreed tests and analyses in respect of which the manner of conduct has not been agreed shall be conducted in such manner as each expert considers appropriate in the presence of the other expert(s); and
   (iii) any test and analyses which have not been agreed shall be conducted in such manner as the expert requiring them to be conducted considers appropriate in the presence of the other expert(s).

(d) Following such statement, and such tests and analyses (if any), each expert shall produce a written opinion in accordance with the provisions of Article 4 dealing only with those issues upon which there is disagreement.

(e) Such written opinions shall be exchanged simultaneously.

(f) Following such exchange, each expert shall be entitled, should the expert so wish, to produce a further written opinion dealing only with such matters as are raised in the written opinion(s) of the other expert(s).

(g) Such further written opinions shall be exchanged simultaneously.

(h) Each expert who has provided a written opinion in the Arbitration shall give oral testimony at an Evidentiary Hearing unless the Parties agree otherwise and the Arbitral Tribunal confirms that agreement.

(i) If an expert who has provided an opinion in the Arbitration does not appear to give testimony at an Evidentiary Hearing without a valid reason, unless the Parties agree otherwise and the Arbitral Tribunal confirms that agreement, the Arbitral Tribunal shall disregard the expert's written opinion unless, in exceptional circumstances, the Arbitral Tribunal determines otherwise.

2. The contents of the discussion referred to at Article 6.1(a) shall be without prejudice to the Parties' respective positions in the Arbitration and, unless all the Parties agree otherwise, and save as provided in Article 6.1(b), the content of that discussion shall not be communicated to the Arbitral Tribunal.

3. Any agreement by the Parties pursuant to Article 6.1(h) that an expert need not give oral testimony at an Evidentiary Hearing shall not constitute agreement with, or acceptance by a Party of, the content of the expert's written opinion.

Article 7 – Testimony by Experts

1. The manner in which an expert gives testimony shall be as directed by the Arbitral Tribunal. The expert's testimony shall be given with the purpose of assisting the Arbitral Tribunal to narrow the issues between the experts and to understand and efficiently to use the expert evidence.

2. The Arbitral Tribunal may at any time, up to and during the hearing, direct the experts to confer further and to provide further written reports to the Arbitral Tribunal either jointly or separately.

3. The Arbitral Tribunal may at any time hold preliminary meetings with the experts.

4. If the Arbitral Tribunal is satisfied that either written opinion or testimony of an expert is not in accordance with the expert declaration contained in Article 8 of the Protocol, the Arbitral Tribunal shall disregard the expert's written opinion and testimony either in whole or in part, as it considers appropriate in all the circumstances.

Article 8 – Expert Declaration

1. The expert declaration referred to in Article 4.5(n) shall be in the following form:

"(a) I understand that my duty in giving evidence in this arbitration is to assist the arbitral tribunal decide the issues in respect of which expert evidence is adduced. I have complied with, and will continue to comply with, that duty.

(b) I confirm that this is my own, impartial, objective, unbiased opinion which has not been influenced by the pressures of the dispute resolution process or by any party to the arbitration.

(c) I confirm that all matters upon which I have expressed an opinion are within my area of expertise.

(d) I confirm that I have referred to all matters which I regard as relevant to the opinions I have expressed and have drawn to the attention of the arbitral tribunal all matters, of which I am aware, which might adversely affect my opinion;

(e) I confirm that, at the time of providing this written opinion, I consider it to be complete and accurate and constitute my true, professional opinion.

(f) I confirm that if, subsequently, I consider this opinion requires any correction, modification or qualification I will notify the parties to this arbitration and the arbitral tribunal forthwith."

Appendix 4

The Chartered Institute of Arbitrators Guideline 10 on the Use of Tribunal-Appointed Experts, Legal Advisers and Assessors

The Chartered Institute of Arbitrators

Guideline 10: Guideline on the Use of Tribunal-Appointed Experts, Legal Advisers and Assessors

1 INTRODUCTION

1.1 In many if not most systems of arbitration there is provision for the arbitral tribunal to appoint experts to report to it on technical matters outside its own expertise and experience.

1.2 As regards arbitrations in England and Wales, Section 37 of the Arbitration Act 1996 (which is based on Article 26 of the Model Law) provides:

"(1) Unless otherwise agreed by the parties –
(a) the tribunal may –
(i) appoint experts or legal advisers to report to it and the parties, or
(ii) appoint assessors to assist it on technical matters, and may allow any such expert, legal adviser or assessor to attend the proceedings; and

(b) the parties shall be given a reasonable opportunity to comment on any information, opinion or advice offered by any such person.

(2) The fees and expenses of an expert, legal adviser or assessor appointed by the tribunal for which the arbitrators are liable are expenses of the arbitrators for the purposes of this Part."

1.3 In this Guideline it is proposed to deal separately with tribunal-appointed experts, legal advisers and assessors. Before doing so, however, three general features of Section 37 need to be mentioned.

1.4 First, Section 37 (which is prefaced by the words "unless otherwise agreed by the parties") is not mandatory. In common with Section 34, it proceeds on the footing that it is for the tribunal to decide all procedural and evidential matters but that this is subject to the right of the parties to reach agreement on those matters. There is only one mandatory aspect of Section 37. Sub-section (2) is made mandatory to avoid the risk of the parties disabling the tribunal from recovering from the parties expenses properly incurred.

1.5 Second, before appointing an expert, legal adviser or assessor under this Section the tribunal must first consider whether this is consistent with its duty under Section 33(1)(b) to adopt procedures suitable to the circumstances of the particular case, avoiding unnecessary delay or expense, so as to provide a fair means for the resolution of the matters falling to be determined.

1.6 Third, if the tribunal does decide to appoint an expert legal adviser or assessor the procedure to be followed must be closely defined in an order made by the tribunal at or about the stage of the appointment. Section 37 leaves the details of that procedure to the discretion of the tribunal save in one respect, that is, that any information, opinion or advice offered by any person appointed by the tribunal must be communicated to the parties and the parties must be given a reasonable opportunity to comment on it. A failure to provide such an opportunity is equivalent to a failure by the tribunal to perform its duty under Section 33(1)(a).

2 COMPARATIVE VIEW

2.1 Article 26 of the Model Law itself reads:

"1. Unless otherwise agreed by the parties, the arbitral tribunal

(a) may appoint one or more experts to report to it on specific issues to be determined by the arbitral tribunal;

(b) may require a party to give the expert any relevant information or to produce, or to provide access to, any relevant documents, goods or other property for his inspection.

2. Unless otherwise agreed by the parties, if a party so requests or if the arbitral tribunal considers it necessary, the expert shall, after delivery of

his written or oral report, participate in a hearing where the parties have the opportunity to put questions to him and to present expert witnesses in order to testify on the points at issue."

2.2. Article 1042 of the Dutch Burgerlijke Rechsvordering contains an equally detailed provision which operates on similar lines to the UNCITRAL Model Law. It says:

"1. The arbitral tribunal may appoint one or more experts to give advice. The arbitral tribunal shall communicate as soon as possible to the parties a copy of the appointment and the terms of reference of the experts.
2. The arbitral tribunal may require a party to provide the experts with the information required by them and to give them the necessary cooperation.
3. Upon receipt of the expert's report, the arbitral tribunal shall provide a copy of the report to the parties without delay.
4. At the request of either party, the experts shall be examined at a hearing. A party wishing to make such a request shall inform the arbitral tribunal and the opposing party thereof without delay.
5. The arbitral tribunal shall give the parties an opportunity to examine the experts and to produce their own experts."

2.3. In other countries, notably Switzerland, France, Belgium, the USA, the parties and, in default, the tribunal's power to determine the arbitral procedure has always been interpreted as permitting the appointment of experts.

2.4. Overall, there is very little if any difference between the position under the 1996 Act and the law prevailing in the countries considered in these guidelines.

3 TRIBUNAL-APPOINTED EXPERTS

3.1 Introduction

3.1.1 In cases where the parties have not excluded the power of the Tribunal to appoint an expert, the Tribunal should exercise care in deciding:

(1) whether or not the case is suited to the use of a tribunal appointed expert;
(2) if so, what are to be the expert's terms of reference;
(3) who is to be appointed and on what terms;
(4) what material is to be provided initially to the expert;
(5) whether the expert is to be able to seek further material or information from the parties;
(6) the time-table for the production of the expert's report;
(7) whether or in what circumstances the parties are to be entitled to call their own expert evidence or to serve their own experts reports;
(8) the procedure for enabling the parties to comment on the expert's report; and
(9) the procedure to be adopted at the hearing.

It is normally wise to provide for such matters in a procedural order at an early stage in the arbitration though some aspects may be reserved and dealt with later.

3.2 Cases Suited to the Use of a Tribunal-Appointed Expert

3.2.1 Where an arbitration raises technical issues these may be resolved in a number of ways eg by ensuring that at least one member of the tribunal has expertise in the relevant discipline, by adopting the familiar procedure that each party commissions an expert to produce a report and that each expert subsequently gives evidence at the hearing, by using a tribunal-appointed expert or by appointing one or more assessors to consider the evidence and to assist the tribunal on technical matters. Two or more of these methods may be used in combination.

3.2.2. At a relatively early stage in most arbitrations it should become clear whether or not there are technical issues upon which expert evidence will be required. Either the tribunal may be called upon to give procedural directions, including directions for the service of experts' reports or, on consideration of the papers, the tribunal may see the need to give directions as regards expert evidence. It is always the duty of the tribunal to ensure that technical issues are fairly resolved and that this is done without unnecessary delay or expense. At this stage the tribunal may wish to consider appointing a single tribunal-appointed expert. Before doing so, however, it is always advisable to enquire from the parties how they propose to deal with any technical issues which may arise and to canvass with them the possible use of a single tribunal-appointed expert. This should enable the possible advantages and disadvantages of the proposal to be brought out into the open and to be properly discussed.

3.2.3. A situation in which the use of a tribunal-appointed expert is obviously called for can arise where the dispute raises technical issues outside the expertise of the tribunal and where neither party has it in mind to call its own expert evidence. But the situation is rarely so clear-cut. In many cases the parties may wish to commission their own expert reports or to adduce evidence from their own experts. If so, a wise arbitrator will hesitate long before excluding such evidence, if it is otherwise admissible, since this might constitute a ground for challenging the eventual award under Section 33(1)(a). It can then be a serious question whether it will serve any useful purpose to use, in addition, a tribunal-appointed expert. In some cases such an appointment may be justified, eg because the tribunal considers that the party-appointed experts are not sufficiently qualified or not sufficiently independent to deal objectively with the issues. In other cases the tribunal may perhaps take the view that the party-appointed experts are likely to investigate all the technical issues in their reports and that the tribunal will be able to decide between them; alternatively that, should any difficulty arise in resolving any technical issues that remain in dispute after the two experts have met in an attempt to agree or narrow the issues, then, in case of need, it will always be possible for the tribunal to appoint an assessor at a later stage. Questions of cost and convenience are likely to arise and no hard and fast rules can be formulated.

3.2.4. Should it be contemplated that both a tribunal appointed expert is to be used and that the parties are to be free to commission their own expert reports, then care should be taken to lay down the respective functions of each type of expert and the time-table for dealing with them. Duplication of cost can sometimes be avoided or minimised if it is ordered or agreed that in the first instance only a single expert report (commissioned by the tribunal) will be produced and that if, on receipt of that report, either party should wish to challenge or supplement it, that party may apply to the tribunal to be allowed to adduce evidence from its own expert on particular defined issues. The need for such evidence can then be assessed on its merits.

3.3 Terms of Reference

3.3.1 It is one of the advantages of employing a tribunal-appointed expert that he or she can be involved at an early stage in the arbitration and can be invited by the tribunal to assist in the preparation of terms of reference which will serve to define the question or questions to be addressed and the type of investigation to be performed. The tribunal should try to ensure that the expert's terms of reference will result in the key issues being fully considered by the expert.

3.3.2 Terms of reference should be established by the tribunal in consultation with the parties. In some cases the parties may create their own terms of reference and offer them for the tribunal's comments or approval. In the more complex type of case it can be useful to ask the expert to look at the draft and to make suggestions before it is finalised.

3.3.3 It should be borne in mind when drafting terms of reference that the expert is being employed to give evidence of opinion or fact related to the specialised discipline in which his experience lies. This may involve him in carrying out investigations or tests. Both the questions to be addressed by him and the type of investigations or tests should be clearly defined. It is important that the expert should not be invited to draw inferences or to express opinions on matters outside his expertise. Its equally important that the terms of reference should seek to draw a distinction between matters on which the expert can properly give evidence and those matters which are for the tribunal to decide.

3.4 Selection of Expert

3.4.1. In many cases the search for a suitably qualified and independent expert can be difficult. Relevant specialist institutions (such as the Chartered Institute of Arbitrators, the Expert Witness Institute, the Society of Expert Witnesses and the Academy of Experts) can be consulted. The tribunal should involve the parties in the selection process and may consider asking each party to offer suggestions or to indicate approval or disapproval of possible appointees.

3.4.2. The tribunal-appointed expert should be asked, before accepting appointment, to submit to the tribunal and to the parties a statement of his or her independence from the parties and the tribunal. The tribunal should invite the parties to state whether they have any objections to the proposed expert's independence.

3.4.3. The tribunal-appointed expert can also be asked, before accepting appointment, to provide a copy of his or her C.V. (and of his or her hourly charging rate) to the parties and the tribunal. The tribunal can then invite the parties to state whether they have any objections to the proposed expert's qualifications to perform the tasks in question, or to the proposed charging rate.

3.5 Material to be Furnished to Expert

3.5.1 The tribunal should specify either in its order for directions or in the expert's terms of reference precisely what documentation or other material is to be provided to the expert initially as the basis upon which his report is to be made.

3.5.2 The tribunal should also consider including a provision in its order requiring each party to give the expert any further information or to produce any further documentation or material that the expert may require. Similarly the tribunal may require the parties to provide the expert with access to any relevant documents, goods, or other property for his or her inspection.

3.5.3 Where the expert is authorised to communicate with the parties so as to obtain documentation or material relevant to his or her task the tribunal should lay down a clear procedure designed to ensure that any material provided by one party is seen by the other and that both sides and the tribunal know precisely what material has been provided to the expert for the purposes of drawing up his or her report.

Procedure after the Report is Received

3.5.4 After the expert's report has been delivered it must be sent to the parties and at this stage the tribunal should set a precise time-table for the service of written comments if this has not previously been done. If there is to be an oral hearing any written comments or submissions will have to be served in sufficient time to be considered beforehand.

3.5.5 At this stage the tribunal may have to deal with any request from the parties that the expert should expand or clarify a particular aspect or aspects of his report or even conduct further investigations with a view to making a supplementary report. The tribunal may of its own motion seek further clarification of the report.

3.5.6 Directions may also have to be given with regard any application from the parties to be allowed to adduce supplementary expert evidence from a party-appointed expert.

3.6 Procedure at the Hearing

3.6.1 The procedure to be followed at the hearing should be prescribed in advance. In so doing the tribunal should be mindful of its duty under

Section 33(1)(b) to adopt procedures which are fair and which avoid unnecessary delay and expense.

3.6.2 Section 37 does not go so far as Article 26 of the Model Law in giving the parties the right to put questions to the expert at a hearing or to present their own expert witnesses to testify on the points at issue. Section 37 leaves these matters to be decided by the tribunal subject to any agreement between the parties.

3.6.3 Some caution needs to be exercised before allowing a situation to develop where extensive oral evidence has to be received both from the tribunal appointed expert and also from experts presented by the parties. There may be situations where this cannot be avoided; such situations should be exceptional.

3.6.4 No such objection attaches to a provision that the tribunal-appointed expert is to attend the hearing and that the parties may question him on his report either directly or through the tribunal. Such a procedure has certain advantages, not least in ensuring that each party has an opportunity to put its case and to deal with any opinion or evidence tendered by the expert.

4 LEGAL ADVISERS

4.1 Section 37 enables arbitrators who are not themselves lawyers to appoint legal advisers for the purposes of making a report to the tribunal and the parties. It does not seek to deal with other situations where lawyers are commonly employed to assist arbitral tribunals, as in certain trade arbitrations where the trade association's legal adviser may sit with the tribunal at hearings to give procedural rulings or as when the tribunal instructs a lawyer to draft, or assist in drafting, its award.

4.2 The Section enables a tribunal to appoint legal advisers to report to it but requires that the parties must be given a reasonable opportunity to comment on any information opinion or advice that is offered. This necessarily involves that the information opinion or advice must be made known in sufficient time for the parties to comment.

4.3 While it can be appropriate, and even desirable in certain situations, for a tribunal to appoint legal advisers to report on a procedural question that has arisen in the reference, or on the substantive law applicable to the dispute, there are dangers involved which it is important to avoid. These include that the lawyer may not be fully informed of the relevant background, that the arguments presented to the tribunal may differ from those communicated to the lawyer, and that the impression may be conveyed that the tribunal has decided the case on the basis of advice provided privately by the lawyer or even that it has been decided by the lawyer himself.

4.4 Section 37 therefore requires that an open procedure be adopted for obtaining information opinion or advice. It sets a standard which should be followed even in those situations where the Section may not strictly apply.

4.5 The important points have been mentioned previously in connection with experts:

(1) Any proposed appointment of a lawyer should be canvassed with the parties before it is made.
(2) The proposed terms of reference, or letter of instruction, should also be communicated in draft to the parties who should be given the opportunity to comment and to suggest amendments so that, if possible, a draft can be agreed.
(3) The identity of the proposed lawyer should similarly be canvassed with the parties.
(4) A clear procedure should be laid down in advance (after being discussed with the parties) covering the information, documents and other material to be supplied to the lawyer, the time within which the report is to be made, the time-limits within which comments are to be made and the procedure at any hearing that may follow.

4.6 It is perhaps worth adding that once an open procedure has been laid down or agreed it should be strictly followed. Private communications between the tribunal and the legal adviser should not occur.

5 ASSESSORS

5.1 The function of an assessor is in many respects similar to that of an expert, namely to give impartial information or advice to the tribunal on technical matters within his or her expertise. There are some differences. An assessor does not normally make a report. He or she commonly sits with the tribunal throughout the hearing or, at all events, those parts of the hearing concerned with matters falling within his or her discipline. The assessor does not give evidence and customarily is not questioned by the parties. An assessor is not part of the tribunal which must make up its own mind on the advice it receives.

5.2 The danger exists that the tribunal may be perceived as deciding an arbitration as a result of private advice given informally by the assessor throughout the hearing or subsequently during informal conversations. Since the danger cannot be wholly avoided and since the tribunal will be mindful of its duty under Section 33(1)(b) to avoid unnecessary expense, it is only in cases where the technical issues are exceptionally complex or difficult that the appointment of assessors should be contemplated.

5.3 Section 37 (like Article 26 of the Model Law and Article 1042(2) of the Dutch Burgerlijke Rechsvordering) requires that the parties must be given a reasonable opportunity to comment on any information, opinion or advice offered by any assessor. This involves that an open procedure must be followed. Whenever possible the role of the assessor and the procedure to be followed should be agreed or laid down in advance.

5.4 In particular, whenever possible any information or advice offered by the assessor should be communicated at the same time to the tribunal and to the parties. Private conversations between the tribunal and the assessor concerning the effect or weight of the technical evidence should be avoided if possible and, if they should occur, the effect of any information or advice given by the assessor should be communicated to the parties immediately. Where assessors give advice to the tribunal following the conclusion of the oral hearing, a convenient mode of ensuring that the parties have an opportunity to comment on that advice is to reduce it to writing and to send it, together with a draft of the proposed technical sections of the award, to the parties for their comments before the award is issued.

Index

B

D

E

J

K

L

M

Q

R

INTERNATIONAL ARBITRATION LAW LIBRARY

1. Moshe Hirsch, *The Arbitration Mechanism of the International Center for the Settlement of Investment Disputes*, 1993 (ISBN 07-923-1993-1).
2. Aida B. Avanessian, *Iran-United States Claims Tribunal in Action*, 1993 (ISBN 18-533-3902-4).
3. Isaak I. Dore, *The UNCITRAL Framework for Arbitration in Contemporary Perspective*, 1993 (ISBN 18-533-3573-8).
4. Vesna Lazić, *Insolvency Proceedings and Commercial Arbitration*, 1998 (ISBN 90-411-1115-8).
5. Joachim Frick, *Arbitration in Complex International Contracts*, 2001 (ISBN 90-411-1662-1).
6. Katherine Lynch, *The Forces of Economic Globalization: Challenges to the Regime of International Commercial Arbitration*, 2003 (ISBN 90-411-1994-9).
7. Christoph Liebscher, *The Healthy Award: Challenge in International Commercial Arbitration*, 2003 (ISBN 90-411-2011-4).
8. Hamid G. Gharavi, *The International Effectiveness of the Annulment of an Arbitral Award*, 2003 (ISBN 90-411-1717-2).
9. Abdulhay Sayed, *Corruption in International Trade and Commercial Arbitration*, 2004 (ISBN 90-411-2236-2).
10. Gabrielle Kaufmann-Kohler & Thomas Schultz, *Online Dispute Resolution: Challenges for Contemporary Justice*, 2004 (ISBN 90-411-2318-0).
11. Christopher R. Drahozal & Richard W. Naimark (eds), *Towards a Science of International Arbitration: Collected Empirical Research*, 2005 (ISBN 90-411-2322-9).
12. Ali Yeşsilirmak, *Provisional Measures in International Commercial Arbitration*, 2005 (ISBN 90-411-2353-9).
13. Christian Bühring-Uhle, *Arbitration and Mediation in International Business*, second revised edition, 2006 (ISBN 978-9-041-12256-8).
14. Bernard Hanotiau, *Complex Arbitrations: Multiparty, Multicontract, Multiissue and Class Actions*, 2006 (ISBN 978-9-041-12442-5).
15. Loukas A. Mistelis & Julian D.M. Lew (eds), *Pervasive Problems in International Arbitration*, 2006 (ISBN 978-9-041-12450-0).
16. Julian D.M. Lew & Loukas A. Mistelis (eds), *Arbitration Insights – Twenty Years of the Annual Lecture of the School of International Arbitration, Sponsored by Freshfields Bruckhaus Deringer*, 2006 (ISBN 978-9-041-12606-1).
17. Mark Kantor, Valuation for Arbitration: *Compensation Standards, Valuation Methods and Expert Evidence*, 2008 (ISBN 978-9-041-12735-8).